Handbook of Strategies and Strategic Processing

Handbook of Strategies and Strategic Processing provides a state-of-the-art synthesis of conceptual, measurement, and analytical issues regarding learning strategies and strategic processing. Contributions by educational psychology experts present the clearest-yet definition of this essential and quickly evolving component of numerous theoretical frameworks that operate across academic domains. This volume addresses the most current research and theory on the nature of strategies and performance, mechanisms for unearthing individuals' strategic behaviors, and both long-established and emerging techniques for data analysis and interpretation.

Daniel L. Dinsmore, Ph.D. is an Associate Professor of Educational Psychology and Research Director for the Northeast Florida Center for STEM Education at the University of North Florida, USA.

Luke K. Fryer, Ph.D. is an Associate Professor in the Centre for the Enhancement of Teaching and Learning at Faculty of Education (CETL), The University of Hong Kong, Hong Kong.

Meghan M. Parkinson, Ph.D. is the Director of Assessment and Research in the College of Education and Human Services at the University of North Florida, USA.

Educational Psychology Handbook Series
Series Editor: Patricia A. Alexander

International Handbook of Research on Teachers' Beliefs
Edited by Helenrose Fives and Michelle Gregoire Gill

Handbook of Test Development, 2nd Edition
Edited by Suzanne Lane, Mark R. Raymond, and Thomas M. Haladyna

Handbook of Social Influences in School Contexts: Social-Emotional, Motivation, and Cognitive Outcomes
Edited by Kathryn R. Wentzel and Geetha B. Ramani

Handbook of Epistemic Cognition
Edited by Jeffrey A. Greene, William A. Sandoval, and Ivar Bråten

Handbook of Motivation at School, 2nd Edition
Edited by Kathryn R. Wentzel and David B. Miele

Handbook of Human and Social Conditions in Assessment
Edited by Gavin T.L. Brown and Lois R. Harris

Handbook of Quantitative Methods for Detecting Cheating on Tests
Edited by Gregory J. Cizek and James A. Wollack

Handbook of Research on Learning and Instruction, 2nd Edition
Edited by Patricia A. Alexander and Richard E. Mayer

Handbook of Self-Regulation of Learning and Performance, 2nd Edition
Edited by Dale H. Schunk and Jeffrey A. Greene

Handbook of Multiple Source Use
Edited by Jason L. G. Braasch, Ivar Bråten, Matthew T. McCrudden

Handbook of Strategies and Strategic Processing
Edited by Daniel L. Dinsmore, Luke K. Fryer, and Meghan M. Parkinson

Handbook of Strategies and Strategic Processing

Edited by
Daniel L. Dinsmore, Luke K. Fryer, and Meghan M. Parkinson

NEW YORK AND LONDON

First published 2020
by Routledge
52 Vanderbilt Avenue, New York, NY 10017

and by Routledge
2 Park Square, Milton Park, Abingdon, Oxon, OX14 4RN

Routledge is an imprint of the Taylor & Francis Group, an informa business

© 2020 Taylor & Francis

The right of Daniel L. Dinsmore, Luke K. Fryer, and Meghan M. Parkinson to be identified as the authors of the editorial material, and of the authors for their individual chapters, has been asserted in accordance with sections 77 and 78 of the Copyright, Designs and Patents Act 1988.

All rights reserved. No part of this book may be reprinted or reproduced or utilised in any form or by any electronic, mechanical, or other means, now known or hereafter invented, including photocopying and recording, or in any information storage or retrieval system, without permission in writing from the publishers.

Trademark notice: Product or corporate names may be trademarks or registered trademarks, and are used only for identification and explanation without intent to infringe.

Library of Congress Cataloging-in-Publication Data
A catalog record for this title has been requested

ISBN: 978-1-138-38993-9 (hbk)
ISBN: 978-1-138-38994-6 (pbk)
ISBN: 978-0-429-42363-5 (ebk)

Typeset in Minion Pro
by Swales & Willis, Exeter, Devon, UK

Dedications

To our children, Coraline and Louisa, who are the light of our lives – *D.L.D.* and *M.M.P.*
To Kaori Nakao for holding down the fort – *L.K.F.*

CONTENTS

Chapter 1 Introduction: What Are Strategies? 1
DANIEL L. DINSMORE, LUKE K. FRYER, AND MEGHAN M. PARKINSON

Section I DEFINITIONS, FORMS, AND LEVELS OF STRATEGIES 9

Chapter 2 Strategic Processing within and across Domains of Learning 11
DENIS DUMAS

Chapter 3 Level of Strategies and Strategic Processing 29
DANIEL L. DINSMORE AND COURTNEY HATTAN

Chapter 4 A Lifespan Developmental Perspective on Strategic Processing 47
AMÉLIE ROGIERS, EMMELIEN MERCHIE, FIEN DE SMEDT, LIESJE DE BACKER,
AND HILDE VAN KEER

Chapter 5 Negotiating Meaning and Engagement: Socially Shared Strategic
Processing 63
DEBORAH L. BUTLER AND LEYTON SCHNELLERT

Chapter 6 Commentary: A Conceptual Framework for Defining Strategies
and Strategic Processing 82
PEGGY VAN METER AND JACQUELINE M. CAMPBELL

Section II STRATEGIES IN ACTION 97

Chapter 7 Reading Comprehension Strategy Instruction 99
PETER AFFLERBACH, MATTHEW HURT, AND BYEONG-YOUNG CHO

viii • Contents

| Chapter 8 | Six Questions Regarding Strategy Use When Learning from Multiple Texts | 119 |
| | ALEXANDRA LIST | |

Chapter 9 Writing Strategies Interventions 141
STEVE GRAHAM, GERARDO BAÑALES, SILZA AHUMADA, PAMELA MUÑOZ, PRISILA ALVAREZ, AND KAREN R. HARRIS

Chapter 10 Mathematics Strategy Interventions 159
KRISTIE NEWTON

Chapter 11 Science Strategy Interventions 177
DOUG LOMBARDI AND JANELLE M. BAILEY

Chapter 12 Strategic Processing in History and Historical Strategy Instruction 195
SUSAN DE LA PAZ AND JEFFERY D. NOKES

Chapter 13 Interplay of Strategic Processes, Executive Functions, and Autonomy Support in Students with Individual Differences 216
ANA TABOADA BARBER, KELLY B. CARTWRIGHT, AND SUSAN LUTZ KLAUDA

Chapter 14 Sharing the Load: A Strategy to Improve Self-regulated Learning 234
MARTINE BAARS, LISETTE WIJNIA, ANIQUE DE BRUIN, AND FRED PAAS

Chapter 15 Commentary: An Analysis of Learning Strategies in Action 248
PHILIP H. WINNE

Section III MEASURING STRATEGIC PROCESSING **257**

Chapter 16 Surveys and Retrospective Self-reports to Measure Strategies and Strategic Processing 259
JAN D. VERMUNT

Chapter 17 Concurrent and Task-specific Self-reports 275
IVAR BRÅTEN, JOSEPH P. MAGLIANO, AND LADISLAO SALMERÓN

Chapter 18 Exploring the Utilization of the Big Data Revolution as a Methodology for Exploring Learning Strategy in Educational Environments 296
KIMBERLY A. LAWLESS AND JEREMY RIEL

Chapter 19 Measuring Processing Strategies: Perspectives for Eye Tracking and fMRI in Multi-method Designs 317
LEEN CATRYSSE, DAVID GIJBELS, AND VINCENT DONCHE

Contents • ix

| Chapter 20 | Commentary: Measuring Strategic Processing in Concert: Reflections and Future Directions | 332 |

DAVID GIJBELS AND SOFIE LOYENS

Section IV **ANALYZING STRATEGIC PROCESSING** **343**

| Chapter 21 | Variable-centered Approaches | 345 |

REBEKAH FREED, JEFFREY A. GREENE, AND ROBERT D. PLUMLEY

| Chapter 22 | Person-centered Approaches to Explaining Students' Cognitive Processing Strategies | 361 |

LUKE K. FRYER AND ALEX SHUM

| Chapter 23 | Qualitative Approaches to the Verbal Protocol Analysis of Strategic Processing | 373 |

BYEONG-YOUNG CHO, LINDSAY WOODWARD, AND PETER AFFLERBACH

| Chapter 24 | Commentary: Analyzing Strategic Processing: Pros and Cons of Different Methods | 393 |

JENNIFER G. CROMLEY

| Chapter 25 | The Future of Strategy Theory, Research, and Implementation: Roads Less Traveled | 406 |

PATRICIA A. ALEXANDER

| Contributor bios | 425 |
| Index | 435 |

1

INTRODUCTION

What Are Strategies?

Daniel L. Dinsmore
UNIVERSITY OF NORTH FLORIDA, USA

Luke K. Fryer
UNIVERSITY OF HONG KONG, HONG KONG

Meghan M. Parkinson
UNIVERSITY OF NORTH FLORIDA, USA

INTRODUCTION: WHAT ARE STRATEGIES?

The purpose of this introductory chapter of the Handbook is two-fold. First, we as co-editors want to lay out the case for the importance of the Handbook. Second, we want this chapter to serve as a guide for the reader to more deeply understand the need for continuing high-quality research on strategies and strategy use.

WHY A HANDBOOK ON STRATEGIES AND STRATEGIC PROCESSING?

Research on strategies and strategic processing has been steadily expanding over the last few decades. This expansion includes increases in the numbers of studies that examine cognitive strategies (Dinsmore, 2017), levels of strategic processing (Asikainen & Gijbels, 2017; Dinsmore & Alexander, 2012), and strategies associated with self-regulation (Dinsmore, Alexander, & Loughlin, 2008; Schunk & Greene, 2017). As many of these cited sources have indicated, the proliferation of this research has far from clarified the relation between strategies, strategy use, and performance. In fact, the past few decades have been marked with numerous calls to clarify these relations in numerous contexts and settings (Block, 2009; Dinsmore & Fryer, 2018) that include higher education (Fryer & Gijbels, 2017).

2 • Daniel L. Dinsmore et al.

Two particular issues with regard to research on the influence of strategies and strategic processing on task and problem-solving performance have emerged that this Handbook is well positioned to address: how strategies and strategy use have been conceptually considered (across domains and contexts as well as levels of processing), and how they have been operationalized and analyzed. We will now turn to how this Handbook addresses each of these two challenging issues as well as additional contributions from the authors of these chapters.

CONCEPTUALIZATIONS OF STRATEGIES AND STRATEGY USE

The editorial decision to position the conceptualizations of strategies and strategy use early in this Handbook underscores the primacy of the issue of poor or misspecified conceptualizations of strategy use in the literature. First, numerous contributions in the first section of this Handbook – *Definitions, Forms, and Levels of Strategies* – explore conceptually and theoretically how strategies and strategic processing have been defined. Dumas (Chapter 2) explores the relations between strategies and their relations to the domains in which they are useful. He provides an overview of how the field has attempted to understand whether or not a strategy is domain general (i.e., useful across a wide number of domains) or domain specific (i.e., useful in one or a limited number of domains). Similarly, Dinsmore and Hattan (Chapter 3) explore how strategies have been stratified with regard to their purpose, or purported purpose – surface-level processing, deep-level processing, or metacognitive processing. Further, Rogiers, Merchie, De Smedt, De Backer, and Van Keer (Chapter 4) overview and offer a new framework to conceptualize strategy use over the lifespan. Finally, Butler and Schnellert (Chapter 5) explore the degree to which a strategy is an individual endeavor, or whether (and how) these strategies and utilization of these strategies may be socially shared across individuals performing a task or solving a problem. Research on strategies and strategic processing must be grounded in terms of how the learner is using them and what the learner is getting out of using them, which in our view is dictated by many factors, chief among them the development of many other cognitive and motivational factors.

Despite the fact that there is a section dedicated to conceptualizations of strategy use, we encourage the reader to consider this issue as they read the remaining three sections of the Handbook. In many cases, the theoretical frameworks from which these expert authors write color how strategies and strategic processing are conceptualized. For some, strategies are subsumed by or heavily influenced by self-regulation (e.g., Baars, Wijnia, de Bruin, & Pass, Chapter 14; Butler & Schnellert, Chapter 5; Winne, Chapter 15). While we as editors do not share this view that strategies should be subsumed in this way, the influence of self-regulation and self-regulated learning on the research regarding strategies and strategy use is undeniable. We strongly encourage readers – especially those new to the field – to keep in mind that the conceptual lines between metacognition, self-regulation, and self-regulated learning themselves have been conceptually muddy for quite some time (Dinsmore et al., 2008) and the role that strategies play within and beyond these three constructs has been even murkier. Additionally, we note that the distinction between *strategies* and *skills* is often blurred. This distinction is made in numerous chapters throughout (Afflerbach, Hurt, & Cho, Chapter 7; Alexander, Chapter 25; Dinsmore & Hattan, Chapter 3; Dumas,

Chapter 2) – an issue of great import since Alexander and Judy's (1988) review article. We hope the chapters in the first section provide the reader with a solid foundation to consider these two issues as they attempt to synthesize these chapters for themselves. Fortunately, the reader is further aided in this synthesis through Van Meter and Campbell's (Chapter 6) illuminating commentary. As we have attempted in this introduction as well, Van Meter and Campbell expertly lay out the case for why strategies should garner special consideration in the literature, in particular given the connections between strategies and problem-solving and task outcomes.

CONCEPTUALIZATIONS OF STRATEGIES IN THE CONTEXT OF INSTRUCTION

Many of the issues alluded to in the previous section may be dependent on the context in which strategies are employed. These issues refer to both the domain and social setting within which strategies and strategy use are considered. The second section – *Strategies in Action* – explores how domain or social setting may change the role of strategies within the broader framework of learning. Strategies and strategy use are considered in the five major academic domains – reading, writing, mathematics, science, and history.

First, Afflerbach et al. (Chapter 7) consider the nature of how strategies and strategic processing both influence the reading situation, as well as how optimal reading strategies can be instructed. Similarly, Graham et al. (Chapter 9) consider domain-specific strategies in writing and how these can be trained. Both of these chapters embed notions of strategy use and their training in contemporary models of reading comprehension (e.g., Kintsch, 2004) and writing (e.g., Graham & Harris, 2006). An important addition to the research on strategy use while reading and writing is undertaken by List (Chapter 8) in her exploration of strategies around multiple text use. The need to employ specific strategies to navigate multiple sources of information is becoming particularly salient with the explosion of information that is prevalent in the age of the Internet and social media. This is especially true as that multitude of information contains conflicting views that the reader must navigate.

Similar explorations of mathematics and science are undertaken by Newton (Chapter 10) and Lombardi and Bailey (Chapter 11) respectively. Given the incredibly broad depth of the field of mathematics, Newton focuses primarily on strategies used to solve algebraic problems and fraction problems – two critical gatekeepers for future mathematical inquiry. Although her chapter focuses on these two areas, we are confident the implications of the chapter could be applied to numerous other areas of mathematical inquiry (e.g., trigonometry) and hopefully give the reader a framework to explore these other areas on their own. Similar to mathematics, the broad range of strategies required across the numerous physical, life, and social science domains are difficult to manage in one chapter. Lombardi and Bailey handle this well by focusing on recent strategies that are common across these sometimes disparate fields – namely, argumentation, science as modeling, and the incorporation of socio-scientific topics to promote strategy use. In the current climate where science is under attack by certain political forces, this chapter provides clear direction with regard to helping the populace use these strategies to better advance science as well as our overall way of life.

4 • Daniel L. Dinsmore et al.

While the preceding domains have a richer history of strategies and strategy instruction, De La Paz and Nokes (Chapter 12) tackle strategies in the domain of history. These authors discuss the intertwined nature of historical inquiry with both the domains of reading and writing. However, as they astutely point out, historians must possess particular strategies that enable them to engage in historical thinking that reaches beyond just those who read and write text. For instance, being able to generate interpretations and knowledge claims are considered a central strategy for historians to have at their disposal.

Next in this section is a primer for understanding how learners' individual differences may influence their strategy use and ultimately their learning outcomes. Taboada Barber, Lutz Klauda, and Cartwright (Chapter 13) explore how language proficiency and atypical reading development (i.e., students with reading comprehension deficits) may influence strategy use. Their key argument is to examine these issues in relation to executive function (i.e., working memory, inhibition, and cognitive flexibility). While they situate this exploration primarily within the domain of reading, we believe this framework could be used equally well to explore strategy use and individual differences across multiple domains and contexts.

However, task completion and problem solving are not always so easily broken down into a single domain or context. Baars, Wijnia, de Bruin, and Pass (Chapter 14) discuss how working across individuals in social settings as well as across domain barriers can be best conceptualized and facilitated. Using an SRL framework, these authors provide the reader with strategies – at the cognitive, metacognitive, and self-regulatory levels – to cope with complex, dynamic problems.

Winne (Chapter 15) takes on the difficult task of trying to synthesize strategy use and training across these multitudes of domains, contexts, and individual differences. Winne provides a framework – situated within self-regulated learning – to tie together these otherwise disparate chapters. This insightful synthesis will no doubt go far in helping the reader construct for themselves a more global view of strategies and strategy use, whether or not that view is more heavily oriented toward SRL, as Winne would argue, or less so, as the editors here would argue for.

OPERATIONALIZATIONS AND ANALYSIS OF STRATEGIES AND STRATEGY USE

While the first two parts of the Handbook explore conceptual and contextual issues of strategies and strategy use, clarifying conceptions is far from the only issue in the contemporary strategies literature. As we hope this Handbook can help lead to some consensus on what strategies are, we are equally concerned with how strategies have been operationalized in the literature. This issue has encompassed both cognitive strategies themselves (e.g., Dinsmore, 2017) as well as metacognitive strategies (e.g., Veenman, Van Hout-Wolters, & Afflerbach, 2006).

The third section – *Measuring Strategic Processing* – begins with the most ubiquitous measurement of strategies and strategic processing (Asikainen & Gijbels, 2017; Dinsmore, 2017; Dinsmore et al., 2008). In this chapter Vermunt (Chapter 16) captures both the historical role of surveys and retrospective self-report as well as the fraught relationship researchers have had with these measures over the past few decades.

While critical of the shortcomings of self-report, Vermunt also offers suggestions for how retrospective self-report and surveys can continue to contribute to the literature. In addition to the arguments in the literature around retrospective self-report, concurrent self-reports have also endured some criticism as well. Bråten, Magliano, and Salmerón (Chapter 17) mirror Vermunt's concerns in discussing both the shortcomings of concurrent self-report, in addition to their future as viable measures of strategies and strategic processing going forward.

These more established measures are recently being challenged by two new paradigms: the emergence of Big Data and the use of physiological measurements of strategic processing. Lawless and Riel (Chapter 18) explore how Big Data is becoming more and more ubiquitous in examining strategies – primarily consumer strategies – in the corporate setting. Behemoth companies like Google employ complex algorithms to examine this strategic behavior (or lack thereof) across Internet search platforms as well as social media platforms. On the one hand, the amount of data is enticing; however, as Lawless and Riel point out, this avalanche of data and the secrecy with which the algorithms are used to examine this data are troubling. In addition to the arrival of Big Data on the scene, the use of physiological measures continues to increase year by year. Catrysse, Gijbels, and Donche (Chapter 19) overview two of these measurements – eye tracking and functional magnetic resonance imaging (fMRI). As with the Big Data chapter, they expose the reader to the promises of these new technologies to better understand strategies and strategic processing, while at the same time critically examining the gaps and difficulties these new approaches represent.

Gijbels and Loyens (Chapter 20) in their commentary weigh the pros and cons of these approaches and offer readers a way to think about designing experiments that leverage the strengths of these particular measurements to best answer their research questions. We certainly agree with Gijbels and Loyens that no one measurement will provide a panacea to investigating strategies and strategic processing. Rather, it will be necessary to smartly employ some combination of these techniques to better help learners become strategic.

The final section – *Analyzing Strategic Processing* – examines the multitude of ways that strategic processing has been examined. Of particular import here is that, similar to the measurement of strategic processing, the analysis or analyses has to first and foremost serve the purpose of the research questions as well as help us better build theories relevant to strategic processing. The Handbook offers three such chapters to help the reader ponder appropriate analytic strategies. The first of these, quantitative variable-centered approaches, are probably most familiar to our readers. Freed, Greene, and Plumley (Chapter 21) not only overview these familiar approaches but also help situate these approaches in the context of analyzing strategic processing, something that not every reader will necessarily have considered. The other quantitative approach – the person-centered approach – is discussed at length by Fryer and Shum (Chapter 22). They offer exciting new ways to analyze strategic processing that have been used primarily in the motivation literature thus far. Finally, with regard to analyses, Cho, Woodward, and Afflerbach (Chapter 23) offer approaches to qualitative examinations of strategic processing. Situated mostly in the context of strategic processing during reading, this chapter provides a framework for qualitative analysis that could certainly be applied in a multitude of contexts.

Of course, being able to select the appropriate analysis is most crucial to effectively analyzing strategic processing. While this is often a difficult endeavor, the reader is aided by Cromley's (Chapter 24) synthesis of these analytic approaches. She deftly describes the pros and cons of these approaches which will undoubtedly aid the reader in selecting an appropriate analysis or analyses.

THE FUTURE OF RESEARCH ON STRATEGIES AND STRATEGIC PROCESSING

While our hope is that this Handbook will help researchers in the field, both experienced and new, to understand the history of strategies in the literature as well as state-of-the-art conceptualizations and methods, we also hope these chapters and commentaries will inspire researchers to challenge existing paradigms, refine and possibly replace theoretical frameworks, and trailblaze new methods to uncover how strategies can help learners overcome challenges and solve the complex, dynamic problems that we face in the 21st century. To help readers synthesize across the four sections of the Handbook, Alexander (Chapter 25) has provided a unique and insightful overview of this history, contemporary research, and a vision for future research that can enable us to employ the vast knowledge that we possess about strategies and strategy use to help learners young and old alike.

This Handbook is a unique collaboration of contributions from researchers across a wide array of theoretical frameworks and disciplinary perspectives. We are indeed fortunate as editors that these authors have shared their wisdom and insights and we hope you agree that they have made this Handbook an informative and inspiring guide for the future.

REFERENCES

Afflerbach, P., Hurt, M., & Cho, B.-Y. (this volume). Reading comprehension strategy instruction. In D. L. Dinsmore, L. K. Fryer, & M. M. Parkinson (Eds.), *Handbook of strategies and strategic processing: Conceptualization, measurement, and analysis*. New York: Routledge.

Alexander, P. A. (this volume). The future of strategies and strategic processing. In D. L. Dinsmore, L. K. Fryer, & M. M. Parkinson (Eds.), *Handbook of strategies and strategic processing: Conceptualization, measurement, and analysis*. New York: Routledge.

Alexander, P. A., & Judy, J. E. (1988). The interaction of domain-specific and strategic knowledge in academic performance. *Review of Educational Research, 58*, 375–404.

Asikainen, H., & Gijbels, D. (2017). Do students develop towards more deep approaches to learning during studies? A systematic review on the development of students' deep and surface approaches to learning in higher education. *Educational Psychology Review, 29*, 205–234.

Baars, M., Wijnia, L., de Bruin, A., & Paas, F. (this volume). Sharing the load: A strategy to improve self-regulated learning. In D. L. Dinsmore, L. K. Fryer, & M. M. Parkinson (Eds.), *Handbook of strategies and strategic processing: Conceptualization, measurement, and analysis*. New York: Routledge.

Block, R. A. (2009). Intent to remember briefly presented human faces and other pictorial stimuli enhances recognition memory. *Memory & Cognition, 37*, 667–678.

Bråten, I., Magliano, J. P., & Salmerón, L. (this volume). Concurrent and task specific self-reports. In D. L. Dinsmore, L. K. Fryer, & M. M. Parkinson (Eds.), *Handbook of strategies and strategic processing: Conceptualization, measurement, and analysis*. New York: Routledge.

Butler, D. L., & Schnellert, L. (this volume). Negotiating meaning and engagement: Socially shared strategic processing. In D. L. Dinsmore, L. K. Fryer, & M. M. Parkinson (Eds.), *Handbook of strategies and strategic processing: Conceptualization, measurement, and analysis*. New York: Routledge.

Catrysse, L., Gijbels, D., & Donche, V. (this volume). Measuring levels of processing: Perspectives for eye tracking and fMRI in multi-method designs. In D. L. Dinsmore, L. K. Fryer, & M. M. Parkinson (Eds.), *Handbook of strategies and strategic processing: Conceptualization, measurement, and analysis*. New York: Routledge.

Cho, B.-Y., Woodward, L., & Afflerbach, P. (this volume). Qualitative approaches to the verbal protocol analysis of strategic processing. In D. L. Dinsmore, L. K. Fryer, & M. M. Parkinson (Eds.), *Handbook of strategies and strategic processing: Conceptualization, measurement, and analysis*. New York: Routledge.

Cromley, J. G. (this volume). Analyzing strategic processing: Pros and cons of different methods. In D. L. Dinsmore, L. K. Fryer, & M. M. Parkinson (Eds.), *Handbook of strategies and strategic processing: Conceptualization, measurement, and analysis*. New York: Routledge.

De La Paz, S., & Nokes, J. (this volume). Strategic processing in history and historical strategy instruction. In D. L. Dinsmore, L. K. Fryer, & M. M. Parkinson (Eds.), *Handbook of strategies and strategic processing: Conceptualization, measurement, and analysis*. New York: Routledge.

Dinsmore, D. L. (2017). Towards a dynamic, multidimensional model of strategic processing. *Educational Psychology Review, 29*, 235–268.

Dinsmore, D. L., & Alexander, P. A. (2012). A critical discussion of deep and surface processing: What it means, how it is measured, the role of context, and model specification. *Educational Psychology Review, 24*, 499–567.

Dinsmore, D. L., Alexander, P. A., & Loughlin, S. M. (2008). Focusing the conceptual lens on metacognition, self-regulation, and self-regulated learning. *Educational Psychology Review, 20*, 391–409.

Dinsmore, D. L., & Fryer, L. K. (2018). The intersection between depth and the regulation of strategy use. *British Journal of Educational Psychology, 88*, 1–8. doi: 10.1111/bjep.12209

Dinsmore, D. L., & Hattan, C. (this volume). Levels of strategies and strategic processing. In D. L. Dinsmore, L. K. Fryer, & M. M. Parkinson (Eds.), *Handbook of strategies and strategic processing: Conceptualization, measurement, and analysis*. New York: Routledge.

Dumas, D. (this volume). Strategic processing within and across domains of learning. In D. L. Dinsmore, L. K. Fryer, & M. M. Parkinson (Eds.), *Handbook of strategies and strategic processing: Conceptualization, measurement, and analysis*. New York: Routledge.

Freed, R., Greene, J. A., & Plumley, R. D. (this volume). Variable-centered approaches. In D. L. Dinsmore, L. K. Fryer, & M. M. Parkinson (Eds.), *Handbook of strategies and strategic processing: Conceptualization, measurement, and analysis*. New York: Routledge.

Fryer, L. K., & Gijbels, D. (2017). Student learning in higher education: Where we are and paths forward? *Educational Psychology Review, 29*, 199–203.

Fryer, L. K., & Shum, A. (this volume). Person-centered approaches to explaining students' cognitive processing strategies. In D. L. Dinsmore, L. K. Fryer, & M. M. Parkinson (Eds.), *Handbook of strategies and strategic processing: Conceptualization, measurement, and analysis*. New York: Routledge.

Gijbels, D., & Loyens, S. (this volume). Measuring strategic processing in concert: Reflections and future directions. In D. L. Dinsmore, L. K. Fryer, & M. M. Parkinson (Eds.), *Handbook of strategies and strategic processing: Conceptualization, measurement, and analysis*. New York: Routledge.

Graham, S., Bañales, G., Ahumada, S., Muñoz, P., Alvarez, P., & Harris, K. R. (this volume). Writing strategy interventions. In D. L. Dinsmore, L. K. Fryer, & M. M. Parkinson (Eds.), *Handbook of strategies and strategic processing: Conceptualization, measurement, and analysis*. New York: Routledge.

Graham, S., & Harris, K. R. (2006). Strategy instruction and the teaching of writing. In C. A. MacArthur, S. Graham, & J. Fitzgerald (Eds.), *Handbook of writing research* (pp. 187–207). New York: The Guilford Press.

Kintsch, W. (2004). The construction-integration model of text comprehension and its implications for instruction. In R. B. Ruddell & N. J. Unrau (Eds.), *Theoretical models and processes of reading* (pp. 1270–1328). Newark, DE: International Reading Association.

Lawless, K. A., & Riel, J. (this volume). Exploring the utilization of the big data revolution as a methodology for exploring learning strategy in educational environments. In D. L. Dinsmore, L. K. Fryer, & M. M. Parkinson (Eds.), *Handbook of strategies and strategic processing: Conceptualization, measurement, and analysis*. New York: Routledge.

List, A. (this volume). Six questions regarding strategy use when learning from multiple texts. In D. L. Dinsmore, L. K. Fryer, & M. M. Parkinson (Eds.), *Handbook of strategies and strategic processing: Conceptualization, measurement, and analysis*. New York: Routledge.

Lombardi, D., & Bailey, J. M. (this volume). Science strategy interventions. In D. L. Dinsmore, L. K. Fryer, & M. M. Parkinson (Eds.), *Handbook of strategies and strategic processing: Conceptualization, measurement, and analysis*. New York: Routledge.

Newton, K. (this volume). Mathematics strategy interventions. In D. L. Dinsmore, L. K. Fryer, & M. M. Parkinson (Eds.), *Handbook of strategies and strategic processing: Conceptualization, measurement, and analysis*. New York: Routledge.

Rogiers, A., Van Keer, H., DeBacker, L., Merchie, E., & De Smedt, F. (this volume). A lifespan developmental perspective on strategic processing. In D. L. Dinsmore, L. K. Fryer, & M. M. Parkinson (Eds.), *Handbook of strategies and strategic processing: Conceptualization, measurement, and analysis*. New York: Routledge.

Schunk, D. H., & Greene, J. A. (2017). *Handbook of self-regulation of learning and performance*. New York: Routledge.

Taboada Barber, A., Lutz Klauda, S., & Cartwright, K. B. (this volume). Interplay of strategic processes, executive functions, and autonomy support in students with individual differences. In D. L. Dinsmore, L. K. Fryer, & M. M. Parkinson (Eds.), *Handbook of strategies and strategic processing: Conceptualization, measurement, and analysis*. New York: Routledge.

Van Meter, P., & Campbell, J. M. (this volume). A conceptual framework for defining strategies and strategic processing. In D. L. Dinsmore, L. K. Fryer, & M. M. Parkinson (Eds.), *Handbook of strategies and strategic processing: Conceptualization, measurement, and analysis*. New York: Routledge.

Veenman, M. V., Van Hout-Wolters, B. H., & Afflerbach, P. (2006). Metacognition and learning: Conceptual and methodological considerations. *Metacognition and Learning, 1*, 3–14.

Vermunt, J. D. (this volume). Surveys and retrospective self-reports to measure strategies and strategic processing. In D. L. Dinsmore, L. K. Fryer, & M. M. Parkinson (Eds.), *Handbook of strategies and strategic processing: Conceptualization, measurement, and analysis*. New York: Routledge.

Winne, P. H. (this volume). An analysis of learning strategies in action. In D. L. Dinsmore, L. K. Fryer, & M. M. Parkinson (Eds.), *Handbook of strategies and strategic processing: Conceptualization, measurement, and analysis*. New York: Routledge.

Section I
Definitions, Forms, and Levels of Strategies

2

STRATEGIC PROCESSING WITHIN AND ACROSS DOMAINS OF LEARNING

Denis Dumas

UNIVERSITY OF DENVER, USA

INTRODUCTION

Educational psychologists observe various aspects of learning and education—whether it be large-scale educational data collected across many schools (e.g., Cameron, Grimm, Steele, Castro-Schilo, & Grissmer, 2015), or more finely grained data collected in a laboratory setting (e.g., Xie, Mayer, Wang, & Zhou, 2019)—and pose a fundamental question: *why do students differ so substantially in their academic outcomes?* (Alexander, 2018). Since the 1890s (James, 1890; Mayer, 2018), educational psychologists have identified and investigated many explanatory factors for the observed student variance in learning outcomes, including but not limited to: intelligence and other cognitive functions (Canivez, Watkins, Marley, Good, & James, 2017), motivation and goals (Linnenbrink-Garcia et al., 2018), self-regulatory abilities (Winne, 2018), and socio-emotional support and development (Wentzel, Muenks, McNeish, & Russell, 2018).

This body of educationally relevant psychological constructs can generally account for hundreds of published educational psychology research studies, but, beginning in the latter part of the 1980s (Alexander & Judy, 1988; Pressley, 1986), educational psychologists began to understand that none of these constructs is the most proximal influence on student performance in school. Instead, the actual procedures that students enact while learning—the specific cognitive actions that students engage in during the learning process—are a much more readily useful predictor of student learning outcomes than are student's pre-existing individual differences or abilities (Alexander, Graham, & Harris, 1998; Dinsmore, 2017). Here, these cognitive procedures are referred to as the *strategies* or *skills* that students employ in order to solve a problem, independently study from text, or regulate their academic activities.

After the identification of strategic or skillful processing as the most proximal influence on student achievement in schools, a number of further patterns emerged in educational psychology data that have complicated this picture. For instance, it had long been understood (e.g., Thorndike, 1913) that student variance existed not only inter-individually in educational outcomes but also intra-individually, meaning that an individual student may be more or less effective at problem solving, studying, or learning in a particular domain of knowledge (e.g., mathematics) than they are in another domain (e.g., reading). But, explaining these intra-individual differences in terms of procedural strategy differences within a student offered some conundrums. For example, some strategic processes used for learning (e.g., self-questioning; King, 1989) appeared to be effective at supporting educational outcomes across a variety of domains, while others were more specific to a single domain (e.g., counting-all in early mathematics; Baroody, 1987). As such, students who more readily use domain-general strategies, or cognitive procedures that are useful across a variety of domains of learning, may have stronger outcomes across a range of academic domains, while those who struggle to use domain-general strategies may have more pronounced intra-individual differences in their learning outcomes across domains because they rely more on strategic processes that are *domain-specific*, or are only useful in one particular domain of learning.

However, even for those strategies that have been identified as *domain-general*, some students are more capable of flexibly utilizing these general procedures across different learning contexts than are other students (Campione & Brown, 1984; Cushen & Wiley, 2018), limiting the degree to which domain-general strategic processes are actually transferred across domains of learning in real-world educational settings. For this reason, being capable of utilizing a strategic process that is theoretically domain-general (e.g., outlining) within one particular domain (e.g., history) does not necessarily mean that a student will be effective at using the exact same strategy within another domain (e.g., biology). This highly limited degree of *strategy transfer* across domains of learning has complicated the degree to which the true domain-generality or domain-specificity of any given cognitive procedure can be identified by researchers. The observed uncommonness of strategic transfer also creates instructional difficulties in that, in some cases, it remains unclear whether the teaching of strategies specific to a given domain or more general strategic procedures is a more effective instructional choice. This is because domain-general strategies may appear to be more widely effective for students to learn, but without the capability of identifying wider learning contexts in which that strategy is useful, students may never actually transfer the strategy across domains. If this occurs more often than not, it may be more prudent for educators to focus on domain-specific strategies with the pre-supposition that strategy transfer will not occur anyway. In this chapter, issues such as this, that center on the degree to which cognitive procedures used for learning and problem solving can be considered transferable across domains of learning (i.e., domain-general), are reviewed and discussed.

CONCEPTUALIZING STRATEGIES IN EDUCATIONAL RESEARCH

The question of whether a given strategy can be considered domain-general or specific relies in critical ways on the definition and conceptualization of strategies themselves. Here, strategies are defined as goal-directed procedures that are planfully and effortfully used to aid in the regulation, execution, or evaluation of a particular problem or task (Alexander & Judy, 1988). In this way, strategies can be useful either within a single domain of learning or across many domains, but all strategies are essentially a special form of procedural knowledge in which a student knows how to enact a given process that improves their capability in problem solving or learning. For example, the study strategy of creating a concept map in order to organize and relate information is, in itself, a form of knowledge because a student has to know what a concept map is and how to create one effectively. But, the procedural knowledge of how to create a concept map can be identified as strategic because such procedural knowledge improves a student's development of the particular academic knowledge (e.g., the civil rights movement within the domain of history) that they are studying when the concept map is used. Of course, a concept map may also be hypothetically helpful when the same student is studying a different topic in a different domain (e.g., taxonomic categories in biology), but there is no guarantee that the same individual student will be capable of evoking the concept map strategy equally effectively across domains.

As stated above, a key component to the definition of strategies is that the procedures enacted by students are done so purposefully, effortfully, and consciously. In contrast, if a strategy is utilized by an individual student enough times that it becomes an automatic habit of mind, it is no longer utilized effortfully and therefore is not referred to as a strategy. Instead, an automated form of procedural knowledge that students may utilize to improve their learning or performance within and across academic settings is referred to as a skill (Afflerbach, Pearson, & Paris, 2008; Alexander et al., 1998). Using this terminology, skills and strategies are often referred to together within the literature (e.g., Vettori, Vezzani, Bigozzi, & Pinto, 2018) because direct instruction of these procedures must begin with the assumption that students will use strategies effortfully before progressing to more automated and rapid utilization of skills. In some areas of educational research that focus on domains or disciplines in which very rapid problem solving is highly valued and a typical instructional goal, e.g., medical education research, Dumas, Torre and Durning's (2018) strategies and skills may be referred to synonymously with the understanding that the fast and automatic deployment of cognitive procedures is the best or only way to utilize particular strategies in the real-world setting, e.g., triaging patients based on visible symptoms. In contrast, educational research that focuses on domains of learning or populations of students in which a slower, more effortful processing typically results in better student outcomes (e.g., multiple-source use; De La Paz & Felton, 2010), shows that the careful theoretical division of strategies and skills is more common within the literature.

One way in which the distinction between strategies and skills complicates the question of domain-generality that is the central focus of this chapter is that, within the same student, certain forms of procedural knowledge may be more or less effortful (i.e., strategic) or automated (i.e., skillful) across domains. In this way, even though a student is capable of using their procedural knowledge to learn more effectively across domains, the actual enactment of that procedural knowledge may appear very different and make domain-general strategic processing difficult to identify. For example, if a student has ample experience in reading informational or persuasive text, they are likely to be familiar with the strategy of questioning the author to improve their comprehension of the text. In fact, they may be so practiced at questioning the author that they do so automatically and rapidly (i.e., skillfully) when reading. However, if the same student visited the more unfamiliar context of an art museum and found themselves tasked with "reading" visual art (i.e., painting or sculpture), they may either not understand that the strategy of questioning the artist was useful, or they may transfer the procedural knowledge effectively, but do so in a slow, effortful (i.e., strategic) way. In this way, the procedure of questioning the author/artist would be a domain-general process, but the enactment of that procedure may appear so different in its pacing and effortfulness that an instructor who worked with the student across domains may not recognize the process as the same.

Such a scenario highlights a fundamental aspect of strategies in that they are something that students *do*. This specifically procedural aspect of strategies and skills separates this area of research from the majority of areas within psychology that focus on mental constructs that individuals *have*. In the educational psychology literature, it is not difficult to identify a number of research foci that are specifically defined as something that students have, or are working to develop, within their minds. For example, creativity is one construct that has historically concerned educational psychologists (Dumas, 2018; Torrance, 1972) and that is typically defined as something that students have in varying amounts and the development of which is supported to varying degrees by particular instruction. However, such a conceptualization of creativity, however interesting and relevant to education, cannot directly describe what students specifically do, in terms of cognitive processes, in order to produce more creative ideas. For that, a much more specific line of research inquiry on strategies for creativity would be needed. This foundational "have vs. do" issue in strategy research is highly relevant to the measurement of strategies (Liu, 2014), because the observation of a cognitive process that students do is much more difficult and specific an undertaking than the quantitative estimation of a cognitive ability that students have. This measurement-related issue will arise again within this chapter during the discussion of the operationalization of domain-generality and specificity, because psychometric procedures designed for the measurement of constructs that students have (e.g., factor analysis) make different predictions about the domain-generality of skills and strategies than does a more specific process-oriented approach. However, before this operationalization problem can be discussed, the meaning of a domain of learning in contrast to other defined areas such as discipline or task must be explained.

AREAS OF LEARNING: DISCIPLINES, DOMAINS, AND TASKS

In educational psychology, the work of the researcher is highly influenced by the general area of learning that is under investigation. For example, research about mathematical education would likely utilize completely different participants, measures, methods, and even theoretical frameworks than research on musical education. For this reason, the careful definition of the area of learning being studied is of critical importance in the literature, especially when questions of the generality or specifically of knowledge are being asked. Here, I review three ways to define an area of learning—by discipline, domain, or task—and highlight the ways in which those definitions may influence the way strategies and skills are understood in the research literature. While these terms are often used synonymously, I will attempt to show how a muddling of these definitions can result in incorrect inferences about the domain-generality of strategic processes.

Based on the root-word *disciple*, a *discipline* is an intellectual lineage or group of people who work in the same area, communicate knowledge to one another, and practice many of the same procedural skills in their work (e.g., Stoecker, 1993). In this way, not only are the forms of procedural knowledge (e.g., strategies and skills) held by a group part-and-parcel of their disciplinary definition, the conceptualization of a discipline as being fundamentally composed of *people* explains how all those individuals developed the same knowledge and practices in the first place: they learned them from their intellectual mentors or shared them with one another. So, a given individual can have an *interdisciplinary* background if they were trained in multiple disciplinary communities, or a given team can be interdisciplinary if members of that team are drawn from differing disciplinary communities.

Given this definition, I would contend that a focus within educational research on differing disciplinary practices lends itself most readily to a more socio-cultural theoretical understanding of learning, in which the communities that work together hold procedural knowledge and the teaching of students constitutes a socialization into a disciplinary community. For example, some researchers who use social network models to study scientists (e.g., Bozdogan & Akbilgic, 2013) take a disciplinary focus in that person-to-person collaborative connections define the borders of the disciplines, and those individuals who learned from the same mentor are assumed to have many attributes in common, especially procedural knowledge. In this way, it is possible for a strategy or skill to be discipline-specific not because it is only theoretically useful to a single group of people, but because it has not been communicated effectively or adopted across disciplinary lines for socio-cultural reasons. For example, the procedural strategy of using machine-learning models to understand open-ended textual data is commonly used within the discipline of the information sciences (Fan, Wallace, Rich, & Zhang, 2006), while it is almost never used in educational psychology. This is not because educational psychologists have no need to understand open-ended text-based data sources, but because machine-learning models have not historically been a part of our disciplinary training. As this example implies, a research focus on disciplinary differences or similarities can be difficult in educational psychology because the school-aged students who are often the focus of our research cannot really be described as members of a particular discipline in the way that those further along the path to expertise can be.

In contrast to a discipline, a domain is an area of *knowledge* that can be studied or taught and therefore developed or constructed through the learning process within an individual (e.g., Greene et al., 2015). So, while a discipline is a unit of intellectual community members, a domain is a unit used to designate the knowledge itself that was created within that discipline, or that is commonly utilized within that discipline, and that individuals operating within that discipline may be likely to hold. What this implies is that, while disciplines and domains are similar enough to potentially have the exact same name (e.g., terms like psychology or mathematics may be simultaneously disciplines or domains), the boundaries of each are based on different criteria. For example, within the discipline of educational psychology—which is defined by our shared intellectual heritage, our communication outlets, and inter-personal collaborations—many of our community members hold and utilize the same declarative and procedural knowledge that supports us as we do our work (i.e., knowledge within the domain of educational psychology). However, many educational psychologists also possess knowledge that is rooted and commonly utilized within a different domain (e.g., statistics). Therefore, we may say that the declarative and procedural knowledge that constitutes the domain of educational psychology overlaps in important ways with other domains of learning. This overlapping knowledge that is useful across multiple domains of learning can be identified as domain-general. If that knowledge that we draw upon is procedural and effortfully evoked, then that knowledge can be defined as strategic, and if a particular strategy is useful for the creation or dissemination of knowledge across multiple domains, it may be described as a domain-general strategy. So, a particular strategy (e.g., using a correlation matrix to understand the relations among variables) may be used to develop or transmit knowledge across a variety of domains (e.g., psychology, sociology, economics), marking it as a domain-general strategy. In this way, it can be seen that experts in a given domain evoke domain-general strategies in their day-to-day work.

One other important note concerning the distinction between disciplines and domains is that, when teaching occurs in schools, especially to younger or less expert students, the knowledge being taught is often separated from the disciplinary community in which it arose. Therefore, the development of domain knowledge, rather than disciplinary acculturation, is often more relevant to educational psychology research with school-aged students (e.g., Bong, 2005). For example, a middle-school student learning about photosynthesis cannot be described as truly joining the discipline of botanists, but instead can be described as learning domain-knowledge in botany. So, if a given cognitive procedure (e.g., note-taking) is effective at improving that student's learning about photosynthesis and is also effective at improving their learning in another domain (e.g., history), then that strategy is effective across domains, and is therefore domain-general. For this reason, that domains of knowledge are often more pertinent to educational psychology research questions than are disciplines of practice, the main focus of most extant research on learning strategies (Alexander, Murphy, Woods, Duhon, & Parker, 1997), as well as the focus of this chapter, is on domains, not disciplines.

Another, more fine-grained way to define an area of learning is through the specific *task* being accomplished by a student, rather than the discipline being participated in or the domain being learned. For example, an elementary-school student may be studying within the domain of geography, but the specific task on which they are working may be labeling a map of the United States with the names of the states and their capitals. Another task that this same student may work on within the same domain of geography may be identifying and defining different types of landforms (e.g., volcano, mesa, peninsula, etc.). Clearly, there would be some strategies that can be effectively used to improve this student's performance on both of these tasks. For example, connecting the new geographic information to their prior knowledge about North America may aid this student in learning related to both tasks, and self-testing may help them evaluate their learning across both tasks. In this way, both of these strategies are clearly generalizable across tasks within the domain of geography. If these strategies were to be helpful in the completion of tasks that arise in a different domain (which they hypothetically would be), they would be domain-general.

In contrast, some well-known strategies are highly specific to a single type of task within a particular domain of learning. For example, the commonly taught First-Outer-Inner-Last (FOIL) strategy for multiplying binomials is a task-specific, and therefore also domain-specific, strategy. Another mnemonic, the Every-Good-Boy-Does-Fine strategy for remembering the notes on a music staff is specific to a single type of task within the domain of music. Such strategies are examples of a more general type (i.e., the mnemonic), but their specific formulation makes them highly task-specific in their usefulness. Despite the very specific nature of these strategies, they are still commonly taught because they allow even novice students to quickly accomplish core tasks within a particular domain, and the successful automatization of such a strategy (i.e., becoming skillful) allows for more advanced learning in the domain. For example, although the Every-Good-Boy-Does-Fine strategy is a time-consuming and task-specific procedure, it may lead to the development of a skillful ability to read a music staff automatically, which in turn allows for further learning of music theory.

Because a strategy is defined as a form of procedural knowledge effortfully evoked for the accomplishment of a particular goal, I would contend that, in their actual real-time enactment, all strategic instances are necessarily task-specific. Students employ strategies to improve their performance on the task at hand, and therefore the specific procedural knowledge evoked must be effective and useful for a particular task in order to be considered strategic. Then, if that task bears enough similarity to other tasks across the domain of the learning, a particular strategy becomes task-general, but may remain domain-specific. Only if the tasks required across domains have enough structural features in common will a particular strategy be effective across those domains and rise to the level of domain-generality. For example, because both the domains of biology and history feature large amounts of novel information that students are expected to memorize and integrate, the tasks students must accomplish across these two domains of learning within schools are at times highly similar. For this reason, the strategy of *outlining* is useful when learning across the domains of biology and history, marking it as a domain-general learning strategy.

Going forward, these definitions of discipline, domain, and task will be used to carefully delineate findings related to the generality and specificity of particular cognitive procedures used for learning and problem solving. In the following section, I turn to a further question: what evidence do researchers use to determine whether a particular strategy is domain-general or domain-specific, and how do those methodological differences influence the conclusions drawn about the generality of particular strategies?

OPERATIONALIZATION OF GENERALITY AND SPECIFICITY

Within the existing research on domain-general and domain-specific strategic processing, an initial operational divide exists between those who identify particular strategic processes as domain-general mainly theoretically based on a conceptualized usefulness of a given strategy across domains (e.g., Niaz, 1994), and those that rely on data (possibly published across multiple studies) to determine if a particular strategy is actually domain-general in its usefulness (e.g., Dinsmore, 2017). One reason why this pattern may be problematic for this area of research is because some sets of strategies can be described as domain general (e.g., help-seeking strategies) because, theoretically, such a type of strategy can easily be conceptualized as useful across a number of tasks and domains of learning. However, in the actual enactment of a strategy such as help-seeking across domains, tasks, learning contexts, or developmental periods, such a strategy may appear very divergently. For this reason, theorizing about the domain- or task-generality of particular strategic processes can sometimes rest upon implicit semantic and ontological categories within the mind of the researcher, making theoretical debates about domain-generality or specificity of a given strategy difficult to resolve (hypertext reading strategies is one recent example of this; Alexander, Grossnickle, Dumas, & Hattan, 2018; Leu et al., 2008).

Help-seeking strategies, and their various specific enactments across contexts, can form a useful illustration of the way in which theorizing about the domain-generality of strategic processes can depend on the ontological categorization of those processes. For example, a young child learning to draw with colored pencils may evoke a highly emotionally charged help-seeking strategy (e.g., crying) while a graduate student learning to do statistical analysis may employ a very different help-seeking strategy, such as reading statistical message boards on the Internet. Are these two very different sets of behaviors both instances of the same strategic process? Because strategies have historically been defined as *goal-oriented* and effortfully used procedural knowledge (Alexander & Judy, 1988), and therefore must be in service of accomplishing a goal, the goal itself (e.g., getting help) may not be the most useful way to define or identify the strategy. Rather, it may be more helpful to theoretically separate a student's goal in enacting a strategy from the strategy itself, as some in the literature have previously done (e.g., Fryer, Ginns, & Walker, 2014). This is because, many human goals are necessarily salient across domains of learning, and a variety of different strategic processes may be useful in achieving those goals (Ames & Archer, 1988). This conceptual issue is relevant to the main focus of this chapter, because the goal of a strategy may be inherently domain-general, but the particular process that an individual student uses to achieve that goal (i.e., the strategy) can be domain-specific in its enactment.

Complicating matters further, it is of course always possible for a student to *attempt* a particular strategy on a task or within a domain or discipline in which it is not appropriate. But does the presence of an attempt indicate the strategy is domain-general? I would argue that some commonly expected effectiveness should be required to mark a particular strategy as domain-general, rather than simply an attempt. To return to the help-seeking example above, the young-child that resorted to crying as a help-seeking strategy while learning to draw with colored pencils may find the same strategy is not effective on another task or within another domain (e.g., learning to play a video game), because care-givers or instructors may respond differently across those contexts. The difference in effectiveness of this particular help-seeking strategy may be even more stark across developmental periods as the child grows up. As a somewhat frivolous example, crying is not likely to be a highly effective help-seeking strategy in graduate level statistics courses, but other forms of help-seeking such as sending an email to an instructor may be effective. In all of these cases, the goal of the procedure is the same (i.e., help-seeking), but the actual process engaged in by the learner is very different both in its enactment and in its effectiveness (Reeves & Sperling, 2015).

The issue of disentangling the strategic process from its goal is related to the further methodological problem of meaningfully connecting the observed behaviors of participants to their underlying cognitive mechanisms or latent structure. For instance, one of the most frequently utilized methods for making inferences about underlying mental attributes from observed data is through latent variable analyses such as factor analysis or item-response theory models (e.g., Dumas & Alexander, 2016). Such models relate to the study of domain-generality and specificity, because they are capable of using the covariance among observed variables to determine whether an observed variable (e.g., an item on a measure) indicates a highly specific latent attribute or a latent attribute that is more generalizable. The well-known and influential theory of general intelligence (g; Spearman, 1904) is one theoretical perspective that posits a body of entirely domain-general cognitive abilities that is based mainly on evidence from factor analytic investigations. In contrast, other theories about the structure of mental attributes include more domain-specific cognitive attributes (e.g., Carroll, 1993), and also base their arguments on factor analytic evidence. Within this factor analytic tradition, the way in which student performance on particular tasks covaries is used to make inferences about the generality of underlying abilities. For example, if student performance on a number of tasks or measures covaries strongly and in a positive direction, an inference can be made that a generalizable underlying latent attribute causes the variation in performance on each task. In contrast, if performance on a number of tasks covaries weakly, the opposite inference—that multiple highly specific latent attributes are present—can be made.

However, one major weakness in linking latent variable research to research on strategic processing is that the actual cognitive processes required for the successful completion of the type of tasks or tests that are conducive to psychometric analysis are seldom known authoritatively enough to infer that the procedural knowledge being measured is actually domain-general or if some other capacity such as processing-speed (Habeck et al., 2015) is driving the covariance. In addition, almost any cognitive task over a certain level of complexity can be solved in multiple ways and using varying strategic processes, so the covariance structure of performance data that is typically used in factor analytic research can rarely point directly to specifically identified strategic processes. In this way, latent variable methods are highly useful for identifying the domain-generality of *abilities*—that consist of both declarative and procedural knowledge evoked in both quantitative and qualitatively different ways across students—but struggle to provide strong evidence for the domain-generality of strategic processes themselves. Please see Greene and colleagues' contribution to this Handbook for a full discussion of variable-centered methodological approaches to strategic processing research.

In contrast to methods that use the covariance among task performance to infer the generality of cognitive functions, other programs of research that have been relevant to the domain-generality and specificity of cognitive strategies have used a process-oriented methodological and measurement approach. In such an approach, the actual processes that participants enact while problem solving are the focus of research. For example, studies in this tradition may utilize think-aloud (Anmarkrud, Bråten, & Strømsø, 2014) or eye-tracking (Catrysse et al., 2018) methods in order to identify not only whether or how well students are able to complete a task but also how they go about it procedurally. Using data such as these, researchers are able to determine whether or not a particular strategy is useful to students across multiple learning tasks, domains of learning, or even across multiple disciplines of practice. For example, if researchers observe students engaging in the same or very similar strategic procedures (e.g., summarizing text) both when they are learning biology and when they are learning psychology, that may indicate that such a strategy is domain-general because it is used across domains.

Of course, the same strategy may be differentially effective across domains and may constitute a highly adaptive or optimal strategy in one domain while it is a relatively weak strategic option in another domain. For example, visualizing may be a highly useful strategy in such domains as chemistry or geometry, but only a somewhat useful strategy within domains such as history. Nonetheless, students may engage in the visualization strategy across both domains, marking it as a domain-general strategy. Such a pattern illustrates a critical point for the direct instruction of strategic processes to students. While an instructor may teach domain-general strategic processes and describe them as such to students, it is likely also critical to carefully explain the particular tasks or learning contexts within those domains for which the strategy may be most appropriate. One example of a strategy that may be over-used, at least by undergraduate students, is highlighting (Cerdán & Vidal-Abarca, 2008). As a support for organizing and remembering what is read, highlighting appears useful across many different types of texts and reading situated in a variety of domains. But, more detailed research has shown that highlighting typically supports only surface-level cognitive processing and can be much more or less effective depending on the elements of the text being read and highlighted (e.g., whether or not the text features technical diagrams; Cromley, Snyder-Hogan, & Luciw-Dubas, 2010). For that reason, a strategy like highlighting may be domain-general, but its effectiveness for learning across domains is far from definite.

In addition, the identification and operationalization of the domain-generality of a given strategy is complicated by the question of whether or not domain-generality presupposes that the same strategy is useful across domains by the same individual student, or whether domain-generality can mean only that the strategy is useful across domains, but not by the same student. This question deals specifically with the relations among strategies and the way ability or performance in a given domain is typically measured, as well as the question of transfer of procedural knowledge across tasks and domains.

GENERALITY AND SPECIFICITY WITHIN AND ACROSS INDIVIDUAL STUDENTS

The focus of this chapter is on the enactment of strategic processes both within and across domains of learning, wherein a strategy that is utilized across multiple domains can be described as domain-general, but a strategy that is only utilized within a single domain can be described as domain-specific. However, such a designation begs a follow-up question: are domain-general strategies utilized across domains *by the same individual student* or are they merely utilized across domains, but by different individual learners? Further, are there individual differences across students in the readiness with which they transfer strategic knowledge to new tasks or domains?

As an example of this general query, take a strategic process that is typically considered to be domain-general, such as connecting to prior knowledge. Theoretically, such a strategy must be considered domain-general because it is easy to imagine that, regardless of the academic situation, new information being presented to a student may be related in some meaningful way to something that the student already knows. Indeed, researchers who have studied students learning across a variety of domains (e.g., Afflerbach, 1990) have observed that connections to prior knowledge can and do arise across domains. However, it is also relevant to consider that, within the same student, certain domains of learning may appear more salient or relevant to their past experiences for a variety of socio-emotional or identity-based reasons (e.g., Hartwell & Kaplan, 2018). Students may be differentially cognitively effective at mapping new information onto their prior knowledge across domains where the relations between prior knowledge and current instruction are not made explicit (Richland & McDonough, 2010), or they may simply possess differential amounts of prior knowledge across domains, limiting the possibility of them connecting new information to that prior knowledge. Therefore, even a highly domain-general strategy such as connecting to prior knowledge can be variant in its generalizability as to its actual usage within a particular student.

This issue is closely related to the question of transfer within the educational and cognitive psychology research area (Marcus, Haden, & Uttal, 2018). In the 2010s, a relatively large quantity of research was published in which researchers attempted to train participants on cognitive functions that are theoretically very domain-general such as working memory (see Melby-Lervag & Hulme, 2013 for a meta-analysis). Of course, the data showed that continued engagement with such cognitive training did substantially improve participants' performance on the tasks or games on which the participants were practicing (Jaeggi, Buschkuehl, Jonides, & Perrig, 2008). Unfortunately, another resounding finding from this area of research was that the gains in ability that participants displayed were limited to the task on which they practiced, or very similar tasks (Sprenger et al., 2013). So, despite the cognitive training taking place on a task that was designed to measure an entirely domain-general ability, learning gains on that ability did not actually influence domain-learning in the way that was hypothesized. So, does that mean that the abilities trained were indeed domain-general or not?

One possible explanation for this effect that is relevant to the topic of this Handbook is that, in order to improve on cognitive training tasks, participants refined their task-specific strategies. These task-specific strategies may have allowed them to improve their performance on those particular tasks but did not allow for general gains on other tasks that were more nested within typical academic domains. Such a hypothesis highlights an interesting paradox concerning the tasks that are often used by psychologists to measure domain-general cognitive abilities (e.g., visuo-spatial reasoning tasks; Dumas & Alexander, 2016). While these tasks are not nested within a particular academic area and are therefore not highly influenced by prior domain-knowledge, they themselves constitute a sort of domain made up of similar tasks. For this reason, some have suggested that the quantification of general capacities should also be undertaken by examining the higher-order patterns among domain-specific measures, as opposed to only abstract tasks (Dumas & McNeish, 2017).

Within educational research on cognitive strategies, this problem is especially salient because, when we make practical recommendations to teachers, we must contend with the possibility that, although a particular cognitive strategy strongly supported student learning in our data, that strategy may not suffice to improve student performance across the range of tasks that students actually encounter in school and in life. For example, relational reasoning strategies are one body of cognitive procedures that have been empirically connected to student learning outcomes across a wide gamut of academic contexts ranging from elementary reading (Farrington-Flint, Wood, Canobi, & Faulkner, 2004) to medical residency (Dumas, Alexander, Jablansky, Baker, & Dunbar, 2014), and many instances in between. However, it is not yet known whether the fact that we can observe students engaging in relational reasoning across those learning contexts means that relational reasoning instruction, if abstracted from domain-specific academic material, would be effective at improving student performance across many domains (Dumas, Alexander, & Grossnickle, 2013). Although future work is necessary to address this research question, I would hypothesize that domain-general relational reasoning instruction would not necessarily improve student performance across all of the domains in which relational reasoning is known to play a role. Instead, it may be that, over the course of domain-learning, students must develop sophisticated strategies for identifying patterns within the information they interact with (i.e., relational reasoning strategies), and that is why the strategies appear so relevant across domains. In this way, a strategy that appears domain-general may actually have developed within a specific domain for a particular student. This issue is related to a further theoretical area that is relevant to the domain-generality of strategies and skills: the way in which the development of expertise influences learners' ability to apply strategies across (as opposed to within) domains.

DOMAIN-GENERALITY AND EXPERTISE DEVELOPMENT

It has been known for decades that experts in a particular domain of learning are more strategic in their thinking within that domain than are novices (see Dinsmore, Hattan, & List, 2018 for a meta-analysis). In addition, as already described, the strategic learning gains made by students who are on the path to expertise are hard-pressed to transfer across domains (Sprenger et al., 2013). However, one aspect of this issue that is less well understood is if, as individuals progress towards expertise, they become more capable of abstracting their developing domain- and task-strategies, or if the inverse is true: that the process of expertise development implies the deepening of strategic processing but does not significantly influence an individual's capacity to apply those strategies across domains.

To use an analogy to explain this point, in their theoretical article on the question of "What is learning anyway?", Alexander, Schallert, and Reynolds (2009) analogically likened the learning process to the process of topographical erosion from a river. In this analogy, learning experiences shape the mind of the learner much as the river erodes a landscape. Using this analogy, it is easy to imagine how certain experiences can have a deep and lasting effect on a student, much as a flood has a deep and lasting effect on a landscape, while other experiences have little effect. Further, it is also clear that certain individual differences within students make them more resistant or sensitive to learning from the environment, much as certain materials (e.g., rocks) are more resistant to influence from the river, while other materials (e.g., mud or sand) are more easily eroded. So, using this analogy, we can ask if the erosion-like process of expertise development must result in a steep domain-specific canyon, or conversely, if a wide domain-general flood-plain is also a possibility. For an individual learner whose knowledge was generalizable so as to analogically resemble a floodplain, would they be recognized as an expert within a particular domain of knowledge, or perhaps more importantly, as an expert participant within a discipline?

One commonly cited proposition that is relevant here comes from the very early days of research on the domain-generality of cognitive skills and abilities. Spearman's law of diminishing returns states that, as expertise develops within a specific domain, the domain-general strategies and skills that supported their earlier thinking and learning (such as those that are applicable to traditional intelligence tests) become less and less relevant. This supposition has been supported by empirical findings many times since (see Blum & Holling, 2017 for a meta-analysis). To incorporate this tenet into Alexander and colleague's erosion analogy, the development of expertise would be likened to the creation of a deep canyon. When a deep canyon is present on the landscape, new environmental forces such as rain are highly likely to be channeled through that canyon, focusing the erosion in one specific area. Following the analogy, if the learning process has created expertise within a particular domain, stimuli from the environment are highly likely to be interpreted in light of that expertise and be processed using strategies and skills that arise within that domain-specific learning. Using this line of theoretical reasoning, I would hypothesize that experts in a particular domain may not be any more likely than more novice students to transfer strategies and skills across domains. One likely exception to this pattern may lie with strategies that are specific to the domains of reading and writing, because they have high relevance across many domains and within nearly any discipline of expert practice (Graham, Harris, Kiuhara, & Fishman, 2017; McNamara, 2012).

FUTURE DIRECTIONS AND CONCLUDING THOUGHTS

Strategies and skills, as forms of procedural knowledge, are the actual processes that students do in order to improve their learning or achievement in school (Dinsmore, 2017). As has been discussed over the course of this chapter, there are a number of caveats that complicate the way that students evoke their procedural knowledge within and across domains learning. For example, procedures can be effortfully utilized (i.e., strategies) or automatized (i.e., skills) and that level of automaticity can vary within a student across domains, even for the same strategy. In addition, even though the same strategy can be identified as useful to students learning one domain as well as different students learning another domain, it may also be that a single student who is capable of successfully applying a strategy in one domain will not be capable of doing so in another domain. Further, the same student, as they develop expertise in a particular domain, may be more or less capable of transferring their strategic processes across domains, or if they do transfer, those strategies may be differentially effective for that learner across those domains. The type of learning context (e.g., task, domain, or discipline) also determines the specificity or generality of strategies wherein some task-specific strategies, if that task arises across domains, may be considered domain-general, and some strategies that can be useful across domains can be enacted very differently across disciplines, leading to a disciplinarily distinct strategic process.

Although the number and complexity of these caveats, and the others discussed in more detail earlier in this chapter, appear to undermine the systematic and empirical study of strategic processes, I would argue that, instead, they point to the richness of this research area and the possible fruitfulness of future inquiries into strategy use. Indeed, any psychological and educational study that goes beyond the quantification of performance or the measurement of ability to a finer grained look at what students actually do when they are thinking and learning, can meaningfully add to the current knowledge about the domain-generality and specificity of strategic processes. For example, it seems apparent that there is a continued need for a longitudinal perspective on strategy and skill development, not just in theorizing but also in empiricism. Most longitudinal work in psychology measures performance on tasks designed to indicate a construct that students have and develop (see Fryer & Vermunt, 2018 for an exception), but the actual procedural shifts students make in order to improve their performance on such tasks may be more interesting and relevant to education than is task performance. One longitudinal perspective that has begun to address this concern is called Dynamic Measurement Modeling (McNeish & Dumas, 2017), and this area of research shows the process for determining the generality of learning strategies, but definitive studies remain in the future.

In addition to a longitudinal or time-series perspective on strategy use, the inclusion of biometric data such as eye-tracking, skin connectivity, or neurological blood flow into studies of strategic processing also appears to be necessary and interesting. When incorporated with cognitive or behavioral data, such biometric markers may aid the field in determining how students evoke strategies when they are engaged in learning. For example, some recent attempts to combine strategic processing codes from think-aloud data, eye-tracking indicators, as well as academic performance, have been able to make novel inferences about reading strategies (Catrysse et al., 2018). In my view, this multi-faceted measurement approach will be particularly useful going forward in this line of inquiry.

For psychologists that study education, a focus on student performance or abilities across domains of learning is not sufficient to determine how students actually engage with tasks to enact their performance. Perhaps even more importantly, a focus on performance and ability does not provide the needed information to determine how instruction can be designed to improve learning outcomes because, without knowing the cognitive procedures by which students improve their performance, we cannot instruct students at the fine-grain procedural level. For this reason, research on strategic processing is absolutely necessary in educational psychology. However, even a sequence of well-designed studies of strategic processing within a single domain of learning cannot determine whether or how strategic knowledge in one domain can transfer to another, or even more so, whether direct instruction on strategies that are designed to be domain-general will actually improve student performance across a variety of domains. For this, targeted work focused on the domain-generality or domain-specificity of strategic processes is necessary.

Throughout the history of educational psychology as a discipline, researchers have sought to identify attributes of learners that would improve their learning and performance not only in one domain of learning but across the gamut of their academic activities (Alexander, 2018). The promise of such domain-general capacities has, in short, been that if students can improve on a domain-general ability, their performance will subsequently increase across multiple domains of learning. However, a finer-grained research approach into the actual cognitive procedures (i.e., strategies and skills) that students enact while thinking and learning has challenged this belief. For example, we now know that even procedures that appear highly generalizable do not readily transfer across domains (Sprenger et al., 2013). For this reason, the research area concerning strategic processing within and across domains, individual students, and expertise development stages currently holds many open questions. But it also remains clear that the evidence-based answers to these educationally relevant questions may be the only way to provide clear and actionable instructional recommendations to practitioners about strategy instruction. Therefore, research attention to the domain-generality and domain-specificity of strategic processes must continue in service of a central disciplinary goal of educational psychology: to support the learning of all students.

REFERENCES

Afflerbach, P., Pearson, P. D., & Paris, S. G. (2008). Clarifying differences between reading skills and reading strategies. *The Reading Teacher, 61*(5), 364–373. doi:10.1598/RT.61.5.1

Afflerbach, P. P. (1990). The influence of prior knowledge and text genre on readers' prediction strategies. *Journal of Reading Behavior, 22*(2), 131–148.

Alexander, P. A. (2005). The path to competence: a lifespan developmental perspective on reading. *Journal of Literacy Research, 37*(4), 413–436. doi:10.1207/s15548430jlr3704_1

Alexander, P. A. (2018). Past as prologue: Educational psychology's legacy and progeny. *Journal of Educational Psychology, 110*(2), 147–162. doi:10.1037/edu0000200

Alexander, P. A., Graham, S., & Harris, K. R. (1998). A perspective on strategy research: Progress and prospects. *Educational Psychology Review, 10*(2), 129–154. doi:10.1023/A:1022185502996

Alexander, P. A., Grossnickle, E. M., Dumas, D., & Hattan, C. (2018). A retrospective and prospective examination of cognitive strategies and academic development: Where have we come in twenty-five years? In A. O'Donnell (Ed.), *Oxford handbook of educational psychology*. Oxford: Oxford University Press.

Alexander, P. A., & Judy, J. E. (1988). The interaction of domain-specific and strategic knowledge in academic performance. *Review of Educational Research, 58*(4), 375–404. doi:10.3102/00346543058004375

Alexander, P. A., Murphy, P. K., Woods, B. S., Duhon, K. E., & Parker, D. (1997). College instruction and concomitant changes in students' knowledge, interest, and strategy use: A study of domain learning. *Contemporary Educational Psychology, 22*(2), 125–146. doi:10.1006/ceps.1997.0927

Alexander, P. A., Schallert, D. L., & Reynolds, R. E. (2009). What is learning anyway? A topographical perspective considered. *Educational Psychologist, 44*(3), 176–192. https://doi.org/10.1080/00461520903029006

Ames, C., & Archer, J. (1988). Achievement goals in the classroom: Students' learning strategies and motivation processes. *Journal of Educational Psychology, 80*, 260–267. doi:10.1037/0022-0663.80.3.260

Anmarkrud, Ø., Bråten, I., & Strømsø, H. I. (2014). Multiple-documents literacy: Strategic processing, source awareness, and argumentation when reading multiple conflicting documents. *Learning and Individual Differences, 30*, 64–76. doi:10.1016/j.lindif.2013.01.007

Baroody, A. J. (1987). The development of counting strategies for single-digit addition. *Journal for Research in Mathematics Education, 18*(2), 141–157. doi:10.2307/749248

Blum, D., & Holling, H. (2017). Spearman's law of diminishing returns A meta-analysis. *Intelligence, 65*, 60–66. doi:10.1016/j.intell.2017.07.004

Bong, M. (2005). Within-grade changes in Korean girls' motivation and perceptions of the learning environment across domains and achievement levels. *Journal of Educational Psychology, 97*(4), 656–672. doi:10.1037/0022-0663.97.4.656

Bozdogan, H., & Akbilgic, O. (2013). Social network analysis of scientific collaborations across different subject fields. *Information Services & Use, 33*(4), 219–233. doi:10.3233/ISU-130715

Cameron, C. E., Grimm, K. J., Steele, J. S., Castro-Schilo, L., & Grissmer, D. W. (2015). Nonlinear Gompertz curve models of achievement gaps in mathematics and reading. *Journal of Educational Psychology, 107*(3), 789–804. doi:10.1037/edu0000009

Campione, J., & Brown, A. (1984). Learning ability and transfer propensity as sources of individual differences in intelligence. In P. Brooks, R. Sperber, & C. McCauley (Eds.), *Learning and cognition in the mentally retarded* (pp. 265–294). Hillsdale, NJ: Psychology Press.

Canivez, G. L., Watkins, M. W., Good, R., James, K., & James, T. (2017). Construct validity of the Wechsler Intelligence Scale for Children—Fourth UK Edition with a referred Irish sample: Wechsler and Cattell–Horn–Carroll model comparisons with 15 subtests. *British Journal of Educational Psychology, 87*(3), 383–407. doi:10.1111/bjep.12155

Carroll, J. B. (1993). *Human cognitive abilities: A survey of factor-analytic studies*. Cambridge, UK: Cambridge University Press.

Catrysse, L., Gijbels, D., Donche, V., De Maeyer, S., Lesterhuis, M., & Van Den Bossche, P. (2018). How are learning strategies reflected in the eyes? Combining results from self-reports and eye-tracking. *British Journal of Educational Psychology, 88*(1), 118–137. doi:10.1111/bjep.12181

Cerdán, R., & Vidal-Abarca, E. (2008). The effects of tasks on integrating information from multiple documents. *Journal of Educational Psychology, 100*(1), 209–222. doi:10.1037/0022-0663.100.1.209

Cromley, J. G., Snyder-Hogan, L. E., & Luciw-Dubas, U. A. (2010). Cognitive activities in complex science text and diagrams. *Contemporary Educational Psychology, 35*(1), 59–74. doi:10.1016/j.cedpsych.2009.10.002

Cushen, P. J., & Wiley, J. (2018). Both attentional control and the ability to make remote associations aid spontaneous analogical transfer. *Memory & Cognition, 46*(8), 1398–1412. doi:10.3758/s13421-018-0845-1

De La Paz, S., & Felton, M. K. (2010). Reading and writing from multiple source documents in history: Effects of strategy instruction with low to average high school writers. *Contemporary Educational Psychology, 35*(3), 174–192. doi:10.1016/j.cedpsych.2010.03.001

Dinsmore, D. L. (2017). Toward a dynamic, multidimensional research framework for strategic processing. *Educational Psychology Review, 29*(2), 235–268. doi:10.1007/s10648-017-9407-5

Dinsmore, D. L., Hattan, C., & List, A. (2018). A meta-analysis of strategy use and performance in the model of domain learning. In H. Fives & D. L. Dinsmore (Eds.), *The Model of Domain Learning: Understanding the Development of Expertise*. New York, USA: Routledge.

Dumas, D. (2018). Relational reasoning and divergent thinking: An examination of the threshold hypothesis with quantile regression. *Contemporary Educational Psychology, 53*, 1–14.

Dumas, D., & Alexander, P. A. (2016). Calibration of the Test of Relational Reasoning. *Psychological Assessment, 28*(10), 1303–1318. doi:10.1037/pas0000267

Dumas, D., Alexander, P. A., Baker, L. M., Jablansky, S., & Dunbar, K. N. (2014). Relational reasoning in medical education: Patterns in discourse and diagnosis. *Journal of Educational Psychology, 106*(4), 1021–1035. doi:10.1037/a0036777

Dumas, D., Alexander, P. A., & Grossnickle, E. M. (2013). Relational reasoning and its manifestations in the educational context: A systematic review of the literature. *Educational Psychology Review, 25*(3), 391–427. doi: 10.1007/s10648-013-9224-4

Dumas, D., Torre, D. M., & Durning, S. J. (2018). Using relational reasoning strategies to help improve clinical reasoning practice. *Academic Medicine: Journal of the Association of American Medical Colleges, 93*(5), 709–714. doi:10.1097/ACM.0000000000002114

Dumas, D. G., & McNeish, D. M. (2017). Dynamic measurement modeling: Using nonlinear growth models to estimate student learning capacity. *Educational Researcher, 46*(6), 284–292. doi:10.3102/0013189X17725747

Fan, W., Wallace, L., Rich, S., & Zhang, Z. (2006). Tapping the power of text mining. *Commun. ACM, 49*(9), 76–82. doi:10.1145/1151030.1151032

Farrington-Flint, L., Wood, C., Canobi, K. H., & Faulkner, D. (2004). Patterns of analogical reasoning among beginning readers. *Journal of Research in Reading, 27*(3), 226–247. doi:10.1111/j.1467-9817.2004.00229.x

Fryer, L. K., Ginns, P., & Walker, R. (2014). Between students' instrumental goals and how they learn: Goal content is the gap to mind. *British Journal of Educational Psychology, 84*(4), 612–630. doi: 10.1111/bjep.12052

Fryer, L. K., & Vermunt, J. D. (2018). Regulating approaches to learning: Testing learning strategy convergences across a year at university. *British Journal of Educational Psychology, 88*(1), 21–41. doi:10.1111/bjep.12169

Graham, S., Kiuhara, S. A., Harris, K. R., & Fishman, E. J. (2017). The relationship among strategic writing behavior, writing motivation, and writing performance with young, developing writers. *The Elementary School Journal, 118*(1), 82–104. doi:10.1086/693009

Greene, J. A., Bolick, C. M., Jackson, W. P., Caprino, A. M., Oswald, C., & McVea, M. (2015). Domain-specificity of self-regulated learning processing in science and history. *Contemporary Educational Psychology, 42*, 111–128. doi:10.1016/j.cedpsych.2015.06.001

Habeck, C., Steffener, J., Barulli, D., Gazes, Y., Razlighi, Q., Shaked, D., … Stern, Y. (2015). Making cognitive latent variables manifest: Distinct neural networks for fluid reasoning and processing speed. *Journal of Cognitive Neuroscience, 27*(6), 1249–1258. doi:10.1162/jocn_a_00778

Hartwell, M., & Kaplan, A. (2018). Students' personal connection with science: Investigating the multidimensional phenomenological structure of self-relevance. *Journal of Experimental Education, 86*(1), 86–104. doi:10.1080/00220973.2017.1381581

Jaeggi, S. M., Buschkuehl, M., Jonides, J., & Perrig, W. J. (2008). Improving fluid intelligence with training on working memory. *Proceedings of the National Academy of Sciences, 105*(19), 6829–6833. doi:10.1073/pnas.0801268105

James, W. (1890). *The principles of psychology.* New York, NY: H. Holt and Company.

King, A. (1989). Effects of self-questioning training on college students' comprehension of lectures. *Contemporary Educational Psychology, 14*(4), 366–381. doi:10.1016/0361-476X(89)90022-2

Leu, D., Zawilinski, L., Castek, J., Banerjee, M., Housand, B., & Liu, Y. (2008). What is new about the new literacies of online reading comprehension? In L. S. Rush, A. J. Eakle, & A. Berger (Eds.), *Secondary school literacy: What research reveals for classroom practices* (pp. 37–68). Urbana: National Council of Teachers of English.

Linnenbrink-Garcia, L., Wormington, S. V., Snyder, K. E., Riggsbee, J., Perez, T., Ben-Eliyahu, A., & Hill, N. E. (2018). Multiple pathways to success: An examination of integrative motivational profiles among upper elementary and college students. *Journal of Educational Psychology, 110*(7), 1026–1048. doi:10.1037/edu0000245

Liu, P. L. (2014). Using eye tracking to understand learners' reading process through the concept-mapping learning strategy. *Computers & Education, 78*, 237–249. doi:10.1016/j.compedu.2014.05.011

MacArthur, C. A., Graham, S., & Fitzgerald, J. (2008). *Handbook of writing research.* New York, NY: Guilford Press.

Marcus, M., Haden, C. A., & Uttal, D. H. (2018). Promoting children's learning and transfer across informal science, technology, engineering, and mathematics learning experiences. *Journal of Experimental Child Psychology, 175*, 80–95. doi:10.1016/j.jecp.2018.06.003

Mayer, R. E. (2018). Educational psychology's past and future contributions to the science of learning, science of instruction, and science of assessment. *Journal of Educational Psychology, 110*(2), 174–179. doi:10.1037/edu0000195

McNamara, D. S. (2012). *Reading comprehension strategies: Theories, interventions, and technologies.* New York, NY: Psychology Press.

McNeish, D., & Dumas, D. (2017). Nonlinear growth models as measurement models: A second-order growth curve model for measuring potential. *Multivariate Behavioral Research, 52*(1), 61–85. doi:10.1080/0027317 1.2016.1253451

Melby-Lervag, M., & Hulme, C. (2013). Is working memory training effective? A meta-analytic review. *Developmental Psychology, 49*(2), 270.

Niaz, M. (1994). Enhancing thinking skills: Domain specific/domain general strategies. *Instructional Science, 22*(6), 413–422. doi:10.1007/BF00897976

Ozuru, Y., Dempsey, K., & McNamara, D. S. (2009). Prior knowledge, reading skill, and text cohesion in the comprehension of science texts. *Learning and Instruction, 19*(3), 228–242. doi:10.1016/j.learninstruc.2008.04.003

Pressley, M. (1986). The relevance of the good strategy user model to the teaching of mathematics. *Educational Psychologist, 21*, 139–161.

Reeves, P. M., & Sperling, R. A. (2015). A comparison of technologically mediated and face-to-face help-seeking sources. *British Journal of Educational Psychology, 85*(4), 570–584. doi: 10.1111/bjep.12088

Richland, L. E., & McDonough, I. M. (2010). Learning by analogy: Discriminating between potential analogs. *Contemporary Educational Psychology, 35*(1), 28–43. doi:10.1016/j.cedpsych.2009.09.001

Spearman, C. (1904). "General intelligence," objectively determined and measured. *The American Journal of Psychology, 15*(2), 201–292. doi:10.2307/1412107

Sprenger, A. M., Atkins, S. M., Bolger, D. J., Harbison, J. I., Novick, J. M., Chrabaszcz, J. S., … Dougherty, M. R. (2013). Training working memory: Limits of transfer. *Intelligence, 41*(5), 638–663. doi:10.1016/j.intell.2013.07.013

Stoecker, J. L. (1993). The Biglan classification revisited. *Research in Higher Education, 34*(4), 451–464. doi:10.1007/BF00991854

Thorndike, E. L. (1913). *Educational psychology*. New York, USA: Teachers College, Columbia University.

Torrance, E. P. (1972). Can we teach children to think creatively? *The Journal of Creative Behavior, 6*(2), 114–143. doi:10.1002/j.2162-6057.1972.tb00923.x

Vettori, G., Vezzani, C., Bigozzi, L., & Pinto, G. (2018). *Frontiers in Psychology*. The mediating role of conceptions of learning in the relationship between metacognitive skills/strategies and academic outcomes among middle-school students, *9*. doi:10.3389/fpsyg.2018.01985

Wanzek, J., Petscher, Y., Al Otaiba, S., & Donegan, R. E. (2019). Retention of reading intervention effects from fourth to fifth grade for students with reading difficulties. *Reading & Writing Quarterly: Overcoming Learning Difficulties*. doi:10.1080/10573569.2018.1560379

Wentzel, K. R., Muenks, K., McNeish, D., & Russell, S. (2018). Emotional support, social goals, and classroom behavior: A multilevel, multisite study. *Journal of Educational Psychology, 110*(5), 611–627. doi:10.1037/edu0000239

Winne, P. H. (2018). Theorizing and researching levels of processing in self-regulated learning. *British Journal of Educational Psychology, 88*(1), 9–20. doi:10.1111/bjep.12173

Xie, H., Mayer, R. E., Wang, F., & Zhou, Z. (2019). Coordinating visual and auditory cueing in multimedia learning. *Journal of Educational Psychology, 111*(2), 235–255. doi:10.1037/edu0000285

3

LEVELS OF STRATEGIES AND STRATEGIC PROCESSING

Daniel L. Dinsmore
UNIVERSITY OF NORTH FLORIDA, USA

Courtney Hattan
ILLINOIS STATE UNIVERSITY, USA

Strategies and the processing that accompanies the use of strategies is generally considered to be dynamic and multidimensional (*Dinsmore, 2017; Dinsmore, Fryer, & Parkinson, this volume). Additionally, the manner in which researchers have conceptualized and operationalized strategies and strategy use has resulted in distinctions between strategies. These distinctions may influence an individual's subsequent performance on the task or problem in which the individual employed a particular strategy. Also, these distinctions may encompass whether those strategies are domain specific or domain general (Dumas, this volume) or the differences between whether those strategies are cognitive, metacognitive, or self-regulatory. The crux of this chapter will be to consider different levels of strategic processing – with a focus on surface-level (i.e., those strategies aimed at understanding or solving a problem; Dinsmore & Alexander, 2106), deep-level (i.e., those strategies aimed at transforming a problem; Dinsmore & Alexander, 2016), metacognitive (i.e., those strategies aimed at monitoring and controlling one's own thinking; Garner, 1988), and self-regulatory strategies (i.e., those strategies aimed at regulating cognition, motivation, or affect; Pintrich & De Groot, 1990) – and how this processing influences individuals' performance in a task or while solving a problem.

Although this task may seem somewhat simplistic, a direct connection between levels of strategy use and performance has been anything but clear (e.g., Block, 2009; Cano, 2007). The long-held notion that those who employ deeper-level strategies over surface-level strategies will perform better (e.g., Phan, 2009b) has not come to fruition across multiple theoretical frameworks or methodologies (e.g., *Asikainen & Gijbels, 2017; *Dinsmore, 2017). Rather, it appears as if there are other mediating and moderating factors that play into how strategy use and performance are linked.

Fortunately, there now exist numerous reviews of the literature, both systematic and non-systematic, that help the field take stock of some of the facets of strategy use – such as levels of processing – and how these other factors might influence performance in conjunction with that strategy use. So, rather than undertake another review to flesh out these issues, we have decided to conduct a review of existing reviews in this relatively mature field of study. A systematic review of reviews is similar to a systematic review in that it is a reproducible review, but rather than reviewing empirical studies, the search criteria identify existing reviews of the literature (see Mills & Fives, 2018, for another example). This review will allow us to provide a picture of how levels of processing have been considered historically, how those historical notions have developed in the current state of the literature, and what limitations remain. These insights will then allow us to provide suggestions for both experienced and new scholars in this area of research, as well as provide practical implications for policymakers and practitioners.

To guide this review of reviews, we pose the following questions:

1. How have theoretical levels of processing been conceptualized and operationalized in literature reviews of strategic processing?
2. Have these levels of processing been shown to influence performance in any systematic manner across these reviews?
3. What other individual and contextual factors have these reviews concluded to be important factors to consider in the relation between levels of processing and performance?

METHODS FOR THE REVIEW

Review Selection

To select relevant reviews for this review we searched PsycINFO and Google Scholar using the terms "strategic processing review" and "cognitive strategy review". These searches resulted in 29 studies that we identified as potential reviews to include in the pool. Additionally, we identified reviews that we were aware of that were not identified in the database search that fit the review criteria. From there, studies were further hand searched by abstract or article to determine whether they would help provide evidence to answer the guiding question for this review of reviews. In this stage we reduced the number of reviews to our final pool, which encompasses 15 total reviews. For example, although *Pintrich's (2004) article, "A conceptual framework for assessing motivation and self-regulated learning in college students," was identified in our search parameters, a thorough inspection of the article indicated that it was primarily an articulation of a theoretical framework, rather than a review of the literature.

We purposefully did not include levels of processing in the search criteria to examine if this facet of strategies in reviews of strategies and strategic processing was scrutinized. The inclusion and conceptualization of levels of processing was subsequently an idea we tracked in our data table, which we will now describe.

Tabling of the Reviews

To gather evidence from these reviews we created a table that recorded the inclusion and conceptualization of levels of processing, whether and how the measurement of levels of processing was addressed, the context or contexts in which levels of processing was examined, which learner individual differences were examined, and what conclusions the review drew regarding the link between levels of strategic processing and performance outcomes. The table is primarily descriptive – rather than a reductive coding process – to provide readers with as much information as possible. In other words, we aim here to provide a resource for those interested in these ideas to find relevant reviews in which they can explore these ideas further.

To begin tabling we first discussed each column in the table and what we thought relevant evidence from a review might look like. Second, we jointly tabled two reviews to ensure that evidence we drew from the reviews into the table was congruent. After tabling and discussing those two reviews, we each independently tabled two additional reviews. Following this independent tabling, we compared the evidence from each of these tables and determined they were sufficiently congruent to divide the remaining reviews between the two of us to table.

FINDINGS AND DISCUSSION OF THE REVIEW

The full table with the descriptive evidence from each review is presented in Table 3.1.

Each of the reviews is listed in the references section with an asterisk preceding the reference. The findings from the reviews in the table will be presented and discussed in accordance with the three guiding questions for the chapter – conceptualization and operationalization of levels of processing, systematic effects of levels of processing on performance, and the influences of contextual and individual factors that mediate or moderate the relation between levels of processing and performance.

Conceptualization and Operationalization of Levels of Processing

Conceptualization. With regard to how levels of processing were conceptualized in these reviews we found that ten of the reviews explicitly discussed levels of processing, while five did not. Of the five reviews that did not discuss levels of processing (*Afflerbach, Pearson, & Paris, 2008; *Alexander & Judy, 1988; *Ashcraft, 1990; *Paris, 1988; Paris, Lipson, & Wixson, 1983), two of these reviews (*Afflerbach et al., 2008; *Alexander & Judy, 1988) were concerned with the definition of a strategy. For instance, Afflerbach and colleagues addressed the confusion between the terms *skill* and *strategy* making the claim that confusion between these two terms could result in less effective instruction for children and adolescents.

Of the reviews that did address levels of processing there were a variety of frameworks from which these levels were addressed. Four of the reviews addressed levels of processing from the perspective of the development of expertise. These perspectives have been forwarded by Alexander and colleagues (Alexander, Grossnickle, Dumas, & Hattan, 2018; *Dinsmore, 2017; *Dinsmore & Alexander, 2012; *Dinsmore, Hattan, & List, 2018). In each of these reviews, conceptualizations of deep- and surface-level processing (strategies to understand the problem versus transforming them respectively) is informed by Alexander's Model of Domain Learning (MDL; Alexander, 1997, 2004). In the MDL, surface-level strategies are those strategies designed to better understand and solve a problem, whereas deep-level strategies are those strategies designed to transform a particular problem. The MDL predicts that those in acclimation (i.e., novices) would rely primarily on surface-level strategies, whereas experts

Table 3.1 Pooled Studies and Codings

Citation	Number of Studies	Conceptualization/Level	Measurement/ Level	Context (i.e., domain, setting)	Task	Learner Ind Diff	Process-Outcome Links
Afflerbach (2008)	N/A	Examined differences between skills and strategies, explicitly looked at definitions of skills/strategies. This article is all about conceptualizing skills and strategies.	N/A	Reading.	N/A	N/A	
Alexander, Graham, and Harris (1998)	N/A	Defines strategies as being procedural, purposeful, effortful, willful, essential, and facilitative. Strategies as a type of procedural knowledge. Contrasts strategies from skillful behavior. Strategies as domain general, domain specific, or task specific. Includes metacognition, self-regulation, learning and instructional strategies.	N/A	Ways teachers can influence strategy growth: explicitly teaching relevant strategies and creating environments in which strategies are required, valued, and rewarded.	Looks at task variables such as nature of the domain, time constraints, mode of response, and perceived value of the task.	Knowledge, motivation, mindfulness, automaticity (does this count) and other individual differences such as short-term memory.	It is implied that being strategic will result in better outcomes from learners, but this is not explicitly examined.
Alexander, Grossnickle, Dumas, and Hattan (2018)	N/A	Skills v. strategies. Types of strategies: domain general and specific; deep v. surface processing; cognitive and metacognitive. Then also mentions meta-strategies, relational reasoning, online learning.	Mentions self-report, assigning conditions, think alouds, eye tracking, and neurophysiological methods	Includes a description of strategies in online settings, as well as strategies in the classroom.	N/A	Considers epistemic beliefs, motivation, and emotion.	Makes some loose links between strategies and learning.

Citation	Number of Studies	Conceptualization/Level	Measurement/ Level	Context (i.e., domain, setting)	Task	Learner Ind Diff	Process-Outcome Links
Alexander and Judy (1988)	N/A	Domain general or specific. Found definitional issues in the studies. No mention of deep v. surface.	N/A	Looked at studies that focused on a particular domain (although found that the studies mentioned a weak articulation of the content). Mentions the importance of social-contextual factors. Found that most studies had participants of college-age or older.	N/A	Knowledge was discussed at length since the focus was on the interaction between domain-specific and strategic knowledge. Also mentions the importance of motivation and social-contextual factors.	Draws the conclusion that both domain and strategic knowledge are central to learning.
Ashcraft	N/A	Strategy defined as how a task is performed mentally. Focus on mental arithmetic. Mentioned that students can use more than one strategy at once. Strategic processes become more automatic.	N/A	Math.	Arithmetic tasks.	N/A	Performance becomes more rapid and accurate as students develop.
Asikainen and Gijbels (2017)	43	Directly examined deep v. surface-level processing.	Looks at self-report measures: ETLA, ASSIST, SPQ, interviews, etc.	Only looked at higher education, longitudinal studies. Domain-specific (several higher education domains were included such as biology, economics, hospitality, etc.).	N/A	Initial approaches.	Ambiguous.

(Continued)

Table 3.1 (Continued)

Citation	Number of Studies	Conceptualization/Level	Measurement/ Level	Context (i.e., domain, setting)	Task	Learner Ind Diff	Process-Outcome Links
Dinsmore (2017)	134	Surface, deep, metacognitive/ self-regulatory.	Examined how quantity, quality, and conditional use were measured.	Reading (45%), mathematics (18%), domain general (17%), science (10%).	Well structured (69%) versus ill structured (24%), both (7%).	Learner goals.	Quality and conditional use explain performance more consistently than simply frequency of strategy use; and numerous person and environmental factors shape the degree to which certain strategies are effective for certain learners.
Dinsmore and Alexander (2012)	221	Directly examined conceptions of levels of processing; explicitly 41.4%, implicitly 50%, and absent 8.6%.	Directly measured levels of processing for studies; 48% self-report, 28.3% by condition; 14.3% coding scheme, 8.1% absent; .9% behavior; .4% by outcome.	Most studies were domain genera (n=117) followed by physical/life science (n=38) and social science (n=36).	60% were task based and 40% were not.	N/A	Mixed/ambiguous links.
Dinsmore, Hattan & List	17	Surface level, deep, metacognitive/ self-regulatory.	Direct observation (1 study), online self-report (24%), offline self-report (71%).	Physical or life science (24%), social sciences (47%), performing arts, physical/ kinesthetic. Generally asked to read rather than tasks specific to the domain.	Lumped task and outcome together – coded as ill-defined (24%) or well-defined (71%).	Stage of development (71% undergraduate students), MDL stage (94% acclimation), domain knowledge, topic knowledge, individual interest, situation interest.	Direct links to performance.

Citation	Number of Studies	Conceptualization/Level	Measurement/Level	Context (i.e, domain, setting)	Task	Learner Ind Diff	Process-Outcome Links
Hattie & Donoghue	228 meta-analyses	Surface, deep, and transfer with an acquiring and consolidation phase for the surface and deep levels.	N/A	Wide variety.	Wide variety.	Degree to which students understand criteria for success influences strategy selection.	The results indicate that there is a subset of strategies that are effective, but this effectiveness depends on the phase of the model in which they are implemented. Further, it is best not to run separate sessions on learning strategies but to embed the various strategies within the content of the subject to be clearer about developing both surface and deep learning, and promoting their associated optimal strategies and to teach the skills of transfer of learning.
Najmaei & Sadeghinejad	N/A	Metacognition as a more abstract level than cognition.	N/A	Business/ marketing.	N/A	N/A	Suggests future directions to link managers' decisions to strategies they use.
Paris (1988)	N/A	Using metaphors to describe learning strategies – Craik and Lockhart's depth versus Anderson "spread of activation" are discussed.	N/A	N/A	N/A	Levels of expertise are discussed.	N/A

(Continued)

Table 3.1 (Continued)

Citation	Number of Studies	Conceptualization/Level	Measurement/Level	Context (i.e., domain, setting)	Task	Learner Ind Diff	Process-Outcome Links
Pintrich (1999)	N/A	Surface, deep following Weinstein and Mayer, metacognitive, self-regulatory. Pintrich, Wolters, and Baxter (1999) have suggested that metacognitive knowledge be limited to students' knowledge about person, task, and strategy variables. Self-regulation would then refer to students' monitoring, controlling, and regulating their own cognitive activities and actual behavior.	N/A	N/A	N/A	Motivational beliefs (self-efficacy, task value, goal orientation).	N/A
Vermunt and Donche (2017)	44 learning patterns studies in which the ILS is used	Deep, stepwise, and concrete strategies, regulation strategies.	All used the Inventory of Learning Styles (ILS).	Teaching strategies, perception of the learning environment, disciplinary differences.	Discussion is much broader than task.	Personality, academic motivation, goal orientation, attributions of academic success, self-efficacy, effort, epistemological and intelligence beliefs, prior education, age, and gender.	Ties the use of strategies to better performance more at the course and semester level rather than a specific task or performance.

would increasingly rely on deep-level strategies and less on surface-level strategies (cf. *Dinsmore et al., 2018). Thus, the MDL does not predict that quantity of strategies should relate directly to performance. Rather, the level or type of strategy could be explained by the individual's development of expertise in a particular domain – such as mathematics – and that that use of the appropriate strategy for that level of expertise should better predict performance in that domain. For example, Dinsmore and Alexander (2016) empirically tested this notion by examining how levels of processing influenced performance on an astronomy task. Those who had low prior knowledge (one of the hallmarks of being a novice) did not perform well using primarily deep-level strategies, whereas those with more prior knowledge performed better on the outcome task using more deep-level strategies. For instance, participants who tried to use elaborative strategies (using one's own prior knowledge to add information in addition to what the author wrote) while reading the text passage in the study only comprehended that passage better when they possessed higher levels of background knowledge. In other words, in these cases, elaborating on a topic when you have little or no prior knowledge – or worse, inaccurate knowledge – can make comprehension *more* difficult.

Two reviews relied instead on the Learning Patterns framework (*Asikainen & Gijbels, 2017; *Vermunt & Donche, 2017). The Learning Patterns framework has evolved quite a bit over time (Richardson, 2015) but began with quasi-experimental investigations by Marton and Säljö (1976a, 1976b). These investigations examined the role that expected assessments changed how individuals processed information for studying. For instance, if the task assessment for a text passage was to memorize important details of the text, individuals would be expected to use surface-level strategies such as rehearsal. Those individuals who were asked to interpret what the text meant would be expected to use deep-level strategies such as making inferences about the message the author is trying to convey. Although Marton and Säljö were examining these effects at the task level, much of the current research using SAL examines students' processing at the course or even semester level. This is evident in *Vermunt & Donche's (2017) review in which he examined a popular instrument used to measure levels of processing in SAL – the Inventory of Learning Styles (ILS; Vermunt, 1998). It should be noted that the levels in this theory go beyond simply surface and deep level with Biggs (1987) adding an *achieving* level as well. Similarly, *Asikainen and Gijbels (2017) also examined self-report instrument yet expanded beyond the ILS and included a wider variety of self-report instruments.

Three reviews did not examine levels of processing with regard to deep and surface; rather these reviews examined cognitive versus metacognitive and self-regulatory levels (*Alexander, Graham, & Harris, 1998; *Najmaei & Sadeghinejad, 2016; Pintrich, 1999). *Alexander et al. (1998) and *Najmaei and Sadeghinejad (2016) relied primarily on Flavell's (1976) conceptualization of metacognition to frame the differences between cognitive and metacognitive strategies. Pintrich (1999), on the other hand, used his self-regulated learning (SRL) framework (Pintrich, 2000) which encapsulated cognitive, metacognitive, self-regulatory, and affective strategy use during performance. Although no such current review of SRL strategies exists to our knowledge, the use of SRL to investigate strategy use is typified by the work of Azevedo, Greene, and colleagues (Greene & Azevedo, 2009; Taub, Azevedo, Bouchet, & Khosravifar, 2014).

For example, Deekens, Greene, and Lobczowski (2018) used an SRL framework to investigate individuals' self-regulatory strategy use (and the levels they defined within that framework) across two academic domains – history and science. Differences between the metacognitive and self-regulatory levels are explored in depth in Dinsmore, Alexander, and Loughlin's (2008) systematic review of those constructs.

An outlier to reviews within the three frameworks previously mentioned was *Hattie and Donoghue's (2016) meta-analysis, which was based on and refined from Hattie's Visible Learning framework (Hattie, 2008). Hattie's visible learning is the perspective that students learn best when they become their own teachers – through, among other ideas, better constructed feedback for students to use (e.g., Hattie & Clarke, 2018). Although this framework is not as tightly constructed as the MDL or SAL – it does not contain the specific mechanisms of how deep and surface strategies influence learning – *Hattie and Donoghue (2016) meta-analysis draws primarily from information-processing views of learning (e.g., Klahr & Wallace, 1976).

Operationalization. Six of the tabled reviews specifically examined the measurement of levels of strategic processing. Two of these reviews were focused solely on retrospective self-report measures (*Asikainen & Gijbels, 2017; *Vermunt & Donche, 2017). Retrospective self-report refers to measures that survey the use of strategies after the task or activity has taken place. As the use of retrospective self-report has been typical in the SAL literature over the past few decades, the prevalence of these retrospective self-reports is not surprising. Given the examination of processing over longer periods of time – such as a course or a semester – the use of retrospective self-reports is easier and less time intensive than some of the concurrent self-report instruments used elsewhere. For example, Vermunt's ILS (Vermunt, 1998) asks how often students are, "Relating elements of the subject matter to each other and to prior knowledge; structuring these elements into a whole."

Three of the reviews examined measurement of levels of processing beyond retrospective self-report (*Alexander et al., 2018; *Dinsmore & Alexander, 2012; *Dinsmore et al., 2018). Across these three reviews it is apparent that retrospective self-report remains the dominant measure of strategy use with *Dinsmore and Alexander (2012) reporting that almost half (48%) of the studies they reviewed used retrospective self-report, with a higher percentage of retrospective self-report (71%) in their review of studies solely using the MDL. Other methods of measurement included concurrent self-report. Concurrent self-report refers to measurements that collect data about strategic processing *during* a task, rather than after a task. Concurrent measurements of strategy use were primarily the use of the think-aloud protocol, eye tracking, and neurophysiological measures such as functional magnetic resonance imaging. Think-aloud protocols refer to the process of asking individuals to verbally report their strategy use as they are engaged in a task (cf., Ericsson, 2006; e.g., Parkinson & Dinsmore, 2018). Eye tracking measurements are those that examine how movement of the eye relative to a task (typically a text) relates to their processing (cf. Rayner, Chace, Slattery, & Ashby, 2006; e.g., Catrysse et al., 2018). Finally, neurobiological measures, such as functional magnetic resonance imaging (fMRI) or functional near infrared spectroscopy (fNIRS) relates the hemoglobin response (i.e., blood flow) of certain regions of the brain to individuals' processing (cf. Kotz, 2009; e.g., Dinsmore, Macyczko, Greene, & Hooper, 2019).

Further, one review examined different facets of strategy use and levels of processing more specifically. In his review, *Dinsmore (2017) examined measures of the quantity (i.e., how often a strategy was used), quality (i.e., how well a strategy was used), and conditional use (i.e., when a strategy was used) to investigate whether these measures and the facets of strategy use better related to performance outcomes – a topic discussed in a subsequent section. In this review, Dinsmore found that 94% of the studies contained some measure of quantity, while only 24% and 19% of those studies contained some measure of quality and conditional use respectively. Since most of the studies reviewed were self-report, capturing the quantity of that strategy use is fairly straightforward. However, capturing the quality and conditional use of strategies requires more time and labor-intensive measures, such as think aloud protocols (TAPs).

Discussion. At issue in the previous two subsections were the conceptualization and operationalization of levels of strategy use. Taken together, findings from these reviews indicate that issues of conceptualization and operationalization have plagued the educational and psychological literature. With regard to the conceptualization of levels of processing, it is clear that how these levels are conceptualized are at worst not explicitly defined (*Dinsmore & Alexander, 2012), and at best researchers in this area have been using competing frameworks with little impetus to collaborate across these frameworks – with some exception (Dinsmore et al., this volume; Gijbels & Fryer, 2017). As Loughlin and Alexander (2012) pointed out, without conceptual clarity, interpreting the findings of these studies – and their accompanying reviews – becomes difficult.

Exacerbating these conceptual issues are measurement issues. The heavy reliance on retrospective self-report has been highly problematic in related areas of the literature such as metacognition and SRL (Dinsmore et al., 2008; Veenman, Van Hout-Wolters, & Afflerbach, 2006). However, the more time and labor-intensive measurements such as TAP are likely not suitable for large, generalizable, longitudinal studies that leverage larger sample sizes over repeated instances across a semester or year of study. Therefore, there has been – and remains – a difficulty with accurately *and* practically assessing levels of cognitive processing. This issue has left us with either measurements that are quite practical in collecting data from hundreds, even thousands, of students that may or may not accurately reflect their strategic or cognitive processing (i.e., retrospective self-report scales), or measurements that may be more accurate but are difficult to collect and analyze at any large scale.

Systematic Effects of Levels of Processing on Performance

Given the issues regarding conceptualization and operationalization mentioned previously, deriving clear links between levels of processing and performance is difficult. However, across these reviews different conclusions were reached. *Hattie and Donoghue's (2016) meta-analysis and *Vermunt and Donche's (2017) review offered perhaps the most targeted interpretation of this relation. Hattie and Donoghue suggest a subset of strategies that are more effective depending on the phase of learning that individuals are in (i.e., acquiring, consolidating, and transferring). Given the data in *Vermunt and Donche's (2017) review, they made an argument that the ILS could be an effective tool to predict processing over a course or semester, which would in turn predict future performance. However, with the issues of retrospective self-report discussed previously in the chapter, there is some doubt whether these claims are justified. If patterns of processing and strategy use are indeed rather stable over time, this could be the case. On the other hand, if processing and strategy use are more attuned to the conditions of the task and change rapidly, this argument may not hold for those particular instances.

Most of the reviews, however, were rather tenuous in speaking about the relation between levels of processing and performance. These reviews often attempted to qualify the relations between levels of processing and performance further than *Hattie and Donoghue (2016). For instance, *Dinsmore (2017) reported that the relations between levels of processing and performance were higher when quality and conditional use of the strategies were measured rather than simply the quantity of that strategy use. *Asikainen and Gijbels (2017) took a dimmer view of the efficacy of self-report instruments used in the SAL framework to predict performance, noting there was little relation between the learning patterns identified using the SAL perspective and learning performance.

In addition to these views, there is also a third perspective of individuals who do not necessarily believe that a direct link to performance is necessary, which comes predominately from the SRL framework (e.g., Pintrich, 1999). The idea that self-regulatory strategy use is a goal in its own right has been a point of major discussion lately, for example at the European Association for Research on Learning and Instruction (EARLI; Molenaar, 2017). Some of these researchers contend that improved self-regulation, even without being linked to performance, should be emphasized. This position subsumes within it the idea that *all* strategies are self-regulatory – one that needs further investigation. As Alexander pointed out in her expositions of the MDL (e.g., Alexander, 1997; 2004), strategies become increasingly metacognitive as one progresses toward higher levels of expertise. Especially in the stage of acclimation (the first stage on the path toward expertise) there is no expectation that the strategies employed are entirely self-regulatory. While we agree that enacting these cognitive strategies (whether surface or deep level) will probably be more successful when enacted alongside self-regulatory strategies, one can certainly employ a reading strategy without being self-regulatory. The degree to which this enaction with, without, or with limited self-regulation is more or less successful for different learners at different stages of expertise needs to be better fleshed out.

Discussion. With regard to the last point – that the link between levels of processing (and strategies more generally) and performance are not of tantamount importance – we disagree. Although we do agree that the ability to engage in self-regulatory strategies is important, this importance is limited if it does not lead to better performance or learning gains. For example, in studies of reading comprehension, there are readers who are termed *effortful* (Alexander, 2005; Dinsmore, Parkinson, Fox & Bilgili, 2019) who employ many strategies and do quite well in terms of performance outcomes. However, they are very inefficient – their reading times a quite a bit higher than readers in other categories, even those that were deemed to be *highly competent readers*. Thus, the relation between regulatory competence – which the *highly competent readers* possess – and reading outcomes is not so straightforward.

Fortunately, evidence supports that strategies – self-regulatory included – should improve performance for a wide range of tasks. Indeed, the MDL in particular proposes that metacognitive and self-regulatory strategies – along with a mix of surface-level and deep-level strategies – are necessary for performance in a domain except for someone who has advanced beyond the novice stage (i.e., in competence or expertise in the MDL). However, we also acknowledge that for some tasks, such as those that are routine or quite straightforward, the degree to which self-regulatory strategies are utilized or required are of much lower import.

Additionally, as a result of these reviews, empirical work that we have conducted, and our practical experience in classrooms with children, adolescents, and adults, we are skeptical of the more targeted view of *Hattie and Donoghue (2016) and *Vermunt and Donche (2017). In the previously mentioned reviews, contextual and individual factors play a key role. We certainly agree with Hattie and Donoghue that some strategies are better than others, but we would posit that the degree to which these strategies are better or worse is far more conditional than they state in their meta-analysis. We dissect this issue now as we turn to the contextual and individual factors that might mediate or moderate the relation between levels of strategy use and performance.

Influences of Contextual and Individuals Factors that Mediate or Moderate the Relation between Levels of Processing and Performance

The last of our three guiding questions examines how each of the reviews in the pool did or did not examine individual and contextual factors during strategy use.

Individual Factors. Eleven of the reviews in the pool specifically discussed individual factors that might influence the relation between level of processing and performance. The largest category of individual differences discussed across these reviews was motivation. Six of these reviews discussed some facet or multiple facets of motivation. For example, *Vermunt & Donche (2017) discussed goal orientations, attributions, effort, and self-efficacy, while Pintrich (1999) discussed self-efficacy, task value, and goal orientation. In general, across both of these reviews, autonomous motivation and positive conceptions of learning (e.g., higher self-efficacy) are more likely to lead to deeper-level strategies employed.

The next largest category was the discussion of prior knowledge or prior performance. Four reviews specifically addressed the importance of prior knowledge on the use of strategies: *Alexander and Judy (1988), *Alexander et al. (1998), *Dinsmore et al. (2018), and Paris et al. (1983). *Asikainen and Gijbels (2017), *Paris (1988), and *Vermunt and Donche (2017) discussed the role of prior performance – or patterns of performance in the case of Asikainen and Gijbels – in the use of strategies and how that influenced performance. As indicated previously, all these reviews support the notion that higher levels of prior knowledge lead to better deep-level processing.

The next set of factors that were mentioned in a few reviews were of epistemic beliefs and emotions. Two studies, *Alexander Grossnickle, Dumas, and Hattan (2018) and *Vermunt and Donche (2017), both discussed how more sophisticated epistemic beliefs might lead to advantageous differences in strategic processing – particularly the use of deeper-level strategies. *Hattie and Donoghue (2016) focused on a related construct, understanding criteria for success in their review. Finally, *Alexander et al. (2018) discussed learner emotions, while *Vermunt and Donche (2017) also addressed personality, age, and gender in his discussion. For Alexander et al. regulation of learner emotions was considered to be beneficial for strategy use, while for Vermunt and Donche they found that the personality factors of openness and conscientiousness were related to patterns of learning they describe as *deep* or *analytic*.

Contextual Factors. The scope of the reviews with regard to contextual factors was also wide ranging. Some of the reviews focused on specific domains such as reading (*Afflerbach et al., 2008; Paris et al., 1983), mathematics (*Ashcraft, 1990), and business (*Najmaei & Sadeghinejad, 2016). Other reviews, however, focused on how domain-general versus domain-specific investigations of strategic processing influenced performance (*Dinsmore, 2017; *Dinsmore & Alexander, 2012; *Dinsmore et al., 2018; *Vermunt & Donche, 2017). Overall, there seems to be consensus among these reviews that while there are some strategies that can be considered domain general, there is certainly quite a bit of evidence to suggest that being conscious of domain when examining strategic processing is important (e.g., Deekens et al., 2018).

Other reviews focused more on the setting in which these investigations of levels of processing took place. For example, *Asikainen and Gijbels (2017) focused solely on students enrolled in higher education, while *Alexander et al. (2018) addressed strategies that students might employ in online versus face-to-face courses. *Alexander et al. (1998) and *Vermunt and Donche (2017) addressed the role of conducive learning environments regarding levels of processing, which is a major area of research in its own right (cf. Gijbels & Loyens, 2008).

Discussion. For us, the discussion in these reviews of the individual and contextual factors that influence the levels of strategic processing and its relation to performance provide additional evidence that a less sophisticated model that posits more deep processing will lead to better performance should indeed be a historical notion. The degree to which there are interrelated constructs such as motivation and epistemic beliefs underscore the interconnected relations between levels of strategic processing and performance. Although many of the individual difference factors have been extensively systematically reviewed, the degree to which contextual factors have been reviewed in this regard is much less extensive.

FUTURE DIRECTIONS

Now that we have addressed the historical and current state of the field, we turn our attention to the future. Although research on levels of processing has spanned nearly a half-century since the work of Marton and Säljö, some progress has been made to create more sophisticated models and frameworks of levels of processing. However, we believe that we have much further to go. We now offer our suggestions for future research and implications for practice.

Future Directions for Research

First, as is evident from these reviews, there has been very little cross-theoretical work in the area of levels of processing. SAL has remained primarily a European and Asian framework, while SRL and the MDL have been primarily used in North America. The SAL tradition, which focuses on the role of the environment on levels of processing, has failed to meaningfully incorporate individual difference factors as well as specific task-level variables in its research agenda. Conversely, both SRL frameworks and the MDL have not taken the role of the learning environment appropriately into account. Some fusion of these primarily endogenous and primarily exogenous approaches to researching levels of processing is needed. As this research continues, it will be vital to continue to refine and adjust our definitions of surface-level and deep-level processing to address the challenges of modeling both individual and contextual factors of depth of processing on performance.

Second, it is also evident that new measures and measurement techniques will be required to propel the field forward. Fortunately, while there is still a long way to go, efforts are already underway to work collaboratively to solve these issues. One such effort is the scientific research network, *Learning Strategies in Social and Informal Learning Contexts*, which has a major focus on measures and measurements that expand our repertoire of tools including eye tracking (Catrysse et al., 2018), heart rate (Sobocinski, Malmberg, Järvelä, & Järvenoja, 2018), and neurobiological tools such as functional near-infrared spectroscopy (Dinsmore, Fox, Parkinson, & Bilgili, 2019). Although these are exciting approaches, it remains to be seen how the plethora of data generated can be effectively analyzed – or, as we will discuss subsequently, how these data may be useful to practitioners. The reader is directed to latter chapters of this Handbook for suggestions on how this might occur (Cho, Woodward, & Afflerbach, this volume; Freed, Greene, & Plumley, this volume; Fryer & Shum, this volume).

Implications for Practice

Past research – and these reviews in particular – offer less guidance on future implications for practice. A notable exception to this trend is offered by *Afflerbach's (2008) review. While not specifically geared toward levels of processing, the review article that was written for reading practitioners (e.g., teachers) would offer a blueprint for discussing the role of levels of strategies for teachers across disciplines. For instance, providing a detailed conception of how different strategies within science (Lombardi & Bailey, this volume) could be considered at the levels of strategies discussed here would provide a service to the field. There are few materials available for practitioners that specifically discuss the issues of levels of strategy use, with a few exceptions (e.g., *Dinsmore et al., 2018).

The bigger issue, however, is providing teachers with tools to measure students' levels of processing in any systematic way or on a more mass scale. The time and labor-intensive processes to collect, transcribe, and code think-aloud protocols are not realistic for teachers; neither are the data-intensive processes to analyze the myriad of strategies used by students on a daily basis approachable for teachers. Again, although we have far to go in this regard, there are potential solutions available in related areas of research.

In two ways, technology can be a helpful asset here. First, technology can be helpful in collecting these data. A good example of this trend is Fryer's application to measure interest (Fryer & Nakao, 2018). The application uses QR codes to scan and record interest levels in participants for certain tasks and activities. This idea has the potential to be exploited for use to measure levels of processing as well. Rather than rely on verbal transcriptions, students could be trained to use an application to concurrently report their strategy use and the levels of that use. Second, some system would be needed to help teachers analyze that data. In many areas of research a promising avenue to solving this problem is with machine learning (Pereira, Mitchell, & Botvinick, 2009). Machine learning uses the powerful computer processing and artificial intelligence to try to analyze patterns in data that humans cannot. However, we certainly have a long way to go with regard to designing and testing systems to analyze students' levels of processing.

Concluding Thoughts

We believe this is an exciting time to be engaged on research dealing with levels of strategy use. The reviews contained in this chapter point to many promising avenues of research that can enable us to better understand how these levels of processing are influenced by individual and contextual differences, how those differences might mediate and moderate the relation between levels of processing and performance, and finally, how those levels of processing might directly relate to performance. We hope this review is helpful to those already engaged in the field, but particularly to those new to this area of research.

REFERENCES

*Reviews included in the review pool are denoted with an asterisk.

*Afflerbach, P., Pearson, P. D., & Paris, S. G. (2008). Clarifying differences between reading skills and reading strategies. *The Reading Teacher, 61*, 364–373.

Alexander, P. A. (1997). Mapping the multidimensional nature of domain learning: The interplay of cognitive, motivational, and strategic forces. In M. L. Maehr & P. R. Pintrich (Eds.), *Advances in motivation and achievement* (Vol. 10, pp. 213–250). Greenwich, CT: JAI Press.

Alexander, P. A. (2004). A model of domain learning: Reinterpreting expertise as a multidimensional, multistage process. In D. Y. Dai & R. J. Sternberg (Eds.), *Motivation, emotion, and cognition: Integrative perspectives on intellectual functioning and development* (pp. 273–298). Mahwah, NJ: Erlbaum.

Alexander, P. A. (2005). The path to competence: A lifespan developmental perspective on reading. *Journal of Literacy Research, 37*, 413–436.

*Alexander, P. A., Graham, S., & Harris, K. R. (1998). A perspective on strategy research: Progress and prospects. *Educational Psychology Review, 10*, 129–154.

*Alexander, P. A., Grossnickle, E. M., Dumas, D., & Hattan, C. (2018). A retrospective and prospective examination of cognitive strategies and academic development: Where have we come in twenty-five years? In A. O'Donnell (Ed.), *Handbook of Educational Psychology*. New York: Oxford University Press.

*Alexander, P. A., & Judy, J. E. (1988). The interaction of domain-specific and strategic knowledge in academic performance. *Review of Educational Research, 58*, 375–404.

*Ashcraft, M. H. (1990). Strategic processing in children's mental arithmetic: A review and proposal. In D. F. Bjorklund (Ed.), *Children's strategies: Contemporary views of cognitive development* (pp. 185–211). Hillsdale, NJ: Lawrence Erlbaum Associates, Inc.

*Asikainen, H., & Gijbels, D. (2017). Do students develop towards more deep approaches to learning during studies? A systematic review on the development of students' deep and surface approaches to learning in higher education. *Educational Psychology Review, 29*, 205–234.

Biggs, J. B. (1987). *Learning process questionnaire manual: Student approaches to learning and studying.* Hawthorn, Australia: Council for Educational Research.

Block, R. A. (2009). Intent to remember briefly presented human faces and other pictorial stimuli enhances recognition memory. *Memory & Cognition, 37*, 667–678. doi:10.3758/MC.37.5.667.

Cano, F. (2007). Approaches to learning and study orchestrations in high school students. *European Journal of Psychology of Education, 22*, 131–151.

Catrysse, L., Gijbels, D., Donche, V., De Maeyer, S., Lesterhuis, M., & Van Den Bossche, P. (2018). How are learning strategies reflected in the eyes? Combining results from self-reports and eye-tracking. *British Journal of Educational Psychology, 88*, 118–137.

Cho, B.-Y., Woodward, L., & Afflerbach, P. (this volume). Qualitative approaches to the verbal protocol analysis of strategic processing. In D. L. Dinsmore, L. K. Fryer, & M. M. Parkinson (Eds.), *Handbook of strategies and strategic processing: Conceptualization, measurement, and analysis*. New York: Routledge.

Deekens, V. M., Greene, J. A., & Lobczowski, N. G. (2018). Monitoring and depth of strategy use in computer-based learning environments for science and history. *British Journal of Educational Psychology, 88*, 63–79.

*Dinsmore, D. L. (2017). Toward a dynamic, multidimensional research framework for strategic processing. *Educational Psychology Review, 29*, 235–268.

*Dinsmore, D. L., & Alexander, P. A. (2012). A critical discussion of deep and surface processing: What it means, how it is measured, the role of context, and model specification. *Educational Psychology Review, 24*, 499–567.

Dinsmore, D. L., & Alexander, P. A. (2016). A multidimensional investigation of deep-level and surface-level processing. *The Journal of Experimental Education, 84*, 213–244.

Dinsmore, D. L., Alexander, P. A., & Loughlin, S. M. (2008). Focusing the conceptual lens on metacognition, self-regulation, and self-regulated learning. *Educational Psychology Review, 20*, 391–409.

Dinsmore, D. L., Fox, E., Parkinson, M. M., & Bilgili, D. (2019). Using reader profiles to investigate students' reading performance. *Journal of Experimental Education, 87*, 470–495. doi:10.1080/00220973.2017.1421519

Dinsmore, D. L., Fryer, L. K., & Parkinson, M. M. (this volume). Introduction: What are strategies? In D. L. Dinsmore, L. K. Fryer, & M. M. Parkinson (Eds.), *Handbook of strategies and strategic processing: Conceptualization, measurement, and analysis*. New York: Routledge.

*Dinsmore, D. L., Hattan, C., & List, A. (2018). A meta-analysis of strategy use and performance in the Model of Domain Learning. In H. Fives & D. L. Dinsmore (Eds.) *The Model of Domain Learning: Understanding the Development of Expertise* (pp. 37–55). New York: Routledge.

Dinsmore, D. L., Macyczko, J., Greene, S., & Hooper, K. (2019, August). Using fNIRS in a multitrait-multimethod investigation of strategic processing during reading. *Paper to be presented at the European Association for Research on Learning and Instruction*, Aachen, Germany.

Ericsson, K. A. (2006). Protocol analysis and expert thought: Concurrent verbalizations of thinking during experts' performance on representative tasks. In K. A. Ericsson, N. Charness, P. J. Feltovich, & R. R. Hoffman (Eds.), *The Cambridge handbook of expertise and expert performance* (pp. 223–241). Cambridge: Cambridge University Press.

Flavell, J. H. (1976). Metacognitive aspects of problem solving. In L. B. Resnick (Ed.), *The nature of intelligence* (pp. 231–235). Hillsdale, NJ: Erlbaum.

Freed, R., Greene, J. A., & Plumley, R. D. (this volume). Variable-centered approaches. In D. L. Dinsmore, L. K. Fryer, & M. M. Parkinson (Eds.), *Handbook of strategies and strategic processing: Conceptualization, measurement, and analysis*. New York: Routledge.

Fryer, L., & Gijbels, D. (2017). Student learning in higher education: Where we are and paths forward. *Educational Psychology Review, 29*(2), 199–203.

Fryer, L. K., & Nakao, K. (2018). Assessing the student course experience "On-Task": Instrument, design, analytical approach and preliminary results. *Presentation conducted for the Second Network Meeting of the Scientific Community on 'Learning Strategies in Social and Informal Learning Contexts'*, Antwerp, Belgium.

Fryer, L. K., & Shum, A. (this volume). Person-centered approaches to explaining students' cognitive processing strategies. In D. L. Dinsmore, L. K. Fryer, & M. M. Parkinson (Eds.), *Handbook of strategies and strategic processing: Conceptualization, measurement, and analysis*. New York: Routledge.

Garner, R. (1988). Verbal-report data on cognitive and metacognitive strategies. In C. E. Weinstein, E. T. Goetz, & P. A. Alexander (Eds.), *Learning and study strategies: Issues in assessment, instruction, and evaluation* (pp. 63–76). San Diego: Academic Press.

Greene, J. A., & Azevedo, R. (2009). A macro-level analysis of SRL processes and their relations to the acquisition of a sophisticated mental model of a complex system. *Contemporary Educational Psychology, 34*, 18–29.

Hattie, J. A. C. (2008). *Visible learning: A synthesis of over 800 meta-analyses relating to achievement*. London: Routledge.

Hattie, J. A. C., & Clarke, S. (2018). *Visible learning feedback*. New York: Routledge.

*Hattie, J. A. C., & Donoghue, G. M. (2016). Learning strategies: A synthesis and conceptual model. *Science of Learning, 1*, 1–13.

Klahr, D., & Wallace, J. G. (1976). *Cognitive development: An information processing view*. Hillsdale, NJ: Lawrence Erlbaum.

Kotz, S. A. (2009). A critical review of ERP and fMRI evidence on L2 syntactic processing. *Brain and Language, 109*, 68–74.

Lombardi, D., & Bailey, J. M. (this volume). Science strategy interventions. In D. L. Dinsmore, L. K. Fryer, & M. M. Parkinson (Eds.), *Handbook of strategies and strategic processing: Conceptualization, measurement, and analysis*. New York: Routledge.

Loughlin, S. M., & Alexander, P. A. (2012). Explicating and exemplifying empiricist and cognitivist paradigms in the study of human learning. In L. L'Abate (Ed.), *Paradigms in theory construction* (pp. 273–296). New York: Springer.

Loyens, S. M., & Gijbels, D. (2008). Understanding the effects of constructivist learning environments: Introducing a multi-directional approach. *Instructional Science, 36*(5–6), 351–357.

Mills, T. M., & Fives, H. (2018). Examining teachers' professional learning: The Model of Domain Learning as an analytic lens to examine exemplary programs. In H. Fives & D. L. Dinsmore (Eds.) *The Model of Domain Learning: Understanding the Development of Expertise* (pp. 175–194). New York: Routledge.

Molenaar, I. (Chair) (2017, August). Measuring and supporting students' self-regulated learning in adaptive educational technologies. *Symposium presented at the biennial conference of the European Association of Research on Learning and Instruction*, Tampere, Finland.

*Najmaei, A., & Sadeghinejad, Z. (2016). Metacognition in strategic decision making. In T. K. Das (Ed.), *Decision making in behavioral strategy* (pp. 49–81). Charlotte, NC: Information Age Publishing.

*Paris, S. G. (1988). Models and metaphors of learning strategies. In C. E. Weinstein, E. T. Goetz, & P. A. Alexander (Eds.), *Learning and study strategies: Issues in assessment, instruction, and evaluation* (pp. 299–322). San Diego, CA: Academic Press.

Paris, S. G., Lipson, J. Y., & Wixson, K. K. (1983). Becoming a strategic reader. *Contemporary Educational Psychology, 8*, 293–316.

Parkinson, M. M., & Dinsmore, D. L. (2018). Investigating the relations between high school students' depth of processing and metacognitive strategy use. *British Journal of Educational Psychology, 88*, 42–62. doi: 10.1111/bjep.12176

Pereira, F., Mitchell, T., & Botvinick, M. (2009). Machine learning classifiers and fMRI: A tutorial overview. *Neuroimage, 45*, S199-S209.

Phan, H. P. (2009b). Exploring students' reflective thinking practice, deep processing strategies, effort, and achievement goal orientations. *Educational Psychology*, 297–313. doi:10.1080/01443410902877988.

Pintrich, P. R. (1999). The role of motivation in promoting and sustaining self-regulated learning. *International Journal of Educational Research, 31*(6), 459–470.

*Pintrich, P. R. (2004). A conceptual framework for assessing motivation and self-regulated learning in college students. *Educational Psychology Review, 16*, 385–407.

Pintrich, P. R. (2000). The role of goal orientation in self-regulated learning. In M. Boekaerts, P. R. Pintrich, & M. Zeidner (Eds.), *Handbook of self-regulation* (pp. 451–502). San Diego, CA: Academic Press.

Pintrich, P. R., & De Groot, E. V. (1990). Motivational and self-regulated learning components of classroom academic performance. *Journal of Educational Psychology, 82*, 33–40.

Pintrich, P. R., Wolters, C., & Baxter, G. (1999). Assessing metacognition and self-regulated learning. In G. Schraw (Ed.), *Issues in the measurement of metacognition: Proceedings from the Tenth Buros-Nebraska symposium on measurement and testing*. Lincoln, NE: The University of Nebraska Press.

Rayner, K., Chace, K. H., Slattery, T. J., & Ashby, J. (2006). Eye movements as reflections of comprehension processes in reading. *Scientific Studies of Reading, 10*, 241–255.

Richardson, J. T. (2015). Approaches to learning or levels of processing: what did Marton and Säljö (1976a) really say? The legacy of the work of the Göteborg Group in the 1970s. *Interchange, 46*, 239–269.

Sobocinski, M., Malmberg, J., Järvelä, S., & Järvenoja, H. (2018, November). *Exploring small-scale adaptation in socially-shared regulation of learning using video and heart rate data*. Presentation conducted for the Second Network Meeting of the Scientific Community on 'Learning Strategies in Social and Informal Learning Contexts', Antwerp, Belgium.

Taub, M., Azevedo, R., Bouchet, F., & Khosravifar, B. (2014). Can the use of cognitive and metacognitive self-regulated learning strategies be predicted by learners' levels of prior knowledge in hypermedia-learning environments? *Computers in Human Behavior, 39*, 356–367.

Veenman, M. V., Van Hout-Wolters, B. H., & Afflerbach, P. (2006). Metacognition and learning: Conceptual and methodological considerations. *Metacognition and Learning, 1*, 3–14.

Vermunt, J. D. (1998). The regulation of constructive learning processes. *British Journal of Educational Psychology, 68*, 149–171.

*Vermunt, J. D., & Donche, V. (2017). A learning patterns perspective on student learning in higher education: State of the art and moving forward. *Educational Psychology Review, 29*, 269–299.

4

A LIFESPAN DEVELOPMENTAL PERSPECTIVE ON STRATEGIC PROCESSING

Amélie Rogiers, Emmelien Merchie, Fien De Smedt, Liesje De Backer, and Hilde Van Keer

UNIVERSITY OF GHENT, BELGIUM

STRATEGIC PROCESSING: FROM A CONDITIONED STATE TO A GROWTH PERSPECTIVE

From the time humans first appeared on earth, we have faced a desire to understand our world and learn what we need to know to survive (Weinstein, Jung, & Acee, 2011). However, it is only from the 1970s onwards that the psychological study of strategies began in earnest. By then, educational research and practice was dominated by the behavioristic theory on learning and instruction, which considered learning merely as a result of certain environmental contingencies (i.e., trial and error, rewards and punishments). Accordingly, the research at that time demonstrated that learners' knowledge could significantly be modified through training (Bryant, Vincent, Shaqlaih, & Moss, 2013). Behavioristic studies, in this respect, targeted observable learning behavior and took a main interest in instructional techniques that contributed to better performance (Bryant et al., 2013). In essence, behaviorists perceived learning as a conditioned state, failing to acknowledge the potential of a growth or developmental orientation on learning.

From the late 1990s onwards, researchers gradually started to recognize learning as a lifelong process, thereby emphasizing the changing nature of individuals' learning behavior with increasing expertise (Alexander, 2003). The work of Alexander and colleagues (1998, 2004) in particular has contributed to our knowledge on the development of learning. As a result, current research on strategic processing (i.e., processing information strategically) continues to extend its focus beyond the initial phases of learning during childhood. From a developmental perspective, individuals are perceived as continuously evolving in the process of learning. Consequently, learning is no longer merely related to young learners, but is rather associated with learners of all ages, including adolescents and adults. In the current 21st century and knowledge society, where lifelong learning is pivotal for active societal participation (Cornford, 2002), this developmental focus started to thrive and found its way into the educational research community. From this perspective, the focus increasingly lies on the complex evolution in strategic processing across the lifespan. This expanded view on learning becomes evident in, for instance, the more recent and increased attention for adolescent and adult learning and education (Alexander & Fox, 2004).

The purpose of this chapter is to elaborate further on this developmental orientation by presenting a framework for strategic processing that encompasses changes in learners' strategy use across the lifespan. A first prerequisite, in this respect, concerns deconstructing how the concept 'strategy' is defined and described in the literature. Surprisingly, although it has been widely used in cognitive research since the 1970s, attempts to unravel the concept 'strategy' mainly stem from the 1990s (e.g., Alexander, Schallert, & Hare, 1991; Dole, Duffy, Roehler, & Pearson, 1991). Even in the current empirical literature, it remains muddled and vague what a strategy precisely entails (Alexander, 2006; Harris, Alexander, & Graham, 2008). This lack of conceptual clarity can be considered as a substantial roadblock for strategy research, a concern that was already strongly expressed in the late 1980s by Alexander and Judy (1988). Therefore, we begin this particular chapter by providing an operational definition of what we constitute as a strategy.

As Harris and colleagues (2008) justly state, the history of strategies in the educational research literature since the mid-1990s has been a story of conceptualization and reconceptualization. Accordingly, differences in the categorization of strategies came to the fore (Harris et al., 2008). Building on the conceptualization of strategies presented by Weinstein and Mayer (1986), we define strategies as mental activities selected by learners to acquire, organize, and elaborate information, as well as to reflect upon and to guide their learning. Specifically, strategies should be understood as procedural, purposeful, effortful, willful, essential, and facilitative by nature (Alexander, Graham, & Harris, 1998). This implies that strategies should be interpreted as procedures or techniques that are employed by learners to bridge the gap between their actual and their potential or desired level of learning, understanding, and performance (Alexander, Grossnickle, Dumas, & Hattan, 2018; Pressley, Graham, & Harris, 2006; Weinstein & Mayer, 1986). Consequently, and taking into account the scope of the present chapter, any consideration of instructional or pedagogical strategies is precluded in this conceptualization (Alexander et al., 2018). While fully acknowledging the importance and added value of instructional strategies for facilitating students' learning process and performance (Alexander et al., 1998), our focus in the remainder of this chapter will be on learners and their applied strategies.

Next to various conceptualizations of the term 'strategies', differences in their categorization also occur in the literature. For instance, they have been distinguished according to their nature, perceptibility, level of depth, and domain of application. First, regarding their nature, strategies can be categorized as either *cognitive* (e.g., paraphrasing), *metacognitive* (e.g., planning), or *motivational-affective* (e.g., using positive self-talk; Pintrich, 2004). Second, some strategies can be applied *overtly* and are consequently easily observable (e.g., schematizing), whereas others take the form of *covert* mental strategies (e.g., monitoring; Wade, Trathen, & Schraw, 1990). Third, a distinction can be made between *deep-level* strategies, aimed at profound understanding and active transformation of information (e.g., elaborating), and more *surface-level* strategies that merely aim at basic comprehension without integrating information (e.g., applying read-and-repeat techniques; Dinsmore & Alexander, 2012; see also Chapter 3). Finally, we discern *general* or *domain-independent* strategies that are applicable in a wide variety of learning contexts (e.g., planning) from *domain-specific* strategies (see also Chapter 2) whose range of applicability is restricted to a particular learning domain (e.g., using problem solving steps for mathematics; Alexander et al., 1998; Weinstein et al., 2011). Taking into account these different conceptualizations, the same strategy can be placed within different categorizations. For example, the *read-and-repeat* strategy is cognitive, overt, surface-level, as well as a domain-independent strategy.

Notwithstanding the value of each separate strategy, it is particularly the ability to flexibly and selectively use a variety of apt strategies that has been shown to be crucial for learning, understanding, and performance across the lifelong journey toward proficiency (Alexander, 2018; Pressley & Harris, 2006). Indeed, effective learning, understanding, and performance requires the orchestration of strategies from different categorizations (Alexander, 2018). Consequently, in view of handling and solving a variety of tasks and problems, having access to a *strategic repertoire* and being able to efficiently make use of it, is indispensable. Different theoretical learning strategy models developed within the 2010s point attention to this strategic repertoire. Four overarching theoretical models are especially relevant here, that is the *Good Strategy User Model* (Pressley, Borkowski, & Schneider, 1987), the *Model of Strategic Learning* (Weinstein et al., 2011), the *Overlapping Waves Model* (Siegler, 1996), and the *Model of Domain Learning* (Alexander, 1998).

Pressley and colleagues (1987) focus in their *Good Strategy User (GSU) Model* on five identified components in good strategy users. According to this model, the good strategy user (1) can exert many strategies to attain goals, (2) has metacognitive knowledge about specific strategies, that is knowing how, when, and where to apply these strategies, (3) understands that good performance is tied to personal effort expended in carrying out appropriate strategies, (4) possesses a non-strategic knowledge base (e.g., the existence of categorizations), and (5) has automatized the first four components and their coordination (Pressley et al., 1987). According to the GSU model, novice learners possess very limited strategy knowledge and tendencies, whereas more proficient learners thoroughly understand and apply a wide range of strategies.

Weinstein and colleagues' (2011) *Model of Strategic Learning (MSL)* summarizes three interacting components of strategic learning that are connected causally with performance (i.e., skill, will, and self-regulation). *Skill* refers to the knowledge of a variety of strategies, and how, when, and where to apply them (i.e., respectively declarative, procedural, and conditional knowledge). *Will* refers to the motivational-affective component within strategic learning, referring to learners' attitudes, beliefs, and goals that drive their learning. *Self-regulation*, the third component according to the MSL, enables learners to monitor and manage their learning process.

Siegler's (1996) *Overlapping Waves Model (OWM)* is predicated on three assumptions: (1) learners employ a variety of strategies when solving a problem, (2) this variety of strategies coexists not only during brief transition periods but also over prolonged periods of time, and (3) gradual changes in the frequency of these applied strategies and more advanced applications of these strategies manifest through experience. Further, this model postulates that the typical pattern of strategy development includes five overlapping dimensions of learning: (1) acquiring the strategy of interest, (2) transferring the strategy to new, unfamiliar problems, (3) strengthening the strategy to assure consistent use across a given type of problem, (4) refining choices among alternative strategies or alternative forms of a single strategy, and (5) executing the strategy of interest increasingly effectively (Chen & Siegler, 2000; Siegler, 1996, 2000).

Finally, the *Model of Domain Learning (MDL)* was described by Alexander (1998) and approaches strategic processing through a developmental lens. In particular, the MDL describes strategic processing through three different stages, that is how learners progress from acclimation through competence to proficiency-expertise. Knowledge, strategies, and interest are identified as three interplaying factors, configuring differently during progression through these stages (Alexander, 1998, 2003). As learners progress from one stage to another, their strategy knowledge increases, and their strategy repertoire extends.

Despite their slightly different focus, the GSU model, MSL, OWM, and MDL show important parallels. On the one hand, all theoretical models point to the importance of having a diverse amount of strategies available (i.e., quantitative dimension). On the other, they also emphasize the efficient and adaptive use of this strategy repertoire (i.e., qualitative dimension). In this respect, all models entail a quantitative and qualitative dimension wherein improvements in strategy use can take place. Furthermore, all models highlight the key role of motivational-affective aspects in strategic processing by considering learners' personal effort (i.e., GSU), will to learn (i.e., MSL), and interest (i.e., MDL and OWM). Next to the abovementioned parallels between the theoretical models, the MDL explicitly distinguishes itself by the predominant focus on strategic processing from a developmental perspective. Before presenting an overarching framework on strategic processing, we therefore take a closer look at this developmental view in the next section.

A DEVELOPMENTAL PERSPECTIVE ON LEARNING

From a developmental perspective, learning is conceptualized as a process wherein change unfolds through different stages. Change is a fundamental characteristic of learning that affects the beginning, middle, and late stages of learning (Alexander, Schallert, & Reynolds, 2009). Accordingly, learning is different at various points in and over time (Alexander et al., 2009).

Change can be understood as arising from the evolved and innate processing capacities of the learner. As Alexander et al. (2009) state: "Being alive means being a learner" (p. 178), thereby referring to learners entering the world in a helpless state but possessing innate capacities or a strategic predisposition enabling them to learn through experience.

Neurological and biological changes enable us to learn differently at different ages, and children generally use increasingly more and effective strategies with age (Bjorklund & Pellegrini, 2000). Although the course of strategy development corresponds to age and years of schooling, it is not strictly aligned with chronological age (Alexander et al., 1998). The fact that children of the same age do not simultaneously develop and use similar strategies (Pressley, 1979, 1986; Pressley et al., 1992; Pressley & Harris, 2006) implies an explicit need to acknowledge individual differences in learners' strategic processing. Rather than with age or grade, the course of strategy development is closely related to learners' experience (Alexander et al., 2009; Chen & Siegler, 2000). As children gain experience and become more competent, their initial signs of strategic behavior are gradually and continuously transformed (Alexander et al., 1998; Siegler, 1996).

In the following sections of this chapter, we elaborate on the developmental stages of strategic processing by presenting a framework that encompasses shifts in learners' strategy use across the lifespan. To develop this conceptual framework, we build on the developmental stages within the MDL (Alexander, 1998, 2003). The presented developmental framework illuminates essential characteristics throughout the distinct stages of strategic processing for diverse individuals who are learning in markedly different contexts. It should, however, be noted that it is not our intention to capture the full nature of the developmental learning process in detail. Our framework provides a general road map of the course of strategy development and highlights important facets in this respect, but it is by no means all encompassing. Rather, it is a way of aligning aspects of learners' strategy development within a coherent and comprehensive overview.

STRATEGIC PROCESSING IN A MULTI-STAGED FRAMEWORK

The developmental framework we present is multi-staged in nature and centers on the evolution in learners' strategy use across time. Over the lifespan, learners' strategic processing systematically changes (Alexander et al., 2009). In accordance with Alexander (1998, 2003), we perceive strategic development as a lifelong journey or process that unfolds across multiple stages: the beginning, middle, and late stages of learning. This continuing development is depicted in the three fusing stages in Figure 4.1.

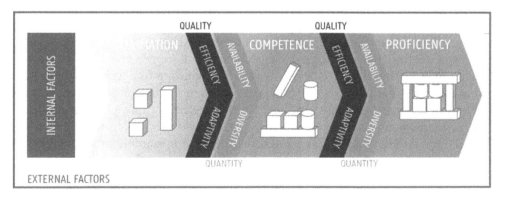

Figure 4.1 The multi-staged framework of the lifespan development of strategic processing, entailing strategies (cf., different building blocks) within three fusing stages of strategic processing (i.e., acclimation, competence, and proficiency) and four shifts in strategic development (i.e., availability, diversity, efficiency, and adaptivity) clustered in two major dimensions (i.e., quantity and quality)

Further, four main characteristics (i.e., availability, diversity, efficiency, and adaptivity) underlying learners' global changes in strategic processing are incorporated in the framework (Figure 4.1). As mentioned earlier, these are derived from the main theoretical models on strategic processing (i.e., GSU, MSL, OWM, MDL) and can be respectively clustered into two major dimensions, wherein *quantity* refers to the availability and diversity of strategies, while *quality* refers to the efficiency and adaptivity of strategies. Over the typical course of learners' strategy development, from acclimation to proficiency, learners' strategic processing undergoes profound changes with respect to each of these four characteristics. More particularly, as learners gain experience and become more competent and proficient in a task or domain, their strategic behavior changes and is characterized by increased availability, diversity, efficiency, and adaptivity (Alexander, 2003; Pressley et al., 1987; Siegler, 1996; Weinstein et al., 2011). In other words, over time, learners' strategy adoption will be characterized by a *quantitative shift*, referring to a more extensive and more diversified strategy repertoire (Alexander et al., 1998; Pressley et al., 1987; Siegler, 1996; Weinstein et al., 2011). Accordingly, a *qualitative shift* in strategic behavior will occur as well, referring to a more efficient, flexible, and apt application of available strategies (Alexander et al., 1998; Pressley et al., 1987; Siegler, 1996; Weinstein et al., 2011). It is important to stress that, although the abovementioned characteristics are considered separately in the theoretical framework, they are interwoven and interactive in reality. Hence, the development of one characteristic might enable the development of another, implying they might evolve symbiotically. We now turn to our framework and elaborate on the influential internal and external factors more in-depth.

As mentioned at the beginning of the chapter, learners can apply various strategies. These strategies are represented as different building blocks in Figure 4.1, which can take different forms or shapes according to how they are conceptualized or categorized (i.e., according to their nature, perceptibility, level of depth, and domain of application). As also can be seen in Figure 4.1, the configuration of these strategies can differ throughout different stages. In this respect, three fusing stages (i.e., acclimation, competence, and proficiency) represent the systematic transformations that unfold in learners' strategic processing (Alexander, 1998, 2003). These systematic transformations occur both within and across developmental stages.

In the early stage of learning (i.e., *acclimation stage*), when learners are first introduced to a task or problem, strategies are primarily used as tools for acquiring task-specific knowledge and for solving problems that are perceived by the learner as challenging and unfamiliar. As learners are just beginning to develop their strategies in this initial stage, their strategic processing is often inefficient, inelegant, and ineffective, whereas their strategy repertoire itself is relatively unsophisticated, limited, fragile, and, disorganized (Alexander, 1998, 2003; Berninger, Fuller, & Whitaker, 1996; Chen & Siegler, 2000). In the context of text-learning, for example, studies in both elementary and secondary education show that a fairly large number of learners possess a very limited initial strategy base (Merchie, Van Keer, & Vandevelde, 2014; Rogiers, Merchie, & Van Keer, 2019a). It was found that only 19% of late elementary graders and 33% of secondary school students respectively addressed a rich strategy repertoire wherein they succeed to effectively combine different text-learning strategies. Students at this acclimation stage apply strategies thus rather superficially (i.e., applying a limited number of strategies in a less efficient, flexible, or qualitative way), showing that their strategic processing is still in its infancy. In addition, learners exhibit minimal strategy transfer, which is restricted to new situations that are similar to the contexts in which these strategies were initially applied (Alexander, Jetton, & Kulikowich, 1995; Garner, 1990). In this stage, learners are mainly concerned with getting through the task, instead of developing competency or proficiency in the task. As such, their interest is classified as more situational (Alexander et al., 1995).

With increased exposure to the domain and related tasks and problems, learners will move to *a stage of competence*. Unlike the acclimated phase, learners in the competence phase have developed a richer and more integrated strategic knowledge base. As this knowledge base grows, their personal investment increases noticeably, and their interest begins to take on a greater role (Alexander, 1997). As learners gain more competence, their strategic repertoire is being expanded steadily and their strategic processing becomes more automatic, sophisticated, effective, and flexible. Existing strategies are modified, upgraded, and fine-tuned to serve new purposes, different strategies are combined in novel ways, and new strategies are learned and acquired (Chen & Siegler, 2000). As illustrated in Figure 4.1, the configuration of strategies becomes more stable and flexible during this stage. When it comes to learning from text, for example, a recent study of Rogiers and colleagues (2019a) shows that a strategy-focused program enabled learners to extend their strategic repertoire considerably. Both learners' self-reported and observed strategy use pointed toward a more strategic and integrated combination of various text learning strategies. As problems and tasks that acquire a strategic solution become more familiar, competent learners approach these by combining a mix of diverse strategies. Finally, their ability to decide whether and when a strategic solution is needed, and which strategies are needed to accomplish this, is growing (Alexander & Judy, 1988; Siegler, 1996). Learners at this stage are more likely to transfer their learned strategies from one situation to another and become less reliant on strategic solutions for solving common problems (Garner, 1990).

Lastly, another shift in strategic behavior occurs as learners acquire expertise and enter the *proficiency stage*. This particular stage is considered the most advanced level of learning and only a few learners actually reach this stage (Alexander et al., 1995). To reach this stage, experts possess a solid and extensive repertoire of highly structured and cohesive strategies (Alexander et al., 1995). This is also illustrated in the configuration of the diverse building blocks – representing strategies – in Figure 4.1. Along with the well-organized strategy base, expert learners demonstrate a deep personal interest in the tasks and the broader field, and a high level of persistence. The shift from competence to expertise is associated with a qualitative shift in the types of strategies learners most commonly rely on. Here, deep-processing strategies become paramount in learners' refined repertoire, while surface-processing strategies become fairly automated (Alexander & Fox, 2004). Even more than in the competence phase, expert learners are able to use the most suitable strategies to tackle problems or tasks as efficiently as possible. In addition, proficient learners exhibit maximal transfer of strategies to novel situations (Garner, 1990; Siegler, 1996).

To conclude, when learners acquire expertise in a task, a shift in their strategic behavior is taking place. This shift can be both quantitative and qualitative by nature, implying changes in the amount and the diversity of strategies becoming available in learners' repertoire as well as in the way strategies are applied by them (Alexander et al., 1998; Siegler, 1996). As learners move forward in their journey toward competence or perhaps even expertise, their strategy repertoire becomes more extensive and their strategic processing becomes more automatic (Alexander, 1998, 2003; Berninger et al., 1996). Accordingly, learners' strategies are configured differently and strengthened gradually across developmental stages. This global path in strategic development looks different, however, depending on both individual and contextual factors.

INTERNAL AND EXTERNAL DIFFERENCES IN LEARNING

Individual differences are inherently connected with human nature. Strategies are always initiated, enacted, and monitored by a learner who approaches tasks or problems in a unique way depending on individual variation in biological, psychological, as well as cognitive factors (Alexander et al., 2018; Chen & Siegler, 2000; Shen & Chen, 2006; Strømsø & Bråten, 2010). Even though there is a generalizable character in the pattern of strategy development, developmental patterns are still truly individual, varying from one person to the other. Learners of the same age and at the same developmental stage within a domain may, for example, still apply different strategies to solve the same problem, even when the context is held constant (Chen & Siegler, 2000; Merchie et al., 2014; Pressley et al., 1990; Rogiers et al., 2019a). For example, in a study of Merchie and colleagues (2014) and Rogiers and colleagues (2019), four learner profiles were identified in both late elementary and secondary school students' text-learning strategy use by means of cluster analysis. Whereas integrated strategy users (ISU) engaged in the strategic combination of different text-learning strategies, limited strategy users (LSU) generally used only a limited number of text-learning strategies. Information organizers (IO) frequently applied text-noting strategies and reported limited use of mental-learning strategies, while mental learners (ML) restricted their repertoire to mental learning strategies without text-noting strategy use. The individual nature of learners' strategic processing is also explicitly acknowledged in Figure 4.1, by positioning *internal factors* in front as an important precondition. Various internal influences, such as learner characteristics (e.g., age, gender, prior knowledge, domain interest, assigned task value, general cognitive capacity, and working memory), might shape a different path *between* individuals. For example, the approaches suitable for young learners taking their first steps toward competence are, therefore, not likely to work for older or more proficient learners (Alexander, 2005).

Next to the inter-individual differences between learners, learning activities are inevitably shaped by the changing conditions *within* individuals (Chen & Siegler, 2000). These intra-individual differences are connected to factors external to the learner. That is, specific task features (e.g., complexity or structure of the task) and context features (e.g., supportive environment, time constraints) as well as the interplay among these features, might shape learners' individual pattern of strategic development (Alexander et al., 2009). These significant differences between and within individuals can set boundaries or create opportunities for learning (Alexander et al., 2018). It is these (inter- or intra-)individual variabilities that determine what the path of strategy development may look like. Furthermore, as learning does not take place in a vacuum but emerges over time and space in a learning context, conditions *external* to the learner play a role in strategy development as well (Alexander et al., 2009). Accordingly, diverse individuals are learning at markedly different places both within and across time. These external factors refer to the ecological context in which learning occurs, which influences learning and is influenced by the learner. In this respect, we particularly refer to the physical and socio-cultural context as well as to the relationships among learners or between the learner and the wider environment. The latter involves the instructional support and guidance offered by educational practitioners or peers to foster learners' strategy use and development. For example, acclimated learners need more support, time, and scaffolding to achieve the advantages that come more easily to expert learners. Additionally, this wider environment can also refer to the classroom or work context in which learning occurs, as well as to the increasingly diverse, online, and rapidly changing learning context 21st-century learners face. In this regard, not only does the learner develop and change over time but also the context in which learning is embedded (e.g., classroom, school, work, society) is subject to continual change as well (Nist & Simpson, 2000). As learners and their learning environment are reciprocally influencing each other, a complex interplay between the two occurs. In fact, learning to become strategic involves becoming responsive to the shifting demands of the learning context (Pressley, Goodchild, Fleet, Zajchowski, & Evans, 1989). By embracing external factors in our developmental framework, it acknowledges the learning context and the accompanying changes and challenges learners in all developmental stages face.

To conclude, we presented a framework of strategic processing that encompasses changes in learners' strategy use across the lifespan. In sum, this conceptual framework is multi-staged in nature, including the configuration of strategies throughout three stages of strategy development (Alexander, 1998, 2003) and the accompanying quantitative (i.e., from less to more available and diverse strategies) and qualitative (i.e., from less to more efficient and adaptive strategies) shifts in learners' strategy use.

ISSUES AND LIMITATIONS IN THE CURRENT FIELD, AND FUTURE DIRECTIONS

We are still facing a number of challenges with regard to the study of learners' strategic development processes. Partly due to the rapidly changing society, there is to date no straightforward answer to the question of how strategic processing systematically changes over the course of a learner's lifespan or academic career (Alexander, 2018). In fact, research into the development of strategic processing is currently still emerging. In line with Alexander (2018), we therefore recommend future studies to explicitly focus on this developmental trajectory. To this end, longitudinal studies on strategic processing, focusing on the transformations that unfold as learners move toward competence or expertise are required. These studies could unravel how learners at different developmental stages internalize the external support they receive, and at which point in time external support can be faded (Alexander, 2018; Chen & Siegler, 2000). Accordingly, a well-established understanding of learners' strategic processing can help curriculum developers and educators in deciding what to emphasize in strategy development and when to teach it (Harris & Graham, 2016). Instead of merely making educated guesses, this enhanced understanding could serve as a sufficient evidence base for effective methods to optimally teach and support learners in all stages (Alexander,

2005). This should not, however, interfere with acknowledging the differences between learners' individual developmental trajectories as indicated above. Given the individual nature of learners' developmental paths, researchers are encouraged to take into account individual differences both between and within learners.

In order to study the development in learners' strategy use over a longer period of time, the adoption of different measurement instruments is recommended (McCardle & Hadwin, 2015; Samuelstuen & Bråten, 2007; Schellings, 2011; Veenman, 2011). To capture this development, both off-line measures, administered prospectively or retrospectively to performance on a task (e.g., self-report data, see also Chapter 16), and on-line measures, gathered concurrently during task performance (e.g., trace data, see also Chapter 17), should be used at different points in time, given their complementary particularities. These multiple instruments enable us to gauge both quality and quantity differences in learners' strategic processing and give us insight into which strategies learners applied (retrospective), are applying (real time), or will apply (prospective) (McCardle & Hadwin, 2015; Schellings, 2011; Veenman, 2011). This implies that researchers need to determine the best way to capture and examine learners' strategic processing at different stages and which measures are most adequate in their specific study. Accordingly, there is an urgent need for appropriate and valid measurement instruments to accurately capture and track learners' strategy use and transfer throughout the developmental course. Currently, more technology-driven measures (e.g., physiological measures, eye tracking measures, keystroke logging tools, etc.) are incorporated into research (e.g., Haataja, Malmberg, & Järvelä, 2018; Leijten & Van Waes, 2013; Malmberg, Järvelä, & Kirschner, 2013). These measures can give insight into factors underlying learners' strategic processing, and which factors provoke or hinder the application of certain strategies. Furthermore, the technological revolution and its associated increase in information sources places new demands on today's learners. Educational researchers acknowledge that this evolving technology has transformed both learning and teaching and may hold both promises and pitfalls (Alexander & Fox, 2004). The growing presence of hypermedia centralizes the question about what it means to be a strategic learner in this digital era. Studies on strategic processing within hypermedia environments are, therefore, recommended.

IMPLICATIONS FOR PRACTICE

Derived from our developmental framework, several implications for practice can be put forward. First, it is important to inform educators and practitioners about the stages and related important shifts in the development of strategic processing. In addition, they should be aware of the obstacles that might arise during that journey, so they can attune their interventions and educational support accordingly (Alexander, 2005).

Second, and as outlined above, strategies are acquired through experience. This implies that we must provide learners with the experiences as well as the tools necessary to move forward in their journey toward competence, and perhaps, proficiency. The different stages of development, however, acquire a different and customized educational approach. For example, learners in the acclimation phase usually demonstrate a strong reliance on surface-level strategies and their strategic processing remains ineffective and inefficient during this phase (Alexander & Judy, 1988; Merchie et al.,

2014; Rogiers et al., 2019a; Vandevelde, Van Keer, & Rosseel, 2013; Vandevelde, Van Keer, Schellings, & Van Hout-Wolters, 2015). Consequently, learners in this phase require more assistance and possess a stronger need for explicit instruction on how to become strategic. During explicit instruction, educators not only model the application of strategies (i.e., explain, verbalize, and demonstrate their thoughts, actions, and reasons while strategic processing) but also provide specific strategy knowledge so that learners become aware of the how, when, why, and where to apply strategies (Kistner et al., 2010; Paris & Paris, 2001; Veenman, van Hout-Wolters, & Afflerbach, 2006; Veenman et al., 2006). More concretely, by focusing on declarative knowledge (i.e., knowing about a variety of strategies), procedural knowledge (i.e., knowing how to use strategies), and conditional knowledge (i.e., knowing when and where to use particular strategies), learners' strategy growth is fostered. Important to notice is, however, that explicit attention to strategies does not solely apply for acclimated learners but for learners in all stages of strategic processing (Alexander et al., 2018). In this regard, strategy instruction requires that educators move beyond a mere "content approach," where the focus is often on facts and learning content. Instead, a "strategies approach," where learners' mental processes are directly targeted, is needed (Alfassi, 2004; Hall-Kenyon & Black, 2010; McKeown, Beck, & Blake, 2009; McNamara, 2011). By means of strategy instruction, strategies are made "transparent" and "transportable" for learners, enabling them to see why a particular strategy is useful, as well as how to apply the strategies in a subject-specific manner to other content areas (Alfassi, 2004; Parris & Block, 2008; Paris, Byrnes, & Paris, 2001; Pressley, 2000). For example, research in secondary education shows that by means of explicit strategy instruction, learners can become more competent in text-learning and extend their strategy repertoire considerably (Rogiers et al., 2019b). Consequently, and in line with several researchers, we recommend strategy instruction as an integral part in the regular instruction course embedded in all content areas (e.g., Alexander et al., 2018; Hamman, Berthelot, Saia, & Crowley, 2000; Harris et al., 2008). Instead of addressing strategy instruction as a separate course, a meta-curricular approach which systematically interweaves strategy adoption with acquiring domain-specific knowledge and skills, appears more valuable for learners' strategy transfer (e.g., Cornford, 2002; Kistner et al., 2010; Veenman, 2011).

Furthermore, as being strategic equally implies that strategies can be employed across a variety of situations, strategy instruction should also explicitly focus on the transfer of strategies. Next to strategy instruction, educators should provide various practice opportunities for learners to strategically solve novel tasks and problems while providing process feedback and gradually fading guidance as learners' proficiency increases (Garner, 1990; Graham & Harris, 1994; Kirschner, Sweller, & Clark, 2006; Weinstein et al., 2011; Pressley et al., 1989). Here, strategies should be practiced and developed in diverse and relevant contexts and learners must be encouraged to modify and combine their strategies according to the task or problem at hand (Alexander, 2003; Alexander et al., 2018). In this respect, learning contexts must be authentic and adaptable to the tasks learners encounter and vice versa. Support for strategy development can be provided by both educators and peers within a collaborative environment that meets the needs of diverse learners (e.g., De Backer, Van Keer, & Valcke, 2015, 2016; De Smedt, Graham, & Van Keer, 2019; De Smedt & Van Keer, 2018).

Third, and perhaps most fundamental, commitment to this lifespan perspective on strategic processing requires a change in the mindset of educators, practitioners, the public, and policy makers to accept strategic processing as a complex process of growth and development. When considering strategic processing from a developmental orientation, we must see the changes and challenges in the initial stages of learning as parts within a larger whole and vice versa (Alexander, 2005; Chen & Siegler, 2000). Within this growth perspective, attention is not exclusively focused on the actual state of one's strategic processing but also on the changes that unfold in the strategic process and the way we can foster them. In essence, good information processing must be perceived as a long-term endeavor (Pressley et al., 1989). In this respect, we can no longer consider strategic development as confined to the early years of schooling, but we are spanning learning readiness to a process of proficient strategic processing. Additionally, we must acknowledge that becoming an expert learner and building up a repertoire of strategies takes considerable time, with several years of strategies' instruction likely necessary for learners to truly take ownership of the strategies, and to apply these adaptively when encountering novel situations (Pressley, 2005; Pressley & Harris, 2006). Within the 21st century where lifelong learning is central, strategic development must, therefore, be seen as an integral responsibility of all educators across all educational levels and far beyond (Pressley et al., 1989).

Further, rather than focusing on the deficiencies, we must direct our attention to the growth opportunities for all learners. Although only a minority will reach the expert stage (Alexander, 1997), our expectations toward all learners should be high, even when they are only taking their first steps toward competence (Jang, Reeve, & Deci, 2010; Vansteenkiste et al., 2012). At the same time, unreasonable expectations might hamper learners' growth as well (Alexander, 2003). Expecting learners to make significant progress in their strategic processing by the time they complete formal education, appears reasonable. This implies that we must be sensitive to see the marked changes and movements in learners' strategic process (Murphy & Alexander, 2002). In addition, strategic development must be seen as an integral part of educators' professional development. Explicit attention to the instruction of strategies can increase teachers' competence to guide learners through this developmental course and equip them with a rich strategic repertoire.

CONCLUDING THOUGHTS

Our overarching intention was to consider the development of strategic processing across the lifespan as well as to offer a framework in which this development is illustrated. We believe the current developmental framework enables us to better understand previously executed empirical studies and to design future studies on mapping and stimulating learners' strategic processing. More particularly, the framework offers a rationale for the use of interventions targeting learners' strategic processing, as well as envisions the paths for strategy research that lies ahead.

As the saying goes, the present belongs to those who have learned but the future belongs to those who are learning (Weinstein et al., 2011). Our 21st century requires us to prepare learners for lifelong learning throughout the different stages of their lifespan. Having an extensive strategy repertoire that can be applied efficiently and flexibly, is a first important step toward becoming an effective learner.

REFERENCES

Alexander, P. A. (1997). Mapping the multidimensional nature of domain learning: The interplay of cognitive, motivational, and strategic forces. In M. L. Maehr & P. R. Pintrich (Eds.), *Advances in motivation and achievement* (Vol. 10, pp. 213–250). Greenwich, CT: JAI Press.

Alexander, P. A. (1998). The nature of disciplinary and domain learning: The knowledge, interest, and strategic dimensions of learning from subject matter text. In C. R. Hynd (Ed.), *Learning from texts across conceptual domains* (pp. 263–287). New York: Routledge.

Alexander, P. A. (2003). The development of expertise: The journey from acclimation to proficiency. *Educational Researcher, 32*(8), 10–14. doi:10.3102/0013189X032008010.

Alexander, P. A. (2005). The path to competence: A lifespan developmental perspective on reading. *Journal of Literacy Research, 37*(4), 413–436. doi:10.1207/s15548430jlr3704_1.

Alexander, P. A. (2006). *Psychology in Learning and Instruction*. Upper Saddle River, NJ: Pearson.

Alexander, P. A. (2018). Looking down the road: Future directions for research on depth and regulation of strategic processing. *British Journal of Educational Psychology, 88*, 152–166. doi:10.1111/bjep.12204.

Alexander, P. A., & Fox, E. (2004). A historical perspective on reading research and practice, redux. In D. E. Alvermann, N. J. Unrau, & R. B. Ruddell (Eds.), *Theoretical models and processes of reading* (6th ed., pp. 3–46). Newark, DE: International Reading Association.

Alexander, P. A., Graham, S., & Harris, K. (1998). A perspective on strategy research: Progress and prospects. *Educational Psychology Review, 10*, 129–154. doi:1023/A:1022185502996.

Alexander, P. A., Grossnickle, E. M., Dumas, D., & Hattan, C. (2018). A retrospective and prospective examination of cognitive strategies and academic development: Where have we come in twenty-five years? In A. O'Donnell (Ed.), *Oxford handbook of educational psychology* (pp. 1–56). Oxford, UK: Oxford University Press.

Alexander, P. A., Jetton, T. L., & Kulikowich, J. M. (1995). Interrelationship of knowledge, interest, and recall: Assessing a model of domain learning. *Journal of Educational Psychology, 87*, 559–575. doi:10.1037/0022-0663.87.4.559.

Alexander, P. A., & Judy, J. E. (1988). The interaction of domain-specific and strategic knowledge in academic performance. *Review of Educational Research, 58*, 375–404. doi:10.3102/00346543058004375.

Alexander, P. A., Schallert, D. L., & Reynolds, R. E. (2009). What is learning anyway? A topographical perspective considered. *Educational Psychologist, 44*, 209–214. doi:10.1080/00461520903029006.

Alexander, P. A., Schallert, D. L., & Hare, V. C. (1991). Coming to terms: How researchers in learning and literacy talk about knowledge. *Review of Educational Research, 61*, 315–343. doi:10.3102/00346543061003315.

Alfassi, M. (2004). Reading to learn: Effects of combined strategy instruction on high school students. *The Journal of Educational Research, 97*(4), 171–185. doi:10.3200/JOER.97.4.171-185.

Berninger, V., Fuller, F., & Whitaker, D. (1996). A process model of writing development across the life span. *Educational Psychology Review, 8*(3), 193–218. doi:10.1007/BF01464073.

Bjorklund, D. F., & Pellegrini, A. D. (2000). Child development and evolutionary psychology. *Child Development, 71*, 1687–1708. doi:10.1111/1467-8624.00258.

Bryant, L. C., Vincent, R., Shaqlaih, A., & Moss, G. (2013). Behaviorism and behavioral learning theory. In B. J. Irby, G. Brown, R. Lara-Alecio, & S. Jackson (Eds.), *Handbook of educational theories* (pp. 133–147). Charlotte, NC: Information Age Publishing.

Chen, Z., & Siegler, R. S. (2000). Overlapping waves theory. *Monographs of the Society for Research in Child Development, 65*, 7–11. doi:10.1111/1540-5834.00075.

Cornford, I. R. (2002). Learning-to-lean strategies as a basis for effective lifelong learning. *International Journal of Lifelong Education, 21*(4), 357–368. doi:10.1080/02601370210141020.

De Backer, L., Van Keer, H., & Valcke, M. (2015). Exploring evolutions in reciprocal peer tutoring groups' socially shared metacognitive regulation and identifying its metacognitive correlates. *Learning and Instruction, 38*, 63–78. doi:10.1016/j.learninstruc.2015.04.001.

De Backer, L., Van Keer, H., & Valcke, M. (2016). Eliciting reciprocal peer tutoring groups' metacognitive regulation through structuring and problematizing scaffolds. *The Journal of Experimental Education, 84*, 804–828. doi:10.1080/00220973.2015.1134419.

De Smedt, F., Graham, S., & Van Keer, H. (2019). "It takes two": The added value of peer-assisted writing in explicit writing instruction. Revised and resubmitted.

De Smedt, F., & Van Keer, H. (2018). Fostering writing in upper primary grades: A study into the distinct and combined impact of explicit instruction and peer assistance. *Reading and Writing, 31*(2), 325–354. doi:10.1007/s11145-017-9787-4.

Dinsmore, D. L., & Alexander, P. A. (2012). A critical discussion of deep and surface processing: What it means, how it is measured, the role of context, and model specification. *Educational Psychology Review, 24*, 499–567. doi:10.1007/s10648-012-9198-7.

Dole, J. A., Duffy, G. G., Roehler, L. R., & Pearson, D. D. (1991) Moving from the old to the new: Research on reading comprehension instruction. *Review of Educational Research, 61*. doi:10.3102/00346543061002239.

Garner, R. (1990). When children and adults do not use learning-strategies - toward a theory of settings. *Review of Educational Research, 60*(4), 517–529. doi:10.3102/00346543060004517.

Graham, S., & Harris, K. R. (1994). The role and development of self-regulation in the writing process. In D. H. Schunk & B. J. Zimmerman (Eds.), *Self-regulation of learning and performance: Issues and educational applications* (pp. 203–228). Hillsdale, NJ, US: Lawrence Erlbaum Associates, Inc.

Haataja, E., Malmberg, M., & Järvelä, S. (2018). Monitoring in collaborative learning: Co-occurrence of observed behavior and physiological synchrony explored. *Computers in Human Behavior, 87*, 337–347. doi:10.1016/j.chb.2018.06.007.

Hall-Kenyon, K. M., & Black, S. (2010). Learning from expository texts: Classroom-based strategies for promoting comprehension and content knowledge in the elementary grades. *Topics in Language Disorders, 30*, 339–349. doi:10.1097/TLD.0b013e3181ff21ea.

Hamman, D., Berthelot, J., Saia, J., & Crowley, E. (2000) Teachers' coaching of learning and its relation to students' strategic learning. *Journal of Educational Psychology, 92*(2), 342–348. doi:10.1037/0022-0663.92.2.342.

Harris, K., & Graham, S. (2016). Self-regulated strategy development in writing: Policy implications of an evidence-based practice. *Policy Insights from the Behavioral and Brain Sciences, 3*(1), 77–84. doi:10.1177/2372732215624216.

Harris, K. R., Alexander, P., & Graham, S. (2008). Michael Pressley's contributions to the history and future of strategies research. *Educational Psychologist, 43*(2), 86–96. doi:10.1080/00461520801942300.

Jang, H., Reeve, J., & Deci, E. L. (2010). Engaging students in learning activities: It is not autonomy support or structure but autonomy support and structure. *Journal of Educational Psychology, 102*, 588–600. doi:10.1037/A0019682.

Kirschner, P., Sweller, J., & Clark, R. E. (2006). Why minimal guidance during instruction does not. Work: An analysis of the failure of constructivist. *Educational Psychologist, 41*(2), 75–86. doi:10.1207/s15326985ep4102_1.

Kistner, S., Rakoczy, K., Otto, B., Dignath-van Ewijk, C., Buttner, G., & Klieme, E. (2010). Promotion of self-regulated learning in classrooms: Investigating frequency, quality, and consequences for student performance. *Metacognition and Learning, 5*(2), 157–171. doi:10.1007/s11409-010-9055-3.

Leijten, M., & Van Waes, L. (2013). Keystroke logging in writing research: Using inputlog to analyze and visualize writing processes. *Written Communication, 30*(3), 358–392. doi:10.1177/0741088313491692.

Malmberg, J., Järvelä, S., & Kirschner, P. A. (2013). Elementary school students' strategic learning: Does task-type matter? *Metacognition and Learning, 9*(2), 113–136. doi:10.1007/s11409-013-9108-5.

McCardle, L., & Hadwin, A. F. (2015). Using multiple, contextualized data sources to measure learners' perceptions of their self-regulated learning. *Metacognition Learning, 10*(1), 43–75. doi:10.1007/s11409-014-9132-0.

McKeown, M. G., Beck, I. L., & Blake, R. G. K. (2009). Rethinking reading comprehension instruction: A comparison of instruction for strategies and content approaches. *Reading Research Quarterly, 44*, 218–253. doi:10.1598/RRQ.44.3.1.

McNamara, D. S. (2011). Measuring deep, reflective comprehension and learning strategies: Challenges and successes. *Metacognition and Learning, 3*, 1–11. doi:10.1007/s11409-011-9082-80.

Merchie, E., Van Keer, H., & Vandevelde, S. (2014). Development of the text-learning strategies inventory: Assessing and profiling learning from texts in fifth and sixth grade. *Journal of Psychoeducational Assessment*, 1–15. doi:10.1177/0734282914525155.

Murphy, P. K., & Alexander, P. A. (2002). What counts? The predictive power of subject matter knowledge, strategic processing, and interest in domain-specific performance. *Journal of Experimental Education, 70*, 197–214. doi:10.1080/00220970209599506.

Nist, S. L., & Simpson, M. L. (2000). College studying. In M. Kamil, P. Mosenthal, P. D. Pearson, & R. Barr (Eds.), *Handbook of reading research, Vol. III* (pp. 645–666). Mahwah, NJ: Lawrence Erlbaum.

Paris, S. G., Byrnes, J. P., & Paris, A. H. (2001). Constructing theories, identities and actions of self-regulated learners. In B. J. Zimmerman & D. H. Schunk (Eds.), *Self-regulated learning and academic achievement* (2nd ed., pp. 253–288). Mahwah, NJ: Lawrence Erlbaum.

Paris, S. G., & Paris, A. H. (2001). Classroom applications of research on self-regulated learning. *Educational Psychologist, 36*(2), 89–101. doi:10.1207/S15326985EP3602_4.

Parris, S. R., & Block, C. C. (2008). Summing Up. In C. C. Block & S. R. Parris (Eds.), *Comprehension Instruction. Research-Based Best Practices* (2nd ed.) (pp. 381–390). New York: The Guilford Press.

Pintrich, P. R. (2004). A conceptual framework for assessing motivation and self-regulated learning in college students. *Educational Psychology Review, 106,* 1854–1878. doi:10.1007/s10648-004-0006-x.

Pressley, M. (1979). Increasing children's self-control through cognitive interventions. *Review of Educational Research, 49,* 319–370. doi:10.3102/00346543049002319.

Pressley, M. (1986). The relevance of the good strategy user model to the teaching of mathematics. *Educational Psychologist, 21,* 139–161. doi:10.1207/s15326985ep2101&2_8.

Pressley, M. (2000). What should comprehension instruction be the instruction of? In M. L. Kamil, P. B. Mosenthal, P. D. Pearson, & R. Barr (Eds.), *Handbook of reading research, Vol. 3* (pp. 545–561). Mahwah, NJ: Lawrence Erlbaum.

Pressley, M. (2005). *Reading Instruction That Works: The Case for Balanced Teaching.* New York: Guilford.

Pressley, M., Borkowski, J. G., & Schneider, W. (1987). Cognitive strategies: Good strategy users coordinate metacognition and knowledge. *Annals of Child Development, 4,* 89–129.

Pressley, M., El-Dinary, P. B., Gaskins, I., Schuder, T., Bergman, J. L., Almasi, J., & Brown, R. (1992). Beyond direct explanation: Transactional instruction of reading comprehension strategies. *Elementary School Journal, 92,* 511–554. doi:10.1086/461705.

Pressley, M., Goodchild, F., Fleet, J., Zajchowski, R., & Evans, E. D. (1989). The challenges of classroom strategy instruction. *The Elementary School Journal, 89,* 301–342. doi:10.1086/461578.

Pressley, M., Graham, S., & Harris, K. R. (2006). The state of educational intervention research. *British Journal of Educational Psychology, 76,* 1–19. doi:10.1348/000709905X66035.

Pressley, M., & Harris, K. R. (2006). Cognitive strategies instruction: From basic research to classroom instruction. In P. A. Alexander & P. Winne (Eds.), *Handbook of educational psychology* (2nd ed., pp. 265–286). New York: Macmillan.

Pressley, M., Woloshyn, V., Lysynchuk, L. M., Martin, V., Wood, E., & Willoughby, T. (1990). A primer of research on cognitive strategy instruction: The important issues and how to address them. *Educational Psychology Review, 2,* 1–58. doi:10.1007/BF01323528.

Rogiers, A., Merchie, E., & Van Keer, H. (2019a). Learner profiles in secondary education: Occurrence and relationship with performance and student characteristics. *The Journal of Educational Research, 112*(3), 385–396. doi:10.1080/00220671.2018.1538093.

Rogiers, A., Merchie, E., & Van Keer, H. (2019b). Stimulating text-learning strategy use in secondary education: A person-centered longitudinal approach. Submitted for publication.

Samuelstuen, M. S., & Bråten, I. (2007). Examining the validity of self-reports on scales measuring students' strategic processing. *British Journal of Educational Psychology, 77,* 351–378. doi:10.1348/0007099 06X106147.

Schellings, G. L. M. (2011). Applying learning strategy questionnaires: Problems and possibilities. *Metacognition and Learning, 6*(2), 91–109. doi:10.1007/s11409-011-9069-5.

Shen, B., & Chen, A. (2006). Examining the interrelations among knowledge, interests, and learning strategies. *Journal of Teaching in Physical Education, 25,* 182–199. doi:10.1123/jtpe.25.2.182.

Siegler, R. S. (1996). *Emerging minds: The process of change in children's thinking.* New York: Oxford University Press.

Siegler, R. S. (2000). The rebirth of children's learning. *Child Development, 71,* 26–35. doi:10.1111/1467-8624.00115.

Strømsø, H. I., & Bråten, I. (2010). The role of personal epistemology in the self-regulation of Internet-based learning. *Metacognition and Learning, 5,* 91–111. doi:10.1007/s11409-009-9043-7.

Vandevelde, S., Van Keer, H., & Rosseel, Y. (2013). Measuring the complexity of upper primary school children's self-regulated learning: A multi-component approach. *Contemporary Educational Psychology, 38*(4), 407–425. doi:10.1016/j.cedpsych.2013.09.002.

Vandevelde, S., Van Keer, H., Schellings, G., & Van Hout-Wolters, B. (2015). Using think-aloud protocol analysis to gain in-depth insights into upper primary school children's self-regulated learning. *Learning and Individual Differences, 43,* 11–30. doi:10.1016/j.lindif.2015.08.027.

Vansteenkiste, M., Sierens, E., Goossens, L., Soenens, B., Dochy, F., Mouratidis, A., … Beyers, W. (2012). Identifying configurations of perceived teacher autonomy support and structure: Associations with self-regulated learning, motivation and problem behavior. *Learning and Instruction, 22,* 431–439. doi:10.1016/j.learninstruc.2012.04.002.

Veenman, M. V. J. (2011). Learning to self-monitor and self-regulate. In R. Mayer & P. Alexander (Eds.), *Handbook of research on learning and instruction* (pp. 197–218). New York: Routledge.

Veenman, M. V. J., van Hout-Wolters, B. H. A. M., & Afflerbach, P. (2006). Metacognition and learning: conceptual and methodological considerations. *Metacognition and Learning, 1*(1), 3–14. doi: 10.1007/s11409-006-6893-0

Wade, S. E., Trathen, W., & Schraw, G. (1990). An analysis of spontaneous study strategies. *Reading Research Quarterly, 25*(2), 147–166. doi:10.2307/747599.

Weinstein, C. E., Jung, J., & Acee, T. W. (2011). Learning strategies. In V. G. Aukrust (Ed.), *Learning and cognition in education* (pp. 137–143). Oxford: Elsevier Limited.

Weinstein, C. E., & Mayer, R. E. (1986). The teaching of learning strategies. In M. C. Wittrock (Ed.), *Handbook of research on teaching* (3rd ed., pp. 315–327). New York: Macmillan.

5

NEGOTIATING MEANING AND ENGAGEMENT
Socially Shared Strategic Processing

Deborah L. Butler and Leyton Schnellert
UNIVERSITY OF BRITISH COLUMBIA, CANADA

NEGOTIATING MEANING AND ENGAGEMENT: SOCIALLY SHARED STRATEGIC PROCESSING

It has long been recognized that collaboration fosters richer forms of learning and innovation than any individual can achieve on their own (e.g., Gillies, 2016). But, given contemporary demands of citizens in the 21st-century's information society, calls to foster learners' collaborative capacities are intensifying in both research and professional literatures. As just one example, Lee, Huh, and Reigeluth, (2015) suggested that, "developing networking skills, maintaining collaborative relationships with people, and making decisions as a team are considered essential skills to be successful in the new era" (p. 562). Correspondingly, researchers and educators alike are currently seeking ways to support learners' developing capacities as collaborative learners.

Unfortunately, research has consistently identified how individuals do not know how to learn with others effectively (e.g., Gillies, 2016; Treff, 2006). For example, students may not know how to engage in the life of a classroom, including the forms of academic discourse required to learn with others (Fisher, Frey, & Pumpian, 2012; Gillies, 2016; Michaels, O'Connor, & Resnick, 2008). Even adults need support to know how to learn and work productively with others in classrooms or workplaces (e.g., Miller, & Hadwin, 2015; Treff, 2006). These findings underline the urgency of finding ways to support students to learn and engage socially.

In this chapter, we contribute by describing how socially shared forms of strategic processing are necessary to, and can be supported within, collaborative activity. To that end, we draw from diverse strands in the literature that have (a) studied collaborative learning processes (e.g., Hadwin, Järvelä, & Miller, 2018; Järvenoja et al., 2015; Miller

& Hadwin, 2015; Volet, Vauras, & Salonen, 2009); (b) surfaced the kinds of norms, expectations, and academic discourse that students need to navigate when learning collaboratively (e.g., Gillies, 2016; Jurkowski & Hänze, 2015; Treff, 2006); (c) identified pedagogical practices that support socially shared forms of strategic processing (e.g., Butler, Schnellert, & Perry, 2017; Perry, Mazabel, & Yee, in press; Schonert-Reichl & Weissberg, 2015); and (d) examined collaborative learning processes in various pedagogical frameworks, such as cooperative learning (e.g., Gillies, 2016; Johnson & Johnson, 2009), computer-supported collaborative learning (CSCL) (e.g., Miller & Hadwin, 2015; Winne, 2015); collaborative problem- or project-based learning (e.g., Kim & Lim, 2018; Lee et al., 2015); and collaborative inquiry (e.g., Hickey et al., 2002; Torre, Van Der Vlueten, & Dolmans, 2016).

To help in identifying convergences and unique contributions across these lines of inquiry, we start by introducing an integrative framework that helped us to pull together ideas relevant to understanding socially shared strategic processing and how to support it. We then build from that framework to identify principles and practices with promise to nurture social forms of strategic processing, including in the kinds of collaborative activities becoming so prevalent in today's schools. We conclude with recommendations for practice and research.

A FRAMEWORK FOR STUDYING STRATEGIC PROCESSING AS SOCIALLY AND CULTURALLY SITUATED

In this section we introduce a framework that we have used previously to characterize individual and social forms of strategic processing from a self-regulated learning (SRL) point of view (Butler, 2015; Butler & Cartier, 2018; Butler & Schnellert, 2015; Butler et al., 2017; Cartier & Butler, 2016). We draw on this framework to (a) conceptualize socially shared strategic processing, and (b) identify individual and social influences that need to be considered when supporting students' capacities as strategic learners (see Figure 5.1).

Situating Strategic Processing in a Model of SRL

As early as the 1980s researchers recognized the power of teaching strategies to students as a means of promoting academic learning (e.g., Brown, Campione, & Day, 1981; Palincsar & Brown, 1988). Findings were consistently that making learning processes visible enabled students to learn *how to* engage more successfully. Still, the challenge at that time was that, while students were learning to use taught strategies capably when cued to do so, they were not taking up those strategies independently, flexibly, or adaptively in other tasks or contexts (Butler, 2002). Thus, researchers set out to solve this transfer problem (e.g., Borkowski & Muthukrishna, 1992; Harris & Graham, 1996; Pressley et al., 1992; Wong, 1994).

At that time, researchers realized that focusing on strategy use per se was not enough to encompass all of the processes involved in the kind of adaptive, situated, and flexible performance required of students across contexts and tasks (e.g., Pressley et al., 1992). To give a fuller picture of strategic processing, models of self-regulation emerged that located strategy use in a cycle of strategic action which requires first generating a clear

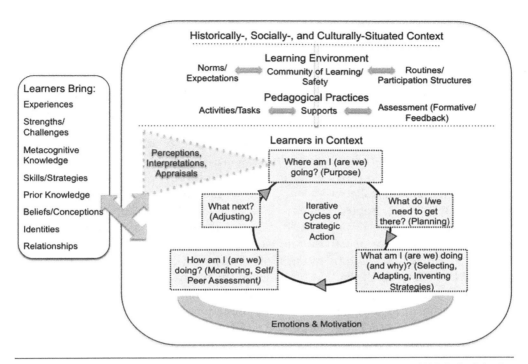

Figure 5.1 Strategic Processing as Socially and Culturally Situated (adapted from Butler et al., 2017; Butler & Cartier, 2018; Cartier & Butler, 2016)

sense of purpose, then choosing strategies best able to achieve goals in a particular situation (e.g., Harris & Graham, 1996; Zimmerman, 1989). Alongside others, Butler (1998, 2002) demonstrated the value of this broader view of strategic processing. For example, Butler's (1998) research with struggling learners found that, while many students lacked knowledge about effective strategies, challenges in "task interpretation" were even more detrimental (Butler & Cartier, 2004). Students who held misconceptions about assigned tasks were derailed in their strategic processing before they even began to work.

Where, then, does strategic processing fit within a model of SRL? Our framework characterizes strategic processing as involving flexible, adaptive, and iterative cycles of strategic action (Butler & Cartier, 2018; Butler et al., 2017; Cartier & Butler, 2016). Strategic action requires being alert to environmental demands and building from one's knowledge and experience in order to interpret expectations, establish a clear sense of purpose, choose strategies well matched to task demands, monitor how things are progressing, and flexibly and adaptively shift goals or approaches as needed. In other words, to be successful, students need to know how to select, adapt, or even invent personalized strategies that enable them to navigate the demands of learning in any given context adaptively and flexibly.

Over time, models of SRL have also evolved to highlight how engaging strategically is not just a cognitive endeavor. Contemporary models of self-regulation define how students' strategic attention needs to focus simultaneously on cognitive, motivational, emotional, behavioral, and social processes (e.g., Boekaerts, 2011; Butler et al., 2017; Zimmerman, 2011). For example, Zimmerman (2008) argued that self-regulating learners know how to control their thoughts, feelings, and actions to achieve personal goals and respond to environmental demands. Butler et al. (2017) suggested that, as part of socially shared strategic processing, students need to orchestrate not just cognitive processes but also their emotions, motivation, and relationships in the service of learning. Correspondingly, supporting collaborative forms of strategic processing requires that pedagogical practices support active, reflective, adaptive, and strategic processing along these multiple dimensions.

Finally, it is key to note that the term "self" in self-regulation is not intended to signify independent learning divorced from social contexts or interaction. Instead, the *self* in self-regulation provides an important reminder of how individuals exercise individual and/or collective agency in how they interpret and respond to the socially and culturally rooted contexts (Bandura, 2000). Over time, work on SRL has been informed by varying socially grounded theoretical perspectives, including socio-cultural, socio-constructivist, and situated points of view (Butler et al., 2017; Hadwin & Oshige, 2011; Zimmerman, 1989, 2008). Our discussion in this chapter is informed by SRL research that has investigated the interplay between individual and social forms of strategic processing (e.g., Anyichie & Butler, 2018; Hadwin et al., 2018; Kaplan, Lichtinger, & Margulis, 2010; Kim & Lim, 2018; McCaslin & Burrows, 2010; McInerney & King, 2018; Perry, Yee, Mazabel-Ortega, Lisaingo, & Määttä, 2017; Volet et al., 2009; Winne, 2015).

Individual and Social Influences on Socially Shared Strategic Processing

Figure 5.1 provides a high level overview of individual and social influences on socially shared strategic processing. Overall the framework suggests that learning emerges from a complex interplay between what students are bringing to a learning environment and the opportunities and constraints afforded by the contexts in which they are learning.

Individual Influences on Socially Shared Strategic Processing. In recognition of individual influences on learning, Figure 5.1 suggests that *what learners bring* to contexts influences their *perceptions, interpretations, and appraisals* of the learning environment and the demands within it (Boekaerts, 2011). These perceptions, interpretations, and appraisals in turn influence whether and how students choose to engage in learning on their own or with others.

Recognizing individual influences is important for understanding and supporting socially shared strategic processing. For example, what learners are bringing to contexts, such as their personal funds of knowledge (Barton & Hamilton, 2012; Moje, 2013; Moll, Amanti, Neff, & Gonzalez, 1992) or socio-emotional competencies (e.g., Lee et al., 2015), can serve as affordances to their own and others' collaborative learning processes. Strategic processing in collaborative contexts can also be enhanced if educators recognize and build on the wide range of experiences, strengths, challenges, knowledge (metacognitive, content-related), skills, and strategies that diverse learners bring to the classroom (e.g., Pushor, 2012). By supporting effective forms of strategic action, educators can, in turn, influence learners' development of beliefs, conceptions, relationships, and identities that positively influence their engagement in subsequent forms of strategic learning (e.g., see Butler & Cartier, 2004; Kozleski & Waitoller, 2010; McCaslin, 2009; Zimmerman, 2011).

When thinking about individual influences, it is particularly important to recognize that students' prior culturally and socially situated experiences shape their understandings about how schools, classrooms, and learning work (Anyichie & Butler, 2018; McCaslin & Burrows, 2010; McInerney & King, 2018). Diverse learners' success in classrooms can be undermined if their understanding about expectations or goals (i.e., their sense of purpose) does not match those of educators and/or peers. To support effective forms of strategic processing, educators need to ensure that all learners, whatever their backgrounds, are supported to discern how classrooms work (Perry et al., 2017). Beyond that, many researchers and educators are also arguing for the creation of culturally responsive environments which enable students to build from their cultural and linguistic backgrounds to inform their learning processes (e.g., Anyichie, 2018; Anyichie & Butler, 2018; Gay, 2010; Ladson-Billings, 1995).

Social Influences on Socially Shared Strategic Processing. Our integrative model of SRL also identifies three layers of social influences on socially shared forms of strategic processing. At the broadest level, learning activity is *historically, socially, and culturally situated*. That broader context influences how norms, routines, and participation structures are constituted within *learning environments* (Leinhardt, Weidman, Hammond, 1987; Perry et al., in press). Finally, within learning environments, *pedagogical practices* provide different kinds of opportunities and supports for strategic processing. Supporting strategic processing requires attending to the influence of these multiple layers of contexts in which learning is invariably situated. Given our focus in this chapter on socially shared strategic processing, pedagogical practices that are particularly influential include (a) activities that are created to invite/require collaboration and co-learning; (b) supports that help students learn how to participate effectively in activities alone and with others; and (c) formative assessment and feedback activities that invite teachers and learners to think and learn collaboratively (Heritage, 2018; Hickey et al., 2002; Nicol & Macfarlane-Dick, 2006).

How individuals engage with others creates a key social influence on learning. SRL literature has shown that productive forms of collaborative activity emerge when students engage in cycles of strategic action together (Butler & Schnellert, 2012). Strategic processing with others involves purposeful thinking and action that is negotiated in context (Kaplan et al., 2010). Building from SRL and formative assessment literatures (e.g., Butler et al., 2017; Hattie & Timperley, 2007; Heritage, 2018), our integrative model highlights key questions that strategically oriented learners need to ask themselves as they work through strategic action cycles alone and/or together (see Figure 5.1).

Many contemporary SRL researchers have studied how students regulate learning together within collaborative activities (i.e., how they engage in cycles of strategic action together). Their research has identified the complexity of "regulation" in collaborative forms of learning. For example, findings have been that individuals engage dynamically in both self- and social forms of regulation within a collaborative task (Hadwin et al., 2018; Hadwin & Oshige, 2011; Volet et al., 2009). Further, social forms of regulation can include dynamically evolving combinations of both *co-regulation* and *socially shared regulation*.

Co-regulation is typically associated with a more knowledgeable person providing instrumental support for another person's self-regulated engagement within the context of an activity (e.g., a teacher facilitating a student to think through a problem strategically). Co-regulation can involve influences from teacher to student, student to teacher, and peer to peer (Hadwin et al., 2018; Volet et al., 2009). Research on co-regulation has identified how educators and students can support each other's learning through cycles of strategic action (e.g., creating a sense of purpose; planning; choosing and enacting strategies; monitoring; adjusting). Findings have shown that one way to support socially shared strategic processing is for teachers to create conditions for themselves or peers to co-regulate a learner's participation (e.g., by asking metacognitive questions that spur a student's thinking about the questions embedded in Figure 5.1; by offering constructive feedback).

Hadwin et al. (2018) defined *socially shared regulation* as "a group's deliberate, strategic, and transactive planning, task enactment, reflection, and adaption" (p. 86). When sharing regulation within collaborative forms of learning, individuals engage in transactive exchanges through which they negotiate meaning, learning processes, and relationships. When engaged in rich forms of socially shared regulation, diverse learners can add their various points of view to co-construct a richer sense of purpose and work iteratively, flexibly, and dynamically through cycles of strategic action together (e.g., taking up the "we" version of the questions in Figure 5.1). Thus, another way in which educators can support social forms of strategic processing is by creating conditions for peers to learn how to engage in productive forms of socially shared regulation with others.

Pulling It All Together. In sum, in this section, we introduced an integrative, situated model of SRL. We built from that framework to define strategic processing as encompassing iterative cycles of strategic action. We also identified how contemporary SRL researchers have characterized socially shared strategic processing as dynamically interacting forms of self- and social regulation (e.g., co-regulation; socially shared regulation). Building on our SRL model, we identified that understanding and supporting strategic processing requires recognizing how individual and social processes intertwine to shape learners' engagement. On the one hand, students bring to contexts a diversity of experiences (e.g., personal, academic), funds of knowledge (e.g., cultural, content, metacognitive), beliefs (e.g., agency), and conceptions (e.g., about academic work) that shape their interpretations of and choices about how to engage in classroom-based activities. On the other, contexts define norms, discourses, and expectations that students need to discern and respond to generatively. To participate successfully in socially shared strategic processing, learners need to know how to build from their personal resources to interpret demands and navigate not just the requirements of academic tasks but also the expectations of how to learn within socially and culturally situated classrooms.

In the rest of this chapter, we build on this framework to consider further what educators can do to support socially shared forms of strategic processing. To begin, we identify foundational approaches educators can take up to empower learners to navigate classrooms. Next, we draw across literatures to distill principles and practices for supporting social forms of strategic learning. Finally, we identify whether and how those principles and practices are, or could be, brought to life to foster socially shared strategic processing within a variety of increasingly common collaborative learning frameworks (e.g., collaborative learning; computer assisted collaborative learning).

SUPPORTING STRATEGIC PROCESSING IN THE LIFE OF THE CLASSROOM

The literature we reviewed consistently suggested how learning environments require social forms of strategic processing, not just within structured collaborative learning activities but also within learning communities as they are instantiated day to day (McCaslin & Burrows, 2010). Thus, a key question is, if they are to engage in strategic processing as "social," how must learners come to be personally aware and adaptive given the dynamically shifting learning environments in which they are participating together?

Setting the Stage for Social Forms of Strategic Processing

Learning environments are highly influential in how students engage in collaborative forms of learning (Woolfolk, Winne, & Perry, 2015). To support students' willingness to take risks and learn together, it is important to create a safe, non-threatening learning environment in which students feel they are 'in it together' (e.g., Noddings, 1992). Educators can do that by developing a *community of learners* that recognizes, values, and builds on diverse learners' strengths, interests, challenges, and histories (Schnellert, Kozak, & Moore, 2015). In communities of learning, students perceive their role, not just to best others or achieve on their own but also to contribute to others' learning. This perspective is consistent with a call for creating positive interdependence as an essential condition for collaborative learning (Gillies, 2016; Johnson & Johnson, 2009), or a "culture of collaboration and interdependence" (Ertmer & Simons, 2006, p. 40). Similarly, Hutchinson (2013) argued for the importance of fostering socially responsible self-regulation, where students deliberately and intentionally manage engagement in prosocial ways that support their own and others' learning. Hymel, McClure, Miller, Shumka, and Trach (2014) added that, in classrooms where cooperative learning and interdependence are supported, "prosocial values can become normative" (p. 20).

Supporting Learners to Recognize and Participate in the Life of the Classroom

Educators typically establish all sorts of norms, routines, and participation structures that help in orchestrating students' engagement in the busy life of the classroom (e.g., morning meetings, sharing circles, "ask three before me") (Leinhardt et al., 1987; Woolfolk et al., 2015). Perry et al. (in press) suggested that these "enable independent and social forms of learning" (p. 40). But, if students are to work successfully with others in classroom contexts, they need to "read" expectations and direct their activities accordingly. Referring to the kinds of norms, routines, and participation structures prevalent in classrooms, Butler et al. (2017) asked: (a) do students know what they are?; (b) do they own them?; and (c) do they know how to participate? Correspondingly, to support effective forms of strategic processing, where all students have a clear sense of purpose and can channel their strategic action effectively, they recommended (a) naming them explicitly (i.e., making them visible); (b) building them with students; and (c) providing supports for all learners to know how to navigate them (see also Perry et al., in press). Doing so enables students, on their own and with others, to work through cycles of strategic action effectively.

Learning to Learn Together: Qualities of Discourse

> Classroom discourse is structured by socially accepted ways in which knowledge is presented and by established procedures for carrying out educational activities. However, the underlying linguistic and social ground rules are usually implicit, for students as well as for teachers. The implicitness of these ground rules has been attributed to students' failure to successfully participate in educational discourse.
>
> (Staarman, 2009, p. 79)

Schoenfeld (2004) suggested that in learning, communities engage students in rich forms of thinking and learning together around "matters of substance" (p. 251). Thus, to support socially shared strategic processing, it is key to identify the quality of discourse in which students are expected to participate together in different classrooms and activities. To that end, Staarman (2009) built on a "thinking together" approach to study forms of educational discourse involved in collaboration (p. 80); Jurkowski and Hänze (2015) studied benefits for cooperative learning when teaching students to engage in "transactive communication" (p. 358); and Michaels et al. (2008) considered how classroom practices can support "academically productive talk" (p. 283). Gillies (2016) focused on how students can be supported to reason together and engage in the kinds of high level talk required in collaborative learning. There is also ample research describing discipline-based forms of discourse that students need to learn how to navigate in texts and conversation (e.g., Hickey et al., 2002; Moje, 2013; Seixas & Morton, 2012). These various discussions combine to suggest how, to engage in socially shared strategic action effectively in classroom environments, students need to learn how to recognize and participate effectively in multiple kinds of academic discourse.

In terms of enriching collaborative learning, research has also suggested how classroom diversity contributes to the quality of discourse within a learning community (Schnellert & Kozak, 2019). As Torre et al. (2016) argued, "cognitive diversity, where group members have different yet overlapping levels of knowledge and expertise results in more effective and innovative individual and group achievements" (p. 192). Kahiigi, Hansson, Danielson, and Tusubira (2012) suggested that students co-construct richer understandings about concepts when they have to negotiate different perspectives. Similarly, Lee et al. (2015) found that task-related conflict created a need to reconcile contrasting views and led to greater learning. This research suggests again that in classrooms students need to build capacities to engage in rich forms of discourse with others. Further, Lee et al. concluded that, to successfully navigate task, process, and relationship conflicts that arise during collaboration, students need to mobilize social skills as they engage in activities, particularly at the group level.

SUPPORTING SOCIAL SHARED STRATEGIC PROCESSING: PEDAGOGICAL PRINCIPLES

How can learners be supported to engage effectively in socially shared strategic processing in classrooms and collaborative activities? In this section, we pull together pedagogical principles and practices from across literatures on social-emotional learning (SEL), SRL, and formative assessment (FA) (see Table 5.1).

Negotiating Meaning and Engagement • 71

Table 5.1 Principles and Practices for Supporting Socially Shared Strategic Processing

Principles	Practices
Create communities of learners that… (SEL, SRL)	• are respectful, welcoming, caring, safe, and inclusive • foster positive interdependence • engage teachers and students in rich forms of co-learning • build from the diversity learners bring to classrooms • create groups in ways that foster safety and mutual respect.
Establish ways of working that enable rich forms of collaboration and learning (SRL)	• create supportive norms, expectations, routines, and participation structures • design activities to invite self- and social forms of regulation • engage learners together in rich forms of academic talk • make ways of working "visible" for all community members • ensure all members know how to participate.
Weave supports for social forms of learning into classrooms and schools (SEL, SRL, FA)	• identify competencies and processes needed in contexts • explicitly support learners' development of those capacities • empower learners to mobilize competencies within activities • sustain focus on competencies and process goals over time • bridge from guiding learning toward independence.
Support learners to engage in full cycles of strategic action (SRL/FA)	• support learners to negotiate a sense of "purpose" • support learners to learn how to purposefully, adaptively, and flexibly engage in planning, reflecting, and adjusting • engage learners in self- and peer-assessment.
Foster agency (SRL/FA)	• position students as owners of their learning and action • engage learners in co-creating the life of the classroom • give students influence (e.g., meaningful choices) • nurture strategic action as a "way of working."

Social Emotional Learning

Earlier we argued that working with others strategically requires navigating cognition, motivation, emotion, behavior, and relationships in the service of learning (Butler et al., 2017). As a result, it is increasingly being recognized that students need to build social-emotional competencies as part of what they bring to contexts (see Figure 5.1). For example, social-emotional competencies, such as self- and social-awareness and relationship skills, are particularly important to negotiating meaning and learning processes in the midst of collaboration. Skills for understanding and managing one's emotions are also necessary to navigate conflicts that invariably arise when negotiating meaning and action.

Fortunately, a burgeoning literature has identified how learners can be supported to develop social-emotional competencies (see CASEL, 2015; Schonert-Reichl & Weissberg, 2015). Two broad recommendations are common across that literature. The first, which converges with our earlier discussion, is to create *communities of learners* that are respectful, welcoming, caring, safe, and nurture positive interdependence (Hymel, McClure, Miller, Shumka, & Trach, 2014; Schonert-Reichl & Weissberg, 2015). The second is to teach social-emotional competencies explicitly, and also *weave support for the development of competencies into classrooms and schools*. To explicitly teach social-emotional competencies, SEL programs have been developed, and research has convincingly demonstrated their effectiveness in terms of advancing both social and emotional competence and achievement (CASEL, 2015; Durlak, Weissberg, Dymnicki, Taylor, & Schellinger, 2011). Still, the contemporary challenge for SEL practice and research is to find ways to help learners mobilize what they are learning through SEL programs into their work with others in classrooms (i.e., bring to bear relationship skills in the context of working collaboratively with peers). Doing so is essential to enabling students to take up effective forms of strategic processing in the context of activities.

Self-Regulated Learning

In this section we build on our prior discussion to specify further how SRL-promoting practices can also support socially shared strategic processing (e.g., Perry, 2013; see Table 5.1). For example, aligned with SEL research, and as we described earlier, SRL researchers are also stressing the importance of creating safe, non-threatening *communities of learners* if students are to be comfortable taking risks and pushing their learning forward together.

Earlier we identified how educators *enable rich forms of learning and collaboration* when they develop and surface norms, routines, and participation structures, ideally with students. In addition, SRL research has suggested that educators need to design activities that create rich opportunities for self-, co-, and socially shared regulation (e.g., Butler et al., 2017; Perry, 2013). Students cannot develop capacities for socially shared strategic processing if they do not have opportunities to collaborate with others. This recommendation is consistent with current calls to engage learners in the kinds of open-ended, authentic problem-solving activities they will face going into adulthood (e.g., project-based learning, design-based learning, collaborative inquiry), where peers and teachers engage together as co-constructors of meaning and tasks (e.g., Dumont, Istance, & Benavides, 2012; Hickey et al., 2002; Kim & Lim, 2018).

As in the SEL literature, SRL researchers have emphasized the importance of *weaving support for students' development of capacities into activities*. Fostering adaptive forms of strategic processing requires dedicated support for students to both (a) negotiate an understanding of purposes and processes, and (b) mobilize those understandings adaptively and flexibly while engaged in academic work. Perry et al. (in press) suggested that teachers and students can scaffold or support each other's engagement in strategic processing by using modeling, questioning, and feedback. Using these and other approaches (e.g., thinking tools or guides), teachers and peers can co-regulate each other's learning within activities (Hadwin, Oshige, Gress, & Winne, 2010).

From an SRL point of view, it is particularly important for educators to move from guiding students' engagement toward supporting students to learn how to *engage in full cycles of strategic action* intentionally and deliberately. For example, with that goal in mind, Butler, Schnellert, and Cartier (2013) investigated how secondary-level teachers were working together to nurture students' effective engagement in self- and social forms of SRL when learning through reading (LTR) in subject area classrooms. Learners in their study achieved the greatest gains when educators (a) focused explicitly on thinking, reading, and learning processes; (b) integrated support for those processes into content area learning; (c) sustained attention to process goals over time; and (d) bridged from structuring students' effective engagement (e.g., using an advance organizer or thinking tool) toward empowering them to take more ownership over how they were engaging in activities (e.g., by creating a personalized version of a planning tool, or by co-constructing criteria with peers). Butler et al. (2013) found that it was a combination of these approaches that most powerfully predicted gains in students' self-regulated engagement in LTR.

A final principle emerging from the SRL literature is to *foster agency* in learners' work alone and with others. To that end, Perry et al. (in press) recommended giving students influence by providing opportunities for them to make learning-related decisions and choices (e.g., about what and how they will learn). When students are engaged in making decisions over "matters of substance" (Schoenfeld, 2004, p. 251), like how learning in their classroom should work or what they want to investigate together, students take ownership of their learning. Also, when learners have to engage in dialogue about purposes or processes, they have to articulate their ideas and negotiate meaning with others in ways that foster metacognition, deeper forms of learning, and a sense of collective efficacy (Bandura, 2000).

Formative Assessment (FA)

Recently researchers have identified how SRL processes and FA practices are intertwined and converging (e.g., Butler et al., 2017; Heritage, 2018; Panadero, Andrade, & Brookhart, 2018). FA involves weaving assessment practices into activities in ways that inform both teaching and learning. In multiple respects, FA practices are optimally designed to support learners' engagement in deliberate, reflective cycles of strategic action, either on their own or with others. For example, FA involves engaging learners in identifying, interpreting, and working with criteria, so that they have a clear sense of purpose (e.g., Andrade, Du, & Mycek, 2010; Nicol & Macfarlane-Dick, 2006). Then, building from criteria, learners engage in both self- and peer-assessment, where they have opportunities to judge progress toward criteria, and adapt performance to reduce gaps between progress and goals (see Table 5.1).

Contemporary research on feedback aligns well with FA practices. For example, in their review, Hattie and Timperley (2007) identified three questions that effective forms of feedback should help learners to answer: Where am I (are we) going? (establishing purpose); How am I (are we) doing? (self-assessing); and Where to Next? (adjusting).

These questions align with a call to support learners' flexible and adaptive engagement in cycles of strategic action. To more fully support socially shared strategic processing, Figure 5.1 adds two additional questions. When collaborating, learners also have to negotiate how they will work together toward goals, both when planning ("What do we need to get there?") and when selecting, adapting, or inventing strategies for getting there ("What are we doing (and why)?"). SRL-promoting practices, FA, and productive feedback can combine to nurture socially shared strategic processing, and at the same time foster agency, metacognition, and deeper forms of collaborative learning.

Supporting Socially Shared Strategic Processing in Collaborative Learning Frameworks

In the previous section we distilled pedagogical principles and practices from the literatures on SEL, SRL, and FA. In this section, we consider how those principles and practices are being, or could be, implemented to support strategic processing in the context of some of the most actively researched collaborative learning frameworks.

Supporting Socially Shared Strategic Processing within Cooperative Learning

Cooperative learning (CL) is a pedagogical framework that has been researched since the 1970s (Gillies, 2016; Johnson & Johnson, 2009). Research has consistently shown benefits of CL for learning, peer relationships, and motivation (Gillies, 2016). Johnson and Johnson (2009) identified five conditions that support effective collaboration during CL. The first is to structure positive interdependence into activities, so that learners feel that success depends on them all contributing to a common goal. This condition aligns well with calls in both the SEL and SRL literatures to build communities of learning in which students feel like they are "in it together" (Perry et al., in press). The second condition for effective CL is to foster promotive interaction, or the willingness of group members to support each other to achieve shared goals. This condition is well aligned with recommendations from the SEL and SRL literatures to support prosocial values (e.g., Hymel et al., 2014) and socially responsible self-regulation (Hutchinson, 2013). The third condition necessary for successful CL is individual accountability, where learners feel responsible for their particular role in achieving a collective goal. This condition is consistent with descriptions of collaboration as involving dynamic coordination between self-, co-, and socially shared forms of regulation (Hadwin et al., 2010). That said, it adds an important focus on ensuring that individuals perceive themselves as having personal accountability within collaborative work. The fourth condition for effective CL is that students know how to participate together. This fourth condition aligns directly with the many calls across the literature to provide explicit support for students to build capacities for collaboration. The final condition necessary for productive CL is effective forms of group processing. Aligned with the SRL and FA literatures, CL research suggests that, to work together effectively, groups need *to learn how to* negotiate their engagement as members of a group through cycles of strategic action.

Many researchers have identified ways to support effective forms of CL. For example, Farivar and Webb (1994) argued that group work is most effective when "students are prepared in stages, and when group skills have been taught and practiced" (p. 51). Their four stages of support for cooperative learning include (1) community building; (2) developing skills for working with others in small groups; 3) developing communication and cooperation skills; and (4) developing helping skills. We interpret these suggestions as calls to surface the kinds of strategic processing required to navigate social dimensions of learning. As part of her review of research on CL, Gillies (2016) advocated for engaging students in dialogic exchanges in which peers probe and clarify each other's thinking, identify and confront discrepancies, provide suggestions, and encourage each other. By integrating supports for productive academic discourse into activities, learners can be supported to take up those ways of thinking on their own. We interpret these suggestions as focusing more on the cognitive dimensions of learning collaboratively with others. Similarly, Jurkowski and Hänze (2015) developed a model for teaching students explicitly how to engage in "transactive communication" (TC) (p. 358). To that end, they provided explanations about TC to university-level students, showed videos with positive and negative examples, provided opportunities for students to identify TC within those examples, engaged students in practice with feedback, and asked students to complete a learning journal to describe TC in their interactions. They found that students who received TC instruction outperformed peers in both TC and knowledge acquisition. Jurkowski and Hänze's (2015) study illustrated how explicit support for collaboration can be woven into activities to support both collaborative learning processes and knowledge construction.

Supporting Socially Shared Strategic Processing in Computer-Supported Collaborative Learning (CSCL)

Technologically supported environments provide a unique opportunity to both host and support socially shared strategic processing. In this section, we highlight just a small fraction of the wide range of research emerging in this area (e.g., Alharbi, Athauda, & Chiong, 2018; Hadwin et al., 2010; Miller & Hadwin, 2015; Winne, 2015).

Miller and Hadwin (2015) provided a conceptual analysis of the qualities of self-, co- and shared regulation in collaborative activity. Building from that analysis, they identified the potential benefits of two kinds of tools that are being built into CSCL environments: scripting tools, which structure and guide learners' engagement in socially shared strategic action, and awareness tools, which "collect, aggregate, and reflect information back to learners to facilitate collaboration" (p. 573). Using examples from a first year undergraduate course, they illustrated how different kinds of tools can support effective forms of collaborative activity. In terms of the pedagogical principles and practices in Table 5.1, notable is how the tools they described create the potential to bridge from guiding learners' engagement through cycles of socially shared regulation (e.g., using scripts) toward fostering more ownership over collaborative reflection, self and shared group assessment, and adjusting (e.g., using awareness tools).

Other researchers are also working to extend from the guiding potential of CSCL to fostering rich forms of learning, agency, and ownership (e.g., Hadwin et al., 2010). For example, Staarman (2009) sought to surface the implicit linguistic and social ground rules for participation in an online discussion forum with primary students. To that end, she negotiated ground rules with students. Consistent with recommendations from the SRL literature to make visible "how things work" in classrooms, this study suggested how social forms of engagement often remain implicit, and how negotiating an understanding of ground rules can help in supporting diverse learners in having a sense both of purpose and of how to achieve expectations.

As a final example, Hickey et al. (2002) developed an approach to assessing collaborative scientific inquiry in genetics within a technologically supported learning environment. Consistent with recommendations in the FA literature (e.g., Nicol & Macfarlane-Dick, 2006), their goal was to help students engage in effective "assessment conversations" (p. 2). They started by building a rubric for assessing collaborative activity, then assessed students' collaboration in groups using the rubric. Finally, they asked groups to review their assessment together. They found that asking students to interpret their assessment together inspired "spirited discourse and argumentation around both the performance assessment and collaboration standards" (p. 7). As they negotiated a shared meaning about their assessment, learners co-constructed a fuller understanding about collaborative inquiry processes. Further, all students, including those who had not been actively engaged in the original collaborative work, negotiated meaning about the problem they had been addressing. The result was that all students learned more about the problem too. In this respect, Hickey et al.'s (2002) study showed how engaging students in FA practices can nurture both socially shared strategic processes and learning.

Supporting Socially Shared Strategic Processing in Open-Ended Collaborative Activities

Given contemporary demands to nurture the development of learners who know how to work well with others, a variety of other kinds of open-ended pedagogical frameworks are being revitalized, developed, and championed. These include, for example, collaborative forms of project-based learning (PBL) (e.g., Alharbi et al., 2018; Kim & Lim, 2018; Lee et al., 2015; Torre et al., 2016), design-based learning (DBL) (e.g., Boix-Mansilla & Gardner, 2007; Edelson, Gordin, & Pea, 1999), and collaborative inquiry (e.g., Hickey et al., 2002). These open-ended frameworks engage learners in authentic forms of goal-directed activity, involve collaboration, and require learners to engage together in cycles of intentional, deliberate action (i.e., forms of self-, co- and socially shared regulation).

Current literature on these open-ended forms of engagement echoes themes we have identified so far throughout this chapter. These include the ubiquitous call to explicitly support learners to learn how to engage successfully together through these activities. But in more open-ended activities, researchers are grappling with how to dovetail scaffolds for collaboration (e.g., guides or tools) with demands for flexible, dynamic, and learner directed and derived forms of engagement (e.g., Alharbi et al., 2018; Lee et al., 2015). For example, in collaborative PBL in K-12 classrooms, Ertmer and Simons (2006) suggested scaffolding learning processes in ways that guide learners rather than telling them what to do. They also made distinctions between hard scaffolds, like handouts, which can be prepared in advance and guide learning in a structured way, and soft scaffolds, which are more dynamic (like conferencing) and can be used to support learning as it unfolds. Ertmer and Simons also suggested introducing shorter versions of PBL first, before introducing a more extended project, developing rituals (i.e., routines) for thinking and learning, whole class debriefings on group processes, incorporating tools that enable students to record group goals and how things are progressing, and scaffolding supports for reflective thinking. Like the combination of scripting and self-awareness tools described by Miller and Hadwin (2015), the various strategies suggested by Ertmer and Simons have great potential to both guide learning and then bridge toward fostering agency and independence.

In their study on PBL, Lee et al. (2015) explored how individual and group level social skills were implicated in generating and resolving intragroup conflict (i.e., linking to the social dimensions of strategic processing in collaboration). As a backdrop to their study, Lee et al. (2015) suggested that the kinds of scripts being used in CSCL can be useful but may be limited given the dynamic forms of engagement required in collaborative PBL. Thus, as an alternative, they argued that students need to develop social skills (i.e., aligned with social-emotional competencies) that they can draw on flexibly and adaptively in social forms of engagement. They found that social skills enacted at the group level were most supportive of successful collaboration. Their findings resonate with the principles and practices included in Table 5.1, which suggest coupling explicit support for competency development (i.e., social-emotional competencies) with opportunities for learners to mobilize, reflect on, and adjust what they are learning within activities. This combination can help them learn how to navigate shifting expectations in different settings over time.

CONCLUSIONS AND FUTURE DIRECTIONS

In this chapter we reviewed literature relevant to understanding and supporting socially shared strategic processing. As we assessed the literature, we found multiple lines of inquiry exploring collaborative processes and how to support them. To help in discerning themes from this wide-ranging research, we relied on an integrative SRL-informed framework that allowed us to identify individual and social influences on learning (McCaslin & Burrows, 2010). Building on that framework, our literature analysis suggested that, not only are students being engaged in more open-ended pedagogical frameworks that require collaboration (e.g., CL, CSCL, PBL), but they are also expected to navigate culturally and socially situated norms, routines, participation structures, and discourse patterns that are instantiated into the life of a classroom. Simultaneously, in article after article, researchers identified how students (and often educators) are not clear on what it looks like to learn collaboratively. We conclude that teachers and students alike can benefit greatly from support to help them discern the socially shared strategic processing expectations of tasks and interactions. Further, learners need to build capacities for socially shared forms of strategic processing that they can carry forward into their futures.

Fortunately, the wide array of research we examined converged to identify productive principles and practices for supporting socially shared strategic processing. For example, in Table 5.1 we pulled together principles and practices from across literatures on SEL, SRL, and FA. We also identified how similar principles and practices are being mobilized to support strategic processing in various kinds of collaborative learning frameworks. Through this review, it became clear that it is not enough to support the development of social engagement in a single kind of collaborative activity. Instead, learners need to know how to read and navigate socially and culturally co-constructed environments adaptively, not only through activities but also in the day-to-day interactions (e.g., transitions, discussions) that form the social life of the classroom.

The literature is rich in examples of how educators and researchers can support socially shared strategic processing. Readers will find many helpful recommendations, not just in the articles we have highlighted here but in the depth of each literature strand and associated discussion. Still, if we were to summarize key recommendations for practice, based on our analysis, they would be to (a) create opportunities for students to participate in social forms of learning that require them to negotiate meaning across diverse beliefs, experiences, and perspectives; (b) offer support for socially shared strategic processing that is attuned to the dynamic cultural and social requirements in a given environment; (c) focus explicit attention on how things work to make purposes and associated thinking and learning processes visible; (d) weave support for learners' developing social-emotional capacities, not just by teaching them explicitly (e.g., in SEL programs) but also in ways that support students to metacognitively employ their developing SEL capacities as activities unfold, as part of strategic processing; (e) bridge from guiding learning toward helping students learn how to navigate social forms of learning flexibly and adaptively; (f) ask students to articulate their interpretation of tasks, possible plans of action, strategies undertaken, and reflections regarding progress in their own words and with peers, to help in negotiating meaning and action with others; and finally (g) empower students by creating opportunities for agency and co-construction of norms, routines, participation structures, expectations, activities, and meaning. Our corresponding recommendation to researchers would be to continue researching the generativity of these kinds of pedagogical principles and practices in terms of supporting socially shared forms of strategic processing.

REFERENCES

Alharbi, N. M., Athauda, R. I., & Chiong, R. (2018). Empowering collaboration in project-based learning using a scripted environment: Lessons learned from analyzing instructors' needs. *Technology, Pedagogy, and Education, 27*(3), 381–397.

Andrade, H. L., Du, Y., & Mycek, K. (2010). Rubric-referenced self-assessment and middle school students' writing. *Assessment in Education: Principles, Policy & Practice, 17*(2), 199–214.

Anyichie, A. C. (2018). Supporting all learners' engagement in a multicultural classroom using a culturally responsive self-regulated learning framework. (*Unpublished doctoral dissertation*). University of British Columbia, Vancouver. Retrieved from https://open.library.ubc.ca/cIRcle/collections/ubctheses/24/items/1.0375773

Anyichie, A. C., & Butler, D. L. (2018, April). Culturally responsive teaching and self-regulated learning: An integrated approach to supporting engagement in inquiry-based learning. Paper presented at the annual meetings of the American Educational Research Association (AERA), New York, NY. Retrieved from www.researchgate.net/publication/324605557

Bandura, A. (2000). Exercise of human agency through collective efficacy. *Current Directions in Psychological Science, 9*(3), 75–78.

Barton, D., & Hamilton, M. (2012). *Local literacies: Reading and writing in one community* (2nd Linguistics Classics Ed.). London: Routledge.

Boekaerts, M. (2011). Emotions, emotion regulation, and self-regulation of learning. In B. J. Zimmerman & D. H. Schunk (Eds.), *Handbook of self-regulation of learning and performance* (pp. 408–425). New York: Routledge.

Boix-Mansilla, V., & Gardner, H. (2007). From teaching globalization to nurturing global consciousness. In M. Suarez Orozco (Ed.), *Learning in the global era: International perspectives on globalization and education* (pp. 47–66). Oakland: University of California Press.

Borkowski, J. G., & Muthukrishna, N. (1992). Moving metacognition into the classroom: "Working models" and effective strategy teaching. In M. Pressley, K. R. Harris, & J. T. Guthrie (Eds.), *Promoting academic competence and literacy in school* (pp. 477–501). Toronto: Academic Press.

Brown, A. L., Campione, J. C., & Day, J. D. (1981). Learning to learn: On training students to learn from texts. *Educational Researcher, 10*(2), 14–21.

Butler, D. L. (1998). The strategic content learning approach to promoting self-regulated learning: A summary of three studies. *Journal of Educational Psychology, 90*, 682–697.

Butler, D. L. (2002). Individualizing instruction in self-regulated learning. *Theory into Practice, 41*, 81–92.

Butler, D. L. (2015). Metacognition and self-regulation in learning. In D. Scott & E. Hargreaves (Eds.), *The SAGE handbook on learning* (pp. 291–309). London, UK: Sage.

Butler, D. L., & Cartier, S. (2004). Promoting students' active and productive interpretation of academic work: A Key to successful teaching and learning. *Teachers College Record, 106*, 1729–1758.

Butler, D. L., & Cartier, S. C. (2018). Case studies as a methodological framework for studying and assessing self-regulated learning. In D. Schunk & J. Greene (Eds.), *Handbook of self-regulation of learning and performance* (2nd ed., pp. 352–369). New York: Routledge.

Butler, D. L., & Schnellert, L. (2012). Collaborative inquiry in teacher professional development. *Teaching and Teacher Education, 28*, 1206–1220.

Butler, D. L., & Schnellert, L. (2015). Success for students with learning disabilities: What does self-regulation have to do with it? In T. Cleary (Ed.), *Self-regulated learning interventions with at-risk youth: Enhancing adaptability, performance, and well-being* (pp. 89–111). Washington, DC: APA Press.

Butler, D. L., Schnellert, L., & Cartier, S. C. (2013). Layers of self- and co-regulation: Teachers' co-regulating learning and practice to foster students' self-regulated learning through reading. *Education Research International*. Retrieved from www.hindawi.com/journals/edu/2013/845694/.

Butler, D. L., Schnellert, L., & Perry, N. E. (2017). *Developing self-regulating learners*. Don Mills, ON: Pearson.

Cartier, S. C., & Butler, D. L. (2016). Comprendre et évaluer l'apprentissage autorégulé dans des activités complexes [Understanding and assessing self-regulated learning in complex activities]. In B. Noël & S. C. Cartier (Eds.), *De la métacognition à l'apprentissage autorégulé* (From metacognition to self-regulated learning, pp. 41–54). Brussels: DeBoeck.

Collaborative for Academic, Social and Emotional Learning (CASEL). (2015). *Effective social and emotional learning programs: Middle and high school edition*. Chicago, IL: Author. Retrieved January 29, 2019, from http://secondaryguide.casel.org/.

Dumont, H., Istance, D., & Benavides, F. (Eds.). (2012). *The nature of learning: Using research to inspire practice. Practitioner guide from the innovative learning environments Project*. Paris: OECD Publishing.

Durlak, J. A., Weissberg, R. P., Dymnicki, A. B., Taylor, R. D., & Schellinger, K. B. (2011). The impact of enhancing students' social and emotional learning: A meta-analysis of school-based universal interventions. *Child Development, 82*(1), 405–432.

Edelson, D. C., Gordin, D. N., & Pea, R. D. (1999). Addressing the challenges of inquiry-based learning through technology and curriculum design. *Journal of the Learning Sciences, 8*(3–4), 391–450. doi:10.1080/1050840 6.1999.9672075

Ertmer, P. A., & Simons, K. D. (2006). Jumping the PBL Implementation Hurdle: Supporting the efforts of K-12 teachers. *Interdisciplinary Journal of Problem-Based Learning, 1*(1). doi:10.7771/1541-5015-1005.

Farivar, S. H., & Webb, N. M. (1994). Are your students prepared for group work? *Middle School Journal, 25*, 51–54.

Fisher, D., Frey, N., & Pumpian, I. (2012). *How to create a culture of achievement in your school and classroom*. Alexandria, VA: ASCD.

Gay, G. (2010). *Culturally responsive teaching: Theory, research and practice*. New York: Teachers College Press.

Gillies, R. M. (2016). Cooperative learning: Review of research and practice. *Australian Journal of Teacher Education, 41*, 3. doi:10.14221/ajte.2016v41n3.3

Hadwin, A. F., Järvelä, S., & Miller, M. (2018). Self-regulation, co-regulation, and shared regulation in collaborative learning environments. In D. H. Schunk & J. A. Greene (Eds.), *Handbook of self-regulation of learning and performance* (2nd ed., pp. 83–106). New York: Routledge.

Hadwin, A. F., & Oshige, M. (2011). Self-regulation, co-regulation, and socially shared regulation: Exploring perspectives of social in self-regulated learning theory. *Teachers College Record, 113*(2), 240–264.

Hadwin, A. F., Oshige, M., Gress, C. L. Z., & Winne, P. H. (2010). Innovative way for using *gStudy* to orchestrate and research social aspects of self-regulated learning. *Computers in Human Behavior, 26*, 794–805.

Harris, K. R., & Graham, S. (1996). *Making the writing process work: Strategies for composition and self-regulation.* Cambridge, MA: Brookline.

Hattie, J., & Timperley, H. (2007). The power of feedback. *Review of Educational Research, 77*(1), 81–112.

Heritage. (2018). Assessment for learning as support for student self-regulation. *Australian Educational Researcher, 45*, 51–63.

Hickey, D. T., DeCuir, J., Hand, B., Kyser, B., Laprocina, S., & Mordica, J. (2002). *Technology-supported formative and summative assessment of collaborative scientific inquiry.* ED466693. Arlington, VA: National Science Foundation.

Hutchinson, L. R. (2013). Young children's engagement in self-regulation at school. (*Unpublished doctoral dissertation*). University of British Columbia, Vancouver. Retrieved from https://circle.ubc.ca/handle/2429/44401

Hymel, S., McClure, R., Miller, M., Shumka, E., & Trach, J. (2014). Addressing school bullying: Insights from theories of group processes. *Journal of Applied Developmental Psychology, 37*, 16–24.

Järvenoja, H., Järvelä, S., & Malmberg, J. (2015). Understanding regulated learning in situative and contextual frameworks. *Educational Psychologist, 50*(3), 204–219.

Johnson, D. W., & Johnson, R. T. (2009). An educational psychology success story: Social interdependence theory and cooperative learning. *Educational Researcher, 38*(5), 365–379.

Jurkowski, S., & Hänze, M. (2015). How to increase the benefits of cooperation: The effects of training in transactive communication on cooperative learning. *British Journal of Educational Psychology, 85*, 357–371.

Kahiigi, E. K., Hansson, H., Danielson, M., & Tusubira, F. F. (2012). Modeling a peer assignment review process for collaborative e-learning. *Journal of Interactive Online Learning, 11*(2), 67–79.

Kaplan, A., Lichtinger, E., & Margulis, M. (2010). The situated dynamics of purposes of engagement and self-regulation strategies: A mixed-methods case study of writing. *Teachers College Record, 113*(2), 284–324.

Kim, D., & Lim, C. (2018). Promoting socially shared metacognitive regulation in collaborative problem-based learning: A framework for the design of structured guidance. *Teaching in Higher Education, 23*(2), 194–211.

Kozleski, E. B., & Waitoller, F. R. (2010). Teacher learning for inclusive education: Understanding teaching as a cultural and political practice. *International Journal of Inclusive Education, 14*(7), 655–666.

Ladson-Billings, G. (1995). Toward a theory of culturally relevant pedagogy. *American Educational Research Journal, 32*(3), 465–491.

Lee, D., Huh, Y., & Reigeluth, C. M. (2015). Collaboration, intragroup conflict, and social skills in project-based learning. *Instructional Science, 43*, 561–590.

Leinhardt, G., Weidman, C., & Hammond, K. M. (1987). Introduction and integration of classroom routines by expert teachers. *Curriculum Inquiry, 17*(2), 135–176.

McCaslin, M. (2009). Co-regulation of student motivation and emergent identity. *Educational Psychologist, 44*, 137–146.

McCaslin, M., & Burrows, H. L. (2010). Research on individual differences within a sociocultural perspective: Co-regulation and adaptation of learning. *Teachers College Record, 113*(2), 325–349.

McInerney, D. M., & King, R. B. (2018). Culture and self-regulation in educational contexts. In D. H. Schunk & J. A. Greene (Eds.), *Handbook of self-regulation of learning and performance* (2nd ed., pp. 485–502). New York: Routledge.

Michaels, S., O'Connor, C., & Resnick, L. B. (2008). Deliberative discourse idealized and realized: Accountable talk in the classroom and in civic life. *Studies in Philosophy of Education, 27*, 283–297.

Miller, M., & Hadwin, A. (2015). Scripting and awareness tools for regulating collaborative learning: Changing the landscape of support in CSCL. *Computers in Human Behavior, 52*, 573–588.

Moje, E. B. (2013). Hybrid literacies in a post-hybrid-world: Making a case for navigating. In K. Hall, T. Cremin, B. Comber, & L. C. Moll (Eds.), *International handbook of research on children's literacy, learning, and culture* (pp. 359–372). Malden, MA: Wiley-Blackwell.

Moll, L. C., Amanti, C., Neff, D., & Gonzalez, N. (1992). Funds of knowledge for teaching using a qualitative approach to connect homes and classrooms. *Theory into Practice, 31*(2), 132–141.

Nicol, D. J., & Macfarlane-Dick, D. (2006). Formative assessment and self-regulated learning: A model and seven principles of good feedback practice. *Studies in Higher Education, 31*(2), 199–218.

Noddings, N. (1992). *The challenge to care in schools: An alternative approach to education.* New York: Teachers College Press.

Palincsar, A. S., & Brown, A. L. (1988). Teaching and practicing thinking skills to promote comprehension in the context of group problem solving. *Remedial and Special Education, 9*, 53–59.

Panadero, E., Andrade, H., & Brookhart, S. (2018). Fusing self-regulated learning and formative assessment: A roadmap of where we are, how we got here, and where we are going. *Australian Educational Researcher*, *45*(1), 13–31. doi:10.1007/s13384-018-0258-y

Perry, N. E. (2013). Classroom processes that support self-regulation in young children. *British Journal of Educational Psychology, Monograph Series II: Psychological Aspects of Education—Current Trends, 10*, 45–68.

Perry, N. E., Mazabel, S., & Yee, N. (in press). Using self-regulated learning to support students with learning disabilities in classrooms. To appear. In A. J. Martin, R. A. Sperling, & K. J. Newton (Eds.), *Handbook of educational psychology and students with special needs*. New York: Routledge.

Perry, N. E., Yee, N., Mazabel-Ortega, S., Lisaingo, S., & Määttä, E. (2017). Using self-regulated learning as a framework for creating inclusive classrooms for ethnically and linguistically diverse learners in Canada. In N. J. Cabrera & B. Leyendecker (Eds.), *Handbook of Positive Development for Minority Children* (pp. 361–377). New York: Springer.

Pressley, M., El-Dinary, P. B., Gaskins, I. W., Schuder, T., Bergman, J. L., Almasi, J., & Brown, R.(1992). Beyond direct explanation: Transactional instruction of reading comprehension strategies. *Elementary School Journal, 92*, 513–555.

Pushor, D. (2012). Tracing my research on parent engagement: Working to interrupt the story of school as protectorate. *Action in Teacher Education, 34*(5–6), 464–479.

Schnellert, L., & Kozak, D. (2019). Exploring diversity and nurturing generativity through in situ teacher education. *Exceptionality Education International, 29*(1), 72–96.

Schnellert, L., Kozak, D., & Moore, S. (2015). Professional development that positions teachers as inquirers and possibilitizers. *LEARNing Landscapes, 9*(1), 217–236.

Schoenfeld, A. H. (2004). Multiple learning communities: Students, teachers, instructional designers, and researchers. *Journal of Curriculum Studies, 36*(2), 237–255.

Schonert-Reichl, K. A., & Weissberg, R. P. (2015). Social and emotional learning: Children. Chapter to appear. In T. P. Gullotta & M. Bloom (Eds.), *The encyclopedia of primary prevention and health promotion* (2nd ed., pp. 936–949). New York: Springer Press.

Seixas, P., & Morton, T. (2012). *The big six historical thinking concepts*. Toronto: Nelson Education Canada.

Staarman, J. K. (2009). The joint negotiation of ground rules: Establishing a shared collaborative practice with new educational technology. *Language and Education, 1*, 79–95.

Torre, D. M., Van Der Vlueten, C., & Dolmans, D. (2016). Theoretical perspectives and applications of group learning in PBL. *Medical Teacher, 38*, 189–195.

Treff, M. (2006). Participation Training. *Adult Learning, 17*(1), 46–48.

Volet, S., Vauras, M., & Salonen, P. (2009). Self- and social regulation in learning contexts: An integrative perspective. *Educational Psychologist, 44*(4), 215–226.

Winne, P. W. (2015). What is the state of the art in self-, co- and socially shared regulation in CSCL? *Computers in Human Behavior, 52*, 628–631.

Wong, B. Y. L. (1994). Instructional parameters promoting transfer of learned strategies in students with learning disabilities. *Learning Disability Quarterly, 17*, 110–120.

Woolfolk, A. E., Winne, P. H., & Perry, N. E. (2015). Chapter 12: Creating learning environments. In *Educational psychology* (Canadian 6th ed., pp. 437–472). Toronto: Pearson Canada.

Zimmerman, B. J. (1989). A social cognitive view of self-regulated academic learning. *Journal of Educational Psychology, 81*, 329–399.

Zimmerman, B. J. (2008). Investigating self-regulation and motivation: Historical background, methodological developments and future prospects. *American Educational Research Journal, 45*(1), 166–183.

Zimmerman, B. J. (2011). Motivational sources and outcomes of self-regulated learning and performance. In B. J. Zimmerman & D. H. Schunk (Eds.), *Handbook of self-regulation of learning and performance* (pp. 49–64). New York: NY: Routledge.

6

COMMENTARY

A Conceptual Framework for Defining Strategies and Strategic Processing

Peggy Van Meter and Jacqueline M. Campbell
PENNSYLVANIA STATE UNIVERSITY, USA

In this chapter, we have been asked to comment on the four proceeding chapters in this section of the Handbook. As a whole, the goal of this section is to forward a definition and conceptualization of strategies and strategic processing that can shed light on the past as well as illuminate a path to the future. Each chapter contributes to this goal by presenting a particular lens through which to consider these definitions. From these four chapters, we come to see strategic processing as it develops with time and experience, shifts across domains, varies across levels, and is embedded in both individual and socially collaborative tasks and environments. In this chapter, we present a definition of strategies and strategic processing derived through a synthesis of these views. The resulting definition is rich and the latter half of this chapter focuses on unpacking this richness. We begin, however, with a discussion of the fundamental questions that initiated our thinking about this chapter and the section as a whole.

COMING TO TERMS WITH TERMS: A RATIONALE FOR DEFINING STRATEGIC PROCESSING

The questions that drove our initial thinking about this chapter began by challenging the assumption that underlies this section of the Handbook. Namely, the assumption that not only are definitions themselves worthy of our time and effort but also that strategic processing in particular warrants such concern. Two specific questions arose from this challenge: (1) why is it necessary to attend so closely to the definitions of some terms? and (2) why is strategic processing particularly deserving of this attention?

The Need to Define Terms

Our thinking with regard to the first question was guided by our training as Educational Psychologists. From this perspective, the need for careful definitions is understood by considering their role within the scholarly community of educational researchers. In this role, one reason that clear definitions are needed is because they provide the shared understandings needed to advance the science of learning and instruction. We were reminded of a seminal piece by Alexander, Schallert, and Hare (1991) that called for a "coming to terms" with the proliferation of labels and meanings that surrounded the study of knowledge. At that time, the educational research literature was awash with studies of both prior knowledge effects and knowledge acquisition, but inconsistencies in how terms were used made it difficult to synthesize across the literature. Alexander et al. (1991) undertook the task of organizing this literature into a single definitional framework and justified this effort by arguing that "labels function as an epistemological shorthand for researchers and practitioners [but] the spawning of terms without thoughtful exploration of the assumptions underlying the terms or the relationships of the terms to existing terminology may have serious theoretical and practical consequences" (p. 315).

In short, terms and definitions allow for the communication between members of a scholarly community that is necessary for the advancement of scientific knowledge. And, when this communication rests on murky grounds where the meanings and boundaries across terms is unclear, the outcome of this communication will be murky as well. Unfortunately, *strategy* and *strategic processing* are examples of such murky terms (Dinsmore & Hattan; Rogier et al., this volume). The chapters in this section draw attention to two particular areas within the study of strategic processing where there is a lack of clarity around terms. First, Rogier et al. distinguish between strategies that teachers use and strategies that students use. The former are pedagogical, or instructional, strategies while the latter are learning strategies. It is these learning strategies that are the focus of this Handbook and, as will be addressed later in this chapter, these strategies come in a variety of forms. A second area that lacks clarity is the distinction between skills and strategies. Skills and strategies are typically distinguished by their degree of automaticity. Skills are deployed automatically under the right conditions and strategies require effort (Dinsmore & Hattan, this volume). As pointed out in the chapter by Dumas, however, this distinction is inconsistently applied, particularly as one looks across domains of learning.

The need to clarify boundaries between pedagogical and learning strategies and between strategies and skills were both explicitly addressed in the chapters of this Handbook section. In addition, there is a need to clarify the boundary between strategy and strategic processing, and this boundary was only implicitly addressed in these chapters. Nonetheless, we can reason through these terms to clarify their distinction. Strategy is a noun and, as such, it can be used to identify a class of things. How we define strategy determines what does and does not belong within the class of things labeled as a strategy. Processing, or strategic processing, by contrast, is a verb. Strategic processing then refers to an action or something that one does. In some respects, this distinction parallels that drawn between the quantitative and qualitative properties of strategies addressed by the chapters in this section. As Rogier et al. (this volume) wrote, "*quantity* refers to the availability and diversity of strategies, while quality refers to the efficiency and adaptivity of strategies" (p. 52). Rather than focusing on this quantity/quality distinction here, however, we address this more strongly in terms of what students *have* and what students *do* (Dumas, this volume) because this distinction provides a productive framework for synthesizing the contents of the chapters in this section. We found this distinction useful as we read these chapters because each differed in whether the focus was on strategies or strategic processing. Dinsmore and Hattan, for example, emphasize how we can understand strategy when they discuss different types of strategies according to levels of processing. Butler and Schnellert, by contrast, place a greater emphasis on strategic processing when they discuss strategies as enacted within a regulatory cycle. Ultimately, this distinction provides the framework for the definitions we derived from these chapters, a definition we will return to in a later section.

A second reason for defining and discussing the meaning of the terms used in our field is because our understanding of the constructs they represent evolve and change over time. This evolution means that, when efforts to define constructs are limited in time and evidentiary foundations, the resulting definitions will, likewise, be limited. Warding off these limitations requires that definitions be revisited over time with recognition that the resulting discussions may lead to revised understandings of a term's definition. Evolution in meaning occurs even for terms that seem clearly defined, and the definition of strategic processing is just such a case. One could argue that there is no need for chapters defining strategic processing because this term was defined long ago. In fact, authors in this section pointed out that the study of strategies in its current form has, more or less, been present in our field since the 1980s and 1990s (Butler & Schnellert, this volume; Rogier et al., this volume). In fact, the single most oft-cited definition of strategy found in these chapters was published back in the 1980s (i.e., Alexander & Judy, 1988). While we concede that the words of older definitions are still relevant today, what justifies the need to revisit definitions is that our understanding of what the words represent has evolved over time.

With respect to strategic processing, this evolution can be traced to both theoretical and practical developments and these developments were illustrated in the chapter by Butler and Schnellert. Theoretical developments since the 1990s, for example, have brought both self-regulated learning and socio-cultural frameworks to the study of strategic processing. As Butler and Schnellert show, strategic processing is now understood as occurring in culturally and socially situated self-regulated cycles. This, we conclude, is a substantial theoretical evolution from earlier research that was just beginning to uncover the role of metacognition in strategy use and transfer (e.g., Ghatala, Levin, Pressley, & Lodico, 1985; Paris, Newman, & Mcvey, 1982; Pressley, Ross, Levin, & Ghatala, 1984).

Butler and Schnellert also address the practical developments that have taken place over the last decades. Namely, the evolution to a 21st-century knowledge society where technological developments drive the need for strategic processing. In particular, these authors address the need for effective socially shared strategic processing in technology-supported and/or informationally rich collaborative environments such as Computer Supported Collaborative Learning and Problem Based Learning. Again, these current day learning environments look far different than those that were the subject of early strategy research, including the early research on strategy use in group settings (e.g., Brown, Pressley, Van Meter, & Schuder, 1996; McDonald, Larson, Dansereau, & Spurlin, 1985; Palinscar & Brown, 1984).

The Need to Define Strategic Processing

The previous section established why key terms in our field need to be defined. In short, terms serve as an epistemological shorthand (Alexander et al., 1991) that undergirds communication across a scholarly community. When these definitions are unclear and evolving over time, the potential for miscommunication is great and can undermine scientific progress. The previous section also established that the potential for miscommunication is present for the terms strategy and strategic processing because their definitions have been both unclear and evolving over time. These points alone, however, are not sufficient to answer the question, "Why are strategies and strategic processing particularly important to define?" Of course, one obvious answer is to point out that strategic processing is consistently tied to learning outcomes, e.g., students' self-reported strategy use predicts learning outcomes (Bråten & Strømsø, 2011; Cantrell, Almasi, Carter, Rintamaa, & Madden, 2010; Credé & Phillips, 2011). These relationships are not sufficient to justify special attention to strategic processing, however, because there are many other variables that show similar, predictive relationships to academic performance (e.g., motivation, Pintrich & Schunk, 2002; spatial ability, Carter, Larussa, & Bodner, 1987; intellectual ability, Sternberg & Kaufman, 1998). Given that other factors are relevant to learning, what is it about strategic processing that warrants special attention? To answer this question, we turn to two characteristics of strategic processing, namely the proximity to learning outcomes and the responsiveness to instruction.

First, with respect to proximity, we agree with Dumas' (this volume) argument that strategic processing is centrally important to the study of learning because how a student processes some learning materials, strategically or otherwise, is immediately and directly tied to what is learned. This has been demonstrated many times in the research literature, but we will share just two examples from our own work. In a study by Firetto and Van Meter (2018), college biology students read to learn about two different physiological systems and the goal of the study was to test instructional conditions that would promote students' integration across the two systems. In the integration instruction condition, students were prompted to directly compare the two systems while the comprehension instruction condition prompted comprehension of each system. These two experimental conditions were compared to a control condition and all participants completed a self-report measure of strategy use and an essay post-test that was scored for both accuracy and cross-system integration. Participants in the integration condition did achieve higher post-test scores, which demonstrates that the instructional intervention was effective. Responses to the strategy measure, however, revealed that these intervention effects were mediated by participants' strategic processing. In a second study, Van Meter et al. (2016) had college engineering students complete an intervention exercise designed to support understanding the First Law of Thermodynamics. An experimental test showed that intervention condition participants had higher conceptual reasoning scores than did control condition participants.

Most relevant to the current point are the findings obtained from a small group of students who thought aloud while completing the intervention exercises. Analysis of these protocols revealed significant relationships between conceptual reasoning scores at post-test and the frequency of strategic processes (e.g., elaboration) while completing the exercise.

A conclusion that can be drawn across these two studies is that, although instructional interventions can and do improve learning, these improvements are tied to the influence of the intervention on students' strategic processing. In both studies, despite the benefit of the intervention overall, participants in experimental conditions who were less strategically engaged in the task benefitted less from the intervention than their more strategic peers. These findings are consistent with other research demonstrating that strategic processing has a direct influence on performance across diverse tasks such as learning from multiple documents (e.g., Bråten & Strømsø, 2011), worked examples (e.g., Chi, Bassok, Lewis, Reimann, & Glaser, 1989), and multimedia (e.g., Cromley, Snyder-Hogan, & Luciw-Dubas, 2010). In sum, students' strategic processing is a proximal cause of learning outcomes.

A second reason that strategies and strategic processing warrant attention is because they are amenable to instruction. While studies of students' independent, naturally occurring use of strategies has shown significant relationships between strategy use and learning (e.g., Chi et al., 1989; Cromley et al., 2010), the evidence also shows that students can be taught to use strategies effectively. One example is McNamara and colleagues' research on training students to use self-explanation. In this training, students learn to generate explanations through the use of five strategies (e.g., bridging, paraphrasing) and practice applying these strategies to expository text. Whether learning through face-to-face tutoring (i.e., SERT; McNamara, 2004, 2017) or via an online strategy trainer (i.e., iSTART; McNamara, Levinstein, & Boonthum, 2004; McNamara, O'Reilly, Best, & Ozuru, 2006), comparisons between trained and untrained students reveals a benefit for self-explanation instruction. In the context of multimedia learning, Mason and colleagues (Mason, Pluchino, & Tornatora, 2015; Mason, Scheiter, & Tornatora, 2017) have trained students to process text and diagrams by having them watch a video replay of a successful student's eye movements. This eye movement modeling example (EMME) shows the model using effective strategic processing such as attending to the diagram and transitioning between corresponding parts of the text and diagram. These EMME studies show that students who were exposed to the model not only score higher on learning outcome measures but also demonstrate more effective multimedia learning patterns in their own eye movements.

Altogether then, there is ample evidence that strategic processing is both a proximal cause of individual variations in learning and addressable through instruction. Moreover, the causal relations between strategies and learning outcomes is robust. This robustness is evidenced, on the one hand, by the range of domains, tasks, and learners that are discussed just within the four chapters of this Handbook section. Dumas, for example, draws attention to the role of strategic processing across domains while Rogier et al. point out that strategy use influences learning and performance across all developmental levels. The robustness of the causal relations is also evidenced by a number of empirical demonstrations that there is a direct and significant path between the application of strategic processing to some material and what is learned from that material (e.g. Berthold, Nückles, & Renkl, 2007; Bråten, Anmarkrud, Brandmo, & Strømsø, 2014; Firetto & Van Meter, 2018; Murphy & Alexander, 2002). Furthermore, although variations in methodologies used makes it difficult to quantify these effects across studies, meta-analytic reviews have concluded that strategy training programs have a positive effect on students' learning (de Boer, Donker, Kostons, & van der Werf, 2018; Dignath & Büttner, 2008; Donker, De Boer, Kostons, Van Ewijk, & van der Werf, 2014).

On these grounds, we argue that the efforts to define strategies and strategic processing are not only justified, they are necessary. Although the chapters in this section advance our understanding of these important learning processes, there are differences in how each conceptualizes strategies and strategic processing. Consequently, these chapters do not present a single agreed upon definition, but rather a call to consider a broad range of related issues. These differences present an opportunity to synthesize across perspectives to generate definitions of strategies and strategic processing that capture not only the essence of this Handbook section but also the direction of this field of study as a whole.

DEFINING TERMS: THE MEANING OF STRATEGIES AND STRATEGIC PROCESSING

We began our task of defining strategies and strategic processing by pulling definitional elements from each of the four chapters in this section. A conceptualization of these terms emerged as we sorted those elements and worked to synthesize across the chapters. As explained above, one critical feature that emerged was the need to distinguish between what is a strategy and strategic processing. With that distinction in mind, we offer the following definitions.

A strategy is an *effortful, goal-directed* form of *procedural knowledge* that is stored in *long-term memory*. There are different *types of strategies* and these strategies must be *coordinated* with one another during complex tasks.

Strategic processing is the *planful, effective enactment* of strategies. Strategies are *flexibly and adaptively* applied to *achieve goals* in *self-regulated cycles*.

Before proceeding to an explanation of these definitions, two features should be pointed out here. First, the repetition of *goal* in these two definitions is intentional. Though we explain this in more detail below, for now we share that goals sit between strategies and strategic processing because it is the student's goal that moves a strategy from what one knows to what one does. That is not to say that the goal itself determines or identifies the strategy. Indeed, goals must be separated from strategies because one goal can be achieved through different strategies and a single strategy can support progress toward different goals (Dumas, this volume). Yet, at the same time, it is not possible to understand either a strategy or strategic processing event without consideration of the student's goal(s). The second feature concerns the use of italics for some of the words in the definitions. The italicized words represent essential features of these definitions. The remainder of this section is dedicated to explaining those features and unpacking the complexity of strategies and strategic processing.

What Is a Strategy?

Effortful, Goal-Oriented, Procedural Knowledge. Identifying a strategy as a form of *procedural knowledge* invokes some of the known characteristics of this knowledge form. As such, we can say that one's knowledge of a particular strategy is knowledge of *how* to do something. And, just like one's knowledge of how to tie a tie or make coffee, this knowledge is stored in *long-term memory* and lies dormant until called upon for some task. Unlike simpler procedures like coffee-making and tie-tying, the conditions for invoking a strategy can be less certain and, thus, strategy transfer is less certain. This can be attributed, at least in part, to the conditional knowledge that is associated with strategies. Conditional knowledge is knowledge of when and why a strategy should be used and this knowledge is directly tied to the *goal-oriented* nature of strategy knowledge: the goal identifies what needs to be achieved (e.g., memorization, attention maintenance) and the conditions identify the strategies that align with that goal. Goals are discussed in greater depth below but, with respect to strategy knowledge, goals and conditional knowledge effect strategy transfer in two ways. First, the flexibility of strategies means that conditions for using a particular strategy may not be as well specified as the conditions for other forms of procedural knowledge. There really is, for example, only one set of conditions under which one must tie a tie, but there are many different conditions under which strategies such as outlining, brainstorming, or self-explanation may be useful.

On the other hand, the conditional knowledge associated with a strategy may be too well specified; that is, too narrowly defined. Dumas (this volume) illustrates this in his discussion of task-specific strategies. A task-specific strategy is one that may be very powerful, but is useful for only one specific task., e.g., the FOIL strategy for remembering how to multiply binomials, Every-Good-Boy-Does-Fine for remembering the notes on a musical staff. While it is true that these specific examples are useful for only a single task, we disagree that the strategy itself is task specific because both are examples of the first-letter mnemonic strategy to support memory (Levin, 1993). A student whose procedural knowledge represents these examples as specific instances of this broader memory strategy is likely to use the strategy across tasks in which remembering both elements and their order matters, e.g., to remember Piaget's developmental stages. This student's procedural knowledge representation will connect the strategy procedures with a broader, more flexible set of conditions, thereby increasing the probability that the strategy will transfer to new contexts. The issue of conditional knowledge in the learning of strategies is important and one that we found to be under-addressed within the chapters of this section.

In addition to drawing attention to students' knowledge of the conditions for strategy use, recognizing a strategy as a form of procedural knowledge also points out the potential for a strategy to be practiced to the point of automaticity. Just as one can automatize coffee-making and tie-tying, one can automatize the use of (at least some) strategies. It is this automaticity that distinguishes between a strategy and a skill. A skill is automatic; a strategy is *effortful*. Strategies then, require that cognitive resources be expended toward not just the material that is the target of the strategy, such as learning Piaget's developmental stages, but also toward the strategy itself. For this reason, teachers must take care not to overload students' cognitive resources by asking them to learn both challenging new content and a new strategy at the same time (Reynolds, 2000).

Types of Strategies

Another essential feature in the definition of strategy that emerged from these chapters is that there are not only different specific strategies, but there are different ways to taxonomize these strategies. Each chapter did present some categorical list of strategies, but no two chapters used the same one. The chapter by Dinsmore and Hattan, for example, identified four categories of strategy: surface, deep, metacognitive, and self-regulatory. Butler and Schnellert, by contrast, offered five: cognitive, motivational, emotional, behavioral, and social. In some respects, these differences are an out-growth of the focus of the chapter. Whereas Dinsmore and Hattan were concerned with specifying the differences in levels of strategies (i.e., surface vs. deep), Butler and Schnellert were concerned with explaining socially shared, self-regulated strategic processing. Though the chapters do use different taxonomies, these categorizations are not in conflict with one another. In fact, synthesizing across these chapters leads to some clarity in the taxonomy that can be used to classify and discuss strategies. We did such a synthesis and the taxonomy that emerged identified three distinct dimensions: self-regulatory, domain, and depth. These dimensions, which are described below, are also fully crossed so that every category from any one dimension can be located within the categories of the other dimensions, e.g., each self-regulatory category includes strategies at varying levels of depth and that can be applied across different domains.

Self-Regulatory Dimension. The first dimension of strategy type is a self-regulatory dimension. Categories in this dimension identify the aspect of the self that the strategy intends to regulate. A cognitive strategy, for instance, intends to regulate cognition while a motivational-affective strategy intends to regulate one's motivational state. Across the chapters, we identified five regulatory categories: cognitive, metacognitive, motivational-affective, behavioral, and social. These categories are described in Table 6.1 and, as these descriptions show, the categories in this dimension are quite broad. These categories are not broad because there are many different strategies that can be classified within each, although this is true. Instead, these categories are broad because the regulatory dimensions themselves are broad. Motivation, for example, encapsulates such constructs as interest, self-efficacy, and goals (Schunk & Zimmerman, 2012). Accordingly, the motivation-affective category includes strategies appropriate for each of these motivational factors.

Domain Dimension. Domain is the second dimension in our taxonomic system for classifying strategies. A "domain is an area of knowledge that can be studied or taught" (Dumas, this volume, p. 15), such as math, history, or music theory. The first category in the domain dimension is domain-general, which captures those strategies that can be applied across multiple domains. Examples of domain-general strategies include using an outline to take notes, sending the instructor an email to seek help, and asking your partner a question to promote collaborative learning. In addition to this domain-general category are the categories of domain-specific strategies. Domain-specific

90 • Peggy Van Meter and Jacqueline M. Campbell

Table 6.1 Categories within Self-Regulatory Dimension

	Description	Examples
Cognitive	• Influences how internal mental operations are applied toward learning material • May include covert, observable behavior, but the causal mechanism lies in the internal cognitive processes • Intended to support performance on academic tasks such as problem solving, reading comprehension, and knowledge acquisition	• Memory strategies (e.g., 1st letter mnemonic) • Problem-solving strategies (e.g., draw a diagram) • Self-explanation • Outlining
Metacognitive	• Guides and directs cognitive processes • Intended to support planning, monitoring, evaluation • Includes knowing how, when, and where to apply strategies	• Choosing a strategy you think will work best • Rereading when you sense you did not understand something • Self-assessment
Motivational-Affective	• Influences a learner's personal effort toward a task or willingness to learn • Includes strategies to manage affective responses and engagement • May include attitudes, beliefs, or interests that drive learning	• Positive self-talk • Monitoring emotional responses • Risk-taking
Behavioral	• Controls behaviors that influence learning • Intended to support behaviors that affect learning positively and discourage behaviors that have a negative effect on learning	• Setting a timer to work for an extended period of time • Rewarding yourself for reading a certain number of pages
Social	• Influences interaction patterns in social settings • Intended to support pro-social behaviors that support learning • Collaboration with others is key • Includes norms or routines in a learning environment	• Co-regulation between teacher and student • Peer-assessment • Asking clarification questions • Elaborative bridging statements

strategies are those that apply to only specific domains such as a timeline in history or solve-it-another-way in mathematics. There are a countless number of domain-specific categories in this taxonomic dimension because there are a countless number of domains in which one might need to be strategic. The nature of the knowledge and ways of thinking vary across domains and, thus, each domain has its own set of effective strategies.

In the chapters of this Handbook section, authors conceptualized the domain-general/specific dimension according to Alexander's Model of Domain Learning

(MDL; Alexander, 1998). The MDL describes phases of development as one moves from a novice to expert and the concomitant shifts in students' knowledge, interest, and strategy use. A hallmark of this development is a move away from domain-general to domain-specific strategies. And, because domain-specific strategies are more specialized to the content and tasks of a domain, these strategies are more powerful than those that generalize across domains. This developmental perspective on strategy use highlights two issues related to the conceptualization of strategies and strategic processing, namely intra-individual differences and the role of conditional knowledge. Intra-individual differences refer to variations within a person regarding both the use and effectiveness of strategies. Rogier et al. (this volume) point out that any single student's location within developmental phases of the MDL will vary across domains. As a result, the student's ability to use domain-specific strategies will also vary across domains. The mathematics major may have developed fairly sophisticated mathematics strategies, but this same student must resort to domain-general strategies in a music theory course. In short, a student's strategy knowledge must be understood in the context of specific learning domains.

With respect to conditional knowledge, our argument is that the degree to which a strategy may be domain-general or domain-specific resides more in the student's knowledge about the strategy than the strategy itself, at least for some strategies. Take for example, the earlier described scenario of the student who understood the FOIL strategy as a task-specific example of the first-letter mnemonic strategy for memorizing ordered elements. In this instance, the strategy is domain-general because the student possesses the conditional knowledge to support transfer across domains (see Dumas, this volume for more discussion on this point). As this example illustrates, there is potential to stretch some strategies across domains. The point remains, however, that there are differences in the strategies that are most effective across domains. Because domain-specific strategies are more powerful than domain-general strategies, an explicit goal of instruction should be to facilitate students' development of the domain-specific strategies that best support learning.

Depth Dimension. The third dimension for categorizing strategies that emerged from this section is depth. This dimension includes two categories. Surface strategies, which are designed to understand, and deep strategies, which are designed to transform (Dinsmore & Hattan, this volume). Paraphrasing, for example, is a surface strategy, while self-explaining, in which the student generates causal inferences, is a deep strategy. In general, deep strategies are preferred because they promote deeper understanding. This is not a universal truth, however, because the effectiveness of either type of strategy is determined by how well matched the strategy is to the task. If a student need only recall Piaget's stages, the first-letter mnemonic is effective. This surface-level strategy will be inadequate, however, if one must be able to explain the differences between stages.

Strategy Coordination. A point made clear by the chapters in this section is that it is not sufficient for a student to know a strategy. The student must also know how that strategy can be used in *coordination* with other strategies (Pressley, Borkowski, & Schneider, 1987). Although it is possible to identify a singular strategy, effective learning requires that these strategies be combined to achieve desired outcomes.

Butler and Schnellert (this volume) address this coordinated use of strategies in the context of socially shared processing by claiming that, in a social context, strategies for managing social-emotional processes are a prerequisite for engaging other forms of strategy use. Strategy coordination is also required even for comparatively simple learning tasks, such as a student independently working to acquire some discrete knowledge. Consider again the student using the first-letter mnemonic to remember Piaget's stages. The assessment of this knowledge is likely to require that the student cannot only recall these stages but also explain or apply them. Under these assessment conditions, the student would best be served by combining the surface-level memory strategy with a deep strategy aimed at explaining and applying the knowledge; a strategy such as self-explaining or self-questioning. Recognition that strategies must be coordinated has led to recommendations that strategy instruction includes opportunities for students to practice this coordination in the context of complex tasks (e.g., reading comprehension, Pressley & Gaskins, 2006).

Summary. The definition of strategy offered here was derived from the chapters of this section of the Handbook and informed by the larger theoretical and empirical literature. In this definition, a strategy is a form of procedural knowledge but, in order to be considered a strategy, use of this knowledge must be effortful. There are different types of strategies and we have offered here a taxonomy for thinking about these types. This taxonomy includes three dimensions: self-regulatory, domain, and depth; and these can categorize both broad classes of strategies (e.g., notetaking) and specific strategic routines (e.g., outlining). Knowledge of individual strategies is not sufficient, however. Learning requires coordinated use of strategies and, thus, students must also have knowledge of how strategies can be combined.

What Is Strategic Processing?

Goals and the Planful, Effective Enactment of Strategies. We begin the discussion of strategic processing with *goals* because goals mobilize a strategy from something a student knows – a procedural knowledge representation – to something a student does – some strategic process. Goals are the internal objectives a student holds for a particular task. The student learning Piagetian stages, for example, might hold the goals of remembering the stages and being able to explain and apply the stages. Goal formulation starts when the student uses information about the task, including any provided instructions, to construct a representation of what the task requires (Rouet, Britt, & Durik, 2017; Winne & Hadwin, 2008). This construction is based on the student's perception of the task and the broader context. As such, the task representation will be influenced by the student's prior culturally and socially situated experiences (Butler & Schnellert, this volume). The task representation is translated into a set of task goals that include the standards a student will use for judging progress and goal attainment (Winne & Hadwin, 1998, 2008).

From the chapters in this Handbook section, goals emerged as central to strategic processing. First, as presented in the definition of strategy, strategic procedural knowledge includes knowledge of the goals, or conditions, for which a strategy is effective. Students select strategies by matching the goals of the task to the strategies suited for meeting those goals. Given a memory task, a student may select the first-letter mnemonic; given an explain and apply task, a student may select self-explanation. This selection leads to the *planful enactment* of the strategy. In other words, during ideal strategic processing, the student plans how the strategy will be deployed with this plan corresponding to task goals. A second issue regards the criteria of *effectiveness* in evaluating qualitative aspects of strategic processing. Dinsmore and Hattan (this volume) argued that only when a process achieves a goal should it be considered strategic; Dumas (this volume) agreed and added the qualification that performance may fall short of the goal, but there must be some "commonly expected effectiveness" (p. 18). Goals then are central to the definition of strategic processing because effectiveness can only be evaluated in light of goal attainment.

Flexible and Adaptive Self-regulated Cycles

The tasks that students undertake are rarely exact matches to the context in which a strategy is learned. The student who learns self-explanation to support problem solving may find herself in a collaborative problem-solving task; the student who learns to write a paper using a plan-write-revise strategy may be under time constraints that do not permit such a lengthy effort. These examples showcase the need for the *flexible and adaptive* application of strategies. Students, that is, must adapt their strategies to the conditions at hand in order to successfully achieve their goals. Indeed, "it is particularly the ability to flexibly and selectively use … apt strategies that [is] crucial for learning, understanding, and performance" (Rogier et al., this volume, p. 49).

This flexible adaptation occurs in the context of *self-regulated cycles* that shift between applying strategies and monitoring their effectiveness (Winne & Hadwin, 1998, 2008). Consequently, the flexible application of strategies does not end with the initial selection and adaptation of strategies. When the student perceives that a strategy is ineffective, a good strategy user (Pressley et al., 1987) will adjust their plan, either making further adaptations to the current strategy or discarding that strategy in favor of another. The self-regulation component of strategic processing is also responsible for the coordinated use of strategies. Complex tasks require the use of more than one strategy and self-regulation permits the student to manage and coordinate these strategies. The student learning Piaget's stages, for example, may first focus only on remembering the names of each stage and later allocate attentional resources to understanding them. Self-regulation demands are further complicated in socially shared strategic processing. Here, the student must not only incorporate social strategies but also coordinate her own strategic processing with that of others (Butler & Schnellert, this volume). Regardless of the specific context, a hallmark of effective strategic processing is engagement in, and management of, self-regulated cycles of adaptive strategy use.

Summary. Goals play a central role in the definition of strategic processing because goals drive both the selection and application of strategies. Once selected, a student is able to plan how the strategies can be applied toward the goal and, ultimately, evaluate the effectiveness of that strategic process according to whether the goal has been achieved. Furthermore, this flexible adaptation allows a student to adjust known strategies to meet the specific conditions and demands of the task at hand.

The selection, adaptation, and monitoring of strategic processing is embedded in self-regulated cycles as a student works toward goals and it is this self-regulation that permits the successful use of strategies during complex tasks.

CONCLUSIONS AND FUTURE DIRECTIONS

The four chapters in this Handbook section each offered a particular conceptualization of strategic processing that is both deep and limited. The depth derives from the close examination of a specific conceptual frame regarding strategies while the limitations result from the boundaries of those frames. Rogier et al., for example, offer a thorough view of strategy development but are silent on questions concerning socially shared strategic processing. By contrast, Butler and Schnellert do take on the complex issue of strategic processing during collaborative tasks but do not address strategy development. Our goal in this commentary was to synthesize across these chapters to provide a broad conceptualization that incorporates the major definitional features that arose from the full set of chapters. This synthesis resulted in the definitions of strategy and strategic processing we have offered here. Despite our efforts to present a broad conceptualization, we must acknowledge that even this effort was limited. Specifically, there are several important issues presented in the chapters of this section and elsewhere that we did not address; issues such as inter-individual differences, instruction and assessment needs, and the distinction between co-regulation and socially shared regulation. Our failure to address these issues here is due primarily to space limitations and we encourage future efforts to more fully incorporate these issues into conceptual understandings of strategies and strategic processing.

We close by underlining a direction for future work that was raised in the chapters throughout this section, an area that we agree is one of great need. This is the need for longitudinal work that examines strategic processing and strategy instruction as it develops over time. Longitudinal research is needed to better understand how students not only acquire and deploy strategies but also how this develops over time and in response to shifting task demands. Long-term examinations of strategy instruction are also needed. This work would consider how students learn strategies not when they are taught at some particular point in time or situated within the academic year of a single classroom, but how they are learned when a strategy curriculum is deployed over years of schooling. Given the life-long learning demands of the 21st-century knowledge society, the development of strategic processing is also a life-long endeavor. Our research agendas should mirror this demand with the goal of supporting students' strategic processing at all stages of life and in all learning endeavors.

REFERENCES

Alexander, P. A. (1998). The nature of disciplinary and domain learning: The knowledge, interest, and strategic dimensions of learning from subject-matter text. In C. Hynd (Ed.), *Learning from text across conceptual domains* (pp. 263–287). Mahwah, NJ: Lawrence Erlbaum.

Alexander, P. A., & Judy, J. E. (1988). The interaction of domain-specific and strategic knowledge in academic performance. *Review of Educational Research, 58*(4), 375–404.

Alexander, P. A., Schallert, D. L., & Hare, V. C. (1991). Coming to terms: How researchers in learning and literacy talk about knowledge. *Review of Educational Research*, *61*(3), 315–343.

Berthold, K., Nückles, M., & Renkl, A. (2007). Do learning protocols support learning strategies and outcomes? The role of cognitive and metacognitive prompts. *Learning and Instruction*, *17*(5), 564–577. doi:10.1016/j.learninstruc.2007.09.007

Bråten, I., Anmarkrud, Ø., Brandmo, C., & Strømsø, H. I. (2014). Developing and testing a model of direct and indirect relationships between individual differences, processing, and multiple-text comprehension. *Learning and Instruction*, *30*, 9–24. doi:10.1016/j.learninstruc.2013.11.002

Bråten, I., & Strømsø, H. I. (2011). Measuring strategic processing when students read multiple texts. *Metacognition and Learning*, *6*(2), 111–130.

Brown, R., Pressley, M., Van Meter, P., & Schuder, T. (1996). A quasi-experimental validation of transactional strategies instruction with low-achieving second-grade readers. *Journal of Educational Psychology*, *88*(1), 18.

Cantrell, S. C., Almasi, J. F., Carter, J. C., Rintamaa, M., & Madden, A. (2010). The impact of a strategy-based intervention on the comprehension and strategy use of struggling adolescent readers. *Journal of Educational Psychology*, *102*(2), 257.

Carter, C. S., Larussa, M. A., & Bodner, G. M. (1987). A study of two measures of spatial ability as predictors of success in different levels of general chemistry. *Journal of Research in Science Teaching*, *24*(7), 645–657.

Chi, M. T., Bassok, M., Lewis, M. W., Reimann, P., & Glaser, R. (1989). Self-explanations: How students study and use examples in learning to solve problems. *Cognitive Science*, *13*(2), 145–182.

Credé, M., & Phillips, L. A. (2011). A meta-analytic review of the motivated strategies for learning questionnaire. *Learning and Individual Differences*, *21*(4), 337–346.

Cromley, J. G., Snyder-Hogan, L. E., & Luciw-Dubas, U. A. (2010). Cognitive activities in complex science text and diagrams. *Contemporary Educational Psychology*, *35*(1), 59–74.

de Boer, H., Donker, A. S., Kostons, D. D., & van der Werf, G. P. (2018). Long-term effects of metacognitive strategy instruction on student academic performance: A meta-analysis. *Educational Research Review*, *24*, 98–115. doi:10.1016/j.edurev.2018.03.002

Dignath, C., & Büttner, G. (2008). Components of fostering self-regulated learning among students. A meta-analysis on intervention studies at primary and secondary school level. *Metacognition and Learning*, *3*(3), 231–264. doi:10.1007/s11409-008-9029-x

Donker, A. S., De Boer, H., Kostons, D., Van Ewijk, C. D., & van der Werf, M. P. (2014). Effectiveness of learning strategy instruction on academic performance: A meta-analysis. *Educational Research Review*, *11*, 1–26. doi:10.1016/j.edurev.2013.11.002

Firetto, C. M., & Van Meter, P. N. (2018). Inspiring integration in college students reading multiple biology texts. *Learning and Individual Differences*, *65*, 123–134.

Ghatala, E. S., Levin, J. R., Pressley, M., & Lodico, M. G. (1985). Training cognitive strategy-monitoring in children. *American Educational Research Journal*, *22*(2), 199–215.

Levin, J. R. (1993). Mnemonic strategies and classroom learning: A twenty-year report card. *The Elementary School Journal*, *94*(2), 235–244. Retrieved from www.jstor.org/stable/1001972

Mason, L., Pluchino, P., & Tornatora, M. C. (2015). Eye-movement modeling of integrative reading of an illustrated text: Effects on processing and learning. *Contemporary Educational Psychology*, *41*, 172–187.

Mason, L., Scheiter, K., & Tornatora, M. C. (2017). Using eye movements to model the sequence of text–picture processing for multimedia comprehension. *Journal of Computer Assisted Learning*, *33*(5), 443–460.

McDonald, B. A., Larson, C. O., Dansereau, D. F., & Spurlin, J. E. (1985). Cooperative dyads: Impact on text learning and transfer. *Contemporary Educational Psychology*, *10*(4), 369–377.

McNamara, D. S. (2004). SERT: Self-explanation reading training. *Discourse Processes*, *38*(1), 1–30.

McNamara, D. S. (2017). Self-explanation and reading strategy training (SERT) improves low-knowledge students' science course performance. *Discourse Processes*, *54*(7), 479–492.

McNamara, D. S., Levinstein, I. B., & Boonthum, C. (2004). iSTART: Interactive strategy training for active reading and thinking. *Behavior Research Methods, Instruments, & Computers*, *36*(2), 222–233.

McNamara, D. S., O'Reilly, T. P., Best, R. M., & Ozuru, Y. (2006). Improving adolescent students' reading comprehension with iSTART. *Journal of Educational Computing Research*, *34*(2), 147–171.

Murphy, P. K., & Alexander, P. A. (2002). What counts? The predictive powers of subject-matter knowledge, strategic processing, and interest in domain-specific performance. *The Journal of Experimental Education*, *70*(3), 197–214. Retrieved from www.jstor.org/stable/20152679

Palinscar, A. S., & Brown, A. L. (1984). Reciprocal teaching of comprehension-fostering and comprehension-monitoring activities. *Cognition and Instruction*, *1*(2), 117–175.

Paris, S. G., Newman, R. S., & Mcvey, K. A. (1982). Learning the functional significance of mnemonic actions: A microgenetic study of strategy acquisition. *Journal of Experimental Child Psychology, 34*(3), 490–509.

Pintrich, P. R., & Schunk, D. H. (2002). *Motivation in education: Theory, research, and applications.* Englewood Cliffs, NJ: Prentice Hall.

Pressley, M., Borkowski, J. G., & Schneider, W. (1987). Cognitive strategies: Good strategy users coordinate metacognition and knowledge. In R. Vasta & G. Whitehurst (Eds.), *Annals of child development* (Vol. 4, pp. 89–129). Greenwich, CT: JAI Press.

Pressley, M., & Gaskins, I. W. (2006). Metacognitively competent reading comprehension is constructively responsive reading: How can such reading be developed in students? *Metacognition and Learning, 1*(1), 99–113.

Pressley, M., Ross, K. A., Levin, J. R., & Ghatala, E. S. (1984). The role of strategy utility knowledge in children's strategy decision making. *Journal of Experimental Child Psychology, 38*(3), 491–504.

Reynolds, R. E. (2000). Attentional resource emancipation: Toward understanding the interaction of word identification and comprehension processes in reading. *Scientific Studies of Reading, 4*(3), 169–195.

Rouet, J. F., Britt, M. A., & Durik, A. M. (2017). RESOLV: Readers' representation of reading contexts and tasks. *Educational Psychologist, 52*(3), 200–215. doi:10.1080/00461520.2017.1329015

Schunk, D. H., & Zimmerman, B. J. (Eds.). (2012). *Motivation and self-regulated learning: Theory research, and applications.* New York: Routledge.

Sternberg, R. J., & Kaufman, J. C. (1998). Human abilities. *Annual Review of Psychology, 49*(1), 479–502.

Van Meter, P. N., Firetto, C. M., Turns, S. R., Litzinger, T. A., Cameron, C. E., & Shaw, C. W. (2016). Improving students' conceptual reasoning by prompting cognitive operations. *Journal of Engineering Education, 105*(2), 245–277.

Winne, P. H., & Hadwin, A. F. (1998). Studying as self-regulated learning. In D. J. Hacker, J. Dunlosky, & A. C. Graesser (Eds.), *The educational psychology series. Metacognition in educational theory and practice* (pp. 277–304). Mahwah, NJ: Lawrence Erlbaum.

Winne, P. H., & Hadwin, A. F. (2008). The weave of motivation and self-regulated learning. *Motivation and Self-Regulated Learning: Theory, Research, and Applications, 2,* 297–314.

Section II
Strategies in Action

7

READING COMPREHENSION STRATEGY INSTRUCTION

Peter Afflerbach and Matthew Hurt
UNIVERSITY OF MARYLAND, USA

Byeong-Young Cho
UNIVERSITY OF PITTSBURGH, USA

READING COMPREHENSION STRATEGIES: CLARIFICATIONS AND CHALLENGES TO EFFECTIVE INSTRUCTION

Prior to our consideration of reading comprehension strategy instruction, we want to make several points related to the term *strategies*. First, *strategies* are not consistently defined or characterized in the professional literature, in theoretical models and in related reading instruction materials. In fact, the words *strategies* and *skills* are sometimes substituted for one another. Consider how *strategies* is used interchangeably with *skills* in the influential National Reading Panel Executive Summary Report (National Institute of Child Health and Human Development, 2000):

> The rationale for the explicit teaching of *comprehension skills* is that comprehension can be improved by teaching students to use specific *cognitive strategies* or to reason strategically when they encounter barriers to understanding what they are reading.
>
> (p. 14; italics added)

There are important differences between strategies and skills (although they are closely related) and consistency of use of these words should be a goal. This can contribute to clarity in theoretical constructs, models of reading comprehension and the instruction that derives from them. In this chapter, we use the following definitions of strategies and skills (Afflerbach, Pearson, & Paris, 2008):

Reading strategies are deliberate, goal-directed attempts to control and modify the reader's efforts to decode text, understand words, and construct meanings of text. *Reading skills* are automatic actions that result in decoding and comprehension with speed, efficiency, and fluency and usually occur without awareness of the components or control involved.

(p. 368)

A further concern is the conflation of reading strategies, teaching strategies and classroom supports related to students' reading comprehension strategy development. For example, the National Reading Panel (NICHD, 2000) states:

The seven individual strategies that appear to be effective and most promising for classroom instruction are (in alphabetical order) comprehension monitoring, cooperative learning, graphic and semantic organizers including story maps, question answering, question generation, and summarization.

(pp. 4–42)

Several notes are in order—the first being that not all of the above are strategies. For example, "graphic and semantic organizers including story maps" may be used in concert with students' reading comprehension strategies (or teachers' instructional strategies), but they are not strategies—they are tools. "Cooperative learning" is a means of constructing knowledge that typically involves classmates and that may involve reading activities, but it is not a strategy. "Comprehension monitoring" is certainly comprised of strategies and actions (e.g., goal setting, calibration, progress tracking, using fix it strategies), as is "summarization." "Question generation" is possibly a strategy. Question answering typically involves the demonstration that comprehension has occurred; how it qualifies as a strategy needs explication. Finally, there is a lack of distinction between reading comprehension instruction strategies (used by teachers) and reading comprehension strategies (used by student readers). When archival, research-related documents are unclear as to the nature of reading comprehension strategies, we may expect confusion in related realizations of instruction.

The Report of the National Reading Panel was a major influence on reading policy, including the No Child Left Behind and Reading First legislation. The fact that reading comprehension strategies were not clearly and consistently defined (nor suitably distinguished from other important aspects of reading instruction) has contributed to confusion in related reading comprehension strategy instruction. Consider information provided on the Reading Rockets website, which is frequented by many teachers seeking ideas for reading instruction, and which describes itself as:

Reading Rockets is a national multimedia project that offers a wealth of research-based strategies, lessons, and activities designed to help young children learn how to read and read better.

(Available from www.readingrockets.org/)

Reading Rockets proposes "Seven Strategies to Teach Students Text Comprehension:" the strategies are monitoring comprehension, metacognition, graphic and semantic organizers, answering questions, generating questions, recognizing story structure and summarizing. This list of "Strategies to Teach" raises concerns similar to those of the National Reading Panel report—lack of clarity on what a strategy is (e.g., how is "answering questions" a strategy?), and conflation of reading strategies with teaching and learning tools (again, how are "graphic and semantic organizers" a strategy?). "Monitoring comprehension" is an integral aspect of "metacognition," and it is not apparent why the two are listed separately. Further, teaching reading strategies divorced from specific purposes for reading, the disciplines in which reading occurs, and particular reading-related tasks, fuels criticism that generic reading comprehension strategy instruction is insufficient for students' needs.

In the extreme, a "more is better" perspective informs recommendations for reading comprehension strategy instruction. Consider the following claim that it is possible to teach the following "25 reading strategies that work in every content area:"

> Reread, activate prior knowledge, use context clues, infer, think aloud, summarize, locate key words, make predictions, use word attack strategies, visualize, use graphic organizers, evaluate understanding, question the text, stop!, monitor & repair understanding (while reading), paraphrase, annotate the text, adjust reading rate, prioritize information, use graphic notetaking, predict, set a reader purpose, text-connections (text-to-self, text-to-text, text-to-world), skim, and SSQ (Stop, Summarize, Question).
>
> (Retrieved from www.teachthought.com/literacy/
> 25-reading-strategies-that-work-in-every-content-area/)

While acknowledging that the effective use of reading comprehension strategies is context-dependent, the website also provides erroneous prescriptions of student readers' strategy use for particular reading situations. If reading comprehension strategy instruction is to be based on research findings, what research suggests the following?

> This all makes reading strategies somewhat content area specific. *Stopping* (maybe the most undervalued strategy ever) and *Rereading* might make more sense in science, while *Visualization* and *Text Connections* may make more sense reading literary works. *Questioning the Text* may make equal sense in both.
>
> (Retrieved from www.teachthought.com/literacy/
> 25-reading-strategies-that-work-in-every-content-area/)

In summary, while reading comprehension strategy instruction is present in most all elementary classrooms, there may be accompanying confusion. Reading strategies are variously defined, mischaracterized, used interchangeably with reading skills, and conflated with teaching strategies and teaching tools. Tying comprehension strategies to instruction, but leaving them untethered to specific reading contexts and tasks, limits the value of instruction. Going forward, clarity as to what strategies are, the role of particular strategies in acts of reading and how strategies are supported by readers' knowledge is necessary to realize the promise of comprehension strategy instruction.

AN OVERVIEW OF READING COMPREHENSION STRATEGY RESEARCH AND INSTRUCTION

The achievement of reading is considered among humankind's loftiest (Huey, 1908) and it has the potential to greatly impact individuals' life accomplishments. Successful reading results in the comprehension of text. Over centuries, with different language systems, and across varied instructional approaches, readers have learned to comprehend text. We note that comprehension strategy instruction is a relative newcomer to reading pedagogy, and that vast numbers of readers have developed fully without the benefit of a single reading comprehension strategy lesson. Nevertheless, we propose that strategy instruction makes more efficient the process of becoming an accomplished reader, as well as the process of reading (Edmonds et al., 2009; Goldman, Snow, & Vaughn, 2016; Pressley et al., 1992).

Our understanding of reading comprehension, like the construct of reading, evolves. In parallel, reading comprehension strategy instruction should reflect these changes. Durkin (1978) investigated reading comprehension instruction in upper elementary (grades 3 through 6) social studies classrooms. A predominant finding was that instruction consisted largely of teachers asking students questions about text content—as if posing a question somehow taught students how to understand text, and to answer the question. The questioning that Durkin observed was not Socratic questioning—with which students might gain new insights, or be led to use complex, higher-order strategies by the vector of the question. Rather, the questions focused on literal recall of facts: names, dates, places and actions as stated explicitly in the text. One conclusion drawn from Durkin's study was the need to rethink how reading comprehension was "taught," and what was taught.

The determination that asking questions is not an adequate teaching approach served as impetus for research intended to inform effective reading comprehension strategy instruction. What would comprise this instruction? How might comprehension be taught? Since the late 1970s, research has provided considerable insights into the nature of expert readers' comprehension strategies, including how, when, where, and why they are used. This has contributed detail needed to develop instruction, including the classification of reading strategies and how they are used. For example, Pressley and Afflerbach (1995) examined think-aloud studies of expert readers' and identified three overarching categories of reading strategy: *identifying and remembering important information, monitoring acts of reading*, and *evaluation* (Table 7.1).

Afflerbach and Cho (2009) and Cho and Afflerbach (2017) introduced a fourth category, *realizing and constructing potential texts*, which included the strategies used by readers as they negotiate the multiple texts, spaces and reading choices encountered in Internet and multimedia reading. Within these general groups of strategy reside specific strategies such as inferencing, summarizing and comprehension monitoring. The understanding of reading comprehension strategies gained through think-aloud protocols maps well onto detailed models of comprehension (Kintsch, 1998; Van Den Broek, Young, Tzeng, & Linderholm, 1999).

In many cases, reading comprehension strategy instruction derives from walking backwards on the path to expertise. That is, developmental trajectories and milestones

Reading Comprehension Strategy Instruction · 103

Table 7.1 A Thumbnail Sketch of Constructively Responsive Reading Strategies

- Overviewing before reading (determining what is there and deciding which parts to process).
- Looking for important information in text and paying greater attention to it than other information (e.g., adjusting reading speed and concentration depending on the perceived importance of text to reading goals).
- Attempting to relate important points in text to one another in order to understand the text as a whole.
- Activating and using prior knowledge to interpret text (generating hypotheses about text, predicting text content).
- Relating text content to prior knowledge, especially as part of constructing interpretations of text.
- Reconsidering and/or revising hypotheses about the meaning of text based on text content.
- Reconsidering and/or revising prior knowledge based on text content.
- Attempting to infer information not explicitly stated in text when the information is critical to comprehension of the text.
- Attempting to determine the meaning of words not understood or recognized, especially when a word seems critical to meaning construction.
- Using strategies to remember text (underlining, repetition, making notes, visualizing, summarizing, paraphrasing, self-questioning, etc.).
- Changing reading strategies when comprehension is perceived not to be proceeding smoothly.
- Evaluating the qualities of text, with these evaluations in part affecting whether text has an impact on reader's knowledge, attitudes, behavior, and so on.
- Reflecting on and processing text additionally after a part of text has been read or after a reading is completed (reviewing, questioning, summarizing, attempting to interpret, evaluating, considering alternative interpretations and possibly deciding between them, considering how to process the text additionally if there is a feeling it has not been understood as much as it needs to be understood, accepting one's understanding of the text, rejecting one's understanding of a text).
- Carrying on responsive conversation with the author.
- Anticipating or planning for the use of knowledge gained from reading.

Source: *Verbal protocols of reading: The nature of constructively responsive reading* (p. 105), by M. Pressley and P.Afflerbach, 1995, Mahwah, NJ: Erlbaum Associates. Copyright 1995 by Lawrence Erlbaum Associates, Inc. Reprinted with permission.

for student readers' growth are deduced from research data on experts' reading, including think-aloud protocols and retrospective accounts of strategy use. Instruction is developed around these markers and includes strategies like previewing, clarifying, summarizing, predicting text contents (and other forms of inferencing), re-reading and varying the rate of reading dependent on the reading task. More recently, research describes the nature of reading comprehension strategies beyond the reading of a single, traditional print text, including those involved in multimedia reading (Mayer, 2014), Internet reading (Cho, 2014) and the reading of multiple documents (Rouet & Potocki, 2018).

Thus, expert reader research informs our understanding of reading comprehension strategies in mature and successful form (Afflerbach & Johnston, 1984) and suggests critical foci for reading comprehension strategy instruction. Detailed accounts of successful strategy use inform approaches to comprehension instruction (Dole, Duffy, Roehler, & Pearson, 1991; Duke, Pearson, Strachan, & Billman, 2011; Wilkinson & Son, 2011). We can theorize about how these strategies develop, their relative complexity, and the timing and sequencing of comprehension instruction to best help student readers (Pressley, 1990).

In addition to providing detail on the *what* of reading strategy instruction, there is ample guidance on the *how* of this instruction which focuses on the pedagogical means to introduce, explain, think-aloud, model and scaffold ephemeral comprehension strategies, so that their nature and use is tangible to students (Almasi & Fullerton, 2012; Palincsar & Brown, 1984). For example, explanation and modeling are at the center of successful reading comprehension strategy instruction. Winograd and Hare (1988) proposed five elements that comprise effective teacher explanation: what the strategy is, why a strategy should be learned, how to use the strategy, when and where the strategy should be used, and how to evaluate use of the strategy. Detailed understanding of the nature of reading strategies, combined with effective instruction, improves reading comprehension (Rosenshine & Meister, 1994) and does so for both younger and older students (Edmonds et al., 2009).

Evolving Ideas about the Nature of Reading and Reading Comprehension Ongoing research contributes to continuous theory building and the evolving understanding of the reading comprehension construct. This knowledge should, ultimately, inform strategy instruction. Consider the case of the Reading Framework of the National Assessment of Educational Progress (National Assessment Governing Board, 2017). This Framework is regularly updated based on consensus, relevant research findings. Examination of current and prior NAEP conceptualizations of *reading* and *reading comprehension* illustrates this evolution. An earlier iteration of the NAEP Reading Framework (1992–2000) proposed that reading comprehension was comprised of the following "Reading Stances" for both expository and narrative texts:

- *initial understanding*, the preliminary consideration of the text as a whole
- *developing an interpretation*, discerning connections and relationships among ideas within the text
- *personal reflection and response*, relating personal knowledge to text ideas
- *critical stance*, standing apart from the text to consider it objectively.

(National Assessment Governing Board, 1992)

The above depiction of reading reflects the influence of research and theories from the fields of information processing, cognition (van Dijk & Kintsch, 1983) and literary criticism (Rosenblatt, 1938). It is notable that the reading processes and stances described above sum to a relatively constrained set of reading products. That is, acts of reading are deemed complete when comprehension of text is attained and readers reflect on their understanding, or position themselves in relation to their understanding of text. This conceptualization of reading implies that reading comprehension strategies and related instruction should focus on the construction of meaning from text.

In contrast, the current NAEP Reading Framework (2017) adds the results of recent research and theory building, and reflects the evolution of our understanding of comprehension. The Framework maintains a focus on reading comprehension as the construction of meaning with text, but adds a major new component:

Reading is an active and complex process that involves:

- understanding written text
- developing and interpreting meaning
- *using meaning as appropriate to type of text, purpose, and situation.*

(Retrieved from www.nagb.gov/content/nagb/assets/documents/ publications/frameworks/reading/2017-reading-framework.pdf, italics added)

The above definition represents a significant change: reading involves not only *the construction of meaning* but also *the use of the meaning that is constructed*. Readers, including student readers, are expected to do things with the meaning that they construct. This "use of comprehension" is demonstrated as students analyze text contents (Bazerman & Prior, 2004), identify claims and supporting evidence (Wineburg, 2001), apply what they learn from the text to solve problems (Hinchman & Appleman, 2017), establish epistemic stances towards the processes and contents of reading (Bråten & Strømsø, 2010), synthesize information within and across texts (Coté, Goldman, & Saul, 1998), interrogate author motive (Beck & McKeown, 2006) and critique text contents and structures (Vasquez, Harste, & Albers, 2010). Each of the above signals the use of higher order thinking strategies during reading.

The expanded notion of reading—including readers' use of what is comprehended—has important implications for reading comprehension strategy instruction. Namely, it forces a focus on what reading comprehension "is" and what strategies are appropriately situated under the umbrellas of reading comprehension and reading comprehension instruction. If reading does not "end" with a reader's establishment of understanding (i.e., constructing a situational model of text; Kintsch, 1998), then comprehension can be considered a mid-point in many acts of reading. And, the strategies involved in using the meaning that is constructed through reading become instructionally important. Determining where comprehension of text "ends" and where related, reading task strategies "begin" is important for both theory and reading comprehension strategies instruction.

To address contemporary accounts of reading, including the model of reading proposed by NAEP, we believe the traditional foci of reading comprehension strategy instruction, including prediction, summarization and comprehension monitoring, should be complemented by instruction that focuses on strategies to use that which is comprehended. Students construct meaning and then use that meaning with related strategies, such as those for analyzing claims and supporting evidence, applying what is learned from text to solve problems, establishing appropriate epistemic stances towards texts, synthesizing information from within and across texts, interrogating author motive and craft, and critiquing and evaluating texts. Instruction should be situated so that these natural counterparts of strategy instruction are taught, learned and practiced together.

COMPREHENSION STRATEGIES ARE NECESSARY FOR STUDENTS TO SUCCEED WITH INCREASINGLY CHALLENGING TEXTS AND RELATED READING TASKS

That current reading comprehension strategy instruction is not helping all students develop into accomplished readers is a near inference we can make from reading achievement performance on national and international assessments, including the NAEP (2017) and the PISA (Programme for International Student Assessment). We possess considerable knowledge about reading comprehension strategies and comprehension development, but this knowledge is not consistently translated into reading comprehension instruction that boosts students' reading performance. NAEP Reading scores in grades 4, 8 and 12, as well as NAEP scores in content areas that require substantial student reading, do not describe a nation of consistently comprehending readers. Consider that 4th and 8th-grade students' reading comprehension performances on NAEP in 2017 (with both grades mean reading achievement scores situated between "basic" and "proficient" levels) were not measurably different from the 2015 scores. Students' performance on NAEP tests in content domains that require considerable amounts of reading is unsettling:

[o]nly 17% of eighth graders demonstrated proficiency in the area of United States History according to the most recent National Assessment of Educational Progress.
(Retrieved from www.nationsreportcard.gov/)

In both reading and content domains that demand significant amounts of student reading, NAEP scores are at best stagnant. Substantial numbers of students struggle to achieve basic levels of reading comprehension, and fewer still reach proficient or advanced levels.

While test results indicate flat or declining reading achievement, many students face increased reading comprehension demands in school. The Common Core State Standards and other standards-based initiatives are intended to influence what students do and learn in classrooms. The Standards reflect a conceptualization of reading in common with the NAEP Reading Framework (National Assessment Governing Board, 2017). Namely, they share the idea that reading involves reader, text, activity and context, and the expectation that readers will use that which they comprehend in related tasks. In both the current NAEP Reading Framework and the Common Core State Standards, comprehension is the salient outcome of reading. However, the evolution of our conceptualization of reading is reflected in the fact that comprehension is no longer considered an end in itself, but rather a requisite component of larger acts of literacy. This places new and often complex demands on students' strategy use.

Consider the following Common Core State English/Language Arts Standard for informational reading, and the reading strategies that are implied for students' success:

Integration of Knowledge and Ideas:

CCSS.ELA-LITERACY.RI.6.8

Trace and evaluate the argument and specific claims in a text, distinguishing claims that are supported by reasons and evidence from claims that are not.
(Retrieved from www.corestandards.org/ELA-Literacy/RI/6/)

A task analysis of the above grade 6 Common Core State Standard indicates the assumption of strategy use that allows students to construct literal and inferential understanding of text—the situational model of text (Kintsch, 1998). However, comprehension is but a prerequisite for further strategic reading performance on the standard. In this case, readers' strategic behavior requires the higher order thinking of identifying claims made in the text, and evaluating claims to determine if they have sufficient evidence to warrant them (Afflerbach, Cho, & Kim, 2015). The implications for reading comprehension strategy instruction are considerable—more, and more complex strategies are needed for student success in reading.

In summary, as our conceptualizations of reading evolve, so too should our ideas related to teaching reading strategies. A prominent example of this evolution is evident in the current definition of reading that anchors the National Assessment of Educational Progress (2017). According to this contemporary view of reading, readers construct meaning and then use this constructed meaning to perform tasks that involve complex reasoning and problem solving. This idea is woven into contemporary standards initiatives, including the Common Core State Standards. A resulting need is development of students' comprehension strategies to both construct meaning and use that meaning in a reading-related task.

WHICH APPROACH TO READING COMPREHENSION STRATEGY INSTRUCTION?

There is substantial knowledge that can inform reading comprehension strategy instruction, and a clear need for effective instruction. However, there is no agreement on the optimal means of this instruction. We noted earlier that much of the detail of reading comprehension strategy instruction derives from analyses of expert readers' strategy use. This research has been situated in specific disciplines, or content domains, including anthropology and chemistry (Afflerbach, 1990), law (Lundeberg, 1987) and history (Wineburg, 2001). A tendency in the development of reading comprehension instruction has been to identify the strategies that are used by accomplished readers "across" disciplines. The apparent universality of a reading comprehension strategy, across readers and texts, becomes an argument for inclusion of that strategy, and it is taught. Thus, while important information about the nature of reading comprehension strategies has been gained through examination of expert readers, derivative instruction has tended to ignore the discipline-specific nature of strategy use and has focused on commonalities across disciplines.

A result is the prevalence of strategies such as prediction, summarization and inferencing—regularly used by accomplished readers, regardless of discipline—in most reading instruction programs (Dewitz, Jones, & Leahy, 2009). These strategies are assumed to be of value to students whose primary reading tasks are to learn and remember literal information from the text, and they are typically taught with a "one size fits all" approach. However, this approach may overlook what can be subtle or more obvious differences in the nature of strategies and how they are used within particular disciplines.

Students' general reading comprehension strategies may not work in more nuanced content area reading, including history, science and literature (Goldman et al., 2016). For example, a generic strategy that serves a student well in summarizing the contents of a textbook chapter on the Revolutionary War is not sufficient when the student attempts to summarize and reconcile two opposing accounts of a related, historic event (e.g., the Boston Tea Party; the Boston Massacre; VanSledright, 2014). Rather, the accomplished student reader must be able to (among other demands) source the different texts, determine their trustworthiness, note similarities and differences in factual and rhetorical information, and render judgment on which text (if either) is more reliable.

108 • Peter Afflerbach et al.

The fact that different disciplines may demand appropriately distinctive strategies, or different "takes" on the same strategy, has prompted a focus on disciplinary approaches to promoting student understanding of text. With such an approach, comprehension strategies are viewed as tied to the reading, reasoning and culture of particular disciplines or content domains, including history, science and literature (Afflerbach & VanSledright, 2001; Kim et al., 2016; Lee, Goldman, Levine, & Magliano, 2016). Unfortunately, the discipline-based aspect of reading comprehension strategy instruction often competes for instructional time with coverage of content—say, World War Two, ecosystems, or novels and short stories. Teachers whose students may not be reading at grade level expectation are fully engaged with trying to cover curricular content and help students meet more basic reading achievement levels, so attending and teaching more complex, discipline-related reading strategies is not always possible.

A second concern with reading comprehension strategy instruction relates to the claim that strategies are given more time and instructional focus than is needed, and that content area knowledge is a more important factor than strategy use in students' successful comprehension of texts (Willingham & Lovette, 2014). From this perspective, having students front-load considerable amounts of content area knowledge may be more effective than extended instruction and practice time with reading strategies, if comprehension of content area text is the goal. Student exposure to key ideas and concepts (and the vocabulary that represents them) is proposed as a superior means for preparing students to learn from reading (Willingham, 2017). A difficulty with this view is that the *raison d'etre* for school is student learning, and much of this learning emanates from reading. As noted by Goldman and colleagues (2016):

> A significant challenge is that the texts they (students) will be asked to read contain unfamiliar content in complex language forms. Many school texts intentionally introduce new topics and concepts to teach new content knowledge. Precisely because the content is new, students' familiar strategy of using their prior knowledge to make inferences and connections, effective for texts about familiar topics and situations, fails.
>
> (p. 2)

It is not clear how students, without reading, are to gain the requisite content area knowledge that would allow them to learn the remaining, new content area knowledge. Willingham's suggestions amount to radical change in how content area information might be learned by students—with a major emphasis on imparting knowledge by means other than student reading. This, of course, stands as able argument for reducing attention to reading strategy instruction because reading itself assumes a considerably lesser role in learning in school (Greenleaf & Valencia, 2017). However, we approach the issue with the idea that learning comprehension strategies that allow us to read independently and successfully in areas replete with new information is of utmost value.

A final concern with reading comprehension instruction is the tendency to introduce, teach and have students practice single comprehension strategies. Students are taught, in a strategy-by-strategy manner (Dewitz et al., 2009), how to make inferences and predictions, how to determine important information and summarize text, and how to set goals and monitor progress towards goals. That these important but individually taught strategies will eventually sum to successful strategic reading may be wishful thinking, because accomplished reading demands both a suitable array of strategies and the ability to carefully coordinate them in relation to the specifics of the reading situation. Consider the following account of strategic reading provided by Pressley and Afflerbach (1995):

> [s]killed readers know and use many different (strategies) in coming to terms with text: They proceed generally from front to back of documents when reading. Good readers are selectively attentive. They sometimes make notes. They predict, paraphrase, and back up when confused. They try to make inferences to fill in the gaps in text and in their understanding of what they have read. Good readers intentionally attempt to integrate across the text. They do not settle for literal meanings but rather interpret what they have read, sometimes constructing images, other times identifying categories of information in text, and on still other occasions engaging in arguments with themselves about what a reading might mean. After making their way through text, they have a variety of ways of firming up their understanding and memory of the messages in the text, from explicitly attempting to summarize to self-questioning about the text to rereading and reflecting. The many [strategies] used by skilled readers are appropriately and opportunistically coordinated, with the reader using the processes needed to meet current reading goals, confronting the demands of reading at the moment, and preparing for demands that are likely in the future (e.g., the need to recall text content for a test).
>
> (pp. 79–80)

Successful reading strategy instruction should contribute to the development of the strategic readers described above, and such successful reading is tied to students' opportunities to learn and practice diverse strategies as they are coordinated in real-time reading.

To summarize, there are several critiques of contemporary reading comprehension strategy instruction worthy of consideration. First, there is the claim that strategy instruction is too generic and not context specific. This is a result of choosing comprehension strategies to be taught based on their omnipresence in strategy reports from expert readers, and not necessarily in relation to the discipline-specific reading topics, tasks and contexts found in school. Second, there is the claim that reading strategies are over taught, and that the key to content area reading success lies in providing students with ample prior knowledge in the content areas, as this helps students read best. Prior knowledge is essential for comprehension, yet reliance on non-reading sources to gain knowledge can lead to further avoidance of reading and strategy development. Further, students are in school to learn, and the vast stores of information that students are expected to comprehend, learn and remember are delivered by texts. How to draw the line between the prior knowledge necessary to learn new information and the new information itself remains unspecified. A third concern is that reading comprehension strategy instruction is marked by the teaching and learning of single, often unconnected strategies, while reading comprehension demands coordinated suites of strategies to succeed. Certainly, the development of accomplished strategic reading is the result of extensive use and practice of sets of strategies.

THE KNOWLEDGE NEEDED FOR SUCCESSFUL READING COMPREHENSION STRATEGY INSTRUCTION AND LEARNING

In the section that follows and in relation to the above concerns, we propose that instruction can be optimized as we consider five types of knowledge related to students' reading comprehension strategy development and use. These types of knowledge should be considered essential to successful reading comprehension strategy instruction. Reading comprehension strategy instruction typically focuses on helping students learn and use procedural knowledge. This procedural knowledge provides students with strategic approaches to reading that should yield declarative knowledge—most often the "stuff" of content area curricula, and the focus on high-stakes tests. This knowledge has a wide range and can include letter names, dictionary definitions of words, a list of genre names for memorization, events and figures in history, prey and predator in science, or distinguishing characteristics of sonnets, epic poems and haiku in literature.

However, we suggest that effective reading comprehension strategy instruction attends to five types of knowledge—*declarative, procedural, conditional, epistemic* and *disciplinary*—that support and ultimately shape students' ongoing strategy use and development. While these types of knowledge may overlap in particular circumstances of reading (e.g., the construction of literal meaning from text involves declarative, procedural and conditional knowledge), we believe that they merit separate consideration due to their role in students' strategy use.

Declarative Knowledge

The knowledge gained from the majority of school reading tasks is *declarative knowledge*. Declarative knowledge involves knowing things: that lions, cheetahs and leopards are cats, that the Declaration of Independence was signed in Philadelphia in 1776, and that haiku typically have a 5-7-5 syllable structure. Knowing that prediction is a reading strategy also qualifies as declarative knowledge. Much schooling focuses on students' acquisition of declarative knowledge. Students are expected to read and learn, and declarative knowledge is the product of the learning processes that students employ. Most tests, local and high stakes, focus on declarative knowledge—the product (and not the processes) of comprehension. As students matriculate through school, the accumulation of declarative knowledge from reading is taken as indication that procedural knowledge (i.e., students' comprehension strategies) is operating, and operating well.

Increased declarative knowledge is the primary result of much school reading: students learn new information in the content areas. However, declarative knowledge is also a prerequisite for comprehension itself. Student readers' existing declarative knowledge serves as a bridge from known to new. As described by Marzano (2004), "What students *already know* about the content is one of the strongest indicators of how well they will learn new information relative to the content." Readers who bring such prior knowledge to acts of reading possess the means to interpret and understand text (Anderson & Pearson, 1984). Moreover, prior knowledge provides a cognitive "place" for the new knowledge gained through reading to be stored (Bartlett, 1932).

Thus, successful reading strategy instruction will be based on a foundation of requisite declarative knowledge that helps students construct meaning. For example, students learning about predators and prey in a savannah environment need a rudimentary understanding of ecosystems for comprehension to occur and have a meaningful afterlife. As meaning is constructed, a reader's existing declarative (or "prior") knowledge serves as the bridge between prior learning and newly learned material. Thus, declarative knowledge is a prerequisite for, and result of, successful reading.

Procedural Knowledge

Learning and accumulating declarative knowledge through reading is enabled by readers' *procedural knowledge*—including the comprehension strategies that readers use to construct meaning. Paris, Lipson, and Wixson (1983) define procedural knowledge as knowing how a "strategy operates and how to use various steps or procedures that are part of the strategy." By making inferences, identifying and remembering important information, monitoring comprehension and summarizing texts, readers use procedural knowledge in the form of strategies to construct the model of text (or texts) that they are reading (Kintsch, 1998; Pressley & Afflerbach, 1995; Rouet & Britt, 2011).

In relation to contemporary accounts of reading (National Assessment Governing Board, 2017) and reading standards initiatives (Common Core State Standards, 2010), successful student readers must possess two types of procedural knowledge: that which pertains to reading comprehension strategies, and that which pertains to strategies used in reading-related tasks. The former are strategies for constructing meaning; the latter for using that constructed meaning. For example, establishing literal understanding of a content area text is a universal reading demand, one regularly met by many students using reading comprehension strategies. Related, identifying a claim-evidence structure in that same text, and determining whether or not the text is trustworthy, is an important reading task strategy. Both rely on students' procedural knowledge.

With reading, procedural knowledge in the form of strategies may be assigned "reading comprehension" or "reading comprehension-related" labels. Whatever the formalities of assigning terms and labels to these related strategy groups, it is sensible to teach them in tandem. This allows students to develop strategies as they are related in the real time of reading and using what is understood from reading. Both types of strategy—to construct meaning and to use constructed meaning—are amenable to teachers' modeling and explaining. As noted earlier, an expected benefit of the development of students' procedural knowledge of reading is growth in declarative knowledge—successful use of reading strategies begets the construction of meaning, which results in new knowledge in the content areas or disciplines.

Conditional Knowledge

A third influence on learning and using reading comprehension strategies is *conditional knowledge*, which often relates to knowing when, why and how to use declarative and procedural knowledge (Alexander, 2008). In the case of reading, conditional knowledge is used to mediate reader-text interactions, and it provides executive control over the strategies for constructing meaning (Bakracevic-Vukman & Licardo,

2010). For developing readers, managing reading comprehension strategies can be a taxing proposition. There is only so much bandwidth (working memory resource) for students to determine what strategy (or strategies) to use, deploy them and then monitor their appropriateness and success, and gain declarative knowledge. A result is that developing readers have much to attend to as they endeavor to learn new content, new reading strategies and the means to manage their acts of reading.

Conditional knowledge is reflected in a reader's situational understanding of reading, and involves metacognition, as decisions are made to set goals, calibrate performance, apply strategies and assess progress (Baker, 2009). Conditional knowledge reflects a student's understanding of why a strategy is important and when it should be used (Paris et al., 1983). Conditional knowledge is necessary to inform student readers' increasingly independent actions—as they initiate reading, monitor comprehension and conclude acts of reading (Dinsmore, Alexander, & Loughlin, 2008). In addition, conditional knowledge is necessary for students' appropriate framing of the epistemological nature of reading—if a text or author is to be challenged, or if the contents of text is trustworthy. With the advent of the Common Core State Standards, and with increasingly complex reading and reading-related tasks demanded of students, the centrality of conditional knowledge for success is apparent.

Epistemic Knowledge

A fourth type of knowledge is *epistemic knowledge*. Kuhn and Park (2005) describe four levels of epistemic development, and related stances towards knowledge. The *realist stance* assumes that "knowledge comes from an external source and is certain"—a reader assuming this stance has no need for critical thinking and related strategies. The *absolutist stance* assumes that "knowledge comes from an external source and is certain but not directly accessible, producing false beliefs." Accordingly, critical thinking strategies are a vehicle for comparing assertions to reality and determining their truth or falsehood. The *multiplist stance* assumes that "knowledge is generated by human minds and therefore uncertain," and readers' critical thinking is irrelevant. The *evaluativist stance* assumes that "knowledge is generated by human minds and is uncertain but susceptible to evaluation," and critical thinking strategies are necessary for readers to construct and evaluate meanings (Kuhn & Park, 2005, p. 113).

The development of student readers' critical and evaluative reading strategies must be accompanied by epistemics: an understanding of the nature of knowledge (Cho, Woodward, & Li, 2018; Elby & Hammer, 2010; Greene, Sandoval, & Braten, 2016). Specific to reading, epistemic knowledge helps the reader develop an appropriate stance towards texts and tasks, and this stance influences reading strategy choice. Epistemic knowledge also helps readers "frame" their approach to both texts and tasks.

Consider the interactions of reading strategies with epistemic knowledge related to two texts: political propaganda and a chapter about an unfamiliar topic. Students, using conditional knowledge, must determine the strategic and epistemic approach they will adopt with each text. Skepticism related to propaganda may trigger a student reader to take an evaluative stance with a series of analytical strategies that focus on constructing meaning *and* determining if there is evidence to support a series of outrageous claims. With the second text containing unfamiliar content, student readers are reduced to using comprehension strategies to construct literal understanding, and information will be taken at face value. Students are unable to conduct critical appraisal of text because they have an insufficient declarative knowledge base with which to make judgment of the text's accuracy and trustworthiness, and their epistemic stance-taking is therefore limited.

Disciplinary Knowledge

The fifth and final type of knowledge that figures in reading comprehension strategy use is *disciplinary knowledge*. This knowledge may be required of students when they read in school content areas. For example, history as a school subject and discipline has evolved in some classrooms to include "reading like a historian"—wherein students focus on interpreting different texts, identifying text sources, determining the trustworthiness of the texts, constructing understanding within and across texts, and making judgments about which historical accounts contained in the text are most reliable. Students' ability to do so is tied to the strategies particular to the discipline:

> Successful readers of history are aware of the intertextual nature of history and are adept at noting conflicting accounts, reconciling contrasting views, and synthesizing information from complementary sources.
> (Afflerbach & VanSledright, 2001, p. 697)

Disciplinary knowledge guides this inquiry—student readers employ reading comprehension strategies in accordance with the culture and established practices of the discipline. The more "true" to the discipline, the more need for discipline-specific reading strategies. And, the more discipline-dependent, the more we should expect curriculum and instruction to help acculturate students to the discipline (Moje, 2015). Goldman et al. (2016), reporting on their work with reading comprehension and disciplinary knowledge, describe this as such:

> [t]he members constitute a discourse community and share a set of conventions and norms regarding valid forms of argument and communication. These norms reflect the field's epistemology—the nature of the disciplinary knowledge and how new knowledge claims in that discipline are legitimized and established ... Thus, in addition to knowing the concepts and principles of their discipline, community members have knowledge about their discipline that supports engaging in the reading, reasoning, and argumentation practices.
> (p. 6)

Disciplinary knowledge is based on students' experiences and learning, and represents the broadest set of understandings that student readers must have and use to be successful with reading comprehension strategies. Disciplinary knowledge involves declarative, procedural, conditional and epistemic knowledge. For example, beginning a unit on ecosystems, students must have a rudimentary knowledge for science—a bridge between what students already know and what they must learn in the unit. Procedural knowledge is evinced as students use the scientific method to investigate predator-prey relationships in a nearby pond. Conditional knowledge assists students in choosing appropriate strategies, using them as necessary, and monitoring the construction of meaning and the related task work. Epistemic knowledge guides students as they approach science—is the content of reading selections comprised of undisputed facts, models and examples of predators and prey?

In summary, different types of knowledge operate in concert with students' reading comprehension strategies, and this knowledge is necessary in all acts of reading. Our theoretical perspective suggests that identification and characterization of these different types of knowledge will benefit reading comprehension strategy instruction. Each of these types of knowledge develops as students learn. Thus, determining the presence of these types of knowledge and their level of development is essential for reading success.

CONCLUSIONS

Effective reading comprehension strategy instruction fosters student development and contributes to independence in reading. There is a considerable lack of consistency in defining and describing reading comprehension strategies, and there is sometimes conflation of these strategies with teaching strategies and teaching tools. This can contribute to a lack of clarity in instructional goals and approaches.

A core of well-researched and widely taught reading comprehension strategies derives from research that documents the use and utility of identifying and remembering important information, monitoring all aspects of the act of reading, and evaluating—progress towards goal, veracity of text and author ability. While many comprehension strategies are used universally, their utility may be limited if they are introduced and taught as generic strategies—usable in each and any act of reading. Instead, it is sensible to consider nuanced strategy use as situated in different content areas or disciplines. Reading and reading-related tasks typically increase in complexity as students matriculate, and research demonstrates that students' reading comprehension strategy must develop in at least two ways: increased sophistication of the core, universal strategies and development of additional strategies that are central to reading and learning in particular content areas or disciplines.

The question of "how much reading comprehension strategy instruction is sufficient?" does not have a conclusive answer. Learning and application and the opportunity to practice and transfer strategies from general to discipline-specific reading tasks is important. As well, describing instruction with optimal combinations of strategy and prior knowledge is necessary, especially when reading is the main vehicle for learning.

There are diverse types of knowledge that surround reading comprehension strategy development and use. Much of contemporary schooling is built on the "procedural knowledge begets declarative knowledge" premise: reading strategies help students gain knowledge in the content areas. Yet, this is only a partial portrayal of the knowledge involved in successful strategy use. Conditional knowledge, in the form of metacognition and executive functioning, is necessary for students' independent initiation, working through and completion of reading tasks. Epistemic knowledge and disciplinary knowledge also come into play as students matriculate towards increasingly complex content area reading demands.

A final note is that the development of strategic student readers is not solely attributable to the effectiveness or quality reading strategy instruction. The fact that not all students read strategically and successfully may be taken as prima facie evidence that strategy instruction is not fully effective. However, there are numerous factors that influence reading development—indeed, human learning in general—including prior reading experiences and related knowledge and experience, and students' affective and conative profiles related to motivation and engagement, and self-efficacy. Further, the influence of factors such as poverty or English learner status can skew perceptions of success or failure of particular approaches to reading comprehension strategy instruction.

FUTURE DIRECTIONS

An important focus for future research is identifying developmental progressions in students' reading comprehension strategies. We noted that most strategy instruction is based on accomplished or expert reader performance. From these performances we better understand an individual strategy's function and contribution to comprehension. However, we lack understanding of the progression of student readers' strategy development. Likewise, we have not identified which strategies might be best candidates for teaching first, or if such sequencing makes sense. An additional area of research should focus on the development of suites of strategies—how students gain the ability to coordinate and use multiple strategies. A further focus for future research should be determination of complementary strategies—those for constructing meaning and those that are involved in using that constructed meaning. Should determination of claim and evidence accompany or follow strategy instruction that focuses on constructing accurate literal understanding? Finally, should strategies be taught based on seeming universality of use (and usefulness) and then be followed by discipline-specific application?

A second general area is determination of the optimal blend of reading comprehension strategy instruction and related knowledge—including knowledge for the content or topic of text, knowledge for managing acts of reading, knowledge for taking appropriate stances towards particular texts and tasks, and knowledge of how strategies operate within the culture of particular learning disciplines. These types of prior knowledge can surround and enhance reading comprehension strategy use. Relevant research can investigate how that prior knowledge is gained and established, to what extent prior knowledge should be provided, activated and used as a scaffold and resource for productive and engaged meaning making, and how instruction helps students learn to spontaneously monitor the construction of meanings, and to constantly revise and elaborate what they know as they construct meaning.

An ongoing challenge relates to strategy instruction within content areas or disciplines. Many content area teachers are not familiar with reading strategy instruction, yet it is in content area reading that powerful and nuanced reading strategies should be introduced, encouraged and grown. In addition, most school curricula in the content areas are already full. This works against the idea of teachers in middle and upper grades finding the time and developing the means to effectively teach reading comprehension strategies. We described five types of knowledge that should surround strategy instruction, yet addressing these types of knowledge as appropriate to the reading situation places further burden on content area teachers. That said, a research focus should include when and how strategy instruction helps students learn, consult and reason about multiple texts and sources of knowledge for content learning in discipline-specific ways. Also, it would be valuable to examine how strategy instruction in and across content areas and the strategic reading experiences may help students assess which strategy may or may not work as they are working on a particular knowledge problem beyond subject-matter classrooms.

REFERENCES

Afflerbach, P. (1990). The influence of prior knowledge on expert readers' main idea construction strategies. *Reading Research Quarterly, 25*, 31–46.

Afflerbach, P., & Cho, B. (2009). Identifying and describing constructively responsive comprehension strategies in new and traditional forms of reading. In S. Israel & G. Duffy (Eds.), *Handbook of reading comprehension research* (pp. 69–90). Mahwah, NJ: Lawrence Erlbaum.

Afflerbach, P., Cho, B., & Kim, J. (2015). Conceptualizing and assessing higher order thinking in reading. *Theory into Practice, 54*, 203–212.

Afflerbach, P., & Johnston, P. (1984). On the use of verbal reports in reading research. *Journal of Reading Behavior, 16*, 307–322.

Afflerbach, P., Pearson, D., & Paris, S. (2008). Clarifying differences between reading skills and reading strategies. *The Reading Teacher, 61*, 364–373.

Afflerbach, P., & VanSledright, B. (2001). Hath? Doth? What! The challenges middle school students face when reading innovative history text. *Journal of Adolescent and Adult Literacy, 44*, 696–707.

Alexander, P. A. (2008). Why this and why now? Introduction to the special issue on metacognition, self-regulation, and self-regulated learning. *Educational Psychology Review, 20*, 369–372.

Almasi, J., & Fullerton, S. (2012). *Teaching strategic processes in reading* (p. 2e). New York: Guilford Press.

Anderson, R. C., & Pearson, P. D. (1984). *A schema—theoretic view of basic processes in reading comprehension* (Report No. 306). Champaign, IL: University of Illinois.

Baker, L. (2009). Metacognitive processes and reading comprehension. In S. Israel (Ed.), *Handbook of research on reading comprehension* (pp. 373–388). New York: Routledge.

Bakracevic-Vukman, K., & Licardo, M. (2010). How cognitive, metacognitive, motivational and emotional self-regulation influence school performance in adolescence and early adulthood. *Educational Studies, 36*, 259–268. doi:10.1080/03055690903180376

Bartlett, F. C. (1932). *Remembering: A study in experimental and social psychology*. Cambridge, UK: Cambridge University Press.

Bazerman, C., & Prior, P. (2004). *What writing does and how it does it*. Hillsdale, NJ: Lawrence Erlbaum.

Beck, I., & McKeown, M. (2006). *Improving comprehension with questioning the author*. New York: Scholastic.

Bråten, I., & Strømsø, H. I. (2010). Effects of task instruction and personal epistemology on the understanding of multiple texts about climate change. *Discourse Processes, 47*, 1–31.

Cho, B. (2014). Competent adolescent readers' use of Internet reading strategies: A think-aloud study. *Cognition and Instruction, 32*, 253–289.

Cho, B., & Afflerbach, P. (2017). An evolving perspective on constructively responsive reading comprehension strategies in multilayered digital text environments. In S. Israel (Ed.), *Handbook of reading comprehension research, 2e* (pp. 109–134). New York: Guilford.

Cho, B.-Y., Woodward, L., & Li, D. (2018). Epistemic processing when adolescents read online: A verbal protocol analysis of more and less successful online readers. *Reading Research Quarterly, 53*, 197–221. doi:10.1002/rrq.190.

Coté, N., Goldman, S. R., & Saul, E. U. (1998). Students making sense of informational text: Relations between processing and representation. *Discourse Processes, 25*, 1–53.

Dewitz, P., Jones, J., & Leahy, S. (2009). Comprehension strategy instruction in core reading programs. *Reading Research Quarterly, 44*, 102–126.

Dinsmore, D., Alexander, P., & Loughlin, S. (2008). Focusing the conceptual lens on metacognition, self-regulation, and self-regulated learning. *Educational Psychology Review, 20*, 391–409.

Dole, J., Duffy, G., Roehler, L., & Pearson, P. (1991). Moving from the old to the new: Research on reading comprehension instruction. *Review of Educational Research, 61*, 239–264.

Duke, N., Pearson, P., Strachan, S., & Billman, A. (2011). Essential elements of fostering and teaching reading comprehension. In S., Samuels, & A. Farstrup (Eds.), *What research has to say about reading instruction* (Vol. 4e, pp. 51–93). Newark, DE: International Reading Association.

Durkin, D. (1978). What classroom observations reveal about reading comprehension instruction. *Reading Research Quarterly, 14*, 481–533.

Edmonds, M., Vaughn, S., Wexler, J., Reutebuch, C., Cable, A., Tackett, K., & Schnakenberg, J. (2009). A synthesis of reading interventions and effects on reading comprehension outcomes for older struggling readers. *Review of Educational Research, 79*, 262–300.

Elby, A., & Hammer, D. (2010). Epistemological resources and framing: A cognitive framework for helping teachers interpret and respond to their students' epistemologies. In L. Bendixen & F. Feucht (Eds.), *Personal epistemology in the classroom: Theory, research, and implications for practice* (pp. 409–433). Cambridge, UK: Cambridge University Press.

Goldman, S., Snow, C., & Vaughn, S. (2016). Common themes in teaching reading for understanding. *Journal of Adult and Adolescent Literacy, 60*, 255–264.

Greene, J., Sandoval, W., & Braten, I. (2016). *Handbook of epistemic cognition.* New York: Routledge.

Greenleaf, C., & Valencia, S. (2017). Missing in action: Learning from texts in subject- matter classrooms. In K. Hinchman & D. Appleman (Eds.), *Adolescent literacies: A handbook of practice-based research* (pp. 235–256). New York: Guilford Press.

Hinchman, K., & Appleman, D. (2017). *Adolescent literacies: A handbook of practice-based research.* New York: Guilford Press.

Huey, E. (1908). *Psychology and pedagogy of reading.* New York: Macmillan.

Kim, J., Hemphill, L., Troyer, M., Thomson, J., Jones, S., & LarRusso, M. (2016). Engaging struggling adolescent readers to improve reading skills. *Reading Research Quarterly, 52*, 352–387.

Kintsch, W. (1998). *Comprehension: A paradigm for cognition.* New York: Cambridge University Press.

Kuhn, D., & Park, S. (2005). Epistemological understanding and the development of intellectual values. *International Journal of Educational Research, 43*, 111–124.

Lee, C. D., Goldman, S. R., Levine, S., & Magliano, J. (2016). Epistemic cognition in literary reasoning. In Greene, J., Sandoval, W. & Braten, I. (Eds.), *Handbook of epistemic cognition* (pp. 165–183). New York: Taylor & Francis.

Lundeberg, M. A. (1987). Metacognitive aspects of reading comprehension: Studying understanding in legal case analysis. *Reading Research Quarterly, 22*, 407–432.

Marzano, P. (2004). The developing vision of vocabulary instruction. In J. Baumann & E. Kameenui (Eds.), *Vocabulary instruction: Research to practice* (pp. 100–117). New York: Guilford Press.

Mayer, R. (2014). *Multimedia learning* (Vol. 3e). Cambridge, UK: Cambridge University Press.

Moje, E. (2015). Doing and teaching disciplinary literacy with adolescent learners: A social and cultural enterprise. *Harvard Educational Review, 85*, 254–278.

National Assessment Governing Board. (1992). *Reading Framework for the 1992 National Assessment of Educational Progress.* Washington, DC: Author.

National Assessment Governing Board. (2017). *Reading Framework for the 2017 National Assessment of Educational Progress.* Washington, DC: Author.

National Institute of Child Health and Human Development. (2000). Report of the National Reading Panel. *Teaching children to read: An evidence-based assessment of the scientific research literature on reading and its implications for reading instruction (NIH Publication No. 00-4769).* Washington, DC: U.S. Government Printing Office.

National Governors Association Center for Best Practices, Council of Chief State School Officers. (2010). *Title: Common Core State Standards.* Washington, DC: National Governors Association Center for Best Practices, Council of Chief State School Officers.

Palincsar, A., & Brown, A. (1984). Reciprocal teaching of comprehension fostering and comprehension-monitoring activities. *Cognition and Instruction, 1*, 117–175.

Paris, S., Lipson, M., & Wixson, K. (1983). Becoming a strategic reader. *Contemporary Educational Psychology, 8*, 293–316.

Pressley, M., & Afflerbach, P. (1995). *Verbal protocols of reading: The nature of constructively responsive reading.* Hillsdale, NJ: Lawrence Erlbaum.

Pressley, M. & Harris, K. (1990). What We Really Know about Strategy Instruction. *Educational Leadership, 48*, 31–34.

Pressley, M., El-Dinary, P., Gaskins, I., Schuder, T., Bergman, J., Almasi, J., & Brown, R. (1992). Beyond direct explanation: Instruction of reading comprehension strategies. *The Elementary School Journal, 92*, 513–555.

Rosenblatt, L. (1938). *Literature as exploration*. New York: Appleton-Century.

Rosenshine, B., & Meister, C. (1994). Reciprocal teaching: A review of the research. *Review of Educational Research, 64*, 479–530.

Rouet, J., & Britt, M. (2011). Relevance processes in multiple document processing. In M. McCrudden, J. Magliano, & G. Schraw (Eds.), *Text relevance and learning from text* (pp. 19–52). Charlotte, NC: Information Age Publishing.

Rouet, J., & Potocki, A. (2018). From reading comprehension to document literacy: Learning to search for, evaluate and integrate information across texts. *Journal for the Study of Education and Development, 41*, 415–446.

Van Den Broek, P., Young, M., Tzeng, Y., & Linderholm, T. (1999). The landscape model of reading: Inferences and the online construction of a memory representation. In H. Oostendorp & S. Goldman (Eds.), *The construction of mental representations during reading* (pp. 62–87). Hillsdale, NJ: Lawrence Erlbaum.

Van Dijk, T., & Kintsch, W. (1983). *Strategies of discourse comprehension*. New York: Academic Press.

VanSledright, B. A. (2014). *Assessing historical thinking and understanding: Innovative ideas for new standards*. New York: Routledge.

Vasquez, V., Harste, J., & Albers, P. (2010). From the personal to the Worldwide Web: Moving teachers to positions of critical interrogation. In Baker, E., & Leu, D. (Eds.), *The new literacies: Multiple perspectives on research and practice*. New York: Guilford Press.

Wilkinson, I., & Son, E. (2011). A dialogic turn in research on learning and teaching to comprehend. In M. Kamil, P. Pearson, E. Moje, & P. Afflerbach (Eds.), *Handbook of reading research* (Vol. IV, pp. 359–387). New York: Taylor & Francis.

Willingham, D. (2017, November 25). How to get your mind to read. *New York Times*. Retrieved from www.nytimes.com/2017/11/25/opinion/sunday/how-to-get-your-mind-to-read.html?utm_source=pocket&utm_medium=email&utm_campaign=pockethits&_r=0

Willingham, D., & Lovette, G. (2014). Can reading comprehension be taught? *Teachers' College Record*. ID Number: 17701. Retrieved from www.tcrecord.org.proxy.its.virginia.edu

Wineburg, S. (2001). *Historical thinking and other unnatural acts: Charting the future of teaching the past*. Philadelphia, PA: Temple University Press.

Winograd, P., & Hare, V. (1988). Direct instruction of reading comprehension strategies: The nature of teacher explanation. In Weinstein, C., Goetz, E., Alexander, P., & Edwards, A. (Eds.) *Issues in assessment, instruction, and evaluation* (pp. 121–139).

8

SIX QUESTIONS REGARDING STRATEGY USE WHEN LEARNING FROM MULTIPLE TEXTS

Alexandra List
THE PENNSYLVANIA STATE UNIVERSITY, USA

Multiple text use, whereby students access and consider information introduced across multiple documents to understand a particular topic, has been described as a complex, challenging, effortful, goal-directed, and contextualized process (Goldman & Scardamalia, 2013; List & Alexander, 2018b; Rouet & Britt, 2011; Rouet, Britt, & Durik, 2017). These characterizations, in and of themselves, point to the central role of strategic processing in students' learning from multiple texts. In this chapter addressing strategic processing in multiple text use, I have three goals. I first overview prior work on strategic processing and introduce a central framework that may be used to conceptualize strategy use when students learn from multiple texts. Second, I suggest future directions in strategy research. I do this by asking six questions. In particular, I make the case in the first section of this chapter that much prior work has focused on *what* strategies students may engage when learning from multiple texts. In the second part of this chapter, I further suggest that the *where, when, who, why,* and *how* of strategy use ought to be considered as well. In the final section of this chapter, I extend the strategy framework introduced in the first to consider how strategies may be applied when students learn from multiple, multimedia documents, presenting a plurality of textual and non-textual information (e.g., diagrams, tables, videos) side by side.

WHAT STRATEGIES DO STUDENTS USE WHEN LEARNING FROM MULTIPLE TEXTS?

Research on strategy use has been an integral part of the multiple text use literature since its inception. Indeed, in one of the first studies to examine multiple text use, Wineburg (1991) compared the strategy use of expert historians and Advanced Placement history students presented with multiple historical documents. Wineburg (1991) found historians' multiple text use to be characterized by the use of three heuristics absent among the document use of Advanced Placement history students. In particular, historians engaged in (a) sourcing, (b) contextualization, and (c) corroboration, whereas high school students did not (see also De La Paz & Nokes, this volume). Sourcing included looking at a document's meta information (e.g., author, publisher) to determine document origin and trustworthiness. Contextualization reflected the application of prior knowledge to situate documents within a historical context. Finally, corroboration reflected the comparison of information across texts, one to another. Since Wineburg's (1991) study, these strategies, and sourcing in particular, have received considerable attention in the literature (Braasch, Rouet, Vibert, & Britt, 2012; Britt & Aglinskas, 2002; De La Paz et al., 2014; De La Paz & Nokes, this volume; Nokes, Dole, & Hacker, 2007; Rouet, Favart, Britt, & Perfetti. 1997) and have been targeted for intervention, to varying extents (Brante & Strømsø, 2018; Nokes et al., 2007; Reisman, 2012).

Likewise, as the literature on multiple text use has progressed, investigations of strategy use have expanded to consider strategies associated with (a) elaboration to support text comprehension (e.g., Wolfe & Goldman, 2005), (b) information accumulation and linking across multiple texts (e.g., Bråten & Strømsø, 2011), (c) notetaking (e.g., Kobayashi, 2009a, 2009b), (d) cross-textual navigation (List & Alexander, 2017b), (e) metacognitive monitoring (Stadtler & Bromme, 2007, 2008), and more (see Afflerbach, Hurt, & Cho, this volume). To systematize this strategic breadth, two frameworks have been introduced (Cho, Afflerbach, & Han, 2018; List & Alexander, 2018b). In the first section of this chapter, I integrate these two frameworks to classify strategies according to two dimensions: their functions (Cho et al., 2018) and referents (List & Alexander, 2018b) when learning from multiple texts. In this case, *functions* reflect the particular aims of strategy deployment, while *referents* capture their targets or foci.

Strategy Functions When Learning from Multiple Texts

A key framework describing strategic processing during multiple text use defines strategies as conscious and controllable efforts to achieve some cognitive purpose and multiple text use as a constructive, meaning-making process (Afflerbach & Cho, 2008; Cho et al., 2018, p. 135). This reflects definitions of strategy use found in earlier work on single text comprehension. This work defines strategy use as intentional and purposeful on the part of the learner (Paris, Lipson, & Wixson, 1983) and strategic processing for comprehension as active and constructive in nature (Baker & Brown, 1984). When engaging in meaning-making based on multiple texts, then, Cho et al. (2018) suggested that students engage in processes falling into one of three general, strategy clusters reflecting: (a) constructive-integrative processing, (b) critical-analytic processing, and (c) metacognitive-reflective processing. *Constructive-integrative* processing, which includes the search for and identification of information in texts, reflects learners' efforts to construct a singular, coherent, cognitive representation of multiple texts, including both content and document information from across texts (Britt, Perfetti, Sandak, & Rouet, 1999; Cho et al., 2018, p. 140; Perfetti, Rouet, & Britt, 1999). *Critical-analytic* processing reflects students' efforts to determine the value, quality, or veracity of texts or text-based information, with such determinations rendered based on sourcing (i.e., consideration of document information) and source evaluation.

Finally, *metacognitive-reflective* processing is focused on the deployment and control of strategies falling into the previous two strategy clusters and includes the reciprocal processes of comprehension monitoring, self-regulation, and metacognition (Cho et al., 2018, p. 143). Across these strategy clusters, Cho et al. (2018) emphasized the interactive nature of strategy use, with the engagement of some strategies (e.g., metacognitive monitoring) eliciting the engagement of others (e.g., information search).

In describing strategic processing as serving "diverse functions and purposes," Cho et al. (2018, p. 144) adopted a *functional* view of strategic engagement. That is, they classified strategies according to their aims or purpose. The three general, strategic aims that may be served during multiple text use are presented in each row of Table 8.1.

Strategy Referents When Learning from Multiple Texts

The second strategy framework I consider in this chapter comes from the *Integrated Framework of Multiple Texts* (IF-MT; List & Alexander, 2018b). The IF-MT conceptualizes multiple text use as a three-stage process, including preparation, execution, and production. In the execution stage, List and Alexander (2018b) classified the strategies that students engage during multiple text use as behavioral, cognitive, or metacognitive in nature. They defined behavioral strategies, including information search, selection, and navigation, as intentional actions performed during the course of engaging with multiple texts. Cognitive strategies, then, are defined as the mental processes that students use when trying to learn from multiple texts. These are further distinguished as intra-textual or inter-textual in nature. *Intra-textual* processes refer to those strategies that are deployed in reference to only a single text; whereas, inter-textual processes refer to strategies that require the simultaneous consideration of more than one text at a time. Finally, metacognitive strategies are regulatory processes engaged based on students' monitoring of their comprehension, epistemic standards, and task satisfaction. As such, our view of metacognitive strategy use is embedded in Schraw and Moshman's (1995) framework, which suggests that metacognition includes both (a) *metacognitive knowledge* (i.e., knowledge of cognition, such as strategy knowledge) and the (b) *regulation of cognition* (i.e., planning, monitoring, and evaluation). In this chapter, due to my focus specifically on strategy use during task completion, I am particularly concerned with students' metacognitive monitoring (i.e., reflection and evaluation of their cognition during task completion) and any regulation (i.e., deliberate efforts to control cognition or affect during task completion) that may result.

The framework suggested by List and Alexander (2018b) may be said to adopt a *directed* view of strategy use. In other words, they classified the strategies that students engage according to the referents at which they are directed or the content they address (i.e., a single text, multiple texts, or learners' knowledge and beliefs). The possible targets or referents for strategy use are reflected in each column of Table 8.1.

Comprehensive Strategy Framework

By overlapping the strategy functions and referents described by Cho et al. (2018) and List and Alexander (2018b), I introduce the *Comprehensive Strategy Framework* (CSF), presented in Table 8.1. Each row of the CSF (Table 8.1) identifies one of three

Table 8.1 Sample Strategies Corresponding to the Functions and Referents Identified in the Comprehensive Strategy Framework

Strategy Functions *See Cho et al. (2018)*	Strategy Referents *See List and Alexander (2018b)*		Inter-modal *Co-referents are a text and another source including non-textual content (e.g., diagram, table, video)*
	Intra-textual *Referent is information in a single text*	**Inter-textual** *Co-referents are more than one text*	**Personal** *Co-referents are a text and learners' prior knowledge or beliefs*
Constructive-integrative processing *Strategies focused on meaning-making within and across texts*	Summarizing content in one text (Anmarkrud et al., 2013) Paraphrasing or restating the content of one text to aid understanding (Wolfe & Golfman, 2004)	Elaborating information in one text by connecting ideas across texts (Anmarkrud et al., 2013)	Elaborating information in one text by connecting it with prior knowledge (Anmarkrud et al., 2013) Introduction of personal associations to text content, in a way that does not support comprehension (Wolfe & Goldman, 2004)
Critical-analytic processing *Strategies focused on determining source and information quality, credibility, and veracity*	Sourcing (Wineburg, 1991) or using document information from one text to predict or interpret text content (Anmarkrud et al., 2013) Positive or negative judgments of some aspect(s) of a text (Wolfe & Goldman, 2004)	Corroboration (Wineburg, 1991) or the comparison of trustworthiness across texts Comparing author benevolence and authority across texts to decide whom to believe (Stadtler & Bromme, 2014)	Contextualization (Wineburg, 1991) or the application of prior knowledge to interpret text content or to aid in text evaluation
Metacognitive-reflective processing *Strategies focused on monitoring and regulating comprehension*	Monitoring the comprehension of a single text (Anmarkrud et al., 2013; Stadtler & Bromme, 2007) Determinations of comprehension success/failure, in reference to a single text (Wolfe & Goldman, 2004)	Trying to solve a comprehension problem in one text by searching for information in other texts (Anmarkrud et al., 2013)	Using information in prior knowledge to address a problem with text comprehension Awareness and monitoring of the biasing role of prior beliefs on reading (Maier & Richter, 2014)

general strategy functions, as specified by Cho et al. (2018). These functions include (a) constructive-integrative processing, (b) critical-analytic processing, and (c) metacognitive-reflective processing. Each column of the CSF corresponds to a strategy referent, as identified by List and Alexander (2018b). Referents include a single text, multiple texts, or learners themselves, including their prior knowledge and beliefs. Jointly, the rows and columns of the CSF introduce the idea that any strategy that students engage during multiple text use may be decomposed according to its function and referent, and that any strategic function that students carry out (e.g., identifying important information) may be executed in reference to a single text, to multiple text, or to students' own knowledge and beliefs. In the sections that follow, I present examples of various strategic functions carried out across the variety of referents possible during students' learning from multiple texts.

Constructive-Integrative Processing. As conceptualized by Cho et al. (2018), constructive-integrative processing involves students' attempts to make meaning from multiple texts and includes strategies such as searching for and locating information, identifying and learning important ideas, and building new knowledge. Adopting List and Alexander's (2018b) directional view of strategy use, the primary distinction in constructive-integrative processing may be whether students are trying to make sense of information presented only within a single text, occurring across multiple texts, or arising from students' prior knowledge.

This difference in foci as the referents for processing is highlighted in Wolfe and Goldman (2005) think-aloud study of adolescents reading conflicting texts about the fall of the Roman Empire. Specifically, Wolfe and Goldman coded students' think-aloud utterances both for the type of processing evidenced (i.e., referred to as a think-aloud event) and for the information source(s) targeted, with four information sources examined (i.e., information from the same text; information from a previous text; prior knowledge; and information from a previous think-aloud comment). In total, 58% of students' utterances reflected elaborations, or attempts to make meaning from information in texts. These included strategies aimed at developing: (a) causal (25.24%) or comparative (8.61%) (i.e., connections that enriched the meaning of texts) self-explanations, (b) surface associations (45%) (i.e., prior knowledge-based connections that did not contribute to textual understanding); (c) predictions (2%) (i.e., expectations), and (d) surface-text connections (12%) (i.e., superficial connections based on semantic overlap). These various elaborative functions were able to be carried out in reference to a single text, to multiple texts, or to students' prior knowledge. Specifically, 49% of elaborations referred to students' prior knowledge, 16% of elaborations focused on a single text, while 18% of elaborations were focused on a previously read text. As such, only a minority of the elaborative utterances that students produced referred to multiple texts. Moreover, few identified causal, comparative relations of any kind, making the intersection of these, or the number of utterances identifying relations across multiple texts, all the more limited.

Wolfe and Goldman (2005) further found that the nature of the connections that students formed differed by referent. In particular, when elaborations referred to a single text, 75% of the connections formed were causal in nature, while 15% were comparative. As a contrast, when elaborations were developed across texts, 46% were causal, while 40% were comparative. In part, this reflects an increase in comparative relations formed when students reason about multiple texts. This differential pattern in think-aloud utterances points to the need to examine not only the function of students' strategic engagement (i.e., formation of causal or comparative connections) but also its referent (e.g., a single text or multiple texts).

Anmarkrud, Bråten, and Strømsø (2014) adopted a similar approach to coding undergraduate students' think-aloud utterances reported during multiple text use. Specifically, in addition to coding for the strategy clusters specified by Afflerbach and Cho (2008), they coded for linking strategies, capturing students' consideration of more than one text at a time, rather than a single text. All told, Anmarkrud et al. (2014) found 31.29% of students' strategic processing involved cross-textual linking. When considering more than one text at a time, they found 47.1% of strategies to be aimed at learning important information, 16.7% of strategies to be aimed at monitoring, and 36.3% of strategies to be focused on evaluation (i.e., critical analytic processing). In this case, the majority of strategies executed across multiple texts focused on connecting ideas across texts to improve comprehension. In examining the nature of cross-textual linking, they further found the majority of such linking to be backward, rather than forward, directed, drawing connections to previously read texts. Moreover, they found linking to identify conflicts between texts, rather than points of concurrence or corroboration. Both different types of strategies (i.e., identifying and learning important information strategies vis-à-vis evaluation strategies) and linking strategies, in particular, were found to have distinct associations with multiple text task performance. In keeping with the differential strategy use, both in function and in referent, documented by Wolfe and Goldman (2005) and Anmarkrud et al., 2014), Table 8.1 includes descriptions of the constructive-integrative strategies that may be engaged in reference to a single text, to multiple texts, or to learners' prior knowledge and beliefs.

Integrative Processing Across Multiple Texts. As strategies that may be used to construct meaning from a single text have been much more extensively examined in prior work (Afflerbach & Cho, 2008; McNamara, 2004; McNamara & Magliano, 2009), here I provide a more detailed discussion of how students may make meaning across multiple texts or engage in cross-textual integration. Cho et al. (2018) and List and Alexander (2018b) recognized that multiple text integration involves the connecting and cognitive representation of texts that are both consistent with and in conflict with one another. For texts that are consistent, providing corroborative (e.g., redundant) or complementary information, the cross-textual strategies engaged may be described as synthesis. These are strategies focused on additively connecting texts and organizing such connections. To make sense of texts that are conflicting, reconciliation-focused strategies are required. Reconciliation is the umbrella term applied to the processes involved in the representation of discordant texts as in conflict with one another, and associated efforts to understand and possibly resolve such conflicts. The joining and organization of the mental representations that arise through synthesis and reconciliation results in integration, or students' holistic conceptualization of multiple texts (Britt et al., 1999; Goldman, Lawless, & Manning, 2013; Perfetti et al., 1999).

List and colleagues (List, 2019; List & Alexander, 2018b) specified four steps involved in both students' synthesis and reconciliation of multiple texts. Specifically, students connect multiple complementary and conflicting texts through: (a) identification,

(b) separate representation, (c) simultaneous relation, and (d) relational elaboration. *Identification* involves students' initial search for possible corroborative or related information across texts or attendance to potential conflict. *Separate representation* involves students' separate mapping or elaboration of related information within each text. *Simultaneous relation* involves students conceptually linking information from separate texts via a single statement, typically using a relational modifier (i.e., a linking term such as and, but, or therefore). Finally, *relational elaboration* involves students classifying the type of cross-textual connections formed, and elaborating these to various extents. This may include students generally specifying that texts agree or conflict with one another or determining a more specific point of comparison across texts (e.g., texts disagree with one another in their estimate of projected causalities as a result of overpopulation).

When texts are classified as being in conflict with one another, Stadtler and Bromme (2014) outlined at least three strategies that students may use to not only represent conflicting information but also to resolve conflicts as well. These included (a) ignoring the conflict, by dismissing one of the texts that conflicts, (b) inferring an (often incorrect) resolution to the conflict based on prior knowledge or other information in texts, or (c) deliberately choosing a side of a conflict to defer to by evaluating and comparing either author (i.e., whom to believe?) or information (i.e., what to believe?) quality. Of course, when students are presented with conflicting information from similarly expert or trustworthy sources, they are left unable to easily determine whom to believe. In such instances, other strategies, including relying on their prior attitudes, making plausibility judgments based on world knowledge, or searching for additional information, may be required (Hepfer, List, & Du, 2019; Lombardi, Seyranian, & Sinatra, 2014). Nevertheless, the comparison and evaluation of discrepant sources remains a key mechanism that students can use to resolve conflicts when these are identified across texts (Braasch et al., 2012). The processes used to evaluate texts' sources (e.g., author) and content were termed critical analytic strategies by Cho et al. (2018).

Critical-Analytic Strategies. Cho et al. (2018) described critical analytic strategies as focused on the evaluation of information and its source(s). The leading evaluation strategy examined within the context of multiple text use has been *sourcing*. As Stadtler and Bromme (2014) explained, sourcing is key because when trying to understand a complex and unfamiliar topic by reading multiple texts, students often do not have the requisite knowledge, resources, and skills necessary to directly evaluate the knowledge claims introduced (i.e., to decide what is true). Rather, students are left to make second-order sourcing judgments or assumptions about information quality based on source characteristics, including author benevolence (i.e., intention to provide accurate and quality information) and expertise (i.e., authoritativeness). Making such judgments is, nevertheless, a complex process. Brante and Strømsø (2018), in a review of sourcing interventions, found sourcing to include students' (a) attendance to and identification of document information, including author, publisher, date of publication, (b) recall of document information (i.e., its storage in memory or in an external representation, like students' notes), (c) use of document information to predict and interpret content in texts, and (d) evaluation of source credibility.

Beyond sourcing, the other strategies identified by Wineburg (1991) may also serve evaluative functions, albeit less frequently considered in prior work. Rouet et al. (1997)

examined the sourcing, corroboration, and contextualization of graduate students classified as either experts or novices in the domain of history. Sourcing included specific references to study documents reflected in students' essays, but was not found to differ across expert and novice graduate students in the domain of history. Corroboration, or comparing information across texts, was classified in one of four ways. Specifically, students developed (a) *argument models* (i.e., recognizing different texts as forwarding conflicting interpretations), (b) *positive connections* (i.e., grouping similar texts), (c) *negative connections* (i.e., identifying conflicting texts), and (d) *general references* (i.e., identifying a group of consistent sources) across texts. Corroboration was limited, with less than one corroborative instance occurring in students' essays, but uniformly so across expert and novice graduate students. Finally, students' engagement in contextualization was classified according to the type of knowledge implicated. Specifically, students made (a) *problem context statements*, drawing on topic-specific prior knowledge; (b) *historical context statements*, using prior knowledge at the domain level; and (c) *general context statements*, reflecting the contribution of general, world knowledge to multiple text evaluation. It was in the engagement in contextualization that expert-novice differences emerged, with expert students including more contextual information overall and more historical contextual statements in their essays, in particular. Elsewhere, the use of sourcing, corroboration, and contextualization by high school history students has been found to be quite limited, with the engagement of the latter two strategies found to be especially rare (Nokes et al., 2007; Stahl, Hynd, Britton, McNish, & Bosquet, 1996).

Nevertheless, all three of these critical-analytic strategies are presented in the second row of Table 8.1. As demonstrated in Table 8.1, critical-analytic strategies may be intra-textually, inter-textually, or personally directed. For instance, students engaging in sourcing may consider the document information in one text (i.e., an intra-textually directed strategy) or can compare author credentials across texts (i.e., an inter-textually directed strategy). Likewise, students may apply prior knowledge to contextualize a particular text (i.e., a personally directed strategy) or may use information in one text to contextualize or situate another (i.e., an inter-textually directed strategy). An exception to this may be the corroborative strategy for text evaluation, which necessarily requires the simultaneous consideration of more than one text and is therefore a strategy that is inter-textual in nature. At the same time, even this strategy may be engaged to compare information in a text with students' prior knowledge, thereby evaluating its content. The intra-textual, inter-textual, and personal-directedness of various critical-analytic strategies is reflected in Table 8.1.

Metacognitive-Reflective Strategies. The final strategy cluster defined by Cho et al. (2018) is termed metacognitive-reflective and includes students' regulation of their own sense-making of multiple texts and monitoring, or self-assessments of comprehension. Although Cho et al. (2018) identified metacognitive-reflective strategy use as necessary for the deployment of the constructive-integrative and critical-analytic strategies necessary for learning from multiple texts, this strategy cluster has, nevertheless, received the least attention in the literature on learning from multiple texts. Wolfe and Goldman (2005) found evidence of metacognitive monitoring among students' think-aloud utterances. These were coded as either reports of comprehension success or comprehension problems; however, each of these accounted for only 3% of all reported think-aloud utterances. Likewise, Anmarkrud, Bråten, and Strømsø (2014) found strategies belonging to the metacognitive-reflective cluster to be the least commonly reported (16.56%), as compared to constructive-integrative (34.36%) and critical-analytic strategies (49.08%). As demonstrated in Table 8.1, these strategies can nevertheless be executed in reference to a single text (e.g., *detecting a comprehension problem with a particular text*), to multiple texts (e.g., *trying to solve a detected comprehension problem ... by searching for clarifying information in other available texts*, Anmarkrud et al., 2014, p. 70), or to students' prior knowledge (e.g., if students are conscious of knowledge revision or belief change; Richter & Maier, 2017).

Other work has sought to explicitly elicit metacognition and comprehension monitoring, in particular, during the course of students' learning from multiple texts. For instance, Stadtler and Bromme (2007, 2008) developed *met.a.ware* as a platform to prompt students' metacognitive monitoring and source evaluation. To spur monitoring, students were asked to rate: *how well do you comprehend the information*, *how much do you know about the topic right now*, and *how much information do you still need on the topic*, after accessing each text. At post-test, students assigned to the monitoring condition were found to have higher factual knowledge as compared to a control group.

Maier and Richter (2014) examined an expanded set of three metacognitive monitoring strategies that students could use when learning from multiple texts. The first involved students monitoring the *biasing influence* of their prior beliefs on their processing of multiple texts. The second involved students identifying inconsistencies across texts, violating standards for internal coherence among information sources (i.e., *internal consistency standard*). Finally, the third standard involved students evaluating information in texts relative to their prior knowledge (i.e., *external consistency standard*). Although not specifically examining the differential effects of these various metacognitive monitoring strategies, instruction on these various strategies and the provision of feedback were found to result in improved situation model construction, corresponding to a more accurate cognitive representation of information presented across texts, and improved text recall. Noteworthy for the development of the CSF is that Maier and Richter (2014) specify monitoring strategies that use both multiple texts and learners' prior knowledge and beliefs as strategy referents. Indeed, as was the case with evaluative strategy use, metacognitive monitoring and regulatory strategies may be deployed in reference to a single text, to multiple texts, or to learners' prior knowledge and beliefs.

Overview

Thus far, we have explicated the strategy clusters identified by Cho et al. (2018) by demonstrating how these may be applied in the service of students' understanding, evaluating, and monitoring their comprehension of single texts or multiple texts or the development of their knowledge. Among the strategies classified in the CSF are processes identified through (a) think-aloud reports (Anmarkrud et al., 2014; Wolfe & Goldman, 2005); (b) students' endorsement of strategy inventories (e.g., *Multiple Text Strategy Inventory* [MTSI], Bråten and Strømsø, 2011); (c) the comparison of the strategic performance of better and poorer learners (Goldman, Braasch, Wiley, Graesser, & Brodowinska, 2012; Wiley et al., 2009); and (d) the elicitation of certain strategies during processing (Maier & Richter, 2014; Stadtler & Bromme, 2007). Nevertheless, underlying these diverse methods for capturing strategy use is a central focus on *what strategies* students engage during multiple text use. That is to say, across these various approaches to capturing and studying strategy use, there has been the underlying assumption that the use of certain strategies over others results in particular benefits for multiple text comprehension and integration. Although this has often been found to be the case (e.g., Bråten, Anmarkrud, Brandmo, & Strømsø, 2014), such findings are hardly universal. For instance, while Bråten and Strømsø (2011) found the information accumulation dimension of the MTSI to be negatively associated with multiple text task performance, List, Du, Wang, and Lee (2019) found students' reports of strategies aimed at both information accumulation and cross-textual elaboration to be positively associated with multiple text integration. Hagen, Braasch, and Bråten (2014) found students' connection formation in their written notes to be associated with multiple text comprehension when asked to write an argument, but not a summary; while Kobayashi (2009a) found students' note-taking, or external strategy use, to have no effect on performance, regardless of task assignment. Wiley et al. (2009) found some justifications for source reliability to differ across students deemed more or less successful at multiple text task completion (e.g., attending to explanation quality), while others did not (e.g., considering cross-textual corroboration). At the same time, Stadtler and Bromme (2007) did not find students assigned to a prompted source evaluation intervention condition to differ in their comprehension of multiple texts, relative to a control group, although some benefits for source recall were identified.

Of course, these mixed findings can be explained in a number of ways, stemming from the variety of methods used to capture students' multiple text use across studies, including differences in the task assignment, texts provided, and outcome measures used. Nevertheless, in this chapter, I argue that these mixed results stem, in part, from limitations in the ways that strategy use has been examined. In particular, I suggest that prior work has focused almost exclusively on *what* strategies students employ during multiple text use, failing to fully capture the dynamic and contextualized nature of strategy use during learning from multiple texts. In the second section of this chapter, I call on researchers leading the next phase of strategy research to move beyond questions addressing *what* strategies students use to conceptualize strategy use in a multidimensional fashion, one that more explicitly considers the where, when, whom, why, and how of strategy use, in addition to the what. I do this by reviewing work already addressing each of these focal questions, in turn.

WHERE ARE STRATEGIES DIRECTED DURING MULTIPLE TEXT USE?

In addition to considering what strategies students deploy during multiple text use, there is a need to consider where, or toward what referent, such strategies are directed. The need to consider the where or referent of students' strategy use is, in part, suggested by the CSF, which explicitly asks that strategy functions be understood as intra-textual, inter-textual, or personally directed in nature. Nevertheless, these represent only general referents, with many more specific referents needing to be considered to understand what features students attend to when strategically using multiple texts.

Two primary referents have been considered in prior work. The first has been students' attendance to document information or source features during text use. For instance, Gerjets, Kammerer, and Werner (2011) used eye-tracking and think-aloud data to examine learners' attendance to specific areas of search results produced on a search engine results page. They found that instructing students to engage in source evaluation increased attendance to document information (e.g., publisher) and user ratings in search results, as compared to a control condition. Examining students' attendance to sources in texts, Braasch et al. (2012) focused on students' gaze patterns and think-aloud utterances in reference either to source information (e.g., an art critic) or to text content. They found that the presentation of conflicting information across texts stimulated attendance to source information but not to content, as compared to the introduction of consistent information.

Examining texts more holistically, Kammerer and Gerjets (2012) considered differences in students' selection of objective (i.e., fact based), subjective (i.e., opinion based), or commercial (i.e., promotional) websites during Internet searches. Likewise, Wiley et al. (2009) found that students learning disproportionately much or little from a multiple text task were distinguishable according to their time allocation, navigation, rereading, and rankings of reliable vis-à-vis unreliable websites.

In addition to directing strategies at source information, some studies have distinguished students' strategy use when directed toward relevant vis-à-vis irrelevant information, with relevance defined as pertinence to task assignment (Cerdán & Vidal-Abarca, 2008; Rouet, Ros, Goumi, Macedo-Rouet, & Dinet, 2011). For instance, Anmarkrud et al. (2013) found students to be able to both distinguish more relevant from less relevant information presented across texts and to more frequently use cross-textual linking strategies when processing relevant vis-à-vis irrelevant information. Collectively these findings point to the need to consider *where*, or at what specific texts or text components, students direct their strategic efforts during multiple text use (e.g., rereading reliable versus unreliable websites; Wiley et al., 2009).

Nevertheless, considerably more work is needed to understand the *where* aspect of strategy use. This includes further examining whether targeting a given strategy referent is specifically associated with task performance, both on its own and in interaction with a particular strategy function engaged (e.g., Braasch et al., 2012; Wiley et al., 2009), and considering an expanded set of strategy referents as potential targets during multiple text use. These referents can include the central arguments forwarded in texts, the evidence provided, and other content-related factors (e.g., List et al., 2019).

Expanding beyond students' learning from documents that are only textual in nature, examining *where* strategies are directed may be particularly important when understanding students' learning from multiple, multimedia documents, or documents including textual information alongside non-textual content, like diagrams, tables, or videos (List & Alexander, 2018a).

Within the context of learning from multimedia documents, students' iterative attendance to textual and non-textual features in textbooks (e.g., diagrams) has been associated with improved learning (Mason, Pluchino, & Tornatora, 2015; Mason,

Pluchino, Tornatora, & Ariasi, 2013; Schwonke, Berthold, & Renkl, 2009). For instance, Cromley, Snyder-Hogan, and Luciw-Dubas (2010) found that while many students skip over diagrams in science textbooks entirely (22%) or attend to a relatively limited set of diagram features (34% of the features possible), those students who do study diagrams, alongside textual content, demonstrate a greater number of inferences and high-level strategies engaged during processing as well as improved task performance. More recent studies examining students' learning from various textual and non-textual sources have found students to engage different strategies in response to different types of documents. For instance, Van Meter and Cameron (2018) found students to take fewer notes on political cartoons than on historical documents, presented during a multiple text task, with the character of notes differing as well (i.e., more affective notes taken in response to political cartoons). All told, these findings point to the need to examine a variety of referents and their elicitation of strategy use during students' learning from multiple, multimedia documents.

WHEN ARE STRATEGIES DEPLOYED DURING MULTIPLE TEXT USE?

While prior work has provisionally considered where students direct strategies during multiple text use, *when* during text use strategies may be deployed has received considerably more limited attention in the literature. Nevertheless, some studies indicate that when during text use students deploy particular strategies matters for their efficacy. For instance, Wineburg (1991), in describing experts' use of the sourcing strategy, specifically notes that experts looked to document information *first*, prior to reading, with sourcing serving as the interpretive lens for the textual information to follow. Emphasizing sourcing prior to reading a text seems in line with research identifying the activation of prior knowledge as a central strategy to support reading comprehension, more generally (Alvermann & Hynd, 1989; Spires & Donley, 1998; Wetzels, Kester, & Van Merrienboer, 2011). In addition to certain strategies needing to be activated prior to multiple text use, other strategies may be more effective when deployed during or after engagement with multiple texts. For instance, across two experiments, Britt and Sommer (2004) examined the effectiveness of intervening tasks on students' integration of multiple texts. They found that composing brief summaries after reading a first text (Experiment 1) improved its integration with a second text, as did answering questions related to text macro-structure (i.e., questions about why events occurred), rather than micro-structure (i.e., questions asking where and when events occurred; Experiment 2).

Within the context of learning from multiple, multimedia documents, Lee and List (2019) compared students' strategic processing when learning information that was presented either as two texts or as two videos. An interesting finding to emerge from this work is that, in addition to some similar and some different strategies engaged during reading vis-à-vis video viewing, video viewing resulted in strategic front-loading in ways that reading did not. That is to say, when viewing videos students engaged disproportionately more strategies during the first quintile of viewing, with strategic engagement during reading found to be more proportionally distributed in nature. While Lee and List attribute these distributional differences in strategy use to the linear nature of videos, rendering non-sequential navigation difficult, these findings point to the need to consider the when of strategy deployment both when students read texts and when they seek to process other media, including videos. A further consideration in determining the when of strategy use may be not only the point of strategy initiation but also its duration.

WHO BENEFITS FROM STRATEGY USE DURING MULTIPLE TEXT USE?

A wide variety of individual difference factors have been examined within the context of learning from multiple texts. These include cognitive factors, like epistemic beliefs and need for cognition (e.g., Bråten, Strømsø, & Samuelstuen, 2008; Ferguson & Bråten, 2013), as well as affective factors, like interest and attitudes (e.g., Bråten & Strømsø, 2006; McCrudden & McTigue, 2018), and, more recently, psychophysiological factors like heart rate variability (Mason, Scrimin, Zaccoletti, Tornatora, & Goetz, 2018; see Brante & Strømsø, 2018 for a review; List & Alexander, 2017a, 2018b for a central framework).

In one research tradition, individual differences on various learner characteristics have been associated with the differential ability to take advantage of the various affordances or features of multiple text environments. For instance, Gil, Bråten, Vidal-Abarca, and Strømsø (2010), while not examining strategy use per se, did find that students with high prior knowledge were able to take advantage of a task assignment asking them to compose an argument, rather than a summary, while students low in prior knowledge were not able to do so. Le Bigot and Rouet (2007) similarly distinguished the performance of students comparatively low and high in prior knowledge, assigned to write either arguments or summaries within hypertext environments that varied according to their format of text presentation (i.e., by topic or by author and topic). Results included that students high in prior knowledge performed better on comprehension questions than their low knowledge counterparts and that argument tasks resulted in students composing more sophisticated written responses than did summary tasks. However, interactions among prior knowledge and hypertext affordances were limited.

A second research approach has examined how individual difference factors may function more directly in interaction with students' strategy use during learning from multiple texts. For instance, Bråten, Strømsø, Brandmo, and Anmarkrud (2014) found prior knowledge, epistemic beliefs, and need for cognition to be associated with students' deeper level strategy use (i.e., engagement in cross-textual elaboration), resulting in improved multiple text comprehension. List, Stephens, and Alexander (2019) found the relation between situational interest and students' multiple text task performance to be mediated by the time that students devoted to text access, considered to be a proxy for persistence and the more effortful processing of multiple texts. Beyond these investigations, few studies have examined how strategies might interact with individual difference factors to result in variations in performance. In particular, there has been limited consideration of the extent to which different strategies may be beneficial for learners differing in prior knowledge, multiple text use skills, or motivation.

Within the context of multimedia learning, a wider range of individual difference factors may need to be considered (Moreno, 2002). These include verbal and visuospatial working memory (Gyselinck, Jamet, & Dubois, 2008; Schüler, Scheiter, & van Genuchten, 2011 for a review), visuospatial reasoning (Hegarty & Waller, 2005; Höffler, 2010; Wu & Shah, 2004), and multimedia/graphic comprehension knowledge and skills (Canham & Hegarty, 2010; Cromley et al., 2013; delMas, Garfield, & Ooms, 2005). Indeed, these individual difference factors in conjunction with affordances in multimedia learning environments have been found to result in differences in performance. For instance, Brucker, Scheiter, and Gerjets (2014) examined how students with high versus low visuospatial reasoning learned from graphics that varied in realism (i.e., realistic versus schematic) and dynamism (i.e., dynamic versus static). Learners with high visuospatial abilities were found to perform better when presented with realistic visualizations, while learners low in visuospatial ability were found to benefit from more schematic graphics. Cook, Wiebe, and Carter (2008) compared the diagrammatic reasoning of students low and high in prior knowledge, learning about diffusion and osmosis. While low knowledge students tended to focus on the surface features of diagrams (e.g., noticing differences in color and shape), high knowledge students were better able to interpret these features, forming inferences based on prior knowledge. Moreover, when asked how diagrams can be improved, students low in prior knowledge expressed a desire for more labeling and verbal explanation, while students high in prior knowledge were satisfied with the more parsimonious diagrams provided. These findings suggested that differences in prior knowledge result not only in attentional differences during processing but in strategic differences as well, with prior knowledge supporting greater inferencing during diagrammatic learning. These results further echo findings from expert-novice studies which have found novice learners to treat diagrams more discretely, grouping them based on surface features, while experts reason more holistically and, crucially, are able to reason across multiple diagrams to develop understanding (Chi, Feltovich, & Glaser, 1981; Kozma, 2003). The next step within this body of work, then, is to further consider how learners' individual differences alongside design features in various multimedia environments might jointly result in differences in strategic processing and ultimately, in improvements in task performance.

WHY DO STUDENTS DEPLOY STRATEGIES DURING MULTIPLE TEXT USE?

The identification of metacognitive-regulatory strategies in Cho et al.'s (2018) strategy framework is, in part, an effort to consider *why* particular strategies may be engaged by learners. In particular, Cho et al. (2018) conceptualized strategy use as the result of learners' metacognitive monitoring and regulation. In the broader literature on multiple text use, two general categories of mechanisms to elicit strategy use have been identified. These are initiating mechanisms that are *internal* (e.g., resulting from metacognitive monitoring) or *external* to the learner, prompted by extrinsic features in the task environment. Indeed, these strategic triggering mechanisms may be said to operate throughout multiple text use, including prior to, during, and following task completion.

Prior to a multiple text task being initiated, students' intentions for strategy use may be elicited by the task assignment (i.e., an external factor, Hagen et al., 2014;

Marton & Säljö, 1976; McCrudden & Schraw, 2007) as well as by students' interpretations of task demands and their cognitive representation via a task model (List, Du, Wang, & Lee, 2019; Rouet & Britt, 2011). Indeed, among the most robust findings in the field of multiple text use is the role that task assignment plays in students' learning from texts (McCrudden & Schraw, 2007; Wiley & Voss, 1999). Nevertheless, most commonly the strategy-driven link between task assignment and actual performance has only been implied rather than directly investigated. This is largely the case for studies determining the facilitative role of argument tasks for multiple text integration, as compared to other multiple text tasks (Bråten & Strømsø, 2011), with Wiley and Voss (1999) attributing this to a difference between argument tasks prompting students to engage in *knowledge-transforming* vis-a-vis *knowledge-telling.*

Informing this literature is a study by Cerdán and Vidal-Abarca (2008) that directly examined students' processing when responding to two different types of tasks, requiring either intra-textual or inter-textual integration. Among differences in processing identified, Cerdán and Vidal-Abarca found that writing an essay to demonstrate global understanding (i.e., an inter-textual task) resulted in students reading relevant information more slowly than irrelevant information. This reflected more strategic processing and stood in contrast to students in the intra-textual task condition, who read both relevant and irrelevant information at the same rate. Moreover, students in the inter-textual task condition engaged in more integrative processing (i.e., defined as the consecutive reading of separate relevant paragraphs in text, one after the other) than students belonging to the intra-textual task condition, and produced more think-aloud utterances when processing relevant segments of text. These processing variables, particularly those related to integration, were later found to be associated with performance on a transfer task, corresponding to deep-level learning, even though no differences in superficial learning emerged, as assessed via performance on a statement verification task. Within the context of learning from multimedia documents, Schwonke et al. (2009) found many students to be ignorant regarding the functions and purpose of multiple representations. They, therefore, found that simply instructing students as to the functions of representations in multimedia environments served to improve learning, particularly for students with low prior knowledge.

Beyond task instructions, during the course of multiple text use, strategy use may be initiated both by students' metacognitive monitoring (Cho et al., 2018) and by features of the task environment, including the texts themselves and their presentation. Introducing a framework of conflict-driven validation, Richter and Maier (2017) argued that students constantly monitor text consistency both with their prior beliefs and in relation to other texts, throughout the course of processing, with the detection of conflict considered to potentially spur elaborative strategy use. Such monitoring may be considered to be an internal, learner factor triggering strategy use and can be contrasted with more external mechanisms examined in prior work. These include the arrangement of search results either as a list or as an ontologically organized, graphical overview resulting in differences in text selection (Kammerer & Gerjets, 2012; Salmerón, Gil, Bråten, & Strømsø, 2010) and the presentation of conflicting, rather than consistent, information across texts spurring attendance to document information (Braasch et al., 2012; Kammerer, Kalbfell, & Gerjets, 2016; Stang Lund, Bråten, Brante, & Strømsø, 2017). More intensively prompting students' strategic processing has been work that explicitly designed multiple text interfaces to cue sourcing, source evaluation, or metacognition (Britt & Aglinskas, 2002; Stadtler & Bromme, 2007, 2008).

Within the context of learning from multimedia representations, Renkl and Scheiter (2017) reviewed the material-oriented (e.g., dynamic versus static representations; realistic versus schematic pictures) and learner-oriented (e.g., inference training) factors that may be used to trigger strategic processing and to improve students' learning from visual displays. One external trigger used by Seufert (2003) to stimulate text and visual integration was to provide students with directive help by explicitly identifying relevant points of connection across representations. Seufert (2003) found such directive help to be particularly useful for students with moderate prior knowledge, while have a slight deleterious effect for low knowledge learners. Such mixed results point to the need to further determine not only whether external triggers do, indeed, elicit certain types of processing but also to ascertain whether externally eliciting certain strategies results in the same benefits for learning as does such strategic processing when it is internally triggered. This latter point is demonstrated by Gerjets, Kammerer, and Werner's (2011) examination of spontaneous versus cued source evaluation during web search. Specifically, while Gerjets et al. (2011) did find that explicitly instructing students to evaluate texts increased the number of evaluation-related think-aloud utterances students reported, the instructed evaluation condition did not result in students' improved justifications for choice of diet (i.e., the topic of the task).

Following task completion, feedback (i.e., an external factor, Llorens, Cerdán, & Vidal-Abarca, 2014; Maier & Richter, 2014; Moreno, 2004) as well as students' self-assessments of task performance (i.e., an internal factor, List & Alexander, 2015; Rouet & Britt, 2011, Wang & List, 2019) can be mechanisms that prompt learners' revisiting of multiple texts and strategy re-engagement. Although these post-task aspects of strategy use have received perhaps the least attention in the literature, these do constitute strategy triggers likely to occur in real-world task contexts. More generally, given the research reviewed up to this point in the chapter, the pertinent question with regard to strategy triggers ought not be what these are, but rather which triggers may be beneficial for whom (i.e., which learners) and when during task completion. In other words, within the context of learning from multiple texts and multiple, multimedia representations it remains essential to ask under what conditions strategies ought to be externally triggered vis-à-vis under what conditions internal, metacognitive triggering is sufficient.

HOW CAN WE DETERMINE THE EFFECTIVENESS OF STRATEGY USE DURING MULTIPLE TEXT TASK COMPLETION?

The final question we are left to grapple with when considering students' strategic engagement with multiple texts is how we can determine whether strategy use is effective. To date, strategy effectiveness has been determined according to whether strategy use increases particular multiple text outcomes or not. Although this constitutes an intuitive approach to evaluating strategy effectiveness, the reality of strategy use is that strategies, even when appropriately engaged, are oftentimes not successful, requiring students to adjust their strategic approaches throughout the course of task completion (Winne & Hadwin, 2008). Currently there have been few, if any, studies to specifically examine this type of dynamic strategy use, wherein students deploy, adapt, and discontinue using strategies, recursively, to accomplish task goals. At the same time, emergent work in the field of self-regulation suggests that microanalytic techniques that specifically ask students why they engage certain strategies may be a promising avenue for gaining more insight into the metacognitive and regulatory decisions underlying students' processing (Callan & Cleary, 2018; Cleary, Callan, Schunk, & Greene, 2018).

Another route to considering the effectiveness of strategy use is to consider the effectiveness with which strategies are engaged. That is to say, just because students deploy a particular strategy does not mean that they do so successfully. As demonstrated by Wolfe and Goldman, (2005), for example, engaging prior knowledge, while effective for some students (Anmarkrud et al., 2014), can lead to irrelevant associations made by students, detracting from learning. Likewise, Kühl, Scheiter, Gerjets, and Gemballa (2011) found students to report more positive monitoring (i.e., reporting successful comprehension) when studying dynamic, rather than static, visuals. At the same time, Kühl et al. (2011) attribute such positive monitoring to an illusion of understanding, rather than to comprehension benefits per se. Beyond these examinations, limited attention has been paid to the effectiveness with which students may deploy particular strategies during task completion. However, such an approach to determining strategy effectiveness can be said to align with efforts to examine students' strategy use in reference to expert processing (e.g., historians, Rouet et al., 1997; Wineburg, 1991; chemists, Kozma, 2003).

A final path to determining strategy effectiveness is tied to theoretical understandings of learning from multiple texts (Rouet & Britt, 2011). Theories of learning from multiple texts specify that much of task completion is guided by students' personal representations of how a task ought to be carried out (i.e., students' task models, Rouet & Britt, 2011). A means of determining strategy effectiveness, then, would be to evaluate strategies relative to the goal(s) and sub-goals that students set for task completion. Nevertheless, the quality, rather than quantity, of students' strategy use remains a fundamentally unexplored area of students' learning from multiple texts.

Thus far, in this section, I have posed a series of questions that may be essential to understanding learners' strategy use when learning from multiple texts. These questions can add additional nuance and interpretive power to understanding students' strategic processing. In the final section of this chapter I briefly discuss how the CSF and the five strategy-directed questions that follow can be used to understand students' processing when learning not only from multiple texts but from multiple, multimedia documents as well, or documents containing textual information alongside non-textual content (e.g., diagrams, tables, videos).

CONCLUSION

In this chapter I ask six questions that I consider to be foundational to understanding students' strategy use in a multidimensional fashion and as it manifests in real or authentic contexts for learning. In such real contexts, strategy use is (a) oriented toward the materials available, or in response to the *where* question, purposefully focused on a variety of stimuli; (b) in response to the *when* question, engaged throughout the course of task completion, (c) to answer the *who* question, variably beneficial to different learners, (d) in response to the *why* question, metacognitively motivated, and (e) to answer the *how* question, recursive and differentially effective. Recognizing this reality necessarily suggests that investigations focused only on the *what* of strategy use, or just which strategies are deployed, to the exclusion of where these strategies are directed, when they are used during processing, who uses these strategies and why, and how effective these are, is insufficient. As such, investigating answers to these various questions is both essential to understanding strategy use and the imperative of future work in this field.

ACKNOWLEDGMENTS

I would like to sincerely thank Jonna Kulikowich for her invaluable feedback on the ideas in this chapter on drives from Pennsylvania to Maryland.

REFERENCES

Afflerbach, P., Hurt, M., & Cho, B.-Y. (this volume). Reading comprehension strategy instruction. In D. L. Dinsmore, L. K. Fryer, & M. M. Parkinson (Eds.), *Handbook of strategies and strategic processing: Conceptualization, measurement, and analysis*. New York: Routledge.

Afflerbach, P. A., & Cho, B. Y. (2008). Identifying and describing constructively responsive comprehension strategies in new and traditional forms of reading. In S. Israel & G. Duffy (Eds.), *Handbook of reading comprehension research* (pp. 69–90). Mahwah, NJ: Erlbaum.

Alvermann, D. E., & Hynd, C. R. (1989). Effects of prior knowledge activation modes and text structure on nonscience majors' comprehension of physics. *The Journal of Educational Research, 83*(2), 97–102.

Anmarkrud, Ø., Bråten, I., & Strømsø, H. I. (2014). Multiple-documents literacy: Strategic processing, source awareness, and argumentation when reading multiple conflicting documents. *Learning and Individual Differences, 30*, 64–76.

Anmarkrud, Ø., McCrudden, M. T., Bråten, I., & Strømsø, H. I. (2013). Task-oriented reading of multiple documents: Online comprehension processes and offline products. *Instructional Science, 41*(5), 873–894.

Baker, L., & Brown, A. L. (1984). Metacognitive skills and reading. In D. Pearson, M. Kamil, R. Barr, & P. Mosenthal (Eds.), *Handbook of reading research* (pp. 353–394). New York: Longman.

Braasch, J. L., Rouet, J. F., Vibert, N., & Britt, M. A. (2012). Readers' use of source information in text comprehension. *Memory & Cognition, 40*(3), 450–465.

Brante, E. W., & Strømsø, H. I. (2018). Sourcing in text comprehension: A review of interventions targeting sourcing skills. *Educational Psychology Review, 30*(3), 773–799.

Bråten, I., Anmarkrud, Ø., Brandmo, C., & Strømsø, H. I. (2014). Developing and testing a model of direct and indirect relationships between individual differences, processing, and multiple-text comprehension. *Learning and Instruction, 30*, 9–24.

Bråten, I., & Strømsø, H. I. (2006). Epistemological beliefs, interest, and gender as predictors of Internet-based learning activities. *Computers in Human Behavior, 22*(6), 1027–1042.

Bråten, I., & Strømsø, H. I. (2011). Measuring strategic processing when students read multiple texts. *Metacognition and Learning, 6*(2), 111–130.

Bråten, I., Strømsø, H. I., & Samuelstuen, M. S. (2008). Are sophisticated students always better? The role of topic-specific personal epistemology in the understanding of multiple expository texts. *Contemporary Educational Psychology, 33*(4), 814–840.

Britt, M. A., & Aglinskas, C. (2002). Improving students' ability to identify and use source information. *Cognition and Instruction, 20*(4), 485–522.

Britt, M. A., Perfetti, C. A., Sandak, R., & Rouet, J.-F. (1999). Content Integration and source separation in learning from multiple texts. In S. R. Goldman, A. C. Graesser, & P. van Den Broek (Eds.), *Narrative comprehension, causality, and coherence: Essays in honor of Tom Trabasso* (pp. 209–233). Mahwah, NJ: Lawrence Erlbaum Associates, Inc.

Britt, M. A., & Sommer, J. (2004). Facilitating textual integration with macro-structure focusing tasks. *Reading Psychology, 25*(4), 313–339.

Brucker, B., Scheiter, K., & Gerjets, P. (2014). Learning with dynamic and static visualizations: Realistic details only benefit learners with high visuospatial abilities. *Computers in Human Behavior, 36*, 330–339.

Cairo, A. (2015). Graphics lies, misleading visuals. In Bihanic, D. (Eds.), *New challenges for data design* (pp. 103–116). London: Springer.

Callan, G. L., & Cleary, T. J. (2018). Multidimensional assessment of self-regulated learning with middle school math students. *School Psychology Quarterly, 33*(1), 103–111.

Canham, M., & Hegarty, M. (2010). Effects of knowledge and display design on comprehension of complex graphics. *Learning and Instruction, 20*(2), 155–166.

Cerdán, R., & Vidal-Abarca, E. (2008). The effects of tasks on integrating information from multiple documents. *Journal of Educational Psychology, 100*(1), 209–222.

Chi, M. T., Feltovich, P. J., & Glaser, R. (1981). Categorization and representation of physics problems by experts and novices. *Cognitive Science, 5*(2), 121–152.

Cho, B. Y., Afflerbach, P., & Han, H. (2018). Strategic processing in accessing, Comprehending, and using multiple sources online. In J. L. G. Braasch, I. Bråten, & M. T. McCrudden (Eds.), *Handbook of multiple source use* (pp. 133–150). New York: Routledge.

Cleary, T. J., Callan, G. L., Schunk, D. H., & Greene, J. A. (2018). Assessing self-regulated learning using microanalytic methods. In D.H. Schunk & B. Zimmerman (Eds.), *Handbook of self-regulation of learning and performance* (pp. 338–351). New York: Routledge.

Cook, M., Wiebe, E. N., & Carter, G. (2008). The influence of prior knowledge on viewing and interpreting graphics with macroscopic and molecular representations. *Science Education, 92*(5), 848–867.

Cromley, J. G., Bergey, B. W., Fitzhugh, S., Newcombe, N., Wills, T. W., Shipley, T. F., & Tanaka, J. C. (2013). Effects of three diagram instruction methods on transfer of diagram comprehension skills: The critical role of inference while learning. *Learning and Instruction, 26*, 45–58.

Cromley, J. G., Snyder-Hogan, L. E., & Luciw-Dubas, U. A. (2010). Cognitive activities in complex science text and diagrams. *Contemporary Educational Psychology, 35*(1), 59–74.

De La Paz, S., Felton, M., Monte-Sano, C., Croninger, R., Jackson, C., Deogracias, J. S., & Hoffman, B. P. (2014). Developing historical reading and writing with adolescent readers: Effects on student learning. *Theory & Research in Social Education, 42*(2), 228–274.

De La Paz, S., & Nokes, J. (this volume). Strategic processing in history and historical strategy instruction. In D. L. Dinsmore, L. K. Fryer, & M. M. Parkinson (Eds.), *Handbook of strategies and strategic processing: Conceptualization, measurement, and analysis.* New York: Routledge.

delMas, R., Garfield, J., & Ooms, A. (2005). Using assessment items to study students' difficulty in reading and interpreting graphical representations of distributions. In K. Makar (Ed.), *Reasoning about distribution: A collection of current research studies.* Proceedings of the Fourth International Research Forum on Statistical Reasoning, Thinking and Literacy. Brisbane, Australia: University of Queensland.

Ferguson, L. E., & Bråten, I. (2013). Student profiles of knowledge and epistemic beliefs: Changes and relations to multiple-text comprehension. *Learning and Instruction, 25*, 49–61.

Gerjets, P., Kammerer, Y., & Werner, B. (2011). Measuring spontaneous and instructed evaluation processes during Web search: Integrating concurrent thinking-aloud protocols and eye-tracking data. *Learning and Instruction, 21*(2), 220–231.

Gil, L., Bråten, I., Vidal-Abarca, E., & Strømsø, H. I. (2010). Summary versus argument tasks when working with multiple documents: Which is better for whom?. *Contemporary Educational Psychology, 35*(3), 157–173.

Goldman, S. R., Braasch, J. L., Wiley, J., Graesser, A. C., & Brodowinska, K. (2012). Comprehending and learning from Internet sources: Processing patterns of better and poorer learners. *Reading Research Quarterly, 47*(4), 356–381.

Goldman, S. R., Lawless, K., & Manning, F. (2013). Research and development of multiple source comprehension assessment. In M. A. Britt, S. R. Goldman, & J.-F. Rouet (Eds.), *Reading: From words to multiple texts* (pp. 180–199). New York, NY: Routledge/Taylor & Francis Group.

Goldman, S. R., & Scardamalia, M. (2013). Managing, understanding, applying, and creating knowledge in the information age: Next-generation challenges and opportunities. *Cognition and Instruction, 31*(2), 255–269.

Gyselinck, V., Jamet, E., & Dubois, V. (2008). The role of working memory components in multimedia comprehension. *Applied Cognitive Psychology: The Official Journal of the Society for Applied Research in Memory and Cognition, 22*(3), 353–374.

Hagen, Å. M., Braasch, J. L., & Bråten, I. (2014). Relationships between spontaneous note-taking, self-reported strategies and comprehension when reading multiple texts in different task conditions. *Journal of Research in Reading, 37*(1), 141–157.

Hegarty, M., & Waller, D. A. (2005). Individual differences in spatial abilities. In P. Shah & A. Miyake (Eds.), *The cambridge handbook of visuospatial thinking* (pp. 121–169). New York: Cambridge University Press.

Hepfer, M., List, A., & Du, H. (2019). Developing a measure of conflict recognition, conflict-related reasoning, and resolution (C3R): Establishing the reliability and validity of the C3R. *Manuscript submitted for publication.*

Höffler, T. N. (2010). Spatial ability: Its influence on learning with visualizations—a meta-analytic review. *Educational Psychology Review, 22*(3), 245–269.

Kammerer, Y., & Gerjets, P. (2012). Effects of search interface and Internet-specific epistemic beliefs on source evaluations during Web search for medical information: An eye-tracking study. *Behaviour & Information Technology, 31*(1), 83–97.

Kammerer, Y., Kalbfell, E., & Gerjets, P. (2016). Is this information source commercially biased? How contradictions between web pages stimulate the consideration of source information. *Discourse Processes, 53*(5–6), 430–456.

Kobayashi, K. (2009a). Comprehension of relations among controversial texts: Effects of external strategy use. *Instructional Science, 37*(4), 311–324.

Kobayashi, K. (2009b). The influence of topic knowledge, external strategy use, and college experience on students' comprehension of controversial texts. *Learning and Individual Differences, 19*(1), 130–134.

Kozma, R. (2003). The material features of multiple representations and their cognitive and social affordances for science understanding. *Learning and Instruction, 13*(2), 205–226.

Kühl, T., Scheiter, K., Gerjets, P., & Gemballa, S. (2011). Can differences in learning strategies explain the benefits of learning from static and dynamic visualizations?. *Computers & Education, 56*(1), 176–187.

Le Bigot, L., & Rouet, J. F. (2007). The impact of presentation format, task assignment, and prior knowledge on students' comprehension of multiple online documents. *Journal of Literacy Research, 39*(4), 445–470.

Lee, H. Y., & List, A. (2019). Processing of texts and videos: A strategy-focused analysis. *Journal of Computer Assisted Learning, 35*(2), 268–282.

List, A., & Alexander, P. A. (2015). Examining response confidence in multiple text tasks. *Metacognition and Learning, 10*(3), 407–436.

List, A., & Alexander, P. A. (2017a). Cognitive affective engagement model of multiple source use. *Educational Psychologist, 52*(3), 182–199.

List, A., & Alexander, P. A. (2017b). Text navigation in multiple source use. *Computers in Human Behavior, 75,* 364–375.

List, A., & Alexander, P. A. (2018a). Postscript: In pursuit of integration. *Learning and instruction, 57, 82–85.*

List, A., & Alexander, P. A. (2018b). Cold and warm perspectives on the Cognitive Affective Engagement Model of Multiple Source Use. In J. L. G. Braasch, I. Bråten, & M. T. McCrudden (Eds.), *Handbook of multiple source use* (pp. 46–66). New York: Routledge.

List, A., & Alexander, P. A. (2019). Toward an integrated framework of multiple text use. In *Educational Psychologist, 54*(1), 20–39.

List, A., Du, H., & Lee, H. Y. (2019). How do students integrate multiple texts?: An investigation of top-down processing. *Manuscript submitted for publication.*

List, A., Du, H., Wang, Y., & Lee, H. Y. (2019). Toward a typology of integration: examining the documents model framework. *Contemporary Educational Psychology, 58,* 228–242.

List, A., Stephens, L. A., & Alexander, P. A. (2019). Examining interest throughout multiple text use. *Reading and Writing, 32*(2), 307–333.

Llorens, A. C., Cerdán, R., & Vidal-Abarca, E. (2014). Adaptive formative feedback to improve strategic search decisions in task-oriented reading. *Journal of Computer Assisted Learning, 30*(3), 233–251.

Lombardi, D., Seyranian, V., & Sinatra, G. M. (2014). Source effects and plausibility judgments when reading about climate change. *Discourse Processes, 51*(1–2), 75–92.

Maier, J., & Richter, T. (2014). Fostering multiple text comprehension: How metacognitive strategies and motivation moderate the text-belief consistency effect. *Metacognition and Learning, 9*(1), 51–74.

Marton, F., & Säljö, R. (1976). On qualitative differences in learning: I—Outcome and process. *British Journal of Educational Psychology, 46*(1), 4–11.

Mason, L., Pluchino, P., & Tornatora, M. C. (2015). Eye-movement modeling of integrative reading of an illustrated text: Effects on processing and learning. *Contemporary Educational Psychology, 41,* 172–187.

Mason, L., Pluchino, P., Tornatora, M. C., & Ariasi, N. (2013). An eye-tracking study of learning from science text with concrete and abstract illustrations. *The Journal of Experimental Education, 81*(3), 356–384.

Mason, L., Scrimin, S., Zaccoletti, S., Tornatora, M. C., & Goetz, T. (2018). Webpage reading: Psychophysiological correlates of emotional arousal and regulation predict multiple-text comprehension. *Computers in Human Behavior, 87*, 317–326.

Mayer, R. E. (2009). *Multimedia learning*. New York: Cambridge University Press.

McCrudden, M. T., & McTigue, E. M. (2018). Implementing integration in an explanatory sequential mixed methods study of belief bias about climate change with high school students. *Journal of Mixed Methods Research, 13*(3), 381–400.

McCrudden, M. T., & Schraw, G. (2007). Relevance and goal-focusing in text processing. *Educational Psychology review, 19*(2), 113–139.

McNamara, D. S. (2004). SERT: Self-explanation reading training. *Discourse Processes, 38*(1), 1–30.

McNamara, D. S., & Magliano, J. (2009). Toward a comprehensive model of comprehension. *Psychology of Learning and Motivation, 51*, 297–384.

Moreno, R. (2002). Who learns best with multiple representations? Cognitive theory predictions on individual differences in multimedia learning. In *EdMedia: World Conference on Educational Media and Technology* (pp. 1380–1385). Association for the Advancement of Computing in Education (AACE).

Moreno, R. (2004). Decreasing cognitive load for novice students: Effects of explanatory versus corrective feedback in discovery-based multimedia. *Instructional Science, 32*(1–2), 99–113.

Nokes, J. D., Dole, J. A., & Hacker, D. J. (2007). Teaching high school students to use heuristics while reading historical texts. *Journal of Educational Psychology, 99*(3), 492–505.

Paris, S. G., Lipson, M. Y., & Wixson, K. K. (1983). Becoming a strategic reader. *Contemporary Educational Psychology, 8*(3), 293–316.

Perfetti, C. A., Rouet, J.-F., & Britt, M. A. (1999). Toward a theory of documents representation. In H. van Oostendorp & S. R. Goldman (Eds.), *The construction of mental representations during reading* (pp. 99–122). Mahwah, NJ: Lawrence Erlbaum Associates, Inc.

Reisman, A. (2012). Reading like a historian: A document-based history curriculum intervention in urban high schools. *Cognition and Instruction, 30*(1), 86–112.

Renkl, A., & Scheiter, K. (2017). Studying visual displays: How to instructionally support learning. *Educational Psychology Review, 29*(3), 599–621.

Richter, T., & Maier, J. (2017). Comprehension of multiple documents with conflicting information: A two-step model of validation. *Educational Psychologist, 52*(3), 148–166.

Rouet, J., & Britt, M. A. (2011). Relevance processes in multiple document comprehension. In M. T. McCrudden, J. P. Magliano, & G. Schraw (Eds.), *Text relevance and learning from text* (pp. 19–52). Charlotte, NC: Information Age.

Rouet, J. F., Britt, M. A., & Durik, A. M. (2017). RESOLV: Readers' representation of reading contexts and tasks. *Educational Psychologist, 52*(3), 200–215.

Rouet, J. F., Favart, M., Britt, M. A., & Perfetti, C. A. (1997). Studying and using multiple documents in history: Effects of discipline expertise. *Cognition and instruction, 15*(1), 85–106.

Rouet, J. F., Ros, C., Goumi, A., Macedo-Rouet, M., & Dinet, J. (2011). The influence of surface and deep cues on primary and secondary school students' assessment of relevance in Web menus. *Learning and Instruction, 21*(2), 205–219.

Salmerón, L., Gil, L., Bråten, I., & Strømsø, H. (2010). Comprehension effects of signaling relationships between documents in search engines. *Computers in Human Behavior, 26*(3), 419–426.

Schüler, A., Scheiter, K., & van Genuchten, E. (2011). The role of working memory in multimedia instruction: Is working memory working during learning from text and pictures?. *Educational Psychology Review, 23*(3), 389–411.

Schwonke, R., Berthold, K., & Renkl, A. (2009). How multiple external representations are used and how they can be made more useful. *Applied Cognitive Psychology, 23*(9), 1227–1243.

Seufert, T. (2003). Supporting coherence formation in learning from multiple representations. *Learning and Instruction, 13*(2), 227–237.

Schraw, G., & Moshman, D. (1995). Metacognitive theories. *Educational Psychology review, 7*(4), 351–371.

Spires, H. A., & Donley, J. (1998). Prior knowledge activation: Inducing engagement with informational texts. *Journal of Educational Psychology, 90*(2), 249–260.

Stadtler, M., & Bromme, R. (2007). Dealing with multiple documents on the WWW: The role of metacognition in the formation of documents models. *International Journal of Computer-Supported Collaborative Learning, 2*(2–3), 191–210.

Stadtler, M., & Bromme, R. (2008). Effects of the metacognitive computer-tool met. a. ware on the web search of laypersons. *Computers in Human Behavior, 24*(3), 716–737.

Stadtler, M., & Bromme, R. (2014). The content-source integration model: A taxonomic description of how readers comprehend conflicting scientific information. In D. N. Rapp & J. L. G. Braasch (Eds.), *Processing inaccurate information: Theoretical and applied perspectives from cognitive science and the educational sciences* (pp. 379–402). Cambridge, MA: MIT Press.

Stahl, S. A., Hynd, C. R., Britton, B. K., McNish, M. M., & Bosquet, D. (1996). What happens when students read multiple source documents in history?. *Reading Research Quarterly, 31*(4), 430–456.

Stang Lund, E., Bråten, I., Brante, E. W., & Strømsø, H. I. (2017). Memory for textual conflicts predicts sourcing when adolescents read multiple expository texts. *Reading Psychology, 38*(4), 417–437.

Van Meter, P. N., & Cameron, C. (2018). The effects of presentation format on multiple document notetaking. *Learning and instruction, 57*, 47–56.

Wang, Y., & List, A. (2019). Calibration in multiple text use. *Metacognition and Learning*, 1–36.

Wetzels, S. A., Kester, L., & Van Merrienboer, J. J. (2011). Adapting prior knowledge activation: Mobilisation, perspective taking, and learners' prior knowledge. *Computers in Human Behavior, 27*(1), 16–21.

Wiley, J., Goldman, S. R., Graesser, A. C., Sanchez, C. A., Ash, I. K., & Hemmerich, J. A. (2009). Source evaluation, comprehension, and learning in Internet science inquiry tasks. *American Educational Research Journal, 46*(4), 1060–1106.

Wiley, J., & Voss, J. F. (1999). Constructing arguments from multiple sources: Tasks that promote understanding and not just memory for text. *Journal of Educational Psychology, 91*(2), 301–311.

Wineburg, S. S. (1991). Historical problem solving: A study of the cognitive processes used in the evaluation of documentary and pictorial evidence. *Journal of Educational Psychology, 83*(1), 73–87.

Winne, P. H., & Hadwin, A. F. (2008). The weave of motivation and self-regulated learning. In D.L. Schunk & B. Zimmerman (Eds.), *Motivation and self-regulated learning: Theory, research, and applications* (Vol. 2, pp. 297–314). New York: Lawrence Erlbaum Associates.

Wolfe, M. B., & Goldman, S. R. (2005). Relations between adolescents' text processing and reasoning. *Cognition and Instruction, 23*(4), 467–502.

Wu, H. K., & Shah, P. (2004). Exploring visuospatial thinking in chemistry learning. *Science Education, 88*(3), 465–492.

9

WRITING STRATEGIES INTERVENTIONS

Steve Graham
ARIZONA STATE UNIVERSITY AND UNIVERSITY ANDRES BELLO, CHILE

Gerardo Bañales, Silza Ahumada,
Pamela Muñoz, and Prisila Alvarez
UNIVERSITY ANDRES BELLO, CHILE

Karen R. Harris
ARIZONA STATE UNIVERSITY, USA

When describing how they write, many professional writers indicate they are very strategic. They apply strategic processes to help them manage the writing task, their writing behavior, and the writing environment (Zimmerman & Risemberg, 1997). For instance, John Irving indicated that before writing *Cider House Rules*, he invested a considerable amount of time and effort in planning, gathering information, making notes, observing, witnessing, and studying (Plimpton, 1958). Similarly, when writing *The Naked and the Dead*, Norman Mailer created an extensive dossier and charts on each character, outlining their actions and interactions (Plimpton, 1967). Truman Capote reported that he was constantly monitoring and evaluating what he wrote, repeatedly reworking his papers, creating and revising a first draft by hand, revising again at the typewriter, and revising once again after letting the paper sit for a week or more (Cowley, 1958).

While strategic writing is a trademark of professional writers (Graham & Harris, 2000), it is also evident in the writing of children. Consider below the description from a fifth-grade student of what good writers do when they write. It is reflective of the sophisticated strategies described by more skilled writers above.

> They brainstorm ideas ... then think about it and then write about it ... look it over to see how to make it all fit in right ... then they do a final copy and go over that. And then if it is still not right, they do it again.
>
> (Graham & Harris, 1996, p. 347)

These examples illustrate some of the strategic processes that skilled and developing writers apply: planning, seeking information, record keeping, organizing, monitoring, evaluating, and revising. They are only the tip of the iceberg though (Zimmerman & Risemberg, 1997), as writers also set goals (rhetorical and content goals as well as tactics for achieving them), self-instruct (e.g., telling themselves what needs to be done), rehearse (e.g., try out a scene in their head before writing it), structure the environment (e.g., find a quiet place to write), self-reinforce (e.g., provide themselves with a reward for completing one or more aspects of a writing task), seek help (e.g., ask another person to provide feedback on the text produced so far), emulate models of good writing (e.g., use another piece of writing as a guide), and manage time (e.g., estimate how much time to spend on each aspect of the writing task).

Young children, in contrast, commonly use an approach to writing that minimizes the use of highly demanding strategic behaviors. They convert writing into tasks of telling what one knows (Scardamalia & Bereiter, 1986). They draw information from memory that seems topic appropriate and write it down, with each new phrase or sentence serving as the stimulus for the next idea. They devote little attention to the constraints imposed by the topic, the development of rhetorical goals, the needs of the audience, or the organization of text. The role of planning, revising, and other strategic processes are minimized, as this retrieve-and-write process acts almost like an encapsulated and automated program, operating with little metacognitive control (McCutchen, 1988). This knowledge telling approach is not necessarily thoughtless though, rather it is forward moving, with little to no recursive interplay among writing processes.

While the knowledge telling approach remains a useful and viable option for some types of writing throughout life, an important goal of schooling is to help develop writers to become more strategic writers (Harris, Graham, MacArthur, Reid, & Mason, 2011). The adaptability of the knowledge telling approach is one barrier to this process. Even though it is basically a one-trick pony involving content generation, it serves an adaptive function. It allows children to produce text while minimizing or eliminating other cognitively demanding processes like planning. For beginning writers this is useful, as other aspects of writing like spelling and handwriting, which cannot be eliminated when writing by hand, are also cognitively demanding (Graham & Harris, 2000). Further complicating the situation, the knowledge telling approach works quite well for many of the types of writing assigned to young children in school, such as writing a personal narrative (Cutler & Graham, 2008). Consequently, it can be challenging to get young writers to take up a more demanding and sophisticated approach to composing when they already have a method that is relatively successful and requires less effort.

Another complication in helping developing writers become more strategic is that writing is not a single thing (Bazerman et al., 2018). Stories, arguments, poems, and informative text differ in important ways. They have different purposes, traditions, and organizing elements (Rijlaarsdam et al., 2012). Moreover, how well one writes in one genre is not a good predictor of how well one writes in another genre (Graham, Harris, & Hebert, 2011). Thus, teaching students to be a more strategic story writer does not mean they will automatically become a more strategic informative writer. Making this situation even more challenging is that the same writing task can vary depending on how it is conceptualized within different communities. For example, a biology and social studies teacher may emphasize the same structural elements for building a written argument (claim, grounds, warrant, support, rebuttal, qualifications; Smagorinsky & Mayer, 2014), but these elements may not appear in the same form or even to the same degree in these two classes (e.g., what counts as legitimate support can differ from one discipline to the next). This means that context must also be taken into account when teaching students to be more strategic writers.

This chapter examines how teachers and schools can help writers become more strategic. We first examine the theoretical role of strategies and strategic processing in writing as well as evidence that supports fostering these skills with developing writers. We then examine approaches for teaching developing writers how to become more strategic writers, providing an example using the Self-regulated Strategy Development model (SRSD; Harris & Graham, 2018). Finally, we consider issues that need to be addressed in future research.

THEORETICAL ROLE OF STRATEGIES AND STRATEGIC PROCESSING IN WRITING

The earliest cognitive models of writing (Hayes & Flower, 1980) to the most recent (see Graham, 2018a) emphasize strategies and strategic process as critical elements of writing. The earliest of these conceptualizations, the Hayes and Flower model, provided a description of the mental operations that skilled writers employ when writing (planning [goal setting, generating ideas, organizing ideas], translating plans into text, and reviewing [reading and editing]). A subsequent model by Hayes (2012) took a different approach, focusing on control processes such as goal setting (for planning, drafting, and revising) as well as task schemas for carrying out various aspects of writing such as revising, collaborating, summarizing, and so forth. In contrast, a model by Zimmerman and Risemberg (1997) concentrated on how writers use self-regulation strategies for managing the writing process, writing behaviors, and the writing environment.

The recent Writer(s)-within-Community (WWC) model by Graham (2018b, 2018c) represents a departure from these previous conceptualizations. It places writing and the cognitive resources writers and their collaborators bring to writing within the context of writing communities (consistent with the argument above about the importance of context in strategic writing). It also draws on both executive control and self-regulation to describe the strategic processes writers use when composing. The WWC model proposes that writing is simultaneously shaped and bound by the characteristics, capacity, and variability of the communities in which it takes place and by the cognitive characteristics, capacity, and individual differences of those who produce it as well as the interaction between community and individuals. The model further proposes that writing development is a consequence of participation in writing communities and individual changes in writers' capabilities, which interact with biological, neurological, physical, and environmental factors.

The WWC model conceptualizes writing as a social activity that is situated within specific writing communities. A writing community is defined as a group of people who share a basic set of goals and assumptions and use writing to achieve their purposes. Examples of writing communities include a science class where students use writing as a tool for learning, an online website where writers share and support each other's writing efforts, and a child and grandparent who send emails to each other to keep in touch. Skilled and developing writers are typically members of multiple writing communities at any point in time.

The *purpose* of each writing community determines the type of writing undertaken, its intended audiences and stances, norms for writing, and identity (including the identity of its *members* who will differ in terms of levels of affiliation, participation, roles and responsibilities, presumed value to the community, and power). A writing community further shapes writing through its use of *tools* and *reoccurring typified actions* that members apply to meet a community's writing goals. Moreover, the writing produced by community members does not happen by chance, as it is molded by a *collective history*, the *social and physical context of the community* (e.g., on-line versus brick and mortar) as well as the other writing communities in which members are currently or previously engaged (e.g., writing practices learned at school are brought home). Thus, what is written and how it is written (strategies, schemas, and strategic processes) is embedded and dependent on the context in which it is produced.

While context shapes what is written, the members of a writing community exercise intentionality over what and how they write, including the degree of personal ownership they take for specific writing tasks. In essence, members of a writing community apply their cognitive capabilities and resources to achieve community and personal writing goals. These capabilities and resources include *long-term memory resources* (e.g., specialized writing knowledge and knowledge of the writing community as well as beliefs about the value/utility of writing, one's competence as a writer, and reasons for writing), *text production processes* (conceptualization, ideation, translation, transcription, and reconceptualization), *control mechanisms* for orchestrating and directing the process of writing (attention, working memory, and executive functioning), and *modulators* that influence writing (emotions, personality traits, and physical states).

The *control mechanisms* proposed in the WWC model specify the strategic processes applied during writing. Attentional processes allow writers to choose what is attended to and what is ignored, and involve focusing, maintaining, switching, and inhibiting attention during all stages of the text *production processes*. This includes what a writer does in solitude, in conjunction with the tools selected for writing, and the actions undertaken with collaborators in the writing community.

Working memory provides a limited and temporary storage system where the internal work of writing occurs. It provides a space where all non-automated composing activities take place. Knowledge and beliefs from *long-term memory* and external information are brought into working memory, processed, and acted upon in order to regulate attention, production processes, writing tools, motivations, emotions, personality traits, and the environmental and social context in which writing takes place.

The third *control mechanism* in the WWC model is executive control. This involves the process of setting goals (formulating intentions), initiating actions to achieve them (plans), evaluating goals and their impact (monitor), and modifying each of these as needed (react). These processes are the mechanisms by which writers and collaborators establish agency and control over the writing process, and they are applied to all aspects of writing (e.g., defining the writing assignment, developing a writing plan, gathering possible writing content, organizing it, constructing sentences, transcribing sentences into text, integrating visual and verbal features into text, reading and rereading plans and text for evaluative purposes, reformulating plans or text based on these evaluations, and editing and creating a polished final product). They are not separate from the confines of the writing community but operate in conjunction with them, as they are used to manage interactions with collaborators, use of selected writing tools, and arranging the writing environment.

The WWC model further proposes that communities and writers develop schemas (or strategies) for carrying out the writing process. These include schemas for setting goals, gathering and organizing possible writing content, drafting text, and evaluating and revising plans and text. It also includes schemas for controlling thoughts, behaviors, inclinations, and the writing environment. For example, a writer may use a schema for brainstorming to help generate possible writing ideas. However, if a writer cannot draw the needed schema from *long-term memory* or one is not available in their writing community, a new plan can be generated through problem solving or by modifying an existing schema that appears somewhat relevant. Of course, a writer may also take action with a poorly articulated schema.

As the WWC model illustrates, writers employ specific schemas (which we will refer to as strategies from this point forward) to accomplish community/personal writing goals. These strategies are beneficial for at least three reasons. One, they direct attention to what needs to be done to carry out a particular aspect of writing. Two, they are efficient, as they provide a structure or set of mental operations which can be used repeatedly, as when a professor uses a particular strategy or structure for writing letters of recommendation. Three, they can reduce cognitive load, as they can break a demanding task like writing into smaller and more manageable tasks (e.g., write by planning, drafting, editing, and revising).

The use of writing strategies does not mean that writers stop engaging in strategic processes involving reasoning, monitoring, evaluating, making interpretations, or solving problems. If a known writing strategy is applied, writers can (and hopefully do) monitor, evaluate, and react accordingly to its use. Further, strategies known to a writer do not provide a solution to every problem he or she faces. For instance, the seemingly simple act of forming an idea into a written sentence requires making decisions about which words and sentence structure best convey the writer's intentions. Even though strategic processing can be purposefully reduced, as when a knowledge telling approach is applied, writing always has the potential to be highly strategic, and as the WWC model illustrates, writers need to become strategic writers in multiple communities.

EMPIRICAL EVIDENCE SUPPORTING STRATEGIC WRITING

The road to writing competence is long and never fully achieved (Bazerman et al., 2018), as there are many different forms of writing, approaches to writing, and ways to continually improve as a writer within different communities. Movement along this road arises, at least in part, from changes in strategic writing behaviors. Graham (2006) examined if the available empirical evidence with students in grades 1 to 12 supported this proposition, and has returned to examine it multiple times in the ensuing years (e.g., Graham et al., 2019). He argues that the following tenets should be supported if strategic writing is important to writing development: (1) skilled writers are more strategic than less skilled writers, (2) developing writers become more strategic with age and schooling, (3) individual differences in strategic writing behaviors predict individual differences in writing performance, and (4) instruction designed to increase strategic writing behaviors improves writing performance.

While it is important to remember that Graham's analyses involved school writing and were mostly focused on planning and revising, his review and subsequent analyses provided evidence which supports each of the four tenets. In terms of the first tenet, Graham (2006) found that skilled writers are more planful and better at revising than less skilled writers. For example, in a study by Bereiter and Scardamalia (1987), college students planned their entire composition during a scheduled preplanning period, generating multiple and abbreviated lists of ideas that were connected by lines or arrows. They also included conceptual planning notes, evaluative statements, and structural markers. Less skilled writers primarily generated content when asked to plan. Similarly, less skilled writers devote little attention to revising, and the nature of their revising differs from that of more skilled writers, as their revisions are mostly superficial, aimed at making small word changes and correcting errors (Chanquoy, 2001)

Graham (2006) also found that the planning and revising of developing writers becomes increasingly sophisticated with schooling and experience (tenet two). This was the case in Bereiter and Scardamalia (1987) above, as the number of planning notes students produced between grades four and six doubled, and conceptual planning increased from grades four and eight. Likewise, students' revising becomes more sophisticated over time, as older writers revise more often, revise larger units of text, and make more meaning-based revisions (MacArthur, Graham, & Harris, 2004).

Graham (2006) indicated that the available data mostly supported one aspect of the third tenet: individual differences in planning behavior predict writing performance. He found, however, that revising behavior is generally unrelated to overall writing performance until high school or later, probably because younger children do not revise much (Fitzgerald, 1987). Subsequent research by Graham and colleagues (e.g., Graham et al., 2019) provide even greater support for the positive relation between strategic behavior and writing, showing that intermediate grade students who are more planful and strategic are better writers than students who are less planful and strategic, even after controlling for writing knowledge, writing motivation, writing skills, reading skills, and gender.

The fourth tenet, teaching strategic behaviors improves writing, was strongly supported in Graham (2006) and subsequent analyses (e.g., Graham, Kiuhara, McKeown, & Harris, 2012). In a meta-analysis by Graham and Harris (2017) involving 42 true- and quasi-experiments conducted with students in grades 1 to 12, teaching students strategies for planning, revising, or both had a strong impact on improving overall writing quality (effect size = 1.26). A separate meta-analysis involving 53 single subject-design studies (Graham, Harris, & McKeown, 2013) also found positive effects of writing strategy instruction for writing quality, structural elements, and number of words written.

Another meta-analysis by Santangelo, Harris, and Graham (2013) provided further support for the importance of strategic behavior in writing. They reported that a variety of instructional procedures designed to support or enhance one or more strategic behaviors improved the quality of writing produced by students in grades 1 to 12. This included goal setting (effect size = 0.73), self-evaluation (effect size = 0.51), emulating models of good writing (effect size = 0.30), forming mental images (effect size = 0.76), and prewriting activities for generating and organizing information (effect size = 0.55). Graham and Harris (2017) also found that the process writing approach, which stresses the importance of engaging in planning, drafting, revising, and editing, improved the quality of grade 1 to 12 students' writing (effect size = 0.34).

While the findings from the reviews above do not address all aspects of strategic writing behavior or the impact of such behavior in a broad range of different writing communities (as they are mostly limited to school contexts), they do support the contention that strategies and strategic processes are an important ingredient in becoming a stronger writer. They also provide strong evidence that instructional procedures aimed at enhancing one or more strategic behaviors can lead to better writing, especially when students are taught strategies for carrying out specific aspects of writing. This approach to improving students' strategic writing behavior is commonly called writing strategy instruction, and it is examined next.

WRITING STRATEGY INSTRUCTION

Writing strategy instruction involves teaching developing writers strategies (i.e., schemas) for carrying out one or more aspects of the writing process. According to Alexander, Graham, and Harris (1998), a strategy can be understood as procedural or "how to" knowledge. They can take the form of a heuristic (e.g., general rules for writing a summary) or more step-by-step procedures (i.e., construct an outline of main points and details). Strategies are purposeful (goal-directed or intentional), willful (must be applied), effortful (cognitively demanding), and facilitative (designed to enhance performance). They vary in terms of their generality, as some writing strategies have broad utility (e.g., brainstorming, semantic webs), whereas others are designed for a specific domain (e.g., the science writing heuristic; Hand & Prain, 2002) or task (TREE for writing an opinion essay, see below). Strategies can facilitate metacognition, as when a strategy prompts writers to reflect on their performance and use any acquired awareness to guide subsequent thoughts and actions. Strategies can further be paired together in a variety of ways to help writers initiate, orchestrate, maintain, and evaluate mental operations used to regulate the writing task, behaviors, processes, and environment as well as writers' motivations.

As children learn and grow as writers, the writing strategies they use and the ways they use these strategies change (Alexander, Graham, & Harris, 1998). With experience and schooling, children's strategic behavior becomes more efficient, effective, flexible, and inventive (old writing strategies are modified and new strategies created).

While these shifts in strategic behavior provide a general picture of the course of strategy development, development patterns are truly individualistic, as developing writers with a similar level of writing experience and schooling may use different strategies to solve the same writing task. As the WWC model illustrates (Graham, 2018b, 2018c), strategic behavior and strategy use not only varies from one person to the next but from one writing community to another.

Strategy development does not occur in isolation but happens in conjunction with other aspects of cognitive development, including advances in a writer's knowledge, motivation, and foundational writing skills (Alexander, Graham, & Harris, 1998; Graham & Harris, 2000). Because writing strategies must be intentionally evoked, their use is directly tied to a writer's beliefs, goal, and sense of agency. As developing writers gain a deeper and richer knowledge base about writing, they can use writing strategies more efficiently and effectively. As foundational writing skills such as handwriting and spelling become more automatic, they are less likely to interfere or impede strategy use.

There are multiple ways that developing writers can acquire new writing strategies (Graham, 2018c). They can acquire new writing strategies by participating in a specific writing community, adopting the sanctioned actions the community uses to carry out writing tasks. They can also learn new strategies or adapt old ones through observation (e.g., watching a teacher write), collaborative writing (e.g., adopting a strategy a collaborator uses), as a consequence of action (e.g., deciding to adapt a strategy to make it effective in a new situation), or deliberate agency (e.g., designing a new strategy). To date, the most scientifically tested means for acquiring new writing strategies involves directly teaching them (Graham & Harris, 2017).

Teaching Writing Strategies

Before the cognitive revolution in writing was fully underway, scholars such as Young, Becker, and Pike (1970) promoted the use of heuristics as a mechanism for college students to understand writing topics and audience. With the publication of Hayes and Flower's (1980) cognitive model of writing, researchers began designing intervention studies to determine the effectiveness of explicitly teaching writing strategies to school-aged students. The very first writing strategy instructional studies involved students with special needs (Harris & Graham, 1985; Moran, Schumaker, & Vetter, 1981), but by the 1990s researchers were studying the effects of such instruction on typically developing writers as well (Englert et al., 1991).

Over the course of four decades, writing strategy instruction has become the most empirically investigated teaching approach in writing (Graham, Harris, & McKeown, 2013). Most of the writing strategy studies conducted to date focus on teaching one or more genre specific strategies (starting with Harris and Graham in 1985), but many studies also teach such strategies in conjunction with more general writing strategies and self-regulation procedures (e.g., Harris & Graham, 2008).

There are many similarities in the instructional approaches used to teach writing strategies to grade 1 to 12 students. Most approaches (Deshler & Schumaker, 1986; Englert et al., 1991; Harris & Graham, 2009; Olson & Land, 2007) apply a gradual release model where strategies are first modeled and writers are supported until they can apply the strategies successfully and independently. Dialogue between teacher and students is also commonly used in these approaches as a way of strengthening students' knowledge and control over the writing strategies taught. There are differences, however, as some approaches specifically include instructional procedures for enhancing maintenance and generalization (Deshler & Schumaker, 1986; Harris & Graham, 2009), others teach writing and reading strategies conjointly (Olson & Land, 2007), and still others stress criterion-based learning principles, teaching the knowledge and self-regulation procedures needed to use the target writing strategies successfully, and using procedures to enhance students' beliefs about writing (Harris & Graham, 2009).

The writing strategy instructional approach that has been researched the most often is the SRSD model developed by Karen Harris. Over 100 studies from around the world have tested the effectiveness of this approach to writing strategy instruction (Graham, Harris, & McKeown, 2013). In addition, when compared to other approaches to teaching writing strategies (effect sizes = 0.56), SRSD is more effective in enhancing the quality of writing for school-aged students (effect size = 1.59; Graham & Harris, 2017). Consequently, to illustrate writing strategy instruction, we provide an example involving SRSD. To demonstrate the global reach of this approach, our example involves a case study of SRSD conducted in Chile.

SRSD

Self-regulated strategy development is an approach for teaching learners task-specific strategies for carrying out composing processes like planning, drafting, and revising. Developing writers learn to apply specific writing strategies; acquire the knowledge needed to use these strategies successfully; learn to regulate the use of these strategies as well as the process of writing; and develop positive beliefs about their writing capabilities and the strategies taught (Harris, Graham, Mason, & Friedlander, 2008). SRSD involves six recursive stages of instruction: develop background knowledge, discuss it, model it, memorize it, support it, and independent performance. Teachers first model how to use the target strategies and self-regulation procedures, but move deliberately to independent learner application, and stress maintenance and generalization of the procedures taught.

Context. The case study presented here took place in Chile and involved teaching opinion essay writing to 20 sixth graders in a private school (average age = 11 years, 67% girls). The teacher in this study (the fifth author of this chapter) is 35 years old with nine years teaching experience. She received professional development in how to deliver SRSD over a one-month period. This included an online course on SRSD and a manual with detailed instructions on how to provide SRSD instruction with the target strategies. All instructional materials needed by the students were provided by the school.

The emphasis in this case study of teaching students strategies for planning, drafting, and reviewing their opinion essay is a departure from the learning objectives in many Chilean schools where little emphasis is placed on such instruction. Instruction was also delivered in the context of a private school. Public school classrooms often contain 35 or more students. The smaller number of students in this private school class made it possible for the teacher to be more attentive to individual needs during instruction. Moreover, the families of students in this class were affluent, and enjoyed greater linguistic and material resources than many students in public schools. Additionally, the teacher modified SRSD instruction as specified in Harris, Graham, Mason, and Friedlander (2008) to make instruction fit her classroom and a Chilean context (e.g., emphasis was placed on peer-evaluation as well as self-evaluation). Lastly, instruction was delivered at the end of the school year. This had two consequences, it was necessary at times to extend a writing class beyond the allotted 45 minutes to accommodate SRSD instruction. It also made it impossible to apply a criterion-based approach to SRSD instruction as is recommended. As a result instruction was time-based (i.e., ten lessons), and less time was devoted to two stages of SRSD: support it and independence performance. This was also influenced by other teaching demands in other subject areas. This meant that students had less time to practice applying the strategies learned, use of the graphic organizers for strategy use were not replaced by student designed organizers, and little attention was devoted to strategy maintenance and generalization. As a result, we will address how these would have been addressed if more time had been available.

Writing Strategies. Students were taught a three-step process for planning and drafting their opinion essay (see Table 9.1). This included first thinking about audience and purpose, and then applying a general writing strategy (POW) for planning and drafting as well as a genre-specific strategy (TREE) for generating ideas and notes for their composition based on the basic parts of an opinion essay. These strategies (or schemas) were used in previous SRSD research (e.g., Harris et al., 2012). While they structure or regulate how students carry out the processes of planning and drafting an opinion essay, they require thoughtful use. As they carry out specific steps, students must make and evaluate the decisions they make. For example, when picking an idea to write about they are encouraged to generate possible ideas and make decisions about which will be most suitable given their purpose and audience. Likewise, when organizing their notes, they generate possible reasons to support their ideas, make decisions about which ones are most convincing, and consider how best to organize them to obtain the maximum argumentative effect. Thus, for each step of these two strategies, students are engaged in making multiple decisions, evaluating them, and modifying them as necessary to achieve their goals.

Develop and Activate Prior Knowledge. At the start of the first class, the teacher began asking students what they knew about opinion essays, including the parts of an opinion essay and the differences between arguments and reasons. To facilitate the development and activation of knowledge about these issues, students reviewed examples of daily argumentation, based on two comic vignettes presented by the teacher. Additionally, students read, first individually and later in turn, a model text entitled "What time should we rest?" Then, students were asked to underline the opinions of the author in the text read, and then to give reasons and explanations to justify their opinion. Finally, the teacher proposed that students reflect and briefly write about what they learned during the lesson, the functions of arguments, and the topics they would like to debate or argue.

During the second class, students read and discussed a model text titled "Should children be paid for their homework?" To facilitate the analysis of the parts of this opinion (thesis, reasons, and explanations), the teacher posed a series of questions and had students annotate these parts directly on the text. Afterwards, the teacher asked students to use these parts to write an opinion essay on the topic: "Should homework be sent home?" The generated texts were collected by the teacher as an initial indication of students' opinion writing performance (pretest). Some of the text produced by students was read and analyzed by the class, using an evaluation guide for the parts of an opinion essay. Students evaluated text alone and together. At the end of class,

Table 9.1 Strategies and Steps for Writing of POW + TREE

Step 1: Think, who will read this, and why am I writing it?

Step 2: Plan what to say using POW
- P = Pick an idea to start with – this is an idea in our heads.
- O = Organize my notes
- W = Write and say more

Step 3: Organize my notes using TREE
- T = Topic sentence – tells the reader what you believe
- R = Reasons
- E = Explain – Explain each reason
- E = Ending – Wrap it up right

students completed a reflection activity based on the questions: What was it that you liked most about writing the opinion text? What was the hardest part of writing the opinion essay?

During the third class the teacher presented the students with two "writing tricks" or strategies: POW + TREE (see Table 9.1). These are mnemonics that specify a series of mental activities or steps underlying the target strategies for planning and drafting opinion essays. The teacher presented these strategies on the blackboard in the form of graphic organizers with the meaning of each step specified. Drawing on the analysis of model texts reviewed in previous classes, the teacher described how Carlos, an ideal student, used these strategies to write his opinion essay. During this process, students focused on identifying the parts of each strategy and learned how to use the graphic organizers to generate planning ideas and notes. At the end of class, the class discussed the importance of using the strategies to write good opinion texts.

In the fourth class, the teacher taught and explained the purpose of two additional tricks students would use to improve their essays: million pesos words and self-regulation strategies. For million pesos words, students received a copy of commonly used words to signal opinion essay ideas or connect them when writing an opinion text (e.g., opinion, order, cause, consequence). The teacher also introduced and modeled self-regulation procedures students would use while writing (i.e., goal setting and self-instruction). For example, she generated and modeled with students help self-instructions that can be usefully applied before, during or after writing. To facilitate this process, students had a table illustrating different types of self-instructions "good writers" use: *task definition* ("What do I need to do?"), *task planning* ("I need to make plan"; "If I stay focused, I can do this"), *implementation and strategy use* ("I need to write down my POW + TREE reminder"; "I need to set a goal to include all of the parts"; "I did the first step and now the second step is …"), *self-assessment* ("How am I doing?"), and *self-reinforcing* ("This is pretty good!"; "I'm getting better at this!"). The teacher and students then discussed the importance of using the million pesos words and self-regulation procedures.

The lessons provided during this stage gave students an introduction to POW + TREE strategies as well as how self-talk can direct one's behavior during writing. In subsequent stages (see below), the teacher will model how to use POW + TREE in a flexible and strategic manner, and apply self-talk to direct the use of these strategies as well as their writing behaviors and thoughts. The teachers will further introduce how to use goal setting, self-monitoring, and self-evaluation for these same purposes. Students then receive practice applying these strategic processes as they write their own essays. As they are learning to use these different strategic tools, the teacher emphasizes that these tools can be used flexibly and intelligently, as they will need to be adapted to different writing topics, tasks, and situations.

Discuss It. During the fifth class, the teacher asked students to help her examine an opinion text to identify if all the elements in the TREE strategy were present. Using a previously written opinion essay, the teacher identified each of these parts, with students help, and made notes for each of these parts on the graphic organizer presented during the third class. She also reminded them that it was important to ask who would read the text and if the arguments made sense. The students then analyzed a new opinion essay, placing the parts they identified in note form on the graphic organizer.

At the start of the sixth class, students reviewed an opinion essay that did not include all of the elements included in TREE. Individually, students read the essay and completed the graphic organizer. As students worked, the teacher reminded them to determine if the writer included all the parts, but also to evaluate if provided reasons made sense. Once the task was completed, the class discussed deficiencies in the essay analyzed. Students then worked in pairs to improve the essay they evaluated, adding new arguments and reasons that made sense. At this point students had acquired the knowledge needed to move to the next step: seeing how the target strategies can be applied.

Model It. In the seventh class, the teacher modeled how to use POW and TREE and the other tricks presented to students in previous lessons. She first provided a review of the strategies and self-regulation procedures presented in prior lessons. Next, using the three-step strategy presented in Table 9.1, she identified the writing topic ("The use of social networks and children's sedentary lifestyle"), making her thinking visible while talking aloud, referring to the appropriate step of POW (Pick an idea to start with), and making notes on the graphic organizer (including setting a goal to include all the basic parts of an opinion essay in her composition). She then began planning her essay aloud, referring to the second step in POW (Organize my notes) and using TREE to guide the idea generation process, as she wrote notes on the graphic organizer. Students were encouraged to provide help by letting the teacher know if the arguments being put forward made sense, the order of ideas was logical and appropriate, and if ideas were relevant. While modeling the use of the target strategies, the teacher used self-instructions to regulate the writing strategies, writing task, and her writing behavior (e.g. "How am I doing?"; "Am I following all the steps?"), making visible how the teacher managed the process of writing.

After planning and drafting the essay as well as checking to see if it had all of the parts, the teacher introduced the idea of collaborative planning. Students were asked to work in pairs to apply all of the procedures used by the teacher during the seventh class with one exception. Once they collaboratively planned their text, each student drafted an essay of their own using the collaborative plan. The teacher then modeled how to evaluate the completed essay using a rubric. Students then evaluated their partner's text using the rubric and provided evaluative comments directly on the text.

During the eighth class, students generated self-instructions they would apply to their own writing. After revising the importance of self-statements, the teacher asked students to generate and record in a table self-instructions they each planned to apply.

Writing Strategies Interventions • 153

Memorize It and Support It. At the start of the ninth class, students played games to ensure they had easy mental access to the steps in POW and TREE. For example, they gathered in a circle and the teacher threw a ball indicating the first letter of the POW strategy, the student receiving the ball had to point out the keyword associated with the letter indicated and throw it to another student to explain the purpose of this step. This same activity was repeated for TREE.

The teacher applied a collaborative activity where students were to apply everything they had learned about writing an opinion essay on "Is it appropriate to give technological toys to six-year-olds?" As collaborative writing occurred, the teacher circulated around the room providing the level of support specific children needed.

If more time had been available, students would have practiced writing essays until they could do so without help from the teacher or peers. This would include fading the graphic organizer, with students creating their own personal graphic organizer they could generate on a separate sheet of paper.

Independent Performance. During the tenth class, students planned and wrote an essay on a topic of their choice. The teacher encouraged students to use their self-instructions, the strategies they were taught, million pesos words, and so forth. Students shared their completed essays with the class and conducted assessments of the quality of their work with another student.

If more time had been available, the class would have held a discussion on how what was learned could be modified to make it work better. In addition, students would have identified other situations where they could apply the strategies and identify how they would need to be modified in those situations. Finally, students would have set goals for using what they learned over time and in other situations.

Impact. As a result of SRSD instruction, students evidenced changes in the way they wrote (e.g., planning in advance) and what they wrote. An example illustrating typical changes in students' writing is provided in Table 9.2. Statistically significant improvements were found for the class as a whole from pretest to posttest on essay

Table 9.2 Example of Performance Before and After SRSD Instruction

Pretest

Writing Prompt: Should homework be sent home?

I think not, because probably having problems in the house or even not having time to do them, and not doing homework, we lost out, unable to give our reasons or explain the reasons why we could not do the homework. At the same time, I also think yes because it helps us to continue with our learning because despite the difficult, being willing, we still managed to solve or understand the task. It is also dependent on the amount of the task, such as writing, because if it is too much, not everyone will be motivated to do it.

Posttest

Writing Prompt: Do you think it is useful to wear a uniform at school?

No, since not having a uniform is highly favorable for students. My first reason is that it is very boring for all students, because having dark and opaque colors does not allow us to express ourselves.

Second, I think that by forcing us to do it all week, we have less motivation to do it correctly.

Lastly, I think it is more comfortable to use "colored clothes," since the uniform is tighter because it has a lot of elastic. In conclusion, I think that the school should not force us to wear the uniform, no matter how much it represents the school; no child feels comfortable doing it.

length, number of essay elements (e.g., reasons), and essay quality (using a five-point holistic quality measure). While orally expressing their opinions was a common part of the participating students' daily lives, they evidenced difficulty doing this effectively with writing before SRSD instruction. They found it especially difficult to organize their written argument effectively and make clear connections between ideas. As a result of SRSD instruction, students' writing became progressively more organized and complete (containing all of the basic parts of an opinion essay), with students using discourse markers associated with persuasive texts (e.g., "one reason why ... ") to signal transitions between ideas, resulting in qualitatively stronger text.

ISSUES AND FUTURE RESEARCH

What Writing Strategies Are Applied within and across Contexts?

Presently, we do not have a clear picture of the types of writing strategies applied or valued in different writing communities. Even in schools, where National, State, or local guidelines favor certain types of writing (e.g., Common Core State Standards, 2010), we know very little about how these types of writing are actualized from one classroom to the next, or if students are taught strategies for carrying out one or more aspects of these writing tasks. In addition, we possess only the haziest pictures of the types of writing strategies taught or the form they take across and within schools. There is some evidence, however, from survey and observational studies that many teachers do not spend enough time teaching writing process or strategies (Graham, 2019), even though there is considerable evidence that such instruction is effective (Graham & Harris, 2017).

This lack of evidence about writing tasks, writing strategies, and writing strategy instruction stems in part from the types of questions asked by researchers when they query teachers about their writing practices in surveys (e.g., Graham, Cappizi, Harris, Hebert, & Morphy, 2014). Questions are broad in their orientation asking about the types of writing students are assigned (e.g., story, persuasive, informative) and how frequently planning and revising strategies are taught. This does not allow researchers to develop a fine-grained sense of what writing or strategy instruction looks like on the ground so to speak. Additional research is also needed to determine if teachers and learners view writing strategy instruction as acceptable (e.g., Troia & Graham, 2017), and explore why teachers do and do not apply such instruction.

Future research needs to examine more broadly how writing and writing strategies differ across writing communities as well as cultures. For example, the forms and purposes of persuasive writing differ in China and the United States, with the former using a less direct approach to presenting an argument, resulting in different strategies for writing in the two cultures (Cai, 1993). Greater knowledge about how writing and strategy instruction is conceptualized and viewed in different writing communities and cultures, will provide a richer base for evaluating and advancing writing strategy instruction, including the development and testing of new writing strategies and approaches for teaching them.

Why Is Writing Strategy Instruction Not More Common in Schools?

While most teachers indicate they teach strategies for planning and revising text, neither writing, writing instruction, nor writing strategy instruction in particular are allocated sufficient time in most classrooms (see Graham, 2019). One likely reason for this is that many teachers' worldwide indicate that their preparation to teach writing is not adequate (e.g., De Smedt, Van Keer, & Merchie, 2016). As the SRSD example from Chile illustrated, writing strategy instruction is demanding and complex. Teachers are less likely to apply such teaching techniques if they are not properly prepared to do so or do not have needed support material. In the United States, several organizations now exist that provide teachers and school systems with training and support to carry out writing strategy instruction (e.g., thinkSRSD and SRSD Online).

There is surprisingly little research investigating professional development (PD) methods for teaching writing strategies. In fact most available strategy instructional studies provide little information about PD for writing strategy instruction. One exception is the work of Harris and colleagues (e.g., Harris et al., 2012), where a practice-based professional development model is used to (1) create a supportive community where teachers can learn to apply SRSD effectively; (2) help teachers modify their own classroom environment so that it is conducive to SRSD instruction; (3) provide teachers with the knowledge, understanding, skills, and beliefs needed to teach SRSD effectively and efficiently in their classrooms; (4) create opportunities for active learning, practice, and feedback in applying SRSD with peers before applying it in the classroom; (5) use materials and other artifacts during PD identical to those teachers will use in the classroom; and (6) provide ongoing classroom support in applying SRSD (see Graham and Harris, 2018 for a detailed explanation as well as how this approach is consistent with the WWC model).

If the promise of writing strategy instruction is to be realized, additional attention to teacher preparation must be undertaken. Such preparation may fall mostly on schools and individual teachers, as colleges of education have proven to be unreliable partners in preparing teachers to teach writing (Graham, 2019). Research is also needed to determine how to bring writing strategy instruction to scale, so that it is a more prominent and effective feature of writing instruction in schools.

How Can Flexible and Sustained Use of Writing Strategies Be Promoted?

Three criticisms of writing strategy instruction are that students use strategies in a non-thoughtful and robotic manner, strategy effects fade over time, and generalization of strategy effects are limited (Alexander, Graham, & Harris, 1998). While any strategy can be used in a non-thoughtful and inflexible manner, instructional approaches to teaching writing strategies, like SRSD, stress intelligent and adaptable use of writing strategies. We provide three examples to illustrate ways in which this is done (Graham & Harris, 2018). One, once students learn how to apply strategies, they discuss as a group how they might be modified to make them better. Two, students practice applying the strategies with different relevant tasks. Three, students identify other situations where they can use inculcated strategies and decide how they need to be adapted for those situations.

While concerns about maintaining learning effects are common across education, writing strategy instruction is one of the few areas in writing research where maintenance is commonly measured. While not all students maintain the effects of writing strategy instruction and the overall effects of writing strategy instruction across students diminishes over time, maintenance effects are actually quite promising. This was evident in a meta-analysis of SRSD in writing, where the average effect size for writing quality immediately following instruction was 1.75 and 1.30 at maintenance (Graham, Harris, & McKeown, 2013). The maintenance probes ranged from two weeks to 28 months. The likely reason for these relatively positive effects is that many writing strategy instructional approaches include mechanisms for facilitating maintenance (e.g., making students aware of gains from using taught strategies, setting goals for continued strategy use). Even so, there is a need to investigate the impact of writing strategy instruction over longer time periods, especially when students receive a year or more of writing strategy instruction.

Generalizability of writing strategy instruction can be challenging. Most writing strategies scientifically tested to date are genre specific (e.g., Graham & Perin, 2007). Take for instance the TREE strategy described earlier. It is likely adaptable for other persuasive writing tasks but not suitable for writing most stories. However, generalizability effects are quite robust (effect size for writing quality = 1.00; Graham, Harris, & McKeown, 2013) when generalization is assessed to a similar genre (e.g., story to personal narrative or persuasive to informative writing). These effects are based on a relatively small number of studies though, and there is little information on the instructional mechanisms responsible for such generalizability effects (see Harris, Graham, & Mason, 2006).

Final Considerations

In closing, we would like to identify several other areas in need of additional investigation. While there are many different writing strategies designed and scientifically tested (see Harris, Graham, Mason, & Friedlander, 2008), they address only a small fraction of the possible writing strategies that might be useful at school, work, and home. There is also a need to develop and test a more comprehensive suite of writing strategies that can be applied in schools or other settings where multiple types of writing occur. This should include considering how one or more writing strategies can be usefully adapted to serve multiple purposes (such as how to adapt a persuasive writing strategy so that it can be applied in different content classrooms). Further, writing strategy instruction is one aspect of teaching writing and there is a need to test how it can be effectively integrated into different approaches to teaching writing (see MacArthur, Schwartz, Graham, Molloy, & Harris, 1996).

There has been surprisingly little research examining which components of strategy instruction are responsible for learners' gains in writing. With SRSD, prior research demonstrated that the self-regulation procedures of goal setting and self-monitoring, included in most SRSD studies (but not in Chilean case study shared earlier), account for one-half a standard deviation in SRSD writing gains (see Graham & Perin, 2007). Other studies examined when in SRSD instruction improvements in writing performance start to occur (Danoff, Harris, & Graham, 1993). Given that such analyses are uncommon, more component analysis research is surely needed.

Finally, teaching writing strategies is just one way of improving strategic behavior in writing. We need to examine and test other methods for promoting strategic writing behavior, including students' designing their own strategies. Such an approach was applied by Butler (1988), but little research has occurred since.

REFERENCES

Alexander, P., Graham, S., & Harris, K. (1998). A perspective on strategy research: Progress and prospects. *Educational Psychology Review, 10*, 129–154.

Bazerman, C., Berninger, V., Brandt, D., Graham, S., Langer, J., Murphy, S., … Schleppegrell, M. (2018). *The lifespan development of writing*. Urbana, IL: National Council of English.

Bereiter, C., & Scardamalia, M. (1987). *The psychology of written composition*. Hillsdale, NJ: Lawrence Erlbaum.

Butler, D. (1988). The strategic content learning approach to promoting self-rgulated learning: A summary of three studies. *Journal of Educational Psychology, 90*, 682–697.

Cai, G. (1993). *Beyond "bad writing": Teaching English composition to Chinese ESL students*. ERIC: ED 364 104.

Chanquoy, L. (2001). How to make it easier for children to revise their writing: A study of text revision from 3rd to 5th grades. *British Journal of Educational Psychology, 71*, 15–41.

Common Core State Standards: National Governors Association and Council of Chief School Officers. (2010). Available from http://corestandards.org/.

Cowley, M. (Ed.). (1958). *Writers at work: The Paris review interviews*. London: Vicking.

Cutler, L., & Graham, S. (2008). Primary grade writing instruction: A national survey. *Journal of Educational Psychology, 100*, 907–919.

Danoff, B., Harris, K. R., & Graham, S. (1993). Incorporating strategy instruction into the school curriculum: Effects on children's writing. *Journal of Reading Behavior, 25*, 295–322.

De Smedt, F., Van Keer, H., & Merchie, E. (2016). Student, teacher, and class-level correlates of Flemish late elementary school children's writing performance. *Reading & Writing: An Interdisciplinary Journal, 29*(5), 833–868.

Deshler, D., & Schumaker, J. (1986). Learning strategie: An instructional alternative for low-achieving students. *Exceptional Children, 52*, 583–590.

Englert, C., Raphael, T., Anderson, L., Anthony, H., Stevens, D., & Fear, K. (1991). Making writing strategies and self-talk visible: Cognitive strategy instruction in writng in regular and special education classrooms. *American Educational Research Journal, 28*, 337–372.

Fitzgerald, J. (1987). Research on revision in writing. *Review of Educational Research, 57*, 481–506.

Graham, S. (2006). Writing. In P. A. Alexander & P. H. Winne (Eds.), *Handbook of educational psychology* (pp. 457–478). Mahwah, NJ: Lawrence Erlbaum.

Graham, S. (2018a). Introduction to conceptualizing writing. *Educational Psychologist, 53*, 217–219.

Graham, S. (2018b). The writer(s)-within-community model of writing. *Educational Psychologist, 53*, 258–279.

Graham, S. (2018c). A writer(s)-within-community model of writing. In C. Bazerman, V. Berninger, D. Brandt, S. Graham, J. Langer, S. Murphy, … M. Schleppegrell (Eds.), *The lifespan development of writing* (pp. 272–325). Urbana, IL: National Council of English.

Graham, S. (2019). Changing how writing is taught. *Review of Research in Education, 43*, 277–303.

Graham, S., Cappizi, A., Harris, K. R., Hebert, M., & Morphy, P. (2014). Teaching writing to middle school students: A national survey. *Reading & Writing: An Interdisciplinary Journal, 27*(6), 1015–1042.

Graham, S., & Harris, K. R. (1996). Self-regulation and strategy instruction for students with writing and learning difficulties. In S. Ransdell & M. Levy (Eds.), *Science of writing: Theories, methods, individual differences, and applications* (pp. 347–360). Mahwah, NJ: Lawrence Erlbaum.

Graham, S., & Harris, K. R. (2000). The role of self-regulation and transcription skills in writing and writing development. *Educational Psychologist, 35*, 3–12.

Graham, S., & Harris, K. R. (2017). Evidence-based writing practices: A meta-analysis of existing meta-analyses. In R. Fidalgo, K. R. Harris, & M. Braaksma (Eds.), *Design principles for teaching effective writing: Theoretical and empirical grounded principles* (pp. 13–37). Hershey, PA: Brill Editions.

Graham, S., & Harris, K. R. (2018). An examination of the design principles underlying a Self-Regulated Strategy Development Study based on the Writers in Community Model. *Journal of Writing Research, 10*, 139–187.

Graham, S., Harris, K. R., & Hebert, M. (2011). *Informing writing: The benefits of formative assessment*. Washington, DC: Alliance for Excellence in Education.

Graham, S., Harris, K. R., & McKeown, D. (2013). The writing of students with LD and a meta-analysis of SRSD writing intervention studies: Redux. In L. Swanson, K. R. Harris, & S. Graham (Eds.), *Handbook of learning disabilities* (2nd ed., pp. 405–438). New York: Guilford Press.

Graham, S., Kiuhara, S., McKeown, D., & Harris, K. R. (2012). A meta-analysis of writing instruction for students in the elementary grades. *Journal of Educational Psychology, 104*, 879–896.

Graham, S., & Perin, D. (2007). A meta-analysis of writing instruction for adolescent students. *Journal of Educational Psychology, 99*, 445–476.

Graham, S., Wijekumar, K., Harris, K.R., Lei, P., Fishman, E., Ray, A., & Houston, J. (2019). Writing skills, knowledge, motivation, and strategic behavior predict students' persuasive writing performance in the context of robust writing instruction. *Elementary School Journal*, *119*, 487–510.

Hand, B., & Prain, V. (2002). Teachers implementing writing-to-learn strategies in junior secondary science: A case study. *Science Education*, *86*(6), 737–755.

Harris, K., & Graham, S. (1985). Improving learning disabled students' composition skills: Self-control strategy training. *Learning Disability Quarterly*, *8*, 27–36.

Harris, K. R., & Graham, S. (2018). Self-regulated strategy development: Theoretical bases, critical instructional elements, and future research. In R. Fidalgo, K. R. Harris, & M. Braaksma (Eds.), *Design principles for teaching effective writing: Theoretical and empirical grounded principles* (pp. 119–151). Leiden, The Netherlands: Brill.

Harris, K. R., Graham, S., MacArthur, C., Reid, R., & Mason, L. (2011). Self-regulated learning processes and children's writing. In B. Zimmerman & D. H. Schunk(Eds.), *Handbook of self-regulation of learning and performance* (pp. 187–202). NY: Routledge.

Harris, K. R., Graham, S., & Mason, L. (2006). Improving the writing, knowledge, and motivation of struggling young writers: Effects of Self-Regulated Strategy development with and without peer support. *American Educational Research Journal*, *43*, 295–340.

Harris, K. R., Graham, S., Mason, L., & Friedlander, B. (2008). *Powerful writing strategies for all students*. Baltimore, MD: Brookes.

Harris, K. R., Lane, K., Graham, S., Driscoll, S., Sandmel, K., Brindle, M., & Schatschneider, C. (2012). Practice-based professional development for strategies instruction in writing: A randomized controlled study. *Journal of Teacher Education*, *63*, 103–119.

Hayes, J., & Flower, L. (1980). Identifying the organization of writing processes. In L. Gregg & E. Steinberg (Eds.), *Cognitive processes in writing* (pp. 3–30). Hillsdale, NJ: Lawrence Erlbaum.

Hayes, J. R. (2012). Modeling and remodeling writing. *Written Communication*, *29*(3), 369–388.

MacArthur, C., Graham, S., & Harris, K. R. (2004). Insights from instructional research on revision with struggling writers. In L. Allal, L. Chanquoy, & P. Largy (Eds.), *Revision: Cognitive and instructional processes* (pp. 125–138). Boston, MA: Kluwer.

MacArthur, C., Schwartz, S., Graham, S., Molloy, D., & Harris, K. R. (1996). Integration of strategy instruction into a whole language classroom: A case study. *Learning Disabilities Research and Practice*, *11*, 168–176.

McCutchen, D. (1988). "Functional automaticity" in children's writing: A problem of metacognitive control. *Written Communication*, *5*, 306–324.

Moran, M., Schumaker, J., & Vetter, A. (1981). *Teaching a paragraph organization strategy to learning disabled adolescents*. (*Research Report 54*). Lawrence, KS: Institute for Research in Learning Disabilities.

Olson, C. B., & Land, R. (2007). A cognitive strategies approach to reading and writing instruction for English language learners in secondary school. *Research in the Teaching of English*, *41*(3), 269–303.

Plimpton, G. (1958). *Writers at work: The Paris review interviews. first series*. London: Secker & Warburg.

Plimpton, G. (1967). *Writers at work: The Paris review interviews. Third series*. New York: Viking.

Rijlaarsdam, G., Van Den Bergh, H., Couzijn, M., Janssen, T., Braaksma, M., Tillema, M., ... Raedts, M. (2012). Writing. In K. R. Harris, S. Graham, & T. Urdan (Eds.), *APA educational psychology handbook* (Vol. 3, pp. 189–227). Washington, DC: American Psychological Association.

Santangelo, T., Harris, K. R., & Graham, S. (2016). Self-regulation and writing: An overview and meta-analysis. In C. MacArthur, S. Graham, & J. Fitzgerald (Eds.), *Handbook of writing research* (Vol. 2, pp. 174–193). New York: Guilford Press.

Scardamalia, M., & Bereiter, C. (1986). Written composition. In M. Wittrock (Ed.), *Handbook of research on teaching* (3rd ed., pp. 778–803). New York: Macmillan.

Smagorinsky, P., & Mayer, R. (2014). Learning to be literate. In R. Sawyer (Ed.), *The Cambridge handbook of learning sciences* (2nd ed., pp. 605–625). Cambridge: Cambridge University Press.

Troia, G., & Graham, S. (2017). Use and acceptability of adaptations to classroom writing instruction and assessment practices for students with disabilities: A survey of grade 3-8 teachers. *Learning Disabilities Research & Practice*, *32*, 257–269.

Young, R., Becker, A., & Pike, K. (1970). *Rhetoric: Discovery and change*. New York: Harcourt.

Zimmerman, B., & Risemberg, R. (1997). Becoming a self-regulated writer: A social cognitive perspective. *Contemporary Educational Psychology*, *22*, 73–101.

10

MATHEMATICS STRATEGY INTERVENTIONS

Kristie Newton
TEMPLE UNIVERSITY, USA

In mathematics, a strategy can be defined as "a general approach for accomplishing a task or solving a problem that may include sequences of steps to be executed, as well as the rationale behind the use and effectiveness of these steps" (Star et al., 2015, p. 26). For example, a student may always approach a quadratic equation by using the quadratic formula (which involves a particular sequence of steps), even though some quadratics can be solved in other ways (e.g., by factoring). Some experts prefer to first "clear the denominator" when they encounter a linear equation with a fraction in front of parentheses (e.g., $\frac{1}{3}(x+6)=4$ becomes $x+6=12$), whereas a student struggling to learn algebra may generally prefer to use the distributive property whenever parentheses are involved, because it is familiar and reliable (Newton, Star, & Lynch, 2010; Star & Newton, 2009).

When students hold misconceptions, their general approach may lead to errors. For example, a student may believe that common denominators are always necessary for operating with fractions, leading him or her to use that strategy to multiply two fractions. Studies identifying common errors can help illuminate misconceptions and poor strategies that need to be targeted as part of an intervention. Therefore, in the first part of this chapter I overview major errors documented in the literature, then I present some interventions designed to target these errors.

As illustrated above, sometimes there are multiple valid strategies for solving mathematics problems. Therefore, in the second part of the chapter I focus on interventions that promote flexible problem solving. "Procedural flexibility includes identifying and implementing multiple methods to solve algebra problems, as well as choosing the most appropriate method" (Star et al., 2015, p. 2). As with the strategy of clearing the denominator described above, employing alternative strategies can make problems easier to solve in some way (e.g., fewer steps). Experts demonstrate this kind of flexibility (Star & Newton, 2009), but researchers have found that it is slow to develop in students (Newton, Lange, & Booth, 2019).

Both erroneous and flexible strategy use can be viewed through Siegler's Overlapping Waves Theory (OWT), which helps to explain how strategy use changes over time. Children typically know multiple ways to solve a given problem; with practice, they begin to use more accurate and efficient strategies (Fazio, DeWolf, & Siegler, 2016; Opfer & Siegler, 2007). The development of accurate, efficient strategies is not smooth or linear. For example, to find the total number of objects given two sets, a child might sometimes count all of the objects, whereas other times the child might use a memorized addition fact to find the total. With practice and feedback, correct strategies replace incorrect ones, and more efficient strategies replace less efficient ones. This chapter focuses on both erroneous and alternative strategies, specifically for fractions and early algebra, and it overviews interventions for addressing errors and promoting flexibility. Algebra has been identified as a gatekeeper and a major concern of researchers and educators interested in mathematics learning (National Mathematics Advisory Panel, 2008). Fractions represent critical prerequisite knowledge for algebra learning that cause difficulties for many children, therefore receiving increased attention in the literature in recent years (Siegler, Fazio, Bailey, & Zhou, 2013). Although whole number knowledge and basic arithmetic are foundational to both fractions and algebra, these topics have received significant attention in the strategy literature. Interested readers are encouraged to seek out that work (e.g., Baroody & Dowker, 2003; Carpenter, Fennema, & Franke, 1996; Shrager & Siegler, 1998; Vanbinst, Ghesquière, & De Smedt, 2012; Verschaffel & De Corte, 1993; Verschaffel, Luwel, Torbeyns, & Van Dooren, 2009). Given space limitations, the current chapter is by no means an exhaustive review of the literature on strategies and strategy interventions related to fractions and algebra.

INCORRECT STRATEGIES

Errors with Fractions

The challenge posed by fractions, along with the important role of fractions for learning algebra, has resulted in increased attention for this topic (Siegler et al., 2013). Because fractions do not have all of the same properties as whole numbers, children must adjust their thinking to accommodate this "new" kind of number. If they do not, it may lead to errors based on misconceptions about fractions, even as they try to integrate information from instruction (Siegler, Thompson, & Schneider, 2011; Stafylidou & Vosniadou, 2004).

Knowledge of fraction magnitudes, or relative sizes of fractions, is especially critical for later mathematics learning. It predicts overall mathematics achievement as well as learning in algebra (Booth, Newton, & Twiss-Garrity, 2014; Siegler et al., 2011). In their study of 200 students, ages 10–16, Stafylidou and Vosniadou (2004) analyzed responses and justifications to ordering tasks and identified different categories of misconceptions students held as they learned about fractions. For example, students may believe that ⅓ is smaller than ⅚ because 3 and 4 are smaller than 5 and 6. In this case, they are treating the numbers as if they are all whole numbers. As students learn about the size of fractional parts relative to the denominator, they may erroneously claim that ¾ is smaller than ⅓ because the larger numbers indicate smaller fractions. Fazio et al. (2016) found that low performing students at a community college used the "bigger denominator" strategy frequently for comparing fractions, resulting in many errors. On the other hand, Malone and Fuchs (2017) found the whole number error to be especially pervasive among a group of at-risk fourth graders.

Students also make a variety of errors with fraction arithmetic, often following predictable patterns (Braithwaite, Pyke, & Siegler, 2017; Newton, Willard, & Teufel, 2014; Siegler & Pyke, 2013). As with comparing fractions, they make errors by overgeneralizing their knowledge of whole numbers. A well-documented example is treating fraction addition as two separate whole number addition problems, erroneously adding across numerators and denominators (e.g., $\frac{1}{2} + \frac{2}{3} = \frac{3}{5}$). Students also make errors by overgeneralizing rules for fraction arithmetic. A student using the incorrect strategy above might instead be thinking of fraction multiplication, for which you multiply across numerators and denominators. Another common error in this category would be to find (or keep) a common denominator when it is not appropriate to do so, such as with fraction multiplication (e.g., $\frac{2}{5} \times \frac{3}{5} = \frac{6}{5}$) or fraction division (e.g., $\frac{6}{5} \div \frac{3}{5} = \frac{2}{5}$). Students making this error have most likely learned how to add fractions, in which case a common denominator is needed.

Interventions

The Institute of Education Sciences (IES) practice guide (Siegler et al., 2010) for effective fraction instruction offers several recommendations for targeting the erroneous strategies described above. The two recommendations with moderate (as opposed to minimal) research-based evidence are as follows. First, students need to "recognize that fractions are numbers and that they expand the number system beyond whole numbers" (p. 19). Interventions that make use of number lines in particular are recommended, given they can assist students in understanding the place of fractions within the number system (Siegler et al., 2010; Wu, 2009). The Common Core State Standards for mathematics recommends introducing fractions using number lines to students as early as third grade (NGA Center & CCSSO, 2010). Second, students need to "understand why procedures for computations make sense" (Siegler et al., 2010, p. 26).

Number Lines. Wu (2009) posited that making use of number lines as a teaching tool provides coherence to the study of numbers. "In particular, regardless of whether a number is a whole number, a fraction, a rational number, or an irrational number, it takes up its natural place on this line" (p. 8). Number lines can support students' understanding of magnitude and equivalence, as well as computations with fractions. Unfortunately, research focused on number line interventions has been scarce. Shin and Bryant (2015) synthesized the fraction intervention research that targeted students struggling to learn mathematics. Across 17 studies, most interventions included concrete and visual representations. However, none of them included number lines.

In a recent study, Hamdan and Gunderson (2017) found a causal effect for number line training. Second and third grade students learning about fractions using a number line out-performed students who were introduced to fractions with an area model on a transfer task that involved fraction comparison. Only the students using a number line representation were able to use what they had learned to compare two fractions.

Fuchs and colleagues (Fuchs, Malone, Schumacher, Namkung, & Wang, 2017) recently reported on the impact of a multi-year program to target at-risk students' fraction knowledge by emphasizing fraction magnitude, including the use of number lines. In a series of studies, they compared performance for students involved in the intervention to a business-as-usual condition, where the primary focus was on a part-whole interpretation of fractions. Students in the intervention group outperformed the control each year on the number line estimation task, which asked students to place fractions and mixed numbers on a number line marked 0 and 2 at the endpoints. Students in the intervention group also outperformed control on addition and subtraction of fractions and mixed numbers. Finally, the intervention group outperformed control on a set of released items from the National Assessment of Educational Progress (NAEP) that emphasized magnitude and part-whole equally.

Over several years of the project, Fuchs and colleagues (Fuchs et al., 2017) tested the effect of additional supports beyond the emphasis on magnitude. For example, in year 2 they varied the type of practice students experienced. One group was focused on fluency, while the other was focused on explaining their thinking. Although no significant difference was found for the three fraction measures, they did find a moderating effect for working memory. In particular, students with very low working memory benefited more from the explaining condition, while students with high working memory benefited more from the fluency practice. However, given that a larger proportion of students benefited from fluency practice, this form of practice was included in the program for subsequent years.

In year 3, additive and multiplicative word problem conditions were included using schema-based instruction, where students were taught to recognize the problem type and to represent the type with a number sentence or visual display. A control group focused on identifying key words in the word problems. The multiplicative group outperformed the additive and control groups on multiplicative word problems and outperformed the control group on additive word problems. The additive group outperformed the other two groups on additive problems but performed similarly to the control group on multiplicative word problems (Fuchs et al., 2017).

In year 4, the researchers compared the added effect of *supported* self-explanations compared to training in solving multiplicative word problems (Fuchs et al., 2017, 2016). Rather than requiring at-risk students to produce their own explanations, self-explanations were modeled and the students analyzed, discussed, and elaborated on them. On word problems, students in the word problem group tended to outperform the explanation group. However, for both magnitude comparison and quality of explanations, students in the supported self-explanation group tended to outperform the word problem group. Moreover, students with both high and low working memory performed similarly in this condition.

The work by Fuchs and colleagues (Fuchs et al., 2017, 2016) described above underscores the importance of emphasizing fraction magnitudes, including the use of number lines, to promote early fraction knowledge. As noted by the authors, their program targeted fourth grade standards, and so additional research is needed "to address the challenges associated with multiplying and dividing fractions as well as other complex mathematics curricular targets" (p. 638).

Understanding Why Procedures Work. Mathematics educators have long held an interest in promoting deep understanding of fraction procedures, suggesting that simply knowing how to compute with fractions is insufficient in many ways. Highlighting this distinction, Skemp (1976) referred to knowing "how" as having an *instrumental understanding*, while knowing both "how and why" suggests a *relational understanding*. For adding fractions, this distinction would suggest, on the one hand, knowing that you need to find common denominators to add ½ and ⅓ versus, on the other, knowing that you need to find common denominators so that the fractions are renamed using same-sized parts, making it easy to find out the total number of those parts.

More broadly, Hiebert and Lefevre (1986) characterized *conceptual knowledge* "as knowledge that is rich in relationships" (p. 3). This characterization of knowledge could include the latter example above, as well as other important relationships. For example, you might know that ½ and ⅓ can also be renamed as decimals and then added, and that the sum is equivalent to the one obtained using fractions. You might also be able to estimate the sum, knowing it must be slightly larger than ½, the first addend. Unfortunately, even when students can accurately identify which fraction is the larger one or estimate the magnitude of each fraction, many are unsuccessful at estimating the sum of the two fractions (Braithwaite, Tian, & Siegler, 2018; Cramer & Wyberg, 2007). This lack of understanding, as well as errors such as the overgeneralizations described above, has prompted researchers and educators to search for ways to support students in making sense of fraction computation.

Visual Representations. As indicted above, the number line is an important representation for understanding fractions, and Fuchs and colleagues (2017) have reported good success at integrating this representation into a program designed to strengthen children's understanding of fraction magnitudes. Research is needed to extend this work to fraction computation. On the other hand, extensive research has focused on concrete manipulatives for visually representing fractions, in order to help students make sense of them. Research on the use of manipulatives in mathematics and science generally supports fading from concrete to abstract representations, as suggested by Bruner's modes of representation (Fyfe, McNeil, Son, & Goldstone, 2014). According to Bruner, the use of concrete and pictorial models should precede work with symbols only. Students need support linking these representations, especially the pictorial and symbolic ones. A meta-analysis focused on fraction skills found that a concrete to abstract progression showed promise for students with disabilities, although more research is needed (Ennis & Losinksi, 2019).

Word Problems. Building on extensive research by Carpenter and colleagues that focused on children's strategies for solving whole number problems (Carpenter et al., 1996), Empson and Levy (2011) emphasized word problems as a critical tool for sense-making with fractions. They recommended a progression of problem types with instructional support to help formalize student thinking about these problems. For example, when asked an equal sharing problem about four children sharing three cookies, a student may draw a picture of a cookie, split it into four parts, and distribute each part to a person. Repeating this process for each cookie results in three one-fourths for each person. In response to this strategy, a teacher might provide a number sentence to match the drawing, such as ¼ + ¼ + ¼ = ¾. These researchers emphasized that a key aspect of this approach involves making mathematical ideas and properties explicit by linking students' strategies directly to the mathematical sentences that represent them.

Summary

There is a long history of educators and psychologists promoting sense-making in mathematics. According to the IES practice guide for effective fraction instruction (Siegler et al., 2010), two general areas of sense-making for fractions are well-supported by research. First, students need to understand that fractions are numbers. Second, students need to understand why fraction procedures work the way they do. Without these understandings, students tend to overgeneralize their prior knowledge in ways that are not appropriate. Interventions targeting these errors highlight *representations* as key to fostering understanding and sense-making. Representing fractions on the number line, with concrete manipulatives and within word problems are all important for fostering deep understanding and appropriate strategy use.

Errors with Algebra

Booth and colleagues (Booth, Barbieri, Eyer, & Paré-Blagoev, 2014) analyzed the errors of Algebra I students across five school districts in four states, in order to understand not only which errors were most common but also which ones were most detrimental to algebra achievement as measured by standardized test items. Based on the extant literature, they coded for conceptual errors with variables, fractions, negatives, operations, mathematical properties, and equality/inequality. For comparison, they also coded for errors with arithmetic.

Across the year, the most prevalent errors were those involving negatives, arithmetic, variables, and the equal sign. A more nuanced analysis revealed a time sensitive aspect for the contribution of particular errors to the end of year assessment scores. For example, while negative number errors were prevalent throughout the year, making those errors at the end of the year was predictive of lower scores on the end of year assessment items. A similar result was found for arithmetic. Errors with equal/inequality became increasingly prevalent throughout the year, and making these errors in the middle or end of the year was predictive of lower end of year scores. Making errors with variables, such as combining unlike terms, in the first part of the year also predicted lower end of year scores.

Some errors that were not among the most common ones were still predictive of end of year scores. In particular, students who began the year making errors with operations (e.g., treating $5 + x$ as $5x$) and with properties (e.g., treating $5 - x$ as $x - 5$) were more likely to have lower end of year algebra scores.

Interventions

The IES practice guide for improving algebra knowledge outlines three research-based recommendations (Star et al., 2015). The first recommendation is to use solved problems, also known as worked examples, to help students analyze and reason about algebraic strategies. The second recommendation is to help students to notice and make use of underlying structures, including the presence and placement of variables and symbols, in algebra problems so that they can see similarities across problem types. The final recommendation is for students to learn and choose from multiple strategies when solving algebra problems. These first two, worked examples and noticing structure, are addressed in this section. The recommendation to learn and use multiple strategies is addressed in the following section, which is focused on procedural flexibility.

Worked Examples. The use of worked examples, which includes a problem presented along with solution method, has a long history in the cognitive and educational psychology literature, particularly for learning mathematics (Atkinson, Derry, Renkl, & Wortham, 2000). Research generally supports the use of worked examples early in the skill acquisition process, along with prompts for self-explanations so that the learner is asked to elaborate on what is presented in the example. For optimal learning, worked examples are interleaved with problems for the learners to solve.

Worked examples with self-explanation prompts have been used along with practice problems to effectively support learning in algebra classrooms. Incorrect examples may be especially important for supporting conceptual knowledge of algebra (Booth, Lange, Koedinger, & Newton, 2013), given they are designed to target common errors/misconceptions. Students with low prior knowledge seem to benefit most from either incorrect worked examples (Barbieri & Booth, 2016) or a combination of correct and incorrect examples (Booth et al., 2015). In a recent study, Barbieri, Miller-Cotto, and Booth (2019) found that eighth graders prone to making conceptual errors as they practiced graphing-related skills benefited more from studying correct and incorrect examples with visual signaling cues than from worked examples with self-explanations. These visual cues were designed to signal important conceptual features in the problems, such as identifying slope and y-intercept within the worked example. Students who made fewer errors during practice problems benefited similarly from worked examples with self-explanations and with visual signaling cues.

Noticing and Using Structure. To mathematicians, noticing and using structure is a fundamental aspect of doing mathematics, so fundamental that mathematics can be described as "the science of structure" (Newton & Sword, 2018, p. 33). In algebra, structure can be thought of as "the underlying mathematical features and relationships of an expression, representation, or equation" (Star et al., 2015, p. 6). As noted above, feature knowledge such as knowledge of the equal sign, negatives, and variables is critical to success in algebra. Noticing structure means noticing how these features are arranged in an algebraic representation and being able to see meaning in those arrangements. For example, a student who notices structure can clearly understand that $2+3+x=10$ and $2+3=x+10$ have quite different meanings, despite the surface similarities.

Experts including mathematicians assert that using precise language can support an understanding of structure (Newton & Sword, 2018; National Governors Association Center for Best Practices & the Council of Chief State School Officers, 2010; Star et al., 2015). For example, they caution against imprecise language such as stating, "two negatives make a positive," because although a negative times a negative results in a positive number, a negative plus a negative does not. Students sometimes overgeneralize these kinds of imprecise statements, making errors such as thinking $-5a - 4a$ is $9a$ (Vlassis, 2004).

One way to capture students' noticing of structure is to measure errors while encoding equations (McNeil & Alibali, 2004). Booth and Davenport (2013) measured feature encoding of algebra by displaying an algebraic equation on a screen for 5 seconds and then asking students to recreate the equation on their paper after it disappears from the screen. Their findings confirm that feature knowledge of algebra supports feature encoding and predicts the ability to solve algebraic equations.

Varying the Format. The equal sign is one feature that has received significant attention in the literature. As noted in the example above, the placement of the equal sign matters. Students who view the equal sign as an indication to find an answer may just add all of the constants together no matter their placement in the equation (e.g., erroneously finding 15 as the value of x for $2+3=x+10$). In a study by McNeil and Alibali (2004), fourth graders making this error frequently encoded non-conventional equations as if they were conventional ones, with all to-be-added terms on the left-hand side of the equal sign (e.g., encoding $4 + 5 = 2 + \_\_$ as $4 + 5 + 2 = \_\_$). Although in late elementary school most students have developed a basic relational understanding of the equal sign, where they recognize it as an indication that two expressions have the same value, a robust understanding of equivalence continues to develop through middle school (Fyfe, Matthews, Amsel, McEldoon, & McNeil, 2018; Rittle-Johnson, Matthews, Taylor, & McEldoon, 2011).

A simple, yet effective intervention for addressing equal sign errors is to more frequently pose unconventional arithmetic problems so that students are not overly accustomed to all terms being on the left of the equal sign, with only a blank for the answer on the right. Under the CCSS, students are expected to be presented with simple, unconventional problems as early as first grade (National Governors Association Center for Best Practices & the Council of Chief State School Officers, 2010). McNeil, Fyfe, and Dunwiddie (2015) provided this kind of modified practice as part of an intervention with second graders. Modified practice workbooks in their study included unconventional problems (e.g., $\_\_ = 3 + 5$ and $8 = \_\_ + 5$), whereas students in a control group received conventional problems to practice (e.g., $3 + 5 = \_\_$). To support a relational understanding of equivalence, the equal sign was sometimes replaced with words that conveyed its meaning, such as "is the same amount as". Finally, the problems were organized such that students encountered several in a row with the same sum (e.g., $\_\_ = 3 + 5$ and $\_\_ = 2 + 6$). Students in the modified workbook condition outperformed students in the control, with lasting effects.

Although the modified practice workbooks (McNeil et al., 2015) resulted in positive, long-term effects compared to traditional practice, not all students achieved a robust understanding of the equal sign. Building on that work, McNeil and colleagues designed and tested a more comprehensive intervention for targeting equal sign knowledge (McNeil, Hornburg, Brletic-Shipley, & Matthews, 2019). In their study of 142 second grade students, an active control group was compared to a comprehensive intervention group. The active control group received practice problems similar to the intervention in McNeil et al. (2015). The comprehensive intervention group included three additional elements: (1) introduction of the equal sign in non-arithmetic situations (e.g., $5 = 5$); (2) concreteness fading, where representations became more abstract over time; and (3) prompts for comparing problem formats and strategies (including incorrect ones). Students randomly assigned to the comprehensive intervention improved significantly more in their understanding of equivalence than students assigned to the active control classrooms, with large effect.

Given that students are introduced to the equal sign very early, much of the research on this topic has been conducted with elementary school children. However, as noted by Booth et al. (2014), students taking algebra make errors related to equal sign knowledge, and these errors predict lower end of year algebra scores. Therefore, more research is needed on how to remediate this knowledge for students learning algebra.

Representations. Asking students to discuss, compare, and move between different algebraic representations, such as equations, graphs, word problems, and diagrams, can support student understanding of underlying algebraic structures (National Council of Teachers of Mathematics, 2000; Star et al., 2015). Additionally, some researchers and educators recommend physical models to support student learning. A balance scale, for example, provides students with a model for understanding that the equal sign indicates that two expressions have the same value. Related, it also provides insight into the idea that the same operation is performed to both sides in order to maintain that equivalency. In a study with 40 eighth graders, Vlassis (2002) found that the model was limited, however, in its ability to help students understand negatives within the equation.

As with fractions, number lines are one way to represent negatives. Tsang, Blair, Bofferding, and Schwartz (2015) compared three instructional conditions for fourth graders learning about negatives, and all three conditions incorporated the number line as the primary representation. The Jumping condition included a small figure that moved along the number line in a way that corresponded to an addition problem (e.g., for 5 + −3, starting at 5 and "jumping" to the left three spaces). The Stacking condition included magnetic manipulatives with different colors to represent positives and negatives. For 5 + −3, five blue blocks are placed on the number line, between 0 and 5. Three red blocks are then stacked on top of the blue ones, starting at 5. Each red and blue pair "cancel" each other, so two blue blocks are left. The Folding condition involved place the 5 blue blocks between 0 and 5, and the 3 red blocks between 0 and −3. Then, the blocks were folded toward each other, with three of them "canceling" each other out. The physical movement of folding in this condition was designed to emphasize the underlying symmetrical structure inherent in the number line. Students in the Folding condition outperformed students in the other two groups on items not yet taught, such as negative fractions and algebra readiness problems (e.g., 2 + −3 = __ + −1).

Comparing. The use of worked examples as an effective instructional tool is not limited to single examples paired with prompts for self-explanation. Another approach supported by research is to use two worked examples, presented side-by-side, in order help students to make comparisons and draw important conclusions. In a study that incorporated pairs of side-by-side worked examples into year-long algebra classrooms, greater use of the comparison materials was associated with greater gains in procedural knowledge (Star et al., 2015). These materials included four types of comparisons, often involving one problem worked in two ways. For example, a correct method of solving a problem might be compared to an incorrect method. Alternatively, one method might highlight why the other one works. Or, a general and alternative method might be compared in order to promote flexible problem solving. Other times, two different problems might be compared. For example, two variations of a problem might be compared in order to highlight a particular idea (e.g., slope), or two visually similar problems might be compared in order to highlight an important difference (e.g., $x^3 \cdot x^4$ and $(x^3)^4$).

Ziegler and Stern (2016) studied this last type of comparison in particular and found long-term benefits for sixth graders with little or no prior knowledge of algebra. Rather than studying worked out examples, these students were exposed to direct instruction as a means to compare and contrast problems with similar features (e.g., $3x + 3x + 3x$ and $3x \cdot 3x \cdot 3x$). The contrast group was presented with addition and multiplication problems simultaneously, whereas the sequential group was presented with addition problems followed by multiplication problems. Although the sequential group outperformed the contrast group on immediate learning, the contrast group outperformed the sequential group on follow-up measures at three time points.

Comparison of this kind holds promise for alleviating some of the errors identified by Booth et al. (2014). Specifically, comparing expressions with similar features but different operations (e.g., $5 + x$ and $5x$) or different ordering of terms (e.g., $5 - x$ and $x - 5$) may help students understand and remember important ideas that are critical for success in algebra. It may also be helpful for addressing errors with negative numbers. During interviews with students about integer arithmetic, Bishop, Lamb, Philipp, Whitacre, and Schappelle (2016) found that some students naturally used these kinds of comparisons when they explained their reasoning about integers. In their comparisons, students varied the sign of the numbers (e.g., $6 - 2$ and $6 - (-2)$), the operations (e.g., $-8 + 3$ and $-8 - 3$), and features such as the order of the addends (e.g., $-5 + 2$ and $5 + -2$) in order to logically reason about what must be true or not true for a given problem. For example, a student reasoned that $6 - (-2)$ cannot be 4 because $6 - 2$ is 4.

Although these kinds of comparisons were not prevalent in the Bishop et al. (2016) study, they occurred across a variety of grade levels. The researchers therefore suggested that it may be fruitful to purposefully incorporate comparisons of this sort into instruction, along with prompts to support students' reasoning about them. They also suggested that students have more opportunities to make conjectures about how operations work, to encourage students to think more about the underlying mathematical structures. One teacher who regularly did this found her students were able to correctly conjecture that dividing across numerators and denominators is a valid approach to fraction division (Newton et al., 2014), a fact that is often obscured through traditional instruction. Systematic research is needed to understand the effects of this kind of intervention.

Summary

As with fraction knowledge, knowledge of algebra requires sense-making. Students need to understand algebraic symbols and the meanings that are conveyed by them and the way they are organized. These understandings can support deep and accurate strategy use in algebra. The IES practice guide for algebra learning recommends the use of worked examples to help students understand algebraic strategies.

Incorrect worked examples can be especially helpful for targeting errors based on common misconceptions. A second recommendation includes helping students notice and use structure. Similar to fractions, representations such as number lines, concrete manipulatives, and word problems, can help. Graphs and equations are also critically important representations for understanding algebraic structures. Varying the format of the equations can highlight important structures such as the equal sign. Comparison also supports noticing and using structure, as it can highlight important similarities or differences between representations that might otherwise be obscured.

ALTERNATIVE CORRECT STRATEGIES

Flexibility with Fractions

Research on flexibility with fractions is scarce, but some research suggests that competent students and experts in mathematics are quite flexible with fractions. Smith (1995) interviewed students at the elementary, middle, and secondary levels about several ordering and equivalence tasks, to better understand their strategies and reasoning about fractions. His findings suggested that students skilled with fractions used a variety of strategies for solving problems, not just the traditional ones learned in school. In fact, they tended to use the most general strategy as a last resort, opting for strategies specific to the problem at hand. Their preferred strategies were often ones that made the problem easier in some way (e.g., required less computation).

Newton (2008) found a similar pattern for experts such as mathematicians, engineers, and high school mathematics teachers that took a fraction assessment designed for a study of preservice teachers. When asked to solve fraction computation items, they generally opted for strategies that made the problem easier for themselves. Out of 11 possible points for flexibility, they scored 8.44 points on average, compared to 2.27 for preservice teachers. Although not published as part of the study, one example expert strategy was to solve $6\frac{2}{5} - 2\frac{4}{5}$ by subtracting the whole numbers and then subtracting the fractions. Doing so resulted in a new subtraction problem, $4 - \frac{2}{5}$, which can be mentally calculated to be $3 - \frac{3}{5}$ based on the fact that two-fifths and three-fifths is one whole. A more common strategy was to rename $6 - \frac{2}{5}$ as $5 - \frac{7}{5}$ and then subtract like parts. In contrast, a strategy used frequently by preservice teachers was to rename both mixed numbers as improper fractions and then subtract numerators, keeping the denominator the same. The preservice teachers in this study generally used the strategy of changing mixed numbers to improper fractions whenever mixed numbers were involved, even when it required more steps.

A case study of a small special education classroom revealed that non-experts are capable of learning and using a variety of strategies for solving fraction problems (Newton et al., 2014). Interestingly, for some problems the more general approach led to errors for these students, whereas an efficient, alternative method led to success. For example, on an end-of-unit fraction assessment, 6 out of 11 students correctly solved $\frac{9}{14} \div \frac{1}{7}$ by dividing the numerators and dividing the denominators. On the other hand, three students attempted to solve the problem by multiplying by the reciprocal (i.e., $\frac{9}{14} \times \frac{7}{1}$), but they all made errors converting the product, $\frac{63}{14}$, to a mixed number. On the other hand, seven students correctly multiplied by the reciprocal to solve $\frac{2}{9} \div \frac{3}{8}$, which did not involve simplifying.

Of note is that four students used both methods successfully during the assessment. However, as mentioned previously the teacher in this classroom regularly introduced a new topic by asking students to make conjectures based on their prior knowledge. This atypical practice lends itself to the use of multiple strategies, since not all students will make the same conjectures each time. Based on the work of Bishop et al. (2016), it seems likely that the requests for conjectures about how things might work helped these students to focus on underlying structures and patterns. In the case of dividing across numerators and denominators, students may reason that since division is related to multiplication and fraction multiplication works by multiplying numerators and denominators, then fraction division should work similarly. Research is needed to better understand the role of conjecturing in the development of flexibility.

Representational flexibility with fractions, or an ability to move smoothly between different fraction representations (e.g., circle, rectangle, and number line), has been a focus for some researchers. Deliyianni, Gagatsis, Elia, and Panaoura (2016) examined the relationship between representational flexibility, problem solving with novel tasks, and understanding of fraction addition using confirmatory factor analysis. Findings suggest that problem solving and representational flexibility constitute major components of fraction understanding. Further, representational flexibility with fraction addition is better supported by the number line and rectangle representations than by circles. These results are consistent with standards documents for mathematics education. In particular, the National Council of Teachers of Mathematics (2000) forwarded problem solving and movement between representations as two important processes that students should experience in mathematics classrooms. And as noted above, the Common Core State Standards (National Governors Association Center for Best Practices & the Council of Chief State School Officers, 2010) recently asserted that the number line is a critical representation for learning fractions.

Flexibility with Algebra

Similar to fractions, flexibility in algebraic thinking is also a characteristic of experts. Star and Newton (2009) interviewed experts about their strategy choices when solving algebra problems, and they had a tendency to value and use cognitively efficient strategies. They typically justified strategy choices by saying a particular method was "easier." When prompted to elaborate, "easier" usually involved fewer steps but, more importantly, it referred to less need for written computation.

On the other hand, students struggling to learn algebra may be more concerned with methods that they can successfully use (Newton et al., 2010). This focus on accuracy may or may not involve the most efficient method. For example, a student might prefer clearing the denominator for problems such as $\frac{1}{3}(x+6)=4$ not because it is the method with the fewest steps, but because he or she is not confident about distributing the fraction without errors. This same student may use the distributive property for a problem such as $3(x+6)=15$ because it is most familiar and the student may be confident in using it successfully. These students are more likely to value efficiency when they are equally confident in different problem-solving strategies.

Flexibility in algebra is predicted by both procedural and conceptual knowledge (Schneider, Rittle-Johnson, & Star, 2011). However, students with both low and high prior algebra knowledge seem to appreciate efficiency in problem solving, even when they do not use more efficient methods (Newton et al., 2019). The third recommendation described above, learning and choosing from multiple strategies, is particularly relevant for promoting procedural flexibility with algebra (Star et al., 2015). By comparing and using different ways to solve the same problem, students are encouraged to notice problem features that make a particular strategy more efficient in some cases.

Interventions

Comparing. As noted above, comparing two worked examples presented side by side can help students draw conclusions about important ideas or strategies (Star et al., 2015). In particular, comparing a general strategy to a more efficient alternative can highlight when one strategy might be more efficient than the other one.

Relative to studying examples sequentially, comparing two examples side by side led to improved procedural knowledge and flexibility in a study involving seventh graders learning to solve equations (Rittle-Johnson & Star, 2007). The intervention in this study was specifically designed to help students attend to structural features that might make one method more efficient in some cases. For example, when solving $3(x + 5) + 4(x + 5) = 14$, students might notice the parentheses and then distribute as a first step to solving the equation. An alternative approach would rely on noticing that each set of parentheses contains the same expression; therefore, a first step can to be combine the two like expressions. The compare condition included prompts to help students notice these features and consider when the alternative method might be a good problem-solving choice. Students in another condition studied the same worked examples, but sequentially (on separate pages) and with prompts that avoided comparisons. The fact that both groups were exposed to both multiple solution methods highlights comparison as an effective intervention for accurate and efficient equation-solving strategies during early algebra learning.

In a follow-up study of seventh and eighth graders, Rittle-Johnson and Star (2009) explored the effects of different types of comparisons in algebra. In one condition, students compared different solution methods for the same problem. Students in another condition compared different problem types solved using the same solution method. The third condition involved comparing equivalent problems using the same method. These researchers found that comparing different methods for solving the same problem was more effective for conceptual knowledge and flexibility than the other two types of comparisons.

Some interventions have targeted *representational flexibility* in the context of algebra. Nistal, Van Dooren, and Verschaffel (2014) tested an intervention targeted at improving students' representational flexibility, conceptualized as the ability to make adaptive choices when choosing representations (e.g., table, graph, formula), to solve linear function problems. The intervention was individualized, in that it involved providing students with feedback on their accuracy using different representations to solve problems at pretest. It also included asking students to reflect on their representational choices and compare them to other (example) students' choices and reasons for making those choices. It was emphasized that the best choice may be depend on both the problem as well as the student (given not everyone has the same proficiency with different representations). Students in the intervention group learned and used representations to a similar extent as students in a control group. However, students who received the intervention solved problems with more speed and accuracy at posttest. Further analyses indicate that this improvement was a result of an improved representational flexibility. In other words, students chose representations for themselves that led to better accuracy at posttest compared to pretest.

Generating More than One Strategy. Comparing two worked examples, presented side by side, can lead to increased flexibility with algebra by providing opportunities to learn about and evaluate different solution strategies (Star et al., 2015a). However, "a specific learner's flexibility in using different methods … depends upon the familiarity of the specific problem at hand" (Atkinson et al., 2000, p. 185). One recommendation to help students gain fluency with a particular strategy is to interleave worked examples with practice problems. However, even when students have knowledge of more efficient strategies, they do not always use them regularly (Newton et al., 2019). The ability to generate multiple solution methods to a single algebra problem seems to be a key skill that helps explain the gap between *knowledge* (e.g., being able to recognize valid alternatives) and *use* of efficient strategies for solving algebra problems.

Asking students to generate a new way to solve an equation led to increased flexibility in a study of sixth grade students with no prior experience in algebra, compared to a control group that was asked to solve a new problem in the same way (Star & Seifert, 2006). Despite solving fewer problems overall, the two groups had similar levels of equation-solving accuracy at posttest. In this case, students were generating alternative solution strategies through invention. Another possibility is to ask students to generate more than one way to solve a problem by recalling methods they learned through studying worked examples. Research is needed to confirm whether this kind of activity can effectively support students learning to flexibly use a variety of problem-solving strategies.

LIMITATIONS AND FUTURE DIRECTIONS

Despite the many advances reported here, some gaps remain in our understanding of effective strategy interventions for fractions and algebra. For example, our knowledge of negatives is limited compared to their positive counterparts. Yet, errors with negatives prevent many students from being successful in algebra (Booth et al., 2014). Further, as noted above, more research is needed on ways to promote regular use of flexible strategies in algebra, such as asking students to solve the same problem in two ways once they have learned multiple strategies. Although there has been renewed interest in fraction knowledge recently, much of this research has focused on identifying challenges to learning fractions and finding effective interventions for faulty strategies (e.g., Fuchs et al., 2017; Siegler et al., 2013). Given the difficulties that children and adults have with fractions, this focus is a reasonable and laudable one. Yet, research on flexibility with fractions is scarce and so future directions should include ways to promote flexibility with fractions.

Much of the research reported here has focused on conceptual and procedural knowledge of fractions and algebra, such as the ability to order fractions or to solve linear equations. While this knowledge is clearly important, additional research is needed to understand and support problem solving with fractions and algebra. "Problem solving" sometimes refers to a student calculating an answer, even to a routine exercise, as opposed to studying a worked example (see Newton & Sword, 2018). I am instead referring to opportunities for students to apply knowledge to a new situation, often presented in the form of word problems. Jitendra, Harwell, Dupuis, and Karl (2017) have conducted extensive research on this kind of problem solving, with a focus on proportional reasoning. Proportions and proportional reasoning represent a bridge between fractions and algebra, making it a critical mathematical milestone in late middle school. Their works suggests that schema-based instruction, where students are taught to identify and represent the underlying structure of a problem, has been effective with general and special education students. The work of researchers like Empson and Levy (2011) builds on the premise that problem solving is important as a *means* for understanding fractions (not simply as an application of fraction knowledge). Future research should extend work presented in this chapter by considering the role of problem solving in learning fractions and algebra. For example, is problem solving compatible with the use of worked examples? If so, how can they work together to support learning?

Related, increased efforts to cross the boundaries of psychology and education are needed. Obersteiner, Dresler, Bieck, and Moeller (2019) recently reported on findings in these fields and in neuroscience, leading to recommendations for fraction instruction. Moreover, research in these fields should come together to support development and understanding of effective comprehensive interventions, such as those described by Fuchs et al. (2017) and McNeil et al. (2019). Interventions that are successful in short laboratory studies or controlled classroom studies sometimes fall short in the context of an ongoing and complicated classroom, for a variety of reason, including lack of implementation by teachers (Star et al., 2015). Attention, prior knowledge, fidelity, and many other factors can prevent even empirically supported practices from making the same impact in the classroom. Yet, for research on fractions and algebra to make a difference with students, the findings must be integrated into regular instruction.

REFERENCES

Atkinson, R., Derry, S. J., Renkl, A., & Wortham, D. (2000). Learning from examples: Instructional principles from the worked examples research. *Review of Educational Research, 70*(2), 181–214.

Barbieri, C., & Booth, J. L. (2016). Support for struggling students in algebra: Contributions of incorrect worked examples. *Learning and Individual Differences, 48*, 36–44.

Barbieri, C., Miller-Cotto, D., & Booth, J. L. (2019). Lessening the load of misconceptions: Design-based principles for algebra learning. *Journal of the Learning Sciences, 28*(3), 381–417.

Baroody, A. J., & Dowker, A. (2003). *The development of arithmetic concepts and skills: Constructing adaptive expertise. "Studies in mathematics thinking and learning"* series. (A. Schoenfeld, Ed.). Mahwah, NJ: Lawrence Erlbaum.

Bishop, J. P., Lamb, L. L., Philipp, R. A., Whitacre, I., & Schappelle, B. P. (2016). Leveraging structure: Logical necessity in the context of integer arithmetic. *Mathematical Thinking and Learning, 18*(3), 209–232.

Booth, J. L., Barbieri, C., Eyer, F., & Paré-Blagoev, E. J. (2014). Persistent and pernicious misconceptions in algebraic problem solving. *Journal of Problem Solving, 7*, 10–23.

Booth, J. L., & Davenport, J. L. (2013). The role of problem representation and feature knowledge in algebraic equation-solving. *The Journal of Mathematical Behavior, 32*(3), 415–423.

Booth, J. L., Lange, K. E., Koedinger, K. R., & Newton, K. J. (2013). Using example problems to improve student learning in algebra: Differentiating between correct and incorrect examples. *Learning and Instruction, 25*, 24–34.

Booth, J. L., Oyer, M. H., Paré-Blagoev, E. J., Elliot, A., Barbieri, C., Augustine, A. A., & Koedinger, K. R. (2015). Learning algebra by example in real-world classrooms. *Journal of Research on Educational Effectiveness, 8*(4), 530–551.

Booth, J. L., Newton, K. J., & Twiss-Garrity, L. (2014). The impact of fraction magnitude knowledge on algebra performance and learning. *Journal of Experimental Child Psychology, 118*,110-118.

Braithwaite, D. W., Pyke, A. A., & Siegler, R. S. (2017). A computational model of fraction arithmetic. *Psychological Review, 124*(5), 603–625.

Braithwaite, D. W., Tian, J., & Siegler, R. S. (2018). Do children understand fraction addition? *Developmental Science, 21*(4), 1–9.

Carpenter, T. P., Fennema, E., & Franke, M. L. (1996). Cognitively guided instruction: A knowledge based for reform in primary mathematics instruction. *The Elementary School Journal, 97*(1), 3–20.

Cramer, K. A., & Wyberg, T. (2007). When getting the right answers is not always enough: 2007 National Council of Teachers of Mathematics Y.. In M. Strutchens & W. G. Martin (Eds.), *The learning of mathematics: 2007 national council of teachers of mathematics Y* (pp. 205–220). Reston, VA: NCTM.

Deliyianni, E., Gagatsis, A., Elia, I., & Panaoura, A. (2016). Representational flexibility and problem-solving ability in fraction and decimal number addition: A structural model. *International Journal of Science and Mathematics Education, 14*(2), 397–417.

Empson, S. B., & Levy, L. (2011). *Extending children's mathematics: Fractions and decimals*. Portsmouth, NH: Heinemann.

Ennis, E. P., & Losinksi, M. (2019). Interventions to improve fraction skills for students with disabilities: A meta-analysis. *Exceptional Children, 85*(3), 367–386.

Fazio, L. K., DeWolf, M., & Siegler, R. S. (2016). Strategy use and strategy choice in fraction magnitude comparison. *Journal of Experimental Psychology: Learning, Memory, and Cognition, 42*(1), 1–16.

Fuchs, L. S., Malone, A. S., Schumacher, R. F., Namkung, J., & Wang, A. (2017). Fraction intervention for students with mathematics difficulties: Lessons learned from five randomized controlled trials. *Journal of Learning Disabilities, 50*(6), 631–639.

Fuchs, L. S., Schumacher, R. F., Long, J., Namkung, J., Malone, A., Wang, A., … Changas, P. (2016). Effects of intervention to improve at-risk fourth graders' understanding, calculations, and word problems with fractions. *Elementary School Journal, 116*(4), 625–651.

Fyfe, E. R., Matthews, P. G., Amsel, E., McEldoon, K. L., & McNeil, N. M. (2018). Assessing formal knowledge of math equivalence among algebra and pre-algebra students. *Journal of Educational Psychology, 110*(1), 87–101.

Fyfe, E. R., McNeil, N. M., Son, J. Y., & Goldstone, R. L. (2014). Concrete fading in mathematics and science instruction: A systematic review. *Educational Psychology Review, 26*(1), 9–25.

Hamdan, N., & Gunderson, E. A. (2017). The number line is a critical spatial-numerical representation: Evidence from a fraction intervention. *Developmental Psychology, 53*(3), 587–596.

Hiebert, J., & Lefevre, P. (1986). Conceptual and procedural knowledge in mathematics: An introductory analysis. In J. Hiebert (Ed.), *Conceptual and procedural knowledge: The case of mathematics* (pp. 1–27). Hillsdale, NJ: Lawrence Erlbaum.

Jitendra, A. K., Harwell, M. R., Dupuis, D. N., & Karl, S. R. (2017). A randomized trial of the effects of schema-based instruction on proportional problem-solving for students with mathematics problem-solving difficulties. *Journal of Learning Disabilities, 50*(3), 322–336.

Malone, A. S., & Fuchs, L. S. (2017). Error patterns in ordering fractions among at-risk fourth-grade students. *Journal of Learning Disabilities, 50*(3), 337–352.

McNeil, N. M., & Alibali, M. W. (2004). You'll see what you mean: Students encode equations based on their knowledge of arithmetic. *Cognitive Science, 28*, 451–466.

McNeil, N. M., Fyfe, E. R., & Dunwiddie, A. E. (2015). Arithmetic practice can be modified to promote understanding of mathematical equivalence. *Journal of Educational Psychology, 107*(2), 423–436.

McNeil, N. M., Hornburg, C. B., Brletic-Shipley, H., & Matthews, J. M. (2019). Improving children's understanding of mathematical equivalence via an intervention that goes beyond nontraditional arithmetic practice. *Journal of Educational Psychology*.

National Council of Teachers of Mathematics. (2000). *Principles and standards for school mathematics*. Reston, VA: Author.

National Governors Association Center for Best Practices & The Council of Chief State School Officers. (2010). *Common Core state standards for mathematics*. Washington, DC: Author.

National Mathematics Advisory Panel. (2008). *Foundation for success: The final report of the National Mathematics Advisory Panel*. Washington, DC: U.S. Department of Education.

Newton, K. J. (2008). An extensive analysis of preservice elementary teachers' knowledge of fractions. *American Educational Research Journal, 45*(4), 1080–1110.

Newton, K. J., Lange, K., & Booth, J. L. (2019, April). Mathematical flexibility: Aspects of a continuum and the role of prior knowledge. *Journal of Experimental Education*. https://doi.org/10.1080/00220973.2019.1586629

Newton, K. J., Star, J. R., & Lynch, K. (2010). Understanding the development of flexibility in struggling algebra students. *Mathematical Thinking and Learning, 12*(4), 282–305.

Newton, K. J., & Sword, S. (2018). *Mathematical learning and understanding in education*. New York, NY: Routledge.

Newton, K. J., Willard, C., & Teufel, C. (2014). Struggling sixth grade students' ways of solving fraction computation problems. *Elementary School Journal, 115*(1), 1–21.

Nistal, A. A., Van Dooren, W., & Verschaffel, L. (2014). Improving students' representational flexibility in linear-function problems: An intervention. *Educational Psychology, 34*(6), 763–786.

Obersteiner, A., Dresler, T., Bieck, S. M., & Moeller, K. (2019). Understanding fractions: Integrating results from mathematics education, cognitive psychology, and neuroscience. In A. Norton & M. Alibali (Eds.), *Constructing number: Merging perspectives from psychology and mathematics education* (pp. 135–162). New York: Springer.

Opfer, J. E., & Siegler, R. S. (2007). Representational change and children's numerical estimation. *Cognitive Psychology, 55*, 169–195.

Rittle-Johnson, B., Matthews, P. G., Taylor, R. S., & McEldoon, K. (2011). Assessing knowledge of mathematical equivalence: A construct modeling approach. *Journal of Educational Psychology, 103*, 85–104.

Rittle-Johnson, B., & Star, J. R. (2007). Does comparing solution methods facilitate conceptual and procedural knowledge? An experimental study on learning to solve equations. *Journal of Educational Psychology, 99*(3), 561–574.

Rittle-Johnson, B., & Star, J. R. (2009). Compared to what? The effects of different comparisons on conceptual knowledge and procedural flexibility for equation solving. *Journal of Educational Psychology, 101*(3), 529–544.

Schneider, M., Rittle-Johnson, B., & Star, J. R. (2011). Relations among conceptual knowledge, procedural knowledge, and procedural flexibility in two samples differing in prior knowledge. *Developmental Psychology, 47*(6), 1525–1538.

Shin, M., & Bryant, D. P. (2015). A synthesis of mathematical and cognitive performances of students with mathematics learning disabilities. *Journal of Learning Disabilities, 48*(1), 96–112. doi: 10.1177/0022219413508324.

Shrager, J., & Siegler, R. S. (1998). SCADS: A model of children's strategy choices and strategy discoveries. *Psychological Science, 9*(5), 405–410.

Siegler, R. S., Carpenter, T., Fennell, F., Geary, D., Lewis, J., Okamoto, Y., … Wray, J. (2010). *Developing effective fractions instruction for kindergarten through 8th grade: A practice guide* (NCEE #2010-4039). Washington, DC: National Center for Education Evaluation and Regional Assistance, Institute of Education Sciences, U.S. Department of Education. Retrieved from whatworks.ed.gov/publications/practiceguides

Siegler, R. S., Fazio, L. K., Bailey, D. H., & Zhou, X. (2013). Fractions: The new frontier for theories of numerical development. *Trends in Education, 17*(1), 13–19.

Siegler, R. S., & Pyke, A. A. (2013). Developmental and individual differences in understanding fractions. *Developmental Psychology, 49*, 1994-2004. doi: 10.1037/a0031200.

Siegler, R. S., Thompson, C. A., & Schneider, M. (2011). An integrated theory of whole number and fractions development. *Cognitive Psychology, 62*, 273–296.

Skemp, R. R. (1976). Relational understanding and instrumental understanding. *Mathematics Teaching, 77*, 20–26.

Smith, J. P. (1995). Competent reasoning with rational numbers. *Cognition and Instruction, 13*(1), 3–50.

Stafylidou, S., & Vosniadou, S. (2004). The development of students' understanding of the numerical value of fractions. *Learning and Instruction, 14*, 503–518.

Star, J. R., Caronongan, P., Foegen, A., Furgeson, J., Keating, B., Larson, M. R., … Zbiek, R. M. (2015). *Teaching strategies for improving algebra knowledge in middle and high school students* (NCEE 2014-4333). Washington,

DC: National Center for Education Evaluation and Regional Assistance (NCEE), Institute of Education Sciences, U.S. Department of Education. Retrieved from http://whatworks.ed.gov

Star, J. R., & Newton, K. J. (2009). The nature and development of experts' strategy flexibility for solving equations. *ZDM - The International Journal on Mathematics Education, 41*, 557–567.

Star, J. R., Pollack, C., Durkin, K., Rittle-Johnson, B., Lynch, K., Newton, K., & Gogolen, C. (2015). Learning from comparison in algebra. *Contemporary Educational Psychology, 40*, 41–54.

Star, J. R., & Seifert, C. (2006). The development of flexibility in equation solving. *Contemporary Educational Psychology, 31*(3), 280–300.

Tsang, J. M., Blair, K. P., Bofferding, L., & Schwartz, D. L. (2015). Learning to "see" less than nothing: Putting perceptual skills to work for learning numerical structure. *Cognition and Instruction, 33*(2), 154–197.

Vanbinst, K., Ghesquière, P., & De Smedt, B. (2012). Numerical magnitude representations and individual differences in children's arithmetic strategy use. *Mind, Brain, and Education, 6*(3), 129–136.

Verschaffel, L., & De Corte, E. (1993). A decade of research on word problem solving in Leuven: Theoretical, methodological, and practical outcomes. *Educational Psychology Review, 5*(3), 239–256.

Verschaffel, L., Luwel, K., Torbeyns, J., & Van Dooren, W. (2009). Conceptualizing, investigating, and enhancing adaptive expertise in elementary mathematics education. *European Journal of Psychology of Education, 24*(3), 335–359.

Vlassis, J. (2002). The balance model: Hindrance or support for the solving of linear equations with one unknown. *Educational Studies in Mathematics, 49*, 341–359.

Vlassis, J. (2004). Making sense of the minus sign or becoming flexible in "negativity." *Learning and Instruction, 14*, 469–484.

Wu, H. H. (2009). What's so sophisticated about elementary mathematics? *American Educator, 32*(3), 4–14.

Ziegler, E., & Stern, E. (2016). Consistent advantages of contrasted comparisons: Algebra learning under direct instruction. *Learning and Instruction, 41*, 41–51.

11

SCIENCE STRATEGY INTERVENTIONS

Doug Lombardi
UNIVERSITY OF MARYLAND, USA

Janelle M. Bailey
TEMPLE UNIVERSITY, USA

HISTORY OF STRATEGIES AND STRATEGIC PROCESSING IN SCIENCE EDUCATION

Strategic processing involves the use of cognitive and metacognitive strategies in learning. In science learning, learners use cognitive and metacognitive strategies to understand (a) scientific content in physics, chemistry, biology, Earth science, and other natural science domains; and (b) how scientists construct their understanding within these various domains (e.g., the practices of science or nature of what constitutes valid scientific knowledge). Thus, in science learning strategic processing is related to both the scientific domain or topic (see, for example, Greene et al., 2015) and the scientific tasks of investigating, explaining, and evaluating (see, for example, Dinsmore & Alexander, 2016).

Both scientific topics (e.g., force and motion) and tasks (e.g., conducting an experiment) are found at the task level per Dinsmore's (2017) Adaptive Model of Strategic Processing. Other levels in Dinsmore's model also apply to science learning. At the core of the model are strategic processing factors relating to quantity (i.e., how much deep- or surface-level processing), quality (i.e., how well was a strategy executed), and conditional use (i.e., how appropriate was it to use a particular strategy). Strategic processing interacts dynamically with the person-level characteristics, such as an individual's (a) level of interest in science (or a particular science topic, e.g., interest in astronomy), (b) prior knowledge of scientific content, (c) goal orientation toward learning science (e.g., mastery vs. performance orientation), and (d) epistemic thinking about scientific content (e.g., evaluations about coherency of scientific explanations). The person level also interacts with the task level (nature of the science learning task and scientific domain), which in turn interacts with the broader learning environment (e.g., the instructional climate that shapes a classroom, such as use of normative behaviors and instructional scaffolds promoting use of particular learning strategies).

For the purposes of this chapter, we view strategies as composed of an array of tactics that fit a broader task category. Thus, strategies are at a larger grain size than tactics (Winne, Jamieson-Noel, & Muis, 2002; Winne & Perry, 2000), with tactics being simple actions taken by a learner based on a specific task feature (e.g., using Newton's Second Law to calculate an object's acceleration when a physics problem gives the applied force and object's mass). So, an example of a physics learning strategy that is composed of categorically consistent tactics would be the "working-backward" strategy that learners would use to solve all or most physics problems (Taasoobshirazi & Farley, 2013). Furthermore, we will operate under the well-established and researched position that learners construct their knowledge both cognitively and socially (see, for example, Bransford, Brown, & Cocking, 2000; National Academies of Sciences, Engineering, & Medicine, 2018). This chapter will, therefore, focus on strategy interventions that specifically help promote science learning and/or have been used extensively by educational researchers to understand science learning and by practitioners to facilitate science learning. Certainly, there are generalized strategies that science learners and teachers use, such as those associated with reading comprehension (Dinsmore & Alexander, 2016), motivation (Muis, Ranellucci, Franco, & Crippen, 2013; Taasoobshirazi & Farley, 2013), and self-efficacy beliefs (Kıran & Sungur, 2012). However, other authors discuss these generalized strategies in more detail elsewhere in this volume (see, for example, Dumas, this volume).

Concept Development and Conceptual Change Strategies

Research into science concept development and conceptual change widely emerged in the early 1970s. Piaget's (1954, 1964) notions of cognitive knowledge construction were foundational to this research vein. In particular, Piaget's idea that thinking processes (he called them operations) act to form mental structures (i.e., concepts) and constitute the basis of a person's knowledge was highly influential. Concepts form and change through processes of assimilation (incorporating new information into existing cognitive structures) and accommodation (changing existing cognitive structures in response to new information). Furthermore, Piaget pointed out that the processes of assimilation and accommodation can happen spontaneously, which he termed the development of knowledge, or through provocation, which he termed learning.

Much early conceptual change research was also based on the notion that individuals' conceptual knowledge formed and changed similarly to how scientists constructed and changed scientific explanations (e.g., explanatory hypotheses and theories). In particular, some conceptual change researchers (see, for example, Posner, Strike, Hewson, & Gertzog, 1982) used T. Kuhn's (1962) notion of a paradigm shift as an analogy to laypeople's conceptual change learning. With this view, conceptual change is seen as a relatively radical knowledge construction process, where some kind of cognitive conflict or dissonance provokes the learner to be dissatisfied with their existing conceptual understanding (Posner et al., 1982). These early conceptual change researchers posited that once dissatisfied, a learner could proceed through a rational process of conceptual change if they constructed a replacement conception that was intelligible and understandable, more plausible than the prior conception, and open to the possibility of fruitfully solving future problems and opening new lines of inquiry. Therefore, science learning based on Piaget's (1954) notion of accommodation and Posner et al.'s (1982) rational conceptual change model included strategies that moved learners linearly and rationally through steps that addressed these conditions (i.e., individuals progressing through each step—intelligibility, plausibility, and fruitfulness—through reasoned logic based on evidence).

Strategies that focus on only one part of the linear and rational conceptual change process, however, are generally ineffective. For example, strategies that promote contradiction of misconceptions through dissonance and cognitive conflict (e.g., presenting a discrepant event, such as a demonstration that air has mass and exerts a force) have little likelihood of promoting conceptual change because of a variety of psychological responses, such as ignoring or rejecting novel information that is causing cognitive conflict (Chinn & Brewer, 1993). Furthermore, learner characteristics, such as motivation, interest, and epistemological beliefs, may limit engagement when the conceptual change strategy focuses solely on cognitive conflict (Dole & Sinatra, 1998; Limón, 2001). Use of analogies that endeavor to increase the coherence and comprehensibility of the new conception have also shown limited effectiveness. For example, Harrison and Treagust (1993) found that students took transfer analogs from the base to the target too literally (e.g., thinking that atoms are alive and divide like cells).

Given the general ineffectiveness in one single strategy promoting conceptual change, some researchers have called for combination of strategies. Such combined strategies generally promote more gradual and sustained conceptual change and conceptual development. For example, Clement (2008) proposed that learners engage in repeated criticism and revision of explanatory models to engage in all elements of the linear and rational conceptual change sequence. This process, called model evolution, is more gradual and involves a series of iterative dissonance and analogy strategies to help the learner construct a scientific model of a phenomenon over time. Gradual model evolution may involve empirical investigation strategies (e.g., labs) that have the potential to help learners deeply engage in critiquing and revising their explanatory models over time.

Empirical Investigation Strategies

For over a century, learners' participation in empirical investigations has been integral to science instruction in many types of learning environments. Empirical investigations are a general strategy that includes all sorts of activities and tactics that generally relate to asking questions about, collecting data from, experimenting on and the testing of natural phenomena (National Research Council [NRC], 2012). Traditionally, such empirical investigations have often occurred in settings or classrooms that simulate a laboratory environment (e.g., measuring temperatures of water, contained in a glass beaker, heated through various changes of state; Hofstein & Lunetta, 1982).

Empirical investigations can also include field experiences in the natural environment (e.g., collecting water samples in a creek located near a school). Empirical investigations in laboratory and field settings often involve use and manipulation of equipment and materials via methodologies consistent within a scientific domain (e.g., growing and counting bacteria in a petri dish filled with agar; Hofstein & Lunetta, 2004). In recent decades, empirical investigations also include virtual electronic simulations and environments in which learners collect data and conduct tests and experiments (e.g., observing global temperature changes via computer-based climate change models; Hofstein & Kind, 2012).

Learners' engagement in empirical investigations can achieve many learning goals. The National Academies of Science released a report in the mid-2000s that said when learners participate in empirical investigations, they may: (a) gain mastery of science content, (b) develop scientific reasoning skills, (c) understand the complexity and uncertainty inherent in empiricism, (d) develop practical skills, (e) understand the characteristic nature of science, (f) cultivate interest in science and interest in learning science, and (g) foster a sense of teamwork (National Research Council, 2007). Inherent within these goals is an assumption that participating in laboratory activities will help learners learn about both the processes of the scientific empiricism (i.e., how to do scientific investigations) and the products of the scientific empiricism (i.e., the knowledge produced from scientific investigations). However, much prior research (see, for example, Driver & Easley, 1978) showed that participation in empirical investigations fell far short of these goals because learners and teachers often relied on a stepwise sequence of procedures to arrive at a predetermined outcome (e.g., the six steps of the so-called "scientific method": make an observation, generate a question, form a hypothesis, conduct an experiment, analyze the data, and draw a conclusion). Therefore, learners only superficially engaged in this type of learning strategy and would not deeply understand how the stepwise laboratory activity related to fundamental scientific concepts (Lunetta, Hofstein, & Clough, 2007).

Inquiry-based Strategies

Inquiry-based science learning strategies emerged from research about learning via empirical investigations. Researchers proposed the learning cycle to weave development of understanding about scientific concepts with development of more abstract and complex reasoning that is reflected in empirical investigations (Karplus & Butts, 1977; SCIS, 1974). The learning cycle consisted of three phases: (a) exploration, where teachers introduced a scenario requiring science students to interact with phenomenon by encountering a problem, generating questions, observing, measuring, etc.; (b) concept introduction, where science students and teachers made sense of their interactions with the phenomenon of interest in an explanation; and (c) concept application, where students elaborated and extended the explanation to other contexts and phenomena. The developers designed the learning cycle to act as a strategy to help students self-regulate their science learning through a guided process of scientific inquiry, including discovery, explanation, and elaboration (Karplus & Butts, 1977). Although guided inquiry-based science strategies came under criticism for a variety of reasons (e.g., focusing solely on manipulation of materials and pieces of equipment to arrive at a pre-defined solution; see, for example, Tobin, Tippins, & Gallard, 1994), the learning cycle heavily influenced science interventions in the 1990s and early 2000s, including, among others, predict-observe-explain (White & Gunstone, 1992), authentic science tasks (Songer, 1996), and project-based science (Marx, Blumenfeld, Krajcik, & Soloway, 1997). The learning cycle is currently manifest in many science classrooms as the BSCS 5E Instructional Model (Bybee et al., 2006), consisting of five phases: engagement, exploration, explanation, elaboration, and evaluation.

Scientific Expertise Strategies

Engaging learners in inquiry-based instruction is closely related to the notion that developing learners' scientific expertise is critical for deep science understanding. Strategies for developing expertise aim to develop learners' thinking skills that reflect the core attributes of authentic scientific reasoning (Chinn & Malhotra, 2002). To develop such expert reasoning, learners need to construct, conceptually organize, and retrieve relevant knowledge about phenomena consistent with scientists who practice within a particular topic domain (Bransford et al., 2000). For example, learners who develop astronomy expertise will be able to construct and relate models of celestial motions that can be accurately applied to astronomical systems at planetary, stellar, and galactic scales. As such, strategies that seek to develop expertise should have students engage in cognitive processes and practices that reflect scientific inquiry (e.g., designing experimental conditions to investigate relations among variables; Künsting, Wirth, & Paas, 2011) and scientific epistemic beliefs (e.g., coordinate theoretical models with multiple lines of evidence; Chinn & Malhotra, 2002).

Developing such scientific expertise through tasks that engage students in authentic inquiry has proved to be a daunting task for both educators and educational researchers. Chinn and Malhotra (2002) found that many science inquiry-based tasks were rather simplistic, with the potential to reinforce non-scientific epistemic beliefs (e.g., scientific knowledge is simple, certain, and algorithmic). However, to facilitate learners' development of scientific expertise, learners should engage in tasks that elicit authentic reasoning strategies over sustained periods of time (see, for example, Chen & Wu, 2012). To aid in this sustained strategy of authentic scientific inquiry, the learning sciences and science education research communities called for the development of instructional scaffolds to facilitate cognitive apprenticeship, where "complex tasks can be distributed ... to minimize obstacles and compensate for limitations by providing assistance at opportune moments" (Quintana et al., 2004, p. 340). This call paved the way for contemporary science learning strategies that incorporated argumentation, modeling, and socio-scientific concepts. In fact, a recent report by the NRC (2018) recommended that "science investigation and engineering design should be *the* [emphasis added] central approach for teaching and learning science and engineering" (p. S-4), with scaffolds needed for learners to develop deep understanding of "phenomena and evidence-based solutions to challenges ... over time" (pp. 3–4).

CONTEMPORARY STRATEGIES AND STRATEGIC PROCESSING IN SCIENCE EDUCATION

Strategies and strategic processing associated with scientific inquiry and expertise have set the stage for science education's present state. For example, the NRC (2012) proposed a three-dimensional framework for K-12 science education integrating:

> [s]cientific and engineering practices; crosscutting concepts that unify the study of science and engineering through their common application across fields; and core ideas in four disciplinary areas: physical sciences, life sciences, earth and space sciences, and engineering, technology, and applications of science.
>
> (p. 2)

This conceptual framework served as the foundation for the development of the *Next Generation Science Standards* (NGSS Lead States, 2013), with some aspect of each dimension combined to form a standard (called a "performance expectation" by the NGSS authors). The scientific and engineering practices are particularly connected to the notion of developing learners' scientific expertise through engagement in scientific inquiry during classroom learning. Although the framework includes eight scientific and engineering practices in which students should engage, they reflect two broad strategic processing categories: science learning through argumentation and science as modeling. We will discuss each of these broad contemporary categories in the remainder of this section, and then in the next section, use an example to demonstrate authentic learning via socio-scientific topics that includes these two strategies.

Science Learning through Argumentation Strategies

Learning science through the practice of argumentation has seen increased emphasis since the late 1990s. For example, the *National Science Education Standards* (NRC, 1996) emphasized that a critical component of scientific literacy is "the capacity to pose and evaluate arguments based on evidence and to apply conclusions from such arguments appropriately" (p. 22). More recent reform-based reports, such as *A Framework for K-12 Science Education* (NRC, 2012), have elevated the construction of evidence-based explanations as a scientific practice in which students should engage during classroom learning. This framework featured argumentation within a centralized hub of scientific activity, in which:

> [a]rgumentation and analysis that relate evidence and theory are also essential features of science …[These argumentation processes] include appraisal of data quality, modeling of theories, development of new testable questions from those models, and modification of theories and models as evidence indicates they are needed.
>
> (p. 27)

The framework also included argumentation within the social enterprise of science, and asserted "the norms for building arguments from evidence are developed collectively in a vast network of scientists working together over extended periods" (p. 27).

In short, educational reformers, researchers, and practitioners view scientific argumentation as an authentic scientific practice and a key science learning strategy.

Scientific argumentation is an inherently constructive process, and as a science learning strategy, it builds upon the notion of cognitive and social construction of evidence-based explanations. Toulmin (1958, 2003, p. 87) proposed a domain-general "layout" of argumentation that educators use widely. In this layout, Toulmin positioned argumentation as a process by which people validate a claim via data and backed warrants. Claims are implicit in assertions (i.e., claiming unalienable rights, such as life, liberty, and the pursuit of happiness), and specifically aim to make a "claim on our attention and our beliefs" (Toulmin, 1958, 2003, p. 11). Science education researchers and practitioners often view claims as scientific explanations (e.g., accounts of how phenomena unfold that may lead to a feeling of understanding; Braaten & Windschitl, 2011; Brewer, Chinn, & Samarapungavan, 1998). As an explanation, claims may also answer questions relating to a particular phenomenon (e.g., the cause of current climate change). Toulmin views data as the "facts … [that act] as a foundation to a claim" (p. 90). Toulmin's use of the term data may be somewhat confusing in a science education framework because of the very specific connection of data as a quantifiable signal (e.g., a quantity obtained from a measurement or modeling simulation). Therefore, researchers and science education practitioners often use the term evidence (or evidence lines) in lieu of the term data or facts. Furthermore, in science, backed warrants are generally referred to as scientific reasoning, such as reasoning that evaluates and justifies connections between lines of evidence and claims. In essence, such reasoning would support the scientific "rules, principles, [and] inference[s]" that act as the tools to evaluate connections between evidence and explanations per Toulmin's layout (Toulmin, 1958, 2003, p. 91). Thus, when thinking about the Toulmin model of argumentation within the context of science learning, claims, data, and backed warrants become claims, evidence, and reasoning.

Many science educators use claims-evidence-reasoning (CER) as a strategy to promote their students' engagement in scientific argumentation. McNeill and Krajcik (2008) first introduced this strategy to facilitate students' construction of explanations about a phenomenon. CER is often used in conjunction with classroom-based inquiry activities, such as investigations where students collect and analyze data (e.g., experiments, problem-based learning scenarios). Teachers can use scaffolds to facilitate students' engagement in the CER strategy, such as answering specific questions that relate to each component (McNeill & Martin, 2011). For example, a question prompt could ask students to generate a claim, such as "what statement can you write to describe why X occurred?" where X is a phenomenon observed in the classroom (e.g., an observation that the temperature of boiling water stays the same even when increasing amounts of energy are applied to a hot plate). Another question could ask students to develop a statement of the evidence related to their claim, such as "what scientific data support your claim?" Finally, the scaffold would then use a question asking students to justify their claim by explicitly connecting the evidence to it, such as "how does the evidence support your claim?" Through this scaffolded CER process, students generate a scientific argument.

The CER process can include a fourth element, counterargument. When evaluation of alternative explanations become part of the CER strategy, students are more fully participating in scientific argumentation (Nussbaum & Edwards, 2011). Consideration of alternatives specifically helps students to develop their critical thinking skills (Lombardi, Bailey, Bickel, & Burrell, 2018; Lombardi, Bickel, Bailey, & Burrell, 2018) and deepen their learning on a particular topic through cognitive elaboration (i.e., making multiple connections with their background knowledge; Nussbaum, 2008). Such critical thinking and cognitive elaboration may also facilitate students' scientifically accurate knowledge construction and reconstruction (Nussbaum, Sinatra, & Poliquin, 2008) and metacognition (D. Kuhn, Zillmer, Crowell, & Zavala, 2013). However, consideration of counterarguments and rebuttals is challenging for students. Therefore, developmental scientists suggest that instruction promoting evaluation of alternative explanations should often begin at early adolescence (i.e., after a student has increasing cognitive control over the coordination of lines of evidence and theory; D. Kuhn & Pearsall, 2000).

Engaging in scientific argumentation is difficult for students because coordination of evidence and theory is a challenge. Furthermore, using argumentation to promote science learning is also challenging for teachers. For example, research has shown that students can make claims without justifications, including not using credible lines of evidence and scientific reasoning (Fischer et al., 2014). Therefore, recent research projects have focused on developing and testing instructional scaffolds that promote students' participation in collaborative and productive scientific argumentation in classroom settings (see, for example, D. Kuhn, 2010; Lombardi, Bailey, et al., 2018; Lombardi, Bickel, et al., 2018; McNeil & Krajcik, 2009; Nussbaum & Edwards, 2011; Rinehart, Duncan, Chinn, Atkins, & DiBenedetti, 2016). When viewing argumentation as a process that promotes deep understanding of both scientific content and skills, Manz (2015) says that development of scaffolds should "shift argumentation from a procedure conducted after scientific work has been done, or conducted in the absence of scientific work, and instead embed it in the scientific enterprise" (p. 20). In doing so, these scaffolds may help students to become more critical evaluators of the connection between lines of evidence and explanations, and potentially with more than one alternative explanation in the context of controversial and complex socio-scientific issues (e.g., causes of climate change).

Science as Modeling Strategies

Modeling and argumentation strategies emerged somewhat concurrently in association with 1990s science education reform efforts (American Association for the Advancement of Science, 1993). In the mid-2000s, the NRC (2007) and others (e.g., Windschitl, Thompson, & Braaten, 2008) presented scientific modeling and theory building as a classroom practice that more authentically represented the scientific enterprise than the oft-used, and so-called, scientific method. The NRC (2007) specifically recommended that teachers should present science "as a process of building theories and models using evidence, checking them for internal consistency and coherence, and testing them empirically" (p. 5). Therefore, for many lines of scientific inquiry, modeling is a quintessential process (Nersessian, 2008). The NRC (2012) more recently stated that scientists use models as tools to "visualize and understand a phenomenon under investigation" (p. 56). Furthermore, models that deepen understanding have compatibility among a variety of scientific fields, are parsimonious, are supported by scientific evidence, and have predictive power (i.e., are supported by future lines of empirical evidence; Pluta, Chinn, & Duncan, 2011). In general, scientific models help people understand "the way the natural and human-engineered world operates" and act as "simplifications of complex laws or theories that [people translate] as general ideas" (Moulding, Bybee, & Paulson, 2015, pp. 62–63).

The science as modeling strategy extends the use of models (including physical, pictorial, graphical, mathematical, and computerized replications of phenomena) to the central focus in inquiry-based learning. Schauble (2018) views science as modeling as a bottom-up strategy for science learning, where students develop models in specific domains, even specific topics, through which they then develop a more general set of heuristics for scientific knowledge construction. Therefore, science instruction must include classroom practice in model use, together with the metacognitive aspects of modeling in science. To encompass the two components of practical use and metacognitive reflection of scientific models, Schwarz et al. (2009) proposed that students simulate scientific activities by constructing models via extant evidence and theory, using models to explain and predict, evaluating models through their ability to predict future observations, and revising models to increase their explanatory and predictive power. In doing so, the science as modeling strategy facilitates learners' participation in scientific discourse and reasoning, critical thinking about alternative representations, and reflectivity about their own understanding (Louca & Zacharia, 2012). Promoting deep cognitive and metacognitive engagement with science content has the potential to move learners' model use beyond purely illustrative and demonstrative purposes toward more meaningful scientific knowledge construction.

Researchers and practitioners often link the modeling as science strategy with argumentation. Windschitl et al. (2018) suggested that the evidence-based argumentation strategy informs students' participation in scientific modeling. These researchers see the practice of argumentation in simultaneously developing models that are predictive of a phenomenon and written explanations that provide additional insight into the phenomenon. For example, consider a situation in which students use a simple computer simulation to predict future climate change and develop a written explanation of the causes of current climate change and future impacts. While doing this work, students could also engage in collaborative argumentation that critiques and parameterizes model uncertainties to develop a revised explanation that establishes a range of possible impacts. Mendonça and Justi (2013) found that students can engage in scientific argumentation when they justify their initial model construction, further calibrate the model with extant evidence, test the model with novel evidence, and evaluate the strengths and weaknesses of the model in explaining a phenomenon. Furthermore, their classroom-based research is consistent with others' linking modeling and argumentation (for an overview, see Jiménez-Aleixandre & Erduran, 2008). However, a more recent review of the linkage of modeling and argumentation found relatively few connections between the two strategies in the literature (Campbell, Oh, Maughn, Kiriazis, & Zuwallack, 2015), with classroom implementation also of likely low frequency. One reason for the lack of connection may be that these learning and teaching strategies are challenging to implement. Much like other strategies that require higher-order thinking skills, argumentation, modeling, and scientific inquiry may be quite difficult for students to learn and for teachers to teach (see, for example, Erduran & Dagher, 2014; Klopfer, 1969). Because of this difficulty, instructional scaffolds may be required to help students learn how to fully engage in science learning strategies. Such scaffolds include, but are not limited to, the use of computer-based tools to promote scientific thinking (Greene, Hutchison, Costa, & Crompton, 2012); employment of teacher moves to promote scientific discourse and argumentation (Duschl, 2008; Li et al., 2016); and regular assignment of science journals in which students can build an ongoing record of their investigations (Sandoval & Reiser, 2004).

AN EXAMPLE OF SCAFFOLDS TO FACILITATE SCIENCE LEARNING STRATEGIES

The following is a short discussion about instructional scaffolds that we have adapted and expanded in our projects, called the Model-Evidence Link (MEL) diagram. The original structure and mode of the MEL was developed by a team of educational psychologists, learning scientists, and science education researchers at Rutgers University (see Chinn & Buckland, 2012, for an overview). Lombardi and colleagues (Lombardi, Bailey, et al., 2018; Lombardi, Bickel, et al., 2018; Lombardi, Sinatra, & Nussbaum, 2013) discuss the adaptations and expansions that we made to the MEL in some detail, and we highlight some of the MEL features in the following discussion. However, prior to discussing the MEL, we enthusiastically acknowledge and support similar efforts of other researcher teams who are developing or have developed instructional scaffolds that facilitate argumentation and/or science as modeling strategies (e.g., *Quality Talk in Science*, Murphy et al., 2018; *Promoting Reasoning and Conceptual Change in Science*, Chinn, Duncan, & Rinehart, 2018).

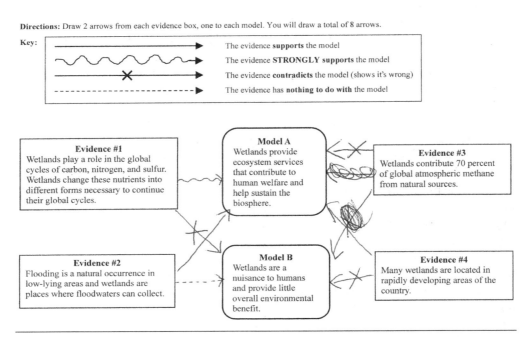

Figure 11.1 A student example of the Wetlands Model-Evidence Link (MEL) diagram

The MEL is an instructional scaffold that facilitates students' scientific evaluations about the connections between multiple lines of scientific evidence and alternative explanatory models about an observed phenomenon (Figure 11.1; Holzer, Lombardi, & Bailey, 2016; Lombardi, 2016). In the context of a particular topic (e.g., causes of current climate change, the link between fracking and earthquakes, the role of wetlands in ecosystem services, and formation of the Moon), the MEL diagram and associated support activities present students with two conceptual models, each providing an explanation for a phenomenon. For example, in the Wetlands MEL, two models provide competing explanations about how wetlands affect humans and the environment: Model A, where wetlands provide ecosystem services that contribute to human welfare and help sustain the biosphere; and Model B, where wetlands are a nuisance to humans and provide little overall environmental benefit. When using the MEL diagram as a scaffold, students draw arrows in one of four different shapes to indicate their evaluation about how well each line of evidence supports each model. Straight arrows indicate that evidence supports the model; squiggly arrows indicate that evidence strongly supports the model; straight arrows with an "X" through the middle indicate the evidence contradicts the model; and dashed arrows indicate the evidence has nothing to do with the model.

The MEL promotes students' cognitive and behavioral engagement in several science learning strategies, including science as inquiry, argumentation, and science as modeling. For example, the MEL diagram prompts students to evaluate the connections between line of evidence and two alternative explanatory models about a phenomenon. This allows students to critique explanatory models much like the scientific community does. Researchers and practitioners have given little attention to critiquing of alternatives in science learning; however, "as all ideas in science are evaluated against alternative explanations and compared with evidence, acceptance of an explanation is ultimately an assessment of what data are reliable and relevant and a decision about which explanation is the most satisfactory" (National Research Council, 2012, p. 44). In fact, our empirical studies show that the MEL results in deeper learning when students consider connections between lines of evidence and alternative explanations, over and above when they consider the same lines of evidence and only one alternative (i.e., the scientific explanation; Lombardi, Bailey, et al., 2018; Lombardi et al., 2013).

The inherent mode of critique initiated by the MEL is also related to students' argumentation and modeling as science strategy use. The NRC (2012) specifically states that "Engaging in argumentation from evidence about an explanation supports students' understanding of the reasons and empirical evidence for that explanation, demonstrating that science is a body of knowledge rooted in evidence" (p. 44). The MEL expands upon this central notion of argumentation involving claims, evidence, and reasoning in argumentation, by introducing claims, evidence, reasoning, *and* critique of alternatives. We have examined both students' depth of reasoning and critique in a task that students complete after drawing their MEL diagram. In this explanation task (Figure 11.2), we prompted students to describe evidence to model links they consider important or interesting. Using a sentence prompt for each explanation, participants indicated the model and evidence number that they chose to discuss, as well as the evidence-to-model connection strength they drew on the diagram (i.e., strongly supports, supports, contradicts, or has nothing to do with). This preface served as the beginning of participants' written explanations, next prompting evaluation with the word "because." For example, a full written explanation from one middle school student participant said, "Evidence #1 strongly supports Model A because atmospheric greenhouse gases have been rising for the past 50 years because of humans" (Lombardi, Bickel, Brandt, & Burg, 2017, p. 319). In our iterative and qualitative content analyses of these written explanations, we found four increasing levels of evaluation from erroneous to critical (Lombardi, Bailey, et al., 2018; Lombardi, Bickel, et al., 2018; Lombardi, Brandt, Bickel, & Burg, 2016), with interesting relations between evaluations and learning when students specifically wrote about lines of evidence that contradicted an explanatory model. These results suggest that contradictory evidence is important in changing students' epistemic judgments (e.g., a plausibility judgment about a particular explanatory model compared to another) to facilitate the process of scientific evaluation in argumentation and collaborative knowledge construction of models (Erduran & Dagher, 2014).

Although our research has shown that the MEL increases students' use of science learning strategies within the course of the activity, we have not yet been able to ascertain whether students transfer their strategy use outside of the classroom context. Our recent development and testing efforts are examining ways to internalize the MEL scaffold into students' mental representations, enabling them to transfer their use of scientific and critical evaluations beyond the specific activities. We are purposely incorporating the idea of conceptual agency (Pickering, 1995), where learners who exercise such agency are authors of their own contributions, accountable to the learning community, and have the authority to think about and solve problems

Please work on this part individually after you complete your diagram. Now that you have completed the diagram, reconsider the plausibility of Models A and B.

Circle the plausibility of each model. [Make two circles, one for each model.]

	Greatly implausible or even impossible									Highly Plausible
Model A	1	2	3	4	5	6	7	8	9	(10)
Model B	1	2	(3)	4	5	6	7	8	9	10

Did the plausibility of Model A and/or Model B change after you completed the diagram? Yes or No [Circle One]

[Note: you may have to look at your previous ratings if you do not remember what they were. Ask your teacher for assistance.]

Which arrows changed your plausibility judgments about the models? If your plausibility judgment did not change, which arrows supported your original plausibility judgments? Use the following steps to provide two explanations for why your plausibility judgments did or did not change.

A. Write the number of the evidence you are writing about. [Note: it is okay to include more than one evidence]
B. Circle the appropriate word (**strongly supports | supports | contradicts | has nothing to do with**).
C. Write which model you are writing about. [Note it is okay to include both models].
D. Then write your reason.

1. Evidence # _1_ (strongly supports) | supports | contradicts | has nothing to do with Model _A_ because:
   Evidence 1 states that wetlands are important in global cycles and help humans through these cycles.

2. Evidence # _2_ strongly supports (supports) contradicts | has nothing to do with Model _A_ because:
   Evidence 2 states that wetlands collect floodwater, therefore saving people from the damages of floods.

Figure 11.2 A student example of the Wetlands MEL Explanation Task

(Nussbaum & Asterhan, 2016). In this newer version of the scaffold, students build their own MEL diagram from a set of lines of evidence and explanatory models. Our hope is that through building and using their own MEL, students will become agents of model evaluation, which is a key component of both the argumentation and science as modeling strategies.

ISSUES AND FUTURE RESEARCH DIRECTIONS

As previous researchers have noted, the implementation of scientific argumentation and science as modeling strategies can be challenging for teachers (e.g., Erduran & Dagher, 2014; Fischer et al., 2014; McNeill & Krajcik, 2008). Teachers may not have the pedagogical knowledge to engage students in argumentation, despite a stated belief that it is an important aspect of student learning in science. In interviews with 30 high school teachers, Sampson and Blanchard (2012) identified a number of perceived barriers to implementing argumentation, such as the achievement level of their students, students' lack of prior experience with argumentation, time and curricular limitations, or teachers' own inexperience with the strategy.

The existence of scaffolds and curricula designed to facilitate either argumentation or science as modeling should support teachers in moving toward using these strategies more often, but there may be additional challenges beyond simply getting such supports into teachers' hands. Once there, what teachers enact in the classroom may not align with what was intended by curriculum developers or researchers (Remillard, 2005). However, Osborne, Erduran, and Simon (2004) demonstrated that directed scaffolds to support argumentation help not only the students improve in their argumentation skills but also the teachers in facilitating argumentation. Lortie (1975) described an "apprenticeship of observation" for teacher education, in that teachers have had 16+ years in the role of students, during which time they have developed ideas and beliefs about what teaching is and what teachers do (Ball, 1988). These ideas may or may not be aligned with the theoretical underpinnings or best practices espoused by either teacher education generally or science education more specifically, and if not, the formal teacher education program may be insufficient for overcoming conflicting beliefs that have developed over this observational period. Explicit and routine inclusion of both science strategies, such as argumentation and science as modeling, and more domain-general strategies and strategic processes in preservice teacher education and inservice professional development programs may be needed to provide teachers with experiences that allow them to carry the strategies forward into their own teaching.

CONCLUDING THOUGHTS

Facilitating widespread use of contemporary science intervention strategies is challenging for many educational researchers and leaders. For deeper cognitive and metacognitive engagement, learners should experience socio-scientific issues (e.g., connections between increased occurrence of extreme weather events and human-induced climate change), which include fundamental science concepts, through argumentation and modeling strategies. Engagement in these deeper science learning strategies is complex, but scaffolding argumentation and modeling instruction may facilitate learners' deep understanding of science. For example, the NRC (2012) suggests that young learners can begin constructing arguments by interpreting observations and collected data. As learners reach adolescence, they can begin to evaluate alternative explanations through gauging how well each is supported by various lines of evidence. Finally, learners should be able to identify flaws in their own arguments, as well as in other arguments, by using scientific norms of logic, analysis, and evaluation. Similarly and relatedly, the NRC (2012) said that:

> [e]ngagement in modeling and evidence-based argumentation invites and encourages students to reflect on the status of their own knowledge and their understanding of how science works ...[and] as they involve themselves in the practices of science ...[e.g., through scientific inquiry], their level of sophistication in understanding how any given practice contributes to the scientific enterprise can continue to develop across all grade levels.
>
> (p. 79)

Therefore, researchers and designers need to create instructional scaffolding that supports effective employment of science learning strategies, as well as teacher education and professional learning opportunities for educators to become well-versed in these strategies. This will enable teachers and learners to develop robust scientific literacy, with deep understanding about what scientists know and how scientists know what they know.

ACKNOWLEDGMENT

The National Science Foundation (NSF), under Grant No. DRL-1316057 and Grant No. DRL-1721041, supported part of this research. Any opinions, findings, conclusions, or recommendations expressed are those of the authors and do not necessarily reflect the NSF's views.

REFERENCES

American Association for the Advancement of Science. (1993). *Benchmarks for science literacy*. New York, NY: Oxford University Press.

Ball, D. L. (1988). Unlearning to teach mathematics. *For the Learning of Mathematics, 8*(1), 40–48. www.jstor.org/stable/40248141

Braaten, M., & Windschitl, M. (2011). Working toward a stronger conceptualization of scientific explanation for science education. *Science Education, 95*(4), 639–669. doi:10.1002/sce.20449

Bransford, J. D., Brown, A. L., & Cocking, R. R. (Eds.). (2000). *How people learn: Brain, mind, experience, and school (expanded edition)*. Washington, DC: National Academy of Sciences.

Brewer, W. F., Chinn, C. A., & Samarapungavan, A. (1998). Explanation in scientists and children. *Minds and Machines, 8*(1), 119–136. doi:10.1023/a:1008242619231

Bybee, R. W., Taylor, J. A., Gardner, A., Vanscotter, P., Powell, J. C., Westbrook, A., & Landes, N. (2006). *The BSCS 5E instructional model: Origins, effectiveness and applications*. Colorado Springs, CO: BSCS.

Campbell, T., Oh, P. S., Maughn, M., Kiriazis, N., & Zuwallack, R. (2015). A review of modeling pedagogies: Pedagogical functions, discursive acts, and technology in modeling instruction. *Eurasia Journal of Mathematics, Science & Technology Education, 11*(1), 159–176. doi:10.12973/eurasia.2015.1314a

Chen, C. H., & Wu, I. C. (2012). The interplay between cognitive and motivational variables in a supportive online learning system for secondary physical education. *Computers & Education, 58*, 542–550.

Chinn, C. A., & Buckland, L. (2012). Model-based instruction: Fostering change in evolutionary conceptions and epistemic practices. In K. S. Rosengren, E. M. Evans, S. Brem, & G. M. Sinatra (Eds.), *Evolution challenges: Integrating research and practice in teaching and learning about evolution* (pp. 211–232). New York, NY: Oxford University Press.

Chinn, C. A., & Brewer, W. F. (1993). The role of anomalous data in knowledge acquisition: A theoretical framework and implications for science instruction. *Review of Educational Research, 63*(1), 1–49. doi:10.3102/00346543063001001

Chinn, C. A., Duncan, R. G., & Rinehart, R. W. (2018). Epistemic design: Design to promote transferable epistemic growth in the PRACCIS project. In E. Manalo, Y. Uesaka, & C. A. Chinn (Eds.), *Promoting spontaneous use of learning and reasoning strategies: Theory, research, and practice for effective transfer* (pp. 242–259). New York, NY: Routledge.

Chinn, C. A., & Malhotra, B. A. (2002). Epistemologically authentic inquiry in schools: A theoretical framework for evaluating inquiry tasks. *Science Education, 86*(2), 175–218. doi:10.1002/sce.10001

Clement, J. (2008). The role of explanatory models in teaching for conceptual change. In S. Vosniadou (Ed.), *International handbook of research on conceptual change* (pp. 417–452). New York, NY: Routledge, Taylor, & Francis Group.

Dinsmore, D. L. (2017). Toward a dynamic, multidimensional research framework for strategic processing. *Educational Psychology Review, 29*, 235–268. doi:10.1007/s10648-017-9407-5

Dinsmore, D. L., & Alexander, P. A. (2016). A multidimensional investigation of deep-level and surface-level processing. *Journal of Experimental Education, 84*, 213–244. doi:10.1080/00220973.2014.979126

Dole, J. A., & Sinatra, G. M. (1998). Reconceptalizing change in the cognitive construction of knowledge. *Educational Psychologist, 33*(2–3), 109–128. doi:10.1080/00461520.1998.9653294

Driver, R., & Easley, J. (1978). Pupils and paradigms: A review of literature related to concept development in adolescent science students. *Studies in Science Education, 5*, 61–84. doi:10.1080/03057267808559857

Dumas, D. (this volume). Strategic processing within and across domains of learning. In D. L. Dinsmore, L. K. Fryer, & M. M. Parkinson (Eds.), *Handbook of strategies and strategic processing: Conceptualization, measurement, and analysis* New York: Routledge.

Duschl, R. (2008). Science education in three-part harmony: Balancing conceptual, epistemic, and social learning goals. *Review of Research in Education, 32*(1), 268–291. doi:10.3102/0091732X07309371

Erduran, S., & Dagher, Z. R. (2014). *Reconceptualizing the nature of science for science education* (pp. 113–135). Netherlands: Springer.

Fischer, F., Kollar, I., Ufer, S., Sodian, B., Hussmann, H., Pekrun, R., ... Strijbos, J. W. (2014). Scientific reasoning and argumentation: Advancing an interdisciplinary research agenda in education. *Frontline Learning Research, 2*(3), 28–45. doi:10.14786/flr.v2i3.96

Greene, J. A., Bolick, C. M., Jackson, W. P., Caprino, A. M., Oswald, C., & McVea, M. (2015). Domain specificity of self-regulated learning processing in science and history. *Contemporary Educational Psychology, 42*, 111–128. doi:10.1016/j.cedpsych.2015.06.001

Greene, J. A., Hutchison, L. A., Costa, L. J., & Crompton, H. (2012). Investigating how college students' task definitions and plans relate to self-regulated learning processing and understanding of a complex science topic. *Contemporary Educational Psychology, 37*(4), 307–320. doi:10.1016/j.cedpsych.2012.02.002

Harrison, A. G., & Treagust, D. F. (1993). Teaching with analogies: A case study in grade-10 optics. *Journal of Research in Science Teaching, 30*(10), 1291–1307. doi:10.1002/tea.3660301010

Hofstein, A., & Kind, P. M. (2012). Learning in and from science laboratories. In B. J. Fraser, K. G. Tobin, & C. J. McRobbie (Eds.), *Second international handbook of science education* (pp. 189–207). New York, NY: Springer.

Hofstein, A., & Lunetta, V. N. (1982). The role of the laboratory in science teaching: Neglected aspects of research. *Review of Educational Research, 52*, 201–217. doi:10.3102/00346543052002201

Hofstein, A., & Lunetta, V. N. (2004). The laboratory in science education: Foundations for the 21st century. *Science Education, 88*(1), 28–54. doi:10.1002/sce.10106

Holzer, M. A., Lombardi, D., & Bailey, J. M. (2016). Wetlands: Good or bad? Evaluating competing models. *The Earth Scientist, 32*(2), 17–21.

Jiménez-Aleixandre, M. P., & Erduran, S. (2008). Argumentation in science education: An overview. In S. Erduran & M. P. Jiménez-Aleixandre (Eds.), *Argumentation in science education: Perspectives from classroom-based research* (pp. 3–27). Dordrecht, Netherlands: Springer.

Karplus, R., & Butts, D. P. (1977). Science teaching and the development of reasoning. *Journal of Research in Science Teaching, 14*(2), 169–175. doi:10.1002/tea.3660140212

Kıran, D., & Sungur, S. (2012). Middle school students' science self-efficacy and its sources: examination of gender difference. *Journal of Science Education and Technology, 21*, 619–630.

Klopfer, L. E. (1969). The teaching of science and the history of science. *Journal of Research in Science Teaching, 6*(1), 87–95. doi:10.1002/tea.3660060116

Kuhn, D. (2010). Teaching and learning science as argument. *Science Education, 94*(5), 810–824. doi:10.1002/sce.20395

Kuhn, D., & Pearsall, S. (2000). Developmental origins of scientific thinking. *Journal of Cognition and Development, 1*(1), 113–129. doi:10.1207/S15327647JCD0101N_11

Kuhn, D., Zillmer, N., Crowell, A., & Zavala, J. (2013). Developing norms of argumentation: Metacognitive, epistemological, and social dimensions of developing argumentive competence. *Cognition and Instruction, 31*(4), 456–496. doi:10.1080/07370008.2013.830618

Kuhn, T. S. (1962). *The structure of scientific revolutions*. Chicago, IL: The University of Chicago Press.

Künsting, J., Wirth, J., & Paas, F. (2011). The goal specificity effect on strategy use and instructional efficiency during computer-based scientific discovery learning. *Computers & Education, 56*, 668–679. doi:10.1016/j.compedu.2010.10.009

Li, M., Murphy, P. K., Wang, J., Mason, L. H., Firetto, C. M., Wei, L., & Chung, K. S. (2016). Promoting reading comprehension and critical-analytic thinking: A comparison of three approaches with fourth and fifth graders. *Contemporary Educational Psychology, 46*, 101–115. doi:10.1016/j.cedpsych.2016.05.002

Limón, M. (2001). On the cognitive conflict as an instructional strategy for conceptual change: A critical appraisal. *Learning and Instruction, 11*(4-5), 357–380. doi:10.1016/S0959-4752(00)00037-2

Lombardi, D. (2016). Beyond the controversy: Instructional scaffolds to promote critical evaluation and understanding of Earth science. *The Earth Scientist, 32*(2), 5–10.

Lombardi, D., Bailey, J. M., Bickel, E. S., & Burrell, S. (2018). Scaffolding scientific thinking: Students' evaluations and judgments during Earth science knowledge construction. *Contemporary Educational Psychology, 54*, 184–198. doi:10.1016/j.cedpsych.2018.06.008

Lombardi, D., Bickel, E. S., Bailey, J. M., & Burrell, S. (2018). High school students' evaluations, plausibility (re) appraisals, and knowledge about topics in Earth science. *Science Education, 102*(1), 153–177. doi:10.1002/sce.21315

Lombardi, D., Bickel, E. S., Brandt, C. B., & Burg, C. (2017). Categorising students' evaluations of evidence and explanations about climate change. *International Journal of Global Warming, 12*(3/4), 313–330. doi:10.1504/IJGW.2017.10005879

Lombardi, D., Brandt, C. B., Bickel, E. S., & Burg, C. (2016). Students' evaluations about climate change. *International Journal of Science Education, 38*(8), 1392–1414. doi:10.1080/09500693.2016.1193912

Lombardi, D., Sinatra, G. M., & Nussbaum, E. M. (2013). Plausibility reappraisals and shifts in middle school students' climate change conceptions. *Learning and Instruction, 27*, 50–62. doi:10.1016/j.learninstruc.2013.03.001

Lortie, D. (1975). *Schoolteacher: A sociological analysis*. Chicago, IL: University of Chicago Press.

Louca, L. T., & Zacharia, Z. C. (2012). Modeling-based learning in science education: Cognitive, metacognitive, social, material and epistemological contributions. *Educational Review, 64*(4), 471–492. doi:10.1080/00131911.2011.628748

Lunetta, V. N., Hofstein, A., & Clough, M. P. (2007). Learning and teaching in the school science laboratory: An analysis of research, theory, and practice. In S. K. Abell & N. G. Lederman (Eds.), *Handbook of research on science education* (pp. 393–441). Mahwah, NJ: Lawrence Erlbaum.

Manz, E. (2015). Representing student argumentation as functionally emergent from scientific activity. *Review of Educational Research, 85*(4), 553–590. doi:10.3102/0034654314558490

Marx, R. W., Blumenfeld, P. C., Krajcik, J. S., & Soloway, E. (1997). Enacting project-based science. *The Elementary School Journal, 97*(4), 341–358. doi:10.1086/461870

McNeil, K. L., & Krajcik, J. (2009). Synergy between teacher practices and curricular scaffolds to support students in using domain-specific and domain-general knowledge in writing arguments to explain phenomena. *The Journal of the Learning Sciences, 18*, 416–460. doi:10.1080/10508400903013488

McNeill, K. L., & Krajcik, J. (2008). Inquiry and scientific explanations: Helping students use evidence and reasoning. In J. Luft, R. Bell, & J. Gess-Newsome (Eds.), *Science as inquiry in the secondary setting* (pp. 121–134). Arlington, VA: NSTA Press.

McNeill, K. L., & Martin, D. M. (2011). Claims, evidence, and reasoning. *Science and Children, 48*(8), 52–56.

Mendonça, P. C. C., & Justi, R. (2013). The relationships between modelling and argumentation from the perspective of the model of modelling diagram. *International Journal of Science Education, 35*(14), 2407–2434. doi:10.1080/09500693.2013.811615

Moulding, B. D., Bybee, R. W., & Paulson, N. (2015). *A vision and plan for science teaching and learning: An educator's guide to A framework for K-12 science education, next generation science standards, and state science standards*. Salt Lake City, UT: Essential Teaching and Learning Publications.

Muis, K. R., Ranellucci, J., Franco, G. M., & Crippen, K. J. (2013). The interactive effects of personal achievement goals and performance feedback in an undergraduate science class. *The Journal of Experimental Education*, *81*, 556–578.

Murphy, P. K., Greene, J. A., Allen, E., Baszczewski, S., Swearingen, A., Wei, L., & Butler, A. M. (2018). Fostering high school students' conceptual understanding and argumentation performance in science through Quality Talk discussions. *Science Education*, *102*, 1239–1264. doi:10.1002/sce.21471

National Academies of Sciences, Engineering, & Medicine. (2018). *How people learn II: Learners, contexts, and cultures.* Washington, DC: The National Academies Press. doi:10.17226/24783.

National Research Council. (1996). *National Science Education Standards.* Washington, DC: National Academy Press. doi:10.17226/4962.

National Research Council. (2007). *Taking science to school: Learning and teaching science in grades K-8.* Washington, DC: The National Academies Press. doi:10.17226/11625.

National Research Council. (2012). *A framework for K-12 science education: Practices, crosscutting concepts, and core ideas.* Washington, DC: National Academies Press. doi:10.17226/13165

National Research Council. (2018). *Science and engineering for grades 6-12: Investigation and design at the center.* Washington, DC: The National Academies Press. doi:10.17226/25216.

Nersessian, N. (2008). Model-based reasoning in scientific practice. In R. A. Duschl & R. E. Grandy (Eds.), *Teaching scientific inquiry: Recommendations for research and implementation* (pp. 57–79). Rotterdam, Netherlands: Sense.

NGSS Lead States. (2013). *Next generation science standards: For states by states.* Washington, DC: The National Academies Press.

Nussbaum, E. M. (2008). Collaborative discourse, argumentation, and learning: Preface and literature review. *Contemporary Educational Psychology*, *33*(3), 345–359. doi:10.1016/j.cedpsych.2008.06.001.

Nussbaum, E. M., & Asterhan, C. S. (2016). The psychology of far transfer from classroom argumentation. In F. Paglieri (Ed.), *The psychology of argument: Cognitive approaches to argumentation and persuasion* (pp. 407–423). London, UK: College Publications, Studies in Logic and Argumentation Series.

Nussbaum, E. M., & Edwards, O. V. (2011). Critical questions and argument stratagems: A framework for enhancing and analyzing students' reasoning practices. *Journal of the Learning Sciences*, *20*(3), 443–488. doi:10.1080/10508406.2011.564567.

Nussbaum, E. M., Sinatra, G. M., & Poliquin, A. (2008). Role of epistemic beliefs and scientific argumentation in science learning. *International Journal of Science Education*, *30*(15), 1977–1999. doi:10.1080/09500690701545919.

Osborne, J., Erduran, S., & Simon, S. (2004). Enhancing the quality of argumentation in school science. *Journal of Research in Science Teaching*, *41*(10), 994–1020. doi:10.1002/tea.20035.

Piaget, J. (1954). *The construction of reality in the child.* New York, NY: Basic Books.

Piaget, J. (1964). Part I: Cognitive development in children: Piaget development and learning. *Journal of Research in Science Teaching*, *2*(3), 176–186. doi:10.1002/tea.3660020306.

Pickering, A. (1995). *The mangle of practice: Time, agency, and science.* Chicago, IL: University of Chicago Press.

Pluta, W. J., Chinn, C. A., & Duncan, R. G. (2011). Learners' epistemic criteria for good scientific models. *Journal of Research in Science Teaching*, *48*(5), 486–511. doi:10.1002/tea.20415.

Posner, G. J., Strike, K. A., Hewson, P. W., & Gertzog, W. A. (1982). Accommodation of a scientific conception: Toward a theory of conceptual change. *Science Education*, *66*(2), 211–227. doi:10.1002/sce.3730660207.

Quintana, C., Reiser, B. J., Davis, E. A., Krajcik, J., Fretz, E., Duncan, R. G., ... Soloway, E. (2004). A scaffolding design framework for software to support science inquiry. *Journal of the Learning Sciences*, *13*(3), 337–386. doi:10.1207/s15327809jls1303_4.

Remillard, J. T. (2005). Examining key concepts in research on teachers' use of mathematics curricula. *Review of Educational Research*, *75*(2), 211–246. doi:10.3102/00346543075002211.

Rinehart, R. W., Duncan, R. G., Chinn, C. A., Atkins, T. A., & DiBenedetti, J. (2016). Critical design decisions for successful model-based inquiry in science classrooms. *International Journal of Designs for Learning*, *7*(2), 17–40. doi:10.14434/ijdl.v7i2.20137.

Sampson, V., & Blanchard, M. R. (2012). Science teachers and scientific argumentation: Trends in views and practice. *Journal of Research in Science Teaching*, *49*(9), 1122–1148. doi:10.1002/tea.21037.

Sandoval, W. A., & Reiser, B. J. (2004). Explanation-driven inquiry: Integrating conceptual and epistemic scaffolds for scientific inquiry. *Science Education*, *88*(3), 345–372. doi:10.1002/sce.10130.

Schauble, L. (2018). In the eye of the beholder: Domain-general and domain-specific reasoning in science. In F. Fisher, C. A. Chinn, K. Engelmann, & J. Osborne (Eds.), *Scientific reasoning and argumentation* (pp. 21–43). New York, NY: Routledge.

Schwarz, C. V., Reiser, B. J., Davis, E. A., Kenyon, L., Achér, A., Fortus, D., … Krajcik, J. (2009). Developing a learning progression for scientific modeling: Making scientific modeling accessible and meaningful for learners. *Journal of Research in Science Teaching*, *46*(6), 632–654. doi:10.1002/tea.20311.

SCIS [Science Curriculum Improvement Study]. (1974). *SCIS teacher's handbook*. Berkeley, CA: Lawrence Hall of Science.

Songer, N. B. (1996). Exploring learning opportunities in coordinated network-enhanced classrooms: A case of Kids as Global Scientists. *Journal of the Learning Sciences*, *5*(4), 297–327. doi:10.1207/s15327809jls0504_1.

Taasoobshirazi, G., & Farley, J. (2013). Construct validation of the physics metacognition inventory. *International Journal of Science Education*, *35*(3), 447–459. doi:10.1080/09500693.2012.750433.

Tobin, K., Tippins, D. J., & Gallard, A. J. (1994). Research on instructional strategies for teaching science. In D. L. Gabel (Ed.), *Handbook of research on science teaching and learning* (pp. 45–93). New York, NY: Macmillan.

Toulmin, S. E. (1958, 2003). *The uses of argument*. Cambridge, UK: Cambridge University Press.

White, R., & Gunstone, R. (1992). *Probing understanding*. London, UK: Routledge.

Windschitl, M., Thompson, J., & Braaten, M. (2008). Beyond the scientific method: Model-based inquiry as a new paradigm of preference for school science investigations. *Science Education*, *92*(5), 941–967. doi:10.1002/sce.20259.

Windschitl, M., Thompson, J., & Braaten, M. (2018). *Ambitious science teaching*. Cambridge, MA: Harvard Education Press.

Winne, P. H., Jamieson-Noel, D., & Muis, K. (2002). Methodological issues and advances in researching tactics, strategies, and self-regulated learning. In P. R. Pintrich & M. Maehr (Eds.), *New directions in measures and methods* (Vol. *12*, pp. 121–155). Oxford, England: Elsevier Science.

Winne, P. H., & Perry, N. E. (2000). Measuring self-regulated learning. In M. Boekaerts, P. R. Pintrich, & M. Zeidner (Eds.), *Handbook of self-regulation* (pp. 531–566). San Diego, CA: Academic Press.

12

STRATEGIC PROCESSING IN HISTORY AND HISTORICAL STRATEGY INSTRUCTION

Susan De La Paz
UNIVERSITY OF MARYLAND, USA

Jeffery D. Nokes
BRIGHAM YOUNG UNIVERSITY, USA

Historians provide insights into who we are as people, and about how humans have functioned in the world over time. Engaging in such work requires deep conceptual understandings about the nature of history, as well as disciplinary ways of thinking. Since the late 1980s, educational researchers have studied strategies used by historians as they investigate the past, uncovering disciplinary norms regarding how history is constructed. Standards exist for gathering and investigating evidence, reconstructing narratives, promoting interpretations, and crafting arguments. Knowing these ways of thinking gives researchers and teachers insights into historical inquiry that impact classroom instruction and teacher preparation.

We begin this chapter with a review of observational studies that have identified core conceptual understandings and strategic processes used by historians as they work with evidence in various genres and within different historical fields. We then describe observational studies of novices' strategic processing in history, with obvious differences that reflect a lack of experience as well as general naiveté about the discipline. Because teachers and researchers have attempted to address these challenges, we consider research on classroom interventions, recognizing the accomplishments as well as issues and limitations in the existing studies. We conclude by suggesting future areas for research on historical strategies, identifying new topics and lines of inquiry, for example, civic engagement.

Throughout this chapter, our focus is on cognitive strategies associated with historical inquiry. We define cognitive strategies as mental processes/processing employed during reading, thinking, speaking, and writing tasks. We address these strategies broadly, making little distinction between what some have considered skills (Afflerbach, Pearson, & Paris, 2008), schematic frameworks (Bransford, Brown, & Cocking,

2000), dispositions (Tishman, Jay, & Perkins, 1993), or social strategies (Gee, 1989). Strategy use often involves metacognitive executive functions and automatic processing (i.e., strategies that have become so habitual that they are used without conscious awareness). Further, we distinguish between cognitive strategies, the thinking processes used by those studying history, and instructional strategies, the teaching methods used by teachers. Additionally, we do not dedicate much time to a discussion of generic cognitive strategies, such as summarizing a text passage, questioning, or monitoring comprehension or pre-writing strategies (see Chapters 7–9, this volume), which are well developed in skilled historians, instead focusing on those strategies that distinguish historical thinking, such as analyzing and using evidence to support in writing a historical interpretation (Monte-Sano, 2010; van Drie & van Boxtel, 2008).

Before considering the strategies historians use to study the past, it is necessary to consider epistemological issues concerning the discipline of history. How is historical knowledge produced? In his landmark work, *The Idea of History*, Collingwood (2005/1993) explained the constructed nature of historical understanding. He suggested that all historical work was imaginative to some degree, with historians weaving a network of interpretations on a framework of agreed upon "facts" and evidence. Just as "it is the artist, and not nature, that is responsible for what goes into the picture," he argued, it is the historian and not the past who constructs history (Collingwood, 2005/1993, p. 236). Holt (1995) provides applications of Collingwood's ideas, discussing the ways historians (and, by extension, history students) might use fragmentary and imperfect evidence to construct defensible interpretations. Thus, the strategies described here are based upon the epistemological stance assumed to construct historical interpretations, with differences in historians' and students' cognitive strategies often traced to epistemological issues.

OBSERVING THE STRATEGIES OF HISTORIANS

What are the strategies associated with historical inquiry and historical thinking, and how have these strategies been identified? Following a tradition of research comparing strategic process of experts and novices (see, for example, Chase & Simon's 1973 comparison of chess players), Wineburg (1991) pioneered research on historians' reading processes. Using think aloud protocols he observed historians as they analyzed a collection of texts associated with the Battle of Lexington. He watched advanced high school students making sense of the same documents. Wineburg found that historians paid attention to the source of the text—seeking source information, noticing the genre, making inferences about the author(s), considering the audience and purpose, and evaluating its reliability and usefulness based upon its source. He labeled this strategy *sourcing*. Additionally, historians noticed similarities and differences between texts. They bounced between documents, cross-checking information. For instance, the historians questioned the accuracy of a textbook account, given the evidence in primary sources included in the document set. Wineburg called this strategy *corroboration*. Further, historians imaginatively considered the physical and social environment, a strategy Wineburg labeled *contextualization*. Students' failure to engage in such thinking supported Wineburg's conclusion that sourcing, corroboration, and contextualization were strategies that distinguished historians as readers. In broader terms, he suggested that experts in different fields may use different strategic processes—a basic assumption of this book.

It should not come as a surprise that professionally trained historians, with advanced degrees and years of experience, read differently than novices. Wineburg contended that this difference was linked to the nature of historical inquiry. Historians understand, for example, that texts represent human accounts and that historical knowledge is constructed by interrogating such evidence. Rouet et al. (1997) tested this hypothesis by comparing the reading of graduate students in psychology and history. In their study, the "novices" were comparable to the "experts" in age, general reading abilities, and academic expertise. These researchers found that individuals' reading strategies differed based upon their purposes for reading. Historians approached the texts as evidence to be interpreted, whereas the psychologists focused on learning basic historical facts. Historians engaged in critical analysis (i.e., sourcing) whereas psychologists engaged in remembering (i.e., paraphrasing).

Building upon Wineburg's (1991) work, other researchers explored strategies that distinguish historians. Shanahan and his colleagues (2008, 2011) met with historians, mathematicians, chemists, and teacher educators and secondary school teachers in these fields for two years. They observed and spoke with them about their reading, seeking implications for classroom instruction and teacher preparation. Like Wineburg, these researchers found that historians thought deeply about the source of the text and evaluated that source's credibility. In addition, historians approached a reading task with *mild skepticism*—viewing texts as fallible and positioned accounts, rather than as bearers of unadulterated information.

Wineburg (1998), too, had questions about the influence of historians' content knowledge on their use of strategies, particularly contextualization. He hypothesized that contextualization required a detailed awareness of historical settings. He wondered whether historians could engage in contextualization in a content area for which they lacked background knowledge. He asked two historians, one with expertise on Lincoln and another without, to use a collection of documents to consider Lincoln's views on race. Wineburg found that the historian who lacked expertise was originally perplexed by the evidence but was gradually able to construct an adequate understanding of the historical context from the content of the documents. This research indicated that rich background knowledge was not a prerequisite for contextualization but that readers could seek out contextual information. Historians are inclined to do so.

Seeking to further understand historians' reading, Leinhardt and Young (1996) observed three historians read two documents—one closely related to their field of expertise and one unrelated. These researchers' purpose was to differentiate historians' textual reading of the document (i.e., comprehending word meanings) from their historical reading (i.e., engaging in interpretation). They hypothesized that historians would first identify the document, categorize it, and employ sourcing, corroboration, and contextualization to evaluate its reliability. Historians would then interpret the document through a textual and a historical read. The researchers found that historians did not consciously employ strategies, as such, but relied on procedural schema—scripts for identifying and interpreting evidence. For example, historians *classify* text genre, and based on this knowledge, use specific reading processes that guide how they read. After classifying a text as a letter, for instance, a historian notes the sender, recipient, and date before reading the body of the message.

Baron (2012) looked at the strategies historians use in a non-traditional setting, considering their analysis of a historical building. She asked five historians to "make meaning of the building" and observed them as they thought aloud during a tour of Boston's Old North Church. Baron identified five strategies that the historians used in that setting. Historians reflected on the origins of the church, how it looked originally, its original purpose, who constructed it, and why its location had been chosen. Baron called this strategy *origination*. Second, these historians used their knowledge of other church buildings to understand the distinctiveness of this particular church, a strategy Baron labeled *intersectionality*. Because the church had been in continual use, it had experienced modifications, renovations, and restorations through the years. Historians considered its multiple contexts, a strategy labeled *stratification*. Additionally, some historians lacked background knowledge about the church, yet used observations to make evidence-based inferences about it. Baron called this heuristic *supposition*, a strategy similar to the contextualization engaged in by the non-expert in Wineburg's 1998 study. Finally, Baron found that some historians engaged in *empathetic insight*, imagining the feelings of historical characters as events unfolded there. Little has been done to follow up on these strategies or to investigate other contexts when historians might employ them. The most important implication of this study is that historians' sense-making strategies appear to be influenced by the nature of the documents they investigate. And because historians use a wide array of evidence (Collingwood, 2005/1993), there may be numerous strategies as yet unidentified associated with the reading of diverse forms of evidence, such as motion pictures, quantitative evidence (e.g., historical records), or photographs.

Just as historians use different strategies for working with different types of evidence, some researchers suggest that they employ different organizing structures within different fields of specialty. For example, Harris (2012) considered whether unique cognitive skills existed for the study of world history. She analyzed articles published in the *Journal of World History* to identify frameworks for considering topics in world history. She determined three tools useful to world historians. First, world historians use *multiple*, sometimes *nested, periodization schemes*, linking periods of continuity segmented by turning points in a manner that constructs meaning out of networks of events. Second, world historians use fluid geographic boundaries that allow *comparisons across regions* and *connections between disparate groups*. World historians situate case studies within larger global trends and highlight transregional contacts. Third, world historians engage in *cross-disciplinary methodologies*, incorporating climate science, anthropology, linguistics, archeology, and other disciplines. The use of these frameworks to conceptualize and study the past represent strategies unique to inquiry in world history. Further evidence exists for the idiosyncratic use of strategies based upon other specializations. For example, in one study, a historian who researched ancient cuneiform tablets, which never explicitly afford source information, did not rely on the source information provided by researchers. Instead, with uncanny accuracy, he used the content of documents to infer their sources (Nokes & Kelser-Lund, 2019). It may be that other fields of history such as family history or social history use unique frameworks and strategies to conduct their investigations.

Nokes and Kesler-Lund's recent study (2019) has replicated and elaborated on many of the findings from Wineburg's (1991) research. In their study, small groups of historians were observed as they collaboratively engaged in a historical investigation, analyzing evidence then writing about the Bear River Massacre. During the early phases of reading, historians spontaneously and quickly evaluated the plausibility of their peers' ideas, building a plethora of possible, though conflicting, interpretations. Nokes and Kesler-Lund labeled historians' strategy *exploring*—the tendency to hold multiple competing, plausible interpretations in mind simultaneously. After some discussion, they began to use evidence to rule out some interpretations and to collectively construct a final, though admittedly tentative, conclusion. In contrast, elementary and secondary students who engaged in the same activity were much less likely to consider plausible explanations that did not match their emerging interpretation. Instead, they honed in on a single interpretation that was resistant to change, even in the face of conflicting evidence and their peers' criticism (Nokes & Kelser-Lund, 2018).

These researchers also highlighted historians' *humility*, a disposition that allowed them to adjust their interpretations in light of new evidence or their peers' insights. Their humility distinguished them from students who engaged in the same activity and were much more certain of the correctness of their conclusions after a much less skillful analysis of the evidence (Nokes & Kelser-Lund, 2018). Leinhardt and Young (1996) found a similar humility in the historians they observed. When historians lacked the knowledge needed to interpret an unfamiliar document, they admitted their inadequacy.

In addition, Nokes and Kelser-Lund (2019) found a connection between historians' reading and writing strategies. They suggested that historians approach a reading task with their written product in mind. The strategies associated with reading (i.e., sourcing) are indistinguishable from pre-writing strategies, as historians formulate a plan for using primary source evidence to defend their interpretation. The same strategies associated with constructing an interpretation (reading) are subsequently used to defend their conclusions (writing/speaking). Further, historians' ways of thinking about a task influenced both their reading and writing in similar ways. For instance, when sourcing, historians considered the intended audience of a document. Similarly, when writing, historians considered the potential audience(s) of their account. *Audience-awareness* distinguished historian readers/writers from elementary and secondary students (Nokes & Kelser-Lund, 2018). Additionally, historians approached texts with *mild skepticism*, a disposition highlighted by others (Shanahan & Shanahan, 2008; Wineburg, 1991). Authors of the documents carried a burden of proof—they had to convince the historians to believe their accounts. As Wineburg (1994) theorized, historians possessed a "line item veto" with the tendency to believe or to discount any tidbit of information based upon their evaluation of the documents.

In sum, and across these studies, historians demonstrate a plethora of strategies such as sourcing, corroboration, contextualization, classification, supposition, skepticism, humility. Table 12.1 lists and defines their strategies, highlights the observational studies that identified the strategies, and cites related intervention research, where existing. Historians are metacognitive in their reading and writing processes (Nokes & Kelser-Lund, 2019). They are goal driven, with a range of strategies to draw from as needs arise. In addition, historians, understanding that the purpose for their work is to

Table 12.1 Historical Reading, Thinking, and Writing Strategies of Historians, and as Found in Intervention Studies

Sourcing	Using information about the source of a document (i.e., its author, audience, purpose, genre) to comprehend and evaluate its content	Wineburg (1991); Shanahan & Shanahan (2008); Shanahan, Shanahan, & Misichia (2011)	Young & Leinhardt (1998); Britt & Aglinskas (2002); De La Paz (2005); Nokes et al. (2007); Goldberg, Schwarz, & Porat (2008); Reisman (2012); De La Paz et al. (2014, 2017); Wissinger & De La Paz (2016); De La Paz & Wissinger (2017)
Corroboration	Comparing, contrasting, and cross-checking evidence found in one document with evidence found in other documents	Wineburg (1991)	Britt & Aglinskas (2002); De La Paz (2005); Nokes et al. (2007); Reisman (2012); De La Paz et al. (2014; 2017); Wissinger & De La Paz (2016)
Contextualization	Imagining the physical, social, political, and technological setting to understand an event and related evidence	Wineburg (1991, 1998)	Britt & Aglinskas (2002); De La Paz (2005); Nokes et al. (2007); Reisman (2012); van Boxtel & van Drie (2012); De La Paz et al. 2014, 2017); Wissinger & De La Paz (2016)
Classifying	Identifying the genre of a text such as a letter, journal entry, or public address, and adjusting reading accordingly	Leinhardt & Young (1996)	
Approaching a text with mild skepticism	Viewing texts as extensions of imperfect and positioned individuals rather than as bearers of unadulterated information	Wineburg (1991); Shanahan & Shanahan (2008); Shanahan et al. (2011)	
Substantiation	Supporting interpretive claims with vetted historical evidence	Goldberg, Schwarz, & Porat (2011)	De La Paz & Felton (2010); De La Paz et al. (2014; 2017); Wissinger & De La Paz (2016); De La Paz & Wissinger (2017); Stoel et al. (2015, 2017)
Building-reading strategies (origination, intersectionality, stratification, supposition, empathetic insight)	Reading buildings as products of a time and setting, comparing them to other buildings, considering how they have changed over time, making inferences based on their features, and considering the feelings of those who used them	Baron (2012)	

Humility	Holding interpretations as tentative, considering alternative interpretations, adjusting interpretations in the face of new evidence	Nokes & Kelser-Lund (2019)	
Exploring	Gathering multiple plausible though conflicting interpretations simultaneously with the intent to later narrow things down to a single interpretation	Nokes & Kelser-Lund (2019)	
Historical empathy or empathetic insight	Attempting to understand the decisions of historical actors by imagining their contexts and anticipating their emotions	Baron (2012)	Levesque (2008)
Structuring inquiries and writing through conceptual frameworks	Using multiple, nested periodization[1] schemes or other structures to impose order and make sense of historical events	Harris (2012)	Young & Leinhardt (1998); Lee (2005); Stoel, van Drie, & van Boxtel (2017)

[1] In studies, teachers attempted to make this visible through the use of syntactic markers (e.g., causal structures or qualifiers) or organizational structures to convey understandings.

construct new interpretations, do so by including perspectives from previously marginalized groups or by looking at old evidence in new ways. Thus, the job of a historian is to raise, then answer, questions, with insights that are both justified and yet still open to further question.

OBSERVING NOVICE'S HISTORICAL THINKING STRATEGIES

As some researchers have identified strategies historians use, other researchers have considered how students approach historical thinking. For example, Lee and Ashby (2000) observed the unsophisticated strategies used by students. When faced with multiple sources that contain conflicting accounts, the youngest students, lacking any strategies, admitted that they could not know what happened in the past. Older, middle-school aged students arbitrarily labeled some accounts as deliberate falsifications, agreeing with others. Slightly older students ruled with the majority of the accounts. Rather than creating a synthesized interpretation that relied on the best evidence from multiple documents, they discounted some accounts and accepted others as factual.

Wineburg (1991) observed gifted high school students as part of his 1991 study. They skillfully applied generic reading strategies such as summarizing, monitoring comprehension, making connections to background knowledge, and rereading. However, the historical thinking strategies they used were as unsophisticated as those Lee and Ashby (2000) observed. For instance, most students sought a non-existent objective source that lacked bias, being enticed by a textbook account. Students' flawed strategies are not confined to traditional historical reading. Seixas (1993) found that when evaluating historical movies, tenth grade students judged as more reliable a movie that portrayed characters who thought and acted like the students would. Movies that showed characters who remained true to the historical context rather than modern norms were considered unrealistic. These studies show that students instinctively apply strategies when engaged in historical reading and viewing, but their strategies focus on present values and fact finding rather than constructing an interpretation—epistemological approaches that interfere with historical thinking.

Stahl and his team of researchers (1996) observed advanced tenth grade students engaged in an investigation of the Gulf of Tonkin Incident. After a series of preassessments, students received 11 documents to choose from. They took notes as they read, then wrote either a description or an opinion essay on the Gulf of Tonkin Incident and resolution. The researchers used students' notes to identify a range of general reading strategies (i.e., copying information verbatim, paraphrasing, reducing multiple ideas into a single thought, or capturing the gist of complex ideas). Aware of Wineburg's (1991) earlier study, the researchers also watched for sourcing, corroboration, and contextualization in students' notes and essays. Researchers found that students frequently chose secondary sources over primary sources. Researchers speculated that students may have valued the seemingly objective account, a finding that corroborates the trust students placed in the textbook in Wineburg's (1991) study. Students' purposeful selection of a seemingly unbiased secondary source demonstrates a strategy, of sorts, though not a strategy that mirrors the thinking of historians. The researchers concluded that students approached the task with an unsophisticated epistemic stance, failing to understand the process of constructing historical knowledge. Presenting students with multiple texts, in the absence of instruction on history's constructed nature, did not spontaneously produce historical thinking.

Some researchers observed novices' reasoning strategies when asked to assume the role of a historian or a juror (Kuhn, Weinstock, & Flaton, 1994). They found that teenage and adult novices faced similar struggles whether playing historian or juror. For example, they were inappropriately certain of their interpretation. Less than half spontaneously cited evidence to support their conclusions. When pressed for evidence, many elaborated on their interpretation but still failed to provide evidence. Kuhn and her colleagues concluded that novices' unsophisticated epistemic stance (i.e., looking for a single, objective interpretation) played a major role in the strategies they employed—a finding common in research on novices' reading in history.

Researchers who studied older novices observed somewhat more mature strategies. For example, Rouet and a team of researchers (1996) found that undergraduate students used a number of strategies to evaluate the reliability of a document. These researchers labeled the students' rationale for trusting or distrusting a text *author justifications*, *document-type justifications*, *content justifications*, and *opinion justifications*, with the latter strategy based on personal opinions. These findings suggest that older students, under the right conditions, classify documents, engage in sourcing, and establish valid criteria for evaluating evidence.

The term "novice" has a wide range of meanings, with one recent study casting history doctoral students engaged in their dissertation work as novices—apprenticing historians. Schneider and Zakai (2016) suggested that doctoral students held some expertise in historical reading, but were novices in historical writing, which if remedied would lead to greater proficiency. The researchers conducted three interviews and two surveys with ten students at various stages of the dissertation writing process. They identified four "tensions" that developed as students wrote.

First, the writing process was complicated by ongoing research. Research and writing were recursive, with the writing process revealing gaps in understandings and promoting new research. Second, students struggled with the concept of historical imagination, aware of their role in constructing interpretations but fearful of taking too great a liberty with evidence. The students were often overwhelmed by the number of conflicting tidbits of evidence, using the strategy of *chunking* to create manageable patterns in the data. Third, dissertation writers struggled to know when to defend an emerging interpretation or to bend to contradictory evidence. Like the historians described above (Nokes & Kelser-Lund, 2019), students recognized the need for humility, knowing that eventually they would have to defend their conclusions with certainty. Finally, the doctoral students understood the foreignness of past contexts but had to make them coherent to modern readers. These expert-novices may have developed an awareness of the epistemology of history but lacked strategies for navigating this novel (for them) way of constructing knowledge. In response, they developed a number of unique strategies including *identifying patterns*, *telling engaging and plausible stories*, *modifying their positions*, and *empathically translating* the actions of historical characters into terms understandable today. This study reveals the problems of classifying research participants as novices or experts, suggesting that further work should be done to map the development of historical expertise.

Ongoing research is lengthening the list of strategies students employ when thinking historically. For example, Kim (2018) explored the strategies high school students used to distinguish between important and trivial historical information, a process sometimes called *ascribing historical significance*. Kim found that students used the narrative template of "tragedy and the struggle for freedom" to appropriately, and sometimes inappropriately, ascribe significance. Events that fit into the narrative of Korea's struggle against Japan, for instance, were deemed to be historically significant, reflecting both omissions and distortions in students' understandings. In a different study, Merkt, Werner, and Wagner (2017) used logs of ninth grade students' moves on a computer platform to observe their behaviors, making inferences about their strategic processing during a historical reading task. Students had to intentionally click on a link to access documents' source information, providing behavioral indicators of their cognitive processing. Researchers found that students who engaged in sourcing and corroboration more skillfully navigated a multiple-document task. In Samuelsson and Wendell's (2016) analysis of sixth grade Swedish students' standardized tests, they found that students critiqued sources, in this case artifacts, by reasoning about time (i.e., when an artifact was created in relation to the era it was being used to study); reasoning about authenticity (i.e., whether an artifact was original); reasoning about usefulness (i.e., whether the artifact helps them understand the past); and reasoning about deficiencies (i.e., weaknesses in the evidence).

To summarize, novices who engage in historical reading, thinking, and writing are strategic in their processes. However, most of the strategies novices use differ markedly from those used by experts, and often inhibit historical thinking. Students' unsophisticated epistemic stance may explain some of the immaturity in strategic processing. To be fair, there is evidence that older students exhibit rudimentary historical thinking strategies such as *classifying* documents and *sourcing*. Yet even doctoral students experience some of the frustrations of novices when engaged in historical writing. Admittedly, with the exception of the doctoral students, the observational studies cited here are dependent upon the students' task. Across studies, novices are especially influenced by the way that they are asked to demonstrate their thinking (Monte-Sano & De La Paz, 2012).

INSTRUCTIONAL APPROACHES FOR TEACHING NOVICES HISTORIANS' COGNITIVE STRATEGIES

Observational research makes clear that historical reading and writing present challenges for novices. Such processes are reliant on the strategies young people use and are contingent upon fragile and emerging understandings of the nature of history as a discipline and upon their epistemic stance. For instance, students might not only lack sophisticated strategies for formulating a compelling historical argument, but they might fail to understand why argumentation is needed in history. Further, students face challenges analyzing and using historical evidence. Finally, students who struggle with literacy in general, such as English-language learners and students with learning disabilities or other disabilities, may have additional linguistic, cognitive, or emotional needs that impact the strategies they use to engage in historical reading, thinking, speaking, and writing.

Fortunately, a growing body of research conducted internationally suggests that teachers can nurture students' historical thinking strategies and improve the resulting products (such as argumentative historical writing) by building background knowledge, teaching skills, and addressing students' understanding of historical inquiry. We now review exemplary studies from this body of research, highlighting instruction developed to teach students historians' cognitive strategies. While less common in the literature, recent work focuses on younger students (e.g., Wissinger, De La Paz, & Jackson, 2017), and on English learners (Monte-Sano, Schleppegrell, Hughes, & Thomson, 2018).

The majority of the instructional approaches reviewed here are complex, often lengthy multi-component interventions, each with more than one heuristic, strategy, or procedural facilitator (e.g., the use of model texts) to teach students more sophisticated historical reasoning. In addition, researchers define the primary focus of their interventions differently. Some study the cognitive frameworks that influence students' conceptual understanding of the processes of historical inquiry. Others attend to cognitive processes (e.g., reading and writing); still others study how class discussions impact student reasoning. We review studies according to the authors' emphasis, theoretical framing, and choice of student learning outcomes, noting at the same time where overlapping methodologies occur.

Instruction on First- and Second-order Concepts

Some educational researchers in the UK (Lee, 2005; Lee & Ashby, 2000), Canada (Seixas & Morton, 2013), the Netherlands (van Drie & van Boxtel, 2008), and the United States (VanSledright, 2002) suggest that students need a cognitive framework for understanding the discipline of history. They label substantive concepts (concrete events, concepts, dates as well as abstract concepts such as nationalism and imperialism) *first-order concepts*. In contrast, *metaconcepts* or *second-order concepts* are related to historical methodologies—*evidence*, *accounts*, *traces*, *significance*, and *perspective*, for instance, carry specialized meanings. As a correct understanding of and fluency with these concepts are foundational in historical inquiry, some researchers have studied how to best foster them.

Because argumentation within history carries certain nuances, van Drie, Braaksma, and van Boxtel (2015) explored the effects of teaching domain general or domain specific argument text structure. They provided advanced 11th-grade students with one of two sample essays during instruction on historical significance. They found a positive effect on historical reasoning for those who viewed the essay that followed nuanced disciplinary norms. Those students were more adept at ascribing *significance*, identifying *causation*, and noting *change*, all historical metaconcepts.

In related studies, Stoel, Van Drie, and Van Boxtel (2015, 2017) explored the effects of explicit instruction or implicit instruction on causal historical reasoning. Explicit instruction, provided by the teacher, focused on causal links between actions and motives of historical actors and contextual factors that explain, limit, or motivate their actions. Students in the implicit condition received no such instruction. Students in both groups were then asked to evaluate the significance of causes and provide arguments for their evaluation. Students in the experimental conditions scored significantly higher at post-test on causal-reasoning strategies and second-order concepts in both studies but no differences were found between conditions in the overall quality of students' written explanations. Small (and inconsistent) changes were found with students' epistemological beliefs. This research suggests that even advanced high school students need instruction in second-order concepts related to causal thinking.

Instruction on Reading Historically

As noted above, historians engage in strategic and purposeful recursive reading and writing processes when engaged in inquiry, critically analyzing the purpose behind texts written by others as they consider their own purposes, plans, and goals for writing (Nokes & Kelser-Lund, 2019). Moreover, intervention researchers outside of the field of history report that teaching students cognitive reading and writing strategies can transfer across processes in a manner that makes it productive to teach them together (Graham & Hebert, 2010). While recognizing benefits to integrating opportunities to read and write about the same historical topic with instruction on each process, some of the earliest studies on nurturing students' historical literacy focus solely on historical reading strategies without attention to writing. Britt and Aglinskas (2002) used cognitive apprenticeships (Brown, Collins, & Duguid, 1989), formed through a computer application called the *Sourcer's Apprentice*, to teach students to source and corroborate when reading multiple documents. This interface modeled how experts analyze documents, then gradually shifted responsibility for completing tasks to students, providing them with structured opportunities to practice. The results indicated that after minimal training, students in an experimental condition demonstrated better sourcing and wrote better essays than those in a control group. Their writing contained more document-based content and more explicit references to sources. This early study demonstrated the potential of providing students with explicit instruction in sourcing and corroboration along with a set of increasingly difficult reasoning tasks. However, few students were involved in the study and no multilevel statistical analyses were conducted.

Nokes, Dole, and Hacker (2007) found that direct instruction on sourcing, corroboration, and contextualization helped high school students use sourcing and corroboration in their writing. The researchers manipulated whether students read multiple texts or a traditional textbook, and whether the instructional focus was on content or historical reasoning. In contrast to prior studies, students engaged in sustained, connected practice, during which they considered critical questions (e.g., which two documents would you rank as the most reliable? Why?). The results showed that the use of multiple texts was the most important factor in learning historical content, and that strategy instruction was central in establishing students' use of sourcing and corroboration. Students showed little improvement in contextualization in spite of multiple lessons, a finding Reisman replicated (Reisman, 2012). Unfortunately, the post-test did not investigate students' overall historical thinking, merely their strategy use.

In 2011, Goldberg, Schwarz, and Porat conducted a descriptive study with Israeli 12th graders. Students grappled with controversial questions about the responsibility and morality of Zionist institutions. The researchers provided a lesson on source reliability and corroboration, similar to Britt and Aglinskas (2002)'s approach. Students then discussed the issues, employing *substantiation*, the use of evidence to support an argument. Students' essays, written after discussions, were evaluated for students' analysis of evidence, sourcing, and epistemological stances. Data revealed that differences in students' ethnic backgrounds were associated with differences in source evaluation, with students less critical of sources that mirrored their personal views. The implications of this finding for history instruction and preparation for civic engagement are profound and considered below.

In a year-long experiment on the effects of document-based activities from the *Reading Like a Historian* curriculum, Reisman (2012) found that explicit strategy instruction in sourcing, contextualization, close reading, and corroboration improved both struggling and proficient students' sourcing and close reading (but not contextualization or corroboration). Reisman proposed that contextualization and corroboration required a deeper epistemological understanding of the discipline, concluding that her instruction was not sufficient for students to internalize these skills. Despite these findings, whole class discussions that were part of the instruction students received gave them opportunities to defend their claims in the face of peer critique. Showing positive effects for sourcing and close reading, Reisman's (2012) work suggests that discussions can bridge everyday and disciplinary arguments if used to critically evaluate evidence.

Historical Discussions and Debates

As reform efforts in teaching history shift away from a dependence on textbooks and teacher lecture to more epistemically mature ways of constructing meaning from primary and secondary source documents, researchers have explored the benefits of discussions as a means for activating student interest and promoting disciplinary thinking (Nussbaum & Edwards, 2011). MacArthur, Ferretti, and Okolo (2002) employed debates on 20th-century immigration to facilitate sixth grade students' historical thinking and content learning. Recognizing the role of *perspective taking* in historical thinking, the researchers hoped the debates would afford opportunities to consider the perspectives of both immigrants and people opposed to immigration. Students showed an improved understanding of multiple perspectives, but their arguments were characteristic of everyday discussions rather than of historical reasoning. Students seldom used specific evidence to substantiate their claims. Researchers concluded that more instruction on historical argumentation was needed. However, findings indicated that students with disabilities participated fully in the debates, suggesting that debates are viable ways to support students' learning.

More recently, Wissinger and De La Paz (2016) examined whether middle school students could use argumentation schemes proposed by Walton, Reed, and Macagno (2008) as heuristics during discussion to learn content and write historical arguments. Though originally conceptualized for philosophers, two common forms of argument are both consistent with strategies that historians use and observed in the historical writing of strong secondary students (De La Paz, Ferretti, Wissinger, Yee, & MacArthur, 2012). The *argument from expert opinion* was therefore used as a model for teaching sourcing and the *argument from consequences* scheme prompted students to consider causal relationships of historical events. Teachers used critical questions to help students test the strength of their argument or its premises (Macagno & Konstantinidou, 2013) similar to those used by Nokes et al. (2007). The researchers found benefits for students in the experimental condition in sourcing, assessing causation, and understanding competing perspectives. They demonstrated increased levels of *substantiation, perspective recognition, contextualization,* and *rebuttal* in their written arguments.

Instruction on Historical Writing

Several studies describe interventions that address argumentative historical writing, ranging from research on the benefits of teacher-provided feedback (Leinhardt, 2000; Young & Leinhardt, 1998) to the general use of explicit strategy instruction (e.g., Stoel et al., 2015, 2017). Across studies, only sustained instruction, such as cognitive apprenticeships, has consistently led to substantive improvements in student writing.

Cognitive Apprenticeships

In a series of studies that focused on historical writing instruction, De La Paz (2005, De La Paz & Felton, 2010; De La Paz et al., 2014, 2017) and her colleagues used cognitive apprenticeships to embed explicit instruction on writing, argument, and thinking. Cognitive apprenticeship became both an instructional model that helped teachers organize the learning environment, and an approach to learning that revealed otherwise hidden cognitive processes to students. Researchers created inquiry lessons that gave students multiple, developmentally appropriate opportunities to practice historical reading and writing. Teachers moved through several stages of instruction, helping students set learning goals and develop metacognitive strategies. In keeping with the cognitive apprenticeship model, teachers taught historical reading and writing heuristics and modeled them by thinking aloud (Collins, Brown, & Holum, 1991), then gradually released responsibility to students who applied the heuristics with reduced scaffolding. Scaffolding included tools to use while reading, planning, and writing, and tools for teachers to monitor students' progress (Monte-Sano, De La Paz, & Felton, 2014a, 2014b).

De La Paz's work collectively shows that when implemented with fidelity, even when controlling for students' entry learning characteristics (e.g., reading proficiency), academically and culturally diverse middle school students improve in their ability to analyze evidence, acknowledge others' perspectives, contextualize, write substantiated historical arguments, and rebut counterclaims. Further, their general writing ability improves. Interviews suggested that many students gained a more sophisticated epistemological approach, though to varying degrees and in ways that correlated with their incoming reading abilities. Although more work needs to be done to replicate this research with different learners and tasks, this program of research clearly establishes the viability of cognitive apprenticeships to teach historical reading, thinking, and writing strategies (De La Paz, 2005; De La Paz & Felton, 2010; De La Paz et al., 2014, 2017).

Recognizing that students learning English often need additional linguistic supports to advance their knowledge of written language, Monte-Sano and a team of researchers

(2018) developed a two-year intervention for sixth and seventh graders with varying academic and linguistic profiles. Their approach, while similar to De La Paz et al.'s use of disciplinary literacy tools to support students, is unique in their use of model essays designed to help English learners develop language structures. These model essays initially provided a fully formed example of the kind of text students were expected to write on the same topic, with blanks to indicate where students were to bring their own claims, evidence, and reasoning. Later, this model became less "template-like," with the writing sample on a related, rather than the same, topic. Older students received only a procedural facilitator, offering options for introducing claims, evidence, and reasoning. Unfortunately, while appearing promising, the authors have yet to disseminate detailed findings on students' linguistic advances (i.e., syntactic development), beyond describing the level of thematic development of ideas.

Wissinger et al. (2017) evaluated the benefits in teaching fourth through sixth graders a reading strategy ("I3C") and a writing strategy ("PROVE IT!") in concert. I3C prompted students to (a) identify the author's stance, (b) identify 3 ideas supporting the author's stance, and to (c) check for limitations in the author's argument. PROVE IT! prompted students to focus on text structure and the skills of historical argumentation, reminding students to (a) provide background information on the historical problem, (b) report their interpretation, (c) offer 3 evidence-based reasons, (d) voice the other side's interpretation, (e) establish a rebuttal, then consider (f) is the argument convincing, and (g) total up what you know by adding a concluding sentence.

This intervention was designed to be developmentally appropriate for younger students. Because elementary students were presumed to know less about history than secondary learners (VanSledright, 2002), the authors integrated timelines, historical cartoons, and excerpts from newspapers into secondary sources. Digital images, audio, and other video media were integrated into the lessons. Each historical investigation was taught in five days, allowing teachers time to provide background information, model, facilitate guided practice, and hold discussions on the qualities of strong writing. After controlling for gender, ethnicity, and pre-test scores, students in the intervention scored higher in historical writing and overall writing quality (a holistic writing measure), and wrote longer essays after instruction and on maintenance probes. Moreover, students with disabilities benefited to the same degree as students without disabilities, after controlling for students' initial reading proficiency.

Summary

A growing body of literature examines instructional strategies that help novices begin to develop the cognitive strategies used by historians. While some posit the importance of new cognitive frameworks to help novices understand the discipline of history, and others provide instruction in multiple cognitive strategies, a common theme is the evaluation of evidence through sourcing. Moreover, with the exception of short intervention studies, students who were taught through a combination of explicit instruction, metacognitive modeling, writing samples, and class or small group instruction improved in their disciplinary reasoning. Additional benefits occur when teachers provide feedback on students' progress in reasoning and writing. While it might be reasonable to hope that such improvements could be realized through a singular focus on one or a few cognitive strategies, this idea is not supported by the research, neither is it likely given the complexity of cognitive processes observed of historians. In fact, the strongest evidence for learning appears when teachers use a cognitive apprenticeship approach to instruction.

ISSUES AND LIMITATIONS IN RESEARCH ON COGNITIVE PROCESSING STRATEGIES

Observational studies of historians and novices have teased out important differences in the types of cognitive strategies that each engage in when making sense of historical evidence. To be clear, not all of the differences can be attributed to procedural knowledge, as historians also possess richer conceptual and factual knowledge. And, the type of cognitive strategies that historians engage in depends, in part, on their evidence, their specialization, and their task (c.f., Nokes & Kelser-Lund, 2019). In contrast to the literature on historians' practices, we know less about how novices can be instructed in historical thinking, in part because it is impossible to frame developmentally appropriate tasks for youngsters without dramatically changing the nature of the historical inquiry. For instance, to our knowledge, no studies consider students' independent research, which is fundamental to true historical inquiry. Further, students in K12 settings learn multiple subjects, which restricts the depth of exploration in history or any other discipline.

The results from intervention studies reveal that students as young as fourth grade can be taught to engage in sourcing and to write interpretations when tasks are structured for younger students and for those who are not fluent speakers in the dominant language, with varying rates for releasing responsibility to the learner. To illustrate, studies investigating cognitive apprenticeships ranged from two lessons with advanced high school students, to 25 lessons with fourth through sixth graders. To be sure, older students are more capable of understanding the goals of historical inquiry. However, the degree to which teachers gave students support and feedback while attempting new tasks has also varied in this literature, with concomitant differences in outcomes. Finally, researchers have yet to consistently parse their findings by type of student learners, so we have limited knowledge about educational outcomes for students with different learning histories.

In addition to the existing quasi-experimental and experimental intervention literature, recent descriptive work illustrates how innovative teachers provide instruction in cognitive processes and strategies in naturalistic settings. Nokes (2014) and VanSledright (2002) each provided instruction to fifth graders that led to more sophisticated understandings of historical inquiry. Nokes introduced 31 document-based activities into an otherwise traditional social studies curriculum, with positive results on students' thinking. After this work, students spontaneously questioned their textbook sources and demonstrated a greater understanding of historians' inquiry processes. Similar, in-depth work with older students has been done by researchers associated with the federally funded, multi-discipline Project READI (Reading, Evidence, and Argumentation in Disciplinary Instruction), which focused on the English language arts, history, and science over a five-year period (Litman et al., 2017; Shanahan, Bolz, Cribb, Goldman, Heppeler, & Manderino, 2016). While Project READI focuses on teachers, without information on learners or learning outcomes, it provides a vision of instruction that nurtures evidence-based argumentation. We anticipate information on outcomes to be forthcoming, and encourage others to explore similar sustained curriculum interventions.

Collectively, current intervention research findings are highly contextualized. Conclusions relate in part to differing levels of access to the curriculum (i.e., whether districts welcome in-depth inquiry or a few lessons), topic, field, level of authenticity in source (e.g., adapted or original documents), text genres (generally argumentation rather than multi-modal texts), and other idiosyncratic factors (e.g., participants' incoming abilities or whether researchers obtained research funding). We expect that the list of cognitive strategies demonstrated by experts and novices will grow as research teams investigate strategies historians use in unexplored authentic settings (e.g., use of print and nonprint, language-based and non-language based representations in Draper et al., 2010). Researchers might explore supporting students' use of digital media (similar to the United States' National History Day inquiry project) or argument-driven webpages, as ways to bridge more sophisticated historical writing. Finally, we recognize the need for continued attention to the topic of assessment of cognitive strategies. Nokes (2017) exploration of eighth grade students' sourcing provides one such example, as does work by Smith and Breakstone (2015), VanSledright (2014), and Seixas, Gibson, and Ercikan (2015) in a variety of educational contexts.

PRESENT AND FUTURE DIRECTIONS

Ample evidence shows that historians are unusually strategic readers. The strategies that they employ, including the way they approach a reading task, sourcing, corroboration, and contextualization, skepticism, perspective-taking, questioning, and others, make them stand out. Increasingly, history education has accepted the objective of helping young people read more like historians. While some have questioned the utility of this (Barton & Levstik, 2004; Heller, 2010), others claim that the strategies associated with historical thinking have numerous applications in an Information Age when online sources must be vetted, information must be cross-checked, and multiple conflicting accounts are becoming the norm. Some assume incorrectly that historical reading transfers easily to the study of current issues using online sources.

Wineburg and colleagues (2018) conducted pioneering work on the application of historical thinking strategies to online reading. They asked Stanford University students, historians, and professional factcheckers to evaluate two webpages on school bullying for accuracy and trustworthiness. The historians struggled. Some judged the website of a small extremist group to be more reliable than that of a large and respected organization. Pressed to justify their evaluation of the webpages, one historian discussed the text font used. Another admitted she had no idea how to identify the source. Citing "negative transfer," Wineburg concluded that the strategies historians applied in reading documents, particularly *vertical reading* (proceeding from the top of the page to the bottom), may interfere with strategic online reading. The university students, a generation raised on the Internet, fared no better than the historians. In contrast to historians and students, the professional factcheckers efficiently aced the task. Using *lateral reading*, the factcheckers opened numerous tabs and used outside sources (including Wikipedia) to investigate the creators of the Internet sites they evaluated. Once the source had been identified, the bias became apparent in the content of the webpage.

Wineburg's (2018) study suggests that the future of teaching historical thinking should include instruction in online reading. Americans increasingly obtain historical knowledge from Internet sources. The strategies of sourcing, corroboration, perspective-taking, humility, and approaching a document with mild skepticism could transfer to online reading. Wineburg concludes, however, that history teachers must intentionally teach for this transfer, with specialized instruction in online searching and reading strategies. Such research is lacking.

In addition, many people see history classrooms as the best place to prepare young people for civic engagement. Civic engagement demands many of the strategies of historical reading, thinking, and writing. For instance, Kuhn et al. (1994) found great overlap between historical reasoning and juror reasoning. Both the historian and juror reconstructed an event, piecing it together from incomplete, biased, and positioned stories of varying credibility. Both processes required sourcing, corroboration, and mild skepticism. Still, questions remain about whether nurturing historical strategies prepares young people for a life of researching issues, making an appeal to government representatives, voting, or serving on a jury.

Ongoing studies identify other strategies that historians use that may have applications for civic engagement. Historians' humility and the manner through which they explore plausible alternatives, even those that do not fit their interpretation at the moment, before arriving at a conclusion, may be useful in civic engagement as citizens work together and with elected officials to find mutually beneficial solutions. Ultimately, argumentation, which is at the heart of historical inquiry, is central to citizenship. In its essence the argumentative process is an ongoing conversation bringing together what multiple voices say in an effort to construct an evidence-based and reasonable interpretation (Graff, Birkenstein, & Durst, 2015). To date we know of no interventions that have explored how to teach students to apply their historical argumentation skills in ways that promote civic engagement. Much work remains to be done on the best ways to prepare young people for 21st-century historical and civic reading, writing, and thinking.

REFERENCES

Afflerbach, P., Pearson, P. D., & Paris, S. G. (2008). Clarifying differences between reading skills and reading strategies. *The Reading Teacher, 61*(5), 364–373.

Baron, C. (2012). Understanding historical thinking at historic sites. *Journal of Educational Psychology, 104*(3), 833.

Barton, K. C., & Levstik, L. S. (2004). *Teaching history for the common good.* New York: Routledge.

Bransford, J. D., Brown, A. L., & Cocking, R. R. (2000). *How people learn: Brain, mind experience and school.* Washington, DC: National Academy Press.

Breakstone, J, McGrew, S, Smith, M, Ortega, T, & Wineburg, S. (2018). Why we need a new approach to teaching digital literacy. Phi Delta Kappan, 99 (6), p27–32. Doi: 10.1177/0031721718762419

Britt, M. A., & Aglinskas, C. (2002). Improving students' ability to identify and use source information. *Cognition and Instruction, 20,* 485–522. doi:10.1207/S1532690XCI2004_2

Brown, J. S., Collins, A., & Duguid, P. (1989). Situated cognition and the culture of learning. *Educational researcher, 18*(1), 32–42. doi:10.3102/0013189X018001032

Chase, W. G., & Simon, H. A. (1973). Perception in chess. *Cognitive Psychology, 4*(1), 55–81.

Collingwood, R. G. (2005/1993). *The idea of history.* New York: Oxford.

Collins, A., Brown, J. S., & Holum, A. (1991). Cognitive apprenticeship: Making thinking visible. *American Educator, 15*(3), 6–11.

De La Paz, S. (2005). Effects of historical reasoning instruction and writing strategy mastery in culturally and academically diverse middle school classrooms. *Journal of Educational Psychology, 97,* 139–156. doi:10.1037/0022-0663.97.2.139

De La Paz, S., Felton, M., Monte-Sano, C., Croninger, R., Jackson, C., Deogracias, J. S., & Hoffman, B. P. (2014). Developing historical reading and writing with adolescent readers: effects on student learning. *Theory & Research in Social Education, 42*(2), 228–274. doi:10.1080/00933104.2014.908754

De La Paz, S., & Felton, M. K. (2010). Reading and writing from multiple source documents in history: Effects of strategy instruction with low to average high school writers. *Contemporary Educational Psychology, 35*(3), 174–192. doi:10.1016/j.cedpsych.2010.03.001

De La Paz, S., Ferretti, R., Wissinger, D., Yee, L., & MacArthur, C. (2012). Adolescents' disciplinary use of evidence, argumentative strategies, and organizational structure in writing about historical controversies. *Written Communication, 29*(4), 412–454.

De La Paz, S., Monte-Sano, C., Felton, M., Croninger, R., Jackson, C., & Piantedosi, K. W. (2017). A historical writing apprenticeship for adolescents: Integrating disciplinary learning with cognitive strategies. *Reading Research Quarterly, 52*(1), 31–52.

De La Paz, S. & Wissinger, D. (2017) Improving the historical knowledge and writing of students with or at-risk for LD. *Journal of Learning Disabilities, 50*(6) 658–671.

Draper, R. J., Broomhead, P., Jensen, A. P., Nokes, J. D., & Siebert, D. (Eds.). (2010). *(Re)imagining content-area literacy instruction.* New York: Teachers College Press.

Gee, J. P. (1989). Literacy, discourse, and linguistics: Introduction. *The Journal of Education, 171*(1), 5–176.

Graff, G., Birkenstein, C., & Durst, R. (2015). *They say, I say: The moves that matter in academic writing.* New York: W. W. Norton & Co.

Goldberg, T., Schwarz, B. B., & Porat, D. (2011). Could they do it differently?: Narrative and argumentative changes in students' writing following discussion of "hot" historical issues. *Cognition and Instruction, 29,* 185–217. http://dx.doi.org/10.1080/07370008.2011.556832.

Graham, S., & Hebert, M. A. (2010). Writing to read: Evidence for how writing can improve reading. *A Carnegie Corporation Time to Act Report.* Washington, DC: Alliance for Excellent Education.

Harris, L. M. (2012). Conceptual devices in the work of world historians. *Cognition and Instruction, 30*(4), 312–358.

Heller, R. (2010). In praise of amateurism: A friendly critique of Moje's "Call for Change" in secondary literacy. *Journal of Adolescent & Adult Literacy, 54*(4), 267–273. doi:10.1598/JAAL.54.4.4

Holt, T. (1995). *Thinking historically: Narrative, imagination, and understanding.* New York: College Board.

Kim, G. (2018). Holding the severed finger: Korean students' understanding of historical significance. *Journal of Curriculum Studies, 50*(4), 508–534.

Kuhn, D., Weinstock, M., & Flaton, R. (1994). Historical reasoning as theory-evidence coordination. In M. Carretero & J. F. Voss (Eds.), *Cognitive and instructional processes in history and the social sciences* (pp. 377–401). Hillsdale, NJ: Lawrence Erlbaum Associates.

Lee, P. J. (2005). Putting principles into practice: Understanding history. In M. S. Donovan & J. D. Bransford (Eds.), *How students learn: History, mathematics, and science in the classroom* (pp. 31–77). Washington, DC: National Academies Press.

Lee, P. J., & Ashby, R. A. (2000). Progression in historical understanding among students age 7-14. In P. N. Stearns, P. Seixas, & S. Wineburg (Eds.), *Knowing, teaching, and learning history. National and international perspectives* (pp. 199–222). New York: New York University Press.

Leinhardt, G. (2000). Lessons on teaching and learning in history from Paul's Pen. In P. N. Stearns, P. Seixas, & S. Winberg (Eds.), *Knowing, teaching, and learning history: National and international perspectives* (pp. 223–245). New York: New York University Press.

Leinhardt, G., & Young, K. M. (1996). Two texts, three readers: Distance and expertise in reading history. *Cognition & Instruction, 14,* 441–486.

Levesque, S. (2008). *Thinking Historically.* Toronto: University of Toronto Press.

Litman, C., Marple, S., Greenleaf, C., Charney-Sirott, I., Bolz, M. J., Richardson, L. K., Hall, A. H., George, M., & Goldman, S. R. (2017). Text-based argumentation with multiple sources: A descriptive study of opportunity to learn in secondary English language arts, history, and science. *Journal of the Learning Sciences, 26*(1), 79–130.

Macagno, F., & Konstantinidou, K. (2013). What students' arguments can tell us: Using argumentation schemes in science education. *Argumentation, 27*(3), 225–243.

MacArthur, C. A., Ferretti, R. P., & Okolo, C. M. (2002). On defending controversial viewpoints: Debates of sixth-graders about the desirability of early 20th century American immigration. *Learning Disabilities Research and Practice, 17*, 160–172.

Merkt, M., Werner, M., & Wagner, W. (2017). Historical thinking skills and mastery of multiple document tasks. *Learning and Individual Differences, 54*, 135–148.

Monte-Sano, C. (2010). Disciplinary literacy in history: An exploration of the historical nature of adolescents' writing. *Journal of Learning Sciences, 19*(4), 539–568.

Monte-Sano, C., & De La Paz, S. (2012). Using writing tasks to elicit adolescents' historical reasoning. *Journal of Literacy Research, 44*(3), 273–299. doi:10.1177/1086296X12450445

Monte-Sano, C., De La Paz, S., & Felton, M. (2014a). Implementing a disciplinary-literacy curriculum for US history: learning from expert middle school teachers in diverse classrooms. *Journal of Curriculum Studies, 46*(4), 540–575. doi:10.1080/00220272.2014.904444

Monte-Sano, C., De La Paz, S., & Felton, M. (2014b). *Reading, thinking, and writing about history: Teaching argument writing to diverse learners in the Common Core classroom, grades 6-12.* New York: Teachers College Press.

Monte-Sano, C., Schleppegrell, M., Hughes, R., & Thomson, S. (2018, April). Middle school students writing in history-social science: Disciplinary and linguistic perspectives. *Presentation at the American Educational Research Association (AERA) annual conference*, New York, NY.

Nokes, J. D. (2014). Elementary students' roles and epistemic stances during document-based history lessons. *Theory and Research in Social Education, 42*(3), 375–413.

Nokes, J. D. (2017). Exploring patterns of historical thinking through eighth-grade students' argumentative writing. *Journal of Writing Research, 8*(3), 437–467.

Nokes, J. D., Dole, J. A., & Hacker, D. J. (2007). Teaching high school students to use heuristics while reading historical texts. *Journal of Educational Psychology, 99*, 492–504. doi:10.1037/0022-0663.99.3.492

Nokes, J. D., & Kelser-Lund, A. (2018, November). An expert/novice/novice comparison of social interactions during document-based history lessons. *Presentation at the College and University Faculty Assembly (CUFA) annual conference*, Chicago, IL.

Nokes, J. D., & Kelser-Lund, A. (2019). Historians' social literacies: How historians collaborate and write during a document-based activity. *The History Teacher, 52*(3), 369–410.

Nussbaum, E. M., & Edwards, O. V. (2011). Critical questions and argument stratagems: A framework for enhancing and analyzing students' reasoning practices. *The Journal of the Learning Sciences, 20*, 443–488.

Reisman, A. (2012). Reading like a historian: A document-based history curriculum intervention in urban high schools. *Cognition and Instruction, 30*(1), 86–112. doi:10.1080/07370008.2011.634081

Rouet, J. F., Britt, M. A., Mason, R. A., & Perfetti, C. A. (1996). Using multiple sources of evidence to reason about history. *Journal of Educational Psychology, 88*(3), 478–493. doi:10.1037/00220663.88.3.478

Rouet, J. F., Favart, M., Britt, M. A., & Perfetti, C. A. (1997). Studying and using multiple documents in history: Effects of discipline expertise. *Cognition and Instruction, 15*, 85–106.

Samuelsson, J., & Wendell, J. (2016). Historical thinking about sources in the context of a standards-based curriculum: a Swedish case. *The Curriculum Journal, 27*(4), 479–499.

Schneider, J., & Zakai, S. (2016). A Rigorous Dialectic: Writing and Thinking in History. *Teachers College Record, 118*(1), 1–36.

Seixas, P. (1993). Popular film and young people's understanding of the history of Native American-White relations. *The History Teacher, 26*, 351–370.

Seixas, P., Gibson, L., & Ercikan, K. (2015). A design process for assessing historical thinking: The case of a one-hour test. In K. Ercikan & P. Seixas (Eds.), *New directions in assessing historical thinking* (pp. 102–116). New York: Routledge.

Seixas, P., & Morton, T. (2013). *The big six: Historical thinking concepts.* Toronto, ON: Nelson Education.

Shanahan, C., Bolz, M. J., Cribb, G., Goldman, S. R., Heppeler, J., & Manderino, M. (2016). Deepening what it means to read (and write) like a historian: Progressions of instruction across a school year in an eleventh grade US history class. *The History Teacher, 49*(2), 241–270.

Shanahan, C., Shanahan, T., & Misichia, C. (2011). Analysis of expert readers in three disciplines: History, mathematics, and chemistry. *Journal of Literacy Research, 43*, 393–429.

Shanahan, T., & Shanahan, C. (2008). Teaching disciplinary literacy to adolescents: Rethinking content-area literacy. *Harvard Educational Review, 78*(1), 40–59. doi:10.17763/haer.78.1.v62444321p602101

Smith, M., & Breakstone, J. (2015). History assessments of thinking: An investigation of cognitive validity. In K. Ercikan & P. Seixas (Eds.), *New directions in assessing historical thinking* (pp. 233–245). New York: Routledge.

Stahl, S. A., Hynd, C. R., Britton, B. K., McNish, M. M., & Bosquet, D. (1996). What happens when students read multiple source documents in history? *Reading Research Quarterly, 31,* 430–456.

Stoel, G. L., Van Drie, J. P., & Van Boxtel, C. A. M. (2015). Teaching towards historical expertise. Developing a pedagogy for fostering causal reasoning in history. *Journal of Curriculum Studies, 47*(1), 49–76.

Stoel, G. L., van Drie, J. P., & van Boxtel, C. A. M. (2017). The effects of explicit teaching of strategies, second-order concepts, and epistemological underpinnings on students' ability to reason causally in history. *Journal of Educational Psychology, 109*(3), 321.

Tishman, S., Jay, E., & Perkins, D. N. (1993). Teaching thinking dispositions: From transmission to enculturation. *Theory into Practice, 32*(3), 147–153.

Van Boxtel, C., & van Drie, J. (2012). "That's in the time of the Romans!" Knowledge and strategies students use to contextualize historical images and documents. *Cognition and Instruction, 30*(2), 113–145.

van Drie, J., Braaksma, M., & van Boxtel, C. (2015). Writing in history: Effects of writing instruction on historical reasoning and text quality. *Journal of Writing Research, 7*(1), 123–157.

van Drie, J., & van Boxtel, C. (2008). Historical reasoning: Towards a framework for analyzing students' reasoning about the past. *Educational Psychology Review, 20,* 87–110.

VanSledright, B. (2002). *In search of America's past: Learning to read history in elementary school.* New York: Teachers College Press.

VanSledright, B. A. (2014). *Assessing historical thinking and understanding: Innovative designs for new standards.* New York: Routledge.

Walton, D., Reed, C., & Macagno, F. (2008). *Argumentation schemes.* New York, NY: Cambridge University Press.

Wineburg, S. S. (1991). On the reading of historical texts: Notes on the breach between school and academy. *American Educational Research Journal, 28,* 495–519.

Wineburg, S. S. (1994). The cognitive representations of historical texts. In G. Leinhardt, I. L. Beck, & C. Stainton (Eds.), *Teaching and learning in history* (pp. 85–136). Hillsdale, NJ: Erlbaum.

Wineburg, S. S. (1998). Reading Abraham Lincoln: An expert/expert study in the interpretation of historical texts. *Cognitive Science, 22,* 319–346.

Wineburg, S. (2018). *Why learn history (when it's already on your phone).* University of Chicago Press.

Wissinger, D., De La Paz, S., & Jackson, C. (2017, November). The effects of the Ic3 for Reading/Prove It! For writing historical reasoning strategy with academically diverse elementary students. *Presentation at the College & University Faculty Assembly (CUFA) annual conference,* San Francisco.

Wissinger, D. R., & De La Paz, S. (2016). Effects of critical discussions on middle school students' written historical arguments. *Journal of Educational Psychology, 108*(1), 43–59.

Young, K. M., & Leinhardt, G. (1998). Writing from primary documents. *Written Communication, 15,* 25–68.

13

INTERPLAY OF STRATEGIC PROCESSES, EXECUTIVE FUNCTIONS, AND AUTONOMY SUPPORT IN STUDENTS WITH INDIVIDUAL DIFFERENCES

Ana Taboada Barber
UNIVERSITY OF MARYLAND, USA

Kelly B. Cartwright
CHRISTOPHER NEWPORT UNIVERSITY, USA

Susan Lutz Klauda
UNIVERSITY OF MARYLAND, USA

Consider Gabriela, a fifth grade student, who is reading a passage about polar bears as part of a science unit on the effects of climate change on animals and their habitats. To comprehend this, or any text, Gabriela must maintain an ever-developing representation of the text meaning in working memory while continuing to decode the words in the text, updating her mental model of text meaning as she proceeds. She must also monitor her understanding of individual words and larger idea units, connecting these to her prior knowledge of the topic, and inferring ideas that the author omits from the text. Gabriela reads:

> Climate change has caused melting of sea ice at the poles, giving rise to smaller areas of frozen land mass and rising sea levels. Polar bears are increasingly endangered because they often have to travel many miles, swimming for long periods, in order to find food.

Gabriela has no difficulty decoding these words. However, to understand the connection between these sentences (i.e., to preserve local text coherence and understand the effects of climate change on an animal species), Gabriela should infer that melting ice reduces the polar bears' habitat, causing them to have to travel longer distances to find food. But, for English Learners (ELs) like Gabriela, who often struggle with reading comprehension despite adequate word decoding abilities, such inferences are often difficult. Similarly, English monolingual children with the same profile of reading skills – adequate word decoding with comparably poor reading comprehension, called specific reading comprehension deficits (RCD) – have difficulty monitoring their understanding (or lack of understanding) of texts and typically fail to make coherence-building inferences to preserve comprehension (Cain & Oakhill, 1999; Cain, Oakhill, Barnes, & Bryant, 2001; Oakhill, Hartt, & Samols, 2005).

In the current chapter, we follow early trends in research on strategic processing and take reading comprehension as our test case for examining relations of executive function (EF) skills, reading comprehension strategies, and autonomy support as a specific practice that fosters motivated and self-regulated behavior. Further, we have identified two groups of students, described in the opening vignette (i.e., ELs, and students with RCD), whose individual differences generate variability in reading comprehension performance, which may enlighten understanding of the relations among the three main variables of interest in the chapter. This chapter converges with that of Afflerbach, Hurt, and Cho (this volume) in focusing on reading strategies, yet diverges from it in centering on the linkages of strategic processing to EF skills and autonomy support, two constructs that are susceptible to improve the learning and reading comprehension of ELs and students with RCD.

EXECUTIVE FUNCTIONS AND STRATEGIC PROCESSES: HISTORICAL OVERVIEW

Strategic Processes in Reading Comprehension

As the opening vignette illustrates, skilled reading comprehension is an incredibly complex task that requires management of multiple, simultaneous, cognitive processes, all directed toward the goal of understanding text. We agree with Wagner, Schatschneider, and Phythian-Sence (2009) that one of the primary purposes for reading is to understand texts. Since the 1970s, the literacy field has seen increased interest in – and research into – the components of reading comprehension processes, particularly the strategic processes used by skilled readers to understand text (see Table 13.1 for numbers of citations by decade). This work has revealed that metacognitive strategies, such as inference making and comprehension monitoring, are at the heart of skilled reading comprehension for children and adults (see Afflerbach, Hurt, & Cho (this volume) for a review). However, monitoring and inference making are difficult for children and develop slowly over the elementary school years (Markman, 1977, 1979; Zabrucky & Ratner, 1986). Fortunately, these strategies can be taught in the context of reading real texts, resulting in improvements in reading comprehension (Brown, Pressley, Van Meter, & Schuder, 1996; Pearson & Dole, 1987), a point we take up later in this chapter.

Interest in children's cognition, including strategy use, expanded in the United States in the 1970s, due in large part to John Flavell's work. Flavell was instrumental in making Piaget's pioneering work in children's cognitive development available in the United States in the 1960s (Flavell, 1963, 1985), making children's cognitive development a valid field of study after a long period of behaviorist perspectives on children's learning. Flavell quickly turned his attention to his now landmark work in metacognition, particularly his emphasis on the deliberate, planful nature of metacognitive strategy use (Flavell, 1979). These developments in understanding children's

218 • Ana Taboada Barber et al.

Table 13.1 Numbers of Citations in Google Scholar by Decade

Decade	Google Scholar Search Terms	
	"Strategy Use" and "Reading Comprehension"	"Development of Executive Function"
1970–1979	20	24
1980–1989	529	15
1990–1999	1,690	67
2000–2009	4,930	1,050
2010–2019	13,900	6,180

thinking were paralleled by work on adults' thinking that highlighted distinctions – and relations – between automatic and effortful, controlled cognitive processes (Shiffrin & Schneider, 1977).

Early research on children's cognitive strategies, inspired by Flavell's work, often focused on reading comprehension because its complexity offered a useful test case for strategy use. For example, Ellen Markman used an inconsistency-detection paradigm in which children read passages that contained deliberate inconsistencies and then were asked whether the passages "made sense." This work revealed first to third grade children (Markman, 1977), and even third to sixth grade children (Markman, 1979), did not actively monitor their own reading comprehension. These data were corroborated by interview findings that indicated 8- to 12-year-old children were often unaware of strategies to repair comprehension failure (Myers & Paris, 1978). Ensuing experimental work indicated that not only did elementary school children have difficulty monitoring comprehension of texts for inconsistencies, they also had difficulty making corrective inferences to repair comprehension after it had broken down (Zabrucky & Ratner, 1986). Noting the need for a comprehensive model of strategy use to guide the growing work in this area, Michael Pressley worked with colleagues Wolfgang Schneider and John Borkowski to develop the Good Strategy User (GSU) model, which described well the nature of strategic processes employed when readers actively comprehend texts. Pressley studied under Flavell in his early years of graduate school, and his ideas about metacognitive strategy use were clearly influenced by Flavell's work, a point he has acknowledged (Pressley, 2005; Pressley, Borkowski, & Schneider, 1987). In the GSU, strategies are defined as:

> [c]omposed of cognitive operations over and above the processes that are a natural consequence of carrying out [a] task, ranging from one such operation to a sequence of interdependent operations. Strategies achieve cognitive purposes (e.g., comprehending, memorizing) and are potentially conscious and controllable activities.
>
> (Pressley, Forrest-Pressley, Elliott-Faust, & Miller, 1985, p. 4)

These can become automatized with practice but are still available for conscious reflection when necessary, such as when comprehension breaks down.

Reading Comprehension Strategies and Executive Functions: Areas of Convergence

The GSU definition of strategies, which focuses on active, goal-directed management of tasks, is similar to definitions of EF that have emerged in the literature. For example, Goldstein and Naglieri (2014, p. 4) indicate "executive functions represent the capacity to plan, to do things, and to perform adaptive actions." EFs are goal-directed cognitive operations that enable the management of thoughts, feelings, and behaviors in order to reach particular goals (Diamond, 2013; Goldstein & Naglieri, 2014). And, although research interest in children's strategy use, particularly with respect to reading comprehension, blossomed beginning in the 1970s, interest in the development of EF is comparatively new to the field (see Table 13.1). The term "executive control" originally emerged in the neuropsychological literature, when Pribram (1973) hypothesized the relation of executive control to frontal lobe functioning; however, research in this area focused primarily on EF deficits in individuals with brain injuries or other neuropsychological problems (Goldstein & Naglieri, 2014). One exception is Myers and Paris (1978, p. 680), in the introduction to their study of children's metacognitive awareness about reading, who noted, "Metacognitive knowledge serves an executive function of coordinating and directing the learner's thinking and behavior." Only recently (i.e., around the year 2000, see Table 13.1) have researchers begun to focus on the development of EF and its relations to other developmental outcomes, such as academic success (e.g., Best, Miller, & Naglieri, 2011), rather than on EF deficits associated with neuropsychological problems or brain injuries (Goldstein & Naglieri, 2014).

Although parallels between metacognitive strategy use and EF are clear (i.e., they both involve goal-directed operations that enable management of behavioral or cognitive processes), little research has investigated the relations between the two. In 2000, Borkowski and colleagues (Borkowski, Chan, & Muthukrishna, 2000) expanded the GSU and suggested links between executive control, motivation, and strategy use. Specifically, Borkowski et al. (2000) hypothesized that EF processes develop because of successful applications of individual strategies. Those successes could lead to motivation for learning which will likely promote application of strategies in new contexts. That is, Borkowski and colleagues suggested that EF emerges only after children have learned and implemented specific strategies. Similarly, Chevalier and Blaye (2016) suggested the development of independent strategy use contributes to the development of children's EF. Finally, Roebers and Feurer (2016) recently argued that both EF and procedural metacognition (i.e., strategy use) contribute to children's developing control over their own cognitive systems, based on reviewing theoretical and empirical work from cognitive, self-regulation, and neuropsychological literatures. More empirical research is needed, however, to disentangle the nature of relations between EF, metacognition, motivation, and engagement in cognitive control processes, such as strategies.

CURRENT WORK ON EFS AND STRATEGIES IN STUDENTS WITH INDIVIDUAL DIFFERENCES

EFs and Reading Comprehension

EFs refer to a set of top-down mental processes required when one needs to guide behavior toward a goal or to coordinate performance in complex tasks (Dawson & Guare,

2010; Diamond, 2013): skills needed to work in a motivated or engaged fashion (e.g., toward a goal that may not be reached immediately; Blaye & Chevalier, 2011; Gillberg & Coleman, 2000), which implicates the involvement of motivational and engagement processes. EFs are important to learning and cognitive and emotional development because they enable children to take time to think, resist temptations or distractions, hold information in memory, and play with ideas while staying focused (e.g., Diamond, 2013). Although there are various conceptualizations of the component skills that make up EF, there is wide agreement that there are three core EFs – inhibition, working memory, and shifting or cognitive flexibility (Diamond, 2013; Miyake et al., 2000). *Inhibition*, or *inhibitory control*, refers to the suppression of dominant, habitual, or prepotent responses when necessary for task completion (Miyake et al., 2000). *Working memory* includes both storage and processing components, and refers to the holding in mind and manipulation of information while performing some operation on it (Diamond, 2013; Miyake et al., 2000). *Cognitive flexibility*, or "shifting," refers to switching back and forth among multiple tasks, operations, or dimensions of tasks (Chevalier & Blaye, 2008; Monsell, 1996) such as shifting attentional focus from an idea or a category to a new one. From the combination of these EFs, higher order EFs are built, such as reasoning, problem solving, and planning (e.g., Collins & Koechlin, 2012). If we consider the three core EFs, each plays a unique role in the prediction of reading comprehension. Working memory (Cain, 2006; Sesma, Mahone, Levine, Eason, & Cutting, 2009), inhibition (Cain, 2006; Kieffer, Vukovic, & Berry, 2013), and cognitive flexibility (Cartwright et al., 2017; Kieffer et al., 2013) all contribute significantly to reading comprehension. Additionally, composite measures of EF (based on factor analyses and theoretical underpinnings for similar functions/skills) made distinct contributions to variance in the reading comprehension of native ESs and ELs in the elementary grades (e.g., Taboada Barber et al., 2019). In sum, the evidence of the direct contributions of EFs to reading comprehension extends to a variety of readers: typically developing readers, students with RCD, and ELs.

However, the question remains: why do EFs relate to reading comprehension? If we think of each of the core EF skills, we can, at least conceptually, understand the roles they play in reading comprehension. *Working memory* plays a critical role in integrating information during comprehension by (a) holding recently processed information to make connections to the latest input (e.g., sentence/idea/word) and (b) maintaining the gist of information for the construction of an overall representation of text (e.g., Cain, Oakhill, & Lemmon, 2004). Cain et al. (2004) also suggest individual differences in inference making and comprehension monitoring are related to working memory. *Inhibition* is important to reading comprehension because it allows readers to forget or suppress information that is no longer relevant, such as inhibition of irrelevant word meanings when activating the meaning of words in a text (Barnes, Faulkner, Wilkinson, & Dennis, 2004; Henderson, Snowling, & Clarke, 2013). Inhibition may also play a role in ignoring irrelevant information at the sentence or paragraph level when building a coherent mental representation of a complete text, such as details not relevant to the overall meaning of the passage (Borella, Carretti, & Pelegrina, 2010; Cain, 2006; Kintsch, 1988). The third core EF skill, *cognitive flexibility*, is particularly important for the flexible coordination of multiple aspects of the comprehension task, such as shifting focus between words, letters, and sounds to their meaning in early childhood (Cartwright et al., 2017; Cartwright, Marshall, Dandy, & Isaac, 2010), middle childhood (Cartwright, 2002; Colé, Duncan, & Blaye, 2014), and adulthood (Cartwright, 2007; Georgiou & Das, 2018), even when controlling for known predictors of reading comprehension. Further, children and adults with RCD are lower in cognitive flexibility than typically developing peers (Cartwright, Bock, Coppage, Hodgkiss, & Nelson, 2017; Cartwright et al., 2017).

Executive Functions and Students with Individual Differences

Given that EFs refer to a family of top-down mental processes that are needed for concentration and control of attention, as well as self-regulation of behavior, their impact on learning goes beyond reading comprehension. Indeed, several areas of achievement are impacted by EFs, such as mathematics and science achievement (Bull & Lee, 2014; Latzman, Elkovitch, Young, & Clark, 2010) and writing (Altemeier, Jones, Abbott, & Berninger, 2006). However, although EFs have been explored in populations with individual differences such as students with RCD (e.g., Cain, 2006; Cartwright et al., 2017), they have been scarcely explored in ELs. Yet, the extant evidence has shown consistently that bilingual children (and adults) perform better on measures of EF skills than English monolingual speakers (e.g., Bialystok, 1999; Bialystok & Martin, 2004; Carlson & Meltzoff, 2008), possibly because bilingualism enhances a general network of executive control, in addition to targeting specific core components such as inhibition (cf. Bialystok & Martin, 2004) or shifting (cf. Meuter & Allport, 1999). Thus, an important outcome of bilingualism may be in managing executive control components to address complex goals (Bialystok, 2015). However, limited research has focused on whether the benefits of EFs found for fully bilingual populations apply to ELs in the elementary grades in the United States.

EFs and Strategies: Relations and State of the Literature

As noted above, although interest in children's strategy use and the development of executive functions has blossomed in recent decades (see Table 13.1), few empirical connections have been made between these literatures (Roebers & Feurer, 2016). Additionally, thinking in this area is mixed, with some scholars suggesting metacognitive strategy use might influence the development of EF (Borkowski et al., 2000; Chevalier & Blaye, 2016), others that EF contributes to strategy use (Gnaedinger, Hund, & Hesson-McInnis, 2016), and yet others holding the view that strategic metacognitive monitoring may be a complex form of EF (Dawson & Guare, 2010; Meltzer, 2010). Given the incipient state of this literature, we consider the relations of EFs and strategy use in the current chapter, paying particular attention to these variables in EL students and students with RCD.

ISSUES AND LIMITATIONS OF THESE TOPICS

EFs and Strategies in Students with Individual Differences

EFs and Poor Comprehenders. Studies comparing poor comprehenders (i.e., students wiZth RCD) with students whose comprehension skills are on a par with their age or grade have shown that less skilled comprehenders struggle with strategic monitoring of reading comprehension, assessed with the inconsistency detection paradigm developed by Markman (1977, 1979). In particular, children with RCD have difficulty detecting inconsistencies in text across pairs of sentences (as required in the comprehension monitoring task), both when the inconsistent sentences are adjacent and when they are separated within the text – increasing the working memory demands of the task (e.g., Oakhill et al., 2005). Sentence comprehension is also more challenging for children who struggle with working memory, such that they have more difficulty understanding sentences with complex syntactic structure than children who don't have challenges with working memory (Wingfield & Grossman, 2006). Further, neurocognitive evidence using fMRI revealed that comprehension of sentences with high working memory demands (i.e., containing additional phrases) was associated with greater inferior parietal cortex activation, evincing a large neural network supporting comprehension tasks that recruit various working memory and planning resources (Novais-Santos et al., 2007)

Sesma et al. (2009) and Follmer (2018) suggest that EF may contribute to reading comprehension because of its possible relations to higher order strategic processing in reading. Indeed, evidence shows that training reading-specific strategic processes improves reading comprehension for struggling comprehenders (e.g., Brown et al., 1996; Yuill & Joscelyne, 1988), which may do so by strengthening underlying EF skills. However, more work is needed in order to substantiate empirically this relation.

EFs and Strategies in ELs. Although there is some research showing the impact of strategy instruction on the reading comprehension of middle-school ELs (e.g., Taboada Barber et al., 2015, 2018; Vaughn et al., 2009), this work does not consider the possible relations between EFs and reading strategies, or EFs and reading comprehension. Precisely because the study of EFs is relatively new within the population of ELs, little is known about the potential interactions or relations between EF skills and achievement, or between EFs and cognitive processes such as comprehension strategies, in this population.

In some of our recent work we found that the two focal reading comprehension strategies of this chapter, inference making and comprehension monitoring, partially mediated the relation of a composite of the three core EF skills (i.e., working memory, inhibition, and cognitive flexibility) at the beginning of the school year with reading comprehension at the end of the year, while controlling for prior reading comprehension in both ELs and ESs in grades 1 through 4 (Taboada Barber et al., 2019). In agreement with others (e.g., Follmer, 2018; Gnaedinger et al., 2016; Sesma et al., 2009), we suggest that the self-regulation and higher order processing entailed in reading comprehension strategies likely necessitate EF skills, which may explain why inferencing and comprehension monitoring act as an explanatory mechanism (mediator) between EF skills and reading comprehension. That is, we suggest that the self-regulatory and intentional nature of strategies, in tandem with the higher order thinking involved in deploying strategic processes, may require or depend on EF skills. For instance, consider inhibitory control (one of the core EFs measured in the aforementioned study) as a required EF for strategic processing during reading comprehension. The capacity for inhibitory control of attention enables a prepotent mental representation (e.g., extraneous thoughts or information acquired earlier) to be resisted (Postle, Brush, & Nick, 2004) in order to attend to other information based on our goals or intention (Diamond, 2013). An association between inhibition and comprehension monitoring can be hypothesized since asking readers to resolve inconsistencies as part of a comprehension monitoring task requires them to (a) attend to the contradictory information, (b) hold it in working memory (inhibitory control is associated with several working memory measures, Diamond, 2013), (c) discard or inhibit the previously acquired (contradictory) information in order to bring the relevant information to the forefront, and (d) establish coherence between the relevant information and the rest of passage. By the same token, inhibitory control can also be strongly related to inferencing as a higher order strategic process, as when one needs to ignore irrelevant inter-sentence information in order to connect two ideas or sentences that are not adjacent to make an inference.

Cognitive flexibility, another of the core EFs we measured in ELs and their ES peers, is also a predictor of concurrent and later reading comprehension performance (Taboada Barber et al., 2019). Indeed, the ability to shift between the twin demands of decoding processes and meaning construction, as required in reading-related cognitive flexibility tasks, is clearly required for reading comprehension (as when we need to switch actively between decoding processes to updating our ever-changing mental model of text meaning in order to read for understanding) but is also likely required for inference making. If we consider that inference making requires that one consider elements from the text as well as our own background knowledge, it is apparent that switching between and coordinating text elements with knowledge we supply is essential to successful inference making. For example, in the opening vignette to the chapter, Gabriela had to coordinate and flexibly switch between ideas in the text and background knowledge about melting ice (i.e., that it gets smaller) in order to correctly infer that the polar bears' habitat was shrinking, causing them to need to travel further to find food. If a reader is unable to flexibly shift between ideas in the text and their own knowledge (while also successfully coordinating phonological, orthographic, and syntactic components of print), then inference making will fail.

Instruction in Inference Making: Benefits for Executive Functions?

As noted previously, it is plausible that instruction in comprehension strategies that require higher order processing, such as inferencing and comprehension monitoring, could result in enhancement of EFs. How might this occur? Some have suggested independent use of strategies might enhance EFs (Borkowski et al., 2000; Chevalier & Blaye, 2016) by providing practice in task-specific application of EF skills. Evidence indicates that although training in general (non-reading-specific) EF skills typically does not enhance reading comprehension (Jacob & Parkinson, 2015; Melby-Lervåg & Hulme, 2013), reading-specific tasks, which provide students with practice in coordinating various elements necessary for successful reading, enhance students' reading comprehension and reading-specific EF (Cartwright, 2002; Cartwright et al., 2017, 2010; García-Madruga et al., 2013; Melby-Lervåg & Hulme, 2013). Thus, it is reasonable to assume inference training may afford similar EF benefits. For example, one instructional activity used in training studies on inference making involves teaching students to identify clue words and using those clue words to infer such information as the setting of a story or the consequences of a character's action (McGee & Johnson,

2003; Yuill & Joscelyne, 1988; Yuill & Oakhill, 1988). For example, here is a story used by Yuill and Joscelyne (1988) to introduce students to making inferences:

> Tommy was lying down looking at a reading book. The room was full of steam. Suddenly Tommy got some soap in his eye. He reached wildly for the towel. Then he heard a splash. Oh no! What would he tell his teacher? He would have to buy a new one. Tommy rubbed his eye and it soon felt better.
>
> (Yuill & Joscelyne, 1988, p. 156)

After reading the story, children were guided in solving the "puzzle" of Tommy's location and of what happened to the book by a trainer who helped them identify clue words in the passage and make inferences based on those words. For the question of Tommy's location, the clue words were *lying down*, *steam*, *soap*, *towel*, and *splash*. Such activities may tap into students' use of the core EFs in multiple ways. For instance, to answer the question regarding Tommy's location, the reader must keep several, if not all, of the clues about the location in mind together and integrate them with their background knowledge to deduce that Tommy was in the bath, thus invoking working memory. At the same time, inhibition is likely entailed as the reader must ignore other associations conjured by the statement that Tommy was "lying down looking at a reading book," such as that he was stretched out on his bed. Cognitive flexibility is required throughout the activity as the reader must shift not only from decoding the words to identifying key (clue) words, but also from reading the passage fluently to strategically making local and global inferences. Local inferences involve linking separate ideas in text, whereas global inferences require that the reader use their prior knowledge to fill gaps in text meaning (Cain & Oakhill, 1999).

Two studies evaluating the effectiveness of inference training have included instruction in using clues to make inferences in concert with instruction in generating and answering "wh" questions (e.g., "who?," "where?," "why?") about a passage and predicting the content of "missing" sentences within a passage (McGee & Johnson, 2003; Yuill & Oakhill, 1988). In these studies, training took place in small groups that met for 6–7 sessions of 20–45 minutes. Yuill and Oakhill (1988), who studied 7- and 8-year-olds, found that those with RCD who received inference training gained 17 months in their comprehension on the Neale Analysis of Reading Ability, compared to 14 months for those who practiced answering comprehension questions orally and 6 months for those who trained in rapid decoding. In their study of 6- to 10-year-olds, McGee and Johnson (2003) found that both inference training and comprehension practice benefited students with RCD, with much greater improvement associated with the former. Additionally, Elbro and Buch-Iversen (2013) found that teaching children, via a visual support, to coordinate their prior knowledge with text elements enabled them to make inferences and improved their reading comprehension after eight 30-minute sessions.

Even shorter-term efforts appear to pay off for poor comprehenders. Yuill and Joscelyne's (1988) study provided 7- and 8-year-olds with individual training in identifying clue words and using them to solve the "puzzle" of missing information in a story, as described above, in just one session including two training stories. Notably, the stories lacked titles and pictures, which ordinarily provide indication of story meaning. Immediately after training, children were tested with eight similar story puzzles and comprehension questions. Students with RCD answered 85% of the test questions correctly, significantly outperforming their counterparts who were not given such training, who answered 72% correctly. These activities would likely strengthen students' EF skills by providing explicit strategies and practice identifying relevant elements (i.e., clues) in text and ignoring irrelevant elements (inhibition), holding multiple relevant elements of text in mind (working memory), and switching between finding missing information and attending to multiple text elements (cognitive flexibility).

Altogether, these training studies suggest that inference making is a malleable skill, especially for students who specifically struggle with reading comprehension. Further, training in higher order strategies appears to entail practice in – and thereby strengthening of – multiple EFs, thus suggesting that inference training may be a fruitful means of promoting reading achievement, as well as the development of EFs, which may itself have far-reaching benefits. How might cognitive strategy instruction facilitate EFs? As others have suggested (Borkowski et al., 2000; Chevalier & Blaye, 2016), independent use of strategies may strengthen EFs. However, students need particular kinds of instructional supports to achieve independence in strategy use (e.g., Brown, 2008), as we discuss in the next section.

FUTURE DIRECTIONS: THE ROLE OF AUTONOMY SUPPORT FOR EFS AND READING COMPREHENSION DEVELOPMENT

Autonomy Support, EFs, Reading Comprehension Strategies and Reading Engagement

Ultimately, beyond their cognitive benefits, strategies are higher order processing tools that should serve a greater good. In this case, the greater good is enhancing students' reading comprehension as well as their EF skills, given that these are malleable factors that have been associated with academic achievement and, broadly, several aspects of well-being (e.g., Best et al., 2011; Diamond, 2013). In addition, cognitive strategy instruction has consistently appeared to promote not just strategy application but also motivated, engaged reading (e.g., Guthrie, McRae, & Klauda, 2007; Souvignier & Mokhlesgerami, 2006). While learning and independently using higher order strategies may directly support students' developing EFs, it is plausible that higher order strategies also indirectly bolster EFs through their linkage with reading engagement (also see Borkowski et al., 2000).

Importantly, research exploring the reading engagement of middle school ELs has shown that engagement is a malleable factor susceptible to teacher influence (e.g., Taboada Barber et al., 2015, 2018), which is in accord with work focused on English monolingual students of varied ages and background characteristics (Guthrie, Klauda, & Ho, 2013; Guthrie et al., 2007). Academic engagement, including reading engagement in particular, is a multidimensional construct – representing students' affective, behavioral, and cognitive involvement in learning (Fredricks, Blumenfeld, & Paris, 2004; Reeve, 2012) – and as such can be affected through several kinds of instructional practices, which influence specific and sometimes multiple aspects of engagement. Such practices include assuring success, arranging opportunities for collaboration, focusing on learning and knowledge goals, incorporating real-world interactions, and providing autonomy support (Guthrie & Klauda, 2016; Guthrie, Wigfield, & You, 2012). Herein we focus especially on autonomy support, as there is burgeoning evidence for its role in the development of EFs outside the school context, which we believe likely extends to academic settings as well. But before considering that research, we briefly examine what autonomy support means, and, especially, how it may be integrated with literacy instruction.

Autonomy Support in Academic Contexts

Autonomy support refers to an interpersonal style for motivating others to learn characterized by behaviors and language that encourage learners' interests and help foster the internalization of the value of learning (Jang, 2008; Reeve, Bolt, & Cai, 1999; Ryan & Deci, 2000), which may be critical for putting forth the effort to use strategic processes. Autonomy support is often contrasted with a controlling style, which entails the teacher, in the school context, or the parent, at home, offering extrinsic rewards for making progress toward goals they've set and, potentially, enforcing consequences for failing to make such progress (Jang, Reeve, & Deci, 2010; Reeve et al., 1999; Reeve & Jang, 2006). Most research on autonomy support has been conducted within the framework of self-determination theory (Ryan & Deci, 2000, 2009), which posits that this form of support, along with support that fosters feelings of competence and relatedness to others, is critical to helping students develop and maintain more internal forms of motivation for learning.

Jang et al. (2010) set forth three general dimensions of autonomy supportive teacher behaviors: nurturing inner motivational resources, relying on noncontrolling informational language, and acknowledging students' perspectives and feelings. Autonomy supportive teachers nurture students' inner motivational resources when they allow students to explore their interests and preferences, work toward personal goals, challenge themselves, and make meaningful choices related to their learning, rather than implement incentives, directives, or deadlines (Jang et al., 2010; Reeve et al., 1999; Reeve, Jang, Carrell, Jeon, & Barch, 2004). In the reading classroom, teachers might nurture inner motivational resources by incorporating students' topic and genre interests when planning assignments and by offering students frequent opportunities to make meaningful choices, such as whether they would like to share knowledge gained through their reading in a presentation, poster, or other mode.

The second way that teachers provide autonomy support – acknowledging the students' perspectives and feelings – means verbally conveying appreciation for students' views about their learning. That is, they seek students' perspectives as well as acknowledge and accept those perspectives as a "potentially valid reaction to classroom demands, imposed structures, and the presentation of uninteresting or devalued activities" (Jang et al., 2010, p. 588). For example, when the teacher notices that students are having difficulty reading an assigned chapter in a novel, they might say "I know this is a long chapter and it contains many unfamiliar words. That can make it hard to stay focused."

The last way that teachers provide autonomy support – relying on noncontrolling informational language – is often used in conjunction with the second dimension. Employing noncontrolling language means that teachers offer explanatory rationales for assigned tasks and generally communicate in ways that are rich in information, including feedback on developing competence, and flexible, rather than evaluative without including feedback, rigid, and pressuring (Jang et al., 2010; Reeve et al., 2004). For instance, to introduce a recreational reading period in a noncontrolling manner, a teacher might say, "There's 20 minutes for free time reading after lunch," rather than "You must read for 20 minutes after lunch." In addition, they would give students a rationale for why this activity is a worthwhile use of their time, as such rationales are particularly important for supporting internalization of the value of an academic task or subject (Reeve et al., 1999; Reeve, Jang, Hardre, & Omura, 2002).

Research on the provision of autonomy support in laboratory and field settings has demonstrated its contributions to engagement and motivation (e.g., Jang et al., 2010) as well as academic performance, including that on reading comprehension tasks that benefit from strategic processing (e.g., Jang, 2008; Vansteenkiste, Simons, Lens, Soenens, & Matos, 2005). In particular, research has demonstrated that learners who received autonomy supportive messages as opposed to those that were controlling, reported greater effort and persistence (Reeve et al., 2002; Vansteenkiste, Simons, Lens, Sheldon, & Deci, 2004), which are key aspects of behavioral engagement and, as such, may energize or reflect high levels of strategic processing. Learners experiencing greater autonomy support have also shown better conceptual learning (Jang, 2008; Vansteenkiste et al., 2005), deeper processing, and higher test performance (Vansteenkiste et al., 2004). Despite the self-regulation promoting characteristics of autonomy supportive practices, they have not been linked explicitly to self-regulatory cognitive processes such as EFs within academic contexts. Such research, however, has emerged within the early childhood developmental literature, pointing toward intriguing future research directions.

Parents' Autonomy Support and EFs

Interestingly, as noted earlier, autonomy support outside the school context has been studied as a possible antecedent or enhancer of EF skills; here we consider this research and, then, in the final section, connect it to our consideration of strategic processes.

Within the developmental literature, maternal autonomy support has been found to be the strongest predictor (compared to maternal sensitivity, or how appropriately and consistently the mother responds to their child's signals, and mind-mindedness, or how much the parent uses mental terms in conversation with their child) of later EFs in 2-year-old children – beyond general cognitive ability and maternal education (e.g., Bernier, Carlson, & Whipple, 2010). Maternal autonomy support in the first three years has also predicted academic achievement in elementary and high school, partially by way of its association with EFs (Bindman, Pomerantz, & Roisman, 2015). Similar findings apply to paternal autonomy support, with paternal support when children were approximately three years old predicting school readiness, a measure including EF, at five years, with child language mediating the relationship (Meuwissen & Carlson, 2018). These findings are significant because they speak of the important role that parent-child relationships may play in children's development of EFs as self-regulatory skills. Given that bodies of research in the child development, neurocognitive, and, lately, education literatures provide compelling support for the idea that individual differences in EFs are meaningful for child cognitive and socioemotional development, it is reasonable to hypothesize that, given the findings within the study of parent-child relations and EFs in early childhood, the study of teacher autonomy support in older children may be associated with individual differences in EFs. That is, the self-regulatory, noncontrolling, and motivation-inducing teacher actions that foster student autonomous learning – including that which transpires through engaged reading – may in turn contribute to the cognitive and self-regulatory nature of EFs.

As Bindman et al. (2015) contended with respect to the parental caregiving context, children with autonomy supportive parents are likely to engage in challenging activities that demand EFs, like solving puzzles more frequently on their own compared to children with more controlling parents. Because of the autonomy support they have consistently received, such children have the motivational resources to persist at those activities, despite the draw of competing activities. As they regularly persevere in such activities, they practice and enhance their EFs. Applied to instructional contexts, it is likely that students who experience autonomy-supportive teachers may not just be more motivated to persist in challenging tasks, but to apply or develop cognitive strategies that assist in those tasks.

Further, as Bindman et al. (2015) suggested, considering how the experience of autonomy may engender more enjoyment of challenging tasks, children with autonomy supportive parents may find using their EFs less enervating – or the enjoyment they experience may energize their continued efforts to use cognitive strategies effectively. Lastly, another avenue through which autonomy support may bolster children's EFs is by promoting language skills, particularly through the provision of explanatory rationales, which are a key aspect of autonomy support (Jang et al., 2010). Children may internalize the language parents and teachers use when guiding them in autonomy supportive ways (Carlson, 2017), increasing their ability to engage in self-talk, which may, in turn, guide their use of such EFs as inhibiting and switching (Bindman et al., 2015; Matte-Gagné & Bernier, 2011; Vallotton & Ayoub, 2011). They may also use such self-talk to encourage their own persistence.

IMPLICATIONS FOR PRACTICE: CLASSROOM AUTONOMY SUPPORT, EXECUTIVE FUNCTIONS, AND STRATEGIC PROCESSES

Might these same processes hypothesized to be at play in the parenting realm be extrapolated to teacher-student interactions and the use of strategic processes for reading comprehension and other academic tasks? It seems likely. However, research is needed to explore whether the outcomes of teacher autonomy support include enhanced reading-specific EFs. In addition, we need research that addresses whether the dynamics among autonomy support and EFs relate to engagement and achievement in different learning contexts. We hypothesize that teacher autonomy support may affect the deployment of EFs in the classroom through the opportunities it affords students for self-determined and self-regulated action, such as solving problems independently, pursuing their own interests through engaged reading, and selecting and applying cognitive strategies to make sense of text. Further, when students effectively regulate their own learning, we suspect that this facilitates more positive teacher-student relationships, compelling teachers to further encourage their students' developing autonomy – and EFs, parallel to how Bernier et al. (2010) suggested positive parent-child interactions may feed back to promote even stronger EFs. Additionally, students may internalize the language that their teachers use when, for instance, providing reading strategy instruction in an autonomy supportive manner and, in turn, translate this language into self-talk that they use when reading independently and deploying their EFs to select and implement cognitive strategies appropriately (Bodrova, Leong, & Akhutina, 2011; Cragg & Nation, 2010).

While we have focused on autonomy support and how it strengthens internalized and intrinsic motivation and engagement, other teacher practices and other aspects of motivation should be examined as contributors to students' strategy usage and strategy selection prior to implementation – processes which necessitate higher order EFs like planning, task analysis, and monitoring (Borkowski et al., 2000). We would love to see future empirical studies consider the relations of teacher practices and motivation in ELs and students with RCD as conduits to effective strategy regulation and thereby, potentially, enhanced EFs and reading comprehension.

REFERENCES

Afflerbach, P., Hurt, M., & Cho, B.-Y. (this volume). Reading comprehension strategy instruction. In D. L. Dinsmore, L. K. Fryer, & M. M. Parkinson (Eds.), *Handbook of strategies and strategic processing: Conceptualization, measurement, and analysis*. New York: Routledge.

Altemeier, L., Jones, J., Abbott, R. D., & Berninger, V. W. (2006). Executive functions in becoming writing readers and reading writers: Note taking and report writing in third and fifth graders. *Developmental Neuropsychology, 29*, 161–173. doi:10.1207/s15326942dn2901_8

Barnes, M. A., Faulkner, H., Wilkinson, M., & Dennis, M. (2004). Meaning construction and integration in children with hydrocephalus. *Brain and Language, 89*, 47–56. doi:10.1016/S0093-934X(03)00295-5

Bernier, A., Carlson, S. M., & Whipple, N. (2010). From external regulation to self-regulation: Early parenting precursors of young children's executive functioning. *Child Development, 81*, 326–339. doi:10.1111/j.1467-8624.2009.01397.x

Best, J. R., Miller, P. H., & Naglieri, J. A. (2011). Relations between executive function and academic achievement from ages 5 to 17 in a large, representative national sample. *Learning and Individual Differences, 21*, 327–336. doi:10.1016/j.lindif.2011.01.007

Bialystok, E. (1999). Cognitive complexity and attentional control in the bilingual mind. *Child Development, 70*, 636–644. doi:10.1111/1467-8624.00046

Bialystok, E. (2015). Bilingualism and the development of executive function: The role of attention. *Child Development Perspectives, 9*(2), 117–121.

Bialystok, E., & Martin, M. M. (2004). Attention and inhibition in bilingual children: Evidence from the dimensional change card sort task. *Developmental Science, 7*, 325–339. doi:10.1111/j.1467-7687.2004.00351.x

Bindman, S. W., Pomerantz, E. M., & Roisman, G. I. (2015). Do children's executive functions account for associations between autonomy supportive parenting and achievement through high school? *Journal of Educational Psychology, 107*, 756–770. doi:10.1037/edu0000017

Blaye, A., & Chevalier, N. (2011). The role of goal representation in preschoolers' flexibility and inhibition. *Journal of Experimental Child Psychology, 108*, 469–483. doi:10.1016/j.jecp.2010.09.006

Bodrova, E., Leong, D. J., & Akhutina, T. V. (2011). When everything new is well-forgotten old: Vygotsky/Luria insights in the development of executive functions. In R. M. Lerner, J. V. Lerner, E. P. Bowers, S. Lewin-Bizan, S. Gestsdottir, & J. B. Urban (Eds.), *Thriving in childhood and adolescence: The role of self-regulation processes* (Vol. 133, pp. 11–28). San Francisco, CA: Jossey-Bass, New Directions for Child and Adolescent Development. doi:10.1002/cd.

Borella, E., Carretti, B., & Pelegrina, S. (2010). The specific role of inhibition in reading comprehension in good and poor comprehenders. *Journal of Learning Disabilities, 43*, 541–552. doi:10.1177/0022219410371676

Borkowski, J. G., Chan, L. K. S., & Muthukrishna, N. (2000). A process-oriented model of metacognition: Links between motivation and executive functioning. In G. Schraw & J. C. Impara (Eds.), *Issues in the measurement of metacognition* (pp. 1–41). Lincoln: Buros Institute of Mental Measurements, University of Nebraska-Lincoln.

Brown, R. (2008). The road not yet taken: A transactional strategies approach to comprehension instruction. *The Reading Teacher*, *61*, 538–547. doi:10.1598/RT.61.7.3

Brown, R., Pressley, M., Van Meter, P., & Schuder, T. (1996). A quasi-experimental validation of transactional strategies instruction with low-achieving second-grade readers. *Journal of Educational Psychology*, *88*, 18–37. doi:10.1037//0022-0663.88.1.18

Bull, R., & Lee, K. (2014). Executive functioning and mathematics achievement. *Child Development Perspectives*, *8*, 36–41. doi:10.1111/cdep.12059

Cain, K. (2006). Individual differences in children's memory and reading comprehension: An investigation of semantic and inhibitory deficits. *Memory*, *14*, 553–569. doi:10.1080/09658210600624481

Cain, K., Oakhill, J., & Lemmon, K. (2004). Individual differences in the inference of word meanings from context: The influence of reading comprehension, vocabulary knowledge, and memory capacity. *Journal of Educational Psychology*, *96*, 671–681. doi:10.1037/0022-0663.96.4.671

Cain, K., & Oakhill, J. V. (1999). Inference making ability and its relation to comprehension failure in young children. *Reading and Writing*, *11*, 489–503. doi:10.1023/A:1008084120205

Cain, K., Oakhill, J. V., Barnes, M. A., & Bryant, P. E. (2001). Comprehension skill, inference-making ability, and their relation to knowledge. *Memory & Cognition*, *29*, 850–859. doi:10.3758/BF03196414

Carlson, S. M. (2017, February). Shaping executive function skills: What can caregivers do? [Video file]. Retrieved from www.simmsmanninstitute.org/projects/videos/#!

Carlson, S. M., & Meltzoff, A. N. (2008). Bilingual experience and executive functioning in young children. *Developmental Science*, *11*, 282–298. doi:10.1111/j.1467-7687.2008.00675.x

Cartwright, K. B. (2002). Cognitive development and reading: The relation of reading-specific multiple classification skill to reading comprehension in elementary school children. *Journal of Educational Psychology*, *94*, 56–63. doi:10.1037/0022-0663.94.1.56

Cartwright, K. B. (2007). The contribution of graphophonological-semantic flexibility to reading comprehension in college students: Implications for a less simple view of reading. *Journal of Literacy Research*, *39*, 173–193. doi:10.1080/10862960701331902

Cartwright, K. B., Bock, A. M., Coppage, E. A., Hodgkiss, M. D., & Nelson, M. I. (2017). A comparison of cognitive flexibility and metalinguistic skills in adult good and poor comprehenders. *Journal of Research in Reading*, *40*(2), 139–152. doi:10.1111/1467-9817.12101

Cartwright, K. B., Coppage, E. A., Lane, A. B., Singleton, T., Marshall, T. R., & Bentivegna, C. (2017). Cognitive flexibility deficits in children with specific reading comprehension difficulties. *Contemporary Educational Psychology*, *50*, 33–44. doi:10.1016/j.cedpsych.2016.01.003

Cartwright, K. B., Marshall, T. R., Dandy, K. L., & Isaac, M. C. (2010). The development of graphophonological-semantic cognitive flexibility and its contribution to reading comprehension in beginning readers. *Journal of Cognition and Development*, *11*, 61–85. doi:10.1080/15248370903453584

Chevalier, N., & Blaye, A. (2016). Metacognitive monitoring of executive control engagement during childhood. *Child Development*, *87*, 1264–1276. doi:10.1111/cdev.12537

Chevalier, N., & Blaye, N. (2008). Cognitive flexibility in preschoolers: The role of representation activation and maintenance. *Developmental Science*, *11*, 339–353. doi:10.1111/j.1467-7687.2008.00679.x

Colé, P., Duncan, L. G., & Blaye, A. (2014). Cognitive flexibility predicts early reading skills. *Frontiers in Psychology: Cognitive Science*, *5*, 1–8. doi:10.3389/fpsyg.2014.00565

Collins, A., & Koechlin, E. (2012). Reasoning, learning, and creativity: Frontal lobe function and human decision-making. *PLoS Biology*, *10*(3). doi:10.1371/journal.pbio.1001293

Cragg, L., & Nation, K. (2010). Language and the development of cognitive control. *Topics in Cognitive Science*, *2*, 631–642. doi:10.1111/j.1756-8765.2009.01080.x

Dawson, P., & Guare, R. (2010). *Executive skills in children and adolescents: A practical guide to assessment and intervention* (2nd ed. ed.). New York, NY: Guilford Press.

Diamond, A. (2013). Executive functions. *Annual Review of Psychology*, *64*, 135–168. doi:10.1146/annurev-psych-113011-143750

Elbro, C., & Buch-Iversen, I. (2013). Activation of background knowledge for inference making: Effects on reading comprehension. *Scientific Studies of Reading*, *17*, 435–452. doi:10.1080/10888438.2013.774005

Flavell, J. H. (1963). *The university series in psychology. The developmental psychology of Jean Piaget*. Princeton, NJ: Van Nostrand. doi:10.1037/11449-000

Flavell, J. H. (1979). Metacognition and cognitive monitoring: A new area of cognitive–developmental inquiry. *American Psychologist*, *34*(10), 906–911. doi:10.1037/0003-066X.34.10.906

Flavell, J. H. (1985). John H. Flavell. *American Psychologist*, *40*, 291–295.

Follmer, D. J. (2018). Executive function and reading comprehension: A meta-analytic review. *Educational Psychologist, 53*, 42–60. doi:10.1080/00461520.2017.1309295

Fredricks, J. A., Blumenfeld, P. B., & Paris, A. H. (2004). School engagement: Potential of the concept, state of the evidence. *Review of Educational Research, 74*, 59–109. doi:10.3102/00346543074001059

García-Madruga, J. A., Elosúa, M. R., Gil, L., Gómez-Veiga, I., Vila, J. Ó., Orjales, I., … Duque, G. (2013). Reading comprehension and working memory's executive processes: An intervention study in primary school students. *Reading Research Quarterly, 48*, 155–174. doi:10.1002/rrq.44

Georgiou, G. K., & Das, J. P. (2018). Direct and indirect effects of executive function on reading comprehension in young adults. *Journal of Research in Reading, 41*, 243–258. doi:10.1111/1467-9817.12091

Gillberg, C., & Coleman, M. (2000). *The biology of the autistic syndromes* (3rd ed.). London, UK: Cambridge University Press.

Gnaedinger, E. K., Hund, A. M., & Hesson-McInnis, M. S. (2016). Reading-specific flexibility moderates the relation between reading strategy use and reading comprehension during the elementary years. *Mind, Brain, and Education, 10*, 233–246. doi:10.1111/mbe.12125

Goldstein, S., & Naglieri, J. A., (Eds.) 2014. *Handbook of executive functioning.* Springer Science & Business Media. doi:10.1007/978-1-4614-8106-5

Guthrie, J. T., & Klauda, S. L. (2016). Engagement and motivational processes in reading. In P. Afflerbach (Ed.), *Handbook of individual differences in reading: Reader, text, and context* (pp. 41–53). New York, NY: Routledge.

Guthrie, J. T., Klauda, S. L., & Ho, A. (2013). Modeling the relationships among reading instruction, motivation, engagement, and achievement for adolescents. *Reading Research Quarterly, 48*, 9–26. doi:10.1002/rrq.035

Guthrie, J. T., Mason-Singh, A., & Coddington, C. S. (2012). Instructional effects of Concept- Oriented Reading Instruction on motivation for reading information text in middle school. In J. T. Guthrie, A. Wigfield, & S. L. Klauda (Eds.), *Adolescents' engagement in academic literacy* (pp. 155–215). Retrieved from www.corilearning.com/research-publications

Guthrie, J. T., McRae, A. C., & Klauda, S. L. (2007). Contributions of Concept-Oriented Reading Instruction to knowledge about interventions for motivations in reading. *Educational Psychologist, 42*, 237–250. doi:10.1080/00461520701621087

Guthrie, J. T., Wigfield, A., & You, W. (2012). Instructional contexts for engagement and achievement in reading. In S. Christensen, A. Reschly, & C. Wylie (Eds.), *Handbook of research on student engagement* (pp. 601–634). New York, NY: Springer Science.

Henderson, L., Snowling, M., & Clarke, P. (2013). Accessing, integrating, and inhibiting word meaning in poor comprehenders. *Scientific Studies of Reading, 17*, 177–198. doi:10.1080/10888438.2011.652721

Jacob, R., & Parkinson, J. (2015). The potential for school-based interventions that target executive function to improve academic achievement: A review. *Review of Educational Research, 85*, 512–552. doi:10.3102/0034654314561338

Jang, H. (2008). Supporting students' motivation, engagement, and learning during an uninteresting activity. *Journal of Educational Psychology, 100*, 798–811. doi:10.1037/a0012841

Jang, H., Reeve, J., & Deci, E. L. (2010). Engaging students in learning activities: It is not autonomy support or structure but autonomy support and structure. *Journal of Educational Psychology, 102*, 588–600. doi:10.1037/a0019682

Kieffer, M. J., Vukovic, R. K., & Berry, D. (2013). Roles of attention shifting and inhibitory control in fourth-grade reading comprehension. *Reading Research Quarterly, 48*, 333–348. doi:10.1002/rrq.54

Kintsch, W. (1988). The role of knowledge in discourse comprehension: A construction– integration model. *Psychological Review, 95*, 163–182. doi:10.1037/0033-295X.95.2.163

Latzman, R. D., Elkovitch, N., Young, J., & Clark, L. A. (2010). The contribution of executive functioning to academic achievement among male adolescents. *Journal of Clinical and Experimental Neuropsychology, 32*, 455–462. doi:10.1080/13803390903164363

Markman, E. M. (1977). Realizing that you don't understand: A preliminary investigation. *Child Development, 48*, 986. doi:10.2307/1128350

Markman, E. M. (1979). Realizing that you don't understand: Elementary school children's awareness of inconsistencies. *Child Development, 50*, 643–655. doi:10.2307/1128929

Matte-Gagné, C., & Bernier, A. (2011). Prospective relations between maternal autonomy support and child executive functioning: Investigating the mediating role of child language ability. *Journal of Experimental Child Psychology, 110*, 611–625. doi:10.1016/j.jecp.2011.06.006

McGee, A., & Johnson, H. (2003). The effect of inference training on skilled and less skilled comprehenders. *Educational Psychology, 23*, 49–59. doi:10.1080/01443410303220

232 • Ana Taboada Barber et al.

Melby-Lervåg, M., & Hulme, C. (2013). Is working memory training effective? A meta-analytic review. *Developmental Psychology*, *49*, 270–291. doi:10.1037/a0028228

Meltzer, L. (2010). *Promoting executive function in the classroom*. New York, NY: Guilford Press.

Meuter, R. F. I., & Allport, A. (1999). Bilingual language switching in naming: Asymmetrical costs of language selection. *Journal of Memory and Language*, *40*, 25–40. doi:10.1006/jmla.1998.2602

Meuwissen, A. S., & Carlson, S. M. (2018). The role of father parenting in children's school readiness: A longitudinal follow-up. *Journal of Family Psychology*, *32*(5), 588–598. doi:10.1037/fam0000418

Miyake, A., Friedman, N. P., Emerson, M. J., Witzki, A. H., Howerter, A., & Wager, T. D. (2000). The unity and diversity of executive functions and their contributions to complex "frontal lobe" tasks: A latent variable analysis. *Cognitive Psychology*, *41*, 49–100. doi:10.1006/cogp.1999.0734

Monsell, S. (1996). Control of mental processes. In V. Bruce (Ed.), *Unsolved mysteries of the mind: tutorial essays in cognition* (pp. 93–148). Hove, UK: Erlbaum.

Myers, M., II., & Paris, S. G. (1978). Children's metacognitive knowledge about reading. *Journal of Educational Psychology*, *70*, 680–690. doi:10.1037/0022-0663.70.5.680

Novais-Santos, S., Gee, J., Shah, M., Troiani, V., Work, M., & Grossman, M. (2007). Resolving sentence ambiguity with planning and working memory resources: Evidence from fMRI. *Neuroimage*, *37*, 361–378. doi:10.1016/j.neuroimage.2007.03.077

Oakhill, J., Hartt, J., & Samols, D. (2005). Levels of comprehension monitoring and working memory in good and poor comprehenders. *Reading and Writing*, *18*, 657–686. doi:10.1007/s11145-005-3355-z

Pearson, P. D., & Dole, J. A. (1987). Explicit comprehension instruction: A review of research and a new conceptualization of instruction. *The Elementary School Journal*, *88*, 151–165. doi:10.1086/461530

Postle, B. R., Brush, L. N., & Nick, A. M. (2004). Prefrontal cortex and the mediation of proactive interference in working memory. *Cognitive, Affective, & Behavioral Neuroscience*, *4*, 600–608. doi:10.3758/CABN.4.4.600

Pressley, M. (2005). Metacognition in literacy learning: Then, now, and in the future. In S. E. Israel, C. C. Block, K. L. Bauserman, & K. Kinnucan-Welsch (Eds.), *Metacognition in literacy learning* (pp. 391–411). Mahwah, NJ: Erlbaum.

Pressley, M., Borkowski, J. G., & Schneider, W. (1987). Cognitive strategies: Good strategy users coordinate metacognition and knowledge. *Annals of Child Development*, *4*, 89–129. Retrieved from www.researchgate. net/publication/47873647_Cognitive_Strategies_Good_Strategy_Users_Coordinate_Metacognition_and_ Knowledge

Pressley, M., Forrest-Pressley, D. L., Elliott-Faust, O. J., & Miller, G. E. (1985). Children's use of cognitive strategies, how to teach strategies, and what to do if they can't be taught. In M. Pressley & C. I. Brainerd (Eds.), *Cognitive learning and memory in children* (pp. 1–47). New York: Springer-Verlag.

Pribram, K. H. (1973). The primate frontal cortex—Executive of the brain. In K. K. H. Pribram & A. R. Luria (Eds.), *Psychophysiology of the frontal lobes* (pp. 293–314). New York, NY: Academic Press.

Reeve, J. (2012). A self-determination theory perspective on student engagement. In S. Christensen, A. Reschly, & C. Wylie (Eds.), *Handbook of research on student engagement* (pp. 149–173). New York, NY: Springer Science.

Reeve, J., Bolt, E., & Cai, Y. (1999). Autonomy-supportive teachers: How they teach and motivate students. *Journal of Educational Psychology*, *91*, 537–548. doi:10.1037/0022-0663.91.3.537

Reeve, J., & Jang, H. (2006). What teachers say and do to support students' autonomy during a learning activity. *Journal of Educational Psychology*, *98*, 209–218. doi:10.1037/0022-0663.98.1.209

Reeve, J., Jang, H., Carrell, D., Jeon, S., & Barch, J. (2004). Enhancing students' engagement by increasing teachers' autonomy support. *Motivation and Emotion*, *28*, 147–169. doi:10.1023/B:MOEM.0000032312.95499.6f

Reeve, J., Jang, H., Hardre, P., & Omura, M. (2002). Providing a rationale in an autonomy-supportive way as a strategy to motivate others during an uninteresting activity. *Motivation and Emotion*, *26*, 183–207. doi:10.1023/A:1021711629417

Roebers, C. M., & Feurer, E. (2016). Linking executive functions and procedural metacognition. *Child Development Perspectives*, *10*, 39–44. doi:10.1111/cdep.12159

Ryan, R. M., & Deci, E. L. (2000). Self-determination theory and the facilitation of intrinsic motivation, social development, and well-being. *American Psychologist*, *55*, 68–78. doi:10.1037/0003-066X.55.1.68

Ryan, R. M., & Deci, E. L. (2009). Promoting self-determined school engagement: Motivation, learning, and well-being. In K. Wenzel & A. Wigfield (Eds.), *Handbook of motivation at school* (pp. 171–195). New York, NY: Routledge/Taylor & Francis Group.

Sesma, H. W., Mahone, E. M., Levine, T., Eason, S. H., & Cutting, L. E. (2009). The contribution of executive skills to reading comprehension. *Child Neuropsychology*, *15*, 232–246. doi:10.1080/09297040802220029

Shiffrin, R. M., & Schneider, W. (1977). Controlled and automatic human information processing: II. Perceptual learning, automatic attending and a general theory. *Psychological Review*, *84*, 127–190. doi:10.1037//0033-295x.84.2.127

Souvignier, E., & Mokhlesgerami, J. (2006). Using self-regulation as a framework for implementing strategy instruction to foster reading comprehension. *Learning and Instruction*, *16*, 57–71. doi:10.1016/j.learninstruc.2005.12.006

Taboada Barber, A., Buehl, M. M., Beck, J. S., Ramirez, E. M., Gallagher, M., & Archer, C. J. (2018). Literacy in social studies: The influence of cognitive and motivational practices on the reading comprehension of english learners and non-english learners. *Reading & Writing Quarterly*, *34*, 79–97. doi:10.1080/10573569.2017.1344942

Taboada Barber, A., Buehl, M. M., Kidd, J., Sturtevant, E., Richey, L. N., & Beck, J. (2015). Reading engagement in social studies: Exploring the role of a social studies literacy intervention on reading comprehension, reading self-efficacy, and engagement in middle school students with different language backgrounds. *Reading Psychology*, *36*, 31–85. doi:10.1080/02702711.2013.815140

Taboada Barber, A., Cartwright, K. B., Stapleton, L., Klauda, S. L., Archer, C., & Smith, P. (2019). *The role of higher order skills, executive functioning, and reading engagement in the reading comprehension of English learners and English speakers.* Manuscript submitted for publication.

Vallotton, C., & Ayoub, C. (2011). Use your words: The role of language in the development of toddlers' self-regulation. *Early Childhood Research Quarterly*, *26*(2), 169–181. doi:10.1016/j.ecresq.2010.09.002

Vansteenkiste, M., Simons, J., Lens, W., Sheldon, K. M., & Deci, E. L. (2004). Motivating learning, performance, and persistence: The synergistic effects of intrinsic goal contents and autonomy-supportive contexts. *Journal of Personality and Social Psychology*, *87*, 246–260. doi:10.1037/0022-3514.87.2.246

Vansteenkiste, M., Simons, J., Lens, W., Soenens, B., & Matos, L. (2005). Examining the motivational impact of intrinsic versus extrinsic goal framing and autonomy- supportive versus internally controlling communication style on early adolescents' academic achievement. *Child Development*, *76*, 483–501. doi:10.1111/j.1467-8624.2005.00858.x

Vaughn, S., Martinez, L. R., Linan-Thompson, S., Reutebuch, C. K., Carlson, C. D., & Francis, D. J. (2009). Enhancing social studies vocabulary and comprehension for seventh-grade English language learners: Findings from two experimental studies. *Journal of Research on Educational Effectiveness*, *2*(4), 297–324.

Wagner, R. K., Schatschneider, C., & Phythian-Sence, C. (Eds.). (2009). *Beyond decoding: The behavioral and biological foundations of reading comprehension.* New York, NY: Guilford Press.

Wingfield, A., & Grossman, M. (2006). Language and the aging brain: Patterns of neural compensation revealed by functional brain imaging. *Journal of Neurophysiology*, *96*, 2830–2839. doi:10.1152/jn.00628.2006

Yuill, N., & Joscelyne, T. (1988). Effect of organizational cues and strategies on good and poor comprehenders' story understanding. *Journal of Educational Psychology*, *80*, 152–158. doi:10.1037//0022-0663.80.2.152

Yuill, N., & Oakhill, J. (1988). Effects of inference awareness training on poor reading comprehension. *Applied Cognitive Psychology*, *2*, 33–45. doi:10.1002/acp.2350020105

Zabrucky, K., & Ratner, H. H. (1986). Children's comprehension monitoring and recall of inconsistent stories. *Child Development*, *57*, 1401–1418. doi:10.2307/1130419

14

SHARING THE LOAD

A Strategy to Improve Self-regulated Learning

Martine Baars
ERASMUS UNIVERSITY ROTTERDAM, THE NETHERLANDS

Lisette Wijnia
ERASMUS UNIVERSITY ROTTERDAM AND HZ UNIVERSITY OF
APPLIED SCIENCES, THE NETHERLANDS

Anique de Bruin
MAASTRICHT UNIVERSITY, THE NETHERLANDS

Fred Paas
ERASMUS UNIVERSITY ROTTERDAM, THE NETHERLANDS,
AND UNIVERSITY OF WOLLONGONG, AUSTRALIA

THE NEED FOR STRATEGIES TO IMPROVE SELF-REGULATED LEARNING

Self-regulated learning (SRL) entails the self-directive and proactive processes that learners can use to achieve academic success (Winne & Hadwin, 1998; Zimmerman, 2008). Examples of those processes are goal-setting, selecting and using learning strategies, and monitoring one's own effectiveness. These and other SRL processes are important for students to be able to regulate their own learning and development, not only during their school and college years but throughout their lives (e.g., Bjork, Dunlosky, & Kornell, 2013). In most models of SRL (for a review, see Panadero, 2017) both monitoring and control processes play an important role. That is, for SRL to succeed, students need to accurately monitor their learning processes and use that information to regulate further learning activities (e.g., Nelson & Narens, 1990).

Yet, research has shown that both children and adults tend to overestimate their own learning processes (e.g., Dunlosky & Lipko, 2007), which is problematic for decisions on their future learning processes and their future learning outcomes (e.g., Dunlosky

& Rawson, 2012). With complex tasks, SRL strategies such as self-monitoring of learning can be too demanding for an individual student. Using collaborative learning as a strategy to divide the demands of the learning task, learners can create a collective cognitive capacity which could potentially lead to a more efficient way of learning with more room for monitoring and regulating the learning process. In this chapter, a cognitive load perspective will be used to discuss how collaborative learning could be a strategy to improve SRL.

SELF-REGULATED LEARNING SKILLS

In order to self-regulate one's own learning processes, an interaction between cognition and metacognition needs to take place (Flavell, 1979). In the model by Nelson and Narens (1990) there are two levels that interact with each other through monitoring and control processes. The first level, the object-level, is the level at which cognitive processes like learning, language processing, or problem solving are going on. The meta-level contains a model of the learner's understanding of the task they are performing. This meta-level is partly informed via monitoring processes but also includes metacognitive knowledge about the task and the learner (i.e., strategies for specific tasks in relation to the experience of the learner; Flavell, 1979). Information gained when monitoring task performance at the object-level is used to update the model of the task at the meta-level. In turn, information from the meta-level is used to influence the activities at the object-level (i.e., control processes). These two levels, and the information flow between them, enable the learner to regulate ongoing learning processes (Dunlosky & Metcalfe, 2009).

Hence, an important strategy for effective SRL is self-monitoring in which learners evaluate their own performance against some standard or goal. Self-monitoring can be measured by asking learners to make monitoring judgments about their own learning process. Monitoring judgments can be made retrospectively (e.g., self-assessment), concurrently (e.g., confidence judgments), or prospectively (e.g., predicting future performance; Baars, Vink, Van Gog, De Bruin, & Paas, 2014; Schraw, 2009b). For example, a judgment of learning (JOL) could be used to have learners judge whether they have understood a text or are able to answers questions about the text on a future test. The accuracy of monitoring judgments is usually operationalized as the correspondence between the judgments and test performance. The correspondence can be expressed as relative accuracy, absolute accuracy, or bias (Schraw, 2009a). Relative monitoring accuracy shows the correspondence between monitoring judgments and performance, and is measured with intra-individual correlations (often the Goodman-Kruskal Gamma correlation, e.g., Maki, 1998; Thiede, Anderson, & Therriault, 2003). Relative accuracy expressed as the gamma correlation shows to what extent participants are able to discriminate between problems on which they perform poorly and problems on which they perform well (Maki, Shields, Wheeler, & Zacchilli, 2005). Absolute accuracy shows how precise the monitoring judgment is and it is measured by the actual deviation between monitoring judgments and performance (e.g., Baars et al., 2014; Baars, Visser, Van Gog, De Bruin, & Paas, 2013). For example, if a student made a monitoring judgment in which (s)he estimates to have five out of ten questions correct but only gets four questions correct on a performance test, the absolute accuracy is one. Bias would measure whether there is an over- or underestimation. In the previous example bias would be one, a positive outcome, indicating overestimation (for a review of accuracy measures, see Schraw, 2009a, 2009b).

When studying word pairs (i.e., paired-associates) both children and adults were found to be able to judge their memory accurately when there was a delay between studying the word pair and the monitoring judgment (for a review of the delayed-JOL effect, see Rhodes & Tauber, 2011). That is, a simple strategy to improve monitoring accuracy when studying word pairs would be to ask learners to make a monitoring judgment after a list of words instead of after each word directly. Yet, this delayed-JOL effect was not found for learning from texts (Maki, 1998) or problem-solving tasks (Baars, Van Gog, De Bruin, & Paas, 2018). Moreover, reviews of research on monitoring judgments when learning from texts (i.e., meta-comprehension) have shown that the accuracy of a single monitoring judgment after reading a text (200–1000 words) is generally very low (average gamma correlation of .27). This indicates that learners cannot accurately monitor their own learning processes when learning from text without any additional instructional support (e.g., Dunlosky & Lipko, 2007; Thiede, Griffin, Wiley, & Redford, 2009).

Similarly, studies on monitoring learning from problem-solving tasks (i.e., meta-reasoning) also found that learners experience difficulties in making accurate monitoring judgments (Ackerman & Thompson, 2017). In educational settings like schools and universities, usually well-structured problems are used in domains such as science, technology, engineering, and mathematics (STEM). In contrast to ill-structured problems that do not have a well-defined goal or solution procedure, well-structured problems are typically solved by applying a limited and known set of concepts and rules (Jonassen, 2011). Research has shown that without additional instructional support, students were found to overestimate themselves when making monitoring judgments about solving well-structured biology problems (Baars, Leopold, & Paas, 2018; Baars, Van Gog, De Bruin, & Paas, 2017; Baars et al., 2014; Baars et al., 2013).

Interestingly, generative strategies were found to improve self-monitoring accuracy when learning from expository text and problem-solving tasks. Generative strategies are learning activities that learners can use to generate (new) information about the learning materials by elaborating on those materials (Fiorella & Mayer, 2016; Wittrock, 1992). Examples of generative strategies that were found to improve monitoring accuracy are generating keywords (e.g., Thiede et al., 2003), making summaries (Thiede & Anderson, 2003), making concept maps (e.g., Redford, Thiede, Wiley, & Griffin, 2012), giving self-explanations (e.g., Griffin, Wiley, & Thiede, 2008), making diagrams (e.g., Van Loon, De Bruin, Van Gog, Van Merriënboer, & Dunlosky, 2014), practicing problems (e.g., Baars, Van Gog, De Bruin, & Paas, 2014), or completing partially worked-out examples (Baars et al., 2013). These generative strategies can provide students with predictive cues on their comprehension of learning materials (i.e., their mental representation), which can help to make more accurate self-monitoring judgments (e.g., Baars et al., 2014; Thiede et al., 2009).

However, in a study by Baars et al. (2018) it was shown that self-explaining during the learning phase or at the posttest did not improve monitoring accuracy or performance when learning to solve problems in secondary education. Furthermore, monitoring accuracy was lower for more complex problem-solving tasks than for less complex problem-solving tasks. These results seem to imply that the complexity of the learning materials plays an important role in monitoring and influences the effectiveness of strategies to improve monitoring.

Looking at SRL models (e.g., Winne & Hadwin, 1998; Zimmerman, 2008), inaccurate monitoring is problematic for the learning process. When monitoring is inaccurate, regulation choices on how to proceed with the learning process will most likely be useless or even harmful for learning. In line with these predictions, Dunlosky and Rawson (2012) found that without additional support, students tend to overestimate their learning, which led to premature termination of study efforts and lower retention. As the consequences of inaccurate monitoring are quite severe and generative strategies do not always suffice in supporting students to make more accurate monitoring judgments, it is important to know why making accurate monitoring judgments is so difficult.

THE COMPLEXITY OF MONITORING LEARNING PROCESSES

One possible explanation of why monitoring one's own learning seems to be difficult and prone to overestimation, is that it takes place at the same time as learning, or directly after learning. Moreover, learning tasks are often complex for students who are novices in a domain, leaving little room for monitoring and regulation processes. According to cognitive load theory (CLT; Sweller, Van Merriënboer, & Paas, 1998, 2019) it can be assumed that the competition for working memory (WM) resources between learning processes and self-regulation processes can have negative effects on either or both of these processes. Understanding the interplay between learning, monitoring, and the role of cognitive load is needed to provide insight into possible strategies to improve SRL processes when learning complex tasks.

According to CLT (Sweller, 2010; Sweller et al., 1998, 2019), complexity of learning tasks can be partially explained by the number of interacting information elements in a task. The higher the number of interacting information elements, the more complex a learning task is. Especially learning more complex materials can place a high demand on limited cognitive resources (Baddeley, 1986; Cowan, 2001). In addition, the expertise of the learner also plays a role in how complex a task is perceived by a learner. That is, with more expertise, information elements can be combined into schemata in long-term memory, and processed as one element in WM, lowering the number of interacting information elements. Therefore, the cognitive load a task imposes will be lower for learners with more expertise than for learners with less expertise (Kalyuga, 2007; Kalyuga & Sweller, 2004). Generally, it can be argued that monitoring one's own learning in education, where typically new, complex tasks have to be learned, is difficult for learners. Moreover, as SRL involves monitoring the object-level and thereby informing the meta-level to control the learning process at the object-level (Nelson & Narens, 1990), SRL presumably causes high element interactivity in and of itself.

Monitoring one's own learning can be seen as a secondary task next to the learning task itself (Griffin et al., 2008; Van Gog, Kester, & Paas, 2011). When tasks are complex and cognitive load is high, it can be hard to perform well on both the learning task and the monitoring task at the same time, because a learner will have to divide cognitive resources between the two tasks (Brünken, Plass, & Leutner, 2003). Due to

WM limitations, performance on one or both of the tasks may suffer when complexity is high and exceeds the learner's processing capacity. Furthermore, the ability to cope with this dual task is dependent on the cognitive resources of the learner. A study by Griffin et al. (2008) showed that reading abilities and working memory capacity (WMC) affected monitoring accuracy. In two experiments, college students read explanatory texts, made monitoring judgments about their comprehension, and took a comprehension test about the texts they read. In the first experiment it was found that re-reading the text improved monitoring accuracy for low-ability readers, but not for high-ability readers. In the second experiment this was confirmed and results further showed that lower-WMC readers benefitted from re-reading in terms of monitoring accuracy whereas high-WMC readers did not. Griffin et al. (2008) concluded that contextual factors such as re-reading and individual differences such as reading abilities are possibly related to the ability of monitoring meta-level cues while reading. They pointed out that monitoring is a secondary process next to the primary task of understanding the text itself. Moreover, monitoring accuracy was assumed to be dependent on the cognitive resources of the reader.

A study by Van Gog et al. (2011) also confirmed the idea that concurrent monitoring can be seen as an additional task demanding resources. In their study, secondary school students had to solve Sudoku problems and rate their mental effort as a measure of cognitive load (see Paas, 1992). There were two conditions: a condition in which students had to keep track of what they were doing (i.e., monitoring) and a condition in which they did not monitor their performance (Van Gog et al., 2011). Using a within-subjects design, the effect of the complexity of the Sudoku problems was investigated. Results showed that the instruction to monitor led to higher cognitive load for the complex problems but not for the simple problems. Also, performance and efficiency of performance (see Paas & Van Merriënboer, 1993) on the complex problems were lower for students in the monitoring condition. Hence, the instruction to monitor performance when solving complex problems increased cognitive load and decreased performance and efficiency (Van Gog et al., 2011).

In sum, SRL, being the combination of monitoring *and* performing a learning task (e.g., Winne & Hadwin, 1998; Zimmerman, 2008), presumably imposes high cognitive load. Monitoring can take place at the same time as learning or directly after a learning task. In both scenarios, the additional task of monitoring demands cognitive resources. Hence, in the case of complex learning tasks, there might be too few resources to accurately monitor and regulate the learning process (Griffin et al., 2008; Van Gog et al., 2011). This could explain why monitoring judgments have been found to be accurate for relatively simple learning materials (e.g., Rhodes & Tauber, 2011) and inaccurate for relatively complex learning materials like expository texts (e.g., Thiede et al., 2009) and problem-solving tasks (e.g., Baars et al., 2018). Yet students are expected to monitor and regulate their own learning to a gradually increasing extent while tasks are getting more complex in (higher) education, especially when learning takes place in digital learning environments in which students operate independently (e.g., Wong et al., 2019). Therefore, it is important to consider strategies to decrease the load of monitoring during learning. One possibility is the use of collaborative learning, which is becoming increasingly popular in many educational settings (Johnson & Johnson, 2009). Collaborative learning could potentially be used as a strategy to reduce the demands on individual cognitive resources when monitoring learning because collaboration creates the opportunity to divide the load between the learners in the group.

COLLABORATIVE LEARNING AS A STRATEGY FOR SRL: SHARING THE LOAD

Students can learn collaboratively by actively working together and putting effort into the attainment of a shared learning goal (e.g., Janssen, Kirschner, Erkens, Kirschner, & Paas, 2010; Johnson & Johnson, 2009; Kirschner, Sweller, Kirschner, & Zambrano, 2018; Slavin, 2014). Several meta-analyses have shown that collaborative learning is related to academic (individual and group) achievement (e.g., Lou, Abrami, & d'Apollonia, 2001; Roseth, Johnson, & Johnson, 2008; Springer, Stanne, & Donovan, 1999). There are several explanations from different disciplines as to why students learn from each other in collaborative settings. For example, social cohesion as a result of working interdependently in collaborative learning can aid learning (O'Donnell & O'Kelly, 1994). Also, collaborative learning can create cognitive conflict and students can question each other's understanding, which can enhance learning (Slavin, 1996). Social interaction and social support are elements in collaborative learning that can create the opportunity for students to develop higher order skills such as reasoning and critical thinking skills (Johnson & Johnson, 2009). Moreover, another explanation for why students can learn from each other in collaborative learning settings is that collaborative learning can facilitate information processing and memory (Topping, 1996).

Strategies to make collaborative learning effective are combining group goals with individual accountability (e.g., grades based on average performance on individual assignments), appealing to student's motivation (e.g., rewards, task attractiveness), and creating interdependence in goals, roles, and tasks (e.g., Slavin, 1996). For collaborative learning to be successful, students need to be able to operate as a team. A meta-analysis by DeChurch and Mesmer-Magnus (2010) showed that team cognition is essential for team effectiveness. Team cognition concerns the manner in which important knowledge for team functioning is organized and distributed within the team. There are two strategies to operationalize team cognition, that is shared mental models and transactive memory. Shared mental models are cognitive understandings of important aspects in the performance context that are shared (i.e., compatible) among the members of a team. Teams with shared mental models can operate efficiently without the need for overt communication, which is important for expert teams. Transactive memory can be seen as a cognitive architecture in which the knowledge of individual group members is included but also knowledge about who possesses what knowledge. Transactive memory is important if there is a degree of specialization or differentiation of knowledge within a team. DeChurch and Mesmer-Magnus (2010) showed that shared mental models and transactive memory were significantly related to team behavioral processes (e.g., planning, goal-setting, coordinating, and team-back-up behavior), motivational state, and team performance.

Similar to the concept of team cognition, it has been proposed that learners in a collaborative learning setting can be seen as an information processing system (Kirschner,

Paas, & Kirschner, 2009a, 2009b). In this system the information in the learning task and the cognitive load associated with the task can be divided among the learners in the group. This way the load can be divided among multiple collaborating working memories. According to the mutual cognitive interdependence principle, this collective WM can be introduced by effective collaborative learning in which students communicate and coordinate the relevant knowledge they have with each other (Kirschner, Paas, & Kirschner, 2011). From a CLT-perspective, dividing the demands of learning a complex task among different learners who are collaborating, can lead to a more effective and efficient way of learning (Paas & Sweller, 2012). That is, the collection of individual WM capacities of the group members can create an expanded processing capacity, which makes it advantageous to work together on more complex tasks (Kirschner et al., 2009a). Especially for complex tasks, sharing the load of high element interactivity across multiple WMs, instead of one, could be effective. Collaboration would serve as a scaffold for the learning process (Kirschner et al., 2018). This will only be effective if WM costs of communication and coordination are decreased by training or by learning in structured or scripted learning environments (Kirschner et al., 2018; Paas & Sweller, 2012). This means that collaboration would be a beneficial approach to learning in which communication and coordination are important strategies to make the collaboration successful.

A study by Kirschner et al. (2009b) investigated groups as information processing systems. Secondary school students learned how to solve biology problem-solving tasks either individually or in small groups. Students indicated their experienced mental effort (i.e., measure of cognitive load; Paas, 1992), and took a test consisting of retention and transfer tasks. The results showed that students who learned in small groups invested less mental effort during the learning phase. Most importantly, an interaction between the type of test (retention or transfer) and condition was found, which indicated that students who learned individually showed more efficient retention performance, and learners who learned collaboratively showed more efficient transfer performance. Presumably, because learners in the small groups could use each other's processing capacity (i.e., information processing system), they were able to process the learning content more deeply and construct higher quality schemata in long-term memory.

To sum up, collaborative learning was found to be successful (e.g., Roseth et al., 2008) and, more importantly, has the potential of ameliorating the limitations of individual WM (e.g., Kirschner et al., 2011). Looking back at the problem of inaccurate monitoring and its effect on the SRL process, possibly collaborative learning could be a way to free up cognitive resources that could then be used to monitor and regulate learning processes more successfully at both the individual and the group level. In order to make collaborative learning effective, several strategies such as training communication and coordination between team members are important. Both from a CLT perspective and the concept of team cognition, one could argue that there is potentially more WMC (Kirschner et al., 2011) in effective collaborative learning, which in turn could affect behavioral processes such as planning and goal-setting if team cognition is achieved (DeChurch & Mesmer-Magnus, 2010). Hence, effective collaborative learning could also be a scaffold for other SRL processes like monitoring and control at the individual level and at the group level.

CO-REGULATION AND SOCIALLY SHARED METACOGNITIVE REGULATION OF LEARNING

Research on co-regulation, socially shared metacognitive regulation (SSMR), and socially shared regulation of learning (SSRL), has looked at SRL processes such as monitoring and regulation during collaborative learning. The terms metacognition, self-regulation, and SRL are often used in parallel to each other (Dinsmore, Alexander, & Loughlin, 2008). This is also the case for studies on shared regulation of learning (Panadero & Järvelä, 2015). The study by Dinsmore et al. (2008) has shown important commonalities in the definitions of metacognition, self-regulation, and SRL. That is, the idea that learners monitor their thoughts and actions during learning, and use that information to regulate or control their learning process, was found to be at the core of each of the three concepts. Similarly, co-regulation, SSMR, and SSRL also seem to have an important commonality, that is, all three fields look at the regulation of learning at the group level (Panadero & Järvelä, 2015). Therefore, all three will be described in this section in order to explore collaborative learning as a strategy to improve SRL processes.

Co-regulation refers to the process of acquiring SRL skills (e.g., monitoring, goal-setting, evaluation) through interactions with others when working on a learning task (Hadwin, Järvelä, & Miller, 2011; Hadwin & Oshige, 2011). Co-regulation is based on emergent temporary interactions with peers or teachers who bring different self-regulatory challenges and expertise into the learning process. In these interactions peers and teachers can prompt each other's regulation processes. The process of co-regulation should lead to the internalization of self-regulation processes. For example, a teacher can co-regulate a learning task together with a student to help improve the student's SRL skills. Research on co-regulation has focused on how learners regulate their learning in interaction with others, how peers can mediate each other's regulation of learning, and how social context or culture constrains co-regulation processes. Hence, co-regulation can be seen as a strategy to learn how to self-regulate one's learning.

SSRL is the collective regulation of learning processes that lead to a shared outcome (Hadwin et al., 2011; Panadero & Järvelä, 2015). It is based on the idea of shared regulation during learning, which provides learners with the opportunity to learn from each other's regulation through modeling (Järvelä et al., 2015). In SSRL the ultimate goal is for individually regulated learners to reach co-constructed planning, monitoring, strategies, evaluation, goal-setting, and beliefs in relation to the learning process with a shared outcome. The process of SSRL could be seen as a strategy to have learners model cognitive and metacognitive strategies during learning in an iterative fashion. This could improve the SRL skills of the other collaborators who in turn can model this behavior to the other learners again. That way, the shared metacognitive regulation of learning is built upon individual's metacognitive regulation (Winne, Hadwin, & Perry, 2013). Research into SSRL has focused on co-constructed SRL knowledge, beliefs, and procedures, and on shared SRL skills such as planning, monitoring, and evaluation (Hadwin et al., 2011). Thus, SSRL describes how groups can use collaborative learning as a strategy to regulate shared learning processes by co-creating and learning from each other.

SSMR refers to self-regulation skills such as planning, monitoring, and evaluation that students can use to control, coordinate, and regulate their learning (De Backer, Van Keer, & Valcke, 2012, 2015; Hadwin et al., 2011). Like in SSRL, students who are working together in a collaborative setting can collectively undertake regulation activities and transfer them to others. This process leads to metacognitive regulation at a social level which promotes successful collaborative learning (De Backer et al., 2012, 2015). According to De Backer et al. (2015), successful collaborative learning requires and, to some extent, also elicits, students to use metacognitive skills (i.e., SSMR). De Backer et al. (2012) found that students who were learning collaboratively in reciprocal peer tutoring groups, increased their use of metacognitive regulation skills such as monitoring and evaluation during the semester.

De Backer et al. (2015) make a distinction between two levels of metacognitive regulation: low-level and deep-level. Low-level metacognitive regulation concerns exploring the demands of the learning task. Deep-level metacognitive regulation refers to processing the task demand and activation of prior knowledge. Students checking the progress of their group can be considered an example of low-level monitoring whereas reflective comments on the quality of the group's progress would be deep-level monitoring. In their study the development and use of SSMR by students in reciprocal peer tutoring groups were investigated. Sessions of reciprocal peer tutoring groups were videotaped, coded, and analyzed. Results showed that from co-regulation by the tutor, students progressed into peer co-regulation and shifted to a socially shared regulation focus. Moreover, this socially shared regulation focus was found to be related to orientation, monitoring, and deep-level regulation. De Backer et al. (2015) suggested it would be interesting to develop and investigate interventions that can support SSMR in collaborative learning. Again, SSMR shows how learners can use collaborative learning as a strategy to regulate their learning by sharing it and transferring regulation from a tutor or more advanced learner to themselves.

In a review study by Panadero and Järvelä (2015), 17 articles addressing SSRL, or SSMR, were analyzed in order to characterize SSRL, levels of social regulation, and relations of SSRL with other learning variables such as performance. The results showed that the studies in the review mostly investigated SSRL using qualitative data (i.e., video-recorded observation data) to investigate the joint regulation of cognition, metacognition, behavior, emotion, and motivation. Furthermore, two types of shared regulation of learning were found: co-regulation in which one or more group members regulated other members' activity, and SSRL in which group members jointly regulated their learning. In addition, a small number of studies in which performance was investigated showed a positive relation between higher levels of SSRL and performance.

Possible interventions to support SSMR and SSRL can be found in work by Järvelä et al. (2015). They identified three strategies to support SSRL: (1) increase learners' awareness of their own and others' learning processes (i.e., Radar Tool), (2) support externalization of students' and others' learning processes and the interaction (i.e., Ourplanner), and (3) prompt acquisition and activation of regulatory processes (i.e., Ourevaluator).

Interestingly, these SSRL supports could theoretically also support team cognition or mutual cognitive interdependence. In addition, this relation between team cognition and SSRL could also be explained the other way around – without team cognition, SSRL would probably be ineffective. Support for awareness of each other's learning process could enhance shared mental models, and externalization of the learning process could enhance transactive memory about who knows what in a team. Using the

SSRL tools could improve communication and coordination of relevant knowledge between students in a collaboration group and thereby introduce a collective WM. Possibly this could free cognitive resources within the group to monitoring their learning process and use this for regulation in an effective way.

To conclude, research on SRL skills and metacognitive skills of learners in groups (e.g., co-regulation, SSMR, SSRL) has shown how learning processes can be regulated in interaction between peers or teachers and peers (De Backer et al., 2012, 2015; Hadwin et al., 2011; Panadero & Järvelä, 2015). Regulation of learning in interaction with others can also lead to acquiring SRL skills as an individual (Hadwin et al., 2011; Järvelä et al., 2015), as well as shifting toward socially shared forms of regulation within a group (De Backer et al., 2015). Collaborative learning settings seem to demand regulation of learning by the learners involved but also to elicit regulation of learning by learners. Hence, there seems to be a relation between team cognition and mutual cognitive interdependence on the one hand, and effective shared regulation of learning, on the other. That means collaborative learning could be an effective strategy to support SRL processes for groups and individuals. Furthermore, instructional supports for SRL or metacognitive processes during collaborative learning could theoretically also support team cognition (DeChurch & Mesmer-Magnus, 2010) and the use of collective WM (Kirschner et al., 2011). Therefore, it would be promising to investigate how the concepts of team cognition, collective WM, and socially shared regulation would overlap, strengthen, or constrain each other. Possibly, team cognition and mutual cognitive interdependence are important prerequisites of shared regulation of learning and could be used to develop interventions to improve shared regulation.

CONCLUSION AND DISCUSSION

SRL concerns the self-directive and proactive processes, such as monitoring and regulation of learning, which learners can use to achieve academic success (Winne & Hadwin, 1998; Zimmerman, 2008). To be successful at self-regulating learning processes, monitoring and control processes need to be accurate. However, making monitoring judgments about complex learning materials such as texts or problem-solving tasks, has been found to be difficult for learners, that is, without additional strategies or instructions monitoring judgments are usually inaccurate (e.g., Baars et al., 2014, 2013; Dunlosky & Lipko, 2007; Thiede et al., 2009). Prior research indicated that task complexity and high demands on cognitive resources can explain why monitoring is difficult for learners (Griffin et al., 2008; Van Gog et al., 2011). A good strategy to improve SRL processes would be to have learners work together and learn collaboratively. That is, collaborative learning could be a scaffold for SRL processes like monitoring and control. In collaborative learning, there is potentially more (collective) WMC (Kirschner et al., 2011) which could affect behavioral processes such as planning and goal-setting (DeChurch & Mesmer-Magnus, 2010). Different strategies can be employed to facilitate effective collaborative learning. For example, combining group goals with individual accountability, appealing to student's motivation, and creating interdependence in goals and roles (e.g., Slavin, 1996). But also, team cognition which consists of shared mental models and transactive memory are necessary for effective collaboration (DeChurch & Mesmer-Magnus, 2010). Moreover, from a

CLT perspective, it is crucial that the communication and coordination demands on WM during collaboration be decreased by training learners in those skills or providing them with carefully structured learning environments to collaborate in (Kirschner et al., 2018; Paas & Sweller, 2012). Especially with instructional support (cf. Järvelä et al., 2015), collaborative learning could elicit regulation of learning potentially leading to socially shared regulation or (improved) individual SRL skills. Informed by research on team cognition, future research could investigate the effect of collaborative learning compared to individual learning on cognitive load, learning outcomes, and SRL skills such as monitoring and regulation.

Yet, to our knowledge, there are no studies on how the concepts of team cognition, collective WM, and socially shared regulation would interact and affect SRL in individuals and groups. This would be an interesting endeavor, especially because it has been suggested that SRL is difficult for an individual and therefore must be even more difficult for a group (Järvelä et al., 2015). Yet based on research about team cognition (DeChurch & Mesmer-Magnus, 2010) and collective WM (e.g., Kirschner et al., 2011), it seems that learning collaboratively in a group would offer better opportunities for learners to monitor and regulate their learning individually or as a group. Future studies could investigate the effect of supporting team cognition in collaborative learning on SRL skills and learning outcomes. Also, the role of (collective) WM could be taken into account. Both qualitative and quantitative approaches would be valuable, as both insights into SRL behaviors in relation to team cognition and collective WM, and empirical evidence about the possible effects of team cognition and collective WM on SRL skills and learning outcomes, are needed.

As previous research on monitoring accuracy (e.g., Baars et al., 2018; Thiede et al., 2009) and collaborative learning (e.g., Kirschner et al., 2009b) has already shown, the type of task and the complexity of the task are important factors to take into account when investigating monitoring accuracy, cognitive load, and collaborative learning. As most tasks in education are new to students, it seems logical to focus on the more complex tasks when investigating collaborative learning, cognitive load, and SRL skills. Also, the development of SRL skills during a course (e.g., De Backer et al., 2015) but also over the years (e.g., Schneider, 2008), in relation to growing expertise (Kalyuga, 2007; Kalyuga & Sweller, 2004) could have important implications for the relation between SRL skills, cognitive load, and collaborative learning. Perhaps studies in different educational settings and with longitudinal design could provide more clarity on this issue. In addition, it seems a fruitful avenue to combine insights from educational studies and organizational studies to investigate SRL in groups of students. Especially the work on the effectiveness of teams (e.g., DeChurch & Mesmer-Magnus, 2010) provides interesting leads to follow up in educational settings.

REFERENCES

Ackerman, R., & Thompson, V. A. (2017). Meta-reasoning: Monitoring and control of thinking and reasoning. *Trends in Cognitive Sciences, 21*, 607–617. doi:10.1016/j.tics.2017.05.004

Baars, M., Leopold, C., & Paas, F. (2018). Self-explaining steps in problem-solving tasks to improve self-regulation in secondary education. *Journal of Educational Psychology, 110*, 578–595. doi:10.1037/edu0000223

Baars, M., Van Gog, T., De Bruin, A., & Paas, F. (2014). Effects of problem solving after worked example study on primary school children's monitoring accuracy. *Applied Cognitive Psychology, 28*, 382–391. doi:10.1002/acp.3008

Baars, M., Van Gog, T., De Bruin, A., & Paas, F. (2017). Effects of problem solving after worked example study on secondary school children's monitoring accuracy. *Educational Psychology, 37,* 810–834. doi:10.1080/014 43410.2016.1150419

Baars, M., Van Gog, T., De Bruin, A., & Paas, F. (2018). Accuracy of primary school children's immediate and delayed judgments of learning about problem-solving tasks. *Studies in Educational Evaluation, 58,* 51–59. doi:10.1016/j.stueduc.2018.05.010

Baars, M., Vink, S., Van Gog, T., De Bruin, A., & Paas, F. (2014). Effects of training self-assessment and using assessment standards on retrospective and prospective monitoring of problem solving. *Learning and Instruction, 33,* 92–107. doi:10.1016/j.learninstruc.2014.04.004

Baars, M., Visser, S., Van Gog, T., De Bruin, A., & Paas, F. (2013). Completion of partially worked examples as a generation strategy for improving monitoring accuracy. *Contemporary Educational Psychology, 38,* 395–406. doi:10.1016/j.cedpsych.2013.09.001

Baddeley, A. D. (1986). *Working memory.* New York: Oxford University Press.

Bjork, R. A., Dunlosky, J., & Kornell, N. (2013). Self-regulated learning: Beliefs, techniques, and illusions. *Annual Review of Psychology, 64,* 417–444. doi:10.1146/annurev-psych-113011-143823

Brünken, R., Plass, J. L., & Leutner, D. (2003). Direct measurement of cognitive load in multimedia learning. *Educational Psychologist, 38,* 53–61. doi:10.1207/s15326985ep3801_7

Cowan, N. (2001). The magical number 4 in short-term memory: A reconsideration of mental storage capacity. *The Behavioral and Brain Sciences, 24,* 87–114.

De Backer, L., Van Keer, H., & Valcke, M. (2012). Exploring the potential impact of reciprocal peer tutoring on higher education students' metacognitive knowledge and regulation. *Instructional Science, 40,* 559–588. doi:10.1007/s11251-011-9190-5

De Backer, L., Van Keer, H., & Valcke, M. (2015). Exploring evolutions in reciprocal peer tutoring groups' socially shared metacognitive regulation and identifying its metacognitive correlates. *Learning and Instruction, 38,* 63–78. doi:10.1016/j.learninstruc.2015.04.001

DeChurch, L. A., & Mesmer-Magnus, J. R. (2010). The cognitive underpinnings of effective teamwork: a meta-analysis. *Journal of Applied Psychology, 95,* 32–53. doi:10.1037/a0017328

Dinsmore, D. L., Alexander, P. A., & Loughlin, S. M. (2008). Focusing the conceptual lens on metacognition, self-regulation, and self-regulated learning. *Educational Psychology Review, 20,* 391–409. doi:10.1007/s10648-008-9083-6

Dunlosky, J., & Lipko, A. R. (2007). Metacomprehension a brief history and how to improve its accuracy. *Current Directions in Psychological Science, 16,* 228–232. doi:10.1111/j.1467-8721.2007.00509.x

Dunlosky, J., & Metcalfe, J. (2009). *Metacognition.* Thousand Oaks, CA: Sage Publications.

Dunlosky, J., & Rawson, K. A. (2012). Overconfidence produces underachievement: Inaccurate self-evaluations undermine students' learning and retention. *Learning and Instruction, 22,* 271–280. doi:10.1016/j.learninstruc.2011.08.003

Fiorella, L., & Mayer, R. E. (2016). Eight ways to promote generative learning. *Educational Psychology Review, 28,* 717–741. doi:10.1007/s10648-015-9348-9

Flavell, J. H. (1979). Metacognition and cognitive monitoring: A new area of cognitive–developmental inquiry. *American Psychologist, 34,* 906–911. doi:10.1037/0003-066X.34.10.906

Griffin, T. D., Wiley, J., & Thiede, K. W. (2008). Individual differences, rereading, and self-explanation: Concurrent processing and cue validity as constraints on metacomprehension accuracy. *Memory & Cognition, 36,* 93–103. doi:10.3758/MC.36.1.93

Hadwin, A. F., Järvelä, S., & Miller, M. (2011). Self-regulated, co-regulated, and socially shared regulation of learning. In D. H. Schunk & B. Zimmerman (Eds.), *Handbook of self-regulation of learning and performance* (pp. 65–84). New York: Routledge.

Hadwin, A. F., & Oshige, M. (2011). Self-regulation, co-regulation, and socially shared regulation: Exploring perspectives of social in self-regulated learning theory. *Teachers College Record, 113,* 240–264.

Janssen, J., Kirschner, F., Erkens, G., Kirschner, P. A., & Paas, F. (2010). Making the black box of collaborative learning transparent: Combining process-oriented and cognitive load approaches. *Educational Psychology Review, 22,* 139–154. doi:10.1007/s10648-010-9131-x

Järvelä, S., Kirschner, P. A., Panadero, E., Malmberg, J., Phielix, C., Jaspers, J., Järvenoja, H. (2015). Enhancing socially shared regulation in collaborative learning groups: Designing for CSCL regulation tools. *Educational Technology Research and Development, 63,* 125–142. doi:10.1007/s11423-014-9358-1

Johnson, D. W., & Johnson, R. T. (2009). An educational psychology success story: Social interdependence theory and cooperative learning. *Educational Researcher, 38,* 365–379. doi:10.3102/0013189X09339057

Jonassen, D. H. (2011). *Learning to solve problems: A handbook for designing problem-solving learning environments.* New York: Routlegde.

Kalyuga, S. (2007). Expertise reversal effect and its implications for learner-tailored instruction. *Educational Psychology Review, 19*, 509–539. doi:10.1007/s10648-007-9054-3

Kalyuga, S., & Sweller, J. (2004). Measuring knowledge to optimize cognitive load factors during instruction. *Journal of Educational Psychology, 96*, 558–568. doi:10.1037/0022-0663.96.3.558

Kirschner, F., Paas, F., & Kirschner, P. A. (2009a). A cognitive load approach to collaborative learning: United brains for complex tasks. *Educational Psychology Review, 21*, 31–42. doi:10.1007/s10648-008-9095-2

Kirschner, F., Paas, F., & Kirschner, P. A. (2009b). Individual and group-based learning from complex cognitive tasks: Effects on retention and transfer efficiency. *Computers in Human Behavior, 25*, 306–314. doi:10.1016/j.chb.2008.12.008

Kirschner, F., Paas, F., & Kirschner, P. A. (2011). Task complexity as a driver for collaborative learning efficiency: The collective working-memory effect. *Applied Cognitive Psychology, 25*, 615–624. doi:10.1002/acp.1730

Kirschner, P. A., Sweller, J., Kirschner, F., & Zambrano, J. (2018). From cognitive load theory to collaborative cognitive load theory. *International Journal of Computer-Supported Collaborative Learning, 13*, 213–233. doi:10.1007/s11412-018-9277-y

Lou, Y., Abrami, P. C., & d'Apollonia, S. (2001). Small group and individual learning with technology: A meta-analysis. *Review of Educational Research, 71*, 449–521. doi:10.3102/00346543071003449

Maki, R. H. (1998). Predicting performance on text: Delayed versus immediate predictions and tests. *Memory & Cognition, 26*, 959–964. doi:10.3758/BF03201176

Maki, R. H., Shields, M., Wheeler, A. E., & Zacchilli, T. L. (2005). Individual differences in absolute and relative metacomprehension accuracy. *Journal of Educational Psychology, 97*, 723–731. doi:10.1037/0022-0663.97.4.723

Nelson, T. O., & Narens, L. (1990). Metamemory: A theoretical framework and new findings. In G. H. Bower (Ed.), *The psychology of learning and motivation* (Vol. 26, pp. 125–173). New York: Academic Press.

O'Donnell, A. M., & O'Kelly, J. (1994). Learning from peers: Beyond the rhetoric of positive results. *Educational Psychology Review, 6*, 321–349. doi:10.1007/BF02213419

Paas, F. (1992). Training strategies for attaining transfer of problem-solving skill in statistics: A cognitive-load approach. *Journal of Educational Psychology, 84*, 429–434. doi:10.1037/0022-0663.84.4.429

Paas, F., & Sweller, J. (2012). An evolutionary upgrade of cognitive load theory: Using the human motor system and collaboration to support the learning of complex cognitive tasks. *Educational Psychology Review, 24*, 27–45. doi:10.1007/s10648-011-9179-2

Paas, F., & Van Merriënboer, J. J. (1993). The efficiency of instructional conditions: An approach to combine mental effort and performance measures. *Human Factors, 35*, 737–743. doi:10.1177/001872089303500412

Panadero, E. (2017). A review of self-regulated learning: six models and four directions for research. *Frontiers in Psychology, 8*(422), 1–28. doi:10.3389/fpsyg.2017.00422

Panadero, E., & Järvelä, S. (2015). Socially shared regulation of learning: A review. *European Psychologist, 20*, 190–203. doi:10.1027/1016-9040/a000226

Redford, J. S., Thiede, K. W., Wiley, J., & Griffin, T. D. (2012). Concept mapping improves metacomprehension accuracy among 7th graders. *Learning and Instruction, 22*, 262–270. doi:10.1016/j.learninstruc.2011.10.007

Rhodes, M. G., & Tauber, S. K. (2011). The influence of delaying judgments of learning on metacognitive accuracy: A meta-analytic review. *Psychological Bulletin, 137*, 131–141. doi:10.1037/a0021705

Roseth, C. J., Johnson, D. W., & Johnson, R. T. (2008). Promoting early adolescents' achievement and peer relationships: The effects of cooperative, competitive, and individualistic goal structures. *Psychological Bulletin, 134*, 223–246. doi:10.1037/0033-2909.134.2.223

Schneider, W. (2008). The development of metacognitive knowledge in children and adolescents: Major trends and implications for education. *Mind, Brain, and Education, 2*, 114–121. doi:10.1111/j.1751-228X.2008.00041.x

Schraw, G. (2009a). A conceptual analysis of five measures of metacognitive monitoring. *Metacognition and Learning, 4*, 33–45. doi:10.1007/s11409-008-9031-3

Schraw, G. (2009b). Measuring metacognitive judgments. In D. J. Hacker, J. Dunlosky, & A. C. Graesser (Eds.), *Handbook of metacognition in education* (pp. 415–429). New York: Routledge.

Slavin, R. E. (1996). Research on cooperative learning and achievement: What we know, what we need to know. *Contemporary Educational Psychology, 21*, 43–69. doi:10.1006/ceps.1996.0005

Slavin, R. E. (2014). Cooperative learning and academic achievement: Why does groupwork work? *Annals of Psychology, 30*, 785–791. doi:10.6018/analesps.30.3.201201

Springer, L., Stanne, M. E., & Donovan, S. S. (1999). Effects of small-group learning on undergraduates in science, mathematics, engineering, and technology: A meta-analysis. *Review of Educational Research, 69*, 21–51. doi:10.3102/00346543069001021

Sweller, J. (2010). Element interactivity and intrinsic, extraneous, and germane cognitive load. *Educational Psychology Review, 22*, 123–138. doi:10.1007/s10648-010-9128-5

Sweller, J., Van Merriënboer, J. J. G., & Paas, F. (1998). Cognitive architecture and instructional design. *Educational Psychology Review, 10*, 251–296. doi:10.1023/A:1022193728205

Sweller, J., Van Merriënboer, J. J. G., & Paas, F. (2019). Cognitive architecture and instructional design: 20 years later. *Educational Psychology Review, 31*, 261–292. doi:10.1007/s10648-019-09465-5

Thiede, K. W., & Anderson, M. C. (2003). Summarizing can improve metacomprehension accuracy. *Contemporary Educational Psychology, 28*, 129–160. doi:10.1016/S0361-476X(02)00011-5

Thiede, K. W., Anderson, M. C., & Therriault, D. (2003). Accuracy of metacognitive monitoring affects learning of texts. *Journal of Educational Psychology, 95*, 66–73. doi:10.1037/0022-0663.95.1.66

Thiede, K. W., Griffin, T. D., Wiley, J., & Redford, J. S. (2009). Metacognitive monitoring during and after reading. In D. J. Hacker, J. Dunlosky, & A. C. Graesser (Eds.), *Handbook of metacognition in education* (pp. 85–106). New York: Routledge.

Topping, K. J. (1996). The effectiveness of peer tutoring in further and higher education: A typology and review of the literature. *Higher Education, 32*, 321–345. doi:10.1007/BF00138870

Van Gog, T., Kester, L., & Paas, F. (2011). Effects of concurrent monitoring on cognitive load and performance as a function of task complexity. *Applied Cognitive Psychology, 25*, 584–587. doi:10.1002/acp.1726

Van Loon, M. H., De Bruin, A. B., Van Gog, T., Van Merriënboer, J. J., & Dunlosky, J. (2014). Can students evaluate their understanding of cause-and-effect relations? The effects of diagram completion on monitoring accuracy. *Acta Psychologica, 151*, 143–154. doi:10.1016/j.actpsy.2014.06.007

Winne, P. H., & Hadwin, A. F. (1998). Studying as self-regulated learning. In D. J. Hacker, J. Dunlosky, & A. C. Graesser (Eds.), *metacognition in educational theory and practice* (pp. 277–304). Mahwah, NJ: Lawrence Erlbaum.

Winne, P. H., Hadwin, A. F., & Perry, N. E. (2013). Metacognition and computer-supported collaborative learning. In C. Hmelo-Silver, A. O'Donnell, C. Chan, & C. Chinn (Eds.), *International handbook of collaborative learning* (pp. 462–479). New York: Taylor & Francis.

Wittrock, M. C. (1992). Generative learning processes of the brain. *Educational Psychologist, 27*, 531–541. doi:10.1207/s15326985ep2704_8

Wong, J., Baars, M., Davis, D., Van Der Zee, T., Houben, G. J., & Paas, F. (2019). Supporting self-regulated learning in online learning environments and MOOCs: A systematic review. *International Journal of Human–Computer Interaction, 35*, 356–373. doi:10.1080/10447318.2018.1543084

Zimmerman, B. J. (2008). Investigating self-regulation and motivation: Historical background, methodological developments, and future prospects. *American Educational Research Journal, 45*, 166–183. doi:10.3102/0002831207312909

15

COMMENTARY

An Analysis of Learning Strategies in Action

Philip H. Winne
SIMON FRASER UNIVERSITY, CANADA

There can be no doubt about significant interest in learning strategies when a Google search for the literal string "learning strategies" returns approximately 7,830,000 results (2019 July 11, 13:45). Given that result, an astonishing finding is the relatively small volume of research about such a popular topic. Searching PsychINFO for academic journal articles with titles containing "learning" and either "strategies" or "strategy" yielded a considerably smaller set of just 1896 items (2019 July 11, 13:44). I speculate there may be much conjecture, hearsay, and even some misinformation about learning strategies populating the Internet. Educational practitioners and scholars can be thankful for chapters in this section of the Handbook that plumb research work on learning strategies.

The range of subject matter domains and diversity of learning contexts surveyed in these chapters reflect multiple conceptions about learning strategies, challenges students face in developing and applying learning strategies, and their value in education. This variety also complicates and tangles understandings about what learning strategies are, how learners use them, which effects are associated with learning strategies, and what should be next steps in research programs. I endeavor to address these issues.

GOOD NEWS AND QUALIFICATIONS

Almost every one of the chapters in this section of the Handbook, with qualifications and some specializations, reports three important findings from research.

First, learners appear to be strategic. Their naturally developed strategies generally are few in number, quite limited in applicability, somewhat naïve, and typically neither well matched to conditions nor particularly effective. The good news is learners appear "naturally inclined" to develop strategies. I interpret this as a strong signal they have engaged in self-regulated learning (SRL). Experience as a self-regulating learner over the span of childhood is quite likely a productive resource educators can tap for students' benefit.

Second, while it is neither easy nor quickly accomplished, learners can be taught new learning strategies. Notably, even quite young learners can be taught. While training may be successful, a downside is the rather severe scarcity of data documenting robust transfer of trained strategies beyond the training setting and the end of training. Successes in helping learners build learning strategies typically yield quite localized and short-lived benefits.

Third, training plus on-the-spot support, e.g., autonomy support (see Taboada Barber, Lutz Klauda, & Cartwright, this volume), which offers learners meaningful choices about how to learn and encourages making choices based on personal motivations like interest and challenge, can help learners to identify when and how to apply a particular strategy, and to persist during early phases of developing a new learning strategy when achieving goals is erratic. But, as often befalls educational research findings, multiple and sometimes overwhelming caveats are appropriate. Isolating specific factors as *the* causes of changes in achievement is very challenging and often not successful. Tamping down excessive optimism about learning strategies needs constant attention not only by Internet surfers but also by researchers and teachers.

WHAT IS A LEARNING STRATEGY?

It is rare to be able to state anything with certainty, but I can report with barely any qualification these chapters concur about one claim: there is a great deal of variance in what a learning strategy is deemed to be and, to a lesser extent, what particular effects a strategy is designed to accomplish (see also Van Meter & Campbell, this volume). Awash in this soup of definitions is moderate consensus about two claims. First, learners should develop or be taught learning strategies. Second, life in school and afterward will be less rewarding if learners are not skilled strategy users. In this context, as I discuss later, there is a missing piece. It is decision-making strategies for choosing which particular learning strategy is most useful in particular circumstances. The broad scope of learning strategies discussed in this section of the Handbook make clear there are many, many strategies. Within subject matter topics, and across disciplines and contexts, teachers are challenged to choose which learning strategies are most appropriate to teach to learners. Then, learners face a daunting task to pick a winning learning strategy from a quite assorted set.

Learning strategies populate a large and multidimensional conceptual space. Each chapter in this section shines differently filtered light on learning strategies. Finding commonality is challenging. In some cases, leaning strategies can be organized along axes of disciplinary schemas for knowledge, various epistemological stances, and even methods researchers use to identify when a learner applies a learning strategy. This can be seen in the chapters focusing on learning strategies differentially appropriate in mathematics, history, and science.

Taking another perspective, a learning strategy refers to how a learner engaged in any task proceeds in a context-sensitive way to stepwise traverse a lattice of cognitive engagements with information in a context where information is updated at each step the strategy is applied. Reading and writing are examples, as would be a set play in basketball or plans for preparing Thanksgiving dinner.

Graham et al. (this volume) and Lombardi and Bailey (this volume) are explicit about how the warp and woof of learning strategies also can be shaped by sociocultural factors in settings where learners live and in which strategies are cued, enacted, and judged. List (this volume) illustrates how even the format of information has a bearing on what learning strategies are considered to be, how learners use them, and what effects they have. Strategies, like chemical isotopes, can vary in minor ways that matter, as Newton (this volume) described.

It is also clear learning strategies can be schemas abstracted from disciplines and represented in content learners are assigned. Strategic readers are described by Afflerbach, Hurt, and Cho (this volume) as, for example, attending to main ideas, synthesizing a summary, creating inferences, forming causal and comparative syntheses. List (this volume) describes learners working with multiple sources as using strategies to seek logical or positional concordance, trustworthiness, and conceptual completeness when mining the internet for ingredients to assemble a term paper. Students reading historical documents approach expertise when they adopt a skeptical stance about the balance and credibility of evidential claims vis-à-vis value-infused and potentially biased interpretations, as De La Paz and Nokes (this volume) discussed. Strategies play roles in how learners conceptualize, act, and react in collaborative work like that illustrated by Baars, Winjia, de Bruiin and Paas (this volume). It may even be the case that learning strategies are expressions of basic features of the cognitive system, namely, capabilities comprising executive functions, a possibility introduced by Taboada Barber et al. (this volume).

All these conceptualizations of what a learning strategy is and what it is for have significant implications in developing an account of what it could mean to be an expert learning strategist. Learners differ in the cognitive operations they apply in tasks, in qualities of those operations and behaviors, in the patterns formed of those constituents, and in temporal and conditional relations among qualitatively textured behaviors. The information one learner draws from memory and assembles with information available in the environment differs from what another learner does. Does this make for different learning strategies or variants of one? Such a multiplex of what a learning strategy "is" leads me to believe a linear continuum is an inept representation of expertise. Learning strategies are better situated within a multidimensional space where axes likely are not orthogonal. For example, an adaptive strategy is likely a complex strategy because adaptivity requires branching points where decisions about what to do next are informed as states of work on a task are successively updated step by step. The more adaptive a strategy, the less likely may be a learner's incentive to use it because the final results of applying the strategy become less predictable. And, because one of those axes is time, a learning strategy is temporally fluid. As time flows and the state of a task is updated, strategies likely flex. In this tangle of descriptions about learning strategies, is there a center? Perhaps.

AN ABSTRACT MODEL FOR A LEARNING STRATEGY

I model a learning strategy as a coordinated set of events with two features. The first feature is that a strategy includes at least two tactics. A tactic is an operation a learner applies if particular conditions arise. It can be abstractly represented as what computer scientists call a production: IF[condition(s)]–THEN[operation(s)]. I point out now and elaborate shortly that every operation generates products which cause the state of the task to be updated.

The second feature of my model for a strategy is the presence of one or more checkpoints between conditions at the start of the task and those at the final state of the task. Checkpoints are spots along the timeline of work on a multistep task where a learner has an opportunity to monitor the state of the task and proceed as planned, per the strategy, or adapt. States of tasks change because operations introduce new products. Those products contribute to new conditions setting the stage for the next IF–THEN production in the strategy. Checkpoints afford options about what to do next. They can be represented as elaborating the earlier and simpler IF–THEN model to take on the form IF[condition(s)]–THEN[operation(s)]–ELSE[different operation(s) if conditions are different].

HOW DOES A LEARNER DECIDE WHICH LEARNING STRATEGY TO USE?

The IF–THEN–ELSE model of a learning strategy begs an important question: how does a learner decide what to do when a tactic that would usually be enacted at a checkpoint in a task is judged inappropriate or is unavailable (e.g., forgotten, precluded by a condition in the environment)? Newton (this volume) references Star, Caronongan et al. (2015, p. 26) who characterize a model like mine as having a "rationale behind the use and effectiveness of these steps." What makes up that kind of rationale?

One element is knowledge about the domain in which a tactic operates. For example, as Newton describes, a learner may know several methods for working with fractions when manipulating arithmetic expressions. How is one chosen over another? I model learners' decision making using five features that blend metacognitive knowledge, motivation, and decision making to form a judgment about utility.

Throughout the timeline of work on a task, learners choose among tactics and learning strategies in the context of current and successively updated conditions. I posit these checkpoints are viewed in light of a personal history. That history includes four fundamental categories of information.

The first category is what the learner predicts will result if a particular learning strategy is applied. Products generated when a learner carries out a learning strategy are not limited to the space of the task's disciplinary domain, e.g., a reduced form of a complex fraction or an inference about the main idea of a text. Carrying out a learning strategy also generates perceptions that are personal. Effort, pace, and affect are examples of personally relevant kinds of information inherently associated with generating a product. As well, social status may be a factor if the learning strategy and its product can be observed by peers or a teacher. Bandura (1977) labeled this kind of information – what a learner predicts will be the result of a tactic or learning strategy – an outcome expectation.

A second category of information enfolded in decisions about using or adapting a learning strategy is the learner's judgment of skill to enact it. The probability an expected product actually will materialize when a learning strategy is applied is inversely proportional to the learner's skill to enact that strategy. This kind of information was labeled an efficacy expectation by Bandura (1977).

A third kind of information I suggest a learner examines is the incentive or "payoff" (see Graham & Weiner, 2012) associated with the predicted product generated by enacting a particular learning strategy. Incentives are reasons to behave, including applying a learning strategy. They can be social (Baars et al., this volume) as well as something "interior" to the learner, what the learner prefers (Karabenick & Collins-Eaglin, 1997) or, in the case of a disincentive, what the learner doesn't like (Bartels, Magun-Jackson, & Kemp, 2009).

The fourth category of information in my list of elements comprising the learner's personal history is an explanation about why a learning strategy succeeds, falters, or fails. According to attribution theory (Weiner, 2010), different attributions, e.g., to luck or to effort, automatically give rise to affect, e.g., worry when a learning strategy seems to have generated the right product by luck, or pride if the learner judges hard work (effort) made a key contribution to generating the right product. Memories about associations between attributions and affect bear on choices about learning strategies in the moment. Procrastination is a good example.

Altogether, these four categories of information – outcome expectations, efficacy expectations, incentives associated with particular products, and attributions explaining success and failure – are input to an unknown calculus the learner uses to determine the utility of a particular learning strategy in particular conditions. The strategy with the greatest marginal utility "wins."

Isolating the first letter of each category of information, including the utility a learner assigns to each strategy, forms an easy to recall mnemonic: AEIOU. Like vowels that add warmth to cold consonant sounds in speech, attributions, efficacy expectations, incentives, outcome expectations, and utilities related to learning strategies imbue cold decision making with warmth when learners choose a strategy to use (Winne & Marzouk, 2019).

Decision-making learners carry out to choose learning strategies is very little addressed in chapters within this section. This is because almost all the primary research available to be reviewed for these chapters investigated effects of only a single learning strategy. To be sure, it is costly and sometimes practically difficult to secure large samples willing to participate in statistically powerful research that examines multiple strategies. Notwithstanding, life in classrooms is more complex than in the lab or in field studies where just one strategy was a focus for research. Learners fortunate enough to know multiple strategies must choose which one to use. Future research should investigate how learners' decisions unfold and how learners can be supported to evolve more productive decision making about learning strategies. Such research is essential to advancing comprehensive theories and fruitful applications of self-regulated learning.

LEARNING STRATEGIES FUSE DOMAIN KNOWLEDGE AND COGNITION

The chapters covering learning strategies in disciplinary domains are explicit that disciplinary knowledge is a key component of learning strategies. Without knowledge such as schemas about key features of an argument, signals about the trustworthiness of online information, allowable operations for manipulating fractions, and so forth, learners lack critical IFS and THENS they need to metacognitively monitor content or targets to aim for in applying cognitive operations that generate knowledge. For example, tasks like self-explaining or locating a main idea are possible because a learner knows what an explanation is and what constitutes a main idea. Put simply, tactics comprising learning strategies are fusions of cognitive operations and information to which operations are applied.

This view of learning strategies and their component IF–THEN tactics makes explicit that learners need disciplinary knowledge as one key to acquiring and applying learning strategies. Taboada Barber et al. (this volume) note working memory plays a role like a valve governing students' opportunity to use learning strategies. While this might appear to emphasize a view of strategies as pure cognition, it actually makes the point that strategies fuse knowledge with cognition. Working memory is where operations are performed on information. Information learners need is curtailed in proportion to how heavily working memory is taxed. Without critical information, cognitive operations are starved for the raw material a strategy needs. This analysis has a direct and important implication, also emphasized in multiple chapters of this section. Students need to be well taught in the subjects they study because disciplinary knowledge is fuel for learning strategies.

CONCERNS ABOUT EXPERIMENTS ON LEARNING STRATEGIES

Features of experimental designs strongly affect the validly of inferences about whether and how learning strategies affect achievement. The "gold standard" design – the randomized controlled trial – randomly assigns to a treatment group a proportion of a sample of learners randomly drawn from a clearly and explicitly defined population. These learners receive instruction about a strategy before engaging in a session where content can be learned using the just-trained strategy. One or more other partitions of the sample form control or comparison groups (randomly assigned if there are more than two groups). These learners may experience a form of placebo "training" or proceed directly to the learning session where they learn using whatever methods they bring with them. The learning session all groups experience may be designed with bias if it includes cues or affordances to use the learning strategy being investigated. This would give an advantage to the treatment group trained to use that strategy for this experiment but greatly limit generalizability beyond the experimental setting. After the learning session ends, all participants take a measure of achievement. Analyses of achievement data examine a hypothesis about the effect of the strategy training.

Interpreting findings from randomized controlled trials is problematic (see Winne, 2017). For example, variables a research reports as "defining" a population commonly have little or no empirical backing as validated moderator variables. Also, the sample is almost never randomly drawn from some population. And, there is rarely a genuine incentive for learners to build knowledge. Beyond these shortcomings, most primary studies reviewed for this section of the Handbook suffer other shortcomings. These could be, but rarely are, reduced in ways that strengthen the validity of inferences about effects of learning strategies.

In studies probing effects of learning strategies, it is helpful to know which students use the strategy being investigated. While it strains the logic of random assignment, inferences about strategy effects could be sharpened by removing achievement data for learners (a) trained to use the strategy but who do not demonstrate skill in using it before the learning session, (b) trained to use the strategy but who do not demonstrate they apply the skill during the learning session, and (c) in the comparison group(s) who already use the strategy or a sufficiently close cousin.

To act on these proposals requires gathering trace data. Trace data are observations of a learner's behavior that are operationally defined to provide a strong signal about which particular cognitive operations a learner applies to which particular information. For instance, a strategy to identify main ideas and relate them to everyday life could be traced by having learners highlight content they judge to be a main idea. This traces metacognitive monitoring for main ideas and can be scored for whether the highlighted content actually is a main idea. Stronger inferences about students' use of the learning strategy can be supported if learners also create a note in which they record a personally generated example of the main idea that was not presented in the source the learner studied, the note traces assembling the learner's prior knowledge, or a schema-relevant instance of the main idea with the main idea developed in the source. Trace data also can be used to examine whether trained students' applications of the learning strategy "wobble" as they engage with content in the learning episode. Such data could be useful in adjusting interpretations of strategy effects as a function of trained participants' fidelity of strategy implementation.

Another feature that can bolster inferences about the effects of learning strategies is to design the measure of achievement to include items in two categories. Strategy-sensitive items require learners to have applied the trained strategy to respond correctly. Scores on these items afford testing a hypothesis about whether the strategy is necessary. If trained students and non-trained students can both answer strategy-sensitive items, the strategy is not necessary. Strategy-insensitive items have no theoretical relation to students' use of the strategy during the learning session. These items afford testing whether the strategy undermines learning in some way or has side effects beyond what current theory forecasts. As best I can judge, primary studies using outcome measures like this were not available to authors of the chapters in this section of the Handbook.

SELF-REGULATED LEARNING MUDDLES FINDINGS

Whatever teachers or researchers add to learning environments by way of instructional designs and treatments, it must not be overlooked that these features are filtered through learners. No matter how careful and detailed features of an instructional design are, learners are not obliged to notice them, to identify the specific tactics and strategies the researcher intended learners to match to those features of instruction, or to diligently and skillfully apply any particular tactics and strategies. In every sense, learners are agents who fully self-regulate learning (Winne, 1995). They strive to meet their goals in ways they judge best for them. We can only hope their activities align to processes and objectives developed set for them. Trace data can test whether hope is satisfied.

Descriptions of self-regulated learning (SRL) abound (e.g., Panadero, 2017; Winne, 2018) and need not be reviewed here. Perspectives acknowledging SRL are scant in these chapters given the argument SRL may be ubiquitous (Winne, 1995). To the extent SRL operates to shape when and which tactics and strategies learners use, interpretations about direct effects of tactics and strategies on outcomes become muddled (Winne, 2017). As just noted, trace data gathered during the learning session could identify whether, how much, and in what ways learners' regulation of trained (and natural) learning strategies affect achievement.

NEXT STEPS AND LEAPS

Strategies are designs for adapting to context as that context evolves over time. Five features need to be realized to create successful opportunities for students to become strategic learners. Students need instruction and support to develop tactics. Thus, one step toward becoming a successful strategic learner is teaching students which conditions in learning scenarios signal that particular operations will be best suited to those conditions. Merely recognizing when a particular action is needed can't help if that action can't be carried out. So, second, students need to be taught what to do to improve learning. Binding Ifs to Thens stocks learners' toolkits with tools they need to succeed. Third, in experiments and in classrooms, learning tasks need to be complex enough so they call for learning strategies but not so complex as to overload cognition. Fourth, like any skill, students need extensive practice to automate strategic learning. While it is difficult to shift balance away from learning a subject matter and toward strategic learning, that is what will be needed and that is what research indicates in comparisons of students trained to use strategies to students who work with naturally developed tactics. Finally, because we are keen for students in classrooms, not just participants in experiments, to become successful strategic learners, teachers will need education and support to make all this happen.

Keys to realizing each of these features are distributed throughout the chapters in this section of the Handbook. Emerging guidelines for realizing research-practice partnerships (e.g., Coburn & Penuel, 2016) provide direction but, as noted by several authors of the chapters, basic theory-exploring research should not be neglected as we push toward practice. Wise funders should take good risks to invest in longer-term projects spanning periods approximately double the usual three- to five-year grant periods. Transforming institutions as inertial as public education is not quick work. As well, sustained attention will be required so students can be introduced to, deliberately practice, and develop multidimensional expertise needed to transfer multifaceted learning strategies across the subjects they study.

REFERENCES

Afflerbach, P., Hurt, M., & Cho, B.-Y. (this volume). Reading comprehension strategy instruction. In D. L. Dinsmore, L. K. Fryer, & M. M. Parkinson (Eds.), *Handbook of strategies and strategic processing: Conceptualization, measurement, and analysis.* New York: Routledge.

Baars, M., Wijnia, L., de Bruin, A., & Paas, F. (this volume). Sharing the load: A strategy to improve self-regulated learning. In D. L. Dinsmore, L. K. Fryer, & M. M. Parkinson (Eds.), *Handbook of strategies and strategic processing: Conceptualization, measurement, and analysis.* New York: Routledge.

Bandura, A. (1977). *Social learning theory.* Englewood Cliffs, NJ: Prentice-Hall.

Bartels, J. M., Magun-Jackson, S., & Kemp, A. D. (2009). Volitional regulation and self-regulated learning: An examination of individual differences in approach-avoidance achievement motivation. *Electronic Journal of Research in Educational Psychology, 7,* 605–626.

Coburn, C. E., & Penuel, W. R. (2016). Research–practice partnerships in education: Outcomes, dynamics, and open questions. *Educational Researcher, 45*(1), 48–54.

De La Paz, S., & Nokes, J. (this volume). Strategic processing in history and historical strategy instruction. In D. L. Dinsmore, L. K. Fryer, & M. M. Parkinson (Eds.), *Handbook of strategies and strategic processing: Conceptualization, measuresment, and analysis.* New York: Routledge.

Graham, S., Bañales, G., Ahumada, S., Muñoz, P., & Alvarez, P., & Harris, K. R. (this volume). Writing strategy interventions. In D. L. Dinsmore, L. K. Fryer, & M. M. Parkinson (Eds.), *Handbook of strategies and strategic processing: Conceptualization, measurement, and analysis.* New York: Routledge.

Graham, S., & Weiner, B. (2012). Motivation: Past, present, and future. In K. R. Harris, S. Graham, & T. Urdan (Eds.), *APA educational psychology handbook, vol 1: Theories, constructs, and critical issues* (pp. 367–397). Washington, DC: American Psychological Association.

Karabenick, S. A., & Collins-Eaglin, J. (1997). Relation of perceived instructional goals and incentives to college students' use of learning strategies. *Journal of Experimental Education, 65,* 331–341.

List, A. (this volume). Six questions regarding strategy use when learning from multiple texts. In D. L. Dinsmore, L. K. Fryer, & M. M. Parkinson (Eds.), *Handbook of strategies and strategic processing: Conceptualization, measurement, and analysis.* New York: Routledge.

Lombardi, D., & Bailey, J. M. (this volume). Science strategy interventions. In D. L. Dinsmore, L. K. Fryer, & M. M. Parkinson (Eds.), *Handbook of strategies and strategic processing: Conceptualization, measurement, and analysis.* New York: Routledge.

Newton, K. (this volume). Mathematics strategy interventions. In D. L. Dinsmore, L. K. Fryer, & M. M. Parkinson (Eds.), *Handbook of strategies and strategic processing: Conceptualization, measurement, and analysis.* New York: Routledge.

Panadero, E. (2017). A Review of self-regulated learning: Six models and four directions for research. *Frontiers in Psychology, 8,* 422.

Star, J. R., Caronongan, P., Foegen, A., Furgeson, J., Keating, B., Larson, M. R., Lyskawa, J., McCallum, W. G., Porath, J., & Zbiek, R. M. (2015). *Teaching strategies for improving algebra knowledge in middle and high school students (NCEE 2014-4333).* Washington, DC: National Center for Education Evaluation and Regional Assistance (NCEE), Institute of Education Sciences, U.S. Department of Education. Retrieved from the NCEE website: http://whatworks.ed.gov.

Taboada Barber, A., Lutz Klauda, S., & Cartwright, K. B. (this volume). Interplay of strategic processes, executive functions, and autonomy support in students with individual differences. In D. L. Dinsmore, L. K. Fryer, & M. M. Parkinson (Eds.), *Handbook of strategies and strategic processing: Conceptualization, measurement, and analysis.* New York: Routledge.

Van Meter, P., & Campbell, J. M. (this volume). A conceptual framework for defining strategies and strategic processing. In D. L. Dinsmore, L. K. Fryer, & M. M. Parkinson (Eds.), *Handbook of strategies and strategic processing: Conceptualization, measurement, and analysis.* New York: Routledge.

Weiner, B. (2010). The development of an attribution-based theory of motivation: A history of ideas. *Educational Psychologist, 45*(1), 28–36.

Winne, P. H. (1995). Inherent details in self-regulated learning. *Educational Psychologist, 30,* 173–187.

Winne, P. H. (2017). Leveraging big data to help each learner upgrade learning and accelerate learning science. *Teachers College Record, 119*(3), 1–24.

Winne, P. H. (2018). Cognition and metacognition within self-regulated learning. In D. Schunk & J. Greene (Eds.), *Handbook of self-regulation of learning and performance.* (2nd ed., pp. 36-48). New York, NY: Routledge.

Winne, P. H., & Marzouk, Z. (2019). Learning strategies and self-regulated learning. In J. Dunlosky & K. Rawson (Eds.), *Cambridge handbook of cognition and education* (pp. 696–715). New York: Cambridge University Press.

Section III
Measuring Strategic Processing

16

SURVEYS AND RETROSPECTIVE SELF-REPORTS TO MEASURE STRATEGIES AND STRATEGIC PROCESSING

Jan D. Vermunt

EINDHOVEN UNIVERSITY OF TECHNOLOGY, THE NETHERLANDS

INTRODUCTION

This chapter is about surveys and retrospective reports as measurement tools for learning strategies, with a focus on strategic processing. The chapter will start with a concise historical overview of the origin of measurement tools, the first generation of surveys and self-report inventories in the area of student learning strategies from the early 1970s onward. The emergence of research on metacognition in the mid-1980s gave rise to the development of a second generation of student learning strategy instruments, broader in nature and including metacognition as a central concept. Two widely used instruments will be discussed. The chapter will continue with very recent developments in this area, characterized by the inclusion of established scales in new instruments, new measurement techniques, new ways of analyzing data, seeking triangulation with other measurement instruments for learning strategies, and extending the research to a wider range of populations and contexts including teachers' learning. This is followed by a critical discussion of the domains of applicability and limitations of inventories and questionnaires on learning strategies. The chapter will close with a discussion of future directions for research and implications for practice.

Learning strategies are conceptualized here as combinations of thinking activities that students employ to learn something (cf. Vermunt & Verloop, 1999). In the literature often three types of learning strategies are discerned: cognitive, affective, and metacognitive strategies (e.g. Zusho, 2017).

Cognitive processing strategies are those combinations of thinking activities that students use to process subject matter and that lead directly to learning outcomes in terms of knowledge, understanding, skill, etc. Affective learning strategies, which students employ to cope with emotions that arise during learning, lead to a mood that may foster or impair the progress of learning processes. Metacognitive regulation strategies are those combinations of thinking activities students use to choose learning

260 · Jan D. Vermunt

goals and contents, to monitor the course and outcomes of their learning processes, and to adjust their learning if needed. Both affective and regulative learning strategies indirectly lead to learning outcomes via their impact on the processing of subject matter (Vermunt & Verloop, 1999).

A FIRST GENERATION OF SURVEYS AND RETROSPECTIVE SELF-REPORTS TO MEASURE STUDENT LEARNING STRATEGIES

Although the origins of the measurement of learning strategies through self-reports probably go back to the middle of the previous century, in the early 1970s the academic literature witnessed the emergence of a first generation of learning strategy self-report measurement tools in different parts of the world. Roughly at the same time Biggs (e.g. 1978) developed the Study Process Questionnaire (*SPQ*) in Australia, Entwistle and his colleagues made the Approaches to Studying Inventory in Europe (*ASI*, e.g. Entwistle, Hanley, & Hounsell, 1979), and Schmeck and colleagues generated the Inventory of Learning Processes in the USA (*ILP*, e.g. Schmeck, Ribich, & Ramanaiah, 1977). Typically, this first generation family of learning strategies inventories included scales on cognitive processing strategies, and some of them also included scales on study motivation.

Biggs' *SPQ* (Biggs, 1978, 1984) is a questionnaire aimed at measuring study processes. The items were written based on variables mentioned in the literature as associated with studying in higher education. These were supplemented with items referring to more general study skills. The first version contained 80 items in the following ten scales: pragmatism, academic motivation, academic neuroticism, internality, study skills, rote learning, meaningful learning, test anxiety, openness, and class dependence (Biggs, 1978). Factor analysis on the data from students from three different countries showed a similar factor structure for the three samples. Three factors explained between 62% and 66% of the variance for the ten scales. The first, *reproductive* factor, was defined by rote learning, pragmatism, test anxiety, neuroticism, and class dependence. The second, *meaningful* factor, was defined by academic motivation, internality, meaningful learning, and openness. The third factor showed more variation, but for all student groups it was associated with *good study skills* and little anxiety. Correlation of the original items with the factor scores showed that each of the three dimensions consisted of two groups of items: an affective or motivational group and a cognitive, strategic group. In the next version of the *SPQ*, that contained 42 items, Biggs (1984) therefore grouped the items into three dimensions, which each consisted of a strategy and a corresponding motive. Students were asked to indicate on a five-point scale the extent to which every item applied to their attitudes towards studying or their usual way of studying. These dimensions and scales are presented in Table 16.1.

Table 16.1 Motives and Strategies in Study Processes (Biggs, 1984)

Dimension	Motive	Strategy
Utilizing (surface)	Instrumental (surface motive)	Reproducing (surface strategy)
Internalizing (deep)	Intrinsic (deep motive)	Meaningful (deep strategy)
Achieving	Achievement (achieving motive)	Organizing (achieving strategy)

Surveys and Retrospective Self-reports • 261

Table 16.2 Scales and Sub-scales of the *ASI* (Entwistle, 1981; Entwistle & Ramsden, 1983)

Scale	Origin
I. Meaning Orientation	
Deep approach	Marton & Säljö (1976)
Use of evidence	Marton & Säljö (1976)
Relating ideas	Marton & Säljö (1976)
Intrinsic motivation	Biggs (1978)
II. Reproducing Orientation	
Surface approach	Marton & Säljö (1976)
Syllabus boundness	Parlett (1970)
Fear of failure	Entwistle & Wilson (1977)
Improvidence	Pask (1976)
III. Strategic Orientation	
Strategic approach	Miller & Parlett (1974), adapted by Ramsden (1979)
Extrinsic motivation	Biggs (1978)
Achievement motivation	Entwistle & Wilson (1977)
IV. Non-Academic Orientation	
Desorganized study methods	Entwistle & Wilson (1977)
Negative atitudes to studying	Entwistle & Wilson (1977)
Globetrotting	Pask (1976)
V. Styles of Learning	
Comprehension learning	Pask (1976)
Operation learning	Pask (1976)

The three dimensions Biggs found show strong similarities with the three main orientations that emerged from Entwistle and Ramsden's (1983) study (see Table 16.2). In his 1984 publication, Biggs proposed to replace the terminology that he had used until then by the concepts of surface, deep, and achieving, to align them with the terminology used in the emerging literature on student learning in higher education at the time.

The *ASI* has been developed by Entwistle and his colleagues in a series of studies. The first research project (Entwistle & Wilson, 1977) aimed to determine the influence of relatively stable personality characteristics on students' study success. The questionnaire on motivation and study methods that was developed in this project turned out to correlate only modestly with students' exam results, on average a Pearson correlation of around .20. Personality characteristics like extraversion, neuroticism and radicalism showed even lower correlations. The researchers concluded that the original motivation and study methods scales were too simple to cover the very different ways in which students approach their studies (Entwistle, 1981; Entwistle et al., 1979).

In 1975 Entwistle and his colleagues started working on the development of a new questionnaire. Factor analysis on the original motivation and study method dimensions yielded five factors that were included as scales in the new questionnaire: organized study methods, achievement motivation, fear of failure, negative attitudes towards studying, and syllabus-boundness. Based on the dimensions that Marton and Säljö

262 • Jan D. Vermunt

(1976) had identified in students' approaches to learning (deep and surface approach) and Pask's (1976) learning styles/strategies (operation and comprehension learning) new scales were developed and new items were written. From Biggs (1976) *Study Behaviour Questionnaire* the scales on intrinsic and extrinsic motivation were taken. Based on Ramsden's (1979) interviews with university students the scale 'strategic approach' was developed. The first version of the *ASI* contained 106 items in 15 scales. After a large scale study with 767 first year students from three universities and a variety of subject areas, the final inventory was composed. Some scales were removed, two new scales were developed based on Pask's (1976) learning pathologies (globetrotting and improvidence) and two components that were thought to be essential for gaining *deep* learning outcomes were added: *relating ideas* and *use of evidence*. The best items from the item pool were selected for inclusion, and most scales were limited to four items. This final version contained 64 items in 16 scales, grouped into five categories (see Table 16.2).

The 64 items were formatted as Likert-type statements and students were asked to indicate on a five-point scale the degree to which each item applied to them. Sometimes students were asked for their general way of studying in their main courses (e.g. Entwistle & Ramsden, 1983), and sometimes they were asked for their way of studying with one particular course (e.g. Watkins, 1982).

Entwistle and his colleagues have since continued developing and updating their inventory. An excellent review of this work and a copy of all inventories are included in Entwistle's (2018) recent book, entitled *Student learning and academic understanding: A research perspective with implications for teaching.*

The Inventory of Learning Processes (*ILP*) is a questionnaire developed by Schmeck et al. (1977) aimed at measuring learning styles. A *learning style* is defined by Schmeck (1983) as 'a disposition on the part of some student to adopt a particular learning strategy regardless of the specific demands of the learning task. Thus, a style is simply a strategy used with some cross-situational consistency' (p. 233). A learning strategy is described by Schmeck as 'a pattern of information-processing activities used to prepare for an anticipated test of memory' (p. 234). In view of the descriptions of learning style and learning strategy, emphasizing the *cognitive processing of subject matter*, the *ILP* does not contain items referring to attitudes, personality, motivation, cognitive style, and preferences for physical and social study environments (Schmeck, 1983).

The items were derived from theories on human information processing and human learning. The three authors (Schmeck et al., 1977) translated cognitive processes as described in the literature into behavior-oriented statements, geared towards the environment and activities of university students. After several development steps and large-scale administrations of intermediate versions of the *ILP*, the final version was composed. This version contained 62 items in four scales that represented the following learning styles or strategies: deep processing, methodical study, fact retention, and elaborative processing. Schmeck (1983) emphasized that what he calls *deep processing* is not the same as the *deep approach* of Marton and Säljö (1984). Deep processing in his conceptualization is a purely information processing strategy of conceptual analysis, classification, and comparison of information. The deep approach as Marton and Säljö view it includes relating information to one's own personal experiences. This last process emerged in Schmeck's analyses as a separate factor which he called *elaborative*

Table 16.3 Scales of the *LASSI* (Weinstein et al., 1988)

Scale
Anxiety
Attitude
Concentration
Information processing
Motivation
Scheduling
Selecting main ideas
Self-testing
Study aids
Test strategies

processing. According to Schmeck, deep and elaborative processing are distinct strategies, although they may be correlated.

The items of the *ILP* are behavior-oriented statements, and students are asked to indicate whether an item applies or does not apply to them (true/false items). Students are asked to think about how they go about studying in general and not in a specific course.

Weinstein and colleagues developed the Learning and Study Strategies Inventory (*LASSI*). A major goal was to develop an instrument that could help educators and trainers diagnose strengths and weaknesses in students' learning and study strategies in order to provide individualized remedial training. The contexts for the development project were the study skills and learning-to-learn courses running at US colleges and universities at the time to help academically underprepared students to remedy student deficiencies (Weinstein, Zimmermann, & Palmer, 1988). The final version of the *LASSI* contains 90 items in ten scales (see Table 16.3). Students are asked to indicate on a five-point Likert scale the extent to which an item is true for them.

THE SECOND GENERATION OF LEARNING STRATEGY INSTRUMENTS AND THE INCLUSION OF METACOGNITION

As noted above, the first generation of learning strategy inventories mainly contained scales on students' cognitive processing strategies and their study motivation/affection. Around the mid-1980s the role of metacognition in student learning became more apparent. The work of Brown and colleagues in the United States (e.g. Brown, 1987) had shown the importance of strategies involved in the regulation and control of student learning processes (e.g. planning, monitoring, control, evaluation strategies). The work of Flavell and colleagues (e.g. Flavell, 1987) had illuminated the role of students' knowledge and awareness of their own cognitive processes and structures (metacognitive knowledge) for their learning. Initially, the focus of metacognitive research was on young children, but later on the research moved to include adolescents and adults as well (e.g. Palinscar & Brown, 1984). Unconnected to the research on metacognition, researchers in Europe had started studying students' conceptions of learning and were able to identify qualitatively different conceptions of what students understood by learning and related phenomena (e.g. Säljö, 1979; Van Rossum, Deijkers, & Hamer, 1985). Students' conceptions of learning turned out to be related to their approaches to learning (e.g. Van Rossum & Schenk, 1984).

These developments gave rise to a second generation of student learning inventories that included metacognitive scales. Two well-known examples of these second generation inventories are the Motivated Strategies for Learning Questionnaire (*MSLQ*) developed by Pintrich and colleagues in the United States (e.g. Garcia & McKeachie, 2005; Pintrich, 2004; Zusho, 2017) and the Inventory of Learning patterns of Students (*ILS*) developed by Vermunt and colleagues in Europe (e.g. Vermunt & Donche, 2017; Vermunt & Vermetten, 2004).

The *MSLQ* was developed by Pintrich and colleagues (Garcia & McKeachie, 2005; Pintrich, 2004; Pintrich, Smith, Garcia, & McKeachie, 1993). It is based on a social-cognitive theoretical framework of motivation and cognition. Motivation and learning strategies are not viewed as traits of the learner, but rather as being dynamic and contextually bound, and learning strategies can be learned and brought under the control of the learner (Garcia & McKeachie, 2005). The final version of the *MSLQ* contains 81 items in 15 scales under two broad headings of motivation and learning strategies (see Table 16.4).

When completing the *MSLQ*, students are asked to think of a specific course. They score items on a seven-point Likert scale, varying from (1) not at all true of me to (7) very true of me. Pintrich (2004) reordered the *MSLQ* scales under a new framework of phases and areas for self-regulated learning. In this framework, he considered the MSLQ scales *rehearsal, elaboration organization, critical thinking*, and *metacognition* as referring to the Cognition area of his model. *Intrinsic goals, extrinsic goals, task value, control beliefs, self-efficacy*, and *test anxiety* he subsumed under the area of Motivation/ Affect. The *MSLQ* scales *effort regulation, help seeking*, and *time/study environment* belong to the area of Behavior in this new model, while *peer learning* and *time/study environment* he considered as relevant for the area of Context.

Table 16.4 Domains and Scales of the *MSLQ* (from Garcia & McKeachie, 2005)

Domains	Scales
Motivation scales	Intrinsic goal orientation
	Extrinsic goal orientation
	Task value
	Control of learning beliefs
	Self-efficacy for learning and performance
	Test anxiety
Learning strategy scales	Rehearsal
	Elaboration
	Organization
	Critical thinking
	Metacognitive self-regulation
	Time and study environment management
	Effort regulation
	Peer learning
	Help seeking

The *ILS* was developed by Vermunt and colleagues (Vermunt, 1996, 1998, 2005; Vermunt & Donche, 2017; Vermunt & Van Rijswijk, 1988; Vermunt & Vermetten, 2004). A learning pattern is conceptualized as a:

> [c]oherent whole of learning activities that learners usually employ, their beliefs about learning and their learning motivation, a whole that is characteristic of them in a certain period of time. It is a coordinating concept, in which the interrelationships between cognitive, affective, and regulative learning activities, beliefs about learning, and learning motivations are united.
>
> (Vermunt & Donche, 2017, p. 270)

The *ILS* covers four domains or learning components: cognitive processing strategies, metacognitive regulation strategies, conceptions of learning, and learning orientations or motivations. The items were derived from interviews with students about these four domains that were analyzed in a phenomenographic, qualitative way (Vermunt, 1996). If necessary, the student quotes were shortened or slightly reformulated. Starting with a pool of 241 items, the number of items was successively reduced through large-scale studies with university students from different universities and various subject areas (Vermunt, 1998).

The final full version of the *ILS* contains 120 items in 20 scales, five scales for each of the four domains. Part A on 'study activities' measures cognitive processing and metacognitive regulation strategies and contains 55 items in ten scales. Here students are asked to indicate on a five-point Likert scale the degree to which they use the described activity in their studies. Part B on 'study views and motives' contains 65 items: 40 on conceptions of learning and 25 on learning orientations/motivations. Here students are asked to indicate on a five-point Likert scale the degree to which they agree with the described view or motive. The shortened version of the *ILS* contains 100 items in 20 scales, 5 scales and 25 items in each domain. Table 16.5 shows the learning components and scales covered by the *ILS*.

Originally the *ILS* was named the Inventory of Learning Styles. However, it soon turned out that the term learning 'style' is often associated with unchangeability, a phenomenon deeply rooted in personality or even one's biological makeup, a hard-to-change human trait. This was contrary to what we meant by learning style, which we see as the result of the interplay between person-bound and environmental influences. Moreover, the term learning style is used for a wide variety of individual differences between learners, so broad that it is almost impossible to define a common meaning of the term (e.g. Coffield, Moseley, Hall, & Ecclestone, 2004). For these reasons, around 2004 we stopped using the term learning 'style' and introduced the concept of learning 'pattern' as a more dynamic term to refer to this interrelated whole of students' learning strategies, views, and motives (Vermunt, 2005; Vermunt & Vermetten, 2004). Initially the name of the *ILS* instrument was kept the same to avoid confusion. However, we now believe that renaming the *ILS* to Inventory of Learning Patterns of Students is more appropriate to avoid confusion with the learning style area.

Research with the *ILS* has repeatedly identified four qualitative different patterns in the way students in higher education learn: reproduction-directed learning,

266 • Jan D. Vermunt

Table 16.5 Learning Components and Scales of the *ILS* (from Vermunt & Vermetten, 2004)

Learning components	Scales of the *ILS*

Processing strategies	Deep processing
	  Relating and structuring
	  Critical processing
	Stepwise processing
	  Memorizing and rehearsing
	  Analyzing
	Concrete processing

Regulation strategies	Self-regulation
	  Learning process and outcomes outcomes
	  Learning contents
	External regulation
	  Learning process
	  Learning outcomes
	Lack of regulation

Conceptions of learning	Construction of knowledge Intake of knowledge Use of knowledge Stimulating education Co-operative learning
Learning orientations	Personally interested Certificate oriented Self-test oriented Vocation oriented Ambivalent

meaning-directed learning, application-directed learning, and undirected learning (e.g. Lonka, Olkinuora, & Makinen, 2004; Richardson, 2000; Vermunt, 1998). For a review of recent research see Vermunt and Donche (2017).

RECENT DEVELOPMENTS IN SELF-REPORT TOOLS TO MEASURE LEARNING STRATEGIES AND RELATED PHENOMENA

Lonka and colleagues (2008) developed the *MED NORD* inventory for measuring medical students' well-being and study orientations. It aimed to measure four domains of student learning: experiences of stress, anxiety, and disinterest; motivational (thinking) strategies; conceptions of learning and knowledge (epistemologies); and approaches to learning. The authors composed the instrument of scales from a variety of other instruments that had previously shown good predictive value, validity, and reliability. For example, students' (motivational) thinking strategies and attributions were measured with items from the Strategy and Attribution Questionnaire (*SAQ*) (Nurmi, Salmela-Aro, & Haavisto, 1995). Students' cognitive strategies were measured with two scales of deep and surface approaches to learning, for which items were taken and modified from Entwistle and Ramsden's (1983) *ASI* and Vermunt and Van Rijswijk's (1988) *ILS*.

The scales showed satisfactory to good internal consistency. Factor analysis yielded five overarching dimensions which the authors called 'study orientations'. These orientations were related to medical students' perception of their learning environment. The authors concluded that the *MED NORD* tool showed consistency and validity and judged it appropriate for measuring medical students' well-being and study orientations. They emphasize that the *MED NORD* is a general instrument that can also be used with other student groups than medical students.

Another group of Finnish researchers took a slightly different approach. For example, Haarala-Muhonen, Ruohoniemi, Parpala, Komulainen, and Lindblom-Ylänne (2017) used an 18-item modified version of the Entwistle and McCune's (2004) Approaches to Learning and Studying Inventory (*ALSI*), measuring deep and surface approaches to learning. The researchers took a person-oriented approach in clustering the students according to their scores on the various variables, which led to four study profiles. They found that both approaches to learning and study success in the first study year predicted Law students' graduation time and the completion of the degree. The authors argue that measuring study approaches in this way can help promote first-year students' awareness of their study practices and support the progress of their studies. In their view, individual students need tailored guidance in transitioning to university studies and identifying the demands of the study programme.

Items from the *ILS* have been incorporated into a tool to measure learning gains in higher education by Vermunt, Ilie, and Vignoles (2018). The funder of their study, the Higher Education Funding Council for England (HEFCE), initiated a series of studies aimed to develop and test different kinds of instruments for their capability to measure university students' learning gains at scale across a variety of disciplines. In their study, Vermunt et al. (2018) first developed a conceptual framework of learning gain. The framework consisted of four components and three cross-cutting dimensions: a cognitive, metacognitive, affective, and socio-communicative component; a view of knowledge and learning dimension; a research dimension; and a moral dimension. Importantly, these components and dimensions were viewed not only, or not primarily, as *prerequisites* for learning (cf. Weinstein et al., 1988), but as important *outcomes* of university studies, or learning gains. In other words, the ability to think critically, learn deeply, self-regulate one's learning and thinking processes, engagement, etc. are viewed as important elements of the espoused aims of higher education institutions, universally around the world.

The authors adapted existing scales and created new scales that covered their conceptual framework as broadly as possible, and that were practical, user friendly, and had the potential for at-scale administration. They took scales from the *ILS* (Vermunt & Vermetten, 2004), a grit scale (Duckworth & Quinn, 2009), emotional and social engagement scales from Fredricks et al. (2016), academic writing difficulties (from Lonka et al., 2013), epistemological beliefs (from Schommer-Aikins, Mau, Brookhart, & Hutter, 2000), and adapted them if deemed necessary. The authors created two new scales on self-management and attitude to research. Moreover, they took items on reasoning ability from the International Cognitive Ability Resource *ICAR* (Condon & Revelle, 2014). With the use of data from a large-scale survey of 11 English universities and over 4,500 students, they tested the reliability and validity of the measurement instrument empirically. Most of the measurement scales turned out to be reliable, and they found evidence for the validity of the conceptual framework as well (Vermunt et al., 2018).

Endedijk, Brekelmans, Sleegers, and Vermunt (2016) developed a Structured Learning Report (*SLR*) that extended the field of self-report tools for learning strategies in three important ways. First, their target group deviated from the traditional first year or undergraduate university student population to include student teachers in the context of professional education, more specifically a postgraduate professional teacher education programme. Second, in their instrument they ask students to report on multiple learning experiences including studying at university and learning from internships. Third, they did not ask students to generalize and report about their normal or average study experience, but they asked them to report on six different but concrete learning experiences. The data from these multiple learning experiences were combined by the researchers in their data analysis. The findings showed that the *SLR* was able to measure student teachers' regulation of their learning in a valid and reliable way. Moreover, individual differences in student teachers' regulation strategies could be identified.

Recently Vermunt, Vrikki, Warwick, and Mercer (2017) developed the Inventory of Teacher Learning (*ITL*), a 32-item instrument to measure in-service and student teachers' professional learning strategies. The development took place in the context of a Lesson Study professional development programme for teachers aimed at supporting the introduction of national innovations in mathematics teaching in England. The items were grounded in qualitative studies on teacher learning in the context of educational innovations. The study drew on longitudinal and cross-sectional data from three waves of data collection from 214 teachers engaged in Lesson Study during one full school year. Three patterns of teacher learning could be identified in this study: meaning-oriented, application-oriented, and problematic learning. The longitudinal study showed the influence of teacher professional development on teachers' use of work-based learning strategies. More specifically, the findings showed positive effects of Lesson Study on meaning-oriented and application-oriented teacher learning and a negative effect on problematic learning (Vermunt, Vrikki, Van Halem, Warwick, & Mercer, 2019). The *ITL* has already been translated into Finnish, Dutch, Swedish, and Chinese for use in research projects on the role of teacher agency in teacher professional learning in Finland, Sweden, the UK, and The Netherlands, and on teachers' adaptations to educational innovations in China (ongoing research). Moreover, the *ITL* has been adapted for use in research on professional development in clinical leadership (Hofmann & Vermunt, 2017).

DOMAINS OF APPLICABILITY AND LIMITATIONS

Inventories and questionnaires on learning strategies as described above have been used for a variety of purposes (Entwistle, 2018; Garcia & McKeachie, 2005). Three important domains of applicability are the following.

First, they have been used to gain scientific knowledge about dimensions and developments in students' use of learning strategies, their motives, and their views and beliefs. This kind of research has, for example, looked into the internal structure of learning strategies, conceptions, and orientations in different educational contexts, developments in students' use of learning strategies during the school career and at transitional phases in that career (e.g. from secondary to higher education), consistency and variability in students' use of learning strategies, relations between learning strategies and personal and contextual factors, and relations between learning strategies and learning outcomes. In this way a rich knowledge base has been built up about the domain of student learning in higher education (for reviews, see for example, Dinsmore, 2017; Entwistle, 2018; Entwistle & McCune, 2004; Fryer, 2017; Gijbels, Donche, Richardson, & Vermunt, 2014; Lonka et al., 2004; Pintrich, 2004; Richardson, 2000; Vermunt & Donche, 2017; Zusho, 2017).

Inventories and questionnaires on learning strategies have also been used to help students reflect on their use of learning strategies, and to help students remedy the weak sides of their approaches to learning and studying (e.g. Donche, Coertjens, Vanthournout, & Van Petegem, 2012; Garcia & McKeachie, 2005; Vermunt, 1995; Weinstein et al., 1988). When completing a self-report strategy inventory, students are encouraged to think about their way of learning and studying, and when they receive feedback on their strategy scale scores they can compare their own use of different learning strategies with that of their peers. The inventory items themselves can give them ideas about potential learning activities they had never thought of before. Sometimes this awareness raising function is embedded into a learning strategy or study skills training programme, in which students receive training to improve learning strategies they are not very proficient in (Weinstein et al., 1988).

Third, learning strategy inventories have also been used to evaluate the effect on students' learning strategies, motives, or views of the teaching environment or a specific course (e.g. Asikainen & Gijbels, 2017; Entwistle & McCune, 2013; Garcia & McKeachie, 2005). Lonka et al. (2008) point to the opportunity their *MED NORD* instrument provides to improve medical education by long-term follow-up studies in which students' well-being, motivational strategies, epistemologies, approaches to learning, and their perception of their learning environment are examined. Vermunt et al. (2018) developed their learning gain instrument to evaluate the impact of different universities, disciplines, and learning environments on students' gains in their use of cognitive and metacognitive learning strategies. Information about the development of students' way of learning in a particular learning environment can give important feedback to lecturers and directors of study to improve the quality of university teaching. If, for example, during a particular course students' use of memorizing strategies increases, this may signal an undesirable effect of the teaching in that course on the quality of student learning.

Discussions we had with policymakers in the context of our learning gain research also revealed some expectations towards the use of learning strategy inventories that we firmly disagree with. In our view these inventories cannot be used for selection purposes of individual students, for example in admission procedures for universities. Neither can they be used for accountability purposes, for example to rank order universities, courses, or lecturers based on the outcomes of comparative analyses of student learning strategy data (e.g. to rank universities that score higher and lower on students' use of critical thinking strategies). The reason for these domains of non-applicability is on our view exactly the self-report nature of these tools. It is vital that students, when they are answering questions about their learning, do not have any other interests than responding as honestly as possible, and that there are no right and wrong answers (Vermunt et al., 2018).

Compared to other research methods on learning strategies, self-reports have their advantages and disadvantages. Advantages are, for example, the possibility to get an overview of large groups of students in a relatively short time, the opportunity to complete the instrument at a time and place that suits individual students, and the possibility to compare a student's individual score on a learning scale with those of other students. The ecological validity is usually high since the questions are geared towards students' studying in their natural study settings. Data collection can be fully digitalized and data analysis can be done easily and quickly with big data files.

But there are also disadvantages. There is the issue of validity, or to what extent can we report validly about the mental processes that occur in our brains (Karabenick et al., 2007; Trevors, Feyzi-Behnagh, Azevedo, & Bouchet, 2016)? Terms used in Likert scales like 'I do this rarely' or 'I do this frequently' may mean different things to different students, or different things to the same students earlier and later in their studies. Especially inventories asking students about their general or average way of learning may impose a difficult task on students to generalize or average their use of learning strategies across a multitude of concrete study experiences. Sometimes the items are not phrased in the language that students use to think about their learning. This is especially the case where items are derived from the scientific literature. We must be cautious to translate or adapt existing inventories for use with other populations than they were originally developed for. Items referring to specific learning activities may not be relevant for new populations, while their actually used learning activities are not represented in these inventories' items (e.g. use the *ASI* to measure work-based learning strategies, use the *ILS* to measure children's learning strategies, use the *SPQ* to measure Indigenous students' learning strategies).

There are alternative methods to measure students' use of learning strategies that may be more suited to specific circumstances or purposes. Thinking aloud, eye-tracking, video-recording observable learning behavior, interviews, learning analytics, performance assessment, fMRI scanning, portfolios, and teacher judgments are some examples of other methods used to measure the cognitive and regulative learning strategies that students use (Endedijk et al., 2016). The other chapters in this book present excellent discussions of some of these methods, so we will not go into detail here (see, for example, Bråten, Magliano, & Salmerón, this volume; Catrysse, Gijbels, & Donche, this volume; Lawless & Riel, this volume). The central problem that all these methods face is that we want to observe or externalize processes that are inherently internal: how students memorize information, relate and structure theories, engage critically with their studies, apply knowledge, think of examples, relate to own experiences, regulate their mental processes, etc. And we want to do that in situations and with tasks that are as similar as possible to their actual learning and study environments and tasks.

All these methods have validity issues. Eye-tracking yields detailed information about where students are looking at in learning or classroom situations, but the correspondence between what students are looking at and where they are thinking about is not straightforward. Thinking aloud yields rich data on students' mental processes while they are doing a study task, but it is labor-intensive, may disrupt 'natural' thinking processes, and may not be representative of the study processes students engage in during their normal studies. The relation between brain processes (for example, fMRI scan data) and learning strategies is still largely to be explored.

FUTURE DIRECTIONS FOR RESEARCH

In my view, the field of research in the area of student learning strategies in higher education should move forward in the following directions. First, it should broaden its scope to incorporate cognitive, regulative, affective, motivational, social/collaborative, communicative, epistemological, and moral components. Second, research should be conducted that focuses on the relation between students' learning and their learning outcomes or gains. Third, more research should be done on the design and effects of powerful learning environments intended to promote active, self-regulated, meaning-oriented, high-quality learning. The incorporation of learning strategy information in learning analytics data gathering to support personalized learning pathways could be an important element of such a research strand. Fourth, the multi-dimensional nature of learning strategies and patterns should be the focus of research more than is the case now. Fifth, more research should be done on the relation between processing and regulation strategies (cf. Dinsmore & Fryer, 2018). Or, to put it more generally, the relation between the various dimensions of the multi-dimensional model should be more in the focus of scientific research in this area (e.g. Fryer & Vermunt, 2018).

Research on strategies should broaden its scope to include different populations and contexts than the traditional focus on undergraduate students at university. One such important population and context is that of teachers' professional learning and development in the context of their work. An important question in this regard is how teachers, or professionals in general, integrate knowledge gained from own experiences, from experienced colleagues, and from 'theory' into a professional theory of practice. We need tools to measure the various components of professional learning. Moreover, we need more knowledge about the impact of various pedagogical approaches to foster high-quality, meaning-oriented teacher learning and deliberate practice. Other important populations and contexts are professionals in other occupations (for example, medical doctors), and secondary and primary school students (Vermunt & Endedijk, 2011; Vermunt et al., 2017, 2019). The relation between student learning and teacher learning and the need for a common conceptual and measurement framework is another important direction for learning strategy research. Finally, we need more triangulation research in which learning strategies are measured by multiple research methods and the evidence is compared and evaluated (cf. Alexander, 2017).

IMPLICATIONS FOR PRACTICE

To maximize the validity of retrospective self-report tools, the items should be phrased in the language that the target population uses to think about their learning. Grounding the items in interviews with students from the target population is the best way to achieve this. Items should be as concrete and specific as possible in view of the purpose of the measurement. Cherry-picking of individual items at face value from validated scales should be discouraged; instead intact scales with good reliabilities should be used. When inventories are used for different populations than they were developed for, often considerable revalidation is necessary.

Surveys and retrospective self-reports occupy an important place in the measurement of learning strategies. The choice for a measurement method depends on the purpose, context, available resources, and practical opportunities. As discussed above, learning strategy inventories can be used to gain scientific knowledge about dimensions and developments in students' use of learning strategies, their motives, and their views and beliefs. They can also be used to help students reflect on their way of learning and to help students to develop the weaker sides of their approaches to learning and studying. A growing field of application of learning strategy inventories is to evaluate the effect of teaching-learning environments or specific courses on the quality of students' learning strategies, motives, or views, with the aim of improving the quality of university teaching. Strategy inventories should in our view not be used for selection purposes of individual students or for accountability purposes of universities, courses, or lecturers.

REFERENCES

Alexander, P. A. (2017). Issues of constructs, contexts, and continuity: Commentary on learning in higher education. *Educational Psychology Review, 29*(2), 345–351.

Asikainen, H., & Gijbels, D. (2017). Do students develop towards more deep approaches to learning during studies? A systematic review on the development of students' deep and surface approaches to learning in higher education. *Educational Psychology Review, 29*(2), 205–234.

Biggs, J. B. (1976). Dimensions of study behaviour: Another look at ATI. *British Journal of Educational Psychology, 46*(1), 68–80.

Biggs, J. B. (1978). Individual and group differences in study processes. *British Journal of Educational Psychology, 48*(3), 266–279.

Biggs, J. B. (1984). Learning strategies, student motivation patterns, and subjectively perceived success. In J. R. Kirby (Ed.), *Cognitive strategies and educational performance* (pp. 111–134). New York: Academic Press.

Bråten, I., Magliano, J. P., & Salmerón, L. (this volume). Concurrent and task specific self-reports. In D. L. Dinsmore, L. K. Fryer, & M. M. Parkinson (Eds.), *Handbook of strategies and strategic processing: Conceptualization, measurement, and analysis*. New York: Routledge.

Brown, A. L. (1987). Metacognition, executive control, self-regulation and other more mysterious mechanisms. In F. E. Weinert & R. H. Kluwe (Eds.), *Metacognition, motivation and understanding* (pp. 65–116). Hillsdale, NJ: Erlbaum.

Catrysse, L., Gijbels, D., & Donche, V. (this volume). Measuring levels of processing: Perspectives for eye tracking and fMRI in multi-method designs. In D. L. Dinsmore, L. K. Fryer, & M. M. Parkinson (Eds.), *Handbook of strategies and strategic processing: Conceptualization, measurement, and analysis*. New York: Routledge.

Coffield, F., Moseley, D., Hall, E., & Ecclestone, K. (2004). *Learning styles and pedagogy in post-16 learning: A systematic and critical review*. London: Learning and Skills Research Centre.

Condon, D. M., & Revelle, W. (2014). The International cognitive ability resource: Development and initial validation of a public-domain measure. *Intelligence, 43*, 52–64.

Dinsmore, D. L. (2017). Toward a dynamic, multidimensional research framework for strategic processing. *Educational Psychology Review, 29*(2), 235–268.

Dinsmore, D. L. D., & Fryer, L. K. (2018). The intersection between depth and the regulation of strategy use. *British Journal of Educational Psychology, 88*, 1–8.

Donche, V., Coertjens, L., Vanthournout, G., & Van Petegem, P. (2012). Providing constructive feedback on learning patterns: An individual learner's perspective. *Reflecting Education, 8*(1), 114–131.

Duckworth, A. L., & Quinn, P. D. (2009). Development and validation of the Short Grit Scale (GRIT–S). *Journal of Personality Assessment, 91*(2), 166–174.

Endedijk, M. D., Brekelmans, M., Sleegers, P., & Vermunt, J. D. (2016). Measuring students' self-regulated learning in professional education: Bridging the gap between event and aptitude measurements. *Quality and Quantity, 50*, 2141–2164.

Entwistle, N. (2018). *Student learning and academic understanding: A research perspective with implications for teaching*. London: Academic Press.

Entwistle, N., Hanley, M., & Hounsell, D. (1979). Identifying distinctive approaches to studying. *Higher Education, 8*(4), 365–380.

Entwistle, N., & McCune, V. (2004). The conceptual bases of study strategy inventories. *Educational Psychology Review, 16,* 325–345.

Entwistle, N., & McCune, V. (2013). The disposition to understand for oneself at university: Integrating learning processes with motivation and metacognition. *British Journal of Educational Psychology, 83*(2), 267–279.

Entwistle, N. J. (1981). *Styles of learning and teaching: An integrated outline of educational psychology.* Chichester: Wiley.

Entwistle, N. J., & Ramsden, P. (1983). *Understanding student learning.* London: Croom Helm.

Entwistle, N. J., & Wilson, J. D. (1977). *Degrees of excellence: The academic achievement game.* London: Hodder & Stoughton.

Flavell, J. H. (1987). Speculations about the nature and development of metacognition. In F. E. Weinert & R. H. Kluwe (Eds.), *Metacognition, motivation and understanding* (pp. 21–29). Hillsdale, NJ: Erlbaum.

Fredricks, J. A., Wang, M. T., Linn, J. S., Hofkens, T. L., Sung, H., Parr, A., & Allerton, J. (2016). Using qualitative methods to develop a survey measure of math and science engagement. *Learning and Instruction, 43,* 5–15.

Fryer, L. K. (2017). Building bridges: Seeking structure and direction for higher education motivated learning strategy models. *Educational Psychology Review, 29*(2), 325–344.

Fryer, L. K., & Vermunt, J. D. (2018). Regulating approaches to learning: Testing learning strategy convergences across a year at university. *British Journal of Educational Psychology, 88,* 21–41.

Garcia, T. D., & McKeachie, W. J. (2005). The making of the motivated strategies for learning questionnaire. *Educational Psychologist, 40*(2), 117–128.

Gijbels, D., Donche, V., Richardson, J. T. E., & Vermunt, J. D. (Eds.). (2014). *Learning patterns in higher education: Dimensions and research perspectives.* New York: Routledge.

Haarala-Muhonen, A., Ruohoniemi, M., Parpala, A., Komulainen, E., & Lindblom-Ylänne, S. (2017). How do the different study profiles of first-year students predict their study success, study progress and the completion of degrees? *Higher Education, 74*(6), 949–962.

Hofmann, R., & Vermunt, J. D. (2017). Professional development in clinical leadership: Evaluation of the chief residents clinical leadership and management programme. *Faculty of Education Working Paper no. 5, 12/2017.* University of Cambridge. Retrieved from https://foeworkingpapers.com/2017/12/08/

Karabenick, S. A., Woolley, M. E., Friedel, J. M., Ammon, B. V., Blazevski, J., Bonney, C. R., ... Kelly, K. L. (2007). Cognitive processing of self-report items in educational research: Do they think what we mean? *Educational Psychologist, 42*(3), 139–151.

Lawless, K. A., & Riel, J. (this volume). Exploring the utilization of the big data revolution as a methodology for exploring learning strategy in educational environments. In D. L. Dinsmore, L. K. Fryer, & M. M. Parkinson (Eds.), *Handbook of strategies and strategic processing: Conceptualization, measurement, and analysis.* New York: Routledge.

Lonka, K., Chow, A., Keskinen, J., Hakkarainen, K., Sandström, N., & Pyhältö, K. (2013). How to measure PhD students' conceptions of academic writing-and are they related to well-being? *Journal of Writing Research, 5*(3), 1–25.

Lonka, K., Olkinuora, E., & Makinen, J. (2004). Aspects and prospects of measuring studying and learning in higher education. *Educational Psychology Review, 16,* 301–331.

Lonka, K., Sharafi, P., Karlgren, K., Masiello, I., Nieminen, J., Birgegård, G., & Josephson, A. (2008). MED NORD–A tool for measuring medical students' well-being and study orientations. *Medical Teacher, 30*(1), 72–79.

Marton, F., & Säljö, R. (1976). On qualitative differences in learning: I - Outcome and process. *British Journal of Educational Psychology, 46*(1), 4–11.

Marton, F., & Säljö, R. (1984). Approaches to learning. In F. Marton, D. Hounsell, & N. Entwistle (Eds.), *The experience of learning* (pp. 36–55). Edinburgh: Scottish Academic Press.

Miller, C. M., & Parlett, M. (1974). *Up to the mark: A study of the examination game.* London: SRHE.

Nurmi, J.-E., Salmela-Aro, K., & Haavisto, T. (1995). The strategy and attribution questionnaire: Psychometric properties. *European Journal of Psychological Assessment, 11,* 108–121.

Palinscar, A. S., & Brown, A. L. (1984). Reciprocal teaching of comprehension-fostering and comprehension-monitoring activities. *Cognition and Instruction, 1*(2), 117–175.

Parlett, M. R. (1970). The syllabus-bound student. In L. Hudson (Ed.), *The ecology of human intelligence* (pp. 272–283). Harmondsworth: Penguin Books.

Pask, G. (1976). Styles and strategies of learning. *British Journal of Educational Psychology, 46*(2), 128–148.

Pintrich, P. R. (2004). A conceptual framework for assessing motivation and self-regulated learning in college students. *Educational Psychology Review, 16,* 385–407.

Pintrich, P. R., Smith, D. A., Garcia, T., & McKeachie, W. J. (1993). Reliability and predictive validity of the Motivated Strategies for Learning Questionnaire (MSLQ). *Educational and Psychological Measurement, 53*(3), 801–813.

Ramsden, P. (1979). Student learning and perceptions of the academic environment. *Higher Education, 8*(4), 411–427.

Richardson, J. T. E. (2000). *Researching student learning: Approaches to studying in campus-based and distance education.* Buckingham: Open University Press and SRHE.

Säljö, R. (1979). Learning in the learner's perspective. *I. Some common-sense conceptions.* Reports from the Department of Education, University of Götenborg no. 76.

Schmeck, R. R. (1983). Learning styles of college students. In R. Dillon & R. R. Schmeck (Eds.), *Individual differences in cognition, 1* (pp. 233–279). New York: Academic Press.

Schmeck, R. R., Ribich, F., & Ramanaiah, N. (1977). Development of a self-report inventory for assessing individual differences in learning processes. *Applied Psychological Measurement, 1*(3), 413–431.

Schommer-Aikins, M., Mau, W., Brookhart, S., & Hutter, R. (2000). Understanding middle students' beliefs about knowledge and learning using a multidimensional paradigm. *Journal of Educational Research, 94*(2), 120–127.

Trevors, G., Feyzi-Behnagh, R., Azevedo, R., & Bouchet, F. (2016). Self-regulated learning processes vary as a function of epistemic beliefs and contexts: Mixed method evidence from eye tracking and concurrent and retrospective reports. *Learning and Instruction, 42*, 31–46.

Van Rossum, E. J., Deijkers, R., & Hamer, R. (1985). Students' learning conceptions and their interpretation of significant educational concepts. *Higher Education, 14*(6), 617–641.

Van Rossum, E. J., & Schenk, S. M. (1984). The relationship between learning conception, study strategy and learning outcome. *British Journal of Educational Psychology, 54*(1), 73–83.

Vermunt, J. D. (1995). Process-oriented instruction in learning and thinking strategies. *European Journal of Psychology of Education, 10*(4), 325–349.

Vermunt, J. D. (1996). Metacognitive, cognitive and affective aspects of learning styles and strategies: A phenomenographic analysis. *Higher Education, 31*, 25–50.

Vermunt, J. D. (1998). The regulation of constructive learning processes. *British Journal of Educational Psychology, 68*, 149–171.

Vermunt, J. D. (2005). Relations between student learning patterns and personal and contextual factors and academic performance. *Higher Education, 49*, 205–234.

Vermunt, J. D., & Donche, V. (2017). A learning patterns perspective on student learning in higher education: State of the art and moving forward. *Educational Psychology Review, 29*(2), 269–299.

Vermunt, J. D., & Endedijk, M. D. (2011). Patterns in teacher learning in different phases of the professional career. *Learning and Individual Differences, 21*(3), 294–302.

Vermunt, J. D., Ilie, S., & Vignoles, A. (2018). Building the foundations for measuring learning gain in higher education: A conceptual framework and measurement instrument. *Higher Education Pedagogies, 3*(1), 266–301.

Vermunt, J. D., & Van Rijswijk, F. A. (1988). Analysis and development of students' skill in selfregulated learning. *Higher Education, 17*, 647–682.

Vermunt, J. D., & Verloop, N. (1999). Congruence and friction between learning and teaching. *Learning and Instruction, 9*, 257–280.

Vermunt, J. D., & Vermetten, Y. J. (2004). Patterns in student learning: Relationships between learning strategies, conceptions of learning, and learning orientations. *Educational Psychology Review, 16*, 359–384.

Vermunt, J. D., Vrikki, M., Van Halem, N., Warwick, P., & Mercer, N. (2019). The impact of Lesson Study professional development on the quality of teacher learning. *Teaching and Teacher Education, 81*, 61–73.

Vermunt, J. D., Vrikki, M., Warwick, P., & Mercer, N. (2017). Connecting teacher identity formation to patterns in teacher learning. In D. J. Clandinin & J. Husu (Eds.), *The SAGE handbook of research on teacher education* (pp. 143–159). London: SAGE.

Watkins, D. (1982). Factors influencing the study methods of Australian tertiary students. *Higher Education, 11*(4), 369–380.

Weinstein, C. E., Zimmermann, S. A., & Palmer, D. R. (1988). Assessing learning strategies: The design and development of the LASSI. In C. E. Weinstein, E. T. Goetz, & P. A. Alexander (Eds.), *Learning and study strategies: Issues in assessment, instruction, and evaluation* (pp. 25–40). New York: Academic Press.

Zusho, A. (2017). Toward an integrated model of student learning in the college classroom. *Educational Psychology Review, 29*(2), 301–324.

17

CONCURRENT AND TASK-SPECIFIC SELF-REPORTS

Ivar Bråten
UNIVERSITY OF OSLO, NORWAY

Joseph P. Magliano
GEORGIA STATE UNIVERSITY, USA

Ladislao Salmerón
UNIVERSITY OF VALENCIA, SPAIN

INTRODUCTION

In their landmark review of research on "learning, remembering, and understanding," Brown, Bransford, Ferrara, and Campione (1983) described a major metaphorical shift occurring during the late 1960s and early 1970s: a shift away from a passive learner responding to environmental influences toward an active learner using strategies in the service of acquiring, retaining, and understanding information. Although those authors acknowledged that it was not particularly clear what was strategic and what was not, their review of the progress made in this area of research during the 1970s and early 1980s focused on "deliberate plans and routines called into service for remembering, learning, or problem solving" (Brown et al., 1983, p. 85).

The defining attributes of strategies were, sometimes fiercely, debated in the following years, especially regarding the attribute of consciousness or intentionality (e.g., Paris, Newman, & Jacobs, 1985; Pressley, Forrest-Pressley, Elliott-Faust, & Miller, 1985). However, more recent views seem to have converged on the idea that strategies involve effortful, intentional, and planful processing (Afflerbach, Pearson, & Paris, 2008; Alexander, Graham, & Harris, 1998; Kendeou & O'Brien, 2018). In this way, strategies are distinguished from skills, which denote automatic, unintentional, and routinized information processing (Afflerbach et al., 2008). In accordance with this distinction, we define strategies as forms of procedural knowledge that individuals intentionally and planfully use for the purpose of acquiring, organizing, or elaborating information, as well as for reflecting upon and guiding their own learning, comprehension, or problem solving (cf., Alexander et al., 1998; Bråten & Samuelstuen, 2004;

Weinstein, Husman, & Dierking, 2000). Thus, when individuals perceive a discrepancy between a desired outcome and their current state of learning, comprehension, or problem solving, and automatic skills cannot get them to the goal, they may decide to invest effort in strategic processing in order to reduce or eliminate that discrepancy (Alexander et al., 1998).

Further, an important distinction has concerned superficial versus deeper processing strategies, with level of processing related to the extent to which information is reorganized or transformed during learning, comprehension, or problem solving. This distinction is consistent with Bereiter and Scardamalia's (1987) classic distinction between knowledge-telling and knowledge-transforming approaches, with the former involving a superficial engagement suitable for reproduction of information in the same or similar form and the latter involving an active transformation of information suitable for generating new meaning or insights. With reference to our definition of strategies, individuals may use superficial strategies, such as selection and rehearsal, to acquire new information, and deeper level strategies, such as constructing summaries and drawing inferences, to organize and elaborate information. The latter part of our definition, referring to reflection and self-guidance, captures metacognitive strategies such as planning, monitoring, control, and evaluation of processing as well as performance (Veenman, 2016).

Needless to say, valid measurement of strategic processing is essential, for example, to understand how the different components or aspects of strategic processing work together with motivation and other forms of cognition, how they come into play and influence task completion and performance within and across domains, and how strategic processing develops over time, both naturally across the lifespan and as a consequence of deliberate strategies instruction. Given the effortful, conscious, and intentional nature of strategic processing, self-report methodologies, indeed, seem applicable in gauging such thinking. Still, there are several caveats concerning some of these methodologies (Tourangeau, 2000; Veenman, 2011), requiring careful consideration of which forms of self-reports may produce results that can be trusted. In this chapter, we generally define self-reports as utterances or answers to prompts or questions provided by an individual about his or her cognitions and actions during learning, comprehension, or problem solving. We discuss concurrent and task-specific self-reports, in particular, focusing on the possibilities and challenges of using such approaches to measuring strategic processing.

The remainder of this chapter is divided into three main sections. In the first, we briefly discuss three theoretical models for understanding the role of strategic processing in learning, comprehension, and problem solving, with an eye to how strategic processing has been measured within these models. In the second, we describe, explain, illustrate, and problematize four different ways to assess strategic processing by means of self-reports. In the third, we summarize the results of our analysis and discuss implications and future directions.

THEORETICAL BACKGROUND

We present and discuss three prominent models focusing on strategic processing. These models were developed within educational psychology decades ago but still influence thinking about strategies and research on strategic processing.

The Good Strategy User Model

This model describes three categories of strategies: goal- or task-specific strategies, monitoring strategies used to control and regulate goal-specific strategies, and higher-order strategies used to plan sequences of goal-specific and monitoring strategies (Pressley, 1986; Pressley, Borkowski, & Schneider, 1987). While the monitoring and planning strategies are considered forms of metacognitive procedures, metacognitive knowledge is represented in the model as specific strategy knowledge, including knowledge about how, when, and where to use particular strategies. Such knowledge also has a motivational aspect because it includes understanding that success is due to the use of task-appropriate strategies and that failure might have been avoided by the use of such strategies. In addition, general metacognitive knowledge about strategies has motivational properties because it includes understanding that strategic effort generally increases the likelihood of success. Finally, the good strategy user has an extensive knowledge base (in addition to the knowledge of and about strategies) that sometimes may make strategic effort superfluous and sometimes prompt strategy use but, most importantly, enables use of particular strategies (Pressley, 1986; Pressley et al., 1987).

Perhaps the most controversial aspect of the Good Strategy User Model is that it posits that good strategy use is often characterized by automaticity, implying that the components described above, including strategic processing, have been automatized or habituated and therefore do not require conscious attention. As noted above, such automatic processing tends to be categorized as skills rather than strategies in more contemporary theorizing.

Because the research leading up to the Good Strategy User Model overwhelmingly relied on randomized experiments, in which participants were trained to perform particular strategies and the effects on outcome variables such as recall of information were measured, the measurement of strategies per se was not a major issue. However, as noted by Levin (2008), Pressley was also eager to use qualitative methods, such as interviews or cued recall techniques, to gain insights into participants' thinking about their cognitive processing (e.g., Pressley & Levin, 1977), and he later became a strong proponent of verbal protocol analysis (e.g., Pressley & Hilden, 2004).

The Model of Domain Learning

This model describes the interplay of knowledge, strategies, and interest across three stages of academic development within a domain, which are termed acclimation, competence, and proficiency/expertise (Alexander, 1997, 2004, 2005, 2012). In addition to changes in the configuration of these main components that occur across the stages, the model acknowledges that there are many phases or episodes of learning within each stage, with these phases or episodes also characterized by certain interplays among knowledge, strategic processing, and interest (Alexander, 1997).

Regarding strategic processing, strategies at different levels of specificity (i.e., domain-general vs. domain-specific) and processing (i.e., surface- vs. deep-processing) are distinguished, as well as cognitive and metacognitive strategies (Alexander, 2004, 2005). Importantly, strategies are conceived of as effortful, intentional, and purposeful procedures directed toward improving learning, comprehension, and problem solving through the acquisition, transformation, and transfer of information (Alexander, 1997, 2004). While learners' dependency on surface strategies to establish a rudimentary knowledge base, gain foundational understanding, and solve elementary problems decreases during the acclimation stage, essentially levels off during the competence stage, and then again decreases during the proficiency/expertise stage, their use of deeper strategies to organize, transform, and critically analyze information increases across the three stages of domain learning and becomes particularly important in the service of knowledge generation, deep comprehension, and problem formulation during the proficiency/expertise stage (Alexander, 2004, 2012).

Of note is that combined shifts in knowledge and interest across the stages are seen as important contributors to the development and increased use of deeper processing strategies (Alexander, 1997). In effect, mutually influential relationships among a large, well-integrated body of knowledge, high individual interest, and a well-established and efficient repertoire of deeper processing strategies are regarded as a hallmark of the most advanced learners in a domain (Alexander, 1997, 2004).

With respect to the measurement of strategies, Dinsmore, Hattan, and List (2018) documented that the research conducted within the Model of Domain Learning overwhelmingly has measured strategic processing by means of offline self-report inventories. However, these offline self-reports have typically been task-specific and collected immediately after task completion (Alexander & Murphy, 1998; Alexander, Murphy, Wood, Duhon, & Parker, 1997; Alexander, Sperl, Buehl, Fives, & Chiu, 2004). For example, Alexander et al. (1997) asked participants to monitor the strategies they used during task completion (i.e., text reading) and immediately afterwards check any strategy they had used to comprehend and remember the text on a list of 20 text-processing strategies, also marking the strategies they had found most helpful. As Dinsmore et al. (2018) showed, the reliability estimates reported for the kind of strategy measures used within the Model of Domain Learning have quite often been lower than desirable, and the relationship between scores on such measures and performance actually seems open to question.

The Cyclical Model of Self-Regulated Learning

This model describes the three cyclical phases of forethought, performance, and self-reflection (Zimmerman (2000, 2013). Forethought includes task analysis and self-motivation used in preparation for efforts to learn. The performance phase involves the execution and monitoring of strategies planned during the forethought phase. Finally, during self-reflection, individuals self-evaluate their learning and reflect on the causes of the outcome, as well as react emotionally to what happened during performance and draw inferences regarding future learning. The cyclical nature of the model involves that processes in one phase influence processes in the next, and that processes during self-reflection influence processes in the forethought phase when individuals continue their efforts to learn (Zimmerman, 2000, 2013).

Within Zimmerman's model, self-regulated strategies are conceived of as purposefully selected or planful cognitive processes and behavioral actions directed at acquiring or displaying knowledge and skills. For example, strategies can facilitate learning and performance by helping students attend to, analyze, and reorganize academic tasks

(Zimmerman, 2000). Of note is also that strategies are considered context-specific within self-regulated learning theory, implying that self-regulated students adjust their strategic choices and activities to different study contexts (Zimmerman, 2000). Finally, Zimmerman's view on self-regulated learning strongly emphasizes that strategic competence is of little value if individuals cannot motivate themselves to use it, with one key source of motivation being their self-efficacy perceptions.

Zimmerman's research on the identification and measurement of self-regulated strategies is strongly associated with the Self-Regulated Learning Interview Schedule (Zimmerman & Martinez-Pons, 1986, 1988, 1990). This methodology consists of a 15-minute individual structured interview during which students are presented with different hypothetical learning contexts (e.g., when completing writing assignments outside class). For each context, students are asked to describe the methods they would use, and if they mention one or more strategies for a learning context, they are also asked to rate the frequency with which each mentioned strategy is used. Zimmerman and Martinez-Pons (1986, 1988, 1990)) have shown substantial positive correlations between students' reports of strategies on this schedule and their academic achievement. However, in addition to using such offline self-reports about hypothetical learning contexts, Zimmerman and colleagues (Cleary & Zimmerman, 2001; Kitsantas & Zimmerman, 2002) have more directly evaluated processes included in the cyclical model by asking individuals close- and open-ended questions during actual task completion. We will return to this methodology in the section termed Task-specific Self-report Inventories.

Summary

To summarize, the three reviewed models provide a foundational understanding of the importance and functioning of strategic processing. Taken together, they describe how strategic processing, functioning within a system of cognitive, metacognitive, and motivational components, can improve learning, comprehension, or problem solving. The models do, however, differ with respect to their adoption of a developmental perspective and the way they conceptualize strategic processing. Thus, while Pressley (1987; Pressley et al., 1987) certainly did not disregard the importance of development, the Good Strategy User Model is not a developmental model of strategic processing. By comparison, both the Model of Domain Learning and the Cyclical Model of Self-Regulated Learning could be described as developmental. These two models differ in terms of the grain sizes on which they focus, however, with the former focusing on comprehensive stages of academic development and the latter focusing on more fine-grained phases that unfold sequentially in a recursive manner over continued efforts to learn. With respect to the conceptualization of strategic processing, Pressley's model differs from the others because it allows for automatic strategic processing, and Alexander's model is unique in distinguishing between surface- and deep-processing strategies. Finally, we note that research conducted within the three models has largely relied on self-reports of strategic processing. In the following section, we further elaborate upon some of these self-report methodologies, ranging from thinking aloud during task completion to answering questions about task-specific processing retrospectively.

MEASURING STRATEGIC PROCESSING THROUGH CONCURRENT AND TASK-SPECIFIC SELF-REPORTS

Self-reports of strategic processing can involve on-line or off-line reporting. On-line approaches refer to measurements taken concurrent to task performance, such as having learners think aloud to create a verbal protocol that subsequently can be analyzed by the researchers. Off-line approaches refer to self-report inventories or interviews administered before or after task performance. In this chapter, we consider on-line measures in the form of concurrent thinking aloud and off-line measures in the form of task-specific self-reports collected immediately after task performance.

Verbal Protocol Analysis

In research on text-based learning and comprehension, individuals can be instructed to think aloud as they read one or more texts (Ericsson & Simon, 1993; Pressley & Afflerbach, 1995; Trabasso & Magliano, 1996). This means that readers are asked to report whatever thoughts come to mind as they read, and the intent is to have them report only those thoughts that are immediately accessible and reportable in language, and therefore represent the contents of working memory (Ericsson & Simon, 1993). This activity can be considered to reflect an effortful search for meaning and, as such, to provide a window on strategic processing (Trabasso & Magliano, 1996). More specifically, verbal protocols resulting from concurrent thinking aloud are considered a valid measure of the metacognitive states that arise during reading and the strategies that respond to these states (Pressley & Afflerbach, 1995), in particular inference processes that support the construction of a mental model (Trabasso & Magliano, 1996). In this section, we describe two approaches to collecting verbal protocol data and discuss available evidence that these approaches are valid measures of comprehension strategies.

Approaches to Collecting Verbal Protocols. One approach is to allow individuals to self-select when and where they think aloud while reading (Goldman, Braasch, Wiley, Graesser, & Brodowinska, 2012; Pressley & Afflerbach, 1995). This approach is viewed as sensitive to metacognitive states that arise during reading and strategies readers employ in response to them (e.g., experiencing confusion after reading a section and then rereading that section in response to that metacognitive state; Pressley & Afflerbach, 1995). That is, readers likely report thoughts that reflect an effortful search for meaning, especially when experiencing challenges understanding the texts.

An alternative approach is to have readers report their thoughts after pre-selected locations, which could be after every sentence, paragraph, or section (Trabasso & Magliano, 1996), or after theoretically determined locations (Kaakinen & Hyönä, 2005; Magliano & Millis, 2003). This approach can be construed as a retrospective protocol because participants are asked to reflect upon cognitive states that have recently occurred but likely remain in working memory (Ericsson & Simon, 1993). Typically, the intent is to reveal thoughts that pertain to mental model construction, in particular (Magliano, 1999; Trabasso & Magliano, 1996). Thus, this approach aims to reveal the products of knowledge activation and inference generation to integrate text constituents in the mental model. This may involve establishing how text constituents are semantically connected (e.g., cause and effect, claim-evidence, and contrastive relationships; Magliano, Trabasso, Graesser, 1999; Ray & Magliano, 2015) or integrating text constituents with background knowledge (Todaro, Magliano, Millis, McNamara, & Kurby, 2008). This approach is suitable for gaining access to processes involved in mental model construction for at least two reasons. First, the sentence prior to a think aloud prompt likely serves as a retrieval cue for knowledge that supports mental model construction, which constrains the contents of working memory that are reported at the prompt. Presumably, these contents reflect the products of the processes that support mental model construction. Second, the instructions typically used with this approach may invoke a strategy to focus on thoughts that are reflective of mental model construction.

Approaches to Coding Verbal Protocols. Verbal protocols can be used to answer research questions regarding strategic processing to the extent that a coding system is developed that is aligned with those research questions. A coding system can be developed through an inductive process that arises from qualitative methodologies, or it can be developed a priori, grounded in theory. In this section, we discuss a few notable examples of these different approaches.

Pressley and Afflerbach (1995) reviewed an extensive list of studies that employed an open-ended prompt methodology (i.e., readers chose when to think aloud) for collecting verbal protocols and a traditional, qualitative analysis. These studies suggested that skilled readers regularly monitor cognitive states as they read, and engage in a number of strategies in response to challenges they face in terms of learning from and comprehending texts (e.g., rereading, paraphrasing, elaborative inferencing).

Trabasso and Magliano (1996) provided an example of developing a coding system a priori inspired by theory. They had college students think aloud after each sentence of short narratives. The coding system was based on the constructionist theory of comprehension (Graesser, Singer, & Trabasso, 1994) and distinguished between three broad categories of inferences: explanations, predictions, and associations. Consistent with the theory, Trabasso and Magliano (1996) found that explanations predominated when examining the inferences produced while thinking aloud. Moreover, explanations based on prior text information provided the primary basis for establishing how distal sentences were related, supporting global coherence. The results were thus consistent with the assumption that comprehension is achieved largely through explanatory reasoning (e.g., Graesser et al., 1994).

A number of researchers have developed coding systems sensitive to such theoretically based distinctions, including a broader range of strategies that can be reflected in verbal protocols (Kaakinen & Hyönä, 2005; Magliano & Millis, 2003; Magliano, Millis, the RSAT Development Team, Levinstein, & Boonthum, 2011; McCarthy & Goldman, 2019; McMaster et al., 2012; Rapp, van den Broek, McMaster, Kendeou, & Espin, 2007; Todaro et al., 2008). These strategies concern paraphrases, episodic recollections, bridging inferences, elaborative inferences, metacognitive judgments, evaluative statements, and affective judgments. Theoretically derived strategies that directly support the construction of a mental model (e.g., bridging inferences, elaborations) tend to be more frequent in verbal protocols than are other strategies (Rapp et al., 2007; Todaro et al., 2008).

However, the frequencies of different strategies vary with reading proficiency (Magliano & Millis, 2003; McMaster et al., 2012). For example, Magliano and Millis (2003) had college students read simple narrative texts and think aloud at selected sentences that afforded bridging inferences based on an a priori, theoretical analysis of the causal structure underlying the story events. They found that proficient readers tended to produce more bridging inferences than less proficient readers, whereas less proficient readers tended to produce more paraphrases than proficient readers. Rapp et al. (2007) and McMaster et al. (2012) compared different profiles of struggling middle school readers who thought aloud at every sentence while reading. While one profile group of struggling readers tended to paraphrase the sentence that was just read, another profile group primarily produced invalid elaborative inferences, both approaches indicating difficulties using deep-processing strategies.

Validating Verbal Protocols. Despite arguments that thinking aloud is minimally subject to task demands (Ericsson & Simon, 1993), it is possible that participants produce thoughts that would not occur during silent reading. Especially, when participants are asked to reconstruct their thoughts, the methodology is prone to fabrication. As such, it is crucial to adopt approaches that help identify which aspects of verbal protocols likely support comprehension and text-based learning in contexts where readers are not asked to think aloud. There are at least three approaches to validating verbal protocols.

The first approach is to demonstrate that the strategies resulting from verbal protocol analysis are correlated with measures of individual differences known to affect comprehension, such as proficiency in reading (McMaster et al., 2012) and comprehension (Kopatich, Magliano, Millis, Parker, & Ray, 2019; Magliano & Millis, 2003; Magliano et al., 2011; Millis, Magliano, & Todaro, 2006), working memory capacity (Whitney, Ritchie, & Clark, 1991), proficiency in a second language (Zwaan & Brown, 1996), or disciplinary expertise (Graves & Frederiksen, 1991). The studies of Magliano and Millis (2003) and McMaster et al. (2012) cited above exemplify this type of validation. Zwaan and Brown (1996) provided a notable example with respect to demonstrating differences in strategic processing as a function of proficiency in a second language. They recruited participants that varied in knowledge of French and had them think aloud (in their native English) while reading narratives written in French or English. While reading in English, both groups of students demonstrated results consistent with Trabasso and Magliano (1996), with the most dominant strategy being explanation. While reading in French, however, only the proficient French readers demonstrated an explanation-based strategy, whereas the less proficient readers engaged in strategies that involved identifying the meaning of lexical items and syntactic relationships. As a final example of this approach, low working memory span readers have been shown to engage in excessive elaboration when thinking aloud compared to high span readers (Whitney et al., 1991).

A second approach to validating verbal protocol analysis is to demonstrate that strategies revealed by thinking aloud are correlated with measures of comprehension outcomes (Goldman et al., 2012; Kopatich et al., 2019; Magliano & Millis, 2003; Magliano et al., 1999, 2011). For example, Magliano, Millis, and colleagues have shown that measures of bridging inferences are positively correlated with comprehension outcomes for texts used in collecting the verbal protocols (Magliano & Millis, 2003;

Magliano et al., 2011; Millis et al., 2006), as well as for other texts (Magliano & Millis, 2003; Magliano et al., 2011). Conversely, the measures of paraphrasing tend to be negatively correlated with comprehension performance (Magliano & Millis, 2003). Magliano and Millis (2003) argued that more proficient readers engage in strategies that promote coherence building, whereas less proficient readers engage in locally focused strategies directed at understanding individual sentences. Kopatich et al. (2019) found that measures of bridging and elaborative inferences partially mediated the effects of general and language processing resources on comprehension outcomes.

A final approach for validating verbal protocols is to demonstrate that they are correlated with moment-to-moment measures of reading, which would suggest that these processes occur during silent reading. The study by Magliano et al. (1999) is an example of this approach. In that study, the explanations, predictions, and associations included in the verbal protocols of one group of students predicted variations in reading times in another group of students who read the same texts silently under different goal conditions (e.g., reading to explain vs. reading to predict). As another example, Kaakinen and Hyönä (2005) collected verbal protocols and eye movement data while participants read expository texts, examining the length of fixations at sentences where participants were asked to think aloud. Those authors found significant correlations between the verbal protocols and eye movement data, with questions and explanations in the protocols, in particular, being positively correlated with fixation times.

Eye Movement Cued Self-reports

One novel approach to eliciting self-reports of strategic processing is to record participants' eye movements while they are performing a task, and afterwards display those eye movements to them to cue reports of their thinking during task performance. Eye movement cued self-reports can be considered a form of retrospective thinking aloud because participants are responding to external cues rather than internal cognitive states. Thus, they are retrospective in the sense that participants are asked to reflect upon strategic processing in the near past, with the products of those strategies likely still in working memory. To elicit these reports, participants are presented with a video of what they just saw while performing a specific task, with the video superimposing participants' eye movements as a small circle indicating where they were looking during task performance. As eye movements are considered to reflect cognitive processes (Rayner, 2009), the rationale is that they may cue participants to report orally on such processes as they were taking place in a specific task environment. In particular, eye movements are assumed to represent an externalization of strategic processes that may be used to cue descriptions of those processes.

Eye movement cued self-reports have been used to measure strategic processing in a variety of learning tasks, including multimedia learning (de Koning, Tabbers, Rikers, & Paas, 2010; Stark, Brünken, & Park, 2018), text reading (Catrysse, Gijbels, & Donche, 2018; Penttinen, Anto, & Mikkilä-Erdmann, 2013; Salmerón, Naumann, García, & Fajardo, 2017), web search (Brand-Gruwel, Kammerer, van Meeuwen, & van Gog, 2017; Muntinga & Taylor, 2018), visual tasks (Jarodzka, Scheiter, Gerjets, & van Gog, 2010), mathematical problem solving (Rau, Aleven, & Rummel, 2017; van der Weijden, Kamphorst, Willemsen, Kroesbergen, & van Hoogmoed, 2018), and interaction with and inspection of complex systems (Ruckpaul, Fürstenhöfer, & Matthiesen, 2015; van Gog, Paas, van Merriënboer, & Witte, 2005; van Meeuwen, Brand-Gruwel, Kirschner, de Bock, & van Merriënboer, 2018).

Issues Concerning the Presentation of Eye Movements. A critical aspect of eye movement videos concerns speed. As eye movements tend to be quick, participants easily may lose track of the fixations. Therefore, Russo (1979) recommended that the replay proceed at a rate compatible with recall and reports. Accordingly, several researchers have used slower speed for video replays, such as 50% (Brand-Gruwel et al., 2017; de Koning et al., 2010; Hyrskykari, Ovaska, Majaranta, Räihä, & Lehtinen, 2008) or 75% of the actual speed (van Meeuwen et al., 2018). Others have replayed the videos at full speed, however (Jarodzka et al., 2010; Salmerón et al., 2017; Stark et al., 2018). While it is evident that eye-movements are faster than verbalizations, it is not so obvious that each fixation represents a unique processing episode that deserves to be commented on. Accordingly, Guan, Lee, Cuddihy, and Ramey (2006) reported that 47% of eye movement visits to particular regions of interest did not elicit any verbal comments. This is especially clear when performing reading tasks, where participants may engage for minutes in reading a long paragraph. Slowing down the replay of this kind of episode may not provide new insights into participants' ongoing processing because they are tapping the same process; rather, it may induce negative reactions toward the task. Researchers also have varied the way videos are replayed as a way to accommodate this issue. Thus, participants have been allowed to change the speed of the recordings (Russo, 1979) or to pause the videos at any time (de Koning et al., 2010; van Gog et al., 2005). Such procedures allow students to report complex thoughts in tasks where a sequence of fixations reflects different cognitive processes. In other cases, such as when a long sequence of fixations reflects a single process (e.g., deep reading), the researcher can just pause the video at points of critical interest (Penttinen et al., 2013; Ruckpaul et al., 2015).

Another relevant issue concerns how eye-movements are represented in the videos. While the major components of eye-movements include both fixations and saccadic movements, the majority of studies have presented eye-movements only as individual fixations, with the size of the circles representing the length of the fixations. During task performance, previous fixations disappear and new ones appear in different locations. This way of representing eye movements thus emphasizes location (i.e., fixation) over orientation (i.e., saccadic movement). It is therefore possible that it increases the likelihood that processing related to objects (e.g., describing objects) are elicited, compared to more dynamic processing (e.g., comparing and contrasting objects). In a rare exception, Ruckpaul et al. (2015) replayed videos representing eye movements during task performance as fixations (i.e., circles) as well as saccadic movements (i.e., lines between circles). Unfortunately, these authors did not include a condition showing only fixations, which made it impossible to address the possibility mentioned above.

Validating Eye Movement Cued Self-reports. Regarding validity, eye movement cued self-reports have been proposed as a less intrusive alternative to concurrent thinking aloud (van Gog et al., 2005). However, as noted earlier, given that participants are asked to reconstruct their thoughts, the methodology is prone to fabrications. Such fabrication may still be less frequent than for retrospective self-reports that do not use eye-movement cues because the reconstruction, at least, must be consistent with the sequence of fixations (Guan et al., 2006).

In the fields of usability and learning research, there have been some attempts to analyze the reliability and validity of this methodology by comparing it to concurrent thinking aloud. Not surprisingly, thinking aloud in response to cues provided by eye movements tends to involve a higher number of verbalizations (Brand-Gruwel et al., 2017; Hansen, 1991; Hyrskykari et al., 2008; Russo, 1979). This may be due, in part, to the fact that participants spend more time reporting when cued by eye movements. Once reporting time is controlled for, however, this difference seems to disappear (Ruckpaul et al., 2015). More importantly, the two methodologies may elicit different types of thoughts (Brand-Gruwel et al., 2017; Hansen, 1991; Hyrskykari et al., 2008; Ruckpaul et al., 2015; van Gog et al., 2005). In usability studies, where participants are assessed as they interact with a system (e.g., when buying products from different web pages), the percentage of manipulative comments (e.g., "I write the name into this field") is lower with eye movement cued than with concurrent thinking aloud, while the difference in terms of cognitive comments (e.g., reflections about the system) is less clear (Hansen, 1991; Hyrskykari et al., 2008). In studies of learning, where participants are engaged in a task to meet a learning goal, the major difference between the two methodologies seems to be the number of metacognitive and evaluative comments produced (i.e., evaluations of the information and the learning process), with higher frequencies observed in eye movement cued verbal protocols (Brand-Gruwel et al., 2017; van Gog et al., 2005). In brief, such comparative studies suggest that protocols from concurrent thinking aloud reflect more processing concerning what participants are doing, while protocols from eye movement cued thinking aloud reflect more processing involving evaluation of their actions.

As mentioned earlier, a major threat for eye movement cued thinking aloud is fabrication. Guan et al. (2006) compared the sequences of verbalizations in such protocols to the actual sequences of problem solving as indicated by participants' eye movements. More than 80% of participants' verbalizations of what they were attending to corresponded to the actual sequences of their eye movements, and less than 3% of the verbalizations corresponded to areas of the task scenario that were not identified by the eye movement data. This pattern of results suggests a low rate of fabrication, but this point should be taken with caution. To the best of our knowledge, no other study has empirically tested the issue of fabrication with eye movement cued self-report data.

Thus far, there also have been few attempts to validate this methodology by testing its predictive power. Elling, Lentz, and de Jong (2011) found that participants thinking aloud concurrently or retrospectively in response to eye movements did not differ in terms of the usability problems detected. Brand-Gruwel et al. (2017) reported a global positive correlation between evaluative verbalizations and performance (i.e., selection of appropriate web pages), but correlations were not reported separately for each methodology (i.e., concurrent and retrospective eye movement cued thinking aloud). Thus, any claim about the validity of this methodology should be considered with caution until further documentation is available.

Task-specific Self-report Inventories

Some self-report inventories measure strategic processing as an aptitude or a trait, by asking respondents "to generalize their actions across situations rather than referencing singular and specific learning events" (Winne & Perry, 2000, p. 542). In a review,

Veenman (2005) showed that correlations between strategy data from such self-report inventories and on-line methodologies, such as concurrent thinking aloud, are generally low, indicating poor convergent validity due to several issues with off-line self-report inventories, such as their decontextualized and retrospective nature. However, as posited by Shellings (2011), low correlations between strategy data from self-report inventories and on-line methodologies may not necessarily indicate the invalidity of data gathered by means of self-report inventories, but reflect the lack of specificity and proximity of many self-report inventories to actual task contexts. Accordingly, she showed that self-reports of strategies on an inventory that was tailored to a particular reading task context yielded scores that were fairly well aligned with on-line strategy data.

Of note is that such task-specific strategy inventories ask learners to make judgments about their strategic activities in a specific task, rather than about what they generally or typically do during learning or comprehension. The logic of this approach is also consistent with Ericsson and Simon's (1993) recommendation that retrospective verbal protocols be provided immediately after task performance, that is, when metacognitive states and strategic activities are still relatively accessible for retrieval in working memory.

In several studies, Bråten and colleagues (Anmarkrud & Bråten, 2009; Bråten & Anmarkrud, 2013; Bråten & Samuelstuen, 2004, 2007; Samuelstuen & Bråten, 2005, 2007), in the context of learning from a single expository text, have demonstrated the possibility to obtain valid measurements when using self-report strategy inventories with items tailored to a specific task context and administered shortly after task performance. These authors have followed the four guidelines for constructing task-specific strategy inventories explicated by Bråten and Samuelstuen (2007). First, a specific task (e.g., to read a text for a particular purpose) must be administered, to which the items on the inventory are referring. Second, the task must be accompanied by an instruction that directs learners to monitor their strategies during task performance and informs them that they will be asked some questions afterwards about how they proceeded. Third, to minimize the retention interval, the strategy inventory must be administered immediately after task completion. Finally, in referring to recent episodes of strategic processing, the wordings of task-specific items must be different from more general statements. This means that general item stems such as "when I study" or "when I read" must be omitted in task-specific items. Moreover, to make it clear that the items refer back to the recently completed task, the verb must be in the past tense (e.g., "I tried to understand the content better by relating it to something I know").

Validating Task-specific Self-report Inventories. Strategy scores on a task-specific self-report inventory based on these guidelines have been validated in several ways. For example, Bråten and Samuelstuen (2007) showed that strategies self-reported in this way corresponded quite closely with strategies traced in the study materials, with correlations between self-reported and traced surface-level strategies exceeding .75 and correlations between self-reported and traced deeper-level strategies exceeding .80. Samuelstuen and Bråten (2005, 2007) demonstrated that students' strategy scale scores accounted for their performance on expository text comprehension tasks, with correlations between deeper-level strategies and performance exceeding .35 (see also, Bråten & Anmarkrud, 2013).

The same type of task-specific self-report inventory was developed by Bråten and Strømsø (2011) to measure strategic processing when individuals read multiple texts on the same topic. Specifically, this measure was constructed to assess a surface strategy involving the accumulation of pieces of information from different texts and a deeper-level strategy involving cross-text elaboration. These two dimensions of multiple text comprehension strategies have been confirmed through factor analysis and scores on these dimensions have been found to predict performance (Bråten, Anmarkrud, Brandmo, & Strømsø, 2014; Bråten & Strømsø, 2011), with the accumulation strategy negatively and the cross-text elaboration strategy positively related to intertextual comprehension performance. Further validation of scores on this inventory was provided by Hagen, Braasch, and Bråten (2014), who compared strategy scale scores with strategies as revealed by students' spontaneous note-taking, and by List, Du, Wang, and Lee (2019), who compared strategy scale scores with multiple text model construction as revealed by students' written responses and with integrative processing as revealed by their think-aloud utterances.

Although valid scores have been obtained on task-specific self-report inventories of strategic processing administered immediately after task performance, such measures may be subject to some of the same errors that seem to plague general, decontextualized strategy inventories. Thus, because individuals in any case have to retrieve strategic episodes after some delay, fallible, biased, and reconstructive memory processes cannot be ruled out. In particular, the social desirability of response alternatives may bias people's self-reports of strategies. Accordingly, people may report more strategic processing than actually executed because they believe this is to be approved by others. It is also possible that people report much use of certain strategies because they believe that those strategies are effective, not because they actually used them to any great extent. Yet another potential problem with task-specific self-report inventories administered after task performance may be a tendency to report using strategies described by the items although other strategies were actually used.

Questioning During Task Performance. Given such potential threats to the validity of scores on task-specific inventories administered after task performance, the procedure used by Zimmerman and colleagues (Cleary & Zimmerman, 2001; Kitsantas & Zimmerman, 2002) may be a viable option. In this approach, participants have been asked a series of task-specific questions about their self-regulatory processes, including their strategies, not only before and after but also during their efforts to learn particular athletic skills. While some of these questions, for example regarding self-efficacy, were close-ended with participants responding on a scale from 0 to 100, others were open-ended with responses coded by the researchers. For example, Kitsantas and Zimmerman (2002), who studied the practice of volleyball overhand serving among college women, stopped the participants during the practice episode and asked them about their strategy for successfully executing the next overhand serve after having missed the target on the two preceding attempts. The self-reported strategies were then coded into the categories of specific techniques, visualization strategies, concentration strategies, both specific techniques and concentration strategies, and practice/no strategy.

This approach was found to be valid in the sense that it differentiated between participants at different levels of expertise with respect to the processes included in the three phases of the cyclical model of self-regulated learning (Zimmerman, 2000,

2013). In the performance phase, in particular, the experts displayed more use of specific technique strategies than did other participants and also monitored their use of specific techniques and outcomes to a greater extent. Further, self-regulatory processes measured in this way were highly correlated with participants' serving performance after the practice (Kitsantas & Zimmerman, 2002). Similar results were obtained by Cleary and Zimmerman (2001), who used task-specific questioning to study self-regulatory processes during participants' practice on a particular basketball skill.

Diary Methods

Diary methods are systematic and structured ways of measuring psychological variables repeatedly in participants' natural learning environment (Iida, Shrout, Laurenceau, & Bolger, 2012). As measures of strategic processing, diaries can be considered standardized instruments used to self-report or self-record strategic activities on a daily basis near the time and in the contexts they occur (Schmitz, Klug, & Schmidt, 2011). While the most common diary method design involves responding to a series of questions about one's own activities once at the same time every day, such recordings sometimes take place several times a day and, at a minimum, after a few days (Iida et al., 2012; Schmitz et al., 2011).

Because diaries are completed in participants' daily environment, diary data can be said to fare well in terms of ecological validity compared to data collected in experimental settings. Moreover, compared to task-specific self-report inventories, which typically refer to one single task context at a single point in time, diaries allow for the measurement of strategies in a range of contexts over time. Because diary methods allow for the aggregation of participant responses over time, they may lead to more valid information than one-shot strategy measurements (Iida et al., 2012). That learners record their strategic activities on a daily basis with reference to specific contexts taking place the same day, may also reduce the chances of retrospective biases (Tourangeau, 2000) and, consequently, increase the validity of such self-reports.

Diary Formats. According to Iida et al. (2012), there are three commonly used diary formats: paper-and-pencil diaries, brief telephone interviews, and electronic diaries. Electronic response formats have become the most common, with participants logging into a secure website daily to complete an online questionnaire, with researchers reminding participants by means of electronic devices if responses are not entered, and with questionnaire data easily transferred to computer programs for statistical analysis.

As an example of a standardized web-based diary in the area of strategic processing, Andreassen, Jensen, and Bråten (2017) constructed a diary that referred to three study contexts: attending lectures, individual study (i.e., studying alone), and social study (i.e., studying with others). Based on a review of the literature on self-regulated study strategies, they identified 20 strategies reportedly used in these three contexts, with six strategies referring to the context of attending lectures (e.g., asking questions to the lecturer during or after lectures), eight strategies referring to the context of individual study (e.g., making drawings or figures to better understand text), and six strategies referring to the context of social study (e.g., consulting fellow students). For each study context that a participant had participated in on a particular day, the participant also recorded in the diary whether he or she had used the strategies associated with that context. For each strategy that was recorded in each study context, the perceived benefit of that strategy was also recorded on a Likert-type scale. Before the data collection started, Andreassen et al. (2017) presented and demonstrated the web-based diaries to the participants, and also had them practice accessing and completing the diaries on their computers or smartphones. During the data collection, which lasted for 12 consecutive days, participants' daily recordings on the diary websites were tracked by the researchers, who contacted every participant who had not completed the diary in the evening with a reminder (via SMS) to enter the diary data for that day.

Validating Diary Data. Several studies have indicated that diary methods may yield valid data on learning processes. For example, Kanfer, Reinecker, and Schmelzer (1996) found high accuracy of diary data when correlating them with data from external observers, and Schmitz and Wiese (2006) demonstrated the effectiveness of an intervention to promote self-regulated learning by means of diary data collected over 35 days. In the Andreassen et al. (2017) study, differences in the reported use and benefits of particular visual and social strategies were observed between college students with and without dyslexia. Still, there are several threats to validity when applying diary methods.

First, depending on the length of the diary questionnaire, the frequency of diary completion, and the length of the diary period, diary methods may burden participants and lead to lack of motivation, non-compliance, and attrition (Iida et al., 2012). Presumably, diary methods are more vulnerable to lack of compliance than other self-report methods because data are essentially collected by the participants themselves, without any researchers present.

Second, completing diaries may produce reactivity effects that confound measurements (Schmitz et al., 2011). That is, daily self-monitoring and reporting may change participant activities, for example, lead to an increase in strategy use because students become more aware of and motivated to change their strategies in desired directions. Moreover, such reactivity may increase when recordings are temporally close to the recorded activities (Schmitz et al., 2011). Thus, on the one hand, recordings that are temporally close to the activities may reduce retrospective biases; on the other, they may compromise validity because of heightened reactivity. According to Iida et al. (2012), however, repeated completion of diaries may lead to a form of habituation that over time will reduce reactivity.

Third, a potential threat to validity concerns construct variability. That is, during a diary period, participants' understanding of a particular construct may change. For example, a participant may start out with a narrow understanding of what constitutes "constructing a summary," but through repeated self-monitoring and reflection and exposure to a diary strategy questionnaire, he or she may come to understand this construct more broadly, with implications for how such strategic activities are recorded in the diary.

Finally, as with task-specific self-report inventories, self-reporting strategic processing on a diary questionnaire where certain strategies are prelisted likely will restrict strategy measurements to those strategies. Thus, although diaries also may allow participants to report on strategies that are not prelisted (Andreassen et al., 2017), they

CONCLUSIONS, IMPLICATIONS, AND FUTURE DIRECTIONS

may be less likely to do so because the prelisting makes them more aware of those strategies and less sensitive to other forms of strategic processing that they actually may engage in.

CONCLUSIONS, IMPLICATIONS, AND FUTURE DIRECTIONS

The theoretical and empirical work discussed in this chapter highlights the important role of strategic processing in learning, comprehension, and problem solving, as well as the need to measure this complex construct in a valid way. We reviewed three theoretical models that have strongly influenced thinking and research on strategic processing within educational psychology. This review clarified the pivotal role of strategic processing within an interactive system of cognitive, metacognitive, and motivational components. Moreover, it showed that the authors of these models, to a large extent, have relied on concurrent and task-specific self-reports in attempting to measure strategic processing. This is not peculiar, given the emphasis on strategies as effortful, conscious, and intentional activities in the service of learning, comprehension, and problem solving. Simply stated: If people are aware of what they do when striving to achieve a particular goal, why not ask them to report what they do, either while doing it or immediately afterwards? As our subsequent discussion of such self-report methodologies showed, however, there are lingering issues with some of these methodologies that may represent challenges for the interpretation of data and replication of results.

First and foremost, a general lack of studies that compare strategy data across different methodologies makes it difficult to say with any degree of certainty whether what is captured (or missed) with respect to strategic processing is unique to particular methodologies. Thus, although data obtained with the concurrent and task-specific self-report methodologies that we discussed in this chapter to some degree have been compared with data from more objective methodologies, such as reading time, eye movements, and traces, such information is sparse and essentially lacking for most of the methodologies. Accordingly, this is an issue that needs further clarification. To involve meaningful comparisons, however, it is important that future researchers in this area try to ensure that more objective measurements (e.g., reading times or eye movements) actually reflect effortful strategic processing, as data from such methodologies are not self-explanatory and also may reflect bottom-up automatic processing or skills (Salmerón, Gil, & Bråten, 2018).

In addition, the different concurrent and task-specific methodologies that we discussed have seldom been compared with one another. Therefore, it is currently not known, for example, to what extent eye movement cued self-reports and task-specific self-report inventories administered immediately after task performance capture the same aspects of strategic processing, or to what extent task-specific self-report inventories and diary methods yield comparable data with respect to strategy use. Consequently, further research including more than one of these measures is needed to probe their concurrent validity.

Finally, different approaches to collecting data with each of the concurrent and task-specific self-report methodologies may yield different findings regarding strategic processing. For example, whether concurrent thinking aloud is self-directed or researcher-directed (i.e., prompted to occur at pre-selected locations), whether eye movement cued self-reports are based on fixations alone or both fixations and saccadic movements, whether task-specific self-report inventories are administered during or immediately after task performance, and whether diaries are completed once or several times a day may provide somewhat different windows on strategic processing. More systematic knowledge about how strategy data may differ with variants of the same type of self-report methodology is therefore also needed.

Taken together, the issues just discussed make it hard to interpret and compare findings from different studies because it is difficult, if not impossible, to determine how much variation is due to researchers' methodological choices or preferences. Given current concerns about failures to replicate findings in psychological and cognitive science (Lindsay, 2015), this problem is not trivial. That is, as it now stands, failure to replicate findings across studies of strategic processing and how it independently and interactively contributes to learning, comprehension, and problem solving may, at least in part, be due to different approaches to strategy measurement across studies. Likewise, varying results of instructional efforts to improve strategic functioning across studies may be due to strategy measures that are differentially sensitive to such efforts or capture different aspects of strategic processing. Hopefully, this chapter will provide an impetus for much further multiple method research including one or more of the self-report methodologies that we discussed in combination with other types of strategy measures to clarify the similarities and differences between those measures.

REFERENCES

Afflerbach, P., Pearson, P. D., & Paris, S. G. (2008). Clarifying differences between reading skills and reading strategies. *The Reading Teacher, 61*, 364–373.

Alexander, P. A. (1997). Mapping the multidimensional nature of domain learning: The interplay of cognitive, motivational, and strategic forces. In M. L. Maehr & P. R. Pintrich (Eds.), *Advances in motivation and achievement* (Vol. 10, pp. 213–250). Greenwich, CT: JAI.

Alexander, P. A. (2004). A Model of Domain Learning: Reinterpreting expertise as a multidimensional, multistage process. In D. Y. Dai & R. J. Sternberg (Eds.), *Motivation, emotion, and cognition: Integrative perspectives on intellectual functioning and development* (pp. 273–298). Mahwah, NJ: Erlbaum.

Alexander, P. A. (2005). The path to competence: A lifespan development perspective on reading. *Journal of Literacy Research, 37*, 413–436.

Alexander, P. A. (2012). Reading into the future: Competence for the 21st century. *Educational Psychologist, 47*, 259–280.

Alexander, P. A., Graham, S., & Harris, K. R. (1998). A perspective on strategy research: Progress and prospects. *Educational Psychology Review, 10*, 129–154.

Alexander, P. A., & Murphy, P. K. (1998). Profiling the differences in students' knowledge, interest, and strategic processing. *Journal of Educational Psychology, 90*, 435–447.

Alexander, P. A., Murphy, P. K., Woods, B. S., Duhon, K. E., & Parker, D. (1997). College instruction and concomitant changes in students' knowledge, interest, and strategy use: A study of domain learning. *Contemporary Educational Psychology, 22*, 125–146.

Alexander, P. A., Sperl, C. T., Buehl, M. M., Fives, H., & Chiu, S. (2004). Modeling domain learning: Profiles from the field of special education. *Journal of Educational Psychology, 96*, 545–557.

Andreassen, R., Jensen, M. S., & Bråten, I. (2017). Investigating self-regulated study strategies among postsecondary students with and without dyslexia: A diary method study. *Reading and Writing, 30*, 1891–1916.

Anmarkrud, Ø., & Bråten, I. (2009). Motivation for reading comprehension. *Learning and Individual Differences, 19*, 252–256.

Bereiter, C., & Scardamalia, M. (1987). *The psychology of written composition.* Hillsdale, NJ: Erlbaum.

292 • Ivar Bråten et al.

Brand-Gruwel, S., Kammerer, Y., van Meeuwen, L., & van Gog, T. (2017). Source evaluation of domain experts and novices during Web search. *Journal of Computer Assisted Learning, 33*, 234–251.

Bråten, I., & Anmarkrud, Ø. (2013). Does naturally occurring comprehension strategies instruction make a difference when students read expository text?. *Journal of Research in Reading, 36*, 42–57.

Bråten, I., Anmarkrud, Ø., Brandmo, C., & Strømsø, H. I. (2014). Developing and testing a model of direct and indirect relationships between individual differences, processing, and multiple-text comprehension. *Learning and Instruction, 30*, 9–24.

Bråten, I., & Samuelstuen, M. S. (2004). Does the influence of reading purpose on reports of strategic text processing depend on students' topic knowledge?. *Journal of Educational Psychology, 96*, 324–336.

Bråten, I., & Samuelstuen, M. S. (2007). Measuring strategic processing: Comparing task- specific self-reports with traces. *Metacognition and Learning, 2*, 1–20.

Bråten, I., & Strømsø, H. I. (2011). Measuring strategic processing when students read multiple texts. *Metacognition and Learning, 6*, 111–130.

Brown, A. L., Bransford, J. D., Ferrara, R. A., & Campione, J. C. (1983). Learning, remembering, and understanding. In J. H. Flavell & E. M. Markman (Eds.), *Handbook of child psychology. Volume III: Cognitive development* (pp. 77–166). New York: Wiley.

Catrysse, L., Gijbels, D., & Donche, V. (2018). It is not only about the depth of processing: What if *eye* am not interested in the text?. *Learning and Instruction, 58*, 284–294.

Cleary, T., & Zimmerman, B. J. (2001). Self-regulation differences during athletic practice by experts, non-experts, and novices. *Journal of Applied Sport Psychology, 13*, 185–206.

de Koning, B. B., Tabbers, H. K., Rikers, R. M. J. P., & Paas, F. (2010). Attention guidance in learning from a complex animation: Seeing is understanding?. *Learning and Instruction, 20*, 111–122.

Dinsmore, D. L., Hattan, C., & List, A. (2018). A meta-analysis of strategy use and performance in the Model of Domain Learning. In H. Fives & D. L. Dinsmore (Eds.), *The Model of Domain Learning: Understanding the development of expertise* (pp. 37–55). New York: Routledge.

Elling, S., Lentz, L. R., & de Jong, M. (2011). Retrospective think-aloud method: Using eye movements as an extra cue for participants' verbalizations. In *Proceedings of the SIGCHI Conference on Human Factors in Computing Systems* (pp. 1161–1170). New York: Association for Computing Machinery.

Ericsson, K., & Simon, H. (1993). *Protocol analysis: Verbal reports as data*. Cambridge, MA: The MIT Press.

Goldman, S. R., Braasch, J. L. G., Wiley, J., Graesser, A. C., & Brodowinska, K. M. (2012). Comprehending and learning from Internet sources: Processing patterns of better and poorer learners. *Reading Research Quarterly, 47*, 356–381.

Graesser, A. C., Singer, M., & Trabasso, T. (1994). Constructing inferences during narrative text comprehension. *Psychological Review, 101*, 371–395.

Graves, B., & Frederiksen, C. H. (1991). Literary expertise in the description of a fictional narrative. *Poetics, 20*, 1–26.

Guan, Z., Lee, S., Cuddihy, E., & Ramey, J. (2006). The validity of the stimulated retrospective think-aloud method as measured by eye tracking. In *Proceedings of the SIGCHI Conference on Human Factors in Computing Systems* (pp. 1253–1262). New York: Association for Computing Machinery.

Hagen, Å. M., Braasch, J. L. G., & Bråten, I. (2014). Relationships between spontaneous note- taking, self-reported strategies and comprehension when reading multiple texts in different task conditions. *Journal of Research in Reading, 37*, 141–157.

Hansen, J. P. (1991). The use of eye mark recordings to support verbal retrospection in software testing. *Acta Psychologica, 76*, 31–49.

Hyrskykari, A., Ovaska, S., Majaranta, P., Räihä, K. J., & Lehtinen, M. (2008). Gaze path stimulation in retrospective think-aloud. *Journal of Eye Movement Research, 2*, 1–18.

Iida, M., Shrout, P. E., Laurenceau, J. P., & Bolger, N. (2012). Using diary methods in psychological research. In H. Cooper (Ed.), *APA handbook of research methods in psychology* (Vol. 1, pp. 277–305). Washington, DC: American Psychological Association.

Jarodzka, H., Scheiter, K., Gerjets, P., & van Gog, T. (2010). In the eyes of the beholder: How experts and novices interpret dynamic stimuli. *Learning and Instruction, 20*, 146–154.

Kaakinen, J. K., & Hyönä, J. (2005). Perspective effects on expository text comprehension: Evidence from think-aloud protocols, eyetracking, and recall. *Discourse Processes, 40*, 239–257.

Kanfer, R., Reinecker, H., & Schmelzer, D. (1996). *Selbstmanagement-Therapie [Self-management therapy]* (2nd ed.). Berlin: Springer.

Kendeou, P., & O'Brien, E. J. (2018). Reading comprehension theories: A view from the top down. In M. F. Schober, D. N. Rapp, & M. A. Britt (Eds.), *The Routledge handbook of discourse processes* (2nd ed., pp. 7–21). New York: Routledge.

Kitsantas, A., & Zimmerman, B. J. (2002). Comparing self-regulatory processes among novice, non-expert, and expert volleyball players: A microanalytic study. *Journal of Applied Sport Psychology, 14*, 91–105.

Kopatich, R. D., Magliano, J. P., Millis, K. K., Parker, C. P., & Ray, M. (2019). Understanding how language-specific and domain-general resources support comprehension. *Discourse Processes, 56*, 530–552.

Levin, J. R. (2008). The unmistakable professional promise of a young educational psychology researcher and scholar. *Educational Psychologist, 43*, 70–85.

Lindsay, D. S. (2015). Replication in psychological science. *Psychological Science, 26*, 1827–1832.

List, A., Du, H., Wang, Y., & Lee, H. Y. (2019). Toward a typology of integration: Examining the documents model framework. *Contemporary Educational Psychology, 58*, 228–242.

Magliano, J. P. (1999). Revealing inference processes during text comprehension. In S. R. Goldman, A. C. Graesser, & P. van Den Broek (Eds.), *Narrative comprehension, causality, and coherence: Essays in honor of Tom Trabasso* (pp. 55–75). Mahwah, NJ: Erlbaum.

Magliano, J. P., & Millis, K. K. (2003). Assessing reading skill with a think-aloud procedure and latent semantic analysis. *Cognition and Instruction, 21*, 251–283.

Magliano, J. P., & Millis, K. K.; The RSAT Development Team, Levinstein, I., & Boonthum, C. (2011). Assessing comprehension during reading with the Reading Strategy Assessment Tool (RSAT). *Metacognition and Learning, 6*, 131–154.

Magliano, J. P., Trabasso, T., & Graesser, A. C. (1999). Strategic processes during comprehension. *Journal of Educational Psychology, 91*, 615–629.

McCarthy, K. S., & Goldman, S. R. (2019). Constructing interpretive inferences about literary text: The role of domain-specific knowledge. *Learning and Instruction, 60*, 245–251.

McMaster, K. L., van den Broek, P., Espin, C. A., White, M. J., Rapp, D. N., Kendeou, P., … Carlson, S. (2012). Making the right connections: Differential effects of reading intervention for subgroups of comprehenders. *Learning and Individual Differences, 22*, 100–111.

Millis, K., Magliano, J., & Todaro, S. (2006). Measuring discourse-level processes with verbal protocols and latent semantic analysis. *Scientific Studies of Reading, 10*, 225–240.

Muntinga, T., & Taylor, G. (2018). Information-seeking strategies in medicine queries: A clinical eye-tracking study with gaze-cued retrospective think-aloud protocol. *International Journal of Human–Computer Interaction, 34*, 506–518.

Paris, S. G., Newman, R. S., & Jacobs, J. E. (1985). Social contexts and functions of children's remembering. In M. Pressley & C. J. Brainerd (Eds.), *Cognitive learning and memory in children* (pp. 81–115). New York: Springer.

Penttinen, M., Anto, E., & Mikkilä-Erdmann, M. (2013). Conceptual change, text comprehension and eye movements during reading. *Research in Science Education, 43*, 1407–1434.

Pressley, M. (1986). The relevance of the Good Strategy User Model to the teaching of mathematics. *Educational Psychologist, 21*, 139–161.

Pressley, M., & Afflerbach, P. (1995). *Verbal protocols of reading: The nature of constructively responsive reading.* Hillsdale, NJ: Erlbaum.

Pressley, M., Borkowski, J. G., & Schneider, W. (1987). Cognitive strategies: Good strategy users coordinate metacognition and knowledge. In R. Vasta (Ed.), *Annals of child development* (Vol. 4, pp. 89–129). Greenwich, CT: JAI Press.

Pressley, M., Forrest-Pressley, D. L., Elliott-Faust, D., & Miller, G. (1985). Children's use of cognitive strategies, how to teach strategies, and what to do if they can't be taught. In M. Pressley & C. J. Brainerd (Eds.), *Cognitive learning and memory in children* (pp. 1–47). New York: Springer.

Pressley, M., & Hilden, K. (2004). Verbal protocols of reading. In N. K. Duke & M. H. Mallette (Eds.), *Literacy research methodologies* (pp. 308–321). New York: Guilford.

Pressley, M., & Levin, J. R. (1977). Developmental differences in subjects' associative- learning strategies and performance: Assessing a hypothesis. *Journal of Experimental Child Psychology, 24*, 431–439.

Rapp, D. N., van den Broek, P., McMaster, K. L., Kendeou, P., & Espin, C. A. (2007). Higher-order comprehension processes in struggling readers: A perspective for research and intervention. *Scientific Studies of Reading, 11*, 289–312.

Rau, M. A., Aleven, V., & Rummel, N. (2017). Making connections among multiple graphical representations of fractions: Sense-making competencies enhance perceptual fluency, but not vice versa. *Instructional Science, 45*, 331–357.

Ray, M., & Magliano, J. P. (2015, November). *Automatic assessment of moment-to-moment comprehension processes.* Paper presented at the annual meeting for the Society for Computers in Psychology, Chicago, IL.

Rayner, K. (2009). The 35th Sir Frederick Bartlett Lecture: Eye movements and attention in reading, scene perception, and visual search. *Quarterly Journal of Experimental Psychology, 62*, 1457–1506.

Ruckpaul, A., Fürstenhöfer, T., & Matthiesen, S. (2015). Combination of eye tracking and think-aloud methods in engineering design research. In J. S. Gero & S. Hanna (Eds.), *Design computing and cognition'14* (pp. 81–97). Cham, Switzerland: Springer.

Russo, J. E. (1979). A software system for the collection of retrospective protocols prompted by eye fixations. *Behavior Research Methods & Instrumentation, 11*, 177–179.

Salmerón, L., Gil, L., & Bråten, I. (2018). Using eye-tracking to assess sourcing during multiple document reading: A critical analysis. *Frontline Learning Research, 6*, 105–122.

Salmerón, L., Naumann, J., García, V., & Fajardo, I. (2017). Scanning and deep processing of information in hypertext: An eye tracking and cued retrospective think-aloud study. *Journal of Computer Assisted Learning, 33*, 222–233.

Samuelstuen, M. S., & Bråten, I. (2005). Decoding, knowledge, and strategies in comprehension of expository text. *Scandinavian Journal of Psychology, 46*, 107–117.

Samuelstuen, M. S., & Bråten, I. (2007). Examining the validity of self-reports on scales measuring students' strategic processing. *British Journal of Educational Psychology, 77*, 351–378.

Schmitz, B., Klug, J., & Schmidt, M. (2011). Assessing self-regulated learning using diary measures with university students. In B. J. Zimmerman & D. H. Schunk (Eds.), *Handbook of self-regulation of learning and performance* (pp. 251–266). New York: Routledge.

Schmitz, B., & Wiese, B. S. (2006). New perspectives for the evaluation of training sessions in self-regulated learning: Time-series analyses of diary data. *Contemporary Educational Psychology, 31*, 64–96.

Shellings, G. (2011). Applying learning strategy questionnaires: Problems and possibilities. *Metacognition and Learning, 6*, 91–109.

Stark, L., Brünken, R., & Park, B. (2018). Emotional text design in multimedia learning: A mixed-methods study using eye tracking. *Computers & Education, 120*, 185–196.

Todaro, S. A., Magliano, J. P., Millis, K. K., McNamara, D. S., & Kurby, C. A. (2008). Assessing the structure of verbal protocols. In B. C. Love, K. McRae, & V. M. Sloutsky (Eds.), *Proceedings of the 30th Annual Conference of the Cognitive Science Society* (pp. 607–612). Austin, TX: Cognitive Science Society.

Tourangeau, R. (2000). Remembering what happened: Memory errors and survey reports. In A. A. Stone, J. S. Turkkan, C. A. Bachrach, J. B. Jobe, H. S. Kurtzman, & V. S. Cain (Eds.), *The science of self-report: Implications for research and practice* (pp. 29–47). Mahwah, NJ: Erlbaum.

Trabasso, T., & Magliano, J. P. (1996). Conscious understanding during text comprehension. *Discourse Processes, 21*, 255–288.

van der Weijden, F. A., Kamphorst, E., Willemsen, R. H., Kroesbergen, E. H., & van Hoogmoed, A. H. (2018). Strategy use on bounded and unbounded number lines in typically developing adults and adults with dyscalculia: An eye-tracking study. *Journal of Numerical Cognition, 4*, 337–359.

van Gog, T., Paas, F., van Merriënboer, J. J., & Witte, P. (2005). Uncovering the problem- solving process: Cued retrospective reporting versus concurrent and retrospective reporting. *Journal of Experimental Psychology: Applied, 11*, 237–244.

van Meeuwen, L. W., Brand-Gruwel, S., Kirschner, P. A., de Bock, J. J. P. R., & van Merriënboer, J. J. G. (2018). Fostering self-regulation in training complex cognitive tasks. *Educational Technology Research and Development, 66*, 53–73.

Veenman, M. V. J. (2005). The assessment of metacognitive skills: What can be learned from multi-method designs? In C. Arelt & B. Moschner (Eds.), *Lernstrategien und Metakognition: Implikationen für Forschung und Praxis [Learning strategies and metacognition: Implications for research and practice]* (pp. 75–97). Berlin: Waxman.

Veenman, M. V. J. (2011). Alternative assessment of strategy use with self-report instruments: A discussion. *Metacognition and Learning, 6*, 205–211.

Veenman, M. V. J. (2016). Metacognition. In P. Afflerbach (Ed.), *Handbook of individual differences in reading: Reader, text, and context* (pp. 26–40). New York: Routledge.

Weinstein, C. E., Husman, J., & Dierking, D. R. (2000). Self-regulation interventions with a focus on learning strategies. In M. Boekaerts, P. R. Pintrich, & M. Zeidner (Eds.), *Handbook of self-regulation* (pp. 727–747). San Diego, CA: Academic Press.

Whitney, P., Ritchie, B. G., & Clark, M. B. (1991). Working-memory capacity and the use of elaborative inferences in text comprehension. *Discourse Processes, 14*, 133–145.

Winne, P. H., & Perry, N. E. (2000). Measuring self-regulated learning. In M. Boekaerts, P. R. Pintrich, & M. Zeidner (Eds.), *Handbook of self-regulation* (pp. 532–568). San Diego, CA: Academic Press.

Zimmerman, B. J. (2000). Attaining self-regulation: A social cognitive perspective. In M. Boekaerts, P. R. Pintrich, & M. Zeidner (Eds.), *Handbook of self-regulation* (pp. 13–39). San Diego, CA: Academic Press.

Zimmerman, B. J. (2013). From cognitive modeling to self-regulation: A social cognitive career path. *Educational Psychologist, 48*, 135–147.

Zimmerman, B. J., & Martinez-Pons, M. (1986). Development of a structured interview for assessing student use of self-regulated learning strategies. *American Educational Research Journal, 23*, 614–628.

Zimmerman, B. J., & Martinez-Pons, M. (1988). Construct validation of a strategy model of student self-regulated learning. *Journal of Educational Psychology, 80*, 284–290.

Zimmerman, B. J., & Martinez-Pons, M. (1990). Student differences in self-regulated learning: Relating grade, sex, and giftedness to self-efficacy and strategy use. *Journal of Educational Psychology, 82*, 51–59.

Zwaan, R. A., & Brown, C. M. (1996). The influence of language proficiency and comprehension skill on situation-model construction. *Discourse Processes, 21*, 289–327.

18

EXPLORING THE UTILIZATION OF THE BIG DATA REVOLUTION AS A METHODOLOGY FOR EXPLORING LEARNING STRATEGY IN EDUCATIONAL ENVIRONMENTS

Kimberly A. Lawless and Jeremy Riel
PENNSYLVANIA STATE UNIVERSITY, USA

INTRODUCTION

Over the late 20th century and early 21st century, rapid advancements in technology have greatly modified what it means to be a competent citizen in contemporary society. Today, technology permeates almost every sector of our lives. We cannot select a movie on our television without algorithms telling us which shows we should be interested in. Looking to buy a product on Amazon? Here are 20 other products consumers just like you have purchased. Let's also not overlook the constant bombardment of advertising that is customized to our buying histories, online conversations, and internet connection habits. There is no question that industry has leveraged technology to offer personalized and directed services in a very effective, albeit somewhat intrusive manner.

The education sector has not been immune to these changes of course. More and more, new technologies are changing where and how we conduct instruction, engage in learning, and assess outcomes. The rise of online education impacts the geographic footprint of our student catchments. Gamification attempts to harness the motivation and flow states of commercially available games for the purposes of learning. Moreover, the vastness of the internet has caused us to rethink what we teach in the classroom and how we do so. Yet, in all of these changes within the enterprises of teaching and learning, what is still clear is that we in education have not kept up with many of the affordances of technology in the way that industry has. This is critically important as we think about the strategies that students need to acquire for both the current and future worlds they will inhabit and contribute to. It is no longer sufficient to think about how we strategically interact with and learn from off-line resources, or even isolated online resources. As a field, we need to understand how we can strategically interact with technology to allow us to think, learn, and produce in an increasingly complex world that is supported more and more by machine-generated algorithms that automate many of our daily tasks. Moreover, these strategies need to become a larger focal area of how we orchestrate instruction, provide supports for learning, and implement assessment practices that truly target the intended outcomes of education.

This is not to say that no research has been done in the area of technology-mediated strategy learning, instruction, and assessment. Certainly there are studies that have examined the use of learning strategies in the deployment of online learning environments (e.g., Knight, 2010; Tsai & Shen, 2009), computer-supported learning environments (e.g., Mathan & Koedinger, 2005; McNamara, Levinstein, & Boonthum, 2004; Moos & Azevedo, 2009), intelligent tutoring systems (e.g., Biswas, Roscoe, Jeong, & Sulcer, 2009; Koedinger & Aleven, 2007), and even game-based learning environments (Barab et al., 2009; Nietfeld, Hoffmann, McQuiggan, & Lester, 2008). The problem with many of these areas of work, however, is that they remain isolated from the larger enterprise of education. They lack the scale and scope necessary to generate a more generalizable understanding of its implementation, the necessary changes we must consider regarding what and how learning occurs, and how we continue to evolve our perspective on how learners will need to adjust as technology and our world landscape continue to change in the future. Education has yet to fully leverage the plethora of data available on students' learning and strategic processes in instructional environments as a means to automate and leverage the adaptable affordances of technology for *in situ* teaching, learning, and assessment.

Because of the increasing complexity of the internet ecosystem today, the intent of this chapter is not to be a "how to" for engaging in the use of new forms and copious amounts of data for research on the strategic knowledge and processes that students employ during the learning process. Rather, its intent is to provide inspiration regarding where the future of research in education in general and strategic processing, in specific, needs to go. Further, this chapter seeks to heighten awareness of the potential affordances of this trajectory to better understand and support learning strategy research and pedagogy as the field moves forward. To this end, this chapter begins by examining the capture and analysis of data in various commercial applications, and how industry has successfully leveraged this data to better understand user engagement and shaping of consumer behaviors toward a targeted set of outcomes. Next, this chapter presents a summary of research from educational researchers' attempts to generalize data strategies used in industry to inform teaching, learning, and assessment practices. Finally, the chapter concludes with a discussion of where we as a field need to move in terms of our research and the challenges the use of these techniques presents to the enterprise of education.

WHAT IS BIG DATA?

Nowadays, almost every action we take both digitally and physically leaves behind a digital footprint. Whenever we go online, use our smart phones, send an email, or even simply watch our TV, we leave behind a digital bread crumb trail. Additionally, mobile devices, wearable technology, and even everyday objects like refrigerators, thermostats, and front door locks are all increasingly connected to the web and actively share data about our behavior in the physical "real world." Along with these user-generated data points, machine-generated data is also a growing trend. Machine-generated data comes about whenever devices interact with other devices, either directly or through a digital service: think of your Alexa home assistant turning your lights or TV on. There are also ambient sensors in the everyday physical environment that collect data, such as information from traffic signals collecting data about traffic patterns or congestion. When combined, the information that is collected, transmitted, and stored across all of these sources, aggregated into what are referred to as "Big Data." Frequently referred to as the "new oil" (Kennedy & Moss, 2015; Lane, 2014) or a rich "gold mine" (Asay, 2013; Steinberg, 2013), Big Data, like its highly sought-after natural resources analogs, is a coveted asset, and as such, those who control it hold political, social, and financial power (Jones, 2015).

It is important to point out that there is a significant difference between big data with a lower case "b", and Big Data with a capital "B." The former, "big data" merely refers to data sets that are collected across a large set of users, meaning it is a "big data" set. The Census for instance, is an example of "big data". Big Data, however, is often defined by a series of characteristics that indeed include volume, but also velocity, variety, value, and veracity, or the "5 Vs" (Anuradha, 2015). Volume, as the name connotes, deals with the amount of data, both structured and unstructured, that is captured. However, to be considered Big Data, the volume collected and aggregated must surpass that which can be aggregated and analyzed by traditional analysis tools. Velocity is the speed at which data is acquired, often measured in terms of minimizing the gap between collection and real time production of the data. Some argue that the speed at which data comes in, and the tempo at which it is processed, is more important than the volume because it is the essential element for making quick and strategic decisions to aid in goal attainment. In addition to the amount and speed of Big Data, variety of data is also a key attribute. Often, researchers minimize their thinking regarding the type of data that can be collected to understand user intention, process, and progress. for example limiting thinking about data forms to click streams, time stamps, and user input. But when considering Big Data, it is not only about what they are doing in situ but also ancillary information collected about how they access (e.g., mobile versus laptop) and where they access online materials (i.e., GPS), what they are posting in forums (e.g., review sites and discussion forums) and on social media regarding their interactions and comprehension, and other data streams that provide indicators of user intent, strategy selection, and success rate.

While volume, velocity, and variety are indeed key components that define Big Data, any data examined under the umbrella of "Big Data" is meaningless unless there is value to what is being aggregated or analyzed. Value is a proposition that focuses on understanding what the data communicates about the user and how this knowledge can help dictate resources to improve the user's experience, quickly and decisively. Finally, Big Data is only useful if the data has a level of veracity that yields consistency across users and interactions. Thus, key questions that Big Data must address are identifying how clean the data is, how much noise needs to be filtered, and what level of dependability does the data produce. In this chapter, we attempt to focus on the affordances of Big Data and what this means for the future of research examining learners' strategic processing and the design of instruction to improve these strategies in the service of obtaining positive learning outcomes.

While the five "Vs" describe the collection and analysis of data in all its various forms, the operational side of Big Data focuses on how to implement the analysis and interpretation of data into actionable interventions altering behaviors and habits toward desired outcomes of the organization. From this perspective, Big Data can, over time, be channeled into machine-based, learning algorithms that automate the adaptation of digital environments to direct and shape user behaviors and actions toward a specific set of desired outcomes. The combination of mining Big Data, analyzing it, and then operationalizing it, is what industry and business sectors have begun to master. Learning about an individual consumer from a wide and varied set of digital actions, profiling actions, habits, and behaviors across learners to identify common patterns, allows industry to use this knowledge to manipulate the digital experience of this consumer in ways that benefit user experience or further encourage purchasing actions. In the next section, we discuss how industry has been successful across these three linked areas of consumer strategy training.

HOW BIG DATA HAS BEEN LEVERAGED BY INDUSTRY

Ostensibly, the commercial value of tracking and identifying the different strategies that users employ across varied digital spaces lies in the increased ability of a company to improve the user's experience, or to better promote certain actions on the part of the user, such as making a purchase or continuing to use the company's services. The goal of such a robust data collection effort is to build analytic models of each user, or user data profiles. These profiles are largely based on the types of strategies that users employ on websites and other digital spaces (Wang, 2008). Thus, as users continue to interact with digital services, individual user models or profiles are continually refined with the intent of developing databases of robust profiles. Such profiles can be used to identify with what features of a digital service users are engaged, whether users regularly achieve their intended outcomes, whether they have difficulty in completing some or all of their intended actions, or whether the software environment is hard to use or otherwise not intuitively designed based on a user's intentions (Kardan & Ebrahimi, 2013).

The thought of large companies that own comprehensive dossiers on individual users that account for *every single* click and movement might indeed seem a little like science fiction. However, website and app providers actually often allow third parties to track their own users across platforms, devices, and websites. Such broad, multi-platform sharing of data between services and websites occurs on virtually every website today, which can readily reveal the types of various browsing, buying, and content viewing strategies of users to companies who desire such information. In addition, the prospect of only being tracked in digital spaces is increasingly less likely given today's commercial technologies, as many mobile device apps readily relay users' physical location data back to companies.

A common example of multi-platform tracking is highlighted by some web analytics tracking services, which are available for free to website and app providers. Such services find widespread use on websites or mobile apps across all industries today (Clifton, 2012). In two of the most common examples, Google (via Google's Analytics service) and Facebook (via Facebook Pixel tracking) provide small snippets of programming code to website and app providers, which are placed on websites that are outside of Google or Facebook's ownership or control. As a result of embedding these snippets of tracking code, Google and Facebook provide software administrators with robust analytics tools that the administrators can use to better understand visitor behavior, including the strategies that they use on the website (Clifton, 2012). However, in return for the monetarily free cost of providing the tracking service, this data on the behaviors on websites is aggregated and returned to Google and Facebook. Such data from external websites and services allows these companies to enrich the user profiles with greater resolution, which is a hallmark of Big Data.

This type of multi-site tracking is also not just limited to capturing data on the strategies employed by users on websites. For example, mobile phones often collect and transmit a host of data to third parties that is valuable for inferring the types of behaviors and strategies that users perform as they go about their everyday lives. Given that an application on a mobile device has the appropriate level of permissions on the mobile device, various dimensions of data are shared from mobile devices to app providers as they are collected from the device's sensors and interaction with nearby internet-connected devices. These multiple data dimensions include a user's location, a user's physiological attributes (e.g., measuring steps taken, heart rate, and rate of movement as tracked by a device's accelerometer, compass, and gyroscope), and environmental factors (e.g., temperature and ambient sound). As a result, the data that composes a person's digital fingerprint is no longer exclusively digital: physical and digital lives are increasingly bridged in the era of Big Data. As a result, seemingly more daily activities can be observed and analyzed in Big Data contexts.

By collecting comprehensive, cross-platform data on users' tastes in content, the entertainment media industry has embraced Big Data approaches to suggest new content to users. Primarily, home entertainment video and TV streaming media services such as Netflix, YouTube, Hulu, and Amazon Prime have embraced Big Data efforts, such as collection and analysis of user viewing preferences by engaging in large-scale data collection and user modeling efforts (Bennett & Lanning, 2007; Gomez-Uribe & Hunt, 2016). However, other media providers have also used Big Data to make content suggestions to individual users based on their prior viewing patterns and inferences on their interests, such as social media content like Twitter, Facebook, and Snapchat (Gao, Tang, Hu, & Liu, 2015), online bookstores like Amazon, and Apple Books (Chien, Chen, Ko, Ku, & Chan, 2015), music providers like iTunes, Spotify, and Pandora (Bu et al., 2010), and online news providers (Kompan & Bieliková, 2010).

In an example featuring the video streaming service Netflix, movies are largely categorized with metadata that uses word-based descriptions of film genre (e.g., mystery, comedy, action), intended age range (e.g., children, adults), topic (e.g., movies about friendship, super heroes, travel, family life), and other features (e.g., special effects, foreign films) (Titcomb, 2018). As Netflix does a thorough job of categorizing each film in its database, viewers can find movies in the Netflix database through text searches alone. However, the true value in Big Data approaches for content recommendation lies in the ability to capture and analyze a user's viewing patterns, as well as any additional information about their interests and other digital activities. Matching search queries with the metadata tags that are attached to movies is often not enough for an algorithm to infer users' individual interests, and thus will likely provide results that may not be relevant to individual viewers within film genres. As a result of accounting for a viewer's history and preferences, the Netflix recommendation system continues to improve its ability to provide hyper-specific recommendations to users through specialized categories, or "microgenres." These microgenres can sometimes include oddly specific film categories that sometimes only have one or two films in the category, with some examples including "emotional independent drama for hopeless romantics," "Oscar-winning visually striking films," and "goofy dance musicals" (LaPorte, 2019).

Recent advancements in the video game industry also provide an excellent illustration of how interactive environments can be automatically adapted based on data on prior interactions. For years, this industry has accurately assumed that as players gain expertise in a game, they might become easily bored and stop playing if more challenging aspects are not made readily available (Giakoumis, Tzovaras, Moustakas, & Hassapis, 2011; Juul, 2009). To one extreme, some scholars have even compared the continual need to evolve video game play to match players' interests as a "content arms race" (Hastings, Guha, & Stanley, 2009). This is particularly true in modern internet-based and massive multiplayer online games, in which the conditions for "winning" a game are not clearly defined. Instead, winning the game takes secondary precedence to interacting with other players and completing a series of increasingly difficult or time-consuming challenges (Granic, Lobel, & Engels, 2014; Quandt & Kröger, 2013). To address this shift in play style associated with long-term, multiplayer games, game makers have integrated increasingly adaptive and dynamic elements to games to maintain alignment with players' expertise, interests, and play motivations.

Because they are situated solely in digital spaces, the video gaming industry can also easily collect and use player data to refine gameplay, rules, and game interfaces (Etheredge, Lopes, & Bidarra, 2013). By using data on users' previous play in real time, the current generation of multiplayer video games have increasingly provided dynamic ongoing support, delivered timely hints as players complete activities, and enabled the difficulty of games to fluctuate based on players' demonstrated level of skill (Tomai, Salazar, & Salinas, 2012; Yannakakis & Togelius, 2011). To meet the equally important need of retaining player engagement, the use of Big Data has likewise afforded the video game industry with many new tools for adapting gameplay based on each player's demonstrated capabilities, interests, and play styles (Pedersen, Togelius, & Yannakakis, 2010; Tomai, 2012). With these advances in mind, modern video games reveal key design parallels to researchers and instructional designers who are interested in implementing interventions for teaching specific skills and strategies to learners through adaptive learning environments.

Modern adaptive games create dynamic changes to interactive capabilities and play structure in multiple ways. The most prominent adaptive feature that game designers implement is *adaptive difficulty*. Based on the interaction patterns of players, adaptive difficulty games fine-tune challenges of in-game opponents, puzzles, and quests (Dziedzic, 2016; Hunicke, 2005). Such difficulty adjustments are made when interaction patterns reveal a player is stuck or not progressing, or alternatively, progressing too quickly without any challenge (Jennings-Teats, Smith, & Wardrip-Fruin, 2010;

Missura & Gärtner, 2009). These challenge-based adaptations have also included changing the types of options available during puzzle solving (Lavoué, Monterrat, Desmarais, & George, 2018), manipulating the types of actions or quests available to players based on their demonstrated skill with the game (Yannakakis, 2012), and limiting the access to locations within complex multiplayer worlds to make decisions easier for new players as they develop skill with the game (Yan & Natkin, 2011).

Another good example is a recent spur of game research that has demonstrated the success of delivering *differentiated hints and player supports* based on prior play data. For instance, Bommanapally, Subramaniam, Chundi, and Parakh (2018) showed that hints can be custom provided as players demonstrate difficulty or lack of progress with navigating multiplayer game worlds and with game interfaces alike. In another example by Chen and Lei (2006), they acknowledge that interacting within a multiplayer environment with many options can be difficult for new players. Thus, providing hints at critical moments can help focus and enable students to continue play. Similarly, Kang, Kim, and Kim (2010) argued that real-time analytics can drive adaptations to the non-player characters and "artificial intelligence" elements of a game, with non-player characters being able to adjust their dialogue to provide hints based on players' demonstrated skill and current state in the game. As an excellent example of scaffolding, the adaptation of hints is closely aligned with the continual adjustment of players' zones of proximal development and can continually support the development of student skills and strategies (Wauck & Fu, 2017).

This practice of promoting continual support and encouraging player motivation by games provides important insights to educators. The long-term process of learning is often emphasized over simple task completion, reaching the end of a curriculum, or taking tests. An emphasis on supporting the process of learning and continual motivation of students is especially true in open-ended learning activities, such as problem- and project-based learning where the "end" state of the learning experience is not necessarily known when students and teachers begin the process (Ertmer & Simons, 2006). Finding ways to automate data collection for dynamic adaption of learning activities, student supports and help mechanisms, and motivational encouragement presents an achievable challenge for educational technology design in the near future.

EDUCATIONAL DATA MINING AND LEARNING ANALYTICS

Within the discipline of education, two emerging fields related to Big Data have begun to emerge, Educational Data Mining (EDM) and Learning Analytics (LA). At the inception of these two fields, there was differentiation between their general purposes. EDM was conceptualized as work that focused on tools, techniques, and methodologies for collecting, aggregating, and analyzing Big Data related to education. By contrast, LA focused more on the application of findings from these processes to optimize educational interactions and learning. As both fields have grown, however, the differences between the definitions have become a bit muddled, merging into a common vision of extracting information from educational data to help inform and implement instructional decision making (Liñán & Pérez, 2015). To simplify this discussion, within the ensuing sections, we default to using the combine term EDM/LA to describe the use of Big Data within the education sector.

EDM/LA at the mile-high view, targets the collection, analysis, and reporting of data from and about students and the learning environments in which they are embedded (Siemens, 2013). There is variation in the more fine-grained definitions of EDM/LA, with some researchers focusing explicitly on the use of student-generated data for the purpose of personalizing learning (Junco & Clem, 2015; Xing, Guo, Petakovic, & Goggins, 2015). EDM/LA can help to model learner behavior as a means to capture patterns in learner strategy, understanding what learners know, and where misconceptions might lie. Because this data can be captured in real time, it can potentially be used across stakeholders for providing scaffolding for learners, feedback to teachers, or even overall progress indicators for administrators (Bienkowski, Feng, & Means, 2012). However, in order for educational systems to provide personalized learning experiences, students must provide information about themselves and regularly interact with the system to create a wide array of analyzable data (Jones, 2015). Once a system is able to build a model of the learner, which includes a better understanding of the student's cognitive and affective characteristics and common interaction patterns, it models what the student knows (or does not) as a means of illuminating the gap between where the student currently is, and where they need to be to achieve the desired learning outcomes (Bienkowski et al., 2012). This can be used to create a learning pathway that is tailored to the specific needs of individual students rather than a mass instructional design plan that homogenizes learning across an entire group of students.

To date, most of the work operating under this definition of EDM/LA has concentrated on very broad learning metrics to study student retention (Arnold, 2010), engagement, learning outcomes (Hrabowski, Suess, & Fritz, 2011), and return on investment regarding technology procurement and deployment (Norris, Baer, Leonard, Pugliese, & Lefrere, 2008). One of the most well-known EDM/LA systems developed to target these outcomes is the Course Signals (CS) system developed at Purdue University (Arnold & Pistilli, 2012). CS works by extracting data from multiple university sources (e.g., admissions information, course interaction data, etc.) and subsequently analyzing this aggregated data to generate actionable intelligence for each student on campus in the form of a risk assessment (Arnold, 2010). The underlying algorithm used to predict students' risk level is measured through four parameters, performance (credits earned), effort (grade in current courses), comparison to peers, prior academic history, and demographics. The algorithm then categorizes students regarding their likelihood of success from low to high. Instructors are provided with the risk assessment prediction and can respond to the student in several ways to correct the trajectory if needed through computer generated email, text, their course management system, or a referral to a face-to face meeting (Pistilli & Arnold, 2010). Results from investigations of the efficacy of the CS system indicate that on courses in which CS is implemented, students obtain more passing grades and there are fewer dropouts and withdrawals (Arnold, 2010).

Although there is clear merit to the CS system, the level of granularity of both the data and the feedback provided to students is pedagogically limited. While instructors are informed of the risk level of a student in an automated fashion, the information provided does little to help the instructor understand *why* a particular student is faltering. What remains largely untapped in CS, and other systems like it, is the examination of EDM/LA as a tool to examine the strategic knowledge and processes that students enact during learning and how these in situ practices can inform instructors, real or virtual, on real-time intervention supports (Dietz-Uhler & Hurn, 2013). For example, such data could provide guidance on the provision or selection of relevant learning resources and content, the insertion of prompts for reflection and awareness, detection of unproductive learning strategies, delivery of timely hints and instruction, and identification of affective states (e.g., boredom, frustration) of the learner (Verbert et al., 2012).

Other researchers and EDM/LA practitioners focus more squarely on defining the purpose of LA as a tool to aiding in adapting interventions to support productive student learning strategies (Drachsler & Kalz, 2016; Rubel & Jones, 2016). In a sense, this perspective on EDM/LA creates an informed strategy for providing targeted feedback to the learner. Feedback informs individuals about what they did correctly or incorrectly, as well as how close they are to accomplishing desired outcomes. When instructors have a nuanced understanding of student success and failures, they can intervene in much more specific ways and provide students with detailed feedback to help them regulate their learning behaviors and recognize students' strengths and weaknesses. However, examining the types of feedback typically provided to students in online learning environments, Tanes, Arnold, King, and Remnet (2011) noted that instructors rarely provided instructive, elaborated, or process-related feedback. Rather than receiving feedback on how to address deficient strategies in their approach to learning, or misconceptions regarding their understanding, students identified as "off course" tended to receive messages carrying low level, summative feedback (Gašević, Dawson, & Siemens, 2015). The default to summative feedback likely stems from the overwhelming volume of feedback that would be necessary in a large online course setting.

EDM/LA is a possible avenue to better address high quality formative feedback to every student. For example, IBM's "Smarter Education Group" has been working on one such automated EDM/LA system, Personalized Education Through Analytics on Learning Systems (PETALS). PETALS is an automated machine-based learning application that continuously learns through data collected from students' interaction with the learning system, their achievements and failures with individual learning modules, and the changes in their learning behaviors in response to intervention adaptations. In addition to the data created through students' interactions within the PETALS system, data is also culled from external sources to iteratively test and generalize identified patterns and profiles on an independent set of students. (IBM, 2013). The system uses this corpus of data to derive a model of the student in math, for example, with specific attention to the strategies used when attempting to solve problems. For example, it may notice that a student is stuck in a "trial and error" strategy loop and nudge then to review a specific resource pertaining to the current issue they are attempting to address, helping the student to regulate their behavior and learn a more productive approach. While the PETALS system was able to detect specific strategies students were using, ascertain if those strategies were productive, and intervene in cases where student's strategy use was either unproductive or faulty, research examining the implementation of PETALS has indicated that it is no better than standard educational practice on improving student performance in math (Pool, 2015). As we know from psychology and educational research, it seems that more feedback is not necessarily better; the quality and timing of feedback is also critical.

PROMISING RESEARCH WITHIN TECHNOLOGY-MEDIATED LEARNING ENVIRONMENTS

While surveying the literature on the use and application of EDM/LA techniques, what became clear is that while there is a growing pool of work that invokes the sentiments and the terminology of the field, very little of it embraces the full complement of affordances EDM/LA has to offer. In order to provide some insight on how EDM/LA can inform our understanding of the strategic process learners invoke when interacting with digital environments as well as how these actions can be captured and then used to dynamically automate scaffolds to improve learning, the following section reviews findings across a diverse set of studies on technology-mediated teaching and learning. The studies reviewed were extracted from the extant pool of research stemming from an EDM/LA lens but also draw on literature that uses in situ data to examine strategic processes outside of EDM/LA.

Intelligent Tutoring Systems

Well prior to the current EDM/LA movement, research examining the development and utility of intelligence tutoring systems (ITS) began to harness the utility of data for the purpose of developing student models and adapting instructional supports to dynamically meet the needs of learners (Sottilare, Graesser, Hu, & Holden, 2013). A very broad and historical definition of ITS is any computer supported application that contains some "intelligence" that can be used for the purpose of teaching and learning (Freedman, Ali, & McRoy, 2000). This definition has evolved as our technologies have become more sophisticated, and now incorporates a focus on automating and aligning three areas of intelligence: complex modeling of a domain, a students' knowledge base and strategic processing, and the pedagogical strategies of teachers and tutors (Arroyo et al., 2014; Khachatryan et al., 2014).

There are a number of well-known ITS applications (e.g., SQL-Tutor, Mitrovic & Ohlsson, 1999; ALEKS, Craig et al., 2013; ASSISTments, Koedinger, McLaughlin, & Heffernan, 2010) that have large user bases that function to ascertain the system's effectiveness, as well as the refinement of our understanding of how to personalize instruction through data interrogation. Multiple literature syntheses and meta analyses have concluded that, under certain circumstances, ITS can produce, and often even outperform, traditional classroom instruction practices (Kulik & Fletcher, 2016; VanLehn, 2011). From a strategic processing perspective, ITS research has also been useful for exploring the strategic processes necessary to successfully solve presented problems (domain model), collect data on the strategies (or misconceptions) that learners use when engaging with an ITS (student model), and then present feedback in order to reinforce successful strategies or redirect a learner to a more successful strategy when implementing a faulty one (pedagogical model, Anderson & Koedinger; Koedinger

& Corbett, 2006). In ASSISTments, for example, Koedinger and colleagues (2013) used data from engaged learners to successfully ascertain problems/errors within the domain or student models by examining the problem-solving strategies used by engaged learners which led to an iterative, offline redesign of the system to be more sensitive to these types of interactions.

In a slightly different vein, researchers have also isolated a subset of strategies that users engage in an unexpected way. In a strategy generally known as "gaming the system," certain users systematically exploit affordances of an ITS to simply get through a task with minimal effort rather than engage in deep thinking and learning the presented material (Muldner, Burleson, Van de Sande, & VanLehn, 2010). There are two common strategies that learners employ when gaming the system: trial and error, and help abuse (Baker, Corbett, & Koedinger, 2004a). Not surprisingly, learner use of these strategies has a negative correlation with learning (Baker, Corbett, Koedinger, & Wagner, 2004b). What is interesting, however, is that research investigating gaming-the-system behaviors has found that use of these strategies is best predicted by characteristics such as motivation, boredom, and interest rather than a faulty instructional practice (Rodrigo et al., 2008). While some of these characteristics can be captured by an ITS through crude system analytics such as reaction time, other attributes are best captured through external data streams that feed into an ITS, which can supplement system interactions to develop a more robust student model. To these ends, this is an area where EDM/LA approaches can push forward the development of robust machine-learning ITS systems.

Online Courses

The rapid rise of distance-based learning and hybrid, online courses, as well as the general size and scale that these contexts afford, holds some promise for deep use of EDM/LA. Since the early 2000s, students have increasingly been exposed to and opted to enroll in online learning opportunities. Entire colleges have been "built" that offer the full complement of their academic programs online. Recent estimates indicate that nearly 34 percent of students take at least one online course during their undergraduate degree, a percentage that is growing every year (Allen & Seaman, 2014). Simultaneous with the explosion of online learning, research has been quick to investigate the role of learning strategies for successful achievement with online learning. For example, Wallace, Kupperman, Krajcik, and Soloway (2000) and his colleagues highlighted the complexity of online information seeking and the difficulties teachers and students have in negotiating these learning spaces. Ligorio (2001) and Tsai and Tsai (2003) indicated that this difficulty requires awareness and metacognitive strategies when engaging online inquiry learning beyond those required in off-line inquiry.

The rapid emergence of online options for students has been facilitated by the emergence of learning management systems (LMSs). Sixty-three percent of online courses use LMSs to serve the online learning needs of students and instructional goals of their teachers (Green & Hughes, 2013). The rise in computer-mediated and online education has opened up new approaches and avenues for collecting and processing data on students and course activities; every instructional transaction can be immediately recorded and added to a database. Many institutions use some form of basic learning analytics technology as part of their LMS platforms. Some of these data points are low level "count" metrics, such as click and engagement patterns and the timestamps associated with these actions (Jones, 2015). Other metrics offer a more robust window into strategic processing such as resource selection, help seeking, reading and writing habits, and multiple window browsing (Siemens, 2013). When these individual data are examined in isolation, their meaning and interpretation are quite limited, but when aggregated and examined through an EDM/LA framework, these rich data trails offer an opportunity to explore learning strategy and achievement from new and multiple angles (Macfadyen & Dawson, 2012). Toward this goal, EDM/LA provides a potentially powerful set of tools to aid instructors in iterative changes to their course materials to improve their effectiveness and supports for student success (Wang & Kelly, 2017).

Several online learning researchers have investigated the relationships between interaction sequences and learning outcomes using EDM/LA methods such as sequence mining to model learner behavior (Köck & Paramythis, 2011) and sequential pattern analysis (Perera, Kay, Koprinska, Yacef, & Zaïane, 2009). Using these EDM/LA techniques, these researchers have been able to identify various sequences for high- and low-performing learners. Most notably, this research found that poor strategy choice, such as ignoring the intended path sequences designed by the course designers and jumping back and forth between resources as the need for information to complete assessment and activities required, led to lower achievement in the course. Similarly, in a study of more than 43,000 students participating on a Massively Online Open Course (MOOC), Mukala, Buijs, and Van Der Aalst (2015) found that better performing students moved through course materials in a very structured way, following a logical path through video-based material and course assessments and watching videos in "batches."

It is important to note the study of online learning courses and MOOCs through EDM/LA does not just have a one-way function that focuses on student outcomes. It has also presented a robust methodology to examine how the design of learning environments can encourage or impede student learning. Aligning EDM/LA and the design of instructional environments allows researchers to examine if learners are engaging with course materials as the designer intended by examining students' actual behaviors and strategies when engaged in the act of learning (Dalziel et al., 2016; Mor, Ferguson, & Wasson, 2015). This is an important area for research, as we know that reliance on student self-reports of learning behaviors or merely on student outcomes does not necessary paint an accurate picture of student learning. Nguyen, Huptych, and Rienties (2018) examined students' time spend studying and engagement to an instructor's intended learning behaviors, finding that at the macro level there was good alignment, but at the micro level, which was captured through an EDM/LA exploration of trace data, there were significant differences in the behaviors students exhibited and those intended by the learning design. They highlight that instructors that have access to this type of data could be better positioned to reflect on and adjust their teaching practices and instructional activities in the future. Further, they postulate that sharing this information regarding how fellow students are interacting with online course materials through the course, could also help learners to self-regulate their learning more efficiently. Unfortunately, most of the research on the use of EDM/LA to facilitate automated changes instruction and scaffolding in MOOCS and online learning settings has fallen far short of the hype failing to implement robust models of instructional intervention (Baker, 2016).

Serious Games

Since the late 1990s, researchers have increasingly touted the capacity of video games as educational tools to cultivate situated activity, problem solving, and collaboration (Gee, 2003; Hamari et al., 2016; McGonigal, 2011; Squire, 2006). EMD/LA has been a popular methodology for examining learning within serious gaming environments and how students' strategic processes correlate with positive outcomes (Liu, Kang, Liu, Zou, & Hodson, 2017). Within this pool of research, a number of studies have been able to isolate the strategies that students enact in the pursuit of goal attainment. For example, Kerr and Chung (2012), using click stream data, were able to differentiate between gamers who employed a systematic trial and error problem-solving strategy from those who simply guessed solutions randomly. Similarly, Snow, Allen, Jacovina, and McNamara (2015) examined the behavior traces learners left when navigating through an educational game, and found that students who demonstrated more controlled choice patterns generated higher quality learning outcomes compared to students who exhibited more disordered choice patterns.

In a more robust implementation of EDM/LA, Liu, Alexandrova, and Nakajima (2011) collected trace data from interactions within a gaming environment and paired it with survey data regarding students' experience during game play. Their analysis resulted in the identification of five different problem-solving strategies: solution development, experimenting, solution review, solution reuse, and reading the tutorial, that were linked to variations in students' motivation and experience of flow states. Sun, Wang, and Chan (2011) manipulated the amount and type of scaffolding provided in a game to understand the impact these various supports had on student strategy use. Through analysis of user behavior logs, they were able to isolate elimination techniques and trial-and-error approaches to problem solving. Interestingly, they also found that increasing levels of scaffolding within the game also led some learners to game the system. These learners became dependent on the tools, and while they ended up completing more problems, they also learned fewer problem-solving strategies. This finding is not insignificant as it points to the need for systems to detect patterns of strategy use within a game to adapt the learning space in ways that are most productive for different types of learners.

DISCUSSION AND CHALLENGES OF BIG DATA AND THE FUTURE OF STRATEGY RESEARCH

Although commercial industries do not specifically examine the strategic processing of learners, certain non-educational sectors have been effectively leveraging Big Data in recent years in ways that help them maximize services to their customers. To achieve this, multiple sources of data that reflect patterns of both users' behaviors and ambient environmental conditions are used to create detailed profiles for users. Industries that have taken advantage of Big Data have used such comprehensive models of users' unique digital fingerprints to nudge users toward actions that are best predicted to help users achieve both corporate and users' personal interests. For educational researchers, such real-world examples provide design inspiration for those who are seeking to develop EDM/LA, educational interventions that can both readily identify the types of strategies and other behaviors that learners are using to meet their goals, and dynamically adapt and personalize learning environments based on strategy and usage patterns.

There is no question that EDM/LA presents huge potential for research on student and instructor strategic processing and knowledge development in the pursuit of developing robust and adaptive online learning environments. At this point, it should be clear that there is great potential in the harnessing of Big Data for the purposes of facilitating evidenced-based and automated instructional personalization. What should also be clear is that right now, much of what is occurring in the education research sector through EMD/LA is at the "buzz word level." What we mean by this is, much of what is being explored in the EDM/LA literature has either conflated that notion that a data set on a large number of participants is equivalent to the broader context of "Big Data" research, or has simply appropriated research on single-source data forms such as click streams or log files and renamed it EDM/LA. Getting serious about Big Data in education means we need to move past the term *de jour*. The field must understand that Big Data involves not only volumes of data but also the real-time capture and analysis of data from a variety of sources that can then be operationalized to tailor instruction based on a user's interactions, strategies, and learning trajectories. This argument is not meant to slight the extant research in its current nascent stage; rather, it is intended to push research forward to advance our knowledge and current pedagogies in ways that reshape education in the way industry has reformed the online market experience for consumers.

As the field moves forward, however, there are a number of issues that need to be resolved to fully embrace the power of Big Data in education. The prospects of collecting and using information about students also raises a number of ethical and logistical questions, including selection of data streams, system interoperability, issues pertaining to student privacy, and the need to create interdisciplinary research teams (Rubel & Jones, 2016). In the following section, we discuss each of these challenges that the field will need to address as the use of EDM/LA becomes more prevalent and more individuals will be impacted by the data collection protocols and resultant environmental adaptations that will be more increasingly conducted by automated, machine-learning algorithms.

Data Selection and Interoperability

Because it is still in its infancy, most of the research reviewed in this chapter has a limited view of the utilization of EDM/LA and Big Data techniques. Within the ITS literature, for example, while there is the use of learner data modeling, and, in some cases, machine learning to iterate these models, research has inadequately explored the integration of multiple streams of data outside of user interactions (Beck & Mostow, 2008). Similarly, while a great deal of rhetoric has expounded on the potential of online learning and MOOCS to use data as a tool to push forward the future of tailored, personalized learning, in reality the majority of this work has been constrained to user log data derived within the LMS platform used to deliver the courses (Mangaroska & Giannakos, 2017). EDM/LA approaches are only as good as the corpus of data available to extract, aggregate, and analyze. If the data pool is restricted to a single stream or service, this is not as insightful as having access to a wider data pool that is pulled from a variety of sources. Such multi-sourced data streams have the unique potential to reveal a more realistic range of learner strategy use and other behaviors that account for both learners' prior interactions and various environmental or structural factors that can influence learner activity. With so many forms of data available, the questions of which data to collect and which sources best provide this data are critical to answer (Slade & Prinsloo, 2013). Educational research must then begin to integrate and aggregate data across a multitude of sources (Di Mitri, Schneider, Specht, & Drachsler, 2018). By examining a more robust corpus of data streams, researchers interested in understanding the strategies that learners employ can expand beyond navigation trace data and include information on why certain users select these strategies, what determines prompt changes in strategy, and how learning environments can dynamically respond to particular strategies to shape more efficient learning practices. For example, at the post-secondary level, such data sources could include admissions information, geo-tagging of student online habits, capture of online activities in which the student is engaged concurrently with their access to online course materials, bio data provided by wearable technologies, and the list goes on. At the elementary and high school levels, collecting such robust data sets on students could facilitate the transfer of knowledge about a student from teacher to teacher or across grades, creating student educational histories that mirror processes used with medical records.

A big challenge for this comprehensive vision of multi-source Big Data integration in educational research is system interoperability. While the ability to capture data in each of these independent streams is currently available (and widely used in industry), communicating these data across the diverse set of systems is a bit more problematic. Essentially, each system has its own data collection and storage protocols. To port data out of individual systems and to aggregate them into a single repository is typically no small feat. The enterprise of education is going to need to put concerted effort into addressing the issue of interoperability if EDM/LA is to realize its value to research. Despite this challenge, the potential benefits of solving the issue of interoperability far outweigh the required investment of time and resources.

Privacy Issues

When conducting research, we understand the issues related to institutional review and the safe conduct of research to protect the rights of subjects. However, the use of EDM/LA falls into the grey area between educational evaluation and research (Van Wel & Royakkers, 2004). Within the business sector, most practitioners are knowledgeable about the implications of the collection of data to shape consumer behavior, but can the same be said about the collection of student data when EDM/LA is implemented? How transparent should schools and educational institutions be with respect to the collection, aggregation, and use of data? While the use of student data for these purposes is often accepted as part and parcel of education in the 21st century (Land & Bayne, 2005), others have criticized the use of digital student data, questioning its legitimacy (Coll, Glassey, & Balleys, 2011). Domínguez, Chiluiza, Echeverria, and Ochoa (2015) have begun work to develop operable frameworks to deal with issues of student privacy within the architecture of EDM/LA, but there remains a great deal of work to do, especially as we move closer to using EDM/LA for real-time instructional adaptation and more targeted learner supports and feedback (Rodríguez-Triana et al., 2017).

Related to issues of surveilling students' educational trajectories through data, Pariser (2011) argues that the results of these identification algorithms can inadvertently imprison learners in cages designed by their past choices. This phenomenon is not isolated to EDM/LA, but is prevalent across the entire Big Data enterprise. The term "filter bubble" refers to the results of Big Data algorithms that dictate what we encounter online, where users are increasingly unable to access or be exposed to content outside of the bubble that the filtering algorithm has determined is most applicable. In practice, filter bubbles essentially create a set of algorithmically generated restrictions that personalize content for users based on previous interactions without any deliberate user choice. A filter bubble, therefore, can cause users to get significantly less contact with contradicting viewpoints or exposure to the full range of opportunities for interaction, causing the user to potentially become intellectually isolated. Moreover, when used in the context of an educational setting, the automation of instructional scaffolds via EDM/LA methods may also prevent students from taking ownership of various strategies or even learning when specific strategies are appropriate, when to change an unsuccessful strategy and cause learners to become less metacognitively aware and self-regulated in their learning pursuits.

De-Siloing Educational Research

As the educational research community moves forward with the quest to demystify strategic processing, knowledge acquisition and application, and the optimal conditions needed to foster robust learning, we must come to terms with what is becoming an inescapable truth. In this highly complex and interconnected world, where data and information are everywhere, it is no longer sufficient to address educational research issues in isolated, disciplinary silos. The problems we face in education today require a multitude of perspectives and domains of expertise to identify, propose, and test solutions. To understand how strategic processes are employed and how instructional elements can shape and influence them, we must move toward a team-based approach, especially as we venture into the deep waters of Big Data and ED/LA. We need to begin to cultivate diverse teams of experts across education, the content disciplines, and computer science. The opportunity, the technology, and the methodologies to make big strides in both understanding and supporting learning exist, but in isolation, the best we can hope for is to chip away at an iceberg.

REFERENCES

Allen, I. E., & Seaman, J. (2014). *Grade change: tracking online education in the united states*. Babson Park, MA: Babson Survey Research Group and Quahog Research Group.

Anuradha, J. (2015). A brief introduction on Big Data 5Vs characteristics and Hadoop technology. *Procedia Computer Science*, *48*, 319–324.

Arnold, K. E. (2010). Signals: Applying academic analytics. *EDUCAUSE Quarterly*, 33, 1.

Arnold, K. E., & Pistilli, M. D. (2012, April). Course signals at Purdue: Using learning analytics to increase student success. In *Proceedings of the 2nd international conference on learning analytics and knowledge* (pp. 267–270). ACM.

Arroyo, I., Woolf, B. P., Burelson, W., Muldner, K., Rai, D., & Tai, M. (2014). A multimedia adaptive tutoring system for mathematics that addresses cognition, metacognition and affect. *International Journal of Artificial Intelligence in Education, 24*(4), 387–426.

Asay, M. (2013). Q&A. Is open source sustainable?. *Technology Innovation Management Review, 3*(1), 46–49.

Baker, R. S. (2016). Stupid tutoring systems, intelligent humans. *International Journal of Artificial Intelligence in Education, 26*(2), 600–614.

Baker, R. S., Corbett, A. T., & Koedinger, K. R. (2004a). Detecting student misuse of intelligent tutoring systems. In *Proceedings of the International conference on intelligent tutoring systems* (pp. 531–540). Springer, Berlin, Heidelberg.

Baker, R. S., Corbett, A. T., Koedinger, K. R., & Wagner, A. Z. (2004b). Off-Task Behavior in the Cognitive Tutor Classroom: When Students "Game the System". *In Proceedings of ACM CHI 2004: Computer-Human interaction,* 383–390.

Barab, S. A., Scott, B., Siyahhan, S., Goldstone, R., Ingram-Goble, A., Zuiker, S. J., & Warren, S. (2009). Transformational play as a curricular scaffold: Using videogames to support science education. *Journal of Science Education and Technology, 18*(4), 305.

Beck, J. E., & Mostow, J. (2008, June). How who should practice: Using learning decomposition to evaluate the efficacy of different types of practice for different types of students. In *Proceedings of the international conference on intelligent tutoring systems* (pp. 353–362). Springer, Berlin, Heidelberg.

Bennett, J., & Lanning, S. (2007, August). The Netflix prize. *Proceedings of KDD CUP and workshop 2007,* San Jose, California, Aug 12, 2007. (p. 35).

Bienkowski, M., Feng, M., & Means, B. (2012). Enhancing teaching and learning through educational data mining and learning analytics: An issue brief. *US department of education, office of educational technology,* 1–57.

Biswas, G., Roscoe, R., Jeong, H., & Sulcer, B. (2009). Promoting self-regulated learning skills in agent-based learning environments. In *Proceedings of the 17th international conference on computers in education* (pp. 67–74).

Bommanapally, V., Subramaniam, M., Chundi, P., & Parakh, A. (2018). Navigation Hints in Serious Games. In *Proceedings of the 4th annual iLRN conference,* Montana.

Bu, J., Tan, S., Chen, C., Wang, C., Wu, H., Zhang, L., & He, X. (2010, October). Music recommendation by unified hypergraph: combining social media information and music content. In *Proceedings of the 18th ACM international conference on multimedia* (pp. 391–400). ACM.

Chen, K. T., & Lei, C. L. (2006, October). Network game design: Hints and implications of player interaction. *Proceedings of 5th ACM SIGCOMM workshop on network and system support for games.* New York: ACM.

Chien, T. C., Chen, Z. H., Ko, H. W., Ku, Y. M., & Chan, T. W. (2015). My-Bookstore: Using information technology to support children's classroom reading and book recommendation. *Journal of Educational Computing Research, 52*(4), 455–474.

Clifton, B. (2012). *Advanced web metrics with google analytics.* Indianapolis, IN: Wiley.

Coll, S., Glassey, O., & Balleys, C. (2011). Building social networks ethics beyond" privacy": a sociological perspective. *International Review of Information Ethics, 16*(12), 47–53.

Craig, S. D., Hu, X., Graesser, A. C., Bargagliotti, A. E., Sterbinsky, A., Cheney, K. R., & Okwumabua, T. (2013). The impact of a technology-based mathematics after-school program using ALEKS on student's knowledge and behaviors. *Computers & Education, 68,* 495–504.

Dalziel, J., Conole, G., Wills, S., Walker, S., Bennett, S., Dobozy, E., & Bower, M. (2016). The Larnaca Declaration on Learning Design. *Journal of Interactive Media in Education, 7,* 1–24.

Di Mitri, D., Schneider, J., Specht, M., & Drachsler, H. (2018). From signals to knowledge: A conceptual model for multimodal learning analytics. *Journal of Computer Assisted Learning, 34*(4), 338–349.

Dietz-Uhler, B., & Hurn, J. E. (2013). Using learning analytics to predict (and improve) student success: A faculty perspective. *Journal of Interactive Online Learning, 12*(1), 17–26.

Domínguez, F., Chiluiza, K., Echeverria, V., & Ochoa, X. (2015, November). Multimodal selfies: Designing a multimodal recording device for students in traditional classrooms. In *Proceedings of the 2015 ACM on international conference on multimodal interaction* (pp. 567–574). ACM.

Drachsler, H., & Kalz, M. (2016). The MOOC and learning analytics innovation cycle (MOLAC): a reflective summary of ongoing research and its challenges. *Journal of Computer Assisted Learning, 32*(3), 281–290. doi:10.1111/jcal.12135

Dziedzic, D. (2016). Dynamic difficulty adjustment systems for various game genres. *Homo Ludens, 9*(1), 35–51.

Ertmer, P. A., & Simons, K. D. (2006). Jumping the PBL implementation hurdle: Supporting the efforts of K-12 teachers. *Interdisciplinary Journal of Problem-based learning, 1*(1), 5.

Etheredge, M., Lopes, R., & Bidarra, R. (2013, August). A generic method for classification of player behavior. In *Proceedings of the second workshop on artificial intelligence in the game design process* (pp. 1–7).

Freedman, R., Ali, S. S., & McRoy, S. (2000). What is an intelligent tutoring system. *Intelligence, 11*(3), 15–16.

Gao, H., Tang, J., Hu, X., & Liu, H. (2015, January). Content-Aware Point of Interest Recommendation on Location-Based Social Networks. In *Proceedings of the AAAI conference* (pp. 1721–1727).

Gašević, D., Dawson, S., & Siemens, G. (2015). Let's not forget: Learning analytics are about learning. *TechTrends, 59*(1), 64–71.

Gee, J. P. (2003). What video games have to teach us about learning and literacy. *Computers in Entertainment, 1*(1), 1–4.

Giakoumis, D., Tzovaras, D., Moustakas, K., & Hassapis, G. (2011). Automatic recognition of boredom in video games using novel biosignal moment-based features. *IEEE Transactions on Affective Computing, 2*(3), 119–133.

Gomez-Uribe, C. A., & Hunt, N. (2016). The Netflix recommender system: Algorithms, business value, and innovation. *ACM Transactions on Management Information Systems, 6*(4), 13.

Granic, I., Lobel, A., & Engels, R. C. (2014). The benefits of playing video games. *American Psychologist, 69*(1), 66.

Green, R. A., & Hughes, D. L. (2013). Student outcomes associated with use of asynchronous online discussion forums in gross anatomy teaching. *Anatomical Sciences Education, 6*(2), 101–106.

Hamari, J., Shernoff, D. J., Rowe, E., Coller, B., Asbell-Clarke, J., & Edwards, T. (2016). Challenging games help students learn: An empirical study on engagement, flow and immersion in game-based learning. *Computers in Human Behavior, 54*, 170–179.

Hastings, E. J., Guha, R. K., & Stanley, K. O. (2009, September). Evolving content in the galactic arms race video game. In *Proceedings of the 2009 IEEE symposium on computational intelligence and games* (pp. 241–248). IEEE.

Hrabowski, F. A., Suess, J. J., & Fritz, J. (2011). Assessment and analytics in institutional transformation. *EDUCAUSE Review Online, 46*, 5.

Hunicke, R. (2005). The case for dynamic difficulty adjustment in games. In *Proceedings of the 2005 ACM SIGCHI International Conference on Advances in computer entertainment technology* (pp. 429–433). New York: ACM.

IBM. (2013). IBM and Georgia's largest school system bring personalized learning to life. *News Release.* http://www-03.ibm.com/press/us/en/pressrelease/42759.wss. Retrieved on 10 Jan. 2019.

Jennings-Teats, M., Smith, G., & Wardrip-Fruin, N. (2010, June). Polymorph: dynamic difficulty adjustment through level generation. In *Proceedings of the 2010 workshop on procedural content generation in games* (p. 11). ACM.

Jones, K. M. (2015). *All the data we can get: A contextual study of learning analytics and student privacy.* (Doctoral dissertation). The University of Wisconsin-Madison.

Junco, R., & Clem, C. (2015). Predicting course outcomes with digital textbook usage data. *The Internet and Higher Education, 27*, 54–63.

Juul, J. (2009). Fear of failing? The many meanings of difficulty in video games. *The Video Game Theory Reader, 2*, 237–252.

Kang, S. J., Kim, Y., & Kim, C. H. (2010). Live path: adaptive agent navigation in the interactive virtual world. *The Visual Computer, 26*(6-8), 467–476.

Kardan, A. A., & Ebrahimi, M. (2013). A novel approach to hybrid recommendation systems based on association rules mining for content recommendation in asynchronous discussion groups. *Information Sciences, 219*, 93–110.

Kennedy, H., & Moss, G. (2015). Known or knowing publics? Social media data mining and the question of public agency. *Big Data & Society, 2*(2). doi:2053951715611145

Kerr, D., & Chung, G. K. (2012). Identifying key features of student performance in educational video games and simulations through cluster analysis. *Journal of Educational Data Mining, 4*(1), 144–182.

Khachatryan, G., Romashov, A., Khachatryan, A., Gaudino, S., Khachatryan, J., Guarian, K., & Yufa, N. (2014). Reasoning mind Genie 2: An Intelligent learning system as a vehicle for international transfer of instructional methods in mathematics. *International Journal of Artificial Intelligence in Education, 24*(3), 333–382.

Knight, J. (2010). Distinguishing the learning approaches adopted by undergraduates in their use of online resources. *Active Learning in Higher Education, 11*(1), 67–76.

Köck, M., & Paramythis, A. (2011). Activity sequence modelling and dynamic clustering for personalized e-learning. *User Modeling and User-Adapted Interaction, 21*(1-2), 51–97.

Koedinger, K. R., & Aleven, V. (2007). Exploring the assistance dilemma in experiments with cognitive tutors. *Educational Psychology Review, 19*(3), 239–264.

Koedinger, K. R., Brunskill, E., Baker, R. S., McLaughlin, E. A., & Stamper, J. (2013). New potentials for data-driven intelligent tutoring system development and optimization. *AI Magazine*, *34*(3), 27–41.

Koedinger, K. R., & Corbett, A. (2006). Cognitive tutors: Technology bringing learning sciences to the classroom. In R. K. Sawyer (Ed.), *The Cambridge handbook of the learning sciences* (pp. 61–77). New York: Cambridge University Press.

Koedinger, K. R., McLaughlin, E. A., & Heffernan, N. T. (2010). A quasi-experimental evaluation of an on-line formative assessment and tutoring system. *Journal of Educational Computing Research*, *43*(4), 489–510.

Kompan, M., & Bieliková, M. (2010, September). Content-based news recommendation. In *Proceedings of the 2010 international conference on electronic commerce and web technologies* (pp. 61–72). Springer, Berlin, Heidelberg.

Kulik, J. A., & Fletcher, J. D. (2016). Effectiveness of intelligent tutoring systems: a meta-analytic review. *Review of Educational Research*, *86*(1), 42–78.

Land, R., & Bayne, S. (2005). Screen or monitor? Issues of surveillance and disciplinary power in online learning environments. In R. Land & S. Bayne (Eds.), *Education in cyberspace* (pp. 165–178). London: RoutledgeFalmer.

Lane, J. E. (Ed.). (2014). *Building a smarter university: Big data, innovation, and analytics*. New York: SUNY Press.

LaPorte, N. (2019, January 2). How to unlock the codes to all of Netflix's TV and movie categories. Fast Company. Retrieved on 31 January 2019. [www.fastcompany.com/90287199/how-to-unlock-the-codes-to-all-of-netflixs-tv-and-movie-categories]

Lavoué, É., Monterrat, B., Desmarais, M., & George, S. (2018). Adaptive Gamification for Learning Environments. *IEEE Transactions on Learning Technologies*, *12*(1), 16–28.

Ligorio, M. B. (2001). Integrating communication formats: Synchronous versus asynchronous and text-based versus visual. *Computers & Education*, *37*(2), 103–125.

Liñán, L. C., & Pérez, Á. A. J. (2015). Educational Data Mining and Learning Analytics: differences, similarities, and time evolution. *International Journal of Educational Technology in Higher Education*, *12*(3), 98–112.

Liu, M., Kang, J., Liu, S., Zou, W., & Hodson, J. (2017). Learning analytics as an assessment tool in serious games: A review of literature. In M. Ma & A. Oikonomou (Eds.), *Serious games and edutainment applications* (Vol. 2, pp. 537–563). London: Springer.

Liu, Y., Alexandrova, T., & Nakajima, T. (2011, December). Gamifying intelligent environments. In *Proceedings of the 2011 international ACM workshop on ubiquitous meta user interfaces* (pp. 7–12). ACM.

Macfadyen, L. P., & Dawson, S. (2012). Numbers are not enough. Why e-learning analytics failed to inform an institutional strategic plan. *Journal of Educational Technology & Society*, *15*(3), 149–163.

Mangaroska, K., & Giannakos, M. (2017, September). Learning analytics for learning design: Towards evidence-driven decisions to enhance learning. In *Proceedings of the 2017 European conference on technology enhanced learning* (pp. 428–433). Springer, Cham.

Mathan, S. A., & Koedinger, K. R. (2005). Fostering the intelligent novice: Learning from errors with metacognitive tutoring. *Educational Psychologist*, *40*(4), 257–265.

McGonigal, J. (2011). *Reality is broken: Why games make us better and how they change the world*. New York: Penguin.

McNamara, D. S., Levinstein, I. B., & Boonthum, C. (2004). iSTART: Interactive strategy training for active reading and thinking. *Behavior Research Methods, Instruments, & Computers*, *36*(2), 222–233.

Missura, O., & Gärtner, T. (2009, October). Player modeling for intelligent difficulty adjustment. In *Proceedings of the international conference on discovery science* (pp. 197–211). Springer, Berlin, Heidelberg.

Mitrovic, A., & Ohlsson, S. (1999). Evaluation of a constraint-based tutor for a database language. *International Journal of Artificial Intelligence in Education*, *10*, 238–256.

Moos, D. C., & Azevedo, R. (2009). Learning with computer-based learning environments: A literature review of computer self-efficacy. *Review of Educational Research*, *79*(2), 576–600.

Mor, Y., Ferguson, R., & Wasson, B. (2015). Learning design, teacher inquiry into student learning and learning analytics: A call for action. *British Journal of Educational Technology*, *46*(2), 221–229.

Mukala, P., Buijs, J. C. A. M., & Van Der Aalst, W. M. P. (2015). Exploring students' learning behaviour in moocs using process mining techniques. In *Department of mathematics and computer science, university of technology, eindhoven, The Netherlands*. (BPM reports; Vol. 1510). BPMcenter.org. (pp. 179–196).

Muldner, K., Burleson, W., Van de Sande, B., & VanLehn, K. (2010, June). An analysis of gaming behaviors in an intelligent tutoring system. In *Proceedings of the 2010 international conference on intelligent tutoring systems* (pp. 184–193). Springer, Berlin, Heidelberg.

Nguyen, Q., Huptych, M., & Rienties, B. (2018). Using temporal analytics to detect inconsistencies between learning design and student behaviours. *Journal of Learning Analytics*, *5*(3), 120–135.

Nietfeld, J., Hoffmann, K., McQuiggan, S., & Lester, J. (2008, June). Self-regulated learning in a narrative centered learning environment. In *Proceedings of the 2008 EdMedia+ Innovate learning conference* (pp. 5322–5327). Association for the Advancement of Computing in Education (AACE).

Norris, D., Baer, L., Leonard, J., Pugliese, L., & Lefrere, P. (2008). Action analytics: Measuring and improving performance that matters in higher education. *EDUCAUSE Review, 43*(1), 42.

Pariser, E. (2011). *The filter bubble: How the new personalized web is changing what we read and how we think.* New York: Penguin.

Pedersen, C., Togelius, J., & Yannakakis, G. N. (2010). Modeling player experience for content creation. *IEEE Transactions on Computational Intelligence and AI in Games, 2*(1), 54–67.

Perera, D., Kay, J., Koprinska, I., Yacef, K., & Zaïane, O. R. (2009). Clustering and sequential pattern mining of online collaborative learning data. *IEEE Transactions on Knowledge and Data Engineering, 21*(6), 759–772.

Pistilli, M. D., & Arnold, K. E. (2010). Purdue Signals: Mining real-time academic data to enhance student success. *About Campus, 15*(3), 22–24.

Pool, R. M. (2015). *Evaluation of performance of the petals trial in two" at risk" high school math classes: Measurement of student gains.* (Doctoral dissertation) Capella University.

Quandt, T., & Kröger, S. (Eds.). (2013). *Multiplayer: The social aspects of digital gaming.* London: Routledge.

Rodrigo, M., Baker, R., d'Mello, S., Gonzalez, M., Lagud, M., Lim, S., ... Viehland, N. (2008). Comparing learners' affect while using an intelligent tutoring system and a simulation problem solving game. In B. P. Woolf, E. Aïmeur, R. Nkambou, & S. Lajoie (Eds.), *Proceedings of the ITS 2008 Conference* (pp. 40–49). Heidelberg: Springer.

Rodríguez-Triana, M. J., Prieto, L. P., Vozniuk, A., Boroujeni, M. S., Schwendimann, B. A., Holzer, A., & Gillet, D. (2017). Monitoring, awareness and reflection in blended technology enhanced learning: A systematic review. *International Journal of Technology Enhanced Learning, 9*(2-3), 126–150.

Rubel, A., & Jones, K. M. (2016). Student privacy in learning analytics: An information ethics perspective. *The Information Society, 32*(2), 143–159.

Siemens, G. (2013). Learning analytics: The emergence of a discipline. *American Behavioral Scientist, 57*(10), 1380–1400.

Slade, S., & Prinsloo, P. (2013). Learning analytics: Ethical issues and dilemmas. *American Behavioral Scientist, 57*(10), 1510–1529.

Snow, E. L., Allen, L. K., Jacovina, M. E., & McNamara, D. S. (2015). Does agency matter?: Exploring the impact of controlled behaviors within a game-based environment. *Computers & Education, 82*, 378–392.

Sottilare, R., Graesser, A., Hu, X., & Holden, H. (Eds.). (2013). *Design recommendations for intelligent tutoring systems.* Orlando, FL: U.S. Army Research Laboratory.

Squire, K. (2006). From content to context: Videogames as designed experience. *Educational Researcher, 35*(8), 19–29.

Steinberg, J. (2013, Sept. 13). Your new iPhone can put your identity at risk. *Forbes.* Retrieved on 7 Jan. 2019. [www.forbes.com/sites/josephsteinberg/2013/09/13/your-new-iphone-can-put-your-identity-at-risk/#552bfdf648bd].

Sun, C. T., Wang, D. Y., & Chan, H. L. (2011). How digital scaffolds in games direct problem-solving behaviors. *Computers & Education, 57*(3), 2118–2125.

Tanes, Z., Arnold, K. E., King, A. S., & Remnet, M. A. (2011). Using Signals for appropriate feedback: Perceptions and practices. *Computers & Education, 57*(4), 2414–2422.

Titcomb, J. (2018, Sep. 4). Netflix codes: The secret numbers that unlock thousands of hidden films and TV shows. *The Telegraph.* Retrieved on 21 Jan. 2018. [www.telegraph.co.uk/on-demand/0/netflix-codes-secret-numbers-unlock-1000s-hidden-films-tv-shows/]

Tomai, E. (2012). Towards adaptive quest narrative in shared, persistent virtual worlds. *Presented at the eighth Artificial Intelligence and Interactive Digital Entertainment (AIIDE 2012),* 51–56.

Tomai, E., Salazar, R., & Salinas, D. (2012). A MMORPG Prototype for Investigating Adaptive Quest Narratives and Player Behavior. *Presented at the international conference on the foundations of digital games.* Raleigh: North Carolina.

Tsai, C. W., & Shen, P.-D. (2009). Applying web-enabled self-regulated learning and problem-based learning with initiation to involve low-achieving students in learning. *Computers in Human Behavior, 25*(6), 1189–1194.

Tsai, M.-J., & Tsai, C. C. (2003). Information searching strategies in web-based science learning: The role of Internet self-efficacy. *Innovations in Education and Teaching International, 40*(1), 43–50.

Van Wel, L., & Royakkers, L. (2004). Ethical issues in web data mining. *Ethics and Information Technology, 6*(2), 129–140.

VanLehn, K. (2011). The relative effectiveness of human tutoring, intelligent tutoring systems, and other tutoring systems. *Educational Psychologist, 46*(4), 197–221.

Verbert, K., Manouselis, N., Ochoa, X., Wolpers, M., Drachsler, H., Bosnic, I., & Duval, E. (2012). Context-aware recommender systems for learning: A survey and future challenges. *IEEE Transactions on Learning Technologies, 5*(4), 318–335.

Wallace, R. M., Kupperman, J., Krajcik, J., & Soloway, E. (2000). Science on the web: Students online in a sixthgrade classroom. *The Journal of the Learning Sciences, 9*(1), 75–104.

Wang, F. H. (2008). Content recommendation based on education-contextualized browsing events for Web-based personalized learning. *Journal of Educational Technology & Society, 11*(4), 94–112.

Wang, S., & Kelly, W. (2017). Video-Based big data analytics in cyberlearning. *Journal of Learning Analytics, 4*(2), 36–46.

Wauck, H., & Fu, W. T. (2017, March). A data-driven, multidimensional approach to hint design in video games. In *Proceedings of the 22nd international conference on intelligent user interfaces* (pp. 137–147). ACM.

Xing, W., Guo, R., Petakovic, E., & Goggins, S. (2015). Participation-based student final performance prediction model through interpretable genetic programming: Integrating learning analytics, educational data mining and theory. *Computers in Human Behavior, 47*, 168–181.

Yan, C., & Natkin, S. (2011). Adaptive multiplayer ubiquitous games: design principles and an implementation framework. In Y. Wang (Ed.), *Transdisciplinary advancements in cognitive mechanisms and human information processing* (pp. 177–200). Hershey, PA: IGI Global.

Yannakakis, G. N. (2012, May). Game AI revisited. In *Proceedings of the 9th conference on computing frontiers* (pp. 285–292). ACM.

Yannakakis, G. N., & Togelius, J. (2011). Experience-driven procedural content generation. *IEEE Transactions on Affective Computing, 2*(3), 147–161.

19

MEASURING PROCESSING STRATEGIES
Perspectives for Eye Tracking and fMRI in Multi-method Designs

Leen Catrysse, David Gijbels, and Vincent Donche
UNIVERSITY OF ANTWERP, BELGIUM

Many educational researchers argue that the main aims of educational research are understanding and enhancing the quality of learning and processing (Dinsmore, 2017; Vermunt & Donche, 2017) and researchers are therefore looking for appropriate methods in order to capture students' learning and processing. Until now, empirical research on students' processing strategies in higher education has mostly focused on the use of self-report measures (Dinsmore & Alexander, 2012; Fryer, 2017; Vermunt & Donche, 2017). In early work on students' processing strategies during learning from texts, interviews were used (Marton & Säljö, 1976) and, later on, concurrent think-aloud protocols (Fox, 2009; Pressley & Afflerbach, 1995). Following this early work, self-report questionnaires were used to gain insight into students' general disposition towards processing strategies (Biggs, 1987, 1993; Entwistle & Waterston, 1988; Vermunt, this volume). There has thus been a shift from measuring processing strategies at a task-specific level to measuring students' general disposition towards processing strategies. Researchers in the field agree on the variability of processing strategies over learning tasks, but most empirical research is conducted at a more general level, thus ignoring this variability at the task level (Fryer, 2017; Vermunt & Donche, 2017).

More recently, with the advent of new psychophysiological measures, such as eye-tracking and functional magnetic resonance imaging (fMRI), there is a renewed interest in examining the task-specific processing strategies during a learning task. These online measures can be used during the execution of a learning task and are able to capture both conscious and unconscious processing activities. The advantage of these psychophysiological measures is that subjects cannot consciously manipulate their responses in comparison with self-report measures where this could be happening (Dimoka et al., 2012) and that they can register the micro-processes of learning (e.g., how information is integrated between words and sentences). As will be demonstrated later in this chapter, some micro-measures are more strategic and conscious in nature than other micro-measures. Self-report measures are only able to capture these strategic and conscious processes, while psychophysiological measures can capture both strategic and more automatized processes during learning.

In this chapter, we will give an overview on how eye tracking and fMRI can be used to examine students' processing strategies in relation to learning from verbal material (i.e., words, paragraphs and texts). We will discuss the opportunities of these measures and show what they can and cannot tell us about processing strategies. In addition, the challenges will be discussed of using these psychophysiological measures in relation to processing strategies. In a final step, we will give our view on how this field can move forward and what we can take away from this chapter.

OPPORTUNITIES

Can Eye Movements Shed Light on Processing Strategies and Strategy Use?

In eye movement registration the location of the eye gaze is recorded with short time intervals (e.g., a low-precision eye-tracker with a sampling frequency of 60 Hz collects pictures of the eye gaze every 16.67 milliseconds, and a high-precision eye-tracker with a sampling frequency of 1200 Hz collects pictures of the eye gaze every .83 milliseconds). In a next step, the location of the eye gaze is related to the stimulus a participant is looking at (e.g., a text, a picture, a video, a questionnaire). This technique allows us to investigate to what parts of the learning material a student allocates visual attention and for how long (Holmqvist & Andersson, 2017). Eye movement research has been used extensively to better understand reading processes at the word and sentence level, the text level and the level of multiple documents (Hyönä, Lorch, & Rinck, 2003; Jarodzka & Brand-Gruwel, 2017; Rayner, 2009). Eye movement research focuses on the micro-processes of reading (e.g., how much time is needed to process certain words and from which word a reader starts rereading a sentence). Theorists have emphasized that the text-related processing strategy adopted by a reader/student will have strong effects on micro-processes and on the construction of the mental representation (Hyönä, Lorch, & Kaakinen, 2002; Kintsch, 1998; Kintsch & van Dijk, 1978). Focusing on text learning, first pass and second pass reading times are often used as eye movement duration measures (Hyönä et al., 2003; Jarodzka & Brand-Gruwel, 2017). First pass reading time refers to the summed duration of all the fixations on the target region (e.g., a sentence) before exiting it. Second pass reading time refers to the duration of all regressions back to the target region (e.g., a sentence) after the first pass reading time has been terminated (Hyönä et al., 2003). First pass reading times are an indication of early processing and object recognition (Hyönä et al., 2003). Second pass reading times or rereading times reflect processes happening later in comprehension (Holmqvist & Andersson, 2017), such as high-level or deeper cognitive processing (Ariasi & Mason, 2011; Holmqvist & Andersson, 2017; Penttinen, Anto, & Mikkilä-Erdmann, 2013) and attempts to reinstate text information into working memory in order to elaborate on it or rehearse it (Hyönä & Lorch, 2004). Second pass reading times are thus more strategic in nature than first pass reading times.

Different student characteristics shape how students build up their mental representations during text learning (Alexander & Jetton, 1996; Fox, 2009; Jarodzka & Brand-Gruwel, 2017). Influential models on deep and surface processing strategies and strategy use stress the importance of the interplay between learner characteristics and the nature of that processing or strategy use (Alexander, 1997; Dinsmore & Hattan, this volume; Richardson, 2015; Vermunt & Donche, 2017). Important learner characteristics that affect the nature of processing during learning are the students' general disposition towards strategy use, interest, motivation, prior knowledge, working memory capacity, personality, regulation and emotions (Baeten, Kyndt, Struyven, & Dochy, 2010; Vermunt, 2005; Vermunt & Donche, 2017). Students' general disposition towards deep and surface processing strategies can have an important influence on how they learn from texts (Kirby, Cain, & White, 2012), especially on what they perceive to be relevant or important in the text (Kendeou & Trevors, 2012). The study of Catrysse et al. (2018) combined general self-report questionnaires on deep and surface processing strategies with eye tracking data of reading one expository text. They showed that students with a general disposition towards combining deep and surface processing strategies, as measured with self-report questionnaires before reading the text, reread the text more thoroughly than students who were lacking in the use processing strategies, as reflected in longer second pass fixation durations. We believe this reflects the uni-dimensional effect of the students' general disposition towards processing strategies on their actual processing during learning from a text. However, the study of Catrysse, Gijbels, and Donche (2018) provided evidence for the multidimensional nature of strategy use during text learning. In this study, general self-report questionnaires on deep and surface processing strategies, task-specific cued retrospective think-alouds and eye tracking were combined. They showed that highly interested students, who use deep processing strategies (both as measured with a general self-report questionnaires and cued retrospective think-alouds), reread key sentences in a text for longer than detailed sentences and thus process these key sentences more deeply. The study did not take students' learning outcomes into account, so it is unclear whether processing these key sentences more thoroughly was related to better reading comprehension. This study emphasizes the importance of the interplay between processing strategies and other learner characteristics in order to fully understand the micro-processes of learning. In addition, it shows that the selectivity in processing information in the text is the result of a more complex interplay between different learner characteristics and is not solely determined by processing strategies. Although this was already assumed in theoretical frameworks and empirical research focusing on learning outcomes (Alexander & Jetton, 1996; Schiefele, 1996, 1999, 2012; Schiefele & Krapp, 1996), eye movement registration now allows us to show these effects during the online learning and reading process.

Early work on eye movements and vision showed the important influence of the learning task on participants' eye movements (Yarbus, 1967). Also, reading and learning from a text may occur with diverse tasks in mind, such as reading in order to give a presentation, reading in order to answer closed-ended questions, reading in order to answer open-ended questions, reading for entertainment, reading in order to find relevant information, etc. (Kaakinen & Hyönä, 2005, 2007; Kaakinen, Hyönä, & Keenan, 2002; Yeari, Oudega, & van Den Broek, 2016; Yeari, van Den Broek, & Oudega, 2015). In addition, researchers examining students' processing strategies agree that one of the most salient contextual variables influencing processing strategies is the assessment method. This is also known as the backwash-effect of assessment (Baeten et al., 2010; Gielen, Dochy, & Dierick, 2003; Segers, Nijhuis, & Gijselaers, 2006). The study of Catrysse et al. (2016) showed that the assessment demands influence how the students process different types of information in the text. More specifically, students who were expecting reproduction-oriented questions processed the details more thoroughly and repeated these details more often. However, students in the deep condition did not look longer at essentials in the text, but this can be explained by the fact that incorporating key information in the mental representation can be achieved mentally, or can result in overt behavior in which students actively reread essential parts (Hyönä et al., 2003; Kaakinen & Hyönä, 2008). Other research showed that key information or central ideas in the text are learned regardless of strategy use and are necessary for building a mental representation of the text (Lonka, Lindblom-Ylänne, & Maury, 1994; van Dijk & Kintsch, 1983). In other eye-tracking studies on students' processing strategies, all students received the same instruction for learning the text, namely, they needed to learn the text in order to answer questions on the content afterwards. It was not further specified which type of questions students could expect (Catrysse et al., 2018). Therefore, it may come as no surprise that students processed details and key sentences in a similar way in order to prepare for all kinds of questions. In another study, all students received the instruction to study the text material like they would do when preparing for exams. Again, it was no surprise that students using different processing strategies were not selective in processing key sentences and details, as the learning task was quite general (Catrysse et al., 2018).

Is fMRI a Bridge Too Far?

With regard to brain imaging methods, there has been an explosion in neuro-educational research since the beginning of the 21st century (Huettel, Song, & McCarthy, 2014). Brain imaging methods are used to localize deep and surface processing strategies in the brain, more specifically, to examine which brain regions are activated during deep and surface processing strategies (Galli, 2014). In 1997, Bruer published a paper in which he claimed that neuroscience was a bridge too far for educational research (Bruer, 1997), meaning that we cannot draw implications for educational practice directly from neuroscientific research. However, together with other researchers, he believed that a two-way path is possible in which education can be linked to cognitive science in fields such as educational and cognitive psychology, and cognitive science can be linked to neuroscience (Bruer, 1997; Mason, 2009; Mayer, 1998). And as student learning takes place in the brain, neuroscience is a relevant research area to examine further (Mayer, 1998). In the educational psychology literature, researchers have emphasized that we should not see deep and surface processing strategies as a pure dichotomy, but rather as being at the ends of a continuum (Dinsmore & Alexander, 2016; Lonka, Olkinuora, & Mäkinen, 2004). Most of the time students combine several processing strategies while learning, and, consequently, how students learn cannot by characterized by one single processing strategy (Donche & Van Petegem, 2009; Vanthournout, Coertjens, Gijbels, Donche, & Van Petegem, 2013). Previous eye movement studies in the field have also provided evidence for the fact that deep and surface processing strategies are often combined when learning (Catrysse et al., 2016, 2018; Catrysse et al., 2018). Neuroscientific research can provide more insight into whether differences between deep and surface processing strategies are qualitative (i.e., activations in different brain regions) or quantitative (i.e., overlapping brain regions but with differences in the level of activation) in nature (Galli, 2014). More specifically, it has the opportunity to indicate whether deep and surface processing strategies are overlapping constructs or not (Catrysse, Gijbels, & Donche, 2019).

In accordance with what other researchers have mentioned as being challenges for neuroscientific research (Mason, 2009; Mayer, 1998; Varma, McCandliss, & Schwartz, 2008; Willems, 2015), processing strategies have mostly been examined using very basic learning tasks at the word level (Catrysse et al., 2019; Galli, 2014). Subjects receive deep-level and surface-level learning tasks in order to evaluate words when they are being scanned. An example of deep-level tasks is the animacy judgement task in which subjects need to decide whether a word is a living or non-living object. The case judgement task is an example of a surface-level task where subjects need to decide whether a word is printed in uppercase or lowercase (Galli, 2014). The levels-of-processing effect was mostly examined at the word level and we suggest two possible explanations for this. Firstly, the practical constraints of the MRI scanner result in the use of very basic learning tasks. Secondly, Craik and Lockhart's (1972) levels-of-processing framework was extensively investigated in experimental research at the word level on memory (Gallo, Meadow, Johnson, & Foster, 2008; Sporer, 1991; Weinstein, Bugg, & Roediger, 2008). In addition, this line of experimental research provided clear and convergent outcomes; namely, that deep processing strategies lead to better recall performance than surface processing strategies (Richardson, 2015). These robust findings at the behavioral level serve as a good start to setting up neuroscientific research, because clear hypotheses can be tested (Mayer, 1998). We can conclude that fMRI research is no bridge too far when it is used to gain more insight into processing strategies at the word level. However, we want to emphasize that a great variety of encoding tasks is used in this line of research, making it hard to compare studies (Catrysse et al., 2019). The review of Galli (2014) indicated that it is hard to precisely distinguish between deep and surface encoding tasks. Galli (2014) suggested that this is one of the main reasons why neuroscientific research is offering mixed evidence on whether the distinction between deep and surface processing strategies is qualitative or quantitative in nature.

CHALLENGES

As described in the above section, first and second pass reading times are often used as measures in eye movement research but can be an indication of different cognitive processes (Ariasi & Mason, 2011; Holmqvist et al., 2011; Hyönä et al., 2003). With regard to fMRI research, the brain is a busy place with all regions working at the same time (Varma et al., 2008). For both types of psychophysiological measures (eye tracking and fMRI), it is thus not so straightforward to interpret these micro-measures of learning. Therefore, a first challenge that is discussed is the interpretation of these micro-measures. Another point of consideration when using psychophysiological measures is taking the lab setting into account, by which one is limited in using a great variety of learning tasks. The ecological validity of learning tasks is discussed as a second challenge. A last challenge that is described is how to handle the more complex datasets resulting from using psychophysiological measures.

Interpretation of Micro-measures

Eye movement registrations and brain imaging methods are able to capture unconscious processing activities that a student would not be able to report on. Therefore, it is hard for subjects to consciously manipulate their responses (Dimoka et al., 2012). As a consequence, the micro-measures are often described as a more objective measure of processing activities. However, we believe that one of the main challenges in eye movement and brain imaging research is to interpret these micro-measures of processing and we therefore argue that these measures are often not as objective as they are described. For example, eye tracking studies have shown that second pass reading times can be an indication of different cognitive processes, such as comprehension monitoring, deeper processing, difficulty with text passages, multiple use of processing strategies, deeper processing in combination with interest, among others (Ariasi, Hyönä, Kaakinen, & Mason, 2017; Catrysse et al., 2018, Catrysse, Gijbels, Donche et al., 2018; Hyönä & Lorch, 2004; Hyönä et al., 2002, 2003). With regard to brain imaging methods, a point of consideration is that the brain is a busy place, with all regions working at all times. To obtain task-relevant signals, participants need to perform the task of interest and the control task during many trials (Varma et al., 2008). Often cognitive subtraction is than used in which the experimental task is compared with the control task to infer which brain regions are specialized for a particular cognitive component (Ward, 2010). In addition, the collection of behavioral data is a necessary step in most brain imaging studies (De Smedt, 2014; Ward, 2010). In memory research, the subsequent memory paradigm is often used (Cabeza & Nyberg, 2000), in which participants are presented with items that they need to remember and the brain imaging data is later analyzed as a function of whether the items were remembered or forgotten during a memory test (Gazzaniga, Ivry, & Mangun, 2014). Whether a word or word pair will be remembered or not not only depends on the processing strategies that were used but also on the way the memory is probed (Craik & Lockhart, 1972; Galli, 2014; Tulving & Thompson, 1973). In addition, when processing strategies are examined at the text level, recall measures have a stronger relationship with surface processing, such as memorizing the text, than with deep processing, such as trying to understand the underlying meaning of the text (Dinsmore & Alexander, 2012).

Multi-method designs are therefore a crucial step to further interpret these micro-measures (van Gog & Jarodzka, 2013; Veenman, 2005). In eye movement research, self-report measures are often used to further interpret the longer fixation durations (Catrysse et al., 2018; van Gog & Jarodzka, 2013). In fMRI research, memory tests are mostly used in order to distinguish between successful and unsuccessful processing and learning (Cabeza & Nyberg, 2000). These psychophysiological measures cannot be used as stand-alone measures, and one should be careful with the interpretation of longer fixation durations or higher activity in certain brain areas as it can be related to different cognitive processes.

Ecological Validity of Learning Tasks

A consequence of using eye movement and brain imaging methods is that this research is almost always conducted in a lab setting. With regard to eye movement research, screen-based eye-trackers or eye-tracking glasses can be used. A limitation of using eye movements with a screen-based eye tracker (i.e., the eye tracking equipment is integrated into the computer screen) to examine students' processing strategies, is that one is only able to investigate students' mental or covert processing strategies. Overt processing strategies produce physical records, such as text notes, summaries, mind maps, while covert strategies do not produce this kind of record and refer to internal mental learning processes (Kardash & Amlund, 1991; Merchie & Van Keer, 2014). Eye movement glasses are worn as normal glasses and, thus, allow the students to freely inspect and interact with all kinds of learning materials. However, there is a downside on using eye movement glasses because the data is more complex to analyze than with screen-based eye trackers, and the eye movement glasses have a lower sampling frequency than screen-based eye trackers (Holmqvist & Andersson, 2017). The computer overlays the gaze data onto the scene video and shows with a marker where the participant is looking. Even if there is a data file, the coordinates of the data refer to the positions in the video and not to positions in the text. Each dataset for each participant will thus be different, which makes it less straightforward to analyze the data afterwards (Holmqvist & Andersson, 2017). Another important aspect of eye movement research is the eye tracker calibration. During the calibration procedure, a dot is moving on the screen and the participant needs to follow the dot with his/her eyes. After this procedure, it can be verified whether the eye gaze can be recorded on different points on the screen. It is important that the eye-tracker be calibrated before and during longer reading processes in order to assure good data quality (Holmqvist et al., 2011). As a consequence, either shorter learning tasks are used or longer learning tasks are used but need to be interrupted for a calibration procedure. Therefore, questions can be raised on the ecological validity of the learning tasks used in eye movement research.

Concerning brain imaging methods, even greater issues arise with regard to the ecological validity of learning tasks. A typical characteristic of fMRI research is the highly controlled environment (Varma et al., 2008). The magnetic resonance imaging (MRI) scanner is a very noisy environment in which subjects have to lie still and are not allowed to move (De Smedt, 2014; Huettel et al., 2014). During an experiment, participants see stimuli projected on a small hanging mirror and are mostly asked to respond by pressing buttons (Varma et al., 2008). These practical constraints result in the use of restricted paradigms in which very elementary tasks, such as learning words, are used (De Smedt, 2014; Howard-Jones, Ott, van Leeuwen, & De Smedt, 2014; Willems, 2015). Thus, fMRI research is limited on what it can tell us about the contextual aspects that are crucial for learning (Varma et al., 2008). Some studies have already moved into studying differences in reading strategies at the text level (Moss & Schunn, 2015; Moss, Schunn, Schneider, & McNamara, 2013; Moss, Schunn, Schneider, McNamara, & Vanlehn, 2011). However, in our opinion fMRI may be a bridge too far at the moment to examine differences in processing strategies at the text level. We believe this first because, in the studies of Moss and colleagues, participants were not able to look back at the short paragraphs (Moss & Schunn, 2015; Moss et al., 2011, 2013). Short paragraphs of two to four sentences were presented only at one point in time. However, there is a vast tradition of eye movement research that shows that look back behavior is a crucial aspect for strategic and deeper cognitive processing when processing words, sentences and texts (Ariasi et al., 2017; Holmqvist et al., 2011; Jarodzka & Brand-Gruwel, 2017; Penttinen et al., 2013; Rayner, 2009). Especially in text comprehension, it is not only crucial to look back within words or sentences but also within and between paragraphs (Hyönä et al., 2003; Jarodzka & Brand-Gruwel, 2017). However, this is not (yet) possible in fMRI research. A second reason why we believe it is a bridge too far, is that we first need to gain more insight into how processing strategies are reflected in behavioral measures before we move to neuroscientific research. Processing strategies were mostly measured with self-report questionnaires at a more general level by which the learning task was often neglected (Dinsmore & Alexander, 2012; Fryer, 2017; Vermunt & Donche, 2017). It is only more recently that think-aloud protocols (Dinsmore & Alexander, 2016; Dinsmore & Zoellner, 2018) and eye movement registration have been used to investigate differences in processing strategies during text learning (Catrysse et al., 2016, 2018; Catrysse et al., 2018). We agree with the suggestion of Varma et al. (2008) that, in order to move beyond the practical constraints of the MRI scanner, more contextual rich learning tasks could be given outside the scanner. However, in our opinion, fMRI will become an online outcome measure and not an online learning process measure. If students get more complex tasks outside the scanner and are then scanned during memory tests as suggested by Varma et al. (2008), it is not a pure online measure that captures learning during the learning process.

Analysis of Complex Data

A characteristic of psychophysiological measures, such as eye movement registration and brain imaging, is that these techniques sample information with a high temporal precision (Holmqvist & Andersson, 2017; Huettel et al., 2014). This results in huge datasets per subject in comparison with the more traditional methods used in educational sciences. This calls for using other analytical techniques in order to take the complexity of the data into account. With regard to analyzing the eye movement data on learning from a text, we want to emphasize the strengths of applying mixed effects models. Although this analytical technique was described in good practices by different researchers in 2008 (Baayen, 2008; Baayen, Davidson, & Bates, 2008; Quené & van Den Bergh, 2008), it is only very recently that eye tracking researchers have adapted this analysis technique to examine eye movement data on reading/learning from texts (Ariasi et al., 2017; Catrysse et al., 2018; Catrysse et al., 2018). Mixed effects models offer several advantages in comparison with other techniques, such as repeated measures ANOVA (Baayen, 2008; Baayen et al., 2008; Quené & van Den Bergh, 2008). A first advantage is that mixed effects models offer more statistical power by conducting analysis on the sentence level instead of on the subject level. Furthermore, mixed effects models have a lower risk of capitalization on chance, i.e., type I error (Quené & van Den Bergh, 2008). Other advantages of mixed effects models include, among others, better methods for treating continuous responses and better methods for modeling heteroscedasticity and non-spherical error variance. In addition, by treating subjects, sentences and texts (if applicable) as crossed items, results can be jointly generalized over similar subjects, sentences and texts (Baayen, 2008; Quené & van Den Bergh, 2008). Subjects, sentences and texts are sampled from a larger population and it is thus important to take this into account in the analysis. Thus, we highly recommend applying mixed effects models for the analysis of eye movement data.

DISCUSSION AND PATHS FOR FUTURE RESEARCH

Eye movements, and more specifically second pass fixation durations, reflect partly what students report on their processing strategies. Deeper cognitive processing, as referred to in eye movement research (Ariasi & Mason, 2011; Holmqvist & Andersson, 2017; Penttinen et al., 2013), is not the same as deep processing, as defined by theoretical models on students' processing strategies (Dinsmore, 2017; Vermunt & Donche, 2017). Deep processing, as defined in theoretical models on processing strategies, refers to the intention to understand what the author wants to say in the text, to engage in meaningful learning, to relate the content of the text to a wider context and prior knowledge, and to focus on the main themes and key information in the text (Dinsmore, 2017; Vermunt & Donche, 2017). The study of Catrysse et al. (2016) showed that when students received reproduction-oriented questions that they processed details in the text more thoroughly than students who received questions aimed at deeper processing. This study showed that longer second pass fixation durations can also be related to surface processing strategies and, thus, do not always reflect the deep processing strategies as referred to in theoretical models on processing strategies. Other research provided evidence that longer second pass fixation durations do not solely reflect deep processing strategies. Longer second pass fixation durations are an indication of the multiple use of processing strategies, namely, combining both surface and deep processing strategies (Catrysse et al., 2018), and can be a reflection of deeper processing strategies only in combination with a high topic interest for key sentences (Catrysse et al., 2018). These findings are shown in Figure 19.1 and propose a framework for future research with psychophysiological measures. The most central circle represents the focus of attention. The second dotted circle represents task-specific learner and contextual characteristics, such as students' interest for a learning task, their processing strategies used during a learning task and the assessment demands for a learning task, among others. The interplay of these characteristics affects the focus of attention as measured with eye tracking. The outer circle represents more general learner and contextual characteristics such as the general disposition towards processing strategies. Both circles interact with each other and affect the focus of attention. Therefore, the inner circles are represented with dotted lines, because all these characteristics interact and may affect the focus of attention. The findings described in this chapter call for two important and related actions for future research: (1) students' processing strategies is a complex and multidimensional construct and should be measured in that way, and (2) psychophysiological measures need to be applied in multi-method designs. Figure 19.1 can thus be compared with a bull's eye. In order to measure students' processing strategies more accurately, the complexity and multidimensionality of processing strategies need to be taken into account for multi-method designs. We further elaborate on these two points below.

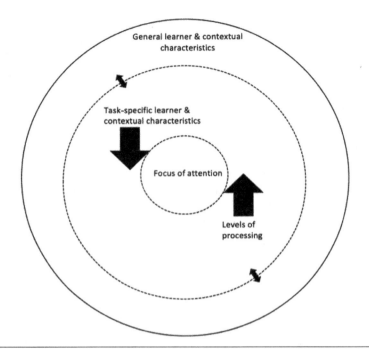

Figure 19.1 Eye Movements and Students' Processing Strategies

Based on the research discussed in this chapter, we want to stress the importance of adapting multi-method designs in order to grasp the full complexity of students' processing strategies and to avoid relying on one single method or instrument. Processing strategies and many learning processes are complex and multidimensional in nature (Alexander, 2017) and, therefore, it is impossible to capture all aspects of processing strategies with one single method. More specifically, research discussed in this chapter demonstrated the added value of applying multi-method designs in order to interpret data from psychophysiological measures. We thus want to stress the importance of combining these measures in order to understand the underlying reasons for processing behavior. By combining different methods, the power of each method is taken to obtain a comprehensive picture and deep insight into students' processing strategies (Schellings, 2011; Schellings & van Hout-Wolters, 2011). We hereby also want to emphasize that no instrument has a greater value than another; however, it is the combination of methods that results in the greatest strength.

Self-report measures such as verbal reports are mostly used in combination with eye movement data (van Gog & Jarodzka, 2013). In the discussed research, the multiple use and the nature of processing strategies was added as a predictor for explaining differences in eye movements. This research showed that both general self-report questionnaires and cued retrospective think-aloud protocols allowed an explanation of the differences in students' eye movements and their learning process. Moreover, a recent review of Dinsmore (2017) indicated that how well a strategy is used and how appropriate the chosen strategy is, are better predictors of learning outcomes than the measures that are mostly used. It would be interesting for future research to see how these aspects of students' processing strategies can explain the differences in eye movements and to verify whether these better predictors for learning outcomes are also good predictors to explain differences in the micro-processes of learning.

In eye movement studies, mostly first pass and second pass duration measures are used to analyze eye movement data (Ariasi et al., 2017; Catrysse et al., 2018; Hyönä et al., 2003; Kaakinen & Hyönä, 2007; Yeari et al., 2016). However, we are convinced that measures other than duration measures would be interesting to examine as well. As indicated in the work of Holmqvist and Andersson (2017), common analyses for reading texts and textbooks are the distribution of fixation times in areas of interest, sequence orders of areas of interest and transitions between areas of interest. Former self-report research has shown that deep processing not only refers to deeper processing of the key information in a text but also to integrating information across the text (Dinsmore & Alexander, 2016; Fox, 2009; Pressley & Afflerbach, 1995). Therefore, analyzing transition matrices would be a promising avenue to further investigate the relation between processing strategies and eye movements. Transitions are movements between areas of interest and are counted for pairs of areas of interest (Holmqvist & Andersson, 2017), for instance the number of transitions from a key sentence to another sentence. Whether key sentences are used as anchor points to process the rest of the text or not could be analyzed. This kind of analysis could clarify whether typically deep processors use key sentences as anchor points and whether, typically, surface processors use detailed sentences as anchor points in order to build up their mental representation of the text. Therefore, we suggest that future research should look further into this kind of analysis as well and go beyond solely analyzing eye movement duration measures.

For future research it would be interesting to further explore the multidimensional nature of students' processing strategies. As shown in Figure 19.1, levels of processing interact with task-specific learner and contextual characteristics. Students' processing strategies are measured in a more dynamic way with psychophysiological measures, but the other learner characteristics, such as for example interest, are up to now mostly measured in a rather static way (Catrysse et al., 2018). Constructs such as students' interest, however, are in fact clearly dynamic in nature and are expected to fluctuate during the learning process (D'Mello, Lehman, Pekrun, & Graesser, 2014). It is assumed that this dynamic response of the reader has an impact on how attentional resources are allocated during reading (Kaakinen, Ballenghein, Tissier, & Baccino, 2018; Kaakinen & Hyönä, 2014). Future research could further explore how task-specific learner characteristics, measured in a dynamic way with psychophysiological measures, interact with processing strategies while reading and/or learning. By doing so, research can shed light on the multidimensional and dynamic nature of processing strategies and its influencing characteristics.

REFERENCES

Alexander, P. A. (1997). Mapping the multidimensional nature of domain learning: The interplay of cognitive, motivational, and strategic forces. In M. L. Maehr & P. R. Pintrich (Eds.), *Advances in motivation and achievement* (pp. 213–250). Greenwich, CT: JAI Press.

Alexander, P. A. (2017). Issues of constructs, contexts, and continuity: Commentary on learning in higher education. *Educational Psychology Review, 29*, 345–351. doi:10.1007/s10648-017-9409-3

Alexander, P. A., & Jetton, T. L. (1996). The role of importance and interest in the processing of text. *Educational Psychology Review, 8*(1), 89–121. doi:10.1007/BF01761832

Ariasi, N., Hyönä, J., Kaakinen, J. K., & Mason, L. (2017). An eye-movement analysis of the refutation effect in reading science text. *Journal of Computer Assisted Learning.* doi:10.1111/jcal.12151

Ariasi, N., & Mason, L. (2011). Uncovering the effect of text structure in learning from a science text: An eye-tracking study. *Instructional Science, 39*(5), 581–601. doi:10.1007/s11251-010-9142-5

Baayen, R. H. (2008). *Analyzing linguistic data: A practical introduction to statistics using R.* Cambridge, UK: Cambridge University Press.

Baayen, R. H., Davidson, D. J., & Bates, D. M. (2008). Mixed-effects modeling with crossed random effects for subjects and items. *Journal of Memory and Language, 59*(4), 390–412. doi:10.1016/j.jml.2007.12.005

Baeten, M., Kyndt, E., Struyven, K., & Dochy, F. (2010). Using student-centred learning environments to stimulate deep approaches to learning: Factors encouraging or discouraging their effectiveness. *Educational Research Review, 5*(3), 243–260. doi:10.1016/J.Edurev.2010.06.001

Biggs, J. (1987). *Student approaches to learning and studying. Research monograph.* Melbourne: Australian Council for Educational Research.

Biggs, J. (1993). What do inventories of students' learning processes really measure? A theoretical review and clarification. *British Journal of Educational Psychology, 63*(1), 3–19. doi:10.1111/j.2044-8279.1993.tb01038.x

Bruer, J. T. (1997). Education and the brain: A bridge too far. *Educational Researcher, 26*(8), 4–16. doi:10.3102/0013189X026008004

Cabeza, R., & Nyberg, L. (2000). Imaging cognition II: An empirical review of 275 PET and fMRI studies. *Journal of Cognitive Neuroscience, 12*(1), 1–47. doi:10.1162/08989290051137585

Catrysse, L., Gijbels, D., & Donche, V. (2019). A systematic review on the conceptualization and operationalization of students' levels of processing in fMRI studies. *Mind, Brain, and Education.* doi:10.1111/mbe.12199

Catrysse, L., Gijbels, D., & Donche, V. (2018). It is not only about the depth of processing: what if eye am not interested in the text?. *Learning and Instruction,* (58), 284–294. doi:10.1016/j.learninstruc.2018.07.009

Catrysse, L., Gijbels, D., Donche, V., De Maeyer, S., Lesterhuis, M., & Van Den Bossche, P. (2018). How are learning strategies reflected in the eyes? Combining results from self-reports and eye-tracking. *British Journal of Educational Psychology, 88*(1), 118–137. doi:10.1111/bjep.12181

Catrysse, L., Gijbels, D., Donche, V., De Maeyer, S., Van Den Bossche, P., & Gommers, L. (2016). Mapping processing strategies in learning from expository text: An exploratory eye tracking study followed by a cued recall. *Frontline Learning Research, 4*(1), 1–16. doi:10.14786/flr.v4i1.192

Craik, F. I. M., & Lockhart, R. S. (1972). Levels of processing: A framework for memory research. *Journal of verbal learning and verbal behavior, 11*, 671–684. doi:10.1016/S0022-5371(72)80001-X

D'Mello, S., Lehman, B., Pekrun, R., & Graesser, A. (2014). Confusion can be beneficial for learning. *Learning and Instruction, 29*, 153–170.

De Smedt, B. (2014). Advances in the use of neuroscience methods in research on learning and instruction. *Frontline Learning Research, 6*, 7–14. doi:10.14786/flr.v2i4.115

Dimoka, A., Banker, R. D., Benbasat, I., Davis, F. D., Dennis, A. R., Gefen, D., … Weber, B. (2012). On the use of neurophysiological tools in IS research: Developing a research agenda for neuroIS. *Mis Quarterly, 36*(3), 679–702.

Dinsmore, D. L., & Hattan, C. (this volume). Levels of strategies and strategic processing. In D. L. Dinsmore, L. K. Fryer, & M. M. Parkinson (Eds.), *Handbook of strategies and strategic processing: Conceptualization, measurement, and analysis.* New York: Routledge.

Dinsmore, D. L. (2017). Toward a dynamic, multidimensional research framework for strategic processing. *Educational Psychology Review.* doi:10.1007/s10648-017-9407-5

Dinsmore, D. L., & Alexander, P. A. (2012). A critical discussion of deep and surface processing: What it means, how it is measured, the role of context, and model specification. *Educational Psychology Review, 24*(4), 499–567. doi:10.1007/s10648-012-9198-7

Dinsmore, D. L., & Alexander, P. A. (2016). A multidimensional investigation of deep-level and surface-level processing. *Journal of Experimental Education, 84*, 213–244. doi:10.1080/00220973.2014.979126

Dinsmore, D. L., & Zoellner, B. P. (2018). The relation between cognitive and metacognitive strategic processing during a science simulation. *British Journal of Educational Psychology, 88*(1), 95–117. doi:10.1111/bjep.12177

Donche, V., & Van Petegem, P. (2009). The development of learning patterns of student teachers: A cross-sectional and longitudinal study. *Higher Education, 57*(4), 463–475. doi:10.1007/s10734-008-9156-y

Entwistle, N., & Waterston, S. (1988). Approaches to studying and levels of processing in university students. *British Journal of Educational Psychology, 58*(3), 258–265. doi:10.1111/j.2044-8279.1988.tb00901.x

Fox, E. (2009). The role of reader characteristics in processing and learning from informational text. *Review of Educational Research, 79*(1), 197–261. doi:10.3102/0034654308324654

Fryer, L. K. (2017). Building bridges: Seeking structure and direction for higher education motivated learning strategy models. *Educational Psychology Review, 29*(2), 325–344. doi:10.1007/s10648-017-9405-7

Galli, G. (2014). What makes deeply encoded items memorable? Insights into the levels of processing framework from neuroimaging and neuromodulation. *Front Psychiatry, 5,* 1–8. doi:10.3389/fpsyt.2014.00061

Gallo, D. A., Meadow, N. G., Johnson, E. L., & Foster, K. T. (2008). Deep levels of processing elicit a distinctiveness heuristic: Evidence from the criterial recollection task. *Journal of Memory and Language, 58*(4), 1095–1111. doi:10.1016/j.jml.2007.12.001

Gazzaniga, M. S., Ivry, R. B., & Mangun, G. R. (2014). *Cognitive neuroscience. The biology of the mind* (4th ed.). New York: W.W. Norton & Company.

Gielen, S., Dochy, F., & Dierick, S. (2003). Evaluating the consequential validity of new modes of assessment: The influence of assessment on learning, including pre-, post- and true assessment effects. In M. Segers, F. Dochy, & E. Cascallar (Eds.), *Optimising new modes of assessment: In search of qualities and standards* (pp. 37–54). The Netherlands: Kluwer Academic Publishers.

Holmqvist, K., & Andersson, R. (2017). *Eye tracking: A comprehensive guide to methods, paradigms and measures.* Lund, Sweden: Lund Eye-Tracking Research Institute.

Holmqvist, K., Nyström, M., Andersson, R., Dewhurst, R., Jarodzka, H., & van de Weijer, J. (2011). *Eye tracking: A comprehensive guide to methods and measures.* Oxford: Oxford University Press.

Howard-Jones, P. A., Ott, M., van Leeuwen, T., & De Smedt, B. (2014). The potential relevance of cognitive neuroscience for the development and use of technology-enhanced learning. *Learning, Media and Technology, 40*(2), 131–151. doi:10.1080/17439884.2014.919321

Huettel, S. A., Song, A. W., & McCarthy, G. (2014). *Functional magnetic resonance imaging* (3rd ed.). Sunderland, Massachusetts U.S.A: Sinauer Associates, Inc. Publishers.

Hyönä, J., & Lorch, R. F. (2004). Effects of topic headings on text processing: Evidence from adult readers' eye fixation patterns. *Learning and Instruction, 14*(2), 131–152. doi:10.1016/j.learninstruc.2004.01.001

Hyönä, J., Lorch, R. F., & Kaakinen, J. K. (2002). Individual differences in reading to summarize expository text: Evidence from eye fixation patterns. *Journal of Educational Psychology, 94*(1), 44–55. doi:10.1037//0022-0663.94.1.44

Hyönä, J., Lorch, R. F., & Rinck, M. (2003). Eye movement measures to study global text processing. In J. Hyönä, R. Radach, & H. Deubel (Eds.), *The mind's eye: Cognitive and applied aspects of eye movement research* (pp. 313–334). Amsterdam: Elsevier Science.

Jarodzka, H., & Brand-Gruwel, S. (2017). Tracking the reading eye: Towards a model of real-world reading. *Journal of Computer Assisted Learning, 33*(3), 193–201. doi:10.1111/jcal.12189

Kaakinen, J. K., Ballenghein, U., Tissier, G., & Baccino, T. (2018). Fluctuation in cognitive engagement during reading: evidence from concurrent recordings of postural and eye movements. *Journal of Experimental Psychology: Learning, Memory, and Cognition.* doi:10.1037/xlm0000539

Kaakinen, J. K., & Hyönä, J. (2005). Perspective effects on expository text comprehension: Evidence from think-aloud protocols, eyetracking, and recall. *Discourse processes, 40*(3), 239–257. doi:10.1207/s15326950dp4003_4

Kaakinen, J. K., & Hyönä, J. (2007). Perspective effects in repeated reading: An eye movement study. *Memory & Cognition, 35*(6), 1323–1336. doi:10.3758/BF03193604

Kaakinen, J. K., & Hyönä, J. (2008). Perspective-driven text comprehension. *Applied Cognitive Psychology, 22,* 319–334. doi:10.1002/acp.1412

Kaakinen, J. K., & Hyönä, J. (2014). Task relevance induces momentary changes in the functional visual field during reading. *Psychological Science, 25,* 626–632.

Kaakinen, J. K., Hyönä, J., & Keenan, J. M. (2002). Perspective effects on online text processing. *Discourse processes, 33*(2), 159–173. doi:10.1207/S15326950DP3302_03

Kardash, C. M., & Amlund, J. T. (1991). Self-reported learning strategies and learning from expository text. *Contemporary Educational Psychology, 16,* 117–138. doi:10.1016/0361-476X(91)90032-G

Kendeou, P., & Trevors, G. (2012). Quality learning from texts we read. What does it take? In J. R. Kirby & M. J. Lawson (Eds.), *Enhancing the quality of learning. Dispositions, instruction, and learning processes* (pp. 251–314). New York: Cambridge university press.

Kintsch, W. (1998). *Comprehension. A paradigm for cognition.* United Kingdom: Cambridge University Press.

Kintsch, W., & van Dijk, T. A. (1978). Toward a model of text comprehension and production.. *Psychological Review, 85*(5), 363–394. doi:10.1037/0033-295X.85.5.363

Kirby, J. R., Cain, K., & White, B. (2012). Deeper learning in reading comprehension. In J. R. Kirby & M. J. Lawson (Eds.), *Enhancing the quality of learning. Dispositions, instruction, and learning processes* (pp. 315–338). New York: Cambridge University Press.

Lonka, K., Lindblom-Ylänne, S., & Maury, S. (1994). The effect of study strategies on learning from text. *Learning and Instruction, 4*, 253–271. doi:10.1016/0959-4752(94)90026-4

Lonka, K., Olkinuora, E., & Mäkinen, J. (2004). Aspects and prospects of measuring studying and learning in higher education. *Educational Psychology Review, 16*(4), 301–323. doi:10.1007/s10648–004–0002–1

Marton, F., & Säljö, R. (1976). On qualitative differences in learning: I - Outcome and process. *British Journal of Educational Psychology, 46*(1), 4–11. doi:10.1111/j.2044-8279.1976.tb02980.x

Mason, L. (2009). Bridging neuroscience and education: A two-way path is possible. *Cortex, 45*(4), 548–549. doi:10.1016/j.cortex.2008.06.003

Mayer, R. E. (1998). Does the brain have a place in educational psychology. *Educational Psychology Review, 10*(4), 389–396. doi:10.1023/A:1022837300988

Merchie, E., & Van Keer, H. (2014). Using on-line and off-line measures to explore fifth and sixth graders' text-learning strategies and schematizing skills. *Learning and Individual Differences, 32*, 193–203. doi:10.1016/j.lindif.2014.03.012

Moss, J., & Schunn, C. D. (2015). Comprehension through explanation as the interaction of the brain's coherence and cognitive control networks. *Frontiers in Human Neuroscience, 9*, 562. doi:10.3389/fnhum.2015.00562

Moss, J., Schunn, C. D., Schneider, W., & McNamara, D. S. (2013). The nature of mind wandering during reading varies with the cognitive control demands of the reading strategy. *Brain Research, 1539*, 48–60. doi:10.1016/j.brainres.2013.09.047

Moss, J., Schunn, C. D., Schneider, W., McNamara, D. S., & Vanlehn, K. (2011). The neural correlates of strategic reading comprehension: Cognitive control and discourse comprehension. *Neuroimage, 58*(2), 675–686. doi:10.1016/j.neuroimage.2011.06.034

Penttinen, M., Anto, E., & Mikkilä-Erdmann, M. (2013). Conceptual change, text comprehension and eye movements during reading. *Research in Science Education, 43*(4), 1407–1434. doi:10.1007/s11165-012-9313-2

Pressley, M., & Afflerbach, P. (1995). *Verbal protocols of reading: The nature of construcitvely responsive reading*. Hillsdale: Erlbaum.

Quené, H., & van Den Bergh, H. (2008). Examples of mixed-effects modeling with cross random effects and with binomial data. *Journal of Memory and Language, 59*(4), 413–425. doi:10.1016/j.jml.2008.02.002

Rayner, K. (2009). Eye movements and attention in reading, scene perception, and visual search. *Q J Exp Psychol, 62*(8), 1457–1506. doi:10.1080/17470210902816461

Richardson, J. T. E. (2015). Approaches to learning or levels of processing: What did Marton and Säljö (1976a) really say? The legacy of the work of the Göteborg group in the 1970s. *Interchange, 46*, 239–269. doi:10.1007/s10780-015-9251-9

Schellings, G. L. M. (2011). Applying learning strategy questionnaires: problems and possibilities. *Metacognition and Learning, 6*(2), 91–109. doi:10.1007/s11409-011-9069-5

Schellings, G. L. M., & van Hout-Wolters, B. (2011). Measuring strategy use with self-report instruments: Theoretical and empirical considerations. *Metacognition and Learning, 6*, 83–90. doi:10.1007/s11409-011-9081-9

Schiefele, U. (1996). Topic interest, text representation, and quality of experience. *Contemporary Educational Psychology, 21*, 3–18. doi:0361-476X/96

Schiefele, U. (1999). Interest and learning from text. *Scientific Studies of Reading, 3*(3), 257–279. doi:10.1207/s1532799xssr0303_4

Schiefele, U. (2012). Interests and learning. In N. M. Seel (Ed.), *Encyclopedia of the sciences of learning* (pp. 1623–1626). New York: Springer.

Schiefele, U., & Krapp, A. (1996). Topic interest and free recall of expository text. *Learning and Individual Differences, 8*(2), 141–160. doi:10.1016/S1041-6080(96)90030-8

Segers, M., Nijhuis, J., & Gijselaers, W. (2006). Redesigning a learning and assessment environment: The influence on students' perceptions of assessment demands and their learning strategies. *Studies in Educational Evaluation, 32*, 223–242. doi:10.1016/j.stueduc.2006.08.004

Sporer, S. L. (1991). Deep - Deeper - Deepest? Encoding strategies and the recognition of human faces. *Journal of Experimental Psychology: Learning, Memory, and Cognition, 17*(2), 323–333. doi:10.1037/0278-7393.17.2.323

Tulving, E., & Thompson, D. (1973). Encoding specificity and retrieval processes in episodic memory. *Psychological Review, 80*, 352–373. doi:10.1037/h0020071

van Dijk, T. A., & Kintsch, W. (1983). *Strategies for discourse comprehension*. New York: Academic Press.

van Gog, T., & Jarodzka, H. (2013). Eye tracking as a tool to study and enhance cognitive and metacognitve processes in computer-based learning environments. In R. Azevedo & V. Aleven (Eds.), *International handbook of metacognition and learning technologies* (pp. 143–156). New York: Springer.

Vanthournout, G., Coertjens, L., Gijbels, D., Donche, V., & Van Petegem, P. (2013). Assessing students' development in learning approaches according to initial learning profiles: A person-oriented perspective. *Studies in Educational Evaluation, 39*(1), 33–40. doi:10.1016/j.stueduc.2012.08.002

Varma, S., McCandliss, B. D., & Schwartz, D. L. (2008). Scientific and pragmatic challenges for bridging education and neuroscience. *Educational Researcher, 37*(3), 140–152. doi:10.3102/0013189x08317687

Veenman, M. V. J. (2005). The assessment of metacognitive skills: What can be learned from multi-method designs?. In C. Artett & B. Moschner (Eds.), *Lernstrategien und metakognition. Implikationen für forschung und praxis* (pp. 77–99). Münster: Waxmann.

Vermunt, J. D. (this volume). Surveys and retrospective self-reports to measure strategies and strategic processing. In D. L. Dinsmore, L. K. Fryer, & M. M. Parkinson (Eds.), *Handbook of strategies and strategic processing: Conceptualization, measurement, and analysis*. New York: Routledge.

Vermunt, J. D. (2005). Relations between student learning patterns and personal and contextual factors and academic performance. *Higher Education, 49*(3), 205–234. doi:10.1007/S10734-004-6664-2

Vermunt, J. D., & Donche, V. (2017). A learning patterns perspective on student learning in higher education: State of the art and moving forward. *Educational Psychology Review, 29*(2), 269–299. doi:10.1007/s10648-017-9414-6

Ward, J. (2010). *The students' guide to cognitive neuroscience* (2nd ed.). New York: Psychology Press.

Weinstein, Y., Bugg, J. M., & Roediger, H. L. (2008). Can the survival recall advantage be explained by basic memory processes?. *Memory & Cognition, 36*(5), 913–919. doi:10.3758/mc.36.5.913

Willems, R. M. (Ed.). (2015). *Cognitive neuroscience of natural language use*. United Kingdom: Cambridge University Press.

Yarbus, A. L. (1967). *Eye movements and vision*. New York: Plenum.

Yeari, M., Oudega, M., & van Den Broek, P. (2016). The effect of highlighting on processing and memory of central and peripheral text information: Evidence from eye movements. *Journal of Research in Reading.* doi:10.1111/1467-9817.12072

Yeari, M., van Den Broek, P., & Oudega, M. (2015). Processing and memory of central versus peripheral information as a function of reading goals: Evidence from eye-movements. *Reading and writing, 28*, 1071–1097. doi:10.1007/s11145-015-9561-4

20

COMMENTARY

Measuring Strategic Processing in Concert: Reflections and Future Directions

David Gijbels

UNIVERSITY OF ANTWERP, BELGIUM

Sofie Loyens

UNIVERSITY COLLEGE ROOSEVELT, UTRECHT UNIVERSITY, AND ERASMUS UNIVERSITY ROTTERDAM, THE NETHERLANDS

In the very first chapter of the Handbook, the editors described the rationale for the section on measuring strategic processing based on the idea that measurements and analyses of strategic processing data are rapidly evolving and that the field is beginning to move away from a reliance on retrospective self-reports and towards finer grained measurements of strategic processing along with new approaches to analyze and visualize the data. The section of the book on measuring strategic processing gives an excellent overview of the different ways strategic processing can be measured today: retrospective self-reports (Vermunt, this volume), concurrent and task-specific self-reports (Bråten et al., this volume), and eye-tracking and fMRI (Catrysse et al., this volume). Finally, the use of Big Data is explored as a way to measure and present strategic processing in educational environments (Lawless and Riel, this volume). In this chapter we will briefly discuss each of these chapters and measurement approaches and aim to provide the reader with suggestions for using these measurement techniques in concert. Therefore, we will first try to sketch a clear overview of what aspects of strategic processing each of the different chapters aims to measure and at what level of granularity. We will dig into the question as to how the different chapters conceptualize and operationalize strategic processing. When thinking about how to use different measurement techniques in concert, getting this picture clear is important because there is, at this moment in time, no strong reason to assume that even when the authors of the different chapters in this volume were invited to write about how they suggest measuring the same concept of strategic processing, this term would convey similar meanings in each of the chapters (cf. Alexander, 2017). The field has for long been dominated by self-report measures to capture strategic processing, and self-reports still play an important role in the field. We will start our chapter with a brief discussion of the two chapters in this volume that focus on self-report measures.

MEASURING STRATEGIC PROCESSING: REFLECTIONS

In his chapter about Surveys and Retrospective Reports to Measure Strategies and Strategic Processing, Vermunt puts the focus on the measurement of learning strategies and conceptualizes them as a combination of cognitive, metacognitive, and affective learning activities that students use to learn (Vermunt, this volume). Vermunt hereby uses the broadest and most general conceptualization of strategic processing of all. He describes two "generations" of student learning inventories to measure this concept: a first generation that focuses on measuring cognitive processing strategies (and to some extent also motivation) and a second generation of student learning inventories that also includes metacognitive scales. Although some of these instruments measure students' processing strategies in a rather general way (e.g., the ILS), the idea of certainly the second generation instruments was and is not that stable constructs are measured. This common misunderstanding has been fed by the faulty association with other trait-based self-report instruments because of the name under which Vermunt's widely used ILS survey is known: the Inventory of Learning Styles. To avoid this misunderstanding, Vermunt (this volume) proposes in his chapter to change the name of his own well-known ILS from "Inventory of Learning Styles" towards 'Inventory of Learning Patterns of Students. Learning patterns is the label Vermunt and other researchers have been using in most of his publications in the 2010s to conceptualize the combination of cognitive, metacognitive, and affective learning activities that students use to learn (see e.g., Gijbels, Donche, Richardson, & Vermunt, 2014). Although the validity of retrospective self-reports and especially inventories asking students about their general or average way of learning has been questioned, Vermunt also stresses some advantages of this technique such as the possibility of gaining an overview of large groups of students in a short time in one place and moment that suits the students, and with high ecological validity. According to Vermunt, all methods to measure strategic processing face the problem that in fact we want to externalize processes that are inherently internal and all methods face validity issues. Hence, more triangulation research is needed in which multiple research methods (including retrospective self-reports) are used (see also Alexander, 2017). Overall, Vermunt (this volume) highlights important issues that played a role (and to some extent still do) in the development of measurement instruments of students' learning strategies. He pointed out the issue of stability, with earlier instruments like the ASI (Entwistle & Wilson, 1977) capturing personality characteristics, typically considered as stable traits. Similarly, the Inventory of Learning Processes (ILP; Schmeck, Ribich, & Ramanaiah, 1977) defines a learning style as a disposition, also suggesting a stable characteristic, although the ILP does not include personality aspects. In contrast, as mentioned above, the later generation of measurement instruments does not start from learning approaches as stable processes anymore and acknowledges variations across (among other things) learning domains and topics. The task/course-specific versus general focus of measurement instruments also relates to some extent to the trait or state dichotomy. This led to different connotations of strategies and styles:

> "Strategy" was used to refer to the preferences shown in tackling an individual task, while "style" related to general preferences more akin to the psychological term cognitive style with its implications of relatively stable behaviour patterns rooted in personality differences or cerebral dominance.
>
> (Entwistle, 1991, p. 201)

A second issue that becomes apparent from Vermunt's chapter is that the self-report instruments developed to capture approaches to learning/students' processing really differed in aim. Although all are concerned with students' learning strategies/activities, some focused on (the frequency of) students' behavior ("How frequently do you do this or that activity?"), while others were mainly concerned with how students perceived aspects of their own learning or the learning environment (usually making use of statements for which students have to indicate their (dis)agreement or "digging deeper" with interviews). This distinction between behavior and perceptions can directly be linked to the three applications of the inventories/questionnaires that Vermunt (this volume) describes: (1) gaining knowledge about dimensions/developments in students' use of learning strategies (i.e., behavior), versus (2) helping students to reflect on their own use of learning strategies and (3) evaluating the teaching environment (i.e., perceptions of learning in the second application and of teaching in the third). Besides measuring behavior versus perceptions, instruments also differ in their inclusive character. For example, the LASSI was designed as a diagnostic instrument and the MED NORD questionnaire maps students' well-being and study orientations, therefore including many aspects of students' learning. These differences in aim of the instruments puts the discussion of conceptual clarity to the fore, which we touched upon above. Since these instruments introduce a wide variety of concepts (see tables in Vermunt's chapter) and some also address relating concepts such as attitudes, personality characteristics, cognitive styles, and preferences for physical and social study environments, conceptual clarity about what we mean with a specific term and how it relates to associated concepts remains the absolute first step. Although we fully agree with Vermunt's call for more focus on relationships, we feel this can only be achieved in a meaningful way when the concepts (used to operationalize strategic processing) that are to be related are sufficiently defined (see also Dinsmore & Alexander, 2012).

The focus of the chapter by Bråten, Magliano, and Salmerón is on concurrent and task-specific self-reports to measure strategic processing. They define (processing) strategies as "forms of procedural knowledge that individuals intentionally and planfully use for the purpose of acquiring, organizing, or elaborating information, as well as for reflecting upon and guiding their own learning, comprehension, or problem solving." Strategies are distinguished from skills, the latter referring to automatic, unintentional, and routinized information processing, while strategies involve effortful, intentional, and planful processing. When automatic skills "fail," strategic processing might lead to the desired outcome.

They distinguish superficial (such as selection and rehearsal) and deeper (such as constructing summaries and drawing inferences) processing strategies. Self-reports are defined as "utterances or answers to prompts or questions provided by an individual about his or her cognitions and actions during learning, comprehension, or problem solving." In the chapter, three different models for understanding the role of strategic processing in learning are discussed: the good strategy user model (Pressley, Borkowski, & Schneider, 1987), the model of domain learning (Alexander, 2004), and the cyclical model of self-regulated learning (Zimmerman, 1998). The authors point out that these models have relied to a large extent on concurrent task-specific self-reports in attempting to measure strategic processing. The most important part of the chapter is where the authors discuss four different ways to assess strategic processing by means of self-reports: verbal protocol analyses, eye movement cued self-reports, task specific self-report inventories, and diary methods. An interesting point raised concerning validation is the issue of priming/cueing by inventories. More specifically, the authors note that:

> Students' reports of strategy use were restricted to strategies prelisted in an inventory even when those strategies did not seem to reflect what the students did during task performance and they were allowed to describe what they actually did in their own words.

Researchers should be aware of this "side-effect" inventories can have. In a similar vein, if "self-monitoring processes" are to be studied and prompting devices are used to keep track of those processes, a critical question to ask is to what extent these processes can still be considered "self." Bråten and colleagues conclude their chapter by stating that there is a general lack of studies that compare strategy data across different methodologies and they call for more multiple method research including one or more of the self-report methodologies that they discussed "in combination with other types of strategy measures to clarify the similarities and differences between those measures." This relates to the point we made earlier in this chapter regarding conceptual clarity. Another observation from Bråten and colleagues' description of the different models is that different aspects of motivation are involved. As Zimmerman pointed out "strategic competence is of little value without motivation," so we clearly understand and support the link with motivational concepts in the different models. Pressley's Good Strategy User Model and Zimmerman's Model of Self-Regulated Learning make links to attributions and self-efficacy respectively, dealing with the motivational question: "Can I do this task?" Alexander's Model of Domain Learning brings interest to the fore, which relates to the question, "Do I want to do this task?" Interestingly, the link with the question, "Why do I want to do this task?" relating to goals and reasons for performing specific activities is not explicitly made in these models (it is made in relation to verbal protocols further in the chapter), while goals seem to be relevant in this discussion as well (for a detailed discussion on the different motivational questions and their related concepts, see Graham & Weiner, 2012; Pintrich, 2003; Wijnia, Noordzij, Arends, Rikers, & Loyens, 2019). Hence, both the chapters of Vermunt and of Bråten et al. end with a similar message: there is still a place for self-report measures, but we need to combine them with other types of measures. The question remains, however, are we indeed talking about data-triangulation when we are combining different ways to measure strategic processing, or should we be talking about triangulation of theories, since the combination of different measures might in fact imply that different (aspects of the same theoretical) constructs are being measured? In addition, Bråten and colleagues also highlighted the importance of the replication of research findings. What is a good moment to start triangulation, when can one be reasonably confident that data from an individual source/instrument are sufficiently stable/reliable?

While both the chapters of Vermunt and of Bråten et al. deal with self-report measures of strategic processing, there is a clear difference in the type of self-report instruments they describe. The instruments discussed by Vermunt are all retrospective self-reports (they ask students to reflect upon and self-report their strategic processing strategies in general, not connected to a specific task). The main part of the chapter by Vermunt deals with surveys, which can be labeled as "off-line" ways to self-report strategic processing. Off-line refers here to self-report inventories or interviews that are not administered while the learning takes place, but before or after the learning task has taken place. The chapter by Bråten et al. deals with both online and off-line self-report instruments but differs from the instruments discussed in Vermunt's chapter because Bråten and colleagues clearly focus on measurement instruments that try to capture students' strategic processing strategies during (online) or immediately after (off-line) the task performance. In the latter case, the self-report questions are formulated in a task-specific way. The difference between Vermunt's and Bråten et al.'s chapters is hence not the difference between online and off-line measures, but between retrospective (Vermunt) and concurrent (Bråten et al.) self-reports. Both Vermunt and Bråten et al. call for self-report instruments to be combined with other types of measures. Combining retrospective and concurrent self-report instruments could also be an interesting suggestion. While far less "fancy" compared to the measurement methods that we will discuss in the next paragraphs, this suggestion already illustrates the types of problems and opportunities triangulation of this type of data (and the "level" of the theories behind the data) could imply.

The chapter by Catrysse et al. (this volume) has a clear focus on "online" and "concurrent" measurement methods. The chapter gives an overview of how eye-tracking and functional magnetic resonance imaging (fMRI) can be used to examine students' levels of processing in relation to learning from verbal material. Catrysse and colleagues describe different theoretical frameworks to conceptualize strategic processing and link the framework to the measurement tool used. Interestingly, the authors speak of a "general disposition towards levels of processing," although the authors do not elaborate on whether they see processing strategies as stable characteristics. What becomes clear from the chapter is that it is not very insightful to categorize students as deep or surface learners, as the authors indicate at several points in the chapter that research points in the direction of a combination of deep and surface processing within students. A strong point of their chapter is that they explicitly mention the role of assessment, acknowledging that assessment demands can steer students' learning activities (see also Loyens, Gijbels, Coertjens, & Coté, 2013). Indeed, the type of assessment and the weight accorded to it, determine students' study activities (e.g., Al Kadri, Al-Moamary, & Van der Vleuten, 2009). fMRI research has used basic learning tasks at word level (e.g., judging whether a word is a living or a non-living object as an example of a surface-level task) to examine students' levels of processing for which mainly Craik and Lockhart's (1972) framework has been used. The word-level at which fMRI can be applied immediately poses a limitation, as learning often involves a text level. Certainly in higher education, understanding, critically evaluating, and being able to integrate different text sources is an all-important skill. Another legitimate question that the authors themselves pose regarding the potential of fMRI in measuring students' levels of processing is how these levels of processing are reflected in behavioral measures. The answer to this important question is still open. The eye-tracking research describes levels of processing during text learning as a multidimensional construct and stresses the importance of the interplay between levels of processing and other learner characteristics such as interest. In addition, contextual characteristics are also of influence, as levels of processing also interact with these characteristics. The importance of the interplay between learner characteristics and the nature of processing is reflected in several theoretical models such as those described by Alexander (1997) and Richardson (2015) but also by Vermunt and Donche (2017). An important reflection that Catrysse and colleagues make, however, is that what is referred to as "deep cognitive processing" in these theoretical models on students' levels of processing is not at all the same as what is understood by "deeper cognitive processing" in the eye-tracking literature. Either longer (eye) fixation durations or higher activity in certain brain areas can be related to different cognitive processing. Catrysse et al. refer therefore to students' levels of processing as complex, multidimensional, and dynamic in nature and stress the importance of adapting multi-method designs to grasp the complexity of students' levels of processing. According to the authors, micro-measures such as eye tracking and fMRI cannot be used as stand-alone measures and hence the use of multi-method designs is advocated. While the suggestion to use multiple methods is very explicitly present in their chapter, the issue of deliberately combining different theories of strategic processing (at different levels) is only implicitly discussed.

Lawless and Riel (this issue) describe the aim of their chapter is to provide inspiration regarding where the future of research in education in general and strategic processing in specific needs to go. In their chapter they examine the capture and analysis of data in various commercial applications and how industry has successfully leveraged these data to better understand user engagement. The authors remark that "we in education have not kept up with many of the affordances of technology in the way that industry has." Given the financial aspects involved, this is, however, not surprising. Nevertheless, it remains an interesting and important issue. The focus of the chapter is on Big Data, which the authors define by a series of characteristics that include volume, but also velocity, variety, value, and veracity. The chapter focuses on "the affordances of Big Data and what this means for the future of research examining learners' strategic processing and the design of instruction to improve these strategies in the service of obtaining positive learning outcomes." While the authors do explain what they understand by Big Data, it is far less clear what "strategic processing" or how "these strategies in the service of obtaining positive learning outcomes" need to be understood. The authors do mention the importance of supporting/scaffolding students' learning processes, especially in open-ended learning activities such as problem- and project-based learning. Indeed, these instructional processes aimed at guiding students' learning processes in student-centered learning environments often remain implicit, but are crucial for the success of those instructional approaches (for an overview of the processes involved in problem-based learning, see Wijnia, Loyens, & Rikers, 2019). The chapter takes a "data-driven" approach towards "strategic processing." Indeed, today, much data about learners is available, both about their digital lives (e.g., clicker data, website viewing patterns) but also data about their physical lives can be traced and made available (e.g., steps taken, heart rate). These daily activities can be observed and analyzed in Big Data contexts and result in learner profiles that reveal, e.g., learners' interests. While the gaming industry already uses this type of data to keep gamers engaged and interested in a game, the step towards introducing adaptive difficulty in learning environments also seems possible.

When it comes to measuring strategic processing based on Big Data, the idea is that "productive strategies" can be detected and that students can be nudged towards using such strategies. This indeed sounds promising, but in order to become pedagogically meaningful, the conceptual question, "What is a strategy?" remains to be answered. Without a clear conceptual idea of what a strategy is or might be, identifying a series of sequences for high- or low-performing learners will probably continue to fall short of the hype and fail to be informative for instructional interventions. In addition, and more generally, one must remain critical of the purpose for which this data is used. On the one hand, it can provide interesting insights for both educators and students themselves. The authors refer to formative feedback for students in this respect to get a better sense of what they are doing and how effective this is. Also, educators can get a better idea based on Educational Data Mining/Learning Analytics (EDM/LA) systems of what better performing students are doing in their courses. However, on the other hand, for systems such as Course Signal, there is also the danger of stereotype threats or, even more severe, exclusion. Similar to Vermunt (this volume) who objected to the use of learning strategy inventories for selection purposes of individual students, Lawless and Riel also indicate that the monitoring of students' educational trajectories "can inadvertently imprison learners in cages designed by their past choices." This is not to say that this type of monitoring making use of big data cannot take place, as prior studies have provided interesting insights into predictors of study success by combining student information from a variety of sources (e.g., De Koning, Loyens, Smeets, Rikers, & van der Molen, 2012; Richardson, Abraham, & Bond, 2012). Hence, the purpose of EDM/LA systems should always be carefully considered. An important observation in this respect is, as the authors acknowledge, that "EDM/LA approaches are only as good as the corpus of data available to extract, aggregate, and analyze."

Another issue that emerged in the present chapter is again the question of self versus other monitoring, when tools/systems are used to help students with their study processes. This is in line with our point related to the chapter by Bråten and colleagues earlier. In the present chapter, we were triggered by the description of the results of Sun and colleagues (2011) who described how students became dependent on the tools presented to them. Nevertheless, we concur with the authors that there is great potential for Big Data to foster automated instructional personalization.

The chapter by Lawless and Riel ends with raising some important theoretical, ethical, and logistical challenges for future research and calls for a more team-based approach (i.e., de-siloing educational research) to the research into strategic processing with diverse teams of experts across education, content disciplines, and computer

MEASURING STRATEGIC PROCESSING: FUTURE DIRECTIONS

Earlier we discussed the different chapters in the section on measuring strategic processing and we paid attention to the relation between the conceptualization and the operationalization of strategic processing. During the discussion of these chapters we raised some salient issues related to the measurement of strategic processing. Most clear of these is the call for triangulation. Triangulation is used to refer to the use of multiple approaches to researching a question and is typically associated with research methods and designs (Haele & Forbes, 2013). The assumption raised at the start of this chapter that the field is beginning to move away from a reliance on self-reports and towards finer grained measures of strategic processing is therefore only partly true. Finer grained approaches are indeed increasingly important, but in the call for triangulation there is still an important place for self-report measures. In the remainder of this chapter, we would like to discuss other variations of triangulation that offer interesting opportunities and new challenges to use the different measurements of strategic processing in concert.

Triangulation of methods and data is probably the most well-known and utilized way to combine methods. While the opportunities are clear, the challenge in mixing methods and data is that different measurement levels and theoretical levels can get mixed and that, in the end, we do not know what we are talking about anymore. At the measurement level, Lonka, Olkinuora, and Mäkinen (2004) made a useful distinction between three levels of granularity in which inventories of strategic processing are used: general, course-specific, and situational. Alexander (1997) distinguishes between micro, mid, and macro levels of theories in which macro-level theories take a lifespan perspective to explain learning, micro-theories explain changes for a specific concept at a specific moment in time, and mid-level theories are situated in between. While the three levels of granularity suggested by Lonka et al. (2004) and the three levels of theories suggested by Alexander (1997) have been successfully used to foster clarity in research in which different types of self-report instruments have been mainly used to triangulate data, the different types of measures that were discussed in the chapters by Catrysse et al. or by Lawless and Riel would probably all be classified in the "situational" or task-specific level of measurement granularity and at the micro-level of theories. In order to foster both empirical and conceptual clarity in the research that uses and combines these types of measures with, e.g., task-specific self-report instruments, we would benefit from finer grained lenses and "nano-theories." In order to stay meaningful for educational practices, these theories at the "nano-level" obviously need to be clearly connected to the theories at the micro-level. This is where the issue of theory-triangulation becomes relevant again. While triangulating different methods and measurement levels is more and more common, the triangulation of levels of theories often lags behind research. Sometimes we have to admit that our theories just fall short in explaining what is happening. In the case of Big Data this results in using a data-driven approach. The idea of triangulation could, however, also be used to combine data-driven approaches with theory-driven approaches. This could also allow triangulating multiple perspectives to students' strategic processing, like student data, teacher data, parent data, peer-data, and Big Data. All these data-streams obviously offer too much information, but in the hands of multidisciplinary teams in which computer scientists and experts in the disciplines and educational psychologists work together, existing theories can be used to give meaning to and dig further into the data and then challenge, stretch, and reshape the existing theories again.

To conclude, we call for future research in which teams of experts in different disciplines work together to triangulate data and theory-driven approaches. Rather than focusing on the opportunities of the different "nano-level" measures of strategic processing and the advantages Big Data can give us to generate fancy but theory-less advice for the educational practice, such collaborations among teams of experts in different disciplines such as computer sciences and educational psychology have the potential to build better theories that can inform students and teachers. In this way, using all different measurement techniques in concert can truly be an added value for all.

REFERENCES

Al Kadri, H. M. F., Al-Moamary, M. S., & Van der Vleuten, C. (2009). Students' and teachers' perceptions of clinical assessment program: A qualitative study in a PBL curriculum. *BMC Research Notes, 2*, 263. doi:10.1186/1756-0500-2-263

Alexander, P. A. (1997). Mapping the multidimensional nature of domain learning: The interplay of cognitive, motivational and strategic forces. In M. L. Maehr & P. R. Pintrich (Eds.), *Advances in motivation and achievement* (Vol. 10, pp. 213–250). Greenwich, CT: JAI Press Inc.

Alexander, P. A. (2004). A model of domain learning: Reinterpreting expertise as a multidimensional, multistage process. In D. Y. Dai & R. J. Sternberg (Eds.), *Motivation, emotion, and cognition: Integrative perspectives on intellectual functioning and development* (pp. 273–299). Mahwah, NJ: Lawrence Erlbaum.

Alexander, P. A. (2017). Issues of constructs, contexts, and continuity: Commentary on learning in higher education. *Educational Psychology Review, 29*, 345–351. doi:10.1007/s10648-017-9409-3

Craik, F. I. M., & Lockhart, R. S. (1972). Levels of processing: A framework for memory research. *Journal of verbal learning and verbal behavior, 11*, 671–684. doi:10.1016/S0022-5371(72)80001-X

De Koning, B. B., Loyens, S. M. M., Smeets, G., Rikers, R. M. J. P., & van der Molen, H. T. (2012). Generation Psy: Student characteristics and academic achievement in a three-year problem-based learning Bachelor program. *Learning & Individual Differences, 22*, 313–323. doi:10.1016/j.lindif.2012.01.003

Dinsmore, D. L., & Alexander, P. A. (2012). A critical discussion of deep and surface processing: What it means, how it is measured, the role of context, and model specification. *Educational Psychology Review, 24*(4), 499–567.

Entwistle, N. J. (1991). Approaches to learning and perceptions of the learning environment. Introduction to the special issue. *Higher Education, 22*, 201–204.

Entwistle, N. J., & Wilson, J. D. (1977). *Degrees of excellence: The academic achievement game*. London: Hodder & Stoughton.

Gijbels, D., Donche, V., Richardson, J. T. E., & Vermunt, J. D. (Eds.). (2014). *Learning patterns in higher education: Dimensions and research perspectives*. New York: Routledge.

Graham, S., & Weiner, B. (2012). Motivation: Past, present, and future. In K. R. Harris, S. Graham, T. Urdan, C. B. McCormick, G. M. Sinatra, & J. Sweller (Eds.), *APA Educational Psychology Handbook, Vol. 1. Theories, constructs, and critical issues* (pp. 367–397). Washington, DC: American Psychological Association. doi:10.1037/13273-013

Haele, R., & Forbes, D. (2013). Understanding triangulation in research. *Evidence-based Nursing, 16*(4), 98. doi:10.1136/eb-2013-101494

Lonka, K., Olkinuora, E., & Mäkinen, J. (2004). Measuring Studying and Learning in Higher Education—Conceptual and Methodological Issues. *Educational Psychology Review, 16*(4), 301–323.

Loyens, S. M. M., Gijbels, D., Coertjens, L., & Coté, D. (2013). Students' approaches to learning in problem-based learning: Taking into account students' behavior in the tutorial groups, self-study time, and different assessment aspects. *Studies in Educational Evaluation*, *39*(1), 23–32. doi:10.1016/j.stueduc.2012.10.004

Pintrich, P. R. (2003). Motivation and classroom learning. In G. E. Miller & W. M. Reynolds (Eds.), *Handbook of psychology: Educational psychology* (Vol. 7, pp. 103–122). New York: John Wiley & Sons.

Pressley, M., Borkowski, J. G., & Schneider, W. (1987). Cognitive strategies: Good strategy users coordinate metacognition and knowledge. In R. Vasta (Ed.), *Annals of child development* (Vol. 4, pp. 89–129). Greenwich, CT: JAI Press.

Richardson, J. T. E. (2015). Approaches to learning or levels of processing: What did Marton and Säljö (1976a) really say? The legacy of the work of the Göteborg group in the 1970s. *Interchange*, *46*, 239–269. doi:10.1007/s10780-015-9251-9

Richardson, M., Abraham, C., & Bond, R. (2012). Psychological correlates of university students' academic performance: A systematic review and meta-analysis. *Psychological Bulletin*, *138*, 353–387. doi:10.1037/a0026838

Schmeck, R. R., Ribich, F., & Ramanaiah, N. (1977). Development of a self-report inventory for assessing individual differences in learning processes. *Applied Psychological Measurement*, *1*(3), 413–431.

Sun, C. T., Wang, D. Y., & Chan, H. L. (2011). How digital scaffolds in games direct problem-solving behaviors. *Computers & Education*, *57*(3), 2118–2125.

Vermunt, J. D., & Donche, V. (2017). A learning patterns perspective on student learning in higher education: State of the art and moving forward. *Educational Psychology Review*, *29*(2), 269–299. doi:10.1007/s10648-017-9414-6

Wijnia, L., Loyens, S. M. M., & Rikers, R. M. J. P. (2019). The problem-based learning process: An overview of different models. In M. Moallem, W. Hung, & N. Dabbagh (Eds.), *The Wiley handbook of problem-based learning* (pp. 273–295). New York: John Wiley & Sons.

Wijnia, L., Noordzij, G., Arends, L. R., Rikers, R. M. J. P., & Loyens, S. M. M. (2019). *A meta-analysis on the effects of problem-based, project-based, and case-based learning on students' motivation*. Manuscript in preparation.

Zimmerman, B. J. (1998). Developing self-fulfilling cycles of academic regulation: An instructional analysis of exemplary instructional models. In D. H. Schunk & B. J. Zimmerman (Eds.), *Self-regulated learning: From teaching to self-reflective practice* (pp. 1–19). New York: Guilford.

Section IV
Analyzing Strategic Processing

21

VARIABLE-CENTERED APPROACHES

Rebekah Freed, Jeffrey A. Greene, and Robert D. Plumley
UNIVERSITY OF NORTH CAROLINA AT CHAPEL HILL, USA

Individuals' strategic processing, or strategy use, is a subject that has fostered increased research in recent years (Dinsmore, 2017). Effective strategic processing is beneficial in accomplishing tasks in a variety of domains. Students intentionally, purposefully, and effortfully use strategies to learn while navigating through content (Cho, Afferbach, & Han, 2018). Strategic processing has been linked to achievement outcomes, though the type and level of strategic processing matters in context (Dinsmore, 2017). Strategic processing is a valuable skill for learners of different ages. For example, in early childhood, learners use strategies to acquire and remember information (Nida, 2015). As another example, children in elementary school demonstrated they were able to respond to feedback in order to enhance strategy use in a dynamic testing situation (Resing & Elliott, 2011). Strategic processing affects learning outcomes for middle school students (Greene & Azevedo, 2009) and high school students, as well (Parkinson & Dinsmore, 2018). Additionally, the results of a recent meta-analysis showed that strategy use is a key variable associated with achievement in higher education (Schneider & Preckel, 2017).

This recent increase in research on strategic processing has led to a growing awareness that cognitive processes are not constrained by developmental stage, but are dynamic and malleable (Dinsmore, 2017). Because strategic processing is malleable, this provides the opportunity for students to learn more beneficial strategies. Researchers studying dynamic strategy use have capitalized on the malleability of strategic processing to identify and encourage students to use more beneficial strategies (e.g., practice testing and distributed practice) that encourage quality learning and achievement outcomes, rather than less beneficial strategies that encourage more shallow processing of the information (e.g., highlighting and rereading; Deekens, Greene, & Lobczowski, 2018; Dunlosky, Rawson, Marsh, Nathan, & Willingham, 2013).

People's strategic processing can change over time within and across learning tasks (Dinsmore, 2017). Given this, research methods that are capable of capturing dynamic processing are necessary (Dinsmore & Zoellner, 2018). However, such methods can produce a lot of data that can be challenging to analyze. Depending on the nature of the data and the research aims, these data may be analyzed in many ways, including variable-centered analyses (Laursen & Hoff, 2006) that allow for an understanding of relations among numerous variables of interest (e.g., strategic processing, motivation, learning). In this chapter, first we outline the differences between variable-centered and person-centered analyses in the context of studying strategy use and strategic processing. Then we discuss the different kinds of variable-centered analyses that can be used to understand and model strategy use and strategic processing data. Then, we conclude with a summary of observations about variable-centered analysis use in the extant literature, as well as practical implications and future directions.

VARIABLE-CENTERED VERSUS PERSON-CENTERED APPROACHES

There are two prevailing approaches to quantitative data analysis: variable- and person-centered. In statistical parlance, researchers employ variable-centered analytical methods to describe the associations between variables within populations that are assumed to be homogeneous regarding those variables' ability to predict a dependent outcome (Laursen & Hoff, 2006). These approaches involve analyses of relations between variables to produce a summarization of these relations, within a given set of parameters, to describe the entire population (Howard & Hoffman, 2018). For example, an R^2 statistic summarizes how much variance in an outcome variable can be explained by a set of predictor variables, for a particular sample assumed to represent a larger population. Variable-centered statistical methods include correlation, regression, path analysis, structural equation modeling, and growth models. Variable-centered methods can be used to investigate the associations between people's anxiety, knowledge of content, and frequency of deep strategy use. The hypotheses for this investigation might be: "There will be a negative relationship between anxiety and frequency of deep strategy use" and "There will be a positive relationship between people's knowledge of content and frequency of deep strategy use." A variety of different kinds of research questions pertaining to strategy use can be studied, including research questions about the efficacy of interventions (Yoon & Jo, 2014), strategy use change over time (Carr, Taasoobshirazi, Stroud, & Royer, 2011), the relation between strategy use and performance or knowledge gains (Greene, Deekens, Copeland, & Yu, 2018), and research questions pertaining to the relationship between strategy use and other learning phenomena (e.g., motivation; Bernacki, Byrnes, & Cromley, 2012).

Alternatively, person-centered methods use the relations between observed variables along with differences between individuals to identify multiple homogeneous subpopulations within a larger heterogenous population (Fryer & Shum, this volume). Also inherent in these methods is the identification of the appropriate number of emergent subpopulations needed to optimize the accuracy of the resulting population summary. Common person-centered approaches include latent class, latent profile, and cluster analysis (Howard & Hoffman, 2018; Laursen & Hoff, 2006). Person-centered analyses might be used to answer research questions such as, "Are there two or more groups of participants in this sample that systematically differ in their use of five common studying strategies?" Person-centered analyses are often preferable to variable-centered analyses when the ratio of participants to strategic processing variables is small, or when researchers are interested in identifying homogeneous subgroups for further analysis. Once these groups have been identified, they can be compared across a number of other covariates or criterion variables, such as prior knowledge or academic performance. Both person- and variable-centered analyses are viable methods for understanding strategic processing. In this chapter we focus on variable-centered approaches.

VARIABLE-CENTERED ANALYSIS TECHNIQUES

Data from a variety of quantitative research designs (e.g., true experimental, quasi-experimental, non-experimental) can be analyzed using variable-centered techniques. Variable-centered analyses can be conducted in studies of strategy use across different time frames as well, including during one learning episode (e.g., Greene et al., 2018) or over multiple episodes (e.g., Carr et al., 2011). Further, variable-centered analyses have been used to understand strategic processing across a variety of contexts, from labs to classrooms to learning online. Strategy use can either be studied as an independent or a dependent variable within variable-centered processes. Before analyses begin, however, it is often necessary to aggregate strategy use data (Greene, Dellinger, Binbasaran Tüysüzoğlu, & Costa, 2013).

Data Aggregation

Researchers who study strategy use and strategic processing sometimes need to utilize data aggregation before analyzing their data. There can be many strategies observed in a sample, often more than ten (e.g., various memorization strategies, higher-order strategies; Dunlosky et al., 2013). In such cases, it can be a challenge to use variable-centered analyses to compare the efficacy of those strategies to one another, due to sample size needs. For example, if 13 strategies are observed in a sample, variable-centered analysis (e.g., research question: which of the 13 strategies is the strongest predictor of learning performance?) guidelines would suggest the need for a relatively large sample (i.e., 117 per Green, 1991). Aggregation can be used to address such challenges, particularly when the use of specific strategies is less important than whether particular types of strategies were used at all. For example, it may not matter whether one participant elaborates, another spaces practice, or a third participant self-tests. What matters is the number of times they invoke any of these effective strategies (Dunlosky et al., 2013). In this situation, it may be useful to create a macro-level aggregate variable (e.g., deep strategy use) comprised of the sum of the frequency of use of these micro-level strategies. In one study, micro-level strategy use data (e.g., frequency of summarizing) were aggregated into surface- and deep-strategy use macro-level variables in order to predict differences in learning outcomes (Deekens et al., 2018). In this study it was less important which specific strategy was used (e.g., taking notes, summarizing, etc.) than the number of times a participant invoked each type of strategy. In another study, the authors aggregated micro-level strategy use variables (e.g., type of note taking strategy) in order to describe the variety of strategies used in their given case or group (Hagen, Braasch, & Bråten, 2014). They found that intertextual knowledge elaboration use statistically significantly predicted deep-level comprehension outcomes when reading to construct an argument, whereas this relationship was not present in participants who used this strategy while reading to summarize.

Aggregation can be used to test posited relations in models of strategy use or self-regulated learning (SRL; Greene & Azevedo, 2009). Many of these models are conceptualized at the macro-level. For example, in Zimmerman's model of SRL, at a macro-level planning in the forethought phase is posited to drive strategy use in the performance phase (Zimmerman, 2013). Yet the data collected are often at the micro-level (e.g., a participant makes a subgoal as one kind of planning, whereas another student calibrates a task definition; one student uses an elaboration strategy during performance, whereas another uses highlighting), thus aggregating to the macro-level is necessary to test whether indeed macro-level planning predicts macro-level strategy use (Greene et al., 2013). In this way, micro-level data can be aggregated into macro-level data to test hypothesized relations in the model (e.g., changes in task understanding can affect the strategies used).

Data can also be aggregated by time or learning phase. For example, data from think-aloud protocols can be aggregated into types of strategies used during learning, as opposed to before or after learning (Greene, Robertson, & Costa, 2011). In sum, data aggregation allows for different, additional, or further analysis of data that can help inform research on strategy use. Once data have been aggregated, they can be analyzed using variable-centered techniques, just as non-aggregated data can be analyzed. In the remainder of this section, we describe various variable-centered analysis techniques, with examples of each to illustrate how they differ.

General Linear Models

The general linear model (GLM) is a term used to encapsulate models that rely on the notion that the relationships between a dependent or outcome variable and independent or predictor variables can be described as a linear function (Rutherford, 2011; Tabachnick & Fidell, 2013). GLM not only includes traditional linear models based on continuous data, like regression, but also incorporates models that utilize categorical data as predictors, such as analysis of variance (ANOVA).

GLM analysis techniques can be used to understand relations between strategy use or strategic processing and other variables of interest, including group membership (e.g., Student's t-test or ANOVA) as well as other continuous variables such as motivation either on their own (i.e., correlation) or in relation to multiple variables (i.e., multiple linear regression). In terms of GLM analyses, strategic processing variables can be either the predictor variable (e.g., how does frequency of strategic processing predict academic achievement?) or the criterion variable (e.g., how do men and women differ in their strategic processing?; what is the relationship between motivation, emotions, and strategic processing?).

Student's t-Test. Student's t-test is a common method used to determine if the difference between the means of two independent samples is statistically significant. However, Student's t-test functions under the assumption that samples are normally distributed and have equal variances. If t-tests are performed on data that do not adhere to these assumptions, the risk of erroneously reporting that the means are statistically significantly different (Type 1 error), and erroneously reporting that the means are statistically equal (Type II error), both increase (Gibbons & Chakraborti, 1991).

Ruffing, Wach, Spinath, Brünken, and Karbach (2015) used t-tests to determine if the use of learning strategies differed based on students' gender. They administered a 77-item inventory to educational science students to collect their self-reported use of learning strategies. The instrument was designed to produce 11 scales of learning strategy use, including effort, attention, time management, literature, learning environment, resource-management, organization, relationships, critical evaluation, cognitive strategies, and metacognition. Then, the data was grouped by gender and mean scores were calculated for each learning strategy scale. The gender-specific scale means could be compared using a t-test to determine if differences between the average male and female strategy use levels were statistically significant. They found female students reported more frequent use of effort, time management, organization, cognitive strategies, and metacognition, whereas male students reported performing the learning strategies of critical evaluation and relationships more often.

Analyses of Variance. ANOVA is used to determine if the differences between means (i.e., dependent variable) of three or more categorical groups (i.e., independent variable) are statistically significant (Rutherford, 2011; Tabachnick & Fidell, 2013). Variance due to additional predictor variables can be controlled by using analysis of covariance (ANCOVA; Rutherford, 2011). When researchers are interested in group differences across a number of dependent variables, a multivariate analysis of variance (MANOVA) should be used to evaluate the mean differences in composites of those dependent variables across independent variable categories (Tabachnick & Fidell, 2013). Finally, when dependent variables are captured from the same participants more than once, repeated-measures ANOVA or MANOVA can be used (Rutherford, 2011).

Anmarkrud, McCrudden, Bråten, and Strømsø (2013) used ANOVA to evaluate university students' think-aloud judgments of text relevance while reading conflicting documents about the scientific evidence regarding the health concerns of cell phone use. Text segments within the documents were coded as containing more or less relevant information and students' comments while reading them were coded as being either positive or negative judgments. To compare the frequency of positive and negative judgements across more and less relevant text segments a 2 (judgment type: positive or negative) × 2 (segment type: more relevant or less relevant) within-subjects ANOVA was performed. Anmarkrud et al. found that while reading more relevant text segments, students expressed a greater number of judgments and those judgments were more frequently rated as positive, whereas the judgments expressed when reading less relevant text were more frequently negative.

Vasilyeva, Laski, and Shen (2015) utilized a MANOVA to determine whether groups based on gender and age differed across multiple outcome measures. The outcomes measured for their study focused on first-graders' answer accuracy and use of four classifications of strategies (retrieval, counting, decomposition, other) while solving addition problems involving single-, mixed-, and double-digit numbers. Vasilyeva et al. found no differences between groups on the five outcome measures, allowing them to exclude those demographic variables from further analysis of the study's data.

Correlation. The bivariate correlation coefficient is used to measure size and directionality of the linear association between two variables. Most commonly reported as Pearson's r, correlation represents the degree to which two variables are related to each other. This measure of relationship ranges from -1 to 1, depending on the degree and valence of their correlation. Measures of variable correlation are omnipresent in reports of statistical findings and provide a foundation for more complex analytical methods, which has led to an underappreciation of their own utility and explanatory value (Lee Rodgers & Nicewander, 1988).

Using bivariate correlation, Askell-Williams, Lawson, and Skrzypiec (2012) evaluated survey responses to study the relationship between Australian secondary school students' self-reported use of cognitive and metacognitive strategies and their self-assessment of how they coped with their homework. Askell-Williams et al. found statistically significant, positive correlations between student's coping status and the use of both cognitive and metacognitive strategies, indicating that "students who reported using higher levels of cognitive and metacognitive strategies were more likely to report that they were coping well with school work" (p. 442). After identifying these positive relationships, the researchers used ANOVA to compare students grouped at the extreme ends of the "coping with homework" scale and found that students who reported coping very well with homework were statistically more likely to report using metacognitive strategies than those students who were not coping well with homework.

Multiple Linear Regression Models. Unlike t-tests and bivariate correlation measures, multiple linear regression (MLR) allows researchers to test multiple predictors at once and look at the unique relationship of each predictor with the criterion variable, over the combined relations of the others. MLR models are used to predict criterion variable values by calculating coefficients for the included predictor variables that minimize the sum of the squared differences between them. Often included in the reported results of a regression is the proportion of variation in the criterion variable that is explained by the model (i.e., R^2; Rutherford, 2011; Tabachnick & Fidell, 2013).

Roelle, Schmidt, Buchau, & Berthold, (2017) described how the use of MLR allowed them to measure an unexpected effect of their experimental intervention that was not initially apparent when they analyzed their data using ANCOVA. In the third experiment discussed in their article, Roelle et al. tested the effects of providing high school students with either information about regulation strategies or the dangers of making overconfident judgments of learning (JOLs), or both. Although the results of ANCOVA indicated that only providing students with information about the use of regulation strategies had a statistically significant positive effect on the number of elaborations students made, the treatment did not have a statistically significant effect on posttest results. In contrast, a statistically significant positive effect on posttest results was found for providing information about the dangers of making overconfident JOLs and additionally the interaction of the two treatments also showed a significant positive effect on posttest scores. To further understand the relationships between their two treatments, the frequency of students' elaboration use, and posttest results, Roelle et al. used MLR. Its ability to test multiple predictors and their interactions made MLR particularly well-suited for this situation.

Using posttest scores as the dependent variable, Roelle et al. (2017) produced an MLR model that included pretest scores, the two treatment groups (i.e., information about regulation strategies and information about the dangers of making overconfident JOLs), an interaction term for the two treatments, the number of elaborations performed, and finally an interaction term between being informed about making overconfident JOLs and elaborations performed. The resulting MLR model produced statistically significant positive coefficients for pretest scores, elaboration use, and the interaction of the JOLs treatment on elaboration use. Though at first an ANCOVA indicated that the overconfident JOLs treatment had no effect on the use of elaboration, the results of an MLR revealed that the JOLs treatment had a statistically significant effect on the use of elaboration. In sum, conducting an MLR revealed that understanding the dangers of making overconfident JOLs was not enough to have a statistically significant effect in this learning situation, and that participants also benefitted from learning regulation strategies in order to produce more effective elaborations. Thus conducting an MLR gave more details of the relationship between having knowledge about overconfident JOLs, strategic processing, and learning outcomes.

Count Data

Many studies of strategic processing have involved self-report data regarding strategy use, which are often normally distributed and amenable to GLM analyses (e.g., Askell-Williams et al., 2012). On the other hand, some studies of strategic processing involve counts of the number of times participants use particular strategies, either via observation (e.g., Hagen et al., 2014), participants' think-aloud verbalizations of strategy use (Greene et al., 2018), or via trace data from computer-based learning environments (Bernacki, 2018). For example, think-aloud protocols conducted during learning events can be coded into behaviors (i.e., monitoring strategy use), and those coded data can be transformed into quantitative data by totaling up or tallying the data (Creswell & Plano Clark, 2018). Researchers can use count data to assess behavior, to compare behavioral measures to self-report measures, and to predict learning and performance outcomes from these data (Gall, Gall, & Borg, 2007; Greene et al., 2011). Often, count data are not normally distributed, and when used as a criterion variable, they violate a basic assumption of GLM analyses. In this case, researchers must use statistical techniques that can compensate for these non-normal distributions of data, such as Generalized Linear Model analyses. In one study, researchers conducted strategy use intervention to see if the instruction received by the students in the intervention group affected subsequent strategy use (Yoon & Jo, 2014). The researchers found that the instructed learning strategy was used more frequently in the treatment group than the comparison group by comparing frequency of count data. In sum, many studies involving strategy use or strategic processing include some measure of the frequency of those behaviors. When the outcome measure is a frequency, it is often the case that the data are non-normally distributed, and in those cases count models should be considered, rather than GLM.

Path Analysis

Compared to GLM, path analysis, also called path model analysis, allows researchers to model and investigate equivalent as well as more complex relations among predictor and outcome variables (Kline, 2014). In regression, all predictors are modeled to correlate with one another, and each predictor has its own unique path modeled as directly connecting the predictor to the outcome variable. Each path has an estimated regression coefficient, which can be tested for statistical significance. Each of these regression coefficients represents the unique relationship between the predictor and the outcome variable, after controlling for all other predictors in the regression. For example, a researcher may be interested in how the frequency of use of two deep strategies, such as elaboration and self-testing, as well as two surface strategies, such as highlighting and summarization, each predict academic achievement (Dinsmore, 2017; Dunlosky et al., 2013). A regression approach can be conducted using an equivalent path model, where the analysis would produce six correlations among the four strategies, as well as four path model coefficients, one for each strategy (see Figure 21.1). In statistical parlance, such a model is saturated, because every variable (i.e., predictors and outcome) is connected to every other variable.

However, in regression models only one formulation of the variables is possible (i.e., all predictors related to the outcome directly). Researchers often have more complex conceptualizations of the relations among phenomena, such as positing mediators between variables (e.g., Pintrich, 2000). For example, rather than assuming that each strategy acts only directly on academic achievement, the researcher may posit instead that the two surface strategies are correlated, with each predicting use of elaboration, which in turn predicts self-testing, which in turn is the only predictor of academic achievement (see Figure 21.2). In this conceptualization, two deep strategies serve as mediators of the relationships between the two surface strategies and academic achievement. To test these ideas, the researcher would use path analysis where the posited model would include only a single correlation (i.e., the two surface strategies), with one path from each surface strategy to elaboration, a single path from elaboration to self-testing, and a single path from self-testing to academic achievement. This more nuanced model, compared to the regression-equivalent path model, is not saturated

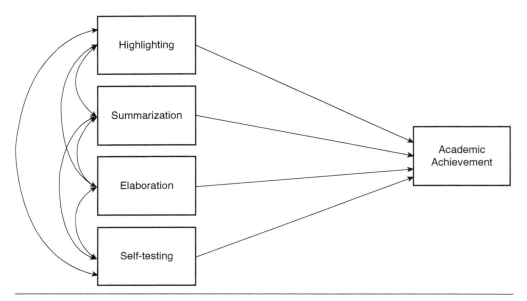

Figure 21.1 Example Path Model of a Regression Analysis

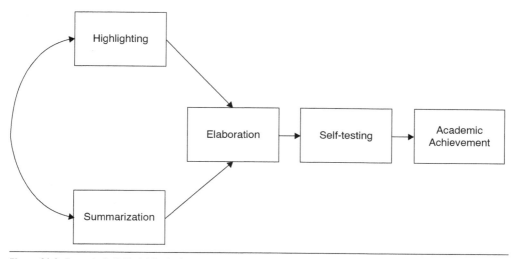

Figure 21.2 Example Path Model Analysis

because there are possible paths that are not specified (e.g., a path from highlighting to self-testing, or from elaboration to academic achievement). Models that are not saturated can be more thoroughly tested for data-model fit than saturated models, and compared to other specifications (e.g., deep strategy use predicting surface strategy use, which in turn predicts academic achievement) to determine which specification best represents relations in the data. Thus, path models and their associated analyses allow researchers to test more complex models than GLM methods such as regression, and often allow for more rigorous tests and comparisons of different conceptualizations of the relations among variables. On the other hand, to be estimated successfully, path model analysis often requires a larger sample size than GLM models (Kline, 2014).

Bernacki et al. (2012) used trace data from college students' use of a technology-enhanced environment to study relations among strategy use, self-reported motivation, and learning performance. The trace data represented counts of college student participants' use of highlighting, note taking, and definition tools, as well as monitoring tools such as accessing a list of learning goals. Bernacki et al. (2012) could have used a regression model in their analysis, but that would not have allowed them to test their hypotheses regarding how motivation predicts strategy use, which they posited would then predict learning, a common consequential order in models of self-regulated learning (SRL; Schunk & Greene, 2018). By using path model analysis, they were able to discover that approach-based motivation was positively related to strategy use, whereas avoidance-based motivation was negatively related. Further, highlighting was the only strategy use variable that predicted learning. Finally, they found acceptable data-model fit for this model, indicating its superiority to a saturated model, adding evidence regarding the validity of their conceptualization.

Deekens et al. (2018) posited a similar model in the second of two studies in their article, arguing that the relationship between pre and posttest measures of learning would be mediated first by the frequency of monitoring, which in turn would predict the frequency of deep and surface strategy use, with both strategy use variables predicting posttest performance. Again, a path analysis model allowed them to examine a common consequential ordering of variables in SRL theory, where prior knowledge positively predicts the frequency of monitoring, which in turn would positively predict deep strategy use while negatively predicting the use of surface strategies. As Dinsmore (2017) and others have argued, Deekens et al. posited that deep strategy use would positively predict posttest performance, whereas surface strategy use would negatively predict performance. These authors found support for their path model, despite a relatively small sample size likely leading to power concerns. A standard regression model would not have allowed for tests of relations between prior knowledge and monitoring, or monitoring and strategy use, as the path model analysis did. In sum, path models allow researchers to more closely adhere to theoretical relations in their analysis and can provide unique insights regarding contingent relations among strategy use and other variables of interest in learning (e.g., motivation, prior knowledge, monitoring; Ben-Eliyahu & Bernacki, 2015).

Structural Equation Modeling

Structural equation modeling is quite similar to path model analysis in that researchers can posit and test complex relations among variables, including mediation (Kline, 2014). However, path model analysis involves only measured variables, which are likely to contain significant amounts of error variance in addition to true score variance. In structural equation modeling, one or more measured variables are replaced with a latent variable constructed of two or more measured variables. The process of estimating the latent variable from the associated measured variables enables researchers to produce an estimate of the error variance in each measured variable, and remove it, thus producing a latent variable that, in theory, is a more accurate and pure representation of the underlying construct (i.e., all true score variance, no error score variance).

For example, many SRL researchers have used the Motivated Strategies for Learning Questionnaire (Pintrich, Smith, Garcia, & McKeachie, 1991) to measure participants' perceptions of their motivation and strategy use (Vermunt, this volume). This questionnaire includes numerous self-report, Likert-type scale items intended to measure motivation (e.g., "In a class like this, I prefer course material that really challenges me so I can learn new things" and "If I study in appropriate ways, then I will be able to learn the material in this course") as well as learning strategy use (e.g., "When studying for this course, I often set aside time to discuss course material with a group of students from the class" and "I ask the instructor to clarify concepts I don't understand well"). In theory, each item is a good but not perfect measure of the underlying latent construct of motivation or learning strategy use. Summing scores across multiple strategy use items would include both true score and error variance in the total. Structural equation modeling allows researchers to estimate and remove the error variance from each individual item, including only true score variance in the estimate of participants' score on the latent variable. This latent variable is a more accurate and statistically stronger estimate than any of its individual measured variable indicators. Structural equation models can be conceptualized, tested, reconceptualized, and compared similarly to path analysis models. However, structural equation modeling often requires even larger sample sizes than path model analysis.

Baas, Castelijns, Vermeulen, Martens, and Segers (2015) used the self-report Children's Perceived Use of Self-Regulated Learning Inventory (Vandevelde, Van Keer, & Rosseel, 2013) to measure elementary school students' surface and deep learning strategies as well as their relations among monitoring, scaffolding, and evaluation. This inventory included two items the authors used to measure perceived use of surface learning strategies, and another eight items used to measure perceived use of deep learning strategies. They used structural equation modeling to determine whether the items appropriately measured each latent perceived strategy use variable, and then they evaluated relations among those latent variables and other phenomena of interest such as scaffolding, monitoring, planning, and product evaluation. They found that scaffolding positively related to perceived use of both surface and deep learning strategies, thus supporting the idea that helping students understand what they need to do next when learning (i.e., scaffolding) is associated with self-reported increases in the perception of strategy use. It is important to note that despite common misconceptions, structural equation modeling does necessarily allow researchers to make causal claims (e.g., scaffolding caused students to perceive greater use of strategies). Causal claims are dependent upon the design of the study (i.e., experimental versus non-experimental designs), rather than the type of analysis technique used (e.g., regression, path model analysis, structural equation modeling; Murnane & Willet, 2010).

Greene, Costa, Robertson, Pan, and Deekens (2010) used a structural equation model to examine relations among college students' knowledge gains while using a computer-based learning environment, SRL processing including strategy use as captured via think-aloud protocol data (Greene et al., 2018), and implicit theories of intelligence (Dweck & Master, 2008). The authors found that planning, monitoring, and strategy use could be used as measured indicators of a latent SRL variable, and that this variable mediated relations between prior knowledge, implicit theory of intelligence, and posttest performance. This posited model allowed these researchers to test common assumptions about SRL (i.e., SRL mediates relations between individual differences and learning performance; Pintrich, 2000) that would have been impossible to assess with a regression model.

Growth Curve Modeling

Often, researchers wish to measure changes in strategy use over time, for example in studies of children's strategic processing as they age through elementary school (Carr & Alexeev, 2011). This change over time can be estimated using growth curve modeling, which is akin to a structural equation modeling approach to GLM repeated measures analysis. In growth curve modeling, the participants' initial performance ability and their rate of change over time are treated as latent variables that can be more accurately estimated after removing error variance from the repeated measures. Carr and Alexeev captured students' use of both cognitive and manipulative mathematics strategies in 2nd, 3rd, and 4th grades and then used growth curve modeling to find statistically significant change in the frequency of observed strategy use over that time period. Their analyses extended beyond the scope of this chapter, revealing previously unobserved differences in students that related to 4th grade mathematics competency, as well. The use of growth curve modeling allowed the authors to more accurately discern how strategy use changed over time, and how that change related to covariates such as fluency, accuracy, gender, and subsequent measures of mathematics competency.

CURRENT AND FUTURE DIRECTIONS FOR VARIABLE-CENTERED APPROACHES TO STRATEGIC PROCESSING RESEARCH

In sum, variable-centered analyses are statistical methods used to prepare or analyze data from previously identified groups (Laursen & Hoff, 2006). Whereas the goal of using person-centered analyses (e.g., cluster analysis and latent class analysis) is to identify previously unobserved groups based upon common patterns within the data, the goal of variable-centered analyses is to explore, compare, or contrast extant groups within the data. Data aggregation prepares data for analyses. The analyses we outlined in this chapter include GLM analyses (i.e., t-tests, ANOVA, multiple linear regression), count models, path analysis, structural equation modeling, and growth curve models.

In this chapter, we explained the purpose of and process for using variable-centered analyses to study strategy use and strategic processing. Researchers were able to answer key research questions about strategy use through variable-centered analytic methods. For example, Bernacki and colleagues' (2012) study used path analysis to analyze trace data from college students' use of a technology-enhanced environment to study relationships among strategy use, self-reported motivation, and learning performance. Using path model analysis meant they were able to discover that approach-based motivation was positively related to strategy use, and avoidance-based motivation was negatively related. Additionally, variable-centered analyses provided other affordances for research, such as analyzing use of count data. Sometimes studies of strategy use involve counts of the number of times participants use particular strategies. These can be counts of strategy use via observation (e.g., Hagen et al., 2014), participants' think-aloud verbalizations of strategy use (Greene et al., 2018), or from trace data from computer-based learning environments (Bernacki, 2018). Researchers can analyze count data that is non-normally distributed through generalized linear model analyses. Also, variable-centered analyses can be used to model complex relations among numerous measured variables (e.g., path analysis), to understand latent variables and structures (e.g., SEM), as well as how strategic processing changes over time (e.g., repeated-measures ANOVA, growth modeling). Variable-centered analyses of strategic processing data have been and likely will continue to be a prominent way of understanding how people enact strategies, as well as the precursors and consequences of such enactment.

Future Directions for Research

There are opportunities to expand the use of variable-centered analyses for strategy use in future research. We identified many researchers who utilized self-report surveys and questionnaires about strategy use (e.g., Askell-Williams et al., 2012; Mirzaei et al., 2014; Ruffing et al., 2015). However, strategy use is dynamic and not stable. Researchers studying strategy use that incorporates behavioral data have an opportunity to capture learning behaviors as they occur, via think-aloud protocols (Anmarkrud et al., 2013), eye fixations on a page (Arya & Feathers, 2012), or other methods. Capturing these strategic processing behaviors as they occur can be more useful than self-report data because it allows for modeling the dynamic nature of strategy use, and can afford an understanding of the sequential and contingent nature of strategic processing (Ben-Eliyahu & Bernacki, 2015; Binbasaran Tüysüzoğlu & Greene, 2015). In the future, variable-centered analyses, such as path modeling, could be used to understand how people leverage feedback to dynamically adjust the depth of their strategy use (Dinsmore, 2017), such as when frequent difficulty with formative assessments leads to participants shifting from surface- to deep-strategy use.

Often, researchers have studied how strategy use predicts achievement or learning outcomes (e.g., Carr et al., 2011). However, there are fewer studies that exist where researchers have considered strategy use itself as the outcome variable (e.g., Greene et al., 2011; Vasilyeva et al., 2015). In the future, researchers may study strategy use as an outcome in itself more often, rather than establishing the relationships between strategy use and other variables (e.g., GPA). Given the established relationship between strategy use and performance outcomes, more research is needed on how to foster effective strategic knowledge and processing among those who would otherwise struggle to enact without support (Bjork, Dunlosky, & Kornell, 2013).

In the future, we encourage diversifying methodological and analytical techniques in the field of strategy use. We identified many studies that utilized quasi-experimental designs (Aghaie & Zhang, 2012) or experimental studies (Cantrell et al., 2014), but fewer case studies. It may be that qualitative research is needed to better understand why people do and do not enact effective strategic processing, and what variables are most important to capture and analyze (e.g., self-efficacy for strategy use; Zimmerman, 2013). Likewise, mixed methods might enhance the knowledge base and research quality in the field of strategy use. For example, researchers might use mixed methods to iterate between what participants actually do when studying (i.e., quantitative data derived from observation) and what they think they are doing (i.e., qualitative investigations of participants' impressions and experience). Such mixed methods research designs may afford greater insight into the variables associated with proper calibration and metacognitive knowledge during strategic processing (Pieschl, Stallmann, & Bromme, 2014).

In addition to methodological and analytical diversification, diversification of samples is also an area of further exploration. For example, Vasilyeva et al. (2015) analyzed cross-cultural differences in strategy use between US and Taiwanese students. They found that Taiwanese children used retrieval practice more than US children. Such research is necessary to understand how strategy use varies across contexts, and why. However, such work must necessarily be conducted from a perspective derived from within the culture, rather than imposing ideas derived from one culture onto another (King & McInerney, 2018).

Conclusion

In conclusion, strategy use data comes in different forms, and some of these data can be analyzed with variable-centered analyses. The variable-centered analyses described here include general linear model approaches such as correlational and regression analyses, path analyses, structural equational models, and growth models. Data aggregation can be used to make strategy use data more amenable to variable-centered analyses, although in some cases count-based analyses must be used. Though the variable-centered analyses most appropriate for a given situation are determined by the research question, the type of data collected, and the goal of the research methods used, we demonstrated in this chapter how variable-centered analyses can be used to answer questions about the nature of strategy use and its relationships with other variables. Specifically, we look forward to seeing how researchers incorporate new applications of analytic methods for understanding strategic processing data.

REFERENCES

Aghaie, R., & Zhang, L. J. (2012). Effects of explicit instruction in cognitive and metacognitive reading strategies on Iranian EFL students' reading performance and strategy transfer. *Instructional Science, 40*(6), 1063–1081.

Anmarkrud, Ø., McCrudden, M. T., Bråten, I., & Strømsø, H. I. (2013). Task-oriented reading of multiple documents: Online comprehension processes and offline products. *Instructional Science, 41*(5), 873–894.

Arya, P., & Feathers, K. M. (2012). Reconsidering children's readings: Insights into the reading process. *Reading Psychology, 33*(4), 301–322.

Askell-Williams, H., Lawson, M. J., & Skrzypiec, G. (2012). Scaffolding cognitive and metacognitive strategy instruction in regular class lessons. *Instructional Science, 40*(2), 413–443.

Baas, D., Castelijns, J., Vermeulen, M., Martens, R., & Segers, M. (2015). The relation between assessment for learning and elementary students' cognitive and metacognitive strategy use. *British Journal of Educational Psychology, 85*(1), 33–46.

Ben-Eliyahu, A., & Bernacki, M. L. (2015). Addressing complexities in self-regulated learning: A focus on contextual factors, contingencies, and dynamic relations. *Metacognition and Learning, 10*(1), 1–13. https://doi.org/10.1007/s11409-015-9134-6

Bernacki, M. L. (2018). Examining the cyclical, loosely sequenced, and contingent features of self-regulated learning: Trace dta and their analysis. In D. H. Schunk & J. A. Greene (Eds.), *Handbook of self-regulation of learning and performance* (2nd ed., pp. 370–387). New York, NY: Routledge.

Bernacki, M. L., Byrnes, J. P., & Cromley, J. G. (2012). The effects of achievement goals and self-regulated learning behaviors on reading comprehension in technology-enhanced learning environments. *Contemporary Educational Psychology, 37*, 148–161.

Binbasaran Tüysüzoğlu, B., & Greene, J. A. (2015). An investigation of the role of contingent metacognitive behavior in self-regulated learning. *Metacognition & Learning, 10*, 77–98. http://dx.doi.org/10.1007/s11409-014-9126-y

Bjork, R. A., Dunlosky, J., & Kornell, N. (2013). Self-regulated learning: beliefs, techniques, and illusions. *Annual Review of Psychology, 64*, 417–444.

Cantrell, S. C., Almasi, J. F., Rintamaa, M., Carter, J. C., Pennington, J., & Buckman, D. M. (2014). The impact of supplemental instruction on low-achieving adolescents' reading engagement. *The Journal of Educational Research, 107*, 36–58.

Carr, M., & Alexeev, N. (2011). Fluency, accuracy, and gender predict developmental trajectories of arithmetic strategies. *Journal of Educational Psychology, 103*(3), 617–631.

Carr, M., Taasoobshirazi, G., Stroud, R., & Royer, J. M. (2011). Combined fluency and cognitive strategies instruction improves mathematics achievement in early elementary school. *Contemporary Educational Psychology, 36*, 323–333.

Cho, B. Y., Afferbach, P., & Han, H. (2018). Strategic processing in accessing, comprehending, and using multiple sources online. In J. L. G. Braash, I. Bråten, & M. T. McCrudden (Eds.), *The handbook of multiple source use* (pp. 133–150). New York: Routledge Publishers.

Creswell, J., & Plano Clark, V. (2018). *Designing and conducting mixed methods research.* (3rd ed). Thousand Oaks, CA: SAGE.

Deekens, V. M., Greene, J. A., & Lobczowski, N. G. (2018). Monitoring and depth of strategy use in computer-based learning environments for science and history. *British Journal of Educational Psychology, 88*(1), 63–79.

Dinsmore, D. L. (2017). *Strategic processing in education.* New York: Routledge.

Dinsmore, D. L., & Zoellner, B. P. (2018). The relation between cognitive and metacognitive strategic processing during a science simulation. *British Journal of Educational Psychology, 88*(1), 95–117.

Dunlosky, J., Rawson, K. A., Marsh, E. J., Nathan, M. J., & Willingham, D. T. (2013). Improving students' learning with effective learning techniques: Promising directions from cognitive and educational psychology. *Psychological Science in the Public Interest, 14*(1), 4–58. https://doi.org/10.1177/1529100612453266

Dweck, C. S., & Master, A. (2008). Self-theories motivate self-regulated learning. In D. H. Schunk & B. J. Zimmerman (Eds.), *Motivation and self-regulated learning: Theory, research, and applications* (pp. 31–51). New York, NY: Lawrence Erlbaum Associates.

Fryer, L. K., & Shum, A. (this volume). Person-centered approaches to explaining students' cognitive processing strategies. In D. L. Dinsmore, L. K. Fryer, & M. M. Parkinson (Eds.), *Handbook of strategies and strategic processing*. New York: Routledge.

Gall, M., Gall, J., & Borg, W. (2007). *Educational research: An introduction* (8th ed.). Pearson: Boston.

Gibbons, J. D., & Chakraborti, S. (1991). Comparisons of the Mann-Whitney, student's t, and alternate t tests for means of normal distributions. *The Journal of Experimental Education, 59*(3), 258–267.

Green, S. B. (1991). How many subjects does it take to do a regression analysis? *Multivariate Behavioral Research, 26*, 499–510.

Greene, J. A., & Azevedo, R. (2009). A macro-level analysis of SRL processes and their relations to the acquisition of a sophisticated mental model of a complex system. *Contemporary Educational Psychology, 34*(1), 18–29.

Greene, J. A., Costa, L.-J., Robertson, J., Pan, Y., & Deekens, V. M. (2010). Exploring relations among college students' prior knowledge, implicit theories of intelligence, and self-regulated learning in a hypermedia environment. *Computers & Education, 55*, 1027–1043.

Greene, J. A., Deekens, V. M., Copeland, D. Z., & Yu, S. (2018). Capturing and modeling self-regulated learning using think-aloud protocols. In D. H. Schunk & J. A. Greene (Eds.), *Handbook of self-regulation of learning and performance* (2nd ed., pp. 323–337). New York, NY: Routledge.

Greene, J. A., Dellinger, K., Binbasaran Tüysüzoğlu, B., & Costa, L. (2013). A two-tiered approach to analyzing self-regulated learning process data to inform the design of hypermedia learning environments. In R. Azevedo & V. Aleven (Eds.), *International handbook of metacognition and learning technologies* (pp. 117–128). New York: Springer.

Greene, J. A., Robertson, J., & Costa, L.-J. C. (2011). Assessing self-regulated learning using think-aloud protocol methods. In B. J. Zimmerman & D. Schunk (Eds.), *Handbook of self-regulation of learning and performance* (pp. 313–328). New York: Routledge Publishers.

Hagen, Å. M., Braasch, J. L., & Bråten, I. (2014). Relationships between spontaneous note-taking, self-reported strategies and comprehension when reading multiple texts in different task conditions. *Journal of Research in Reading, 37*, 141–S157.

Howard, M. C., & Hoffman, M. E. (2018). Variable-centered, person-centered, and person-specific approaches: Where theory meets the method. *Organizational Research Methods, 21*(4), 846–876.

King, R. B., & McInerney, D. M. (2018). Self-regulation in cultural context. In D. H. Schunk & J. A. Greene (Eds.), *Handbook of Self-Regulation of Learning and Performance (2nd Ed.)* (pp. 485–502). New York, NY: Routledge.

Kline, P. (2014). *An easy guide to factor analysis*. New York, NY: Routledge.

Laursen, B., & Hoff, E. (2006). Person-centered and variable-centered approaches to longitudinal data. *Merrill-Palmer Quarterly, 52*(3), 377–389.

Lee Rodgers, J., & Nicewander, W. A. (1988). Thirteen ways to look at the correlation coefficient. *The American Statistician, 42*(1), 59–66.

Mirzaei, A., Rahimi Domakani, M., & Heidari, N. (2014). Exploring the relationship between reading strategy use and multiple intelligences among successful L2 readers. *Educational Psychology, 34*(2), 208–230.

Murnane, R. J., & Willet, J. B. (2010). *Methods matter: Improving causal inference in educational and social science research*. New York, NY: Oxford University Press.

Nida, R. E. (2015). Effects of motivation on young children's object recall and strategy use. *The Journal of Genetic Psychology, 176*(3), 194–209.

OECD. (2013). *Trends shaping education 2013*. Paris, France: Author. 10.1787/trends_edu-2013-en.

Parkinson, M. M., & Dinsmore, D. L. (2018). Multiple aspects of high school students' strategic processing on reading outcomes: The role of quantity, quality, and conjunctive strategy use. *British Journal of Educational Psychology, 88*(1), 42–62.

Pieschl, S., Stallmann, F., & Bromme, R. (2014). High school students' adaptation of task definitions, goals and plans to task complexity–The impact of epistemic beliefs. *Psihologijske teme, 23*(1), 31–52.

Pintrich, P. R. (2000). The role of goal orientation in self-regulated learning. In M. Boekaerts, P. Pintrich, & M. Zeidner (Eds.), *Handbook of self-regulation* (pp. 451–502). San Diego, CA: Academic Press.

Pintrich, P. R., Smith, D. A. F., Garcia, T., & McKeachie, W. J. (1991). *A Manual for the Use of the Motivated Strategies for Learning Questionnaire (MSLQ). Ann Arbor:* University of Michigan, National Center for Research to Improve Postsecondary Teaching and Learning.

Resing, W. C. M., & Elliott, J. G. (2011). Dynamic testing with tangible electronics: Measuring children's change in strategy use with a series completion task. *British Journal of Educational Psychology, 81*, 579–605.

Roelle, J., Schmidt, E. M., Buchau, A., & Berthold, K. (2017). Effects of informing learners about the dangers of making overconfident judgments of learning. *Journal of Educational Psychology, 109*(1), 99.

Ruffing, S., Wach, F., Spinath, F. M., Brünken, R., & Karbach, J. (2015). Learning strategies and general cognitive ability as predictors of gender-specific academic achievement. *Frontiers in Psychology, 6*, 1–12.

Rutherford, A. (2011). *ANOVA and ANCOVA: a GLM approach.* Hoboken, N.J.: Wiley.

Schneider, M., & Preckel, F. (2017). Variables associated with achievement in higher education: A systematic review of meta-analyses. *Psychological Bulletin, 143*(6), 565.

Schunk, D. H., & Greene, J. A. (2018). Historical, contemporary, and future perspectives on self- regulated learning and performance. In D. H. Schunk & J. A. Greene (Eds.), *Handbook of Self-Regulation of Learning and Performance (2nd Ed.)* (pp. 1–15). New York, NY: Routledge.

Tabachnick, B. G., & Fidell, L. S. (2013). *Using multivariate statistics* (6th ed.). Boston, MA: Pearson.

Vandevelde, S., Van Keer, H., & Rosseel, Y. (2013). Measuring the complexity of upper primary school children's self-regulated learning: A multi-component approach. *Contemporary Educational Psychology, 38*, 407–425. doi:10.1016/j.cedpsych.2013.09.002

Vasilyeva, M., Laski, E. V., & Shen, C. (2015). Computational fluency and strategy choice predict individual and cross-national differences in complex arithmetic. *Developmental Psychology, 51*, 1489–1500.

Vermunt, J. (this volume). Surveys and retrospective self-report. In D. L. Dinsmore, L. K. Fryer, & M. M. Parkinson (Eds.), *Handbook of strategies and strategic processing.* New York: Routledge.

Yoon, H., & Jo, J. W. (2014). Direct and indirect access to corpora: an exploratory case study comparing students' error correction and learning strategy use in L2 writing. *Language Learning & Technology, 18*, 96–117.

Zimmerman, B.J. (2013). From cognitive modeling to self-regulation: A social cognitive career path. *Educational Psychologist, 48*(3), 135–147.

22

PERSON-CENTERED APPROACHES TO EXPLAINING STUDENTS' COGNITIVE PROCESSING STRATEGIES

Luke K. Fryer and Alex Shum
THE UNIVERSITY OF HONG KONG

INTRODUCTION

This chapter will present what is, as yet, a very small niche within the strategic processing research literature: the (potential) role of person-centered analyses for strategic processing research. This chapter is organized into three sections. The first aims to situate person-centered quantitative research methodologies within the plethora of analytical approaches that are commonly pursued. Then the reader is introduced to key person-centered research that has been undertaken, establishing the current state of the field and how it might continue to develop. The final section of this chapter makes a case for person-centered analytical approaches as a viable means of relating and integrating some of our processing strategy theories into a more comprehensive picture of how individual differences and the environment interact across a learners' knowledge, skills and motivation-beliefs development.

Having stated the goals, it is important to make clear what the chapter will not attempt to do. It will not be a "how to" guide for researchers who lack sufficient experience with classical statistics. A grounding in statistics, both in "pen and paper knowledge" and experience designing and analyzing research, is necessary for this chapter to be of any real use and is directed at such readers. For readers seeking to brush up on the basics, Howell (2016) is suggested. For readers interested in a firm (detailed) grounding in the analytical methods discussed in this chapter you are referred to Hagenaars and McCutcheon (2002).

As a start, it is important to address the person-centered methods which will be the focus of this chapter. It is therefore relevant to note that all of the research the author has undertaken, and much of the recent research discussed, has been done with Latent Profile Analysis (LPA). LPA is consistent with common factor analysis (FA), whereby the covariation of variables (observed) is explained by continuous variables (latent). Bauer and Curran (2004) sum up the difference between LPA and FA by stating that "the common factor model decomposes the covariances to highlight relationships among the variables, whereas the latent profile model decomposes the covariances to highlight relationships among individuals" (p. 6).

Clustering approaches (i.e., K-mean) are historically (Steinley, 2006), and still currently, more popular, and have a demonstrated propensity for recovering accurate classification patterns (Steinley & Brusco, 2011). However, latent profile analyses have a number of demonstrated strengths which have made it the author's preferred approach to person-centered analysis. Two key strengths of LPAs are allowing partial membership into multiple subgroups rather than a rigid assignment to one and the many longitudinal techniques that a latent profile analysis approach makes possible (for a detailed list of the advantages of latent profile analysis relative to standard clustering approaches, please see the supplement to Morin et al., 2017).

SITUATING PERSON-CENTERED ANALYSES WITHIN QUANTITATIVE APPROACHES TO RESEARCHING COGNITIVE STRATEGIES

Strategic processing is a complex field further complicated by its assortment of isolated theories, each seeking to describe similar cognitive and meta-cognitive processes. There are practical reasons for the lack of interaction between strategic processing theories. The chief of these pragmatics is the way programs of research develop and are then handed down from supervisor to student, generation to generation. Another reason and one this chapter will return to, is that the dominant approach to research design and analysis has for some time been (and remains) variable-centered. As will be discussed later, variable-centered analyses lend themselves to testing hypothetical connections between variables, generally within one theoretical framework. Variable-centered studies depend on these established theoretical connections for both research design and resulting modelling/analysis. Person-centered approaches, while similarly drawing on strong theory for hypothesis development, also have a parallel interest in how a theory or multiple theories are actually expressed in a population. The additional, more recent area of investigation yields more space for cross-theory research.

Strategic processing researchers have an increasingly broad array of variable-centered approaches available to them. Early theories of strategic processing research often relied on difference testing and experimental research design (Craik & Tulving, 1975; Marton & Säljö, 1976a, 1976b). In the more than four decades since these foundational theories were conceived, strategic processing researchers have moved from increasingly complex comparisons of means (e.g., Biggs, 1978; Gadzella, Ginther, & Williamson, 1986), to correlative-based analysis (e.g., Entwistle, 1989; Entwistle & Waterston, 1988) as more large-scale research was carried out in natural settings with surveys. The currents of variable-centered research since the late 1990s have been a slow increase in longitudinal research paired with increasingly complex analytical approaches. There has also been a steady shift towards diversifying the ways in which we collect data about how individuals strategically process information. Some of these include qualitative approaches such as think aloud (for some recent examples, see

Deekens, Greene, & Lobczowski, 2018; Dinsmore & Zoellner, 2018; Parkinson & Dinsmore, 2018) combined with modelling such as path analyses. They also include popular research technologies such as eye-tracking for reading experiences (Catrysse et al., 2018), click traces left from interacting with digital multimedia (Winne & Hadwin, 2013), and functional near-infrared spectroscopy (fNIRS) during tasks (Dinsmore, Hooper, & Macyczko, 2018).

Despite these advances, the field has been hindered from progressing analytically, relative to other areas of educational psychology, for several reasons. For some areas of strategic processing research, such as approaches to learning, context has been largely restricted to higher education. These smaller islands of research have resulted in a kind of Galapagos effect, with scant incoming and outgoing exchange of ideas. Other major strategic processing theories have faced similar growing problems, remaining fixed to specific groups of researchers.

Furthermore, due to the complex, ongoing processes under examination by strategic processing researchers, there is a growing agreement that survey-based self-reports alone are not a data source sufficient to continue to push the field forward (Dinsmore, 2017). This is a research tool that has dominated strategic processing for nearly four decades. Including alternative data sources (such as achievement data) for intensive analytical approaches such as Structural Equation Modelling (SEM) and latent growth analysis can be difficult.

Given the underdeveloped nature (analytically) of the field of strategic processing and pressure to move beyond surveys as the only means of assessing students' strategic processing, our first question is: Where does person-centered research fit in and amongst this somewhat constrained variable-centered field (see Freed et al. this volume for a comprehensive overview of the variable-centered approaches)?

Person-centered and variable-centered approaches to analyses are "considered as complementary approaches, as both provide alternative views of the same reality" (Morin et al., 2017, p. 400). In some respects, person-centered approaches are less restrictive than many variable-centered approaches. Perhaps the most important example of this is that variable-centered approaches assume participants come from a single population and derive mean-based parameters from these participants for analysis. In contrast, person-centered approaches relax this assumption, and allow the possibility that a sample of participants might include subpopulations with different sets of parameters. This difference is particularly important for research with heterogenous samples, and in contexts where sensitive subgroups are the target.

One further critical difference is that person-centered analyses provide a means of examining the interactions among the many psychological and environmental components which are each integral to the research of something as complex as cognitive processing, e.g., the motivations and beliefs which propel (or impede) individuals as well as the affordances and constraints of learning environments. A person-centered approach to research design necessitates that research question framing diverges from standard correlational questions focusing on variables. Research questions need to focus on how variables are expressed together by an individual and groups of individuals and the differences between subgroups' attributes (i.e., level and shape, which are explained in the next section). This is a shift in researching paradigm that needs to be considered prior to embarking on these methods.

The next section will review how person-centered research approaches have and are currently being applied. Examples of recent strategic processing and related research in the area of motivations and beliefs will be discussed along with directions for future research.

LESSONS AND DIRECTIONS FOR PERSON-CENTERED RESEARCH IN STRATEGIC PROCESSING

While many researchers might see person-centered analyses as one more analytical approach that might be applied to a data set, this kind of thinking vastly undervalues its perspective and misjudges the preparation necessary to ensure meaningful results. As an initial guide for strategic processing researchers interested in this approach, three straightforward steps might support appropriate and meaningful use. The first is framing the proposed research appropriately. This includes the theories, resulting selection of constructs and relevant research questions. It is generally the case that person-centered methods are applied when the theory under consideration is well substantiated, with considerable variable-centered research evidence accumulated. This foundation can then be used to extrapolate and develop appropriate hypotheses. Much like variables arising from factor analyses, which cannot be effectively described by theory, subgroups which are unexplainable are unlikely to be replicable and not useful research outcomes. Robust, well-tested theory and constructs that have established construct validity are as essential for person-centered as they are for variable-centered research and must be confirmed first. And as a second step, the potential shape as well as level (Morin & Marsh, 2015) of the hypotheses the chosen theory can generate for different subgroups. Shape refers to qualitative differences across subgroup profiles, in contrast to quantitative difference only (level) (Morin et al., 2017). Some theories, especially those that are narrow and function across a simple continuum of "a lot" = good, and "scant" = bad are not the best theoretical frames for finding meaningful subgroups. Approaches to learning (Marton, Hounsell, & Entwistle, 1984) are an example of this, as surface and deep approaches have been organized as existing on a continuum (i.e., surface to deep; Kember, Biggs, & Leung, 2004; Kember & Leung, 1998). Another theory that describes a broader range of cognitive processing strategies (Learning Patterns; Vermunt, 1994; Vermunt & Donche, 2017) acknowledges the reality of concurrent strategy use that results in subgroups with profiles that demonstrate differences in shape as well as level (Vermetten, Lodewijks, & Vermunt, 1999). A third point for consideration is sample size. The sample size necessary for the effective recovery of subgroups using LPAs varies depending on a number of criteria ranging from the number of indicators, the true number of classes and the inter-class distance (for an in-depth discussion see Tein, Coxe, & Cham, 2013). Increases in any of these can increase the sample size necessary for obtaining a meaningful set of subgroups.

A Review of Person-centered Research in Strategic Processing

Since the late 1990s several strategic processing researchers have applied person-centered analyses within their research programs. Earlier research classically applied clustering techniques, often focusing on an exploration of how a single theory might be expressed across a sample of students. More recent research has focused on complementing or integrating theoretical perspectives and modelling transitions between subgroups across time.

Beginning with the early person-centered strategic processing studies, applications have aimed to examine the convergence of theoretically related constructs. Clustering research by Prosser, Ramsden, Trigwell, and Martin (2003) brought together aspects of the learning environment (course experience questionnaire; Elphinstone, 1989; Ramsden, 1991), and approaches to learning (Biggs, 1987) are an example of applying clustering to a large sample with two indicators (surface and deep approaches to learning; Marton et al., 1984). This analysis resulted in high quality and low quality learning clusters, i.e., clusters based on level differences. Consistent with this study's general approach, but applying latent profile analysis, Abar and Loken (2010) also examined longstanding variable-centered theory and empirical evidence in a student population. A collection of indicators from well-established surveys (Midgley et al., 2000; Pintrich, Smith, Garcia, & McKeachie, 1991) with relevance to self-regulation were used to cluster a sample of high school students. Three subgroups were identified as High, Low and Average SRL subgroups: subgroups again based on level differences. Both studies were modest, largely exploratory studies, essentially aiming to see what their respective theories might look like across a population.

In an early longitudinal person-centered study, Alexander and Murphy (1998) brought together knowledge, interest and strategy measures to cluster students' pre-post experience during a psychology course. One of the aims of this approach was to examine changes in subgroup number and profile shape, while also connecting profiled members with achievement in the course. An increase in the number subgroups (three to four) was found, pointing to changes across the courses. Furthermore, the subgroup that demonstrated a convergence of high interest and strategic processing along with moderate levels of domain knowledge presented the higher achievement. Robust theory and their pre-post approach yielded information about how the theory applied to specific population and subgroup differentiation by shape and level. By connecting the clusters to students' course-end examinations, specific achievement related findings were also made possible.

During the 2010s there has been an explosion of person-centered studies across educational psychology, but scant application to the field of strategic processing. Recent research both within and outside the field of strategic processing will be drawn on here to provide potential direction for future research. There is a growing recognition that if our learning strategy research is to continue to progress, it needs to increase its connections to other aspects of the learning process. Seeking to draw together students' goals for learning (instrumental; Fryer, 2013; Simons, Dewitte, & Lens, 2004), amotivation (Legault, Green-Demers, & Pelletier, 2006) and their strategic processing (approaches to learning; Trigwell & Ashwin, 2006), an LPA was undertaken with these constructs along with annualized GPA as a covariate. The results yielded subgroups that were differentiated by level and shape, suggesting strong connections between distal goals and depth of processing. The person-centered outcomes also highlighted the reality that individuals pursue multiple goals when learning and that it is the balance of these goals (distal vs. proximal) that marks students applying a deep approach to learning. These results contrasted with previous variable-centered (longitudinal SEM) findings in the same research context (Fryer, Ginns, & Walker, 2014), which only highlighted the role of one type of distal goal and failed to demonstrate the fact that students pursue multiple goals simultaneously and that the balance of these goal pursuits, as much as any single goal, might be playing a role in students' strategic processing.

Educational psychology research is primarily concerned with the nature of student learning and how best to support students in being more effective in their learning. From a quantitative perspective, person-centered research is the more effective (relative to variable-centered) means of getting at these experiences, both cross-sectionally and longitudinally. One area of concern receiving considerable attention recently is the student experience across the transition from secondary to higher education (Kyndt, Donche, Trigwell, & Lindblom-Ylänne, 2017) – an area of longstanding concern in Japan (Cummings, 1984). As such, an extension to LPA, Latent Profile Transfer Analysis (LPTA) was employed. This analysis integrates autoregressive modelling to test longitudinal subgroup membership (Nylund, Asparoutiov, & Muthén, 2007). LPTA provides profile information at multiple time points and indicates the stability/variability of these subgroups and the transitions of each student between measurement points. LPTA is therefore a means of establishing how students might change categorically over time, by assessing their movement between established subgroups across as many as five consecutive time points (for an extensive review see Nylund, 2007).

LPTA was applied to a sample of students prior to and after their first year at a Japanese university (Fryer, 2017b). The aim was to reveal latent subgroups based on their learning experiences and strategic processing. Analyses suggested three subgroups were present. Consistent with Prosser et al., (2003) and the broad continuum these experiences and processes were distributed on, only level differentiated the subgroups from one another. The transition analyses that examined how and whether students meaningfully changed across the year-long experience revealed a pattern of students' transition towards subgroups reporting lower quality learning experiences and less overall strategic use. Furthermore, students in the "Low" subgroup presented more dependence on surface strategies between the two time points suggested, a "poor get poorer" downward spiral. This type of analysis provides a unique perspective on students' longitudinal experiences by indicating categorical change (rather than incremental) and highlighting how learning experiences might play a role in the development of these distinct subgroups over time.

A second longitudinal example from recent research touches on an avenue for strategic processing research which person-centered approaches have a potential to contribute to: theoretical convergence. This is a critical issue for strategies researchers (Coertjens, 2018; Dinsmore & Fryer, 2018; Fryer, 2017a) that few research programs meaningfully address. Person-centered analyses are well positioned to explain how different learning strategies combine and develop over time within different subgroups. Using LPTA, Fryer and Vermunt (2018) examined how the regulation of students' learning and their strategic processing of learning materials converge across a year of study at university. Consistent with Alexander and Murphy's early work (Alexander & Murphy, 1998), the longitudinal nature of the data offered an opportunity to look at the stability of subgroups' profiles across time. Rather than two snapshots provided by clustering students in two separate analyses (or as in an LPA at each time point), LPTA determines the subgroups at both time points simultaneously (reducing Type 1 errors) while also indicating students' potential movement between subgroups. Results from this analysis presented four subgroups at both times, with the shape of profiles remaining relatively consistent across time. Transition findings, for example, pointed towards the low quality (i.e., low self-regulation and deep approach to learning relative to higher lack of regulation and surface approaches to learning) strategy group as both growing in size and demonstrating the highest level of stability (i.e., lowest level of students transitioning out and in, relative to "remainers"). The least stable subgroup consisted of students reporting the lowest overall strategy use, with over half of them moving on to subgroups reporting more strategy use. While results suggested paired self-regulation and deep approaches, consistent with theory (Vermunt, 1987), it also highlighted that fact many students reported using relatively consistent amounts of all strategies. This kind of analytical approach is therefore well-disposed to demonstrating where theory seems to work (i.e., for some students) and other areas it might not meaningfully apply to. It is also an excellent means of examining at-risk subgroups that might not be getting the support they need to develop the kinds of strategies necessary to be successful.

To provide additional examples of how person-centered analyses can support our understanding of strategic processing it is necessary to draw on research from the related area of motivation and beliefs for learning. Considerable research has investigated the development of strategic processing skills across time (e.g., Alexander & Murphy, 1998; Gordon & Debus, 2002), but variable-centered research relies on mean-level difference comparisons at worst and latent growth analysis at best. LPTA can provide a clearer, categorical outcome that establishes how many students actually developed (or failed to), while indicating where they started. Oga-Baldwin and Fryer (2018) is an example of a study assessing whether a national initiative – supporting students' intrinsic motivation for learning a foreign language – was actually having any meaningful traction. To demonstrate "traction", a mean increase, regardless of its effect size, is not sufficient evidence. Through LPTA, this study could establish where students started and where they ended up after two years of elementary school. Results from the study demonstrated a clear pattern of students' annual movement towards subgroups with more adaptive motivational profiles (represented by five motivations and beliefs for learning – including intrinsic motivation), thereby suggesting "traction" for the national policy.

Person-centered studies that span multiple learning contexts can indicate how students vary in different learning environments (e.g., Alexander, Jetton, & Kulikowich, 1995). These kinds of studies can also provide external validity for theories, expanding their relevance, or, just as importantly, constraining it. Person-centered studies that bridge domains of learning also have the potential to challenge longstanding beliefs about the differences in studying different subjects. In a recent study with secondary students, Oga-Baldwin and Fryer (2018) have applied this research design to testing the age-old premise that students' motives for studying a new language differ substantially from their reasons for studying their native language. Results from this study demonstrated strong overlap for subgroups – their membership, level and shape – for the same students' motives in these two subjects. Person-centered analysis is the only quantitative means of making a comparison of multiple theoretical components and challenging assumptions about students' learning experience in different contexts.

There are a few examples of how variable (longitudinal latent structural equation modeling) and then person-centered (Latent Profile Transition Analyses) research can be undertaken synergistically within a single study (Fryer & Ainley, 2019; Fryer & Bovee, 2018). Fryer and Bovee initially used SEM to demonstrate the critical longitudinal connections between teacher support and prior computer skills for online learning (controlling for prior knowledge). The examination of transition of students (between the three subgroups revealed at each time point), however, revealed the critical role of students' prior competence and teacher support together for student learning experiences and outcomes, i.e., teacher support was critical but only when students had sufficient prior knowledge. This pair of variable and person-centered approaches can offer a deeper analysis, allowing researchers to step beyond the mean and assess whether there are vulnerable subpopulations in need of additional support.

Person-centered approaches offer researchers a number of choices. Some examples from research in strategic processing and neighboring fields have been presented. It is worth noting that the most common approaches are those taken by early research in this area: examining samples for theoretically consistent groups. The majority of this research employs variance testing (e.g., MANOVAs) and difference testing (e.g., ANOVAs) to assess the validity of subgroups revealed and the impact of group membership on covariates or distal outcomes like achievement.

Mixture Modeling (e.g., Hagenaars & McCutcheon, 2002) incorporates Latent Class Analysis (LCA; Latent Profile Analysis is a type of LCA with continuous indicators) along with a wide range of analytical techniques. Mixture Modeling offers researchers a powerful means of both establishing the validity of subgroups, as well as ascertaining the reasons for and outcomes of membership. For readers familiar with M*plus* (Muthén & Muthén, 1998-2015), Morin (2016) has organized a supplementary instructional document which details in stepwise fashion, increasingly sophisticated levels of person-centered tests. These analyses offer researchers the opportunity to integrate multiple group solutions, mixture regression and growth mixture modeling (linear and non-linear) into person-centered analyses. Through the analyses outlined by Morin and colleagues, subgroups can also be tested for similarity across a broad range of factors, e.g., Configural Similarity, Structural Similarity, Dispersion Similarity and Distribution Similarity. While measurement issues like those addressed by these tests are still just on the horizon for person-centered research, they are certain to become standard practice in the near future.

NUDGING STRATEGIC PROCESSING RESEARCH FORWARD

This chapter has touched on avenues by which person-centered approaches have and have yet to be utilized by strategic processing researchers. Examining how theory, validated by variable-centered research, is expressed by distinct subgroups is an example of an exploratory application (e.g., Prosser et al., 2003). Comparing students' experiences in distinct learning contexts (e.g., two courses at university; Alexander et al., 1995), and retesting cross-theoretical connections suggested by past variable-centered analyses (Fryer et al., 2016) are two more practical uses of cross-sectional research designs.

Person-centered longitudinal studies are much less common but have considerable potential for contribution to our understanding of strategic processing theory and its application to different populations (and subpopulations) across time. In its simplest form, they can track both subgroup membership and profile stability across time, thereby suggesting a pattern of population change (Fryer, 2017b). Findings from these studies derive their strength from the categorical nature (i.e., membership and potential movement between subgroups) focusing on distinct individuals, and vulnerable subpopulations can yield results that speak to popular readership and, potentially, policymakers. Longitudinal person-centered studies can, like cross-sectional studies, be conducted to supplement and support variable-centered findings (Fryer & Ainley, 2019). However, they can also provide a more dynamic and fine-grained perspective on longitudinal variable-centered studies, which might be lost in a focus on the average student experience (Fryer & Bovee, 2018). It is possible to examine not just the separate subgroups at different time points but also the movers (students moving between one subgroup and another over time). Results from this kind of targeted examination might support theory confirmation and building regarding how (as well as whether) students' strategies meaningfully develop. Extensions to this kind of study might include regression as part of the analysis (rather than as an ad hoc addition) to resolve important questions. First the outcomes of membership to a specific group might be assessed and perhaps more interestingly the movement between groups can also be predicted (Morin et al., 2017; Muthén & Muthén, 1998–2015).

Looking to the future and where strategic processing research must go if it is to continue to develop, the gaps and overlaps of our theories are an area in need of attention. This issue has been raised in a recent special issue (Dinsmore & Fryer, 2018) seeking to bring together metacognitive and cognitive strategy research. Unfortunately, it was chiefly in the commentaries for this special issue that these strategies were meaningfully addressed together. Part of the reason for this might be that the special issue was dominated by variable-centered studies in which, due in part to their analytical approach, most contributors applied a single theory to their chosen questions. Person-centered and, in some cases qualitative (See Cho et al., this volume), studies are analytical tools that are in many ways better situated to support potential theoretical integration. Cross-sectional snapshots of how strategies might come together will certainly be useful to researchers interested in contributing to this area. Longitudinal studies, across time and context, are crucial for seeing how individuals apply different strategies concurrently and sequentially. Longitudinal studies will provide perspective on how individuals' strategy use develops, and to the strategy use that signals that development. Again, crucially, the categorical nature of change within longitudinal person-centered studies is both a strength and a weakness. Used in combination with variable-centered analysis like latent curve analysis, however, its weakness is less apparent.

In conclusion, person-centered analyses are a mature area of analysis that is under-exploited by strategic processing researchers. Their potential as a means of support and extension for variable-centered studies, which continue to dominate strategic processing research, has barely been tapped. The most promising uses for some of these analytical techniques have yet to even be considered by strategic processing researchers. A new generation of researchers coming to the field of strategic processing, unbound by loyalty to one or other theory, however, will (I hope) see their potential for the theoretical extension and integration that needs to come.

REFERENCES

Abar, B., & Loken, E. (2010). Self-regulated learning and self-directed study in a pre-college sample. *Learning and Individual Differences, 20*(1), 25–29. doi:https://doi.org/10.1016/j.lindif.2009.09.002

Alexander, P. A., Jetton, T. L., & Kulikowich, J. M. (1995). Interrelationship of knowledge, interest, and recall: Assessing a model of domain learning. *Journal of educational psychology, 87*(4), 559.

Alexander, P. A., & Murphy, P. K. (1998). Profiling the differences in students' knowledge, interest, and strategic processing. *Journal of Educational Psychology, 90*(3), 435. doi:10.1037/0022-0663.90.3.435

Bauer, D. J., & Curran, P. J. (2004). The integration of continuous and discrete latent variable models: Potential problems and promising opportunities. *Psychological Methods, 9*(1), 3–29. doi:10.1037/1082-989X.9.1.3

Biggs, J. B. (1978). Individual and group differences in study processes. *British Journal of Educational Psychology, 48*, 266–279. doi:10.1111/j.2044-8279.1978.tb03013.x

Biggs, J. B. (1987). *Study Process Questionnaire Manual. Student Approaches to Learning and Studying.* Australian Council for Educational Research Ltd., Radford House, Frederick St., Hawthorn 3122, Australia.

Catrysse, L., Gijbels, D., Donche, V., De Maeyer, S., Lesterhuis, M., & Van Den Bossche, P. (2018). How are learning strategies reflected in the eyes? Combining results from self-reports and eye-tracking. *British Journal of Educational Psychology, 88*(1), 118–137. doi:10.1111/bjep.12181

Coertjens, L. (2018). The relation between cognitive and metacognitive processing: Building bridges between the SRL, MDL, and SAL domains. *Journal of Experimental Psychology: General, 88*(1), 138–151.

Craik, F. I. M., & Tulving, E. (1975). Depth of processing and the retention of words in episodic memory. *Journal of Experimental Psychology: General, 104*, 68–294. doi:10.1037/0096-3445.104.3.268

Cummings, W. (1984). *Educational policies in crisis: Japanese and American perpectivies..* New York: Praeger.

Deekens, V. M., Greene, J. A., & Lobczowski, N. G. (2018). Monitoring and depth of strategy use in computer-based learning environments for science and history. *British Journal of Educational Psychology, 88*(1), 63–79. doi:doi:10.1111/bjep.12174

Dinsmore, D. L. (2017). Toward a dynamic, multidimensional research framework for strategic processing. *Educational Psychology Review, 29*(2), 235–268. doi:10.1007/s10648-017-9407-5

Dinsmore, D. L., & Fryer, L. K. (2018). The intersection between depth and the regulation of strategy use. *British Journal of Educational Psychology, 88*, 1–8. doi:http://doi.org/10.1111/bjep.12209

Dinsmore, D. L., Hooper, K. C., & Macyczko, J. (2018). *Exploring the Use of fNIRS in a Multrait-multimethod Investigation of Students' Strategic Processing.* Paper presented at the Second Network Meeting of the Scientific Community on 'Learning Strategies in Social and Informal Learning Contexts', Antwerpen.

Dinsmore, D. L., & Zoellner, B. P. (2018). The relation between cognitive and metacognitive strategic processing during a science simulation. *British Journal of Educational Psychology, 88*(1), 95–117. doi:doi:10.1111/bjep.12177

Elphinstone, L. J. (1989). *Development of the course experience questionnaire.* Masters. Melbourne: Melbourne University.

Entwistle, N. (1989). Approaches to studying and course perceptions: The case of the disappearing relationships. *Studies in Higher Education, 14*, 155–156. doi:10.1080/03075078912331377466

Entwistle, N., & Waterston, S. (1988). Approaches to studying and levels of processing in university students. *British Journal of Educational Psychology, 58*, 258–265.

Fryer, L. K. (2013). *Motivated study and learning strategies: Cross-sectional and longitudinal investigations.* (Ph.D. Educational Psychology), Sydney University.

Fryer, L. K., Van den Broeck, A., Ginns, P. & Nakao, K. (2016). Understanding students' instrumental goals, motivation deficits and achievement: Through the Lens of a latent profile analysis. *Psychologica Belgica, 56*, 226–243, doi: 10.5334/pb.265.

Fryer, L. K. (2017a). Building bridges: Seeking structure and direction for higher education motivated learning strategy models. *Educational Psychology Review, 29*(2), 325–344. doi:10.1007/s10648-017-9405-7

Fryer, L. K. (2017b). (Latent) transitions to learning at university: A latent profile transition analysis of first-year Japanese students. *Higher Education, 73*(3), 519–537. doi:10.1007/s10734-016-0094-9

Fryer, L. K., & Ainley, M. (2019). Supporting interest in a study domain: A longitudinal test of the interplay between interest, utility-value, and competence beliefs. *Learning and Instruction.* doi:10.1016/j.learninstruc.2017.11.002

Fryer, L. K., & Bovee, H. N. (2018). Staying motivated to e-learn: Person- and variable-centred perspectives on the longitudinal risks and support. *Computers & Education, 120*, 227–240. doi:https://doi.org/10.1016/j.compedu.2018.01.006

Fryer, L. K., Ginns, P., & Walker, R. (2014). Between students' instrumental goals and how they learn: Goal content is the gap to mind. *British Journal of Educational Psychology, 84*(4), 612–630. doi:10.1111/bjep.12052

Fryer, L. K., & Vermunt, J. D. (2018). Regulating approaches to learning: Testing learning strategy convergences across a year at university. *British Journal of Educational Psychology, 88*, 138. doi:10.1111/bjep.12169

Gadzella, B. M., Ginther, D. W., & Williamson, J. D. (1986). Differences in learning processes and academic achievement. *Perceptual and motor skills, 62*(1), 151–156. doi:10.2466/pms.1986.62.1.151

Gordon, C., & Debus, R. (2002). Developing deep learning approaches and personal teaching efficacy within a preservice teacher education context. *British Journal of Educational Psychology, 72*(4), 483–511.

Hagenaars, J. A., & McCutcheon, A. L. (2002). *Applied latent class analysis.* Cambridge: Cambridge University Press.

Howell, D. C. (2016). *Fundamental statistics for the behavioral sciences (Ninth Ed.).* Boston, MA: Cengage Learning.

Kember, D., Biggs, J. B., & Leung, D. Y. P. (2004). Examining the multidimensionality of approaches to learning through the development of a revised version of the Learning Process Questionnaire. *British Journal of Educational Psychology, 74*, 261–279. doi:10.1348/000709904773839879

Kember, D., & Leung, D. Y. P. (1998). The dimensionality of approaches to learning: an investigation with confirmatory factor analysis on the structure of the SPQ and LPQ. *British Journal of Educational Psychology, 68*, 395–407.

Kyndt, E., Donche, V., Trigwell, K., & Lindblom-Ylänne, S. (2017). *Higher education transitions.* New York: Taylor & Francis.

Legault, L., Green-Demers, I., & Pelletier, L. (2006). Why do high school students lack motivation in the classroom? Toward an understanding of academic amotivation and the role of social support. *Journal of Educational Psychology, 98*, 567–582. doi:10.1037/0022-0663.98.3.567

Marton, F., Hounsell, D. J., & Entwistle, N. (1984). *The experience of learning: Implications for teaching and studying in higher education.* r. I. edition Ed. Vol. null. Edinburgh: University of Edinburgh, Centre for Teaching, Learning and Assessment.

Marton, F., & Säljö, R. (1976a). On qualitative differences in learning I: Outcome and processes. *British Journal of Educational Psychology, 46*, 4–11. doi:10.1111/j.2044-8279.1976.tb02980.x

Marton, F., & Säljö, R. (1976b). On qualitative differences in learning II: Outcome as a function of the learner's conception of the task. *British Journal of Educational Psychology, 46*, 115–127. doi:10.1111/j.2044-8279.1976.tb02304.x

Midgley, C., Maehr, M. L., Hruda, L. Z., Anderman, E., Anderman, L., Freeman, K. E., & Urdan, T. (2000). Manual for the patterns of adaptive learning scales. *Ann Arbor, 1001*, 48109–41259.

Morin, A. J. S. (2016). Person-centered research strategies in commitment research. In P. M. John (Ed.), *The handbook of employee commitment* (pp. 490–508). UK: Edward Elgar Publishing.

Morin, A. J. S., Boudrias, J.-S., Marsh, H. W., McInerney, D. M., Dagenais-Desmarais, V., Madore, I., & Litalien, D. (2017). Complementary variable- and person-centered approaches to the dimensionality of psychometric constructs: application to psychological wellbeing at work. *Journal of Business Psychology & Health, 32*(4), 395–419. doi:10.1007/s10869-016-9448-7

Morin, A. J. S., & Marsh, H. W. (2015). Disentangling shape from level effects in person-centered analyses: An illustration based on university teachers' multidimensional profiles of effectiveness. *Structural Equation Modeling: A Multidisciplinary Journal, 22*(1), 39–59. doi:10.1080/10705511.2014.919825

Muthén, L. K., & Muthén, B. O. (1998-2015). *Mplus user's guide* (Sixth ed.). Los Angeles, CA: Muthén & Muthén.

Nylund, K. L. (2007). *Latent transition analysis: Modeling extensions and an application to peer victimization.* Los Angeles: Doctoral dissertation, University of California.

Nylund, K. L., Asparoutiov, T., & Muthén, B. O. (2007). Deciding on the number of classes in latent class analysis and growth mixture modeling: A monte Carlo simulation study. *Structural Equation Modeling-a Multidisciplinary Journal, 14*, 535–569. doi:10.1080/10705510701575396

Oga-Baldwin, W. L. Q., & Fryer, L. K. (2018). Schools can improve motivational quality: Profile transitions across early foreign language learning experiences. *Motivation and Emotion, 42*, 527–545. doi:10.1007/s11031-018-9681-7

Parkinson, M. M., & Dinsmore, D. L. (2018). Multiple aspects of high school students' strategic processing on reading outcomes: The role of quantity, quality, and conjunctive strategy use. *British Journal of Educational Psychology, 88*(1), 42–62. doi:doi:10.1111/bjep.12176

Pintrich, P. R., Smith, D. A. F., Garcia, T., & McKeachie, W. J. (1991). *A manual for the use of the motivated strategies for learning questionnaire (MSLQ)* (Vol. null).

Prosser, M., Ramsden, P., Trigwell, K., & Martin, E. (2003). Dissonance in experience of teaching and its relation to the quality of student learning. *Studies in Higher Education, 28*, 37–48. doi:10.1080/03075070309299

Ramsden, P. (1991). A performance indicator of teaching quality in higher education: The course experience questionnaire. *Studies in Higher Education, 16*, 129–150. doi:10.1080/03075079112331382944

Simons, J., Dewitte, S., & Lens, W. (2004). The role of different types of instrumentality in motivation, study strategies, and performance: Know why you learn, so you'll know what you learn!. *British Journal of Educational Psychology, 74*, 343–360. doi:10.1348/0007099041552314

Steinley, D. (2006). K-means clustering: A half-century synthesis. *British Journal of Mathematical and Statistical Psychology, 59*, (1), 1–34. doi:10.1348/000711005X48266

Steinley, D., & Brusco, M. J. (2011). Evaluating mixture modeling for clustering: Recommendations and cautions. *Psychological Methods, 16*, 63–79.

Tein, J.-Y., Coxe, S., & Cham, H. (2013). Statistical power to detect the correct number of classes in latent profile analysis. *Structural Equation Modeling: A Multidisciplinary Journal, 20*(4), 640–657. doi:10.1080/10705511.2013.824781

Trigwell, K., & Ashwin, P. (2006). *Undergraduate students' experience of learning at the University of Oxford.* Unpublished report. University of Oxford. Oxford.

Vermetten, Y. J., Lodewijks, H. G., & Vermunt, J. D. (1999). Consistency and variability of learning strategies in different university courses. *Higher Education, 37*(1), 1–21.

Vermunt, J. D. (1987). Regulation of learning, approaches to studying and learning styles of adult students. In P. R. J. Simons & G. Beukhof. (Eds.), *Regulation of learning* (pp. 1–20). The Hague: S.V.O.

Vermunt, J. D. (1994). *Inventory of learning styles (ILS) in higher education. Tilburg*: University of Tilburg.

Vermunt, J. D., & Donche, V. (2017). A learning patterns perspective on student learning in higher education: State of the art and moving forward. *Educational Psychology Review, 29*, 269–299. doi:10.1007/s10648-017-9414-6

Winne, P. H., & Hadwin, A. F. (2013). Nstudy: Tracing and supporting self-regulated learning in the internet. In R. Azevedo & V. Aleven (Eds.), *international handbook of metacognition and learning technologies* (pp. 293–308). New York: Springer New York.

23

QUALITATIVE APPROACHES TO THE VERBAL PROTOCOL ANALYSIS OF STRATEGIC PROCESSING

Byeong-Young Cho
UNIVERSITY OF PITTSBURGH, USA

Lindsay Woodward
DRAKE UNIVERSITY, USA

Peter Afflerbach
UNIVERSITY OF MARYLAND, USA

In this chapter, we examine qualitative approaches to verbal protocol analysis and their role in constructing detailed accounts of strategic processing. To that end, we draw from diverse studies in the area of reading in which qualitative protocol data is extensively used to catalog and describe the readers' strategies engaged with a variety of texts, tasks, and goals. Thus, our discussion is situated within the domain of reading in an effort to illustrate the potential of qualitative verbal protocol analysis to a wider range of domains of knowledge, problem, and learning through examining the versatility of strategic processing in reading. In the sections that follow, we first argue for the importance of investigating strategic processing in reading. Then, we examine the scientific merits of qualitative verbal protocol analysis in examining such strategic processing. Finally, we discuss critical issues in the qualitative analysis of verbal protocol data and suggest possible means of addressing the issues to undertake rigorous analyses of strategic processing.

THE IMPORTANCE OF ANALYZING STRATEGIC PROCESSING TO UNDERSTANDING THE CONSTRUCT OF READING

Our conception of reading is grounded at the intersection of research literature on *readers* (e.g., knowledge, skills, attitudes, identities), *texts* that they access and process (e.g., genres, structures, purposes, modes), and the *contexts* in which reading takes place (e.g., social influences, task environments) (McNamara & Magliano, 2009; Snow, 2002). We note that these variables interact distinctively in accordance with readers' goals. When reading is successful, the *goals* that readers establish help guide strategies—as text, task, and context comprise the problem space that is demanding of strategic processing. Reading goals are not static. They may change as readers gain knowledge from constructing meaning from text, and as readers reflect on their needs and opportunities related to goals. That is, acts of reading are situated with the specific goals that are planned, revisited, and reformulated along the course of making meaning (Brown, Collins, & Duguid, 1989; Kintsch, 1988).

Readers use cognitive and metacognitive strategies to achieve goals. This process is dynamic, as readers select, adjust, and coordinate different strategies to construct meaning. The use of specific strategies is not a stand-alone cognitive activity. Rather, strategies are interrelated and mutually supportive as reading progresses under control of reader metacognition (McNamara, 2007; Pressley, 1995; Veenman, 2015). Hence, reading is better understood when we identify and describe how strategies are chosen and orchestrated by readers. Verbal protocol analysis is well-suited to the task of providing detailed data related to such strategic reading.

Strategic reading, in particular, involves chains of intentional cognitive actions focused on building a coherent understanding of text (Alexander, Graham, & Harris, 1998; Cho, 2014). Of course, not all reading behaviors are necessarily strategic, neither are all strategies successful (Afflerbach, Pearson, & Paris, 2008). However, cognitive work must be initiated and assessed by the reader for utility and effectiveness in each iteration of strategy use (Afflerbach, Cho, & Kim, 2015). Due to this situational intentionality, determining the nature of strategies in specific reading situations is a challenging task that demands contextualized inferences about the enactment of those processes.

That said, qualitative studies provide a common ground for research that seeks to describe the types and sequences of strategic processes in reading. Research on accomplished reading describes some common features that may distinguish strategic actions from non-strategic behaviors. In their meta-analytic work, Pressley and Afflerbach (1995) reexamined the numerous cognitive and metacognitive strategies taken from the verbal protocols of accomplished readers (e.g., librarians, historians, scientists) observed in 38 primary research studies. Their analysis yielded a compendium of reading comprehension strategies, which were grouped into three categories: (a) identifying and learning text content, (b) self-monitoring of thinking processes, and (c) evaluating different aspects of reading.

For example, Pressley and Afflerbach (1995, pp. 31–62) describe the array of strategic actions that accomplished readers carry out for *identifying and learning text content* in the following manner:

- Before reading, accomplished readers attempt to *construct a goal for reading.* They *overview the content and structure of text* and *determine what to read and where to start* as informed by the overview as well as the goal. Accordingly, these readers *activate prior knowledge* that may help them to better understand text. These prereading activities help readers *generate an initial hypothesis about text.*
- Initially, accomplished readers tend to read text from front to back to *test their text hypotheses.* As reading progresses (once their initial testing of hypotheses tell text relevance), however, they opportunistically *adjust attention and effort by according to the priorities and needs for information processing,* getting involved in a more active and focused reading of text ideas. For example, these readers *use*

both literal and inferential reasoning using text information, *analyze and integrate* different parts of text, and *interpret* text ideas and hidden meanings.

- After the initial reading, accomplished readers *reread* selected parts of text with an eye out for particular information. Rereading and reflection leads them to *construct a cohesive summary of text* (i.e., situated mental representation). They *self-question over text content*, reflecting on text with the possibility of reflection leading to shifts in text interpretation. Consequently, these readers continually *evaluate and reconstruct an understanding of text, change their responses to text* as the understanding is reconstructed as a result of reading and reflection, and *think further* on the mentally represented text in *anticipation of using it later* for real-life purposes.

Strategic processing is a window on our understanding of how reading works. Verbal protocol studies of reading describe successful readers who employ a set of strategic thoughts and processes (*italicized* in the above descriptions from Pressley & Afflerbach, 1995). Although not all strategies are equally prominent in their text processing, these accomplished readers regulate their use of strategies in relation to the construction of meaning and the goals they seek to achieve. In stark contrast, ineffective strategy use is observed in novice readers. These readers might intend to be strategic, but their actions may not be goal-relevant due to multiple challenges such as a lack of domain knowledge, ineffective self-reflection, unspecific (or no) goals, a shortage of metacognitive awareness, and uninformed perspectives on what reading "is." Therefore, observing and evaluating one's strategy use, such as that inferred from verbal reports, is a litmus test for the performance and accomplishment of the reader.

We note that the bullet points above offer only a tangential summary of many strategies for identifying and learning text content—Pressley and Afflerbach (1995) documented a total of 204 interrelated strategies in this category only. That is, a considerable degree of variety, complexity, and uniqueness must be anticipated in the examination of how readers choose and organize among these strategies in different, extended, or novel tasks. We also reiterate that reading is understood in a particular coordination of reader, text, and context, and it is important to consider how manifold interactions among these components may play out in the analysis of readers' goal-directed engagement in strategic processing.

In short, our stance toward reading supports the importance of investigating the nature of strategic processing situated in this complex coordination that must count as an essential consideration for that investigation. It also calls for attention to qualitative analysis of process-oriented data, specifically reader-generated verbal reports, from which detailed accounts of readers' strategies, and their relationship to text, context, and goal that interplay in meaning making, are constructed. Such work can contribute to increasingly fine-grain understandings of the complexities and nuances in strategic reading which might not be revealed otherwise.

THE VALUE OF ANALYZING READER-GENERATED VERBAL DATA IN INQUIRY INTO STRATEGIC READING

In-depth examinations of verbal reports have contributed to advancing theories of learning that cut across diverse traditions of inquiry. Theoretical support for the veracity of verbal report data is fairly broad-based—and this data can inform us critically

376 • Cho et al.

about strategic minds. So as our common sense tells us, for example, vast literature in linguistics suggests that language offers a window into the mind of the speaker (Chomsky, 1975; Lakoff, 1987). The generative language of a person has also long been a major subject for philosophical and psychological investigations to complicate how the mind works in reasoning (Boring, 1953; James, 1890). The language of a learner may be seen as (inner) speech, a form of mediated action through culturally internalized higher-order mental functions (Vygotsky, 1962; Wertsch, 1998).

In cognitive science, however, an initial articulation and defense of verbal reports as data for the scientific studies of human cognition was provided by Ericsson and Simon in 1980. Their motivation reflects reactions to uninformed practices in cognitive studies at that time and their reevaluation of verbal data in the interrogation of cognitive processing:

> For more than half a century, and as the result of an unjustified extrapolation of justified challenge to a particular mode of verbal reporting (introspection), the verbal reports of human subjects have been thought suspect as a source of evidence about cognitive processes ... verbal reports, elicited with care and interpreted with full understanding of the circumstances under which they were obtained, are a valuable and thoroughly reliable source of information about cognitive processes. It is time to abandon the careless charge of "introspection" as a means for disparaging such data ... To omit them [verbal data] when we are carrying the "chain and transit of objective measurement" is only to mark as terra incognita large areas on the map of human cognition that we know perfectly well how to survey.
>
> (p. 247)

Ericsson and Simon (1980) noted that the verbal reports of human subjects historically have been discredited due to the overgeneralized labeling of such language data as a product of introspection, which was denigrated to be a form of informal report that is useful at best for glimpsing a subject's internal state of mind (Nisbett & Wilson, 1977). As a result, such misconception of verbal reports and uninformed research practices (e.g., measuring human thinking exclusively with standardized self-report measures) could not provide authentic information on a subject's cognitive processes in action. Alternatively, Ericsson and Simon argued for the value of verbal reports of human subjects as sense-makers, urging reconsideration of such data as a reliable source of scientific evidence that supports both the exploration and the verification of cognitive theories.

Along with emerging methodological discussions in reading (e.g., Afflerbach, 2000; Afflerbach & Johnston, 1984; Kucan & Beck, 1997; Magliano & Graesser, 1991; Pressley & Afflerbach, 1995; Smagorinsky, 1998) since the work of Ericsson and Simon, verbal protocol analysis has been gaining trustworthiness and popularity as a means of assessing the cognitive processes involved in text comprehension. Pressley and Afflerbach (1995) reached a conclusion that it is valuable to consider the merits of analyzing verbal reporting data, despite several considerations that must be addressed methodologically, because of the theoretical advancement made in part by the studies of readers' verbal protocols:

> On the one hand, the protocol analyses do support various models of comprehension that have been proposed. That is, the processes specified by each of these

models are represented in the think-aloud reports ... On the other hand, the verbal report data ... does more than provide partial verification of theoretical models. In fact, the verbal report data extend these models, leading to a complex description of reading than specified by any of the previously existing models.

(p. 83)

As supported by Pressley and Afflerbach (1995), as well as by Ericsson and Simon (1980), verbal protocol analysis may not only assist in exploration of yet-to-be-examined cognitive processes in novel tasks and contexts of reading, but it can contribute to verification of pre-existing theories by adding evidentiary (counter) examples in detail. Informed analysis of verbal protocols facilitates reasoned judgments concerning what extent of congruence or idiosyncrasy could be found between models of text processing and the aggregate insights from the verbal data.

We endorse the scientific merits of verbal protocol analysis, suggesting that analysis of reader-generated verbal data has several promises for advancing reading theories. Verbal protocol analysis foremost can help the investigation of the architecture of reading—even though it is an unobservable construct (e.g., when, where, and how reading begins, goes on, and ends). A particular strength of verbal protocol analysis relates to detailed description of the cognitive and metacognitive mechanisms through which mental representations are elaborated during text comprehension. Further, the investigation of verbal report data can provide the opportunity to integrate contextualized accounts of strategic processes into a coherent theory that explains the interplay of individual differences, text features, and situational influences.

ACKNOWLEDGING THE INFERENTIAL GAPS BETWEEN WHAT IS HEEDED IN MIND AND WHAT INDEED IS VERBALIZED

As much as we value the scientific merits of verbal protocol analysis, we also acknowledge several limitations that need to be addressed with care. Pressley and Afflerbach (1995) portrayed verbal protocol analysis as a "maturing" methodology (p. 1). We agree with their point that, while much interesting work has been already accomplished with varied verbal protocol analysis approaches, the ongoing development of the methodology parallels the evolution in our understanding of acts of reading. A result can be continued refinement of both.

Perhaps the most difficult task is to identify and narrow the inferential gap that exists between what we desire to understand (describe, reveal, or verify) and what we can do with data (Messick, 1989). Verbal protocol analysis is not free of this concern because what is inferred from verbal data might neither fully nor accurately represent thoughts and processes of readers (Ericsson & Simon, 1998; Smagorinsky, 1998). For example, it is obvious that what we desire to know is a "pure" form of situated processes (i.e., cognitive strategies) and thoughts (i.e., mental representations by the strategy use) which are heeded in mind (i.e., short-term memory) during an authentic cognitive task. These processes and thoughts—namely, first-level cognition "C1" in this discussion—could be those that are not intervened by any additional construct-irrelevant tasks imposed by others. However, psychological realities of C1 processes and thoughts may not be explicitly observed by any research technologies currently available. To address the issue, alternative ways of collecting data which are assumed to best characterize the genuine C1 processes and thoughts are necessitated.

However, this situation (i.e., with the goal of better understanding authentic cognition by adding a somewhat unnatural task or mechanism in order to observe that cognition) may cause researchers to be in a dilemma where the additional data-gathering task, especially when involving extra language generation, may facilitate modifications of strategic processing and thinking at the very moments of data generation—namely, second-level cognition "C2" here. That is, verbal reporting inevitably influences the operation of C1-level processing and thinking and what it captures may be those at the C2-level because language mediates cognitive work (e.g., Davis, Carey, Foxman, & Tarr, 1968; Posner, 1982; Smagorinsky, 1998). Such influences are oftentimes indicated by readers slowing down the reading speed or being disoriented in repeating surface-level comments on thoughts. Also, there is a chance that some of the chains of strategic thinking and related action are non-verbalized for a particular reason (e.g., personality, motivation, verbal proficiency, working memory at capacity, relational factors) and are consequently excluded from the analysis. What matters at this point is with what rigor and in relation to what context the investigator can account for the involvement of task demands, as well as the unexpectedly modified acts of reading, in describing the C2 thoughts and processes to the greatest extent.

In a worst scenario, verbal reports may be an inaccurate and unreliable source of data when participants' verbalizations significantly change the course of thinking and processing. Such uncontrolled interruptions may, in turn, entirely disrupt what readers normally do and think in a task that would otherwise be authentic and ecologically valid. What is verbalized in this case are of third-level cognition "C3," which might not be in our best interests because what we are striving for is to estimate and fill in the data-reality gap while maintaining the substance and sequence of strategic processing and thinking that best resemble those for authentic reading.

Nonetheless, we believe that the major events of strategic text processing, as well as the mental representations that emerge across the moments of processing, can be generally accessible and reportable in a well-designed research task (Fox, Ericsson, & Best, 2011). Figure 23.1 illustrates that it is highly possible that, despite the influences, to some extent, the task of verbal reporting would not significantly change the course of reading strategy use and the properties of represented thoughts (Norris, 1990). It means that the inferences we propose to make from verbal reports should represent the course of cognitive actions, metacognitive controls, and evolving representations at the C2 level without much losing the integrity of C1-level authentic reading.

It is important to note that the integrity of verbal protocols is the result of text- and task- appropriate design. Such design accounts for all relevant experimental variables (e.g., prompts, waiting time, text familiarity, task impressions) as well as the contextual factors (e.g., reading goals, materials and resources, settings and situations, textual scopes and boundaries). A carefully designed verbal-reporting task minimizes the likelihood of over-involvement of automatic processing (e.g., if a reading task is familiar and easy enough for the reader to complete it quickly without much effort) or unnecessary facilitation of vague self-explanations (e.g., the task is too difficult to complete so the reader becomes constantly relying on the help of self-talk without a clear focus and deep engagement in text understanding). When conducting data analysis,

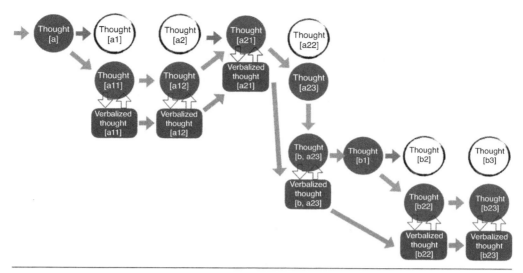

Figure 23.1 A Flow of Thinking in Verbal Reporting during Reading

the investigator should carefully examine the data, progressing into a better situated understanding of the verbalized thoughts while self-questioning whether data makes sense in relation to a particular coordination of reader, text, and context. Depending on the focus of the particular study, researchers may also conduct grounded theorizing (Glaser & Strauss, 1967) in which new insights into reader-text-task-context interactions can be generated from verbal report data.

Opportunity is that acknowledging limitations of a method may fuel the action to design a rigorous research task and data analysis. For verbal protocol analysis, the inferential gap in the verbal data analysis would make it difficult to evaluate the proximity and disparity between what is heeded in mind and what indeed is verbalized. However, considering taken-for-granted challenges seriously may create a new opportunity to generate, test, and apply alternative principles and means to address manifold issues in verbal protocol analysis. When researchers challenge commonplace assumptions, develop alternative strategies, and explore new approaches, informed research processes may contribute to constructing a contextualized account of strategic processing as close as possible to that which is carried out in an authentic task of reading.

In what follows, we focus on the specific merits and major issues in verbal protocol analysis and possible means of addressing the issues, as we seek to undertake rigorous and situated investigations of the strategic processing involved in complex reading tasks. We draw on our own previous work, and that of others, to discuss theoretical and practical considerations for qualitative analysis of verbal report data. Specifically, we focus on:

- how the contextual knowledge of the investigator creates new opportunities for verbal protocol analysis,
- how data saturation contributes to understanding the phenomena being interpreted and is judged in ways that inform the progress of qualitative analysis, and
- how evidentiary reasoning is undertaken rigorously throughout the analysis and contributes to the unique conceptual contributions that a qualitative approach holds.

CONTEXTUAL INFLUENCES IN VERBAL REPORTING AND THE CONTEXTUAL KNOWLEDGE OF THE INVESTIGATOR IN VERBAL PROTOCOL ANALYSIS

As is true in any disciplined investigation, the collection of verbal reports and the analysis of such data are carefully planned and closely related. It is therefore important to develop an understanding of the ways that analysis is intertwined with measurement, and the influence of the context of the study on the data being generated. To illustrate the contextual influence of the research task on the analysis of verbal report data, we present two of our own prior studies that share the same context, but differ because the research questions and subsequent data analyses were guided by different research questions, although both studies were intended to contribute to understanding of strategic processing during reading.

To begin with, the first study (Cho, Woodward, Li, & Barlow, 2017) was informed by literature on strategic processing of internet sources (e.g., Afflerbach & Cho, 2009) and explored how adolescents' internet reading strategies contribute to the quality of their generated questions about a given topic. The research task involved participants thinking aloud during a one-hour information searching session to learn about mountaintop mining, a controversial issue, with a variety of types and sources of text available on the internet. An important element of the research design for this study (Cho et al., 2017) was recognizing the affordances and obstacles created by authentic and unconstrained textual environments. One example is participant-directed source selection, as compared to a more conventional situation of reading in a controlled environment where participants interact with predetermined texts, such as a replication of a search engine with selected texts available. A review of the methods used in previous studies of internet reading strategies indicated that there was potential in creating a task which utilized an unconstrained search environment with an open-ended task in order to best capture how students read in an internet setting (Cho, 2014; Coiro & Dobler, 2007; DeSchryver, 2015).

Therefore, our research design sought to increase ecological validity in the study of strategic processing during internet reading, which involved controlling particular elements of the task (e.g., predetermined task, prompt, and time) in order to collect data that would respond to our research questions while leaving others open (e.g., unconstrained textual space, navigation, choice of text) in order to replicate an authentic reading space. We used analytical rubrics to judge the qualities of individual students' use of four major strategies (i.e., information location, meaning making, self-monitoring, and source evaluation) that are prominent features in internet reading. This scoring procedure allowed us to gain "quality scores" to build a structural model that statistically accounts for the association of those strategies with the outcomes of internet reading such as knowledge gain and question generation on the topic they read about.

During our analysis of verbal protocols, however, it became apparent that there were additional influences, other than the cognitive strategies used by participants, on the information sources chosen by the participants and the related information they learned. We encountered many instances in which readers verbalized their stances, positions, or attitudes toward the task of internet reading, beyond what information they were attending to and how they were comprehending it. For example, while accessing a website run by a group of environmental scientists in the mining-affected Appalachian states, one high school reader reported:

> I'm a science person, not political expert or any … I prefer to use the website of these scientists and the articles here, or whatever it has me to look at … something that is objective and looks scientific. I would not invest my time reading some of the previous articles I found, which were mostly authored by people from interest groups.

Options for coding the above verbal protocol data include self-monitoring, source evaluation, or a hybrid strategy that subsumes both. However, the complicated and idiosyncratic nature of strategy use can evoke further questions about the motivation of the reader pursuing a particular kind of source authority as informed by the reflection of *how I come to know* and *what source to be chosen for my learning*. Although such imposing of personal dispositions toward source authority was not the primary focus of the current study, we, as the investigators, understood that the unconstrained online task setting not only affords the reader freedom of information access but also encourages her to be held accountable in seeking more reliable sources. We cataloged numerous instances of such verbal reports that were deserving of further attention. Consequently a consideration of the task environment, in which adolescent readers were verbalizing their thoughts in an unconstrained setting for locating and processing varied internet sources on a controversial issue, led to our further investigation of the data from an alternative theoretical approach that we believe can assist in examining different aspects of strategic online reading.

Our contextual interpretation of particular verbal protocols extended the scope of the strategic processing we analyzed in online reading. Therefore, in order to better understand why participants engaged in the cognitive processing documented in our first study, we decided to conduct a further qualitative verbal protocol analysis for a subset of the original data. We focused on how verbal report data could demonstrate the enactment of readers' orientations and attitudes toward knowledge (what counts as knowledge) and knowing (how one comes to know) in the vast information space on the internet (Greene, Muis, & Pieschl, 2010; Hofer, 2004). Accordingly, verbal protocol analysis was driven by a research question generated in part by the initial analysis of data which revealed readers' epistemic beliefs: how do adolescent readers activate and engage epistemic beliefs when performing a critical online reading task? That is, we focused on what we refer to as *epistemic processing* in online reading (Cho, Woodward, & Li, 2018).

Because the verbal report data was generated in an authentic space (i.e., participants' internet moves were not restricted, and they could engage in self-selected strategies in relation to their beliefs), our data analysis reflected the richness of the context itself. For example, Figure 23.2 draws on excerpts from two contrasting cases that imply how readers' verbal reports could be interpreted in relation to the context in which they were given. In the first example, the student demonstrated an emotional connection to the topic throughout the session (e.g., "is upsetting"). As she encounters new information—the influence of mountaintop mining on streams—she recalls previously learned information about the mining practices, deforestation, and the greenhouse

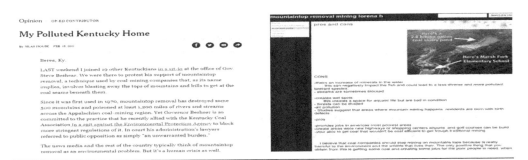

Figure 23.2 Contextualized Coding and Analysis of Verbal Protocols

effect (e.g., "I'm thinking about the sites that I've read today"). She then connects the two ideas, making a knowledge claim that there is a connection between the greenhouse effect and the disappearance and polluting of streams. The ongoing dialogue that this participant created among multiple internet sources and herself contributed to understanding her epistemic engagement in interrelating and reconciling different perspectives. A similar contextual relevance is found when examining the second excerpt in Figure 23.2, but the comment therein is representative of the epistemically naïve process that this participant engaged in throughout his session. Above all things, this reader gets lost in his text-selection (e.g., "I have no idea ... where I have to start"). While he does engage in several strategic approaches, the actions taken fail to demonstrate the depth of knowledge investigation required to learn from the selected texts. This pattern of reading is explained through the epistemic processing analysis, which identifies the confusion he expressed in identifying high-quality sources.

When conducting an analysis of verbal report data, there are a number of influences that the study design and methods employed have on both the data generated and the subsequent data analysis. As glimpsed from our work, however, with the nuanced knowledge of the investigators about the context of research task, verbal protocol analysis may evolve and create a new opportunity to examine different aspects of strategic processing. To highlight, the analyses of verbal reports using different lenses provided by affiliated paradigms can inform our understanding of the broad range of factors that operate with strategic processing at the intersection of cognitive and epistemic engagement.

DATA SATURATION AND DECISION MAKING ABOUT WHEN TO STOP OR GO FURTHER IN VERBAL PROTOCOL ANALYSIS

Analyzing verbal protocols is an iterative process. In particular, a critical aspect of verbal reporting data analysis relates to choosing, revising, or creating a coding framework that is best suited to describing the data (Bogdan & Biklen, 2007). That said, typically, a first consideration is determining how a particular coding framework may be effective in helping to decide the units of analysis that will be used. Chi (1997) recommended the following when considering verbal reports: "(a) the grain size of the segment, (b) the correspondence of the grain size to the questions one is asking, (c) the characteristics in the data used for segmenting, and (d) when it may not be necessary to segment" (p. 284). While it is important to draw on existing literature and the data collected to inform the nature of analysis, the units of analysis may need to be adjusted once coding has begun if the unit used is not sufficient to determine whether or not a particular code describes certain strategic processes underlying the corresponding verbal reports.

Coding frameworks in qualitative data analysis are either established a priori from existing literature or theoretical frameworks, or they are informed by existing theory but emerge from the data itself, typically drawing on grounded theory analysis approaches (Corbin & Strauss, 2015; Glaser & Strauss, 1967). It is important to refine the coding framework until it sufficiently describes the data, especially when verbal reports involve "discovery"—aspects of a phenomenon that have not been previously cataloged. We take an example of this process again from our study of epistemic processing in online reading (Cho et al., 2018). Figure 23.3 shows the structure of epistemic processes involved in online reading that were operated at multiple levels, grounded in the verbal report data of the participating high school students.

In this structure, the top-level categories (i.e., epistemic judgment, epistemic monitoring, epistemic regulation) were not related only to dimensions found in previous literature (Barzilai & Zohar, 2012; Greene, Yu, & Copeland, 2014; Hofer, 2004) but were also supported by our data. The next level of category (e.g., acritical, surface-level, and critical processing within epistemic judgement) describe the qualities of strategy use in relation to judgments of internet sources. The third level categories (e.g., noticing authority and probing authority within surface-level processing) identify specific actions or dispositions and their qualities found in the data. This multilayered structure of coding depicts how the initial framework was further refined, interrelated, and reorganized to best describe the data collected in our study.

This process can be described as data saturation, which Corbin and Strauss (2015) outline as having the following characteristics: "no new or relevant data seem to emerge regarding a category, the category is well developed in terms of its properties and dimensions demonstrating variation, and the relationships among categories are well established and validated" (p. 212).

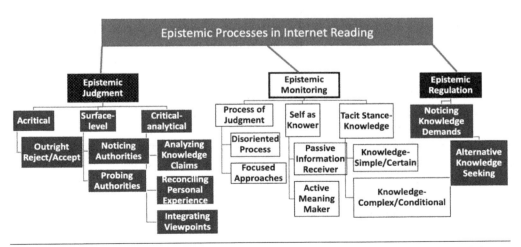

Figure 23.3 Multilayered Coding Structure of the Epistemic Processes in a Critical Internet Reading: A Grounded Theory

In our example, the existing literature and the recursive analysis of our data worked together to inform a robust coding scheme that sufficiently captured the multilayered and multifaceted structure of the epistemic processing apparent in our data set. Therefore, as the coding scheme becomes more developed and represents more of the data, the coding process becomes less challenging as the data more readily fit the descriptive categories of the coding scheme.

While this process is important to describing the data within one study, we note that theoretical saturation may not always occur within a single study. As described in the previous section, the mental models of strategic processing in internet reading have been challenged, questioned, revised, and refined by attending to underexamined aspects of reading (i.e., epistemic processing) and the underlying factors that influenced them (e.g., uncertainties of online information space and readers' responses to the contextual features). This window into previously unresearched phenomena is an important affordance of the verbal protocol analysis and has contributed to the subsequent development of research questions and data analysis. As such, through building on previous works, researchers may be able to seek to foreground the importance of replication and multiple contexts to understanding what a single study contributes, or not, to an overall understanding of strategic processing and the possibility of reaching data saturation within a single study, while recognizing that theoretical saturation requires subsequent research.

ARGUMENTATION AND EVIDENTIARY REASONING IN QUALITATIVE VERBAL PROTOCOL ANALYSIS

Verbal protocol analysis involves an argument process. It requires a logical reasoning concerned with the experiences of human subjects and the processes they engage in to navigate and make sense of the world (Bogdan & Biklen, 2007). Chi (1997) elaborated on this idea within the context of verbal report data regarding the potential of qualitative methods to capture participants' natural behaviors in authentic settings to gain a "richer and deeper understanding of a situation" (p. 280). Central to developing claims in qualitative research are the data analysis procedures used to identify evidence of a particular phenomenon. However, this process is not without challenges because "coding of verbal reports is an interpretive act" and "the richness of language and the constructive nature of understanding language" present both the promise and the challenge of making a legitimate claim substantiated by verbal reports (Pressley & Afflerbach, 1995, p. 122).

Because qualitative research is primarily inductive and grounded in data, rather than deductive or beholden to theory, there is particular importance placed upon the conceptual frameworks that ground the study and contribute to the inferences made from the data (Merriam, 1998). Thus, the coding of qualitative data typically includes a robust explanation of both previous research, related theory, and their contributions to the emerging data coding and analysis schemes. Further, as in quantitative research, the methods of analysis are discussed at due length; however, the involvement of the researcher as an analytical instrument (Patton, 1990) often engages additional discussion on the methodological decisions made (i.e., rationale that supports why a particular method, approach, and procedure is chosen, employed, or modified within the context of its use).

We present the path of argumentation undertaken in our verbal protocol analysis concerning epistemic processing for online reading (Cho et al., 2018). As outlined in Figure 23.4, the diagram (informed by Toulmin's (1958) argument model) unpacks the reasoning process into the following components:

- Claim: The assertions made about the focal aspect of investigation about epistemic processing in online reading.
- Data: The verbal report data collected from a suitably designed research task and the results from the qualitative verbal protocol analysis in relation to codes, categories, and themes of epistemic processing in online reading.
- Warrant: Theoretical framework that describes what epistemic processing means in online reading, why the studies of the topic matter, and how it can be investigated.
- Backing: Empirical studies that use verbal protocol analysis to examine epistemic processing in online reading and therefore elaborate the theoretical framework.
- Qualifiers: Conditions that limit the claim made from evidentiary reasoning.
- Rebuttals: Counterclaims, alternative explanations, or limitations that could be suggested in response to the claiming and reasoning.

We first sought to examine why epistemic processing matters in online environments through an overview of the theoretical literature in the areas of personal epistemology and internet reading, which serves as the *warrant* for our study. We drew on previous work that established theories for understanding how epistemic beliefs influence learning processes (Hofer & Pintrich, 1997), the relationship between epistemic beliefs and cognitive processing (Hofer, 2004), and established what we meant by epistemic processing and addressed relevant concerns regarding measurement issues related to personal epistemology (Cho, 2014; DeBacker, Crowson, Beesley, Thoma, & Hestevold, 2008; Goldman, Braasch, Wiley, Graesser, & Brodowinska, 2012; Greene, Azevedo, & Torney-Purta, 2008). Our exploration of theoretical warrant extended to a discussion of the perspectives informing our understanding of epistemic processing in online reading, which included recognizing the intertextual nature of the internet (Landow, 1992), complexities of identifying sources of information (Lankes, 2008; Metzger & Flanagin, 2013), and the sophisticated and critical mindset needed to seek and gain knowledge from reading online (Greene et al., 2014; Lankshear, Peters, & Knobel, 2000; Ulyshen, Koehler, & Gao, 2015).

We then drew on additional research to expand these theoretical understandings to other studies which sought to utilize verbal reporting methods to investigate the role of epistemic beliefs in online reading, as *backing* for the warrant established in theoretical overview. We discussed the contributions and limitations of the selected empirical studies related to the particular dimensions of epistemic beliefs (Hofer, 2004), how individual differences of readers could interact with epistemic beliefs when reading online (Mason, Boldrin, & Ariasi, 2010a), the relationship among sophisticated epistemic beliefs, searching processes, and understanding (Mason, Boldrin, & Ariasi, 2010b), the influence of a particular topic on the enactment of epistemic beliefs (Ferguson, Bråten, & Strømsø, 2012), the role of self-regulation and epistemic processing in learning from online sources (Greene et al., 2014), and the processing related to

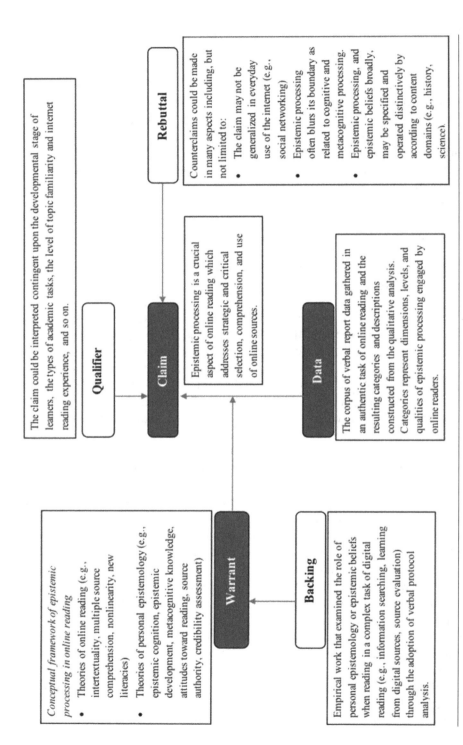

Figure 23.4 A Simple Representation of Argument Reasoning Engaged in Verbal Protocol Analysis of Epistemic Processing in Online Reading

views that readers may hold about the nature of knowledge (Barzilai & Zohar, 2012). Having presented the previous warrant and backing, we argued that in order to build on the existing understanding of epistemic beliefs and online reading, it is also important to understand the epistemic processes readers employ in an unconstrained digital space and which particular processes are undertaken by more and less successful readers. In one way, we hope to build a theoretical net which is capable of capturing and then explaining the phenomena reported in participants' verbalizations.

We used readers' concurrent verbal protocols as *data* that is particularly well-suited for capturing the moment-to-moment processes of readers as they navigate a multi-source text environment. We first identify the context of data collection and detail the types of data and methods used to collect it. Then, we describe how the data was prepared for analysis, which included transcripts of participants' verbal reports along with the screen capture of their actions. The transcripts were then open coded using semantic segmentation of data (Chi, 1997), which allowed for particular thoughts or actions to be contextualized within a larger chain of processing. This initial coding focused on a small sample of data to identify all possible instances of epistemic processing. Subsequent coding involved comparison of the researcher-generated codes to develop superordinate code categories which were then integrated into a coherent coding scheme. The remaining data was analyzed in a process of axial coding with the initial coding scheme to refine and improve it throughout the data analysis process. Because a primary purpose of our study was to investigate the epistemic processes that emerged from the data, the explanation of the categories and related dimensions and actions were the first major *claim*. In addition to descriptions of epistemic judgment, monitoring, and regulation, verbal report data was presented to exemplify each element of the three larger categories (Cho et al., 2018, pp. 209–210).

Our findings were then discussed relative to the nomological network provided by prior theory and research. This also allowed us to *qualify* the context in which our claims were grounded and recognized that our study did not capture students who were not likely to be proficient at thinking aloud, nor the knowledge that is gained when seeking to understand as part of a collaborative effort. However, the study did yield evidence about how the individual epistemic processes of students experienced more and less success during their reading task. Yet, there are other potential limitations of (or counterclaims against) our study that must be addressed in any discussion of our findings. These include the critical questioning task that may not reflect the ways in which students learn from online sources in more personal spaces, the nature of the task design to be situated within a school context, and the non-verbalized beliefs that learners may hold. Further, research on domain expertise indicates that lack of domain knowledge and understanding of disciplinary practices (Maggioni, Fox, & Alexander, 2010; Warren, 2011) may also shape the process of online reading.

In summary, argumentative reasoning is an essential part of the verbal protocol analysis that seeks to achieve a methodological rigor and theoretical contribution to generating new knowledge and insights. Such evidentiary process requires connecting the research work to a robust conceptual framework built upon previous studies of key constructs to be examined, and to a thoughtful consideration of counter claims and alternative explanations. Through the process, researchers may be able to seek to not only establish a clear ground for the claims that emerge from the data but also to clarify the importance of our findings through acknowledging additional and alternative perspectives.

REMAINING ISSUES IN THE QUALITATIVE ANALYSIS OF VERBAL REPORT DATA

As reviewed in this chapter, and in relation to our own research, qualitative analysis of verbal report data has many challenges. These challenges, to name a few, include identifying and accounting for the contextual influences of tasks on verbal reporting, and acknowledging the sometimes ambiguous boundaries within which verbal report data can describe a particular type of strategic processing of interest, but beyond which the inference of strategy or process is not warranted. Finally, the complex argumentative work on a claim made for strategic processing ought to be substantiated by evidence of verbal data and theoretical reasoning to bond the claim and evidence, which should result in a robust understanding of the particular phenomenon being studied. However, we counter that these issues can be addressed with detailed accounts of the variables and their influences involved in research task. We note that qualitative analysis, as opposed to quantitative work, embraces the *complications and interweaving* nature of strategic processing across a series of critical moments. Sophistication about such nuances and complexities and revelation of possible factors that might have affected the process by active use of *contextual knowledge and situated reasoning* is one of the powerful virtues that a rigorous and sophisticated qualitative analysis can achieve.

We support that verbal protocol analysis is *a system of methods* that is useful for the scientific investigation of what strategic processing is and how it works. The purpose of verbal protocol studies of reading is to know what the reader is doing and thinking while performing a cognitive task, which can be achieved through situated inferences that are made from the real-time language data collected through carefully designed procedures for verbal reporting. Such analysis can challenge and help us to detail the nature and process of decision making and thinking engagement in the comprehension of readers with different tasks (e.g., Hartman, 1995; Wolfe & Goldman, 2005), texts (e.g., Eva-Wood, 2004; Gottlieb & Wineburg, 2012), and environments (e.g., Azevedo, Guthrie, & Seibert, 2004; Coiro & Dobler, 2007). This stance is undergirded by accumulated methodological work suggesting verbal reports as a helpful source of information (e.g., Fox et al., 2011) by which we can look into not only readers' conscious, goal-directed, and strategic acts of reading (e.g., Pressley & Afflerbach, 1995; Suh & Trabasso, 1993) but also the mental representations built through such processing (e.g., Chi, 1997; Tenbrink, 2015).

We note that reliable inferences made from verbal data have significant contributions to exploring, building, and refining theoretical models of and perspectives on reading in complex tasks and contexts (Cho & Afflerbach, 2018; Pressley & Afflerbach, 1995). What must be reiterated here is that what could be inferred from a participant's verbal data depends on our acuity with theoretical confidence in response to the subtleties, nuances, and complexities of what verbal utterances mean and represent; all of such inferences are contingent on the task, the context, and the participant. For example, a conclusion drawn from what verbal data tell us about reading can be therefore bolstered in association with, and is often disrupted by, a method of *triangulation* (Denzin, 1970) that interrelates other complementary data sources such as behavioral, biometric, and outcome data that are sensitive to detect the influences of how reading works in that complex coordination of relevant variables on the substance of the verbal data (Bråten, Magliano, & Salmerón, in press; Magliano & Graesser, 1991).

At the same time, we also note that central to the credibility of a qualitative study is *transparency* in data collection and analysis. A robust explanation of the procedures and factors involved in verbal protocol analysis increases the trustworthiness of findings (Lincoln & Guba, 2000). Reporting contextual information about both the participants and the researcher, and the procedures they have been through, is critical to a publishing of qualitative work in general, and verbal data analysis especially. Both verbal protocol experts (Afflerbach, 2000; Chi, 1997) and qualitative methodologists (Cresswell, 2014; Denzin & Lincoln, 2005) address the importance of *disclosure* in qualitative work. Qualitative data produces a rich understanding of particular phenomena, which is closely tied to both the participants and the context in which the data is produced. Thus, it is critical to disclose that information which directly relates to verbal data analysis when reporting the results of a study.

More important is disclosure related to *researcher positionality*, which is shaped by theoretical approaches that inform the design and purpose of the study and securing data sources that best demonstrate the focal aspects of the study (Denzin, 1986; Miles, Huberman, & Saldana, 2014). The theoretical approaches to qualitative verbal data analysis serve to disclose the orientations and perspectives used by the researchers to both design their study and inform their data analysis. Establishing a clear position within the existing literature is an important contribution to the credibility of reports of qualitative verbal data analysis. Therefore, theoretical positioning and orientation of the researcher must be completely disclosed, due to the potential influence that these elements have not only on the process of data collection and analysis but also on the consequent claiming and reasoning about strategic processing in reading.

REFERENCES

Afflerbach, P. (2000). Verbal reports and protocol analysis. In M. J. Kamil, P. B. Mosenthal, P. D. Pearson, & R. Barr (Eds.), *Handbook of reading research* (Vol. 3, pp. 163–179). Mahwah, NJ: Erlbaum.

Afflerbach, P., & Cho, B.-Y. (2009). Identifying and describing constructively responsive comprehension strategies in new and traditional forms of reading. In S. E. Israel & G. G. Duffy (Eds.), *Handbook of research on reading comprehension* (pp. 69–90). New York, NY: Routledge.

Afflerbach, P., Cho, B.-Y., & Kim, J. (2015). Conceptualizing and assessing higher-order thinking in reading. *Theory into Practice, 54*(3), 203–212.

Afflerbach, P., & Johnston, P. (1984). On the use of verbal report in reading research. *Journal of Reading Behavior, 16*(4), 307–322.

Afflerbach, P., Pearson, P. D., & Paris, G. S. (2008). Clarifying differences between reading skills and reading strategies. *The Reading Teacher, 61*(5), 364–373.

Alexander, P., Graham, S., & Harris, K. (1998). A perspective on strategy research: Progress and products. *Educational Psychology Review, 10*, 129–154.

Azevedo, R., Guthrie, J. T., & Seibert, D. (2004). The role of self-regulated learning in fostering students' conceptual understanding of complex systems with hypermedia. *Journal of Educational Computing Research, 30*(1&2), 87–111.

Barzilai, S., & Zohar, A. (2012). Epistemic thinking in action: Evaluating and integrating online sources. *Cognition and Instruction, 30*(1), 39–85. doi:10.1080/07370008.2011.636495

Bogdan, R. C., & Biklen, S. K. (2007). *Qualitative research for education: An introduction to theories and methods* (5th ed.). Boston, MA: Allyn & Bacon.

Boring, E. G. (1953). A history of introspection. *Psychological Bulletin, 50*(3), 169–189.

Bråten, I., Magliano, J. P., & Salmerón, L. (in press). Concurrent and task-specific self-reports. In D. L. Dinsmore, L. K. Fryer, & M. M. Parkinson (Eds.), *Handbook of strategies and strategic processing: Conceptualization, intervention, measurement, and analysis*. New York: Routledge.

Brown, J. S., Collins, A., & Duguid, P. (1989). Situated cognition and the culture of learning. *Educational Researcher, 18*(1), 32–42.

Chi, N. T. H. (1997). Quantifying qualitative analyses of verbal data: A practical guide. *The Journal of the Learning Science, 6*(3), 271–315.

Cho, B.-Y. (2014). Competent adolescent readers' use of internet reading strategies: A think-aloud study. *Cognition and Instruction, 32*(3), 253–289.

Cho, B.-Y., & Afflerbach, P. (2018). An evolving perspective of constructively response reading comprehension strategies in multilayered digital text environments. In *Handbook of research on reading comprehension* (2nd ed., pp. 109–134). New York, NY: Guilford Publications.

Cho, B.-Y., Woodward, L., & Li, D. (2018). Epistemic processing when adolescents read online: A verbal protocol analysis of more and less successful online readers. *Reading Research Quarterly, 53*(2), 197–221.

Cho, B.-Y., Woodward, L., Li, D., & Barlow, E. (2017). Examining adolescents' strategic processing during online reading with a question-generating task. *American Educational Research Journal, 54*(4), 691–724.

Chomsky, N. (1975). *Reflections on language*. New York: Pantheon.

Coiro, J., & Dobler, E. (2007). Exploring the online reading comprehension strategies used by sixth-grade skilled readers to search for and locate information on the Internet. *Reading Research Quarterly, 42*(2), 214–257.

Corbin, J., & Strauss, A. (2015). *Basics of qualitative research: Techniques and procedures for developing grounded theory* (4th ed.). Los Angeles, CA: Sage.

Cresswell, J. W. (2014). *Research design: Qualitative, quantitative, and mixed methods approaches* (4th ed.). Thousand Oaks, CA: Sage.

Davis, J. H., Carey, M. H., Foxman, P. N., & Tarr, D. B. (1968). Verbalization, experimenter presence, and problem solving. *Journal of Personality and Social Psychology, 8*, 299–302.

DeBacker, T. K., Crowson, H. M., Beesley, A. D., Thoma, S. J., & Hestevold, N. (2008). The challenge of measuring epistemic beliefs: An analysis of three self-report instruments. *Journal of Experimental Education, 76*(3), 281–312.

Denzin, N. (1970). *The research act: A theoretical introduction to sociological methods*. Chicago, IL: Aldine.

Denzin, N. (1986). *Interpretive biography*. Newbury, CA: Sage.

Denzin, N., & Lincoln, Y. (2005). *The SAGE handbook of qualitative research* (3rd ed.). Thousand Oaks: Sage Publications.

DeSchryver, M. (2015). Higher order thinking in an online world: Toward a theory of web-mediated knowledge synthesis. *Teachers College Record, 116*, 1–44.

Ericsson, K. A., & Simon, H. A. (1980). Verbal reports as data. *Psychological Review, 87*(3), 215–251.

Ericsson, K. A., & Simon, H. A. (1998). How to study thinking in everyday life: Contrasting think-aloud protocols with descriptions and explanations of thinking. *Mind, Culture, and Activity, 5*(3), 178–186.

Eva-Wood, A. L. (2004). Thinking and feeling poetry: Exploring meanings aloud. *Journal of Educational Psychology, 96*(1), 182–191.

Ferguson, L. E., Bråten, I., & Strømsø, H. I. (2012). Epistemic cognition when students read multiple documents containing conflicting scientific evidence: A think-aloud study. *Learning and Instruction, 22*, 103–120.

Fox, M. C., Ericsson, A., & Best, R. (2011). Do procedures of verbal reporting of thinking have to be reactive? A meta-analysis and recommendation for best reporting methods. *Psychological Bulletin, 137*(2), 316–344.

Glaser, B. G., & Strauss, A. L. (1967). *The discovery of grounded theory: Strategies for qualitative research*. Chicago: Aldine Publishing Company.

Goldman, S. R., Braasch, J. L. G., Wiley, J., Graesser, A. C., & Brodowinska, K. (2012). Comprehending and learning from internet sources: Processing patterns of better and poorer learners. *Reading Research Quarterly, 47*(4), 356–381.

Gottlieb, E., & Wineburg, S. (2012). Between Veritas and Communitas: Epistemic switching in the reading of academic and sacred history. *The Journal of the Learning Sciences, 21*(1), 84–129.

Greene, J. A., Azevedo, R., & Torney-Purta, J. (2008). Modeling epistemic and ontological cognition: Philosophical perspectives and methodological directions. *Educational Psychologist, 43*(3), 142–160.

Greene, J. A., Muis, K. R., & Pieschl, S. (2010). The role of epistemic beliefs in students' self-regulated learning with computer-based learning environments: Conceptual and methodological issues. *Educational Psychologist, 45*(4), 245–257.

Greene, J. A., Yu, S. B., & Copeland, D. Z. (2014). Measuring critical components of digital literacy and their relationships with learning. *Computers & Education, 76*, 55–69.

Hartman, D. K. (1995). Eight readers reading: The intertextual links of proficient readers reading multiple passages. *Reading Research Quarterly, 30*(3), 520–561.

Hofer, B. K. (2004). Epistemological understanding as a metacognitive process: Thinking aloud during online searching. *Educational Psychologist, 39*(1), 43–55.

Hofer, B. K., & Pintrich, P. R. (1997). The development of epistemological theories: Beliefs about knowledge and knowing and their relation to learning. *Review of Educational Research, 67*(1), 88–140.

James, W. (1890). *The principles of psychology*. New York, NY: Holt.

Kintsch, W. (1988). The role of knowledge in discourse comprehension: A construction-integration model. *Psychological Review, 95*(2), 163–182.

Kucan, L., & Beck, I. (1997). Thinking aloud and reading comprehension research: Inquiry, instruction, and social interaction. *Review of Educational Research, 67*(3), 271–299.

Lakoff, G. (1987). *Women, fire, and dangerous things*. Chicago: University of Chicago Press.

Landow, G. P. (1992). *Hypertext: The convergence of contemporary critical theory and technology*. Baltimore, MD: Johns Hopkins University Press.

Lankes, R. D. (2008). Trusting the Internet: New approaches to credibility tools. In M. J. Metzger & A. J. Flanagin (Eds.), *Digital media, youth, and credibility* (pp. 101–122). Cambridge, MA: MIT Press.

Lankshear, C., Peters, M., & Knobel, M. (2000). Information, knowledge and learning: Some issues facing epistemology and education in a digital age. *Journal of Philosophy of Education, 34*(1), 17–39.

Lincoln, Y. S., & Guba, E. G. (2000). Paradigmatic controversies, contradictions, and emerging confluences. In N. K. Denzin & Y. S. Lincoln (Eds.), *The handbook of qualitative research* (2nd ed., pp. 163–188). London: Sage.

Maggioni, L., Fox, E., & Alexander, P. A. (2010). The epistemic dimension of competence in the social sciences. *Journal of Social Science Education, 9*(4), 15–23. doi:10.4119/UNIBI/jsse-v9-i4-1141

Magliano, J. P., & Graesser, A. C. (1991). A three-pronged method for studying inference generation in literary text. *Poetics, 20*, 193–232.

Mason, L., Boldrin, A., & Ariasi, N. (2010a). Epistemic metacognition in context: Evaluating and learning online information. *Metacognition and Learning, 5*, 67–90.

Mason, L., Boldrin, A., & Ariasi, N. (2010b). Searching the Web to learn about a controversial topic: Are students epistemically active? *Instructional Science, 38*, 607–633.

McNamara, D. S. (Ed.). (2007). *Reading comprehension strategies: Theories, interventions, and technologies*. New York: Erlbaum.

McNamara, D. S., & Magliano, J. (2009). Toward a comprehensive model of comprehension. *The Psychology of Learning and Motivation, 51*, 297–384.

Merriam, S. B. (1998). *Qualitative research and case study applications in education*. San Francisco, CA: Josey-Bass Publishers.

Messick, S. (1989). Validity. In R. L. Linn (Ed.), *Educational measurement* (3rd ed., pp. 13–103). London, UK: Collier Macmillan.

Metzger, M. J., & Flanagin, A. J. (2013). Credibility and trust of information in online environments: The use of cognitive heuristics. *Journal of Pragmatics, 59*, 210–220.

Miles, M. B., Huberman, M., & Saldana, J. (2014). *Qualitative data analysis: A methods sourcebook* (3rd ed.). New York, NY: SAGE.

Nisbett, R. E., & Wilson, T. D. (1977). Telling more than we can know: Verbal reports on mental processes. *Psychological Review, 84*(3), 231–259.

Norris, S. P. (1990). Effects of eliciting verbal reports of thinking on critical thinking test performance. *Journal of Educational Measurement, 27*(1), 41–58.

Patton, M. (1990). *Qualitative evaluation and research methods*. Beverly Hills, CA: Sage.

Posner, M. I. (1982). Protocol analysis and human cognition. In G. R. Ungson & D. N. Braunstein(Eds.), *Decision making: An interdisciplinary inquiry* (pp. 78–82). Belmont, CA: Kent (Wadsworth).

Pressley, M. (1995). More about the development of self-regulation: Complex, long-term, and thoroughly social. *Educational Psychologist, 30*(4), 207–212.

Pressley, M., & Afflerbach, P. (1995). *Verbal protocols of reading: The nature of constructively responsive reading*. Hillsdale, NJ: Lawrence Erlbaum Associates.

Smagorinsky, P. (1998). Thinking and speech and protocol analysis. *Mind, Culture, and Activity, 5*(3), 157–177.

Snow, C. (2002). *Reading for understanding: Toward a R&D program in reading comprehension*. Santa Monica, CA: RAND.

Suh, S., & Trabasso, T. (1993). Inferences during reading: Converging evidence from discourse analysis, talk-aloud protocols, and recognition priming. *Journal of Memory and Language, 32*, 279–300.

Tenbrink, T. (2015). Cognitive discourse analysis: Accessing cognitive representations and processes through language data. *Language and Cognition*, *7*, 98–137.

Toulmin, S. E. (1958). *The uses of argument*. Cambridge, UK: Cambridge University Press.

Ulyshen, T. Z., Koehler, M. J., & Gao, F. (2015). Understanding the connection between epistemic beliefs and internet searching. *Journal of Educational Computing Research*, *53*(3), 345–383.

Veenman, M. V. J. (2015). Metacognition. In P. Afflerbach (Ed.), *Handbook of individual differences in reading: Reader, text, and context* (pp. 26–40). New York, NY: Routledge.

Vygotsky, L. S. (1962). *Thought and language*. Cambridge MA: MIT Press.

Warren, J. E. (2011). "Generic" and "specific" expertise in English: An expert/expert study in poetry interpretation and academic argument. *Cognition and Instruction*, *29*(4), 349–374.

Wertsch, J. V. (1998). *Mind as action*. New York, NY: Oxford University Press.

Wolfe, M. B. W., & Goldman, S. R. (2005). Relations between adolescents' text processing and reasoning. *Cognition and Instruction*, *23*, 467–502.

24

COMMENTARY

Analyzing Strategic Processing: Pros and Cons of Different Methods

Jennifer G. Cromley

UNIVERSITY OF ILLINOIS AT URBANA-CHAMPAIGN, USA

The authors in this section reviewed variable-centered (e.g., regression), person-centered (e.g., cluster analysis), and qualitative approaches to analyzing a variety of types of data collected on learning strategies. The authors discussed data collected from questionnaires, think-aloud protocols, eye tracking, and computer log files. Research on strategy use has also considered student discourse in dyads (e.g., Miller, Cromley, & Newcombe, 2015) and coding of gestures as indicative of strategy use (e.g., Alibali & Goldin-Meadow, 1993). The authors clearly laid out the different types of research questions that different analyses are suited for and various assumptions about the data that are required for the analyses. For most analyses, when data meet the assumptions of the test (e.g., normal distribution) the parametric tests are used, and when data fail one or more assumptions, non-parametric tests are used. Although mathematical transformations or bootstrapping are other options, they are not commonly used in education research, so I do not discuss them here.

In this chapter, I lay out some different data analysis options for the researcher working with strategy data. I lay out the options, in each case taking into account a number of considerations: (1) Do the data meet the assumptions for a candidate data analytic approach (e.g., normality, linearity)? (2) Are sample sizes large enough for the candidate data analytic approach? (3) Is data reduction needed (e.g., combining fine-grained codes from think-alouds, creating factor scores)?, and (4) Do large sample sizes need to be planned for in advance (e.g., full structural equation modeling)? Taking these considerations into account allows the analyst to maximize statistical power, while preserving the validity (i.e., trustworthiness) of the results from each analysis.

VARIABLE-CENTERED ANALYSES

Chi Squared Test

In addition to a long tradition of t test and ANOVA analyses to compare strategy treatment groups to control groups, some early work in strategy use during learning used chi squared tests to look for disproportionate use of certain strategies in think-aloud studies between novice/expert (e.g., Ennis & Safrit, 1991) or tutored/untutored participants (e.g., Azevedo & Cromley, 2004). One advantage of the chi squared test is that it takes account of different learners being more or less talkative—some people are simply more chatty than others (see Table 24.1). It is important to take account of these differences, because analyses of raw counts of many types of data will not show the differences that researchers are trying to test; they will simply show effects of talkativeness, and talkativeness is rarely related to learning. One disadvantage of the chi squared test is that, as a non-parametric test, it has low statistical power to detect an association, if an association between variables is indeed present. Another disadvantage is that while a chi squared test may seem to show associations between codes, it merely shows co-occurrence across an entire transcript (or log file, etc.).

Table 24.1 Summary of Uses for, Pros of, and Cons of the Statistics Reviewed in this Chapter

Statistic	Used for	Pros	Cons
chi squared	Associations between 2 categorical variables	EasyAccounts for base rate differences without any extra calculations Few assumptions	Low power Just an association
t test	Comparing means of 2 groups on a continuous outcome	Easy	Must meet 4 assumptions No 'covariate'
ANOVA	Comparing means of 2+ groups on a continuous outcome	Easy	Must meet 4 assumptions No 'covariate'
correlation	Associations between 2 continuous variables	Easy	Must meet 4 assumptions Just an association
regression	Effect of one or more independent variables, simultaneously, on a single, continuous dependent variable	EasyEffect of each independent variable takes account of all other independent variables Can test moderation	Must meet 4 assumptions
path analysis	Effect of one or more independent variables, simultaneously, on continuous dependent variable(s)	Can test mediation Account for measurement error in 'DVs' Multiple DVs simultaneously	Specialized software, steep learning curve Must meet 4 assumptions
structural equation modeling	Effect of one or more independent factors, simultaneously, on continuous dependent factor(s)	'Pure' factors, account for measurement error Can test mediation multiple DVs simultaneously	Specialized software, steep learning curve Multiple variables per construct Must meet 4 assumptions

Statistic	Used for	Pros	Cons
GCM	Shape and rate of change over time on a variable Predictor(s) of intercept and slope(s), outcome(s) of intercept and slope(s)	Power Flexible shape(s) of growth Growth on growth (i.e., multiple DVs simultaneously)	Specialized software, steep learning curve Multiple variables per construct Must meet 4 assumptions Multiple time points High reliability needed measurement invariance over time needed
transition analysis	Sequence of strategy moves during learning	Analyzes the actual sequence	Low power
LCA	Subgroups of participants Predictor(s) of subgroup membership, outcome(s) of subgroup membership	'Pure' factors, account for measurement error Can combat stereotyping	Specialized software, steep learning curve No unique solution Multiple choice points
GMM	Subgroups of trajectories Predictor(s) of intercept and slope(s), outcome(s) of intercept and slope(s)	Can combat stereotyping Multiple routes to similar outcomes	See GCM plus No unique solution Multiple choice points
LTA	Predictors of transitions between levels of a categorical outcome	'Pure' factors, account for measurement error Can combat stereotyping	See GCM plus No unique solution Multiple choice points
Qual TA	Sequences during actual learning	Illuminate how a process works	Good data collection practice is especially important Coding approach needs to be somewhat flexible Coding is effort intensive

T Test, ANOVA

Both the parametric mean comparison tests (independent samples t test, one-way ANOVA, factorial ANOVA) and their non-parametric counterparts (e.g., Mann-Whitney U test, Kruskal-Wallis ANOVA) have been used in learning strategy experiments and group comparisons. For example, in my own work (Cromley et al., 2013), we compared three different types of instruction in diagram comprehension strategies with high school students who had been pre- and posttested on diagram comprehension. We used mixed 2 (between: treatments) × 2 (within: pre- and posttest) ANOVAs to show whether any of the groups showed higher scores at posttest, after accounting for pretest scores. Besides statistical power, the repeated-measures ANOVA has less restrictive assumptions than ANCOVA for analyzing pretest-posttest, treatment-comparison group experiments. For a 2-group comparison, there is no difference in power between an independent-samples t test and an ANOVA.

One disadvantage of these group comparisons noted by Freed et al. (this volume) is that not all participants may participate or engage in the treatment at the same level, which lowers statistical power. Another disadvantage of ANOVAs is that large sample sizes are needed—a minimum of 20 participants per cell (i.e., 4 cells in a 2 × 2 design) is recommended. Non-parametric tests have less power but fewer assumptions, and are an important tool. However, some analyses have non-parametric counterparts only in R (e.g., mixed between- and within-subjects design, Feys, 2016). Finally, if classrooms are assigned to treatments (rather than individual participants being assigned to treatments), then a screening test called the Intraclass Correlation Coefficient (ICC) is needed to check whether the assumption of independence of observations is violated. If so, when large numbers of classes were tested, then multilevel modeling needs to be used; with smaller numbers of classes, alternatives to multilevel modeling need to be used (Huang, 2016).

Correlation

With samples of 60 or larger, correlation has ample statistical power to detect $r > .35$, and a correlation matrix should always be reported with any dataset that has two or more continuous variables. The disadvantage of correlation was also noted by Freed et al.; correlation is simply a measure of association. The non-parametric Spearman rank correlation may be needed if variables are not normally distributed (Hinkle, Wiersma, & Jurs, 1988).

Regression

Linear regression has been frequently used in non-experimental studies, but can be used in experiments. As noted by Freed et al., learning strategy researchers test effects of antecedents (e.g., strategy instruction) on strategy use (e.g., Yoon & Jo, 2014), and also test effects of strategy use on outcome variables (e.g., history learning; Deekens, Greene, & Lobczowski, 2018). Regression has the advantage over correlation that multiple independent variables can be used simultaneously to explain variance in a single dependent variable. Such variables can be variables of substantive interest or 'control' variables to account for variance in the DV that is not of substantive interest (e.g., students of slightly different ages participate, but age might account for some variance in the DV). Independent variables should always be chosen based on theory and prior research; they should not be chosen based on correlations with the outcome variable, and not by the analysis software as in 'forward' or 'backward' regression.

It is quite straightforward to test for interactions in regression—that is, to test whether an independent variable has a different strength of effect in one group than in another group (often termed moderation). For example, Leutner, Leopold, and Sumfleth (2009) compared strategy instruction in using imagery (only) to strategy instruction in drawing-to-learn (only), to a combination of both, or neither, with 10th grade chemistry students. They found that the drawing strategy by itself had no effect and the imagery strategy alone had no effect, but having students draw and use imagery together actually harmed learning (a significant interaction). Imagery moderated the effect of drawing on comprehension; there was an interaction between drawing strategy instruction and imagery strategy instruction.

Linear regression can accommodate any type of predictor variable(s)—continuous or categorical—but the dependent variable must be continuous. If the dependent variable is a category, then various different types of logistic regression are available. For example, Greene and Azevedo (2009) categorized posttest performance into low, medium, and high, and used a form of logistic regression to analyze effects of during-learning monitoring on the posttest category. They found that more metacognitive monitoring during learning was associated with being in a higher category. Note that continuous variables that show a normal distribution should never be re-coded as dichotomous ('high' vs. 'low') variables, as this causes a severe loss in statistical power.

Regression does have some disadvantages, in that missing data on any one variable will cause that participant's data to not be included, measurement error in variables cannot be accounted for, and *either* antecedents *or* consequences of learning strategies can be tested, but not both. In addition, if the normality or equal variances assumptions of regression are not met by the data, non-parametric regression is somewhat challenging to learn. As with ANOVA, the ICC needs to be checked and multilevel modeling may be needed.

Path Analysis

As noted by Freed et al., researchers who are interested in both antecedents *and* consequences of learning strategies can test both simultaneously using path analysis, which is a simplified type of structural equation modeling (SEM). Each effect of one variable on another is called a path, hence path analysis. A set of variables and the paths (or correlations) that connect them are called a model. Path analysis can be used in non-experimental and experimental studies. For example, Cromley and Azevedo (2007) tested effects of background knowledge on strategy use *and* effects of strategy use on comprehension in a single path model. There are many advantages of testing a single path model rather than running many regressions: (1) more statistical power/ lower risk of Type I error, (2) there are statistics available to capture the overall fit of the model rather than multiple F tests, and (3) both the direct (single path, regression) effect of a variable and its indirect effect via the mediator variable can be tested. Path analysis can overcome also the other disadvantages of regression noted above: participants can be included even if they have missing data and measurement error in dependent variables can be accounted for. Path analyses can be used to compare the size of effects across different groups (called multi-group modeling), which allows for more flexibility in modeling. Moderation (interactions) can be tested in path analysis as they can in regression. In most SEM software packages, missing data are handled using Full Information Maximum Likelihood (FIML; confusingly, sometimes simply called ML). FIML uses all data that is present on a pair of variables for the numerator of a relation that is tested (analogous to a regression beta weight), but for the denominator it uses only participants with complete data on all variables in the model. Note that FIML does not involve any kind of estimating what the missing data values might be (the latter is termed imputation). Furthermore, if variables are somewhat non-normal, SEM software can address this (Robust Maximum Likelihood or MLR). The free R package *lavaan* has made SEM more accessible to researchers, at least in terms of software costs.

Path analysis has several disadvantages for the researcher, who has to learn the complexities of SEM and programs/apps (e.g., non-convergence, fit indices, comparing nested models, adding error covariances). Learning the various 'tips and tricks' to handle these issues is not a trivial matter and is typically learned in coursework. In multi-group modeling, having a group with only a small number of participants can cause problems. In addition, when many variables are included in a path model, the researcher cannot claim that his or her model is 'correct,' merely that it shows adequate fit. Despite the term 'effect,' path analysis cannot establish causality—experiments can establish causality, and any of the analyses reviewed here can be used to analyze data from an experiment. As with ANOVA and regression, the ICC needs to be checked and multilevel path modeling may be needed.

Structural Equation Modeling

As noted by Freed et al., SEM has even more advantages over path analysis in terms of removing error variance from measured variables and thus testing relations among more 'pure' factors called latent variables. In SEM, sets of measured variables are hypothesized to be driven by a single, unmeasured factor. These factors are then tested for specific, theory-driven influences on each other. Typically the work of creating latent factors—often referred to as a measurement model—is done in the first step. This is an important difference from MANOVA where a set of dependent variables is combined into a composite(s), and the composite(s) is tested for group differences. In many studies, there is no theoretical or empirical basis for the single composite of all dependent variables involved in MANOVA. Hence the popularity of SEM, where latent factors are defined based on a strong theoretical rationale.

In SEM, testing theory-driven relations among latent factors is done in a second step—sometimes called the structural model. As with regression and path analysis, SEM can be used in non-experimental or experimental research. As with path analysis, moderation (interactions) can be tested in SEM (Marsh, Wen, Nagengast, & Hau, 2012). Like path analysis, SEM programs typically use FIML to account for missing data. One example of SEM with strategy use comes from Ahmed and colleagues (Ahmed et al., 2016), who tested Cromley's model of comprehension using SEM in order to better account for measurement error in each variable and construct. They found that neither a background knowledge factor nor a vocabulary factor had effects on strategy use. Strategy use had small and mostly non-significant direct effects on reading comprehension, except in 7th to 8th grades, and had entirely non-significant indirect effects on comprehension.

In addition to the above disadvantages of SEM, larger samples are required compared to most of the other techniques. Sample sizes for SEM are calculated from the number of loadings from factors onto observed variables, paths, and correlations in the model, and error estimates on all outcome variables. In this sense, SEM requires many measured variables, and more variables in a model is better for power. SEM is considered a large-sample technique; some fit statistics are only suitable for samples of $N > 250$. As with path analysis, the researcher's 'best' model may not be the 'best possible' model. As with ANOVA, regression, and path analysis, the ICC needs to be checked and multilevel SEM may be needed.

Other Latent Variable Models

Latent variable (factor analysis) approaches are important techniques for researchers analyzing strategy data. One reason is the important point brought up by Freed et al.—the need for data reduction. If we gather (or code for) 35 different strategies, we may not be able to conduct 35 different analyses, but we can reduce these 35 codes to a smaller number of high-level codes. However, researcher decisions about these groupings might be biased; hence, more objective data reduction techniques like exploratory factor analysis or multidimensional scaling are used. The disadvantage to these techniques is that they are completely data-driven; results may be specific to the particular sample. Like path analysis and SEM, there may not be a single 'best' model.

Growth Curve Modeling

As noted by Freed et al., there is much interest in how strategy knowledge changes over time, and growth curve modeling (GCM) is a very powerful and flexible approach. GCM can be implemented in either an SEM framework or as a special form of multilevel modeling. The main results of GCM are an average starting score (intercept) and average speed of growth (slope). These are averages because in effect a separate curve is fit for each participant. Intercepts and slopes can be related to antecedent(s) and/or outcome(s) of those strategies. For example, Ahmed and colleagues (Ahmed, Van der Werf, Kuyper, & Minnaert, 2013) modeled growth in three types of learning strategies from students at the beginning, middle, and end of 7th grade: shallow learning strategies, deep learning strategies, and metacognitive learning strategies. Four academic emotions from the beginning of 7th grade (anxiety, boredom, enjoyment, and pride) were tested as antecedents of the strategy growth curves. Patterns were somewhat complex, but students who had higher scores on enjoyment and pride at the beginning of the year also had higher scores on all strategy use scales at that time and grew faster in all of the strategy use scales over the course of the year. GCM can easily handle missing data and non-linear growth (curvilinear or discontinuous) in a way that mixed ANOVA cannot.

If researchers are interested in growth on several strategy variables, growth in one strategy can be related to growth on another strategy. These 'growth on growth' models can be very informative for developmental theories of strategy use (e.g., Siegler, 2005 'overlapping waves' model of strategy development). For example, Ahmed et al. (2013) could have correlated the intercepts and slopes among shallow, deep, and metacognitive learning strategies. These correlations would then suggest how strategies develop in tandem. For example, if shallow learning strategies decline and deep learning strategies increase, these two slopes will have a negative correlation (the more one's shallow learning strategies decline, the more one's deep learning strategies increase). There are many different options for testing growth-on-growth models; correlating intercepts and slopes is only one option (Wickrama, Lee, O'Neal, & Lorenz, 2016).

As with SEM, a disadvantage of GCM is that these require large samples, and having more measured variables (i.e., measuring at more time points) gives more power. With three time points, only the most basic models can be run; with more time points, more complex models can be run. Most published research fits quadratic models, but more types of functions are becoming available in software, packages, and apps (e.g., logistic, exponential, Gompertz) and the common functions may not be the best fitting ones. Measures generally must have very high internal consistency reliability ($\geq$ .90 is ideal), which can be difficult to obtain. In addition, researchers should show that participants interpret the questionnaire or test items similarly over time, called measurement invariance. If factor loadings for items change over time, that suggests the underlying construct does not have the same meaning to participants over time. Visual checks on raw data are critical for GCM, are time consuming, and may show that there is not just one shape of growth (see Growth Mixture Modeling below). GCM also has a steep learning curve for researchers, although those who already know SEM or multilevel modeling will be able to master the technique faster.

Transition Analyses/Data Mining

Briefly mentioned by Cho et al. (this volume), researchers may be interested in specific multiple-strategy patterns within learning process data. For example, after enacting a low-level strategy in a think-aloud, what comes next? There are many statistical approaches to transition analysis, including ones that resemble the chi squared test (e.g., Wampold & Margolin, 1982), hidden Markov models (e.g., D'Mello, Olney, & Person, 2010), and log-linear models (Jadallah et al., 2011). All of these identify pairs of coded variables (such as 'from' monitoring 'to' recalculating) that occur disproportionate to what would be expected if strategy sequences were random. For example, Jadallah et al. found that 23% of the time after a Collaborative Reasoning teacher prompted a 'give evidence' strategy, the next move was a student giving evidence. Furthermore, 17% of the time after giving evidence, the teacher offered praise for using that strategy, and 13% of the time praise led to giving more evidence. These transition analyses showed that the intervention had its effects on achievement because the teacher strategy prompts did in fact result in students using those strategies.

Other approaches to finding patterns in strategy data fall under data mining methods, such as classification trees, neural networks, machine learning, time series analysis, social network analysis, and so on. Other methods discussed here are often referred to as data mining methods, including LCA, hidden Markov models, and even some regression models. In many cases, these approaches are used to seek out transition patterns within strategy use data. Researchers interested in strategy use should stay abreast of these emerging analytical techniques, as they may come into wider use in the coming years.

The advantage of transition analyses is that they are the only technique that can answer questions about sequences rather than about simple co-occurrence within a transcript or log. Transition analyses have the disadvantages of low statistical power, and results may be sample-specific. Researchers need to be clear about which codes will be included in transition analyses (e.g., whether to include an off-task code), as analysis will change substantially from including or excluding even a single code. In addition, having fewer codes is more likely to show meaningful patterns in transition analysis. Moreover, there are challenges in deciding whether to analyze 'the next' turn (lag = 1) and/or 'the next turn after' (lag = 2). Transition analyses using the Wampold and Margolin (1982) method are easy to run using the Multiple Episode Protocol Analysis freeware from Erkens and colleagues (e.g., Janssen, Erkens, & Kanselaar, 2007).

PERSON-CENTERED ANALYSES

Latent Class Analysis (LCA)

As noted by Fryer and Shum (this volume), LCA 'classes' can be tested for differences in antecedents or outcomes of strategy use. For example, in unpublished analyses of data reported in Cromley, Snyder-Hogan, and Luciw-Dubas (2010), think-aloud participants were clustered on percentage of inferences, of high-level strategies, and of low-level strategies. The three-cluster solution suggested (1) a low-level strategies cluster who mostly used highlighting and copying definitions, with almost two-thirds of verbalizations being low-level strategies, (2) a high-level strategies cluster, with more than half of verbalizations being high-level strategies such as summarizing and self-questioning and less than one-third of verbalizations being low-level strategies, and (3) a balanced strategies, high inference cluster with one-tenth of verbalizations being inferences, and about one-third each of high- and low-level strategies. Females were significantly over-represented in the high-level strategies cluster, and the high-inference cluster scored significantly higher on free recall than the low-level strategies cluster.

LCA/cluster analysis has the advantage that it is the only approach to analyzing data where subgroups are evident (e.g., when subgroups are evident in scatterplots). An additional advantage is that a class (subgroup) might have a majority from a particular demographic group (e.g., under-represented minority students), but LCA does not force all people from that demographic to be in a particular class; thus, LCA might be a way to lessen effects of stereotyping in research.

As noted by Fryer and Shum, decisions about the number of latent classes require a mix of theory, statistical expertise, and practical knowledge. A statistically preferable solution that results in an uninterpretable class is not the best solution. In addition, LCA sometimes produces classes such as 'low cognitive strategy-low metacognitive strategy,' 'medium-medium,' and 'high-high' which do not add to our understanding (any more than a simple regression would). LCA is not an exploratory technique; as emphasized by Fryer and Shum; a strong theory needs to guide the choice of variables to cluster on. As with exploratory factor analysis, the researcher needs to carefully document and explain the reasons for each choice made at the various decision points in LCA (How many classes? What findings were taken into consideration?). As with SEM, there is a steep learning curve for researchers in learning the nuances of choosing clustering variables, the order of clustering and entering antecedent or outcome variables, fit indices, interpretability, and so on. In addition, each of these analytic choices needs to be carefully described and well justified for the researcher's audience. A stronger case can be made for LCA if the sample is first split in two, and the analyses are run on both sub-samples to see if they replicate. Thus, by definition, LCA is a large-sample technique.

Growth Mixture Modeling (GMM)

Longitudinal data sometimes show distinct subgroups with quite different shapes of change. For example, some people may show a negative quadratic ('smile') pattern of growth on use of a strategy, whereas others in the same dataset show a positive quadratic ('frown') pattern of growth on use of the same strategy. Growth mixture modeling is a hybrid of GCM and LCA in that each subset of growth trajectories is a latent class. One advantage of GMM is that statistically significant growth can be found for some subsets of participants, whereas an overall analysis might show no growth. A second advantage is theoretical—GMM can reveal multiple, effective routes to similar, positive outcomes. A third advantage is that, as in LCA, different demographics can be shown to be disproportionate in some classes (think of these as clusters), but not all members of that group are forced to have a certain pattern of growth.

As with LCA, there are a number of disadvantages to GMM. As with LCA and cluster analysis, there are many decision points that must be well justified. As with LCA, it is important to identify the latent growth classes (clusters of people showing a similar pattern of growth) *before* adding predictors or outcomes of being in a class. The SEM learning curve is somewhat steeper for GMM than for GCM. Finally, GMM is a rapidly evolving area of GCM, and researchers should seek out recent articles to use the best approaches to sample size, number of time points, fit indices, model convergence, and so on.

Latent Transition Analysis

If participants are in different classes over time (or different categorical developmental states over time, as in different Piagetian stages), various antecedent variables can be analyzed as predictors of these changes. For example, Rinne, Ye, and Jordan (2017) categorized students at various stages of fraction problem-solving strategies at three time points between 4th and 6th grades. They identified three latent classes: (1) a large-number bias class showing the well-known whole number bias (e.g., '1/4 must be larger than 1/3 because 4 is larger than 3'), (2) an intermediate small-number bias class (e.g., '8/9 must be larger than 20/40 because 8 and 9 are smaller than 20 and 40'), and (3) a correct-answer normative group. In the fall of 4th grade, 71% were in class 1, 12% were in class 2, and 17% were in class 3. By spring of 5th grade, only 31% were left in class 1, 26% were in class 2, and 43% had reached class 3. By spring of 6th grade, only 23% were still in class 1, 24% were in class 2, and 53% had reached class 3. Beyond simply describing how many participants were in each class at each time point Rinne et al. (2017) showed that higher number line knowledge at 4th grade significantly predicted making the jump from class 1 to class 3 by 5th grade. Thus, LTA is useful when people are in different categories or classes at each time point (rather than having a score on a continuous variable at each time point as in GCM). All of the advantages of LCA apply to LTA (e.g., avoiding stereotyping). LTA can be thought of as the more statistically powerful SEM (latent variable) version of log-linear analysis.

As with LCA—which is typically used as a first step in LTA—there are a number of decision points, all of which must be well justified. As with GMM, it is important to decide on a number of classes before adding antecedents or outcomes of class membership to the model. Like LCA, LTA is a large-sample technique. As expected, there is a steep learning curve in the SEM (or specialized LCA) software required to conduct LTA.

Commentary • 403

QUALITATIVE ANALYSES OF PROCESS DATA

The strategy data described by Cho et al. (this volume) can be analyzed qualitatively or quantitatively, and different disciplines have different practices. Cho et al. emphasize that with the right tasks, materials, learners, and prompts, the resulting data can be highly informative. Perhaps a disadvantage of think-aloud research is that there are many steps in the design of data collection and during actual data collection where a researcher can go wrong. For example, researchers should not model or demonstrate a think-aloud, as this is known to influence what learners do and do not verbalize. Likewise, prompts need to be very carefully worded, so as not to ask for explanations—otherwise, this becomes a self-explanation prompt rather than a think-aloud protocol.

Likewise, Cho et al. similarly emphasize the importance of careful coding (categorizing) of strategies. The many decision points in coding need to be justified and documented, such as finding a balance between emergent coding (bottom up) and pre-specified codes (top down). As with study design, well-done coded process data can provide insights that are not possible from other analyses, but there are many pitfalls, and re-coding requires a great deal of added effort. In general, it is wise to do initial coding at a more fine-grained level (even though high inter-rater reliability is more difficult, the larger the number of codes that are used), because these fine-grained codes are easy to collapse later on.

SUMMARY

The variable-centered quantitative, person-centered quantitative, and qualitative analysis methods reviewed here answer very different kinds of research questions. The variable-centered analyses ask 'what happens to a variable (on average) when there is a change to another variable?' The person-centered analyses ask 'are there subgroups of participants with similar combinations of scores on two or more variables'? If so, variable-centered analyses are used to compare subgroups on antecedent or consequent variables. The qualitative analyses ask 'what processes happen during learning and in what sequence(s)?'

Beyond those basic divisions, and given that assumptions of a test are met, the advantages and disadvantages of each method largely revolve around five themes: (1) whether directional effects are tested, (2) the number of observed variables which operationalize various measured constructs, (3) the nature of and number of dependent variable(s), (4) whether the researcher wants to test for mediation and/or moderation, and (5) statistical power. Note that all of these issues arise in any kind of data analysis, whether strategic processing is involved or not, and whether the research is in education or some other field of study.

For simple association, the chi square and correlation were discussed; the other tests (t test/ANOVA, regression, SEM) all require stating effects in a certain direction, i.e., independent and dependent variables. For those tests, if variables are switched (a variable that had been mistakenly entered as an independent variable is subsequently entered as a dependent variable) the results will change.

If only a single measure is collected for each construct, then chi square, correlation, t test, ANOVA, or regression are the choices. If multiple measures are collected on at least one construct, then the SEM approaches—SEM, GCM, LCA, GMM—give more statistical power (assuming that sample sizes are large enough to permit SEM).

If dependent variable(s) are continuous, then t test, ANOVA, linear regression, or the SEM approaches are the choices. If dependent variable(s) are categorical, then chi square, logistic regression, or the SEM approaches are the choices. If there is only one dependent variable, then t test, ANOVA, or regression are the choices. If there are multiple dependent variables tapping different constructs, then the SEM approaches—SEM, GCM, LCA, GMM—give more statistical power (assuming that sample sizes are large enough to permit SEM).

If the researcher wants to test for mediation (A affects B, B affects C, therefore A affects C indirectly via B; B mediates the effect of A on C), path analysis or SEM approaches must be used, as by definition there are multiple dependent variables. If the researcher wants to test for moderation (interactions), then regression, factorial ANOVA, path analysis, and SEM are available.

Finally, with regard to statistical power, all of the latent variable approaches—SEM, GCM, LCA, and GMM—require larger samples than the other types of analyses. This is mostly due to the large number of factor loadings, paths, correlations, and error terms that are estimated in these models. On the other hand, the use of FIML increases statistical power compared to dropping all participants missing on any variable.

In summary, the strategy researcher may have more than one option for analyzing strategic processing data, but there are many considerations that must be weighed simultaneously. In practice, screening for assumptions on all independent and dependent variables and then considering the actual sample size(s) obtained will often dictate which specific analysis can be used from among the hypothetical choices. Some kind of data reduction—collapsing codes, creating factor scores, or other composites—might be needed in order to use the non-SEM approaches if SEM approaches had been planned for. At the same time, if latent variable analyses are planned (e.g., collecting multiple indicators of a construct, testing mediation)—and these have many advantages in terms of statistical power and accounting for measurement error—then large sample sizes need to be planned in advance.

REFERENCES

Ahmed, W., Van der Werf, G., Kuyper, H., & Minnaert, A. (2013). Emotions, self-regulated learning, and achievement in mathematics: A growth curve analysis. *Journal of Educational Psychology, 105*(1), 150.

Ahmed, Y., Francis, D. J., York, M., Fletcher, J. M., Barnes, M., & Kulesz, P. (2016). Validation of the direct and inferential mediation (DIME) model of reading comprehension in grades 7 through 12. *Contemporary Educational Psychology, 44*, 68–82.

Alibali, M. W., & Goldin-Meadow, S. (1993). Gesture-speech mismatch and mechanisms of learning: What the hands reveal about a child's state of mind. *Cognitive Psychology, 25*(4), 468–523.

Azevedo, R., & Cromley, J. G. (2004). Does training on self-regulated learning facilitate students' learning with hypermedia? *Journal of Educational Psychology, 96*(3), 523–535. doi:10.1037/0022-0663.96.3.523

Cho, B.-Y., Woodward, L., & Afflerbach, P. (this volume). Qualitative approaches to the verbal protocol analysis of strategic processing. In D. L. Dinsmore, L. K. Fryer, & M. M. Parkinson (Eds.), *Handbook of strategies and strategic processing: Conceptualization, measurement, and analysis.* New York: Routledge.

Cromley, J. G., & Azevedo, R. (2007). Testing and refining the direct and inferential mediation model of reading comprehension. *Journal of Educational Psychology, 99*(2), 311–325. doi:10.1037/0022-0663.99.2.311

Cromley, J. G., Bergey, B. W., Fitzhugh, S. L., Newcombe, N., Wills, T. W., Shipley, T. F., & Tanaka, J. C. (2013). Effects of three diagram instruction methods on transfer of diagram comprehension skills: The critical role of inference while learning. *Learning and Instruction, 26*, 45–58. doi:10.1016/j.learninstruc.2013.01.003

Cromley, J. G., Snyder-Hogan, L. E., & Luciw-Dubas, U. A. (2010). Cognitive activities in complex science text and diagrams. *Contemporary Educational Psychology, 35*, 59–74. doi:10.1016/j.cedpsych.2009.10.002

D'Mello, S., Olney, A., & Person, N. (2010). Mining collaborative patterns in tutorial dialogues. *Journal of Educational Data Mining, 2*(1), 1–37.

Deekens, V. M., Greene, J. A., & Lobczowski, N. G. (2018). Monitoring and depth of strategy use in computer-based learning environments for science and history. *British Journal of Educational Psychology, 88*(1), 63–79.

Ennis, C. D., & Safrit, M. J. (1991). Using a computer simulation to compare expert/novice problem-solving subroutines. *British Journal of Educational Technology, 22*(3), 174–186.

Feys, J. (2016). Nonparametric tests for the interaction in two-way factorial designs using r. *R Journal, 8*(1), 367–378.

Freed, R., Greene, J. A., & Plumley, R. D. (this volume). Variable-centered approaches. In D. L. Dinsmore, L. K. Fryer, & M. M. Parkinson (Eds.), *Handbook of strategies and strategic processing: Conceptualization, measurement, and analysis.* New York: Routledge.

Fryer, L. K., & Shum, A. (this volume). Person-centered approaches to explaining students' cognitive processing strategies. In D. L. Dinsmore, L. K. Fryer, & M. M. Parkinson (Eds.), *Handbook of strategies and strategic processing: Conceptualization, measurement, and analysis.* New York: Routledge.

Greene, J. A., & Azevedo, R. (2009). A macro-level analysis of SRL processes and their relations to the acquisition of a sophisticated mental model of a complex system. *Contemporary Educational Psychology, 34*(1), 18–29.

Hinkle, D. E., Wiersma, W., & Jurs, S. G. (1988). *Applied statistics for the behavioral sciences.* Boston, MA: Houghton-Mifflin.

Huang, F. L. (2016). Alternatives to multilevel modeling for the analysis of clustered data. *The Journal of Experimental Education, 84*(1), 175–196.

Jadallah, M., Anderson, R. C., Nguyen-Jahiel, K., Miller, B. W., Kim, I. H., Kuo, L. J., ... Wu, X. (2011). Influence of a teacher's scaffolding moves during child-led small-group discussions. *American Educational Research Journal, 48*(1), 194–230.

Janssen, J., Erkens, G., & Kanselaar, G. (2007). Visualization of agreement and discussion processes during computer-supported collaborative learning. *Computers in Human Behavior, 23*(3), 1105–1125.

Leutner, D., Leopold, C., & Sumfleth, E. (2009). Cognitive load and science text comprehension: Effects of drawing and mentally imagining text content. *Computers in Human Behavior, 25*(2), 284–289. doi:10.1016/j.chb.2008.12.010

Marsh, H. W., Wen, Z., Nagengast, B., & Hau, K. T. (2012). Structural equation models of latent interaction. In R. Hoyle (Ed.), *Handbook of structural equation modeling* (pp. 436–458). New York: Guilford.

Miller, B. W., Cromley, J. G., & Newcombe, N. S. (2015). Improving diagrammatic reasoning in middle school science using conventions of diagrams instruction delivered in electronic warm-ups. *Journal of Computer Assisted Learning, 32*(4), 374–390. doi:10.1111/jcal.12143

Rinne, L. F., Ye, A., & Jordan, N. C. (2017). Development of fraction comparison strategies: A latent transition analysis. *Developmental Psychology, 53*(4), 713–730.

Siegler, R. S. (2005). Children's learning. *American Psychologist, 60*(8), 769–778.

Wampold, B. E., & Margolin, G. (1982). Nonparametric strategies to test the independence of behavioral states in sequential data. *Psychological Bulletin, 92*(3), 755–765.

Wickrama, K. K., Lee, T. K., O'Neal, C. W., & Lorenz, F. O. (2016). *Higher-order growth curves and mixture modeling with Mplus: A practical guide.* New York: Routledge.

Yoon, H., & Jo, J. W. (2014). Direct and indirect access to corpora: An exploratory case study comparing students' error correction and learning strategy use in L2 writing. *Language Learning & Technology, 18*, 96–117.

25

THE FUTURE OF STRATEGY THEORY, RESEARCH, AND IMPLEMENTATION

Roads Less Traveled

Patricia A. Alexander

UNIVERSITY OF MARYLAND, USA

Since the 1970s, my academic life has been intricately intertwined with strategies—text-processing, cognitive, metacognitive, problem-solving, learning strategies, and more. I was drawn to strategy research because I saw these intentional, effortful, and planful processes as a part of the answer to the question that brought me to graduate school in the first place: How can I help students who struggle to learn, especially when learning requires them to make sense of written language? By serendipity, I became intrigued by this question at a time when certain forces aligned. The Center for the Study of Reading led by Richard Anderson was in its heyday (Anderson, Reynolds, Schallert, & Goetz, 1977), John Flavell (1979, 1987) and Ellen Markman (1977) were unfolding their theory and empirical work on metacognition, and Ruth Garner (1987), my advisor, was a young, brilliant Assistant Professor at the University of Maryland exploring the boundaries between cognitive and metacognitive strategies. When I completed my PhD and headed to Texas A&M, more elements fell into place. I began to collaborate with Claire Ellen Weinstein (Weinstein, Goetz, & Alexander, 1988), a key player in learning and study strategies, along with colleagues like Diane Schallert and Ernest Goetz (Schallert, Alexander, & Goetz, 1988), who were alumnae of the Center for the Study of Reading. In a matter of a few short years, I was set on a path that I hoped would lead to deeper understanding about the very nature of strategies and the component processes they entailed—a path I continue to follow today.

However, this journey since the 1970s has been proven more challenging than I would have initially assumed. Before long, I came to appreciate that what appeared to be a fairly direct and well-demarcated road to understanding in concept was, in reality, meandering, obstructed, and even perilous at times. Nonetheless, the journey has been enlightening and has allowed me to contribute to a more detailed and, I trust, more accurate mapping of strategies and strategic processing than the one that guided my

The Future of Strategy Theory • **407**

initial foray. Along the way, I have attempted to chronicle my journey through the realm of strategy theory, research, and interventions (Alexander, 1997; Alexander & Judy, 1988; Alexander & Kulikowich, 1991; Alexander, Pate, Kulikowich, Farrell, & Wright, 1989). Now I have been given another opportunity to relive that 40-year journey, by reflecting on the diverse and informative collection of chapters populating this Handbook dedicated to strategies and strategic processing.

What I feared the most was that the obstacles to significant progress in strategy theory, research, and intervention that I repeatedly encountered in years past would still be visible, and that the road before me would likely be much the same as the one I had been trekking. Instead, what I discovered in this comprehensive volume was a panoramic and more unimpeded view of strategies and strategic processing. With this clearer vista, I could discern new roads being carved in the landscape of strategy research, and I could envision where these less trodden paths might carry future travelers. Despite these positive developments and the promises they hold, there are still cautionary signs that must be heeded and barriers to progress that have yet to be removed.

My mission in this final chapter is to revisit the impediments to significant progress in the strategy domain that I and others have charted (Dinsmore, 2017; Garner, 1990; Harris, Alexander, & Graham, 2008). Then, I will turn to the contents of this Handbook to illustrate how its contributors have either successfully navigated the barriers that have created problems for others in the past or have actively worked to dismantle them. Finally, with this analysis as the background, I project where those less traveled roads could carry the strategy researchers of today and tomorrow.

STRATEGY RESEARCH'S MEANDERING AND CIRCUITOUS COURSE

What are the persistent or re-emerging barriers within strategy's topography that have hampered progress for theorists, researchers, practitioners, and learners alike. Let me detail six that I have found to be most persistent and problematic.

- conceptual haziness;
- entrenched pathways;
- absence of navigational supports;
- insufficient time and space for maneuvering;
- inadequate preparations;
- outdated or poorly matched equipment.

Conceptual Fogginess

Let us take as a given that individuals' progress will inevitably be thwarted if they cannot determine where they are or where they are headed. Yet, that is precisely one of the more fundamental problems plaguing the terrain of strategy theory, research, and implementation. The conceptual fog that permeates the domain means that those journeying in this area are often operating with only a vague and sometimes distorted sense of what strategies are and what processes they encompass. Why this situation has persisted for decades is an enigma. Even in the 1970s and early 1980s, leading scholars like Ann Brown (Brown & Smiley, 1978), John Bransford (Bransford & Franks, 1976), and Merle Wittrock (Wittrock, Marks, & Doctorow, 1975) were attempting to clear the air as to the nature of strategies and their importance to learning and academic development. These early trailblazers into memory, information-processing, learning, cognitive, and metacognitive strategies took care to specify that what they regarded as *strategies* were intentional, planful, and effortful procedures that aided learners' progress when their default, automatic ways of functioning proved inadequate. In effect, strategies were NOT habituated modes of operation or *skills*.

Despite these early efforts to map the boundaries between strategies and skills, the conceptual fogginess continued to invade the literature and confound instructional practice. This remained true even with repeated attempts to remind the educational community that *strategies* and *skills* were not synonymous terms (Afflerbach, Pearson, & Paris, 2008; Alexander, Graham, & Harris, 1998; Paris, Lipson, & Wixson, 1983). However, these periodic efforts have seemingly had limited effect. Moreover, this problem of conceptual fogginess is not isolated to the boundaries between strategies and skills. It has occurred, as well, in the demarcations between cognitive and metacognitive strategies (Brown & Campione, 1996; Flavell, 1979, 1987; Garner, 1987, 1990), and between metacognitive and self-regulatory strategies (Brown, 1980; Dinsmore, Alexander, & Loughlin, 2008).

Why has this conceptual fog not lifted after so many years and after such concerted efforts? Clearly, there are multiple reasons why this phenomenon persists. Among those reasons, I have argued, are neglect or disregard (Alexander, 2018b). The neglect comes about, in part, from those who are experienced travelers within this realm who simply fail to chronicle the meaning by key terms, perhaps under the mistaken assumption that those terms represent common knowledge. I have witnessed such neglect far too often in the literature (Alexander & Dochy, 1995; Alexander, Schallert, & Hare, 1991; Dinsmore et al., 2008). The consequence of this neglect is that there is increased opportunity for researchers' intentions to be misinterpreted and for actions of those who follow to be ill-informed and misdirected. On the other hand, the problems I am describing may also reflect the disregard of the conceptual markers or explicit linguistic signs that have been put into place. I cannot help but wonder, how many of today's educational researchers and practitioners are aware of the rich history on strategies and strategic processing that exists? Sadly, the lack of such a panoramic view of landscape that encompasses strategy and strategic processing means that obstacles that could have been needlessly avoided continue to impede forward progress.

Set Pathways

In the early 1980s, at a point relatively early in my career, I had a somewhat contentious encounter with a very prominent strategy researcher. This established researcher was sharing results of a strategy intervention study at a national conference, and had presented her findings for participants by grade level. When the chair called for questions, I posed what I regarded as a rather benign question to this researcher. I asked whether she had examined her data to see if any groups of students who received the training demonstrated little or no effects or even some decrement in performance. The researcher responded in a rather terse manner that testing for differential impact of the strategy based on learner characteristics was not of concern to her. Such a statement struck me as illogical given what was known about the power of prior knowledge at that time.

In that researcher's defense, however, the prevailing belief at the time was that strategy training should benefit all students, and that the more strategies students reported using during task performance, the better their outcomes would be. Personally, I was not convinced. After years of teaching middle-schoolers from very diverse backgrounds and with wide-ranging abilities and interests, I had witnessed important differences in why, when, and how they operated strategically. As I saw it, the more knowledgeable certain students were about a specific topic or how familiar they were with a given task, the less they need to operate strategically. Also, the more that students' individualistic approaches to addressing a problem or task were working well, the less likely they would benefit from training in what would be a more rudimentary strategy. For these reasons, I set out to explore the relation between domain-specific knowledge and strategic processing (Alexander & Judy, 1988; Alexander et al., 1989; Pate, Alexander, & Kulikowich, 1989). What I was able to establish was that students' relevant knowledge impacted their need for certain strategies, the manner in which strategies were implemented, and whether training of specific strategies would prove advantageous or disadvantageous.

A survey of more recent strategy training studies suggests that with relatively few exceptions (e.g., Harris & Graham, 2016; Murphy et al., 2018), researchers still cast strategies in rather algorithmic, non-strategic language. Even when individuation or personalization are mentioned, they are infrequently incorporated into the experimental design. Instead, this facet of strategies is relegated to either the limitations or future directions.

Absence of Navigational Supports

Perhaps you have experienced the phenomenon of trying to find your way in some unfamiliar locale equipped with only a rough map of the area to guide you. Navigating the locale can prove quite challenging for you depending on the quality of the map, the complexity of the surroundings, your orientating skills, and your urgency of getting from point A to point B. Personally, if it were not for my GPS, I would find myself hopelessly lost in many cases. Analogously, such navigational problems have been a reoccurring theme within the realm of strategies and strategic processing, especially for novice researchers and practitioners who must rely on often sketchy and incomplete depictions by which to navigate the domain. This unacceptable situation arises in part because those conducting strategy research and devising interventions do not produce renderings of their work that are sufficiently detailed and precise for replication or implementation. There is only so much detail that can be inserted into a research article, after all. So, inevitably, anyone attempting to retrace the steps of strategy researchers will have some unmarked territory to navigate.

Also, there is a scarcity of individuals who are willing and able to serve as the navigational guides that educators require to put strategy research into practice. This scarcity has long existed because of the unique qualifications required of effective navigational guides between empirical research and educational implementation. Specifically, those who play this invaluable role must be quite knowledgeable about strategies and strategic processing and well versed in the academic domain or tasks involved (e.g., mathematics and working fraction problems). These guides must also be quite familiar with contemporary school cultures and skilled at speaking the language of teachers. If the qualifications required of these guides were not enough of an obstacle, there is often little professional incentive or institutional support for those who might take on this demanding role (Murphy, 2015).

One other reason that this navigational problem persists is because too many researchers are not expressly invested in communicating directly with teachers or school leadership. Their audience tends to be members of the research community, their peers. Even those engaged in intervention studies carried on in classrooms rarely leave behind the cache of materials, comprehensible guides, or continued supports that would allow teachers and school leadership to pursue strategy interventions on their own. This situation represents a true paradox. This is because these educational practitioners who are not the primary audience for strategy researchers will be the very individuals responsible for ensuring the success of the interventions these researchers have devised. Thankfully, there are rare exceptions in the field of strategy research, such as Graham and Harris (2016) dedicated work on Self-Regulated Strategy Development (SRSD) or Murphy et al.'s (2018) more recent classroom-based studies of Quality Talk, that serve as models of what can be done to dismantle this imposing barrier. Whether others would be willing and able to assume this mantle of both researcher and navigational guide remains to be seen.

INSUFFICIENT TIME AND SPACE

For the sake of argument, let us assume for a moment that the translational and navigational barriers I just described have been addressed and the methods and procedures for facilitating strategic processing are available. There are still formidable obstacles that impede progress for those that this research are intended to help—students and teachers. Those impediments come in the form of adequate allocation of time and space within the learning environment. As with the other obstructions I have noted, the insufficiency of the time and space students and their teachers need to develop and hone strategies or to function strategically within the classroom context is a longstanding problem. In fact, Garner (1990) identified this situation as one of the reasons why children and adults fail to be strategic. As Garner convincingly argued, educational researchers and practitioners cannot expect to witness strategic processing in schools if the learning environment does not demonstrate a valuing of strategies and strategic processing by the time devoted to scaffolding those procedures or by the mental space allocated for thinking and self-monitoring. Instead, when there is too little time and mental space, students will naturally fall back on their habituated routines, rather than invest in planful, effortful strategic processing.

If anything, since Garner published that insightful review, classrooms have become even more focused on performance goals and school curricula have become even more information dense (Alexander, 2018a). Thus, if time and space are markers of the learning environment that value and support strategic processing, then we have made little, if any, progress in dismantling this particular barrier to optimal strategy use.

Inadequate Preparation

What 40+ years of strategy research has demonstrated time and time again is that effective and efficient strategy use does not simply happen by chance. It happens when learners have a rich repertoire of strategies upon which they can draw, an adequate base of domain or topic knowledge regarding the problems and tasks at hand, and intrinsic or extrinsic reasons to invest the requisite time and energy (Alexander, 1997, 2003). It happens when teachers and educational leaders understand the power of strategic processing not just for their students' learning and development but also for their own pedagogical effectiveness and professional growth. Moreover, it is unlikely to happen spontaneously for either students or teachers, but requires orchestrated experiences, expert models, continuous feedback, and ongoing supports.

So, why is it still the case, after all these decades, that we expect students and teachers to somehow miraculously display efficient and effective strategic behavior when the aforementioned prerequisites have not been assembled? How can we expect students with very little relevant knowledge of the topic or domain, with little explicit instruction in strategies (surface or deep), and with little incentive to abandon their marginally useful approaches to learning or studying, to progress in this realm? How can we look to teachers to be the paragons of strategic behavior or expect them to invest instruction time and valuable curricular space to strategies when they have not been prepared to do so or when the educational climate, professional supports, or incentives do not exist? The simple answer is, *we cannot*. Further, until these aversive conditions are eliminated or greatly reduced, the landscape for strategies and strategic processing for these key players will remain littered with obstacles to optimal learning and academic development.

Outdated or Poorly Matched Equipment

In a special issue of the *British Journal of Educational Psychology* devoted to the complicated relations between depth and regulation of strategic processing (Dinsmore & Fryer, 2018), I remarked about the challenges of unearthing data about strategic processing (Alexander, 2018b). Measurement concerns have consistently complicated any journey into the domain of strategy theory and research. It was certainly an obstacle in the 1970s and 1980s, and required the pioneers into this territory to devise creative tasks that would afford basic insights into when students and teachers were being strategic and what they were actually doing when they were being strategic. Error detection tasks, ambiguous passages, embedded prompts, and other sundry tools were part of the strategy researchers' equipment, along with think-aloud protocols and retrospective interviews (Flavell, 1979; Greene, Robertson, & Costa, 2011; Markman, 1977).

Over the past decades, it is important to appreciate that even as new data-gathering techniques and measures have become available, such as logfiles, eye-tracking, or fMRIs, the domain of strategies and strategic processing has itself expanded. Now, as I will discuss in the subsequent section, we must contend with multiple rather than singular texts, materials that are not just one-dimensional but also multimedia (e.g., print versus mixed media), and with an inundation of information to be processed that is both accurate and inaccurate. Consequently, we have progressed beyond simply struggling to disentangle strategies from skills to wrestling with issues of general versus domain-specific strategies, levels of strategic processing, and the conceptual and operational distinctions between cognitive, metacognitive, and self-regulatory strategies. Thus, it is fair to ask whether the methods, measures, or data-analytic tools required to accurately and richly identify, gauge, or track strategic processing will ever get us to where we need to go in this complex domain.

PROMISING NEW INROADS

As I stated in the opening for this chapter, I have spent a good portion of the last four decades encountering impediments to forward progress in the strategy domain. Thus, I was understandably a bit leery to set out again to travel that very familiar path. Yet, the more I delved into the content of this Handbook and explored the avenues of inquiry laid out by these established experts, visions of where the field is headed become clearer and far more promising than I would have expected. Almost from the outset, it was apparent to me that this foray into what I regarded as familiar terrain was going to be a different experience. Here I discuss four inroads into the domain that I regard as particularly encouraging.

- demarcating boundaries;
- looking wider and going deeper;
- encountering complementary routes;
- experiencing tectonic shifts.

Demarcating Boundaries

From the opening chapter and for various chapters thereafter, contributing authors systematically and thoughtfully established the boundaries for specific concepts they were mapping. Such conceptual demarcations were especially evident in the first section of the Handbook on "Definitions, Forms, and Levels of Strategies," when authors were focused on defining the foundational term, *strategy*. I also found a level of conceptual consistency in the authors' conceptualization, as signified by their use of such descriptors as *effortful*, *intentionally*, or *purposefully* to denote those processes invoked when problems or questions arise that cannot be resolved by students' habituated routines or *skills* (e.g., Afflerbach, Hurt, & Cho, this volume; Dumas, this volume; Newton, this volume; Rogiers, Merchie, de Smedt, DeBacker, & van Keer this volume).

However, evidence of conceptual specificity also extended to discussions of more particularized forms of strategies, including learning, domain-general, domain-specific, and science learning strategies. In his examination of strategic processing within and across domains for example, Dumas (this volume) offers definitions of *domain-general strategies* (i.e., useful across a number of domains) and *domain-specific strategies* (i.e., useful in a single domain). Then, he goes on to explain how the clarity of the theoretical distinction between strategies classified as domain general and domain specific gets muddled when these strategies are enacted in research. Similarly, in their chapter on science strategy interventions, Lombardi and Bailey (this volume) took great care in defining strategies. These authors did so, in part, by differentiating them from tactics. What the authors set out to establish, particularly for the domain of physics, was that strategies, in effect, consist of *tactics*, which they characterize as

The Future of Strategy Theory • 413

an array of simple actions that collectively allow for the completion of specific tasks or activities. Even with this conceptual variation, Lombardi and Bailey still attach the descriptors planfulness, effortfulness, and goal-directed to the concept of strategies.

Further, for their review of reviews on levels of strategic processing, Dinsmore and Hattan (this volume) begin by offering working definitions of surface-level and deep-level strategies, as well as metacognitive and self-regulatory strategies. *Surface-level strategies*, according to the boundaries that Dinsmore and Hattan set, entail intentional actions taken to grasp the problem at hand and to initiate solutions, whereas *deep-level strategies* involve transforming or reframing the problem or approaching its solution in novel or creative ways. Moreover, when learners are engaged in *metacognitive strategies*, they are attempting to actively monitor their thinking or their cognitive processing, whereas *self-regulatory strategies* are broadly applied to the monitoring and control of not only learners' cognition but also to their physical, motivational, and social-emotional actions.

Regrettably, the conceptual precision found in the aforementioned chapters was not evident in all the chapters populating this Handbook. As to why this explication failed to occur in certain contributions, I can only speculate. Perhaps those contributing authors felt those terms were already well established in the literature. Yet, this is not a valid assumption. Maybe those authors were working under the assumption that at least the notions of strategies and strategic processing had been set for this Handbook in the editors' opening chapter (Dinsmore, Fryer, & Parkinson, this volume). Even if this is a more defensible position, it does not free these authors from explicating the concepts guiding their individual contributions. So, improvements in clearing away the conceptual debris that obstructs journeys into strategy theory, research, and interventions are certainly apparent in this volume, even though continued improvements are warranted.

Looking Wider and Going Deeper

A greater specificity was also evident across these contributions that investigated *how*, *when*, *why*, or in *what way* strategies are enacted within academic domains, such as history, science, or mathematic (de la Paz & Nokes, this volume; Lombardi & Bailey, this volume). For example, Newton (this volume) describes the procedural flexibility that students must manifest when they are tackling algebra or fraction problems, while Graham et al. (this volume) specify four tenets of strategic writing derived from decades of theoretical and empirical research, including numerous intervention studies:

- Skilled writers operate more strategically than less skilled writers.
- With age and appropriate experiences, writers can become more strategic.
- The unique behavioral patterns that individuals manifest in their strategic writing predict writing performance differences.
- Writing performance can improve with instruction designed to increase strategic writing.

In both the Newton (this volume) and Graham et al. (this volume) chapters, and in others that target foundational domains of learning (de la Paz & Nokes, this volume; Lombardi & Bailey, this volume), contributors thoughtfully characterize their respective domains and then reveal how strategic processing must yield to the nature of those domains in nontrivial ways. Even while acknowledging the influence of the domain, these authors retain the conceptual core that defines strategies—their planful, effortful, and intentional nature.

What this symbiotic relation between domain and strategic processing brings to light is that the well-marked borders between strategic forms (domain general and domain specific; deep and surface; cognitive and metacognitive) are far more permeable in situ, as Dumas (this volume) suggests. In essence, there are no purely domain-general or domain-specific or cognitive or metacognitive strategies—no true dichotomies—when these contrasting strategies are instantiated in research or practice. Rather, the distinctions between strategic forms are determined, in part, by the features of the immediate environment, including the task at hand, and the degree to which that task requires the transformation or iteration of relevant strategic forms.

When strategies are viewed in this more flexible or fluid light, the notion of what it means to be metacognitive or self-regulatory takes on a somewhat different meaning. It means that part of being "meta" or self-regulatory when strategically engaged requires students to recognize the level of strategy transformation or iteration that needs to be undertaken in Domain A for Problem B versus for Problem D in Domain C. This reframing of differences in strategic forms also has implications for the manner in which strategies are taught. For instance, it has been long understood that strategies cannot be taught or applied rigidly, even in domains such as mathematics or science, as Newton (this volume) reinforces. I appreciate that when a strategy is being introduced, especially with young learners, those with specific learning difficulties, or those for whom the domain or task is especially challenging, it may be necessary to overly simplify its nature. I have done precisely that when training very young children to reason analogically (Alexander et al., 1987; White & Alexander, 1986). But with time and experience and with cognitive maturation, the more fluid nature of the trained strategy must be embraced so as to allow students to personalize the strategy or modulate its character to fit the specific context or task. This is why effective strategy interventions (Harris & Graham, 2009, 2016; Murphy, 2015; Murphy et al., 2018) provide for fading of external support and personalization of the trained procedures. I grant that this proposed permeability of the boundaries between strategic forms demands more investigation, but I regard it as worthy of further exploration, nonetheless.

This novel thought engendered by the chapters in the "Strategies in Action" section gave rise to a related notion. The editors of this Handbook are among the leaders in the field probing the issue of "levels" of strategic processing. I have already commented on the conceptual clarity that Dinsmore and Hattan (this volume) brought to the notions of deeper and more surface-level strategies. However, from my perspective, those pursuing this topic (myself, included) have applied this designation to the degree of problem modulation or transformation in which learners strategically engage (deeper) in contrast to their attention to the features of the problem and potential solution paths (more surface). What I am proposing here is that these levels could also reflect the degree of transformation or iteration the learner envisions in the strategic process itself. Whether this turns out to be a viable addition to the existing concept of levels of processing remains to be seen, of course. Nonetheless, the thought-provoking contributions of this volume were the catalyst for my cognitive ruminations.

Encountering Complementary Routes

Another pleasant excursion that I had when delving into this volume came in the informative section surveying the measurement of strategies and strategic processing. It was not just the richness of the individual contributions that I found appealing, but the alternative and complementary pathways the authors laid out for chronicling and evaluating students' strategic journeys. I have long been frustrated by the limited avenues available for measuring strategies and strategic processing (Alexander, 2018b; Alexander et al., 1998; Alexander, Grossnickle Peterson, Dumas, & Hattan, 2018). However, while the contributing authors in the section did not present me with any wholly new paths for uncovering what remains largely in the minds of individuals or groups, they did expand and extend those paths. Consequently, I was afforded fresh vistas onto the nature and effects of strategic processing. For example, it was delightful to read an entire chapter devoted to person-centered analyses (Fryer & Shum, this volume), accompanied with an up-to-date examination of variable-centered analytic approaches (Freed, Greene, & Plumley, this volume).

The Freed et al. exploration of variable-centered analyses offered a nice synopsis of statistical procedures useful in strategy research; from correlational analyses and structural equation modeling to case studies and mixed methods designs. I certainly concur with these authors that variable-centered approaches hold an important position within the field of strategy research—and will continue to do so well into the future. Further, the number of techniques that can be utilized in person-centered analysis are far fewer in number than exists for variable-centered analyses. Yet, these alternative approaches allow researchers to examine the complex and often intricate interplay between learner characteristics and strategic performance for a given problem within a specific context (Fryer & Shum, this volume). In effect, person-centered approaches provide insights into *what*, strategically, is working for *whom* and under *what conditions.*

However, whether the approach that researchers take in strategy research is variable- or person-centered, the fact remains that the outcomes are only as good as the data analyzed. There is both good news and bad news on this front for strategy researchers. The good news is that new and improved tools for unearthing markers of strategic processing and for making sense of the resulting data have made an appearance since the 1970s. The new tools include more portable and sophisticated eye-tracking devices, and advancements in neuroimaging techniques (e.g., fMRI, functional near-infrared spectroscopy) and biophysiological monitoring (e.g., skin galvanic or electrodermal responses). The proliferation of digital devices also permits researchers to record relevant information (e.g., time stamps, navigation paths) as students engage in academic tasks (Bråten, Magliano, & Salmerón, this volume; Cho, Woodward, & Afflerbach, this volume; List, this volume).

Contributors to this volume expand on these new and improved tools and what they can reveal about strategies and strategic processing. For example, Catrysse, Gijbels, and Donche (this volume) illustrate how eye tracking and fMRI data can offer invaluable clues as to the level of students' strategic engagement. As Catrysse et al. rightly acknowledge, there are still challenges in reaching conclusions from such data sources, including the degree of inferencing and interpretation involved. There is also the concern for ecological validity, since these data are gathered under conditions far different from what students typically experience. Also, Taboada Barber, Cartwright, and Klauda (this volume) detail how data on executive function derived from neuro-imaging techniques can contribute to a richer understanding of what is occurring in the minds of students confronting cognitive or linguistical challenges in the classroom, and the concomitant motivational, emotional, and social issues that co-exist. What this chapter reinforced for me is that strategic processing is not solely a cognitive enter-prise, but is intertwined with motivational, emotional, and social factors that must be considered when devising interventions. As with Taboada Barber et al., my colleagues and I have found the literature on executive function invaluable in our investigations of relational reasoning. Relational reasoning is a higher-order executive function that involves the extraction of meaningful patterns from seemingly unrelated information through the perception of similarities and dissimilarities (Alexander, 2017; Alexander, Jablansky, Singer, & Dumas, 2016).

Despite the progress in measurement tools and data-analytic procedures (Freed et al., this volume; Fryer & Shum, this volume), far too many strategy researchers con-tinue to rely on survey and self-report data without corroborating information. The shortcomings of this practice have been discussed at length (Mayer et al., 2007). For one thing, humans are not the most reliable information source when it comes to their internal operations and the conditions that may have prompted those actions (Alexan-der, 2013). Interestingly, Vermunt (this volume) presents a more positive, contrasting view of survey and self-report data. Beginning in the 1970s and running to the present day, he frames his discussion in a historical context, describing several generations of survey and retrospective self-report instruments. Whether I accept this more optimis-tic view of survey and self-report data, especially in the absence of any direct measures, I found several aspects of Vermunt's discussion intriguing.

For one, the concept of learning styles, which was a focus of the early generations of survey instruments, was explicated. Specifically, *learning styles*, which are now referred to as *approaches to learning*, are conceived as learners' disposition to adopt a learning or studying routine regardless of the specific context or task demands (Schmeck, 1983). From my perspective, and that of other contributors to this volume (Afflerbach et al,, this volume), this conception has more in common with the definition of skills than strategies; more habituated than intentional and more rigid than flexible. That being said, Vermunt offers three rationales for the continued use of surveys and retrospective self-reports. First, the decades of research using these measures has led to a rich litera-ture on college students' learning and study practices. Second, these tools have served as a catalyst for students' reflections on their actions when studying. Third, rather than serving as a self-evaluation tool for students, Vermunt considered the later generations of these survey and self-report measures to be viable for assessing the instructional environment.

Finally, in their chapter, Cho, Woodward, and Afflerbach (this volume) delve into another form of self-reporting, verbal protocols, but they do so through what they classify as a qualitative lens. Consistent with Vermunt's rationale, these authors see merits to employing verbal protocol analyses as a mechanism for probing the thinking and reasoning of students engaged in online reading tasks. I found other aspects of this chapter thought provoking. For one, I was struck by the authors' claim that qualitative research is primarily inductive and informed by the data, "rather than deductive or beholden to theory." This claim was puzzling to me because much of the chapter established how the authors' analysis was, in fact, driven by theories of epistemic beliefs, text comprehension, argument, and more.

Perhaps Cho et al.'s choice of word, beholden, was intended to signal a strict top-down process that allowed for no variability or flexibility based on trends emerging from the data, task, or situation. As a counterargument, I would contend that the distinction between inductive and deductive in strategy research that the authors pose represents a false dichotomy. The complexity of the phenomena being explored almost inevitably forces researchers to move rhythmically between induction and deduction. Otherwise, studies of strategies and strategic processing would either be atheoretical and, thus, uninterpretable, *or* led wholly by the data, in which case, there would be no sense of what might be relevant or whether inferences seemed reasonable or realistic.

Bråten et al. (this volume) also explore verbal protocols in their chapter on concurrent and task-specific self-reports. Addressing the concern that thinking aloud while engaged in a cognitive task alters normal strategic processing by directing students to share what otherwise would be tacit, habituated actions, these authors describe alternative approaches to gathering verbal protocol data. In addition, they discuss the coding of these verbal protocols and consider what steps are required to ensure the validity of those data. One recommendation they offer is to look for correspondence between the strategies identified from the verbal protocol data and what would be expected based on individual differences data. Similarly, there should be a reasonable relation between what individuals verbalize about their processing and the quality of their performance. In effect, more knowledgeable or more competent learners should be more likely to describe deeper-processing and regulatory strategies than those for whom the task at hand is unfamiliar and cognitive demanding. Likewise, the students who verbalize more instances of deeper, regulatory processing should tend to have higher outcomes than those whose strategic processing is limited and surface-level. Another approach to validation could involve corroborating what students report with some objective markers such as logfiles, eye tracking patterns, or neuro-imaging data.

Collectively, what these chapters on methodology revealed is that there are multiple paths that can be traversed in the study of strategies and strategic processing and that researchers should be able to follow one or more of these paths in pursuit of their goals. What I also came to realize is that these paths may diverge as certain junctures in the journey, but they are also apt to cross or even overlap at other times. The bigger question that lingers for me is whether these complementary routes reach similar points in the end. My guess is that they will ultimately afford different vistas onto the strategy landscape, but the topography will be recognizable, nonetheless.

Tectonic Shifts

There is absolutely no denying that the ground upon which educational researchers and practitioners stand has shifted significantly since the 1970s. The picture of this shift I have tried to paint in words cannot do justice to those tectonic movements nor to the seismic effects on learning and development they engendered (Alexander, 2018a). Students populating today's classrooms have never known a world without readily transportable technology, social media, and smartphones that have more computing capacity than the full size computers of past generations. Also, the population of post-industrial countries are truly awash in all manner of information 24/7—a good portion of which can be flawed or intentionally misleading.

Of course, one could argue that inaccurate or misleading information has always been part of human existence and has inevitably contributed to misunderstandings or misconceptions. While that may be true, the situation today is significantly different for various reasons. The first is an exponential increase in the amount of information individuals encounter, and thus a concomitant increase in the amount of erroneous information being communicated. Second, because there is far greater ease and speed of access to information for those living in post-industrial societies, and far fewer filters in place to monitor the quality of that information flow, even young children can be exposed to false, biased, or malicious content. Third, with the enhanced technological savvy that exists and the "innovations" that savvy has produced, such as bots, there are even more opportunities for individuals or groups to intentionally fabricate or distort information for the purpose of misleading or misdirecting others. For these reasons, the need for effective strategic processing seems even greater for those who want to become more knowledgeable and more competent and who, therefore, want to be able to cull the distorted, malicious, and clearly incorrect information from that which is less biased, more factual, and better substantiated (Alexander, & the Disciplined Reading and Learning Research Laboratory, 2012).

Within the pages of this Handbook, there is evidence that many contributors are attuned to these topographical shifts, which is encouraging for the future of strategy theory, research, and interventions. I saw traces of it when Bråten et al. (this volume) were describing the intelligent systems that can be applied to analyze verbal protocols. But, there were several chapters in particular that gave the contemporary nature of strategic processing notable attention. For one, List (this volume) specifically addresses the strategic processing of multiple texts rather than a single text, which is an increasingly common occurrence in students' lives. The very description that she puts to multiple text use (MSU)—a complex, challenging, effortful, goal-directed, and contextualized process—parallels the conception of strategies framing this Handbook. The six core questions that List poses are revealing in terms of what strategies seem especially relevant to MSU and about the nature of strategic engagement when more than one document must be accessed and processed. While the empirical literature and theoretical models of MSU have abounded of late, there is still much to be learned about students' strategic processing of multiple texts that are most often multimedia (text plus pictures or video) in nature.

One reason I feel that the field has only begun to scratch the surface of strategic processing in MSU studies is because current findings have come almost entirely from highly orchestrated studies. In effect, participants are not only presented with specific task parameters and a prescribed topic that researchers deem controversial, but they are typically given a library of more or less credible sources that forward pro *and* con positions on the topic. Thus it is unclear how students free to select their search topic and to locate relevant sources would be engaged strategically. Even in the study described by Cho et al. (this volume) that the researchers labeled an "authentic" task involving "authentic reading," students were expected to research the topic of mountaintop mining the researchers viewed as controversial. Students participating in the

The Future of Strategy Theory • 419

study were required to verbalize their thinking over the course of one hour. Why this qualifies as an "authentic" task encompassing "authentic" reading was not apparent to me. Consequently, until more naturalistic studies of students' processing of multiple documents are undertaken, the *what, when, how,* and *why* of strategic processing of multiple texts remains an open question.

In their contribution to this Handbook, Lawless and Riel (this volume) share research on what they refer to as *technology-mediated strategies* with a particular eye toward extracting meaningful patterns from "big data" about students' strategic processing. Such a topic would have been alien to strategy theorists and researchers 40 years ago, but is in keeping with today's world. As these authors explain it, so much human activity in contemporary society leaves behind digital footprints. When these thousands upon thousands of footprints are amassed for the purpose of examination, they are referred to as *big data*. While the commercial and sociopolitical power of big data is becoming quite evident in this age of bots, trolling, and phishing, the potential value for investigating strategic processing is still underdeveloped. I was especially taken with the authors' statement that: "Education has yet to fully leverage the plethora of data available on students' learning and strategic processes in instructional environments as a means to automate and leverage the adaptable affordances of technology for teaching, learning, and assessment in situ." The authors then set out to illustrate what that leveraging could encompass. The result was a glimpse into the possible future for strategy theory, research, and intervention.

FORGING AHEAD

In bringing this chapter to close, I want to address several sectors within the strategy domain that remain underexplored and underdeveloped. Even with the promising new inroads just described, the disregard of these regions should not be allowed to persist for fear of thwarting further progress. The specific sectors I want to pinpoint relate to:

- focusing greater attention on teachers as strategic guides;
- nesting strategy research in more naturalistic contexts;
- generating multidimensional, developmental representations.

Teachers as Strategic Guides

What was apparent from the contents of this Handbook was that contributors' interests—whether addressing the nature, forms, and levels of strategies, their enactment in academic domains, or their measurement—was squarely on learners. While that is understandable, given researchers' altruistic aim of improved learning and development for all students, it ignores one crucial principle:

> It is ultimately the teachers, through their day-to-day interactions with students, their explicit or implicit instruction, and the learning environment they help create, who routinely mark the strategic paths that their students tend to follow.

However, even though teachers and teaching are mentioned in almost every chapter in this volume, they are most often addressed indirectly. There is not one chapter that

420 • Patricia A. Alexander

puts teachers in the foreground. This is true even for the several chapters that are specifically about interventions. Where are the studies of teachers' strategic processing? What does strategic teaching look like generally or within specific academic domains? How are teachers prepared to assume positions as their students' strategic role models, promoters, appraisers, and navigational guides?

Without more concentrated research attention on teachers' strategic knowledge and behavior both at a general and domain-specific level, and without strategic processing being an explicit component in teachers' professional development, there is no reason to expect significant improvements in students' strategic behaviors. That is because the value that teachers place on strategic processing, and the time and attention it garners within classroom instruction becomes a highly determinative factor in what their students do (Garner, 1990). Moreover, if you change the strategic knowledge and strategic behaviors of teachers, you change the instructional climate that exists for students.

Naturalistic Contexts for Strategy Inquiry

Earlier, I noted my concern over the ecological validity of research into students' strategic behaviors in online environments. Such concern is by no means new or surprising. There has long been tension between basic and applied research within the educational community—between laboratory studies and what transpires in natural settings. This is one of the legacies that traces back to E. L. Thorndike's dismissal of the classroom as a useful context for scientific research (Berliner, 1993). As with many false dichotomies, there is no reason to presume a paradoxical relation between research carried out in a more orchestrated or controlled setting and that which is conducted in situ. Both serve valuable and potentially complementary roles and there are always ways to make experimental research more ecological valid or classroom-based research more controlled.

The point that I make here is that strategy theorists and researchers cannot remain in the sector of highly controlled or contrived investigations if their intentions are to map the entire landscape of strategies and strategic processing. They must venture into the less cultivated and certainly more volatile terrain that students experience daily. By exploring this more dynamic and changeable environment, researchers should be able to more richly and accurately describe the strategic behaviors of the teachers and students who reside there. Further, these researchers should be better equipped to devise interventions that can be sustained within that more dynamic and volatile environment, and to lay out alternative routes that teachers and students can more readily pursue toward improved strategic processing.

Multidimensional, Developmental Models

When discussing the need for navigational supports, I mentioned the struggle of finding one's way when equipped with only a rough sketch of the landscape. The underlying premise of that statement was that: The better the map, the easier the journey. Certainly, the chartings of the strategy domain have improved noticeably since the

1970s. This Handbook is a testament to that fact. Yet, when it comes to the fundamental question of how strategic processing should change over time, current mappings are still in need of enhancement, as Rogiers et al. (this volume) so contended. The features these contributors would add to existing models (my own included) were four characteristic changes that they felt undergirded development: availability, diversity, efficiency, and adaptivity. That is certainly a beginning.

Yet, as was also evident in many chapters in this volume, strategy enactment is not a one-dimensional process, not solely a cognitive enterprise. Therefore, one-dimensional mappings are, by default, incomplete and potentially misdirecting. Rather, what seems required is a multidimensional rendering that incorporates knowledge, motivational, emotional, and sociocultural forces that are continually interacting with the cognitive and metacognitive elements that have long been part of existing strategy models. The Model of Domain Learning (Alexander, 1997, 2003) is a multidimensional mapping that includes individual and situational interest, domain and topic knowledge, along with deeper and more surface-level processing strategies, as driving forces in expertise development. Still there is more to chart. What I have acknowledged is that the MDL is a mid-range topographical rendering. It does not take into account more microlevel or global forces that are also influential in strategy development.

Thus, beyond multidimensionality, mappings of the strategy domain must take into consideration its highly idiosyncratic and dynamic character. No two individuals travel the same strategic terrain in the same way. Further, even the same individual experiences fluctuations in the knowledge and interest that fuel strategic behavior. This almost demands an interactive map that allows learners to pinpoint their current location within the landscape and to plot various courses of action, depending on the immediate conditions. Such an interactive and individualized mapping may seem unrealistic based on the current state of theory and research. But the knowledge base and technological capabilities have advanced so much that more detailed and individualized renderings may not be so far off. At the very least, I remain optimistic that the field will reach a point in the relatively near future where the representations of strategy processing it produces will be richer and more useful than in generations past. The contributors to this volume have already laid the groundwork and set the benchmarks for those who will follow.

IN TRIBUTE

I would like to dedicate this chapter to the pioneers into strategy theory, research, and interventions who have left this plane of existence, but who have, nonetheless, blazed a trail across this landscape for all who follow.

Ruth Garner
Wilbert (Bill) McKeachie
Paul Pintrich
Michael Pressley
Claire Ellen Weinstein
Merle Wittrock

REFERENCES

Afflerbach, P., Pearson, P. D., & Paris, S. G. (2008). Clarifying differences between reading skills and reading strategies. *The Reading Teacher, 61*(5), 364–373. doi.org/10.1598/RT.61.5.1

Afflerbach, P., Hurt, M., & Cho, B. Y. (this volume). Reading comprehension strategy instruction. In D. L. Dinsmore, L. K. Fryer, & M. M. Parkinson (Eds.), *Handbook of strategies and strategic processing: Conceptualization, measurement, and analysis* New York: Routledge.

Alexander, P. A. (1997). Mapping the multidimensional nature of domain learning: The interplay of cognitive, motivational, and strategic forces. In M. L. Maehr & P. R. Pintrich (Eds.), *Advances in motivation and achievement* (Vol. 10, pp. 213–250). Greenwich, CT: JAI Press.

Alexander, P. A. (2003). Profiling the developing reader: The interplay of knowledge, interest, and strategic processing. In C. M. Fairbanks, J. Worthy, B. Maloch, J. V. Hoffman, & D. L. Schallert (Eds.), *The Fifty-first Yearbook of the National Reading Conference* (pp. 47–65). Oak Creek, WI: National Reading Conference.

Alexander, P. A. (2012). the Disciplined Reading and Learning Research Laboratory . Reading into the future: Competence for the 21st century. *Educational Psychologist, 47*(4), 1–22. doi:10.1080/00461520.2012.722511

Alexander, P. A. (2013). Calibration: What is it and why it matters? An introduction to the special issue on calibrating calibration. *Learning and Instruction, 24*, 1–3. doi:org/10.1016/j.learninstruc.2012.10.003

Alexander, P. A. (2017). Relational reasoning in STEM domains: A foundation for academic development. *Educational Psychology Review, 29*, 1–10. doi:org/10.1007/s10648-016-9383-1

Alexander, P. A. (2018a). Information management versus knowledge building: Implications for learning and assessment in higher education. In O. Zlatkin-Troitschanskaia, M. Toepper, H. A. Pant, C. Lautenbach, & C. Kuhn (Eds.), *Assessment of learning outcomes in higher education: Cross national comparisons and perspectives* (pp. 43–56). Dordrecht, Netherlands: Springer.

Alexander, P. A. (2018b). Looking down the road: Future directions for research on depth and regulation of strategic processing. *British Journal of Educational Psychology, 88*, 152–166. doi:org/10.1111/bjep.12204

Alexander, P. A., & Dochy, F. J. R. C. (1995). Conceptions of knowledge and beliefs: A comparison across varying cultural and educational communities. *American Educational Research Journal, 32*, 413–442.

Alexander, P. A., Graham, S., & Harris, K. (1998). A perspective on strategy research: Progress and prospects. *Educational Psychology Review, 10*, 129–154. doi:org/10.1023/A:1022185502996

Alexander, P. A., Grossnickle Peterson, E. M., Dumas, D., & Hattan, C. (2018). A retrospective and prospective examination of cognitive strategies and academic development: Where have we come in twenty-five years? In A. O'Donnell (Ed.), *Oxford handbook of educational psychology* New York: Oxford University Press Online Publication Date: May 2018. doi:10.1093/oxfordhb/9780199841332.013.23

Alexander, P. A., Jablansky, S., Singer, L. M., & Dumas, D. (2016). Relational reasoning: What we know and why it matters. *Policy Insights from the Behavioral and Brain Sciences, 3*(1), 36–44. doi:10.1177/2372732215622029

Alexander, P. A., & Judy, J. E. (1988). The interaction of domain-specific and strategic knowledge in academic performance. *Review of Educational Research, 58*, 375–404. doi:org/10.3102/00346543058004375

Alexander, P. A., & Kulikowich, J. M. (1991). Domain-specific and strategic knowledge as predictors of expository text comprehension. *Journal of Reading Behavior, 23*, 165–190. doi:org/10.1080/10862969109547735

Alexander, P. A., Pate, P. E., Kulikowich, J. M., Farrell, D. M., & Wright, N. L. (1989). Domain-specific and strategic knowledge: Effects of training on students of differing ages or competence levels. *Learning and Individual Differences, 1*, 283–325. doi:org/10.1016/1041-6080(89)90014-9

Alexander, P. A., Schallert, D. L., & Hare, V. C. (1991). Coming to terms: How researchers in learning and literacy talk about knowledge. *Review of Educational Research, 61*, 315–343.

Alexander, P. A., Wilson, A. F., White, C. S., Willson, V. L., Tallent, M. K., & Shutes, R. E. (1987). Effects of teacher training on children's analogical reasoning performance. *Teaching and Teacher Education, 3*(4), 275–285. doi:org/10.1016/0742-051X(87)90020-5

Anderson, R. C., Reynolds, R. E., Schallert, D. L., & Goetz, E. T. (1977). Frameworks for comprehending discourse. *American Educational Research Journal, 14*(4), 367–381. doi:org/10.3102/00028312014004367

Berliner, D. C. (1993). The 100-year journey of educational psychology: From interest, to disdain, to respect for practice. In T. K. Fagan & G. R. VandenBos (Eds.), *Master lectures in psychology. Exploring applied psychology: Origins and critical analyses* (pp. 37–78). Washington, DC, US: American Psychological Association. doi.org/10.1037/11104-002

Bransford, J. D., & Franks, J. J. (1976). Toward a framework for understanding learning. *Psychology of Learning and Motivation, 10*, 93–127. doi:org/10.1016/S0079-7421(08)60465-X

Bråten, I., Magliano, J. P., & Salmerón, L. (this volume). Concurrent and task specific self-reports. In D. L. Dinsmore, L. K. Fryer, & M. M. Parkinson (Eds.), *Handbook of strategies and strategic processing: Conceptualization, measurement, and analysis* New York: Routledge.

Brown, A. L. (1980). Metacognitive development and reading. In R. J. Spiro, B. C. Bruce, & W. F. Brewer (Eds.), *Theoretical issues in reading comprehension: Perspectives from cognitive psychology, linguistics, artificial intelligence, and education* (pp. 453–481). Mahwah, NJ: Lawrence Erlbaum Associates.

Brown, A. L., & Campione, J. C. (1996). Communities of learning and thinking, or a context by any other name. In P. Woods (Ed.), *Contemporary issues in teaching and learning* (pp. 120–126). New York: Routledge.

Brown, A. L., & Smiley, S. S. (1978). The development of strategies for studying texts. *Child Development, 49*, 1076–1088. doi:10.2307/1128747

Catrysse, L., Gijbels, D., & Donche, V. (this volume). Measuring levels of processing: Perspectives for eye tracking and fMRI in multi-method designs. In D. L. Dinsmore, L. K. Fryer, & M. M. Parkinson (Eds.), *Handbook of strategies and strategic processing: Conceptualization, measurement, and analysis* New York: Routledge.

Cho, B. Y., Woodward, L., & Afflerbach, P. (this volume). Qualitative approaches to the verbal protocol analysis of strategic processing. In D. L. Dinsmore, L. K. Fryer, & M. M. Parkinson (Eds.), *Handbook of strategies and strategic processing: Conceptualization, measurement, and analysis* New York: Routledge.

de la Paz, S., & Nokes, J. (this volume). Strategic processing in history and historical strategy instruction. In D. L. Dinsmore, L. K. Fryer, & M. M. Parkinson (Eds.), *Handbook of strategies and strategic processing: Conceptualization, measurement, and analysis* New York: Routledge.

Dinsmore, D. L. (2017). Toward a dynamic, multidimensional research framework for strategic processing. *Educational Psychology Review, 29*, 235–268. doi:org/10.1007/s10648-017-9407-5

Dinsmore, D. L., Alexander, P. A., & Loughlin, S. M. (2008). Focusing the conceptual lens on metacognition, self-regulation, and self-regulated learning. *Educational Psychology Review, 20*, 391–409. doi:org/10.1007/s10648-008-9083-6

Dinsmore, D. L., & Fryer, L. K. (2018). Editorial: The intersection between depth and the regulation of strategy use. *British Journal of Educational Psychology, 88*, 1–8. doi:org/10.1111/bjep.12209

Dinsmore, D. L., Fryer, L. K., & Parkinson, M. M. (this volume). Introduction: What are strategies? In D. L. Dinsmore, L. K. Fryer, & M. M. Parkinson (Eds.), *Handbook of strategies and strategic processing: Conceptualization, measurement, and analysis* New York: Routledge.

Dinsmore, D. L., & Hattan, C. (this volume). Levels of strategies and strategic processing. In D. L. Dinsmore, L. K. Fryer, & M. M. Parkinson (Eds.), *Handbook of strategies and strategic processing: Conceptualization, measurement, and analysis* New York: Routledge.

Dumas, D. (this volume). Strategic processing within and across domains of learning. In D. L. Dinsmore, L. K. Fryer, & M. M. Parkinson (Eds.), *Handbook of strategies and strategic processing: Conceptualization, measurement, and analysis* New York: Routledge.

Flavell, J. H. (1979). Metacognition and cognitive monitoring: A new area of cognitive–developmental inquiry. *American Psychologist, 34*, 906–911. doi:10.1037/0003-066X.34.10.906

Flavell, J. H. (1987). Speculation about the nature and development of metacognition. In F. E. Weinert & R. H. Kluwe (Eds.), *Metacognition, motivation, and understanding* (pp. 21–29). Hillsdale, NJ: Lawrence Erlbaum Associates.

Freed, R., Greene, J. A., & Plumley, R. D. (this volume). Variable-centered approaches. In D. L. Dinsmore, L. K. Fryer, & M. M. Parkinson (Eds.), *Handbook of strategies and strategic processing: Conceptualization, measurement, and analysis* New York: Routledge.

Fryer, L. K., & Shum, A. (this volume). Person-centered approaches to explaining students' cognitive processing strategies. In D. L. Dinsmore, L. K. Fryer, & M. M. Parkinson (Eds.), *Handbook of strategies and strategic processing: Conceptualization, measurement, and analysis* New York: Routledge.

Garner, R. (1987). *Metacognition and reading comprehension.* Norwood, NJ: Ablex.

Garner, R. (1990). When children and adults do not use learning strategies: Toward a theory of settings. *Review of Educational Research, 60*, 517–529. doi:org/10.3102/00346543060004517

Graham, S., & Harris, K. R. (2016). A path to better writing: evidence-based practices in the classroom. *The Reading Teacher, 69*(4), 359–365. doI:10.1002/trtr.1432.

Graham, S., Bañales, G., Ahumada, S., Harris, K. R., Muñoz, P., & Alva, P. (this volume). Writing strategies interventions. In D. L. Dinsmore, L. K. Fryer, & M. M. Parkinson (Eds.), *Handbook of strategies and strategic processing: Conceptualization, measurement, and analysis* New York: Routledge.

Greene, J. A., Robertson, J., & Costa, L. J. C. (2011). Assessing self-regulated learning using think-aloud methods. In B. J. Zimmerman & D. H. Schunk (Eds.), *Handbook of self-regulation of learning and performance* (pp. 313–328). New York: Routledge.

Harris, K. R., Alexander, P. A., & Graham, S. (2008). Michael Pressley's contributions to the history and future of strategies research. *Educational Psychologist, 43*, 86–96. doi:org/10.1080/00461520801942300

Harris, K. R., & Graham, S. (2009). Self-regulated strategy development in writing: Premises, evolution, and the future. *British Journal of Educational Psychology, 113,* 113–135. Monograph Series No. 6 doi: org/10.1348/9 78185409X422542

Harris, K. R., & Graham, S. (2016). Self-regulated strategy development in writing: Policy implications of an evidence-based practice. *Policy Insights from the Behavioral and Brain Sciences, 3,* 77–84. doi: org/10.1177/2372732215624216

Lawless, K. A., & Riel, J. (this volume). Exploring the utilization of the big data revolution as a methodology for exploring learning strategy in educational environments. In D. L. Dinsmore, L. K. Fryer, & M. M. Parkinson (Eds.), *Handbook of strategies and strategic processing: Conceptualization, measurement, and analysis* New York: Routledge.

List, A. (this volume). Six questions regarding strategy use when learning from multiple texts. In D. L. Dinsmore, L. K. Fryer, & M. M. Parkinson (Eds.), *Handbook of strategies and strategic processing: Conceptualization, measurement, and analysis* New York: Routledge.

Lombardi, D., & Bailey, J. M. (this volume). Science strategy interventions. In D. L. Dinsmore, L. K. Fryer, & M. M. Parkinson (Eds.), *Handbook of strategies and strategic processing: Conceptualization, measurement, and analysis* New York: Routledge.

Markman, E. M. (1977). Realizing that you don't understand: A preliminary investigation. *Child Development, 48,* 986–992. doi:10.2307/1128350

Mayer, R. E., Stull, A. T., Campbell, J., Almeroth, K., Bimber, B., Chun, D., & Knight, A. (2007). Overestimation bias in self-reported SAT scores. *Educational Psychology Review, 19,* 443–454. doi:org/10.1007/s10648-006-9034-z

Murphy, P. K. (2015). Marking the way: School-based interventions that "work.". *Contemporary Educational Psychology, 40,* 1–4. doi:org/10.1016/j.cedpsych.2014.10.003

Murphy, P. K., Greene, J. A., Firetto, C. M., Hendrick, B. D., Li, M., Montalbano, C., & Wei, L. (2018). Quality Talk: Developing students' discourse to promote high-level comprehension. *American Educational Research Journal, 55,* 1113–1160. doi:org/10.3102/0002831218771303

Newton, K. J. (this volume). Mathematics strategy interventions. In D. L. Dinsmore, L. K. Fryer, & M. M. Parkinson (Eds.), *Handbook of strategies and strategic processing: Conceptualization, measurement, and analysis* New York: Routledge.

Paris, S. G., Lipson, M. Y., & Wixson, K. K. (1983). Becoming a strategic reader. *Contemporary Educational Psychology, 8*(3), 293–316. doi.org/10.1016/0361-476X(83)90018-8

Pate, P. E., Alexander, P. A., & Kulikowich, J. M. (1989). Assessing the effects of training social studies content and analogical reasoning processes on sixth-graders' domain-specific and strategic knowledge. In D. B. Strahan (Ed.), *Middle school research: Selected Studies 1989* (pp. 19–29). Columbus, OH: Research Committee of the National Middle School Association.

Rogiers, A., van Keer, H., DeBacker, L., Merchie, E., & De Smedt, F. (this volume). A lifespan developmental perspective on strategic processing. In D. L. Dinsmore, L. K. Fryer, & M. M. Parkinson (Eds.), *Handbook of strategies and strategic processing: Conceptualization, measurement, and analysis* New York: Routledge.

Schallert, D. L., Alexander, P. A., & Goetz, E. T. (1988). Implicit instruction of strategies for learning from text. In C. E. Weinstein, E. T. Goetz, & P. A. Alexander (Eds.), *Learning and study strategies: Issues in assessment, instruction, and evaluation* (pp. 193–214). San Diego: Academic Press.

Schmeck, R. R. (1983). Learning styles of college students. In R. Dillon & R. R. Schmeck (Eds.), *Individual differences in cognition* (1 pp. 233–279). New York: Academic Press.

Taboada Barber, A., Cartwright, K. B., & Klauda, S. L. (this volume). Interplay of strategic processes, executive functions, and autonomy support in students with individual differences. In D. L. Dinsmore, L. K. Fryer, & M. M. Parkinson (Eds.), *Handbook of strategies and strategic processing: Conceptualization, measurement, and analysis* New York: Routledge.

Vermunt, J. D. (this volume). Surveys and retrospective self-reports to measure strategies and strategic processing. In D. L. Dinsmore, L. K. Fryer, & M. M. Parkinson (Eds.), *Handbook of strategies and strategic processing: Conceptualization, measurement, and analysis* New York: Routledge.

Weinstein, C. E., Goetz, E. T., & Alexander, P. A. (Eds.). (1988). *Learning and study strategies: Issues in assessment, instruction, and evaluation.* San Diego: Academic Press.

White, C. S., & Alexander, P. A. (1986). Effects of training on four-year-olds' ability to solve geometric analogy problems. *Cognition and Instruction, 3,* 261–268. doi:org/10.1207/s1532690xci0303_6

Wittrock, M. C., Marks, C., & Doctorow, M. (1975). Reading as a generative process. *Journal of Educational Psychology, 67,* 484–489. doi:org/10.1037/h0077017

CONTRIBUTOR BIOS

Peter Afflerbach is Professor of Education at the University of Maryland. Dr. Afflerbach's research interests focus on individual differences in reading, reading comprehension strategies for print and digital reading, reading assessment, and the verbal reporting methodology. He serves on the Reading Committee of the National Assessment of Educational Progress (NAEP) and was elected to the International Literacy Association's Reading Hall of Fame in 2009. He is the editor of the *Handbook of Individual Differences in Reading: Reader, Text, and Context* (2016), and co-editor of the *Handbook of Reading Research*, 4th Edition (2010) and 5th Edition (in press).

Silza Ahumada received a Bachelor of Arts degree in Hispanic language and literature, majoring in Spanish linguistics, from Universidad de Chile. Currently, she is a Ph.D. candidate at the Education and Society doctoral program, Universidad Andres Bello, Chile. Her doctoral research studies the implementation of evidence-based practices for writing instruction in elementary school teachers and how the adoption of these practices is related to personal, classroom, and institutional factors.

Patricia A. Alexander is a Distinguished University Professor, the Jean Mullan Professor of Literacy, and Distinguished Scholar-Teacher in the Department of Human Development and Quantitative Methodology at the University of Maryland. The author of over 300 articles, books, chapters, and monographs, her research focuses on text-based learning, strategic processing, knowledge, and interest. Her *Model of Domain Learning* (1997, 2003, 2018) considers the interaction of these factors in students' academic development. She currently serves as the senior editor of *Contemporary Educational Psychology* and is the Educational Psychology Handbook series editor for Routledge.

Prisila Alvarez received a Master's in Reading Comprehension and Written Production from School of Education and Social Sciences, Andres Bello University, Chile. She currently works as a teacher of basic education in public schools in Chile, where she teaches reading, writing, and speaking strategies to children.

426 • Contributor Bios

Martine Baars is an educational psychologist and her research concerns improving self-regulated learning in primary, secondary, and higher education. She focuses on several aspects of self-regulated learning such as self-monitoring accuracy, motivation, learning strategies, and cognitive load during learning in both offline and online learning environments (e.g., MOOCs) for individuals and groups. As a Researcher Martine is active in the Centre for Education and Learning (CEL) of the Strategic Alliance of Leiden University, Delft University of Technology (TU Delft) and Erasmus University Rotterdam, as well as in the Community of Learning and Innovation (CLI) at the Erasmus University Rotterdam.

Janelle M. Bailey is a faculty member in the Department of Teaching and Learning at Temple University, where she focuses on astronomy and Earth science teaching and learning as well as science teacher education. She is a Past President of the American Association of Physics Teachers (AAPT) and serves as a reviewer for several research and practitioner journals. Janelle earned her Ph.D. in Teaching & Teacher Education (minor in Astronomy) with a focus on astronomy education from the University of Arizona; an M.Ed. in Science Education from the University of Georgia; and a B.A. in Astrophysics from Agnes Scott College.

Gerardo Bañales holds a Ph.D. in Educational Psychology from University Ramon Llull, Spain. He is currently an Associate Professor at the School of Education and Social Sciences, Andres Bello University, Chile. He teaches courses in theory and teaching of writing in master's and doctorate programs. Among his publications is *Teach to Read and Write in Higher Education: Educational proposals based on research*. His current lines of research are related to teacher professional development and the strategic teaching of narrative, expository, and argumentative writing in primary and higher education contexts.

Ivar Bråten is a Professor of Educational Psychology in the Department of Education at the University of Oslo, Norway. His main research interests are epistemic cognition, self-regulated learning, reading comprehension, and multiple document literacy. He is widely published, with international research articles, book chapters, and books in his areas of specialization. He currently serves on six editorial review boards.

Deborah L. Butler is a Professor in the Faculty of Education at the University of British Columbia. Previous roles include Director for the Centre of Cross-Faculty Inquiry, Associate Dean for Graduate Programs and Research, Associate Dean for Strategic Development, and Senior Associate Dean. She is past Co-President of the Canadian Association for Educational Psychology (2012–2014). In her collaborative research with educators, she has studied how to support academic success by students within inclusive classrooms, and how why supporting self-regulated learning (SRL) is so key to empowering learners, and how educators can work together to construct practices that achieve positive outcomes.

Jacqueline M. Campbell received her Bachelor's degree in Chemistry from Shippensburg University and her Master's degree in Educational Psychology from

The Pennsylvania State University. Currently, she is a Ph.D. candidate in Educational Psychology at The Pennsylvania State University. Her research addresses problem-solving issues in undergraduate STEM courses and specifically focuses on developing interventions to improve students' ability to learn from worked examples and use effective learning strategies.

Kelly B. Cartwright is Professor of Psychology, Neuroscience, and Teacher Preparation at Christopher Newport University (CNU) where she directs the Reading, Executive function, And Development Lab (READ Lab). Her research explores the development of skilled reading comprehension and the neurocognitive and affective factors that underlie comprehension processes and difficulties from preschool through adulthood. Her work has appeared in *Journal of Educational Psychology, Contemporary Educational Psychology, Research in Developmental Disabilities*, and a range of other publications. She regularly works with teachers in public and private schools to understand and improve reading comprehension for struggling readers, and these experiences inform her research.

Leen Catrysse (Ph.D.) is a postdoctoral Researcher and Guest Professor at the Department of Training and Education Sciences, Faculty of Social Sciences of the University of Antwerp, Belgium. The focus of her research is on how to measure higher education students' processing strategies and learning in general with eye-tracking in combination with other online and biometric measures.

Byeong-Young Cho (Ph.D.) is an Associate Professor of Language, Literacy and Culture in the School of Education, University of Pittsburgh, and a research scientist at Pitt's Learning Research & Development Center. His research focuses on understanding cognitive, metacognitive, and epistemic dimensions of reading and learning in a complex task environment. His recent work examines classroom practices that support student learning and engagement through accessing, processing, and using multiple texts in disciplinary and digital literacies instruction.

Jennifer G. Cromley is Professor of Educational Psychology at the University of Illinois at Urbana-Champaign. She does basic and applied research in comprehension of illustrated scientific text, as well as research on achievement and retention of undergraduate students in STEM. She has used a wide variety of parametric and non-parametric statistics in her research on outcomes of learning, predictors of learning, and the processes that happen during learning. She has taught graduate statistics for 14 years, ranging from introductory to advanced educational statistics.

Liesje De Backer is a postdoctoral Researcher at the Department of Educational Studies at Ghent University, Belgium. She obtained her Ph.D. in 2015. The main focus of her current research activities is on fostering socially shared regulation processes in face-to-face and computer-supported collaborative learning in higher education, as well as on investigating the relation between collaborative learners' shared regulation behavior and their performance.

428 • Contributor Bios

Anique de Bruin is an Educational Psychologist and Professor in Self-regulation in Higher Education. Her research aims at understanding how students and professionals monitor and regulate their learning when studying texts, during problem solving, and during clinical reasoning, and how these processes can be supported through effective instructional design.

Susan De La Paz is a Professor in the Department of Counseling, Higher Education, and Special Education at the University of Maryland. Her research spans *learning to write* and *writing to learn* – and is driven by the need for effective instruction to facilitate students' planning, translating, and revising skills, as well as to support their use of writing to develop epistemic and disciplinary understanding in academic subjects. She is a co-author of *Reading, Thinking, and Writing about History: Teaching argument writing to diverse learners in the common core classroom, grades 6–12.*

Fien De Smedt obtained her Ph.D. in 2019 and currently works as a postdoctoral Researcher at the Department of Educational Studies at Ghent University, Belgium. Her research focuses on studying cognitive and motivational challenges in writing and on how to overcome these challenges. In this respect, she investigates the effectiveness of explicit writing instruction and peer-assisted writing in elementary and secondary education.

Daniel L. Dinsmore is an Associate Professor and Research Director of the Northeast Florida Center for STEM Education (NEFSTEM) at the University of North Florida. His research mainly encompasses strategy use and strategic processing in multiple academic domains and how this leads to expertise in those domains.

Vincent Donche (Ph.D.) is a Professor at the Department of Training and Education Sciences, Faculty of Social Sciences of the University of Antwerp, Belgium. He conducts research in the domains of learning and instruction, higher education, and educational measurement.

Denis Dumas is an Assistant Professor of Research Methods and Statistics at the University of Denver's Morgridge College of Education. In general, his work focuses on understanding student learning, cognition, and creativity through the application and refinement of latent variable methods. He is widely interested in the mental attributes that contribute to students' academic success across domains and contexts, and has recently been specifically researching the way in which expertise development influences students' strategic processing both individually and in groups.

Rebekah Freed is a doctoral student in the Learning Sciences and Psychological Studies Ph.D. program in the School of Education at the University of North Carolina at Chapel Hill. She has an M.A. in Educational Psychology and a B.A. in Psychology. She previously taught Human Development and Psychology courses at Westminster College and Utah Valley University. She also worked as a research assistant studying social development at the University of Utah. Her current research interests include ways of fostering volition and goal pursuit during self-regulated learning.

Contributor Bios • 429

Luke K. Fryer is an Associate Professor and Assistant Director (Programmes, CETL) within the Faculty of Education at The University of Hong Kong. He is a Researcher in multiple areas of inquiry, from online learning and teaching to learning strategies in higher education, and, more recently, the development of interest during education.

David Gijbels is Full Professor of Learning and Instruction at the Department of Training and Education Sciences in the Faculty of Social Sciences of the University of Antwerp, Belgium. His research is situated in the research group Edubron and focuses on learning and assessment in (higher) education and in the workplace.

Steve Graham is the Warner Professor of Educational Leadership and Innovation at Mary Lou Fulton Teachers College at Arizona State University. He is also a Research Professor at the Institute for Learning Sciences and Teacher Education at Australian Catholic University at Brisbane. He is the current editor of *Journal of Educational Psychology*. He is interested in all aspects of writing, including strategy instruction.

Jeffrey A. Greene is a Professor and Associate Dean for Academic Affairs in the School of Education at the University of North Carolina at Chapel Hill. He has a Ph.D. in Educational Psychology and an M.A. in Educational Measurement, Statistics, and Evaluation. He was awarded the 2016 Richard E. Snow Award for Distinguished Early Contributions in Educational Psychology from Division 15 of the American Psychological Association. Greene's research focuses upon digital literacy, including student cognition, self-regulation, and epistemic cognition in science and history domains.

Karen R. Harris is the Warner Professor of Educational Leadership and Innovation at Mary Lou Fulton Teachers College at Arizona State University. She is also a Research Professor at the Institute for Learning Sciences and Teacher Education at Australian Catholic University at Brisbane. She is the former editor of *Journal of Educational Psychology*. Her research interest focuses on self-regulation and strategy instruction. She is the developer of the Self-Regulated Strategy Development Model, which has been used widely in writing.

Courtney Hattan is an Assistant Professor of Elementary Literacy Education in the School of Teaching and Learning at Illinois State University. She earned her Ph.D. in Educational Psychology from the University of Maryland and her M.S.Ed. with a focus in reading from Johns Hopkins University. Dr. Hattan has worked as an elementary and middle school Language Arts and Social Studies teacher in Baltimore city and rural North Carolina. Her program of research centers on the interplay between readers' knowledge and what they understand and remember from text.

Matthew Hurt began his work in education as a 3rd grade teacher in Oklahoma City after finishing his Bachelor of Arts in Political Science and Public Relations at Virginia Tech. Later, he moved to Nashville to pursue a master's degree in Education Policy at Vanderbilt University. While in Tennessee, he worked for Metro Nashville Public

Schools and then with the Tennessee Department of Education. Matthew is currently a doctoral student at the University of Maryland in the Teaching and Learning, Policy and Leadership Department.

Susan Lutz Klauda is a Faculty Specialist at the University of Maryland and an Adjunct Professor at The Catholic University of America. Her research has centered on the interplay of cognitive, affective, and social dimensions in reading skill development and on the characteristics of effective reading interventions for children and adolescents. Currently, she is focusing on reading comprehension and motivation in elementary school-aged dual language learners. Her work has appeared in such journals as *Reading Research Quarterly*, *Journal of Educational Psychology*, and *Educational Psychology Review*.

Kimberly A. Lawless is the Dean of the College of Education at The Pennsylvania State University. Her research focuses on the meaningful integration of technology in support of interdisciplinary learning and problem solving.

Alexandra List is an Assistant Professor in the Department of Educational Psychology, Counseling, and Special Education at The Pennsylvania State University. Her work examines how students learn from multiple texts, such as when researching information on the Internet. Her work has appeared in leading educational psychology journals, including *Educational Psychologist*, *Learning and Instruction*, and *Computers in Human Behavior*. She teaches undergraduate and graduate courses in Learning and Instruction and Program Evaluation. Alexandra earned her Ph.D. in Educational Psychology and M.A. in Educational Measurement and Statistics from the Department of Human Development and Quantitative Methods at the University of Maryland.

Doug Lombardi is an Associate Professor, Department of Human Development and Quantitative Methodology, University of Maryland. As the Head of the Science Learning Research Group, he conducts research focusing on developing tools to facilitate students' reasoning about socio-scientific topics (i.e., those that pose local, regional, and global challenges, such as climate change). Doug received early career research awards from the American Educational Research Association's Division C, American Psychological Association's Division 15, and NARST: A Worldwide Organization for Improving Science Teaching and Learning Through Research.

Sofie Loyens is a Full Professor of Excellence in Education at University College Roosevelt (UCR), one of Utrecht University's liberal arts and sciences colleges. Her Chair of Excellence in Education is the first (and only) of its kind in the Netherlands. She is also appointed as an Associate Professor in Educational Psychology at Erasmus University Rotterdam (EUR). She is currently an associate editor of *Contemporary Educational Psychology* and serves on various editorial boards. Her research focuses on problem-based learning (or more broadly student-centered/constructivist learning environments), motivation from a Self-Determination Theory perspective, and self-regulated/self-directed learning.

Contributor Bios • 431

Joseph P. Magliano received his Ph.D. in Psychology at the University of Memphis in 1992. He is a Professor of Educational Psychology in the Department of Learning Sciences at Georgia State University. His research focuses on the cognitive mechanisms that support the comprehension of different media (texts, films, comics). He has an interest in understanding why some college students struggle with their academic reading activities, developing ways to assess why they struggle, and interventions to support them. He has published extensively on these topics and received external funding to support this research.

Emmelien Merchie is a postdoctoral Researcher and Lecturer at the Department of Educational Studies at Ghent University, Belgium. She obtained her Ph.D. in 2014. Her research activities focus on measuring and stimulating reading comprehension and learning from text in elementary and secondary education. She also investigates the effectiveness of mind maps in text comprehension and learning.

Pamela Muñoz holds a Master's in Reading Comprehension and Written Production from the School of Education and Social Sciences, Andres Bello University, Chile. She currently works as a teacher of basic education in private schools in Chile, where she teaches reading, writing, and speaking strategies to children.

Kristie Newton has taught both middle and high school mathematics as well as conducted professional development for mathematics teachers at the elementary, middle, and high school levels. Her research has focused on the development of mathematical knowledge, especially related to fractions and algebra. She has explored mathematical thinking across a range of groups, from struggling learners to experts, in order to understand misconceptions as well as productive and flexible ways of problem solving. She is also interested in how this knowledge is related to other significant factors, such as motivation and instruction.

Jeffery D. Nokes is an Associate Professor in the History Department at Brigham Young University. He earned a Ph.D. in teaching and learning from the University of Utah. A former middle school and high school teacher, he researches history teaching and learning, historical literacy, and preparing young people for civic engagement. His scholarship has appeared in several important journals. He is the author of *Building Students' Historical Literacies: Learning to read and reason with historical texts and evidence* and *Teaching History, Learning Citizenship: Tools for civic engagement*. Jeffery has received middle school, high school, and university teaching awards.

Fred Paas is Professor of Educational Psychology at Erasmus University Rotterdam in the Netherlands, and Professorial Fellow at the University of Wollongong, Australia. Since 1990 he has been investigating the instructional control of cognitive load in the training of complex cognitive tasks. In 2016 he was recognized as the world's most productive author in the five best journals in the field of educational psychology for the period 2009–2014. He is editor-in-chief of the journal *Educational Psychology Review*, and editorial board member of the *Journal of Educational Psychology*. He is a fellow of the American Educational Research Association.

Meghan M. Parkinson is the College of Education and Human Services Director of Assessment and Accreditation. She also teaches educational psychology. Meghan was previously an Early Childhood Specialist for the Jacksonville Public Library and an ESOL teacher for Catholic Charities Refugee Resettlement Program. Her research interests include literacy and vocabulary development, metacognitive processes, and preservice teachers' beliefs about the nature of knowledge and learning (epistemic beliefs).

Robert D. Plumley is a doctoral student in the Ph.D. in Education (Learning Sciences & Psychological Studies) program at the University of North Carolina at Chapel Hill. He has also earned an M.S. in Computer Science from Pace University and a B.S. in Business Administration from North Carolina State University. His research focuses on the use of technology-enhanced learning environments and learning analytics methodologies to identify and encourage students' engagement in self-regulated learning strategies.

Jeremy Riel is an Educational Technologist at the University of Illinois at Chicago College of Education. He researches the applicability of emerging technologies for educational uses, designs for online and distance education, and learning analytics.

Amélie Rogiers obtained her doctoral degree in Educational Studies at Ghent University, Belgium, in 2019 after completing her teacher training and obtaining her Master's degree. Her doctoral research focuses on measuring and fostering secondary school students' strategies for learning text. Currently, Amélie is still working as a Researcher at the Department of Educational Studies.

Ladislao Salmerón obtained his Ph.D. in Cognitive Psychology at the University of Granada, Spain. During the academic year 2004–2005 he was a Fulbright visiting scholar at the Institute of Cognitive Science at the University of Colorado, Boulder. He is currently an Associate Professor in the Department of Developmental and Educational Psychology at the University of Valencia, Spain. His research focuses on the assessment of digital literacies and their promotion in different populations.

Leyton Schnellert is an Associate Professor in UBC's Department of Curriculum & Pedagogy. His scholarship attends to how teachers and teaching and learners and learning can embrace student diversity and inclusive education. Dr. Schnellert is the Pedagogy and Participation Research Cluster Lead in UBC's Institute for Community Engaged Research. His community-based collaborative work contributes a counterargument to top-down approaches that operate from deficit models, instead drawing from communities' funds of knowledge to build participatory and culturally responsive practices. His books, films, and research articles are widely referenced in local, national, and international contexts.

Alex Shum is a Lecturer within the Faculty of Science at The University of Hong Kong. He is also currently a Ph.D. candidate undertaking research in formative testing, feedback, and self-efficacy development.

Ana Taboada Barber's work centers on studying the influence of specific cognitive, linguistic, and motivation variables on the literacy and language development students of diverse language backgrounds. As a former English as a Second Language teacher, Ana's work in reading comprehension development is principally concentrated within the population of Dual Language Learners (DLLs) or emergent bilinguals within the United States. More recently, Ana has extended her focus to include Spanish-speaking students in South America. Her work has been published in *Journal of Educational Psychology*, *Reading Psychology*, *Journal of Experimental Education*, *Literacy Research and Instruction*, and *Reading Research Quarterly*, among others.

Hilde Van Keer received her Ph.D. in 2002 and is currently Professor at the Department of Educational Studies at Ghent University, Belgium. Her main research interests include peer learning, measuring and fostering self-regulated learning, and learning and instruction in reading and writing. In these research lines, intervention research in authentic learning environments and close partnership with primary and secondary schools is at the core of the studies.

Peggy Van Meter received her Master's degree in Psychology from Wake Forest University and her doctoral degree, with a specialization in Educational Psychology, from the University of Maryland, College Park. Currently, she is an Associate Professor in the Educational Psychology program at The Pennsylvania State University. Her research addresses college student learning with multiple representations that include both verbal and visual representations. She has conducted a number of studies across different science and engineering courses testing interventions to support student learning from these representations.

Jan D. Vermunt is a Professor of Learning and Educational Innovation at Eindhoven University of Technology, Eindhoven School of Education, The Netherlands. He is also Scientific Director of the School. From 2012 to 2018 he was a Professor of Education at the University of Cambridge and a Fellow of Wolfson College. He served as Editor-in-Chief of *Learning and Instruction*, one of the leading journals in the world in the field of Educational Research, from 2014 to 2018. His research interests focus on teaching and student learning in higher education, and teachers' learning and professional development.

Lisette Wijnia is a Professor of Applied Sciences at HZ University of Applied Sciences in Vlissingen, The Netherlands and Senior Lecturer at Erasmus University College of Erasmus University Rotterdam, The Netherlands. She obtained her Ph.D. in 2014. In her Ph.D. thesis she investigated students' motivation and achievement in problem-based learning, for which she received a best dissertation award from *Stichting Praemium Erasmianum*. Her current research focuses on students' motivation and self-regulated learning in secondary and higher education and the effectiveness of student-centered, collaborative learning methods such as problem-based learning. She is an editorial board member of *Contemporary Educational Psychology*.

Philip H. Winne (Ph.D., Stanford) is Professor at Simon Fraser University and formerly a 2-term Tier I Canada Research Chair. He researches self-regulated learning, metacognition, and learning analytics; and develops software technologies to support learners and gather big data for learning science. He has published more than 185 scholarly books, articles, chapters, and proceedings. Honors include the Robbie Case Memorial Award, Barry J. Zimmerman Award, and Canadian Society for the Study of Education Mentorship Award. He is a Fellow of the American Educational Research Association, American Psychological Association, Association for Psychological Science, Canadian Psychological Association, and Royal Society of Canada.

Lindsay Woodward (Ph.D.) is an Assistant Professor in the School of Education at Drake University in Des Moines, Iowa. Her research focuses on understanding how teachers and students utilize digital texts and tools for literacy learning. Her recent work has appeared in journals such as the *American Educational Research Journal*, *Reading Research Quarterly*, and *Teachers College Record*.

INDEX

Abar, B. 365
acclimation 31, 40, 50, 51, 52–53, 55, 56–57, 277–278
accumulation 287
adaptability 93, 155, 156, 250
adaptive difficulty 301–302
Adaptive Model of Strategic Processing 177
affective strategies 259–260
Afflerbach, Peter 5, 250, 416–417; levels of processing 31, 32, 43; reading comprehension 3, 99–118; verbal protocol analysis 281, 373–392
agency 71, 78; computer-supported collaborative learning 75; conceptual 188–189; self-regulated learning 66, 73; writing 145, 148
Aglinskas, C. 206
Ahmed, W. 399
Ahumada, Silza 141–158
Alexander, P. A.: concept of strategy 3, 48, 147; definition of terms 83; development of learning 47, 51, 55; erosion analogy 22, 23; learner characteristics 337; levels of processing 31–34, 37–42; levels of theories 339; Model of Domain Learning 50, 90–91, 279, 335; multiple text use 121, 123, 131; person-centered study 365, 366; research 6, 406–424
Alexandrova, T. 308
Alexeev, N. 355–356
algebra 160, 164–169, 170–172, 173, 413
algorithms 5, 297, 299, 303, 311
Alibali, M. W. 166
Allen, L. K. 308
ALSI see Approaches to Learning and Study Inventory
Alvarez, Prisila 141–158
analysis of variance (ANOVA) 348, 349, 356, 368, 394, 395–396, 399, 403–404

analytics: learning 302–311, 338; video games 302; web 299–300
Anderson, Richard 406
Andersson, R. 327
Andreassen, R. 288–289
Anmarkrud, O. 124, 127, 129, 131, 286, 349
ANOVA see analysis of variance
Approaches to Learning and Study Inventory (ALSI) 267
Approaches to Study Inventory (ASI) 260, 261–262, 333
argumentation: history 205, 207–208, 209, 211, 212; Project READI 210–211; science 182–184, 185–186, 187, 188, 189–190; verbal protocol analysis 384–387, 388
Arnold, K. E. 304
Ashby, R. A. 202
Ashcraft, M. H. 33
ASI see Approaches to Study Inventory
Asikainen, G. 33, 37–38, 40–42
Askell-Williams, H. 350
assessment: backwash-effect of 320; formative 67, 73–74, 76, 357; history 211; influence on learning 336
ASSISTments 306
Atkinson, R. 172
attributions 41, 252, 266, 335
automaticity 54, 88, 196, 255, 277, 378
autonomy support 225–228, 249
Azevedo, R. 37, 397

Baars, Martine 4, 234–247, 250, 355
Bailey, Janelle M. 3, 177–194, 250, 412–413
Bañales, Gerardo 141–158
Bandura, A. 251

436 • Index

Barbieri, C. 164, 165
Barlow, E. 380
Baron, C. 198
Bauer, D. J. 362
Baxter, G. 36
Becker, A. 148
behavioral strategies: multiple text use 121; self-regulation 89, 90
behaviorism 47
Bereiter, C. 146, 276
Bernacki, M. L. 353, 356
Bernier, A. 228–229
Berthold, K. 350–351
Bieck, S. M. 173
Big Data 5, 296–316, 337–338, 339–340, 419
Biggs, J. B. 37, 260–261, 262
bilingualism 221
Bindman, S. W. 228
biology 17, 85, 236, 240
biometric data 24; *see also* physiological measurements
Bishop, J. P. 168, 170
Blair, K. P. 167
Blanchard, M. R. 189
Blaye, A. 219
Bofferding, L. 167
Bommanapally, V. 302
Booth, J. L. 164, 165, 166, 167, 168
Borkowski, John 218, 219
Bouchet, F. 37
Bovee, H. N. 368
Braaksma, M. 205
Braasch, J. L. G. 128, 287
Brand-Gruwel, S. 285
Brandmo, C. 131
Bransford, John 275, 407–408
Brante, E. W. 125
Bråten, Ivar 338, 349, 418; concurrent and task-specific self-reports 5, 275–295, 334–336, 417; multiple text use 124, 127, 128, 131
Breakstone, J. 211
Brekelmans, M. 268
bridging inferences 281, 282, 283
bridging statements 90
Britt, M. A. 130, 206
Brletic-Shipley, H. 166–167
Bromme, R. 125, 127, 128
Brown, Ann 263, 275, 407–408
Brown, C. M. 282
Brucker, B. 132
Bruer, J. T. 320
Bruner, J. 163
Brünken, R. 349
Bryant, D. P. 161

BSCS 5E Instructional Model 181
Buch-Iversen, I. 224
Buchau, A. 350–351
Buijs, J. C. A. M. 307
Butler, Deborah L. 2, 63–81, 84, 89, 92, 94, 156
Bybee, R. W. 185

Cain, K. 220
Cameron, C. 130
Campbell, Jacqueline M. 3, 82–96
Campione, J. C. 275
Capote, Truman 141
Caronongan, P. 251
Carpenter, T. P. 163
Carr, M. 355–356
Carter, G. 132
Cartier, S. C. 73
Cartwright, Kelly B. 4, 216–233, 416
Castelijns, J. 355
Catrysse, Leen 5, 317–331, 336–337, 339, 415
CER *see* claims-evidence-reasoning
Cerdán, R. 133
Chan, H. L. 308
Chase, W. G. 196
checkpoints 251
chemistry 20
Chen, K. T. 302
Chevalier, N. 219
Chi, N. T. H. 384
chi squared test 394, 400, 403
children 345, 414; executive functions 219; mathematics 160; reading comprehension 217–218, 224–225; strategy development 51, 147; writing 141, 142
Children's Perceived Use of Self-Regulated Learning Inventory 355
Chiluiza, K. 310
Chinn, C. A. 181
Cho, Byeong-Young 5, 250, 400; multiple text use 120–127, 132, 418; qualitative analysis of data 403; reading comprehension 99–118; verbal protocol analysis 373–392, 416–417
Chundi, P. 302
Chung, G. K. 308
chunking 203
civic engagement 212
CL *see* cooperative learning
claims-evidence-reasoning (CER) 183–184
clarification 90, 103
classification 197–198, 199, 200, 204
classroom life 69–70, 78
Cleary, T. 288
Clement, J. 179
CLT *see* cognitive load theory

clue words 223–224
clustering techniques 362, 364–365, 401
co-regulation 67–68, 73, 74, 90, 241, 242
coding of data 399, 400, 403, 417; multiple text use 123, 124; variable-centered approaches 349, 351; verbal protocols 281, 381, 382–384, 387
cognitive apprenticeships 208–209, 210
cognitive flexibility 4, 220–221, 222–223, 224–225
cognitive load theory (CLT) 237–238, 240, 243–244
cognitive processes 14, 19, 24, 25, 250; dynamic nature of 345; eye tracking 318, 321–323, 324, 325, 337; first-level and second-level cognition 377–378; highlighting 20; Inventory of Learning Processes 262; measurement issues 39; person-centered approaches 363; self-regulated learning 235, 278; strategies and skills 13; verbal protocol analysis 374, 376–379, 385
cognitive strategies 4, 48–49; autonomy support 228; children 217–218; conceptual boundaries 414; conceptual fogginess 408, 412; defining 195, 259; gender differences 349; history 195–196, 204–211; ILS 265; multiple text use 121; person-centered approaches 361–372; reading 374; research 1; science 177; self-regulation 89, 90; socially shared regulation of learning 241; surveys and retrospective self-reports 263, 333; verbal protocol analysis 377
collaboration: engagement 225; video games 308; writing 143, 145, 152, 153
collaborative learning 63–64, 66–70, 72, 74–78, 235, 238–244
Collingwood, R. G. 196
Common Core State Standards (CCSS) 106, 107, 112, 161, 166, 170
communication 240, 244
communities of learners 69, 71, 72, 74
comparison 167–168, 169, 171–172
competence 40, 50, 51, 52, 53–54, 277–278
complexity of learning tasks 237, 240, 243, 244, 255
comprehension 37, 40, 99–118; concurrent and task-specific self-reports 290; English Learners 216; executive functions 217–229; eye tracking 318; individual differences 131; intertextual knowledge elaboration 348; Model of Domain Learning 278; multiple text use 120, 124, 127, 128, 131; reading comprehension deficits 216–217, 221–222, 224–225, 229; science 178; sourcing 130; strategy definition 275–276; strategy use 398; task-specific self-report inventories 286; verbal protocol analysis 281–283, 374, 376–377, 388; working memory capacity 238
comprehension monitoring 100–101, 105, 112, 121; Comprehensive Strategy Framework 122; executive functions 222, 223; eye tracking 322; history 202; multiple text use 127

Comprehensive Strategy Framework (CSF) 121–123, 127, 128–129
computer-supported collaborative learning (CSCL) 64, 75–76, 77
concentration strategies 287
concept maps 13, 236
conceptual change 178–179
conceptual frameworks 39, 201, 384, 386, 387
concurrent and task-specific self-reports 38
conditional knowledge 57, 91, 110, 111–112, 114
conflict-driven validation 133–134
conjectures 170
constructive-integrative processing 120, 122, 123–124, 127
context 55, 65; adaptation to 255; Comprehensive Strategy Framework 122; eye tracking 325, 326, 337; levels of processing 42; reading 373–374; self-regulated learning 279; verbal protocol analysis 380–382; writing 143, 144–145
contextualization: history 120, 196–197, 199, 200, 202, 206–207, 208, 211; multiple text use 125–126
control: MSLQ 264; self-regulated learning 234, 235, 240; writing 145
Cook, M. 132
cooperative learning (CL) 74–75, 100
coordination of strategies 91–92
Corbin, J. 383
correlation 350, 362, 394, 396, 403
corroboration: Comprehensive Strategy Framework 122; history 120, 196–197, 199, 200, 202, 204, 206–207, 211, 212; multiple text use 125–126
Costa, L.-J. 355
count data 351, 356, 358
Course Signals (CS) 303, 338
covariance 19
covert strategies 49
Craik, F. I. M. 321, 336
creativity 14
critical-analytic processing 120, 122, 123, 125–126, 127
critical thinking: collaborative learning 239; learning gain 267; MSLQ 264; science 184, 185
critiquing of alternatives 187
Cromley, Jennifer G. 6, 130, 393–405
cross-textual strategies 120, 124–125, 128, 129, 131, 287
CS see Course Signals
CSCL see computer-supported collaborative learning
CSF see Comprehensive Strategy Framework
Cuddihy, E. 284
cultural factors 67, 78, 154, 357
Curran, P. J. 362
cyclical model of self-regulated learning 278–279, 287, 335

438 • Index

Danielson, M. 70

data aggregation 347–348, 356, 358

data analysis 324–325, 378–379, 393–405; *see also* qualitative approaches; quantitative approaches; verbal protocol analysis

data collection 43, 411; Big Data 298, 299–300, 309, 310; cognition 378; diary methods 288–289; diversification of methods 362–363; self-reports 270; verbal protocols 280–281, 380, 382–383, 388, 389; *see also* measurement

data reduction 399, 404

data saturation 379, 383–384

data selection 309–310

Davenport, J. L. 166

De Backer, Liesje 2, 47–62, 242

de Bruin, Anique 4, 234–247, 250

de Jong, M. 285

De La Paz, Susan 4, 195–215, 250

De Smedt, Fien 2, 47–62

DeChurch, L. A. 239

decision making 252

declarative knowledge 16, 19, 57, 110–111, 113, 114

Deekens, V. M. 38, 353–354, 355

deep-level strategies 29, 31–37, 43, 91, 334, 336; brain imaging 320–321; Children's Perceived Use of Self-Regulated Learning Inventory 355; conceptual boundaries 413, 414; definition of strategies 276; developmental perspective 49, 53; eye tracking 322, 325; formative assessment 357; growth curve modeling 399; key sentences 327; learner characteristics 319; Model of Domain Learning 41, 277–278; path model analysis 354; person-centered approaches 367; task-specific self-report inventories 286, 287; verbal protocols 417

deep processing 262–263, 266

Deliyianni, E. 170

developmental perspective 47–48, 50–51, 55–56, 58, 279

diagrams 86, 90, 122, 129–130, 132, 135, 167, 236, 395

diary methods 288–290, 291

Dinsmore, Daniel L. 1–8, 84, 89; Adaptive Model of Strategic Processing 177; goals 93; learning outcomes 326; levels of processing 29–46, 354, 413; Model of Domain Learning 278; self-regulated learning 241

disciplinary knowledge 110, 113–114, 253

disciplines 15–16, 115–116

discourse 70

discussions 207–208

diversity 70

Dole, J. A. 206

domain, definition of 15–16

domain-general strategies 12, 13–14, 16, 17–25, 49, 89–91; conceptual boundaries 412, 414; levels of processing 42, 277; science 189; teachers 420

domain-specific strategies 12, 17–25, 49, 89–91, 409; conceptual boundaries 412, 414; levels of processing 42, 277; meta-curricular approach 57; teachers 420; writing 3

domains 252–253

Domínguez, F. 310

Donche, Vincent 5, 36–42, 265, 317–331, 337, 415

Donoghue, G. M. 35, 38, 39, 41

drafting 147, 149, 150

Dresler, T. 173

Du, H. 128, 287

Dumas, Denis 2, 11–28, 41, 412–413, 414; definitions of strategies/strategic processing 83, 85, 86; goals 93; levels of processing 31, 32; task-specific strategies 88

Dunlosky, J. 237

Dunwiddie, A. E. 166

Dupuis, D. N. 173

Durkin, D. 102

Durning, S. J. 13

Dynamic Measurement Modeling 24

Echeverria, V. 310

Educational Data Mining (EDM) 302–311, 338

educational psychology 11–12, 14, 24–25; deep and surface processing strategies 320; discipline of 15–16; person-centered approaches 363, 365–366; transfer 21

effectiveness 134–135

efficacy expectations 251, 252

effort regulation 264

EFs *see* executive functions

elaboration 37, 350–351; Comprehensive Strategy Framework 122; intertextual knowledge 348; MSLQ 264; multiple text use 123; relational 125; science 184; task-specific self-report inventories 287; verbal protocol analysis 281, 282, 283

elaborative processing 262–263

Elbro, C. 224

Elia, I. 170

Elling, S. 285

emotions 399, 421; affective strategies 259–260; learner characteristics 319; levels of processing 41–42; monitoring emotional responses 90; socially shared strategic processing 66

empathetic insight 198, 200, 201

empirical investigations 179–180

Empson, S. B. 163, 173

emulation 142, 147

Endedijk, M. D. 268

engagement 225–226; autonomy support 227; executive functions 220; learning gain 267; online learning 307; reading comprehension 115

engineering 85–86, 236

English Learners (ELs) 115, 204, 205, 208–209, 216, 221, 223

Entwistle, N. J. 260, 261–262, 266, 267, 334

epistemic beliefs 131, 267, 417; history 206; science 181; verbal protocol analysis 381, 385–387

epistemic knowledge 110, 112–113, 114

epistemic processing 381–382, 383–384, 385–387

Ercikan, K. 211

Erduran, S. 189

Ericsson, K. A. 286, 376, 377

Erkens, G. 400

Ertmer, P. A. 69, 76–77

Every-Good-Boy-Does-Fine mnemonic 17, 88

evidence: claims-evidence-reasoning 183–184; history 195, 196–202, 203–204, 206–207, 208, 209; Model-Evidence-Link diagram 186–189; Project READI 210–211; reading comprehension 105; verbal protocol analysis 385, 388

executive functions (EFs) 4, 114, 196, 217–229, 416

expectations 251, 252

experimental designs 253

expertise 22–23, 54; domain 387; history 197, 203, 250; Model of Domain Learning 31–37, 50, 277–278; science 181; studies 35; task complexity 237; see also proficiency

explanation 104

exploring 201

eye tracking 43, 56, 270, 318–320, 321–327, 336–337, 356–357; advantages of 317–318; concurrent and task-specific self-reports 38; cued self-reports 283–285, 290–291; deep and surface processing strategies 321; domain-general strategies 19; eye movement modeling example 86; multi-faceted measurement 24; multiple text use 129; technological advances 363, 411, 415

Eyer, F. 164

Facebook 300

factor analysis (FA) 19, 361–362

Farivar, S. H. 74–75

Fazio, L. K. 160–161

feedback 72–73; autonomy support 227; continuous 411; EDM/LA 304, 338; history 209; intelligent tutoring systems 305; multiple text use 134; quality and timing of 304

Ferrara, R. A. 275

Ferretti, R. P. 207

Feurer, E. 219

filter bubbles 311

FIML see Full Information Maximum Likelihood

Firetto, C. M. 85

first-order concepts 205–206

First-Outer-Inner-Last (FOIL) strategy 17, 88, 91

Flavell, John 217–218, 263, 406

flexibility: cognitive 220–221, 222–223, 224–225; mathematics 159, 169–172; self-regulated cycles 93; writing strategies 155

Flower, L. 143, 148

fMRI 38, 222, 270, 317–318, 320–324, 336–337, 411, 415

Follmer, D. J. 222

formative assessment (FA) 67, 73–74, 76, 357

fractions 160–164, 169–170, 172–173

Fredricks, J. A. 267

Freed, Rebekah 5, 345–360, 396–399, 415

Friedlander, B. 149

Fryer, Luke K. 1–8, 39, 361–372, 401

Fuchs, L. S. 161, 162, 163, 173

Full Information Maximum Likelihood (FIML) 397, 398, 404

funds of knowledge 66, 68

Fyfe, E. R. 166

Gagatsis, A. 170

Galli, G. 321

gaming the system 306

Garner, Ruth 406, 410

GCM see growth curve modeling

Gemballa, S. 135

gender 349

general linear models (GLMs) 348–351, 353, 357–358

generalizability 16, 23, 25, 156, 285; see also domain-general strategies

generative strategies 236

geometry 20

Gerjets, P. 129, 132, 134, 135

Gibson, L. 211

Gijbels, David 5, 33, 37–42, 317–331, 332–341, 415

Gil, L. 131

Gillies, R. M. 70, 75

GMM see growth mixture modeling

goals: collaborative learning 239; definitions of strategies/strategic processing 87, 88, 92–93; domain-generality and domain-specificity 18; engagement 225; executive functions 219–220; Good Strategy User Model 49, 277; individual differences 11; Model of Strategic Learning 49–50; motivation 89; MSLQ 264; multiple text use 135; person-centered approaches 365–366; reading 373–374, 375; science 177; self-regulated learning 65–66; writing 142, 143, 145, 147, 148

Goetz, Ernest 406

Goldberg, T. 206–207

Goldman, S. R. 108, 113, 123, 126–127, 135

440 • Index

Good Strategy User (GSU) Model 49, 50, 218–219, 277, 279, 335
Google 5, 300
Graham, Steve 3, 32, 37, 141–158, 250, 410, 413
granularity 303, 339, 382
graphic organizers 100–101, 150, 152
Greene, Jeffrey A. 5, 37, 345–360, 397
Griffin, T. D. 238
Grossnickle, E. M. 31, 32, 41
growth curve modeling (GCM) 355–356, 395, 399–400, 403–404
growth mixture modeling (GMM) 395, 401–402, 403–404
GSU see Good Strategy User Model
Guan, Z. 284, 285
Gunderson, E. A. 161

Haarala-Muhonen, A. 267
Hacker, D. J. 206
Hadwin, A. F. 68, 75, 77
Hagen, A. M. 128, 287
Hagenaars, J. A. 361
Hamdan, N. 161
Hansson, H. 70
Hänze, M. 70, 75
Hare, V. C. 83, 104
Harris, Karen R. 32, 37, 48, 141–158, 410
Harris, L. M. 198
Harrison, A. G. 179
Harwell, M. R. 173
Hattan, Courtney 2, 29–46, 89, 93, 278, 413
Hattie, J. A. C. 35, 38, 39, 41, 73, 84
Hayes, J. R. 143, 148
help-seeking strategies 18, 142, 264
heuristics 147, 148, 207, 208
Hickey, D. T. 76
Hiebert, J. 163
highlighting 20
historical empathy 201
history 4, 20, 195–215, 250; disciplinary knowledge 113; multiple text use 119–120, 125–126; outlining 17; reading comprehension strategies 107, 108; self-regulation 38
Holmqvist, K. 327
Holt, T. 196
Hornburg, C. B. 166–167
Howell, D. C. 361
Huh, Y. 63
humility 199, 201, 203, 212
Huptych, M. 307
Hurt, Matthew 99–118, 250
Hutchinson, L. R. 69
Hymel, S. 69
Hyönä, J. 283

IBM 304
ICAR see International Cognitive Ability Resource
IES see Institute of Education Sciences
IF-MT see Integrated Framework of Multiple Texts
Iida, M. 288, 289
Ilie, S. 267
ILP see Inventory of Learning Processes
ILS see Inventory of Learning Patterns of Students
incentives 252
individual differences 4, 11–12, 216–233; developmental perspective 56; domain-general strategies 20–21; expertise development 22–23; learning 54–55; multiple text use 131–132; reading abilities 238; studies 31–36; verbal protocol analysis 282; writing 146
inferencing: as deep strategy 334; reading comprehension 102, 107, 108–109, 216–217, 218, 222–223, 224–225; verbal protocol analysis 280–283, 374–375
information location 380
information processing systems 239–240
inhibition 4, 220, 222–223, 224–225
inquiry-based strategies 180–181, 187, 208
Institute of Education Sciences (IES) 161, 164, 168
instruction 57, 85–86, 94, 249, 337; awareness raising 269; drawing and imagery 396; engagement 225–226; history 204–212; mathematics 173; reading comprehension strategies 99–118, 223–225; science 186–189; teachers as strategic guides 419–420; writing 146–154
instructional strategies 32, 83, 196
Integrated Framework of Multiple Texts (IF-MT) 121
integrative processing 124–125
intelligence 11, 19
intelligent tutoring systems (ITS) 305–306, 309
intentionality 290, 345, 374, 408; definitions of strategies/strategic processing 87, 120, 275, 334, 412; executive functions 222; Model of Domain Learning 277–278; self-regulated learning 73; socially shared strategic processing 76; writing strategies 144, 147, 148
interdisciplinarity 15, 309, 311, 340
International Cognitive Ability Resource (ICAR) 267
internet 296–297; epistemic processes 383, 384; historical strategies 211–212; multiple text use 3; verbal protocol analysis 380–382, 385–387; web analytics 299–300; see also online learning
interoperability 310
intersectionality 198, 200
intra-individual differences 12, 54–55, 91
introspection 376
Inventory of Learning Patterns of Students/Inventory of Learning Styles (ILS) 36, 37, 39–40, 264, 265–266, 267, 270, 333

Inventory of Learning Processes (ILP) 260, 262–263, 333
Inventory of Teacher Learning (ITL) 268
Irving, John 141
ITS *see* intelligent tutoring systems

Jacovina, M. E. 308
Jadallah, M. 400
Jang, H. 226
Järvelä, S. 242
Jensen, M. S. 288
Jitendra, A. K. 173
Johnson, D. W. 74
Johnson, H. 224
Johnson, R. T. 74
JOLs *see* judgments of learning
Jordan, N. C. 402
Joscelyne, T. 224
judgments of learning (JOLs) 235–236, 350–351
Judy, J. E. 3, 31, 33, 41, 48
Jurkowski, S. 70, 75
Justi, R. 185

Kaakinen, J. K. 283
Kahiigi, E. K. 70
Kammerer, Y. 129, 134
Kanfer, R. 289
Kang, S. J. 302
Karbach, J. 349
Karl, S. R. 173
Kelser-Lund, A. 199
Kerr, D. 308
key sentences 327
keywords 236
Khosravifar, B. 37
Kim, C. H. 302
Kim, G. 204
Kim, Y. 302
King, A. S. 304
Kirschner, P. A. 240
Kitsantas, A. 287
knowledge: conceptual 163, 171, 173, 178–179, 210;
    conditional 57, 91; content area 108; declarative
    16, 19, 57, 110–111, 113, 114; disciplinary 110,
    113–114, 253; domains 12, 15–16, 33, 252–253;
    expertise development 22–23; funds of 66, 68;
    Good Strategy User Model 49, 277; history 196,
    202–203, 210; ILS 266; MED NORD inventory
    266–267; metacognitive 121; Model of Domain
    Learning 50, 278; multidimensional models
    421; reading comprehension 110–114, 115–116;
    science 181, 184, 185, 188; strategy development
    148; surveys and retrospective self-reports 334;
    verbal protocol analysis 379, 381, 388; *see also*
    prior knowledge; procedural knowledge

knowledge telling approach 142
Kobayashi, K. 128
Koedinger, K. R. 306
Komulainen, E. 267
Kopatich, R. D. 283
Krajcik, J. 183, 306
Kühl, T. 135
Kuhn, D. 112, 203, 212
Kuhn, T. S. 178
Kupperman, J. 306
Kuyper, H. 399

Lamb, L. L. 168
language 376
Laski, E. V. 349
LASSI *see* Learning and Study Strategies Inventory
Latent Class Analysis (LCA) 368, 395, 400, 401, 402,
    403–404
Latent Profile Analysis (LPA) 361–362, 364
Latent Profile Transfer Analysis (LPTA) 366–367, 368
Latent Transition Analysis (LTA) 395, 402
latent variable analysis 19, 399, 404
Lawless, Kimberley 5, 296–316, 337–339, 419
Lawson, M. J. 350
LCA *see* Latent Class Analysis
Le Bigot, L. 131
learner characteristics 131, 319, 325, 337
learning: areas of 14–16; autonomy support 226;
    behaviorism 47; collaborative 63–64, 66–70,
    72, 74–78, 235, 238–244; concurrent and task-
    specific self-reports 290; cooperative 74–75,
    100; developmental perspective 47–48, 50–51,
    55–56, 58; diagrammatic 132; domains of
    11–28; ILS 266; internal and external differences
    in 54–55; learning gain 267, 269, 271; learning
    patterns 37, 265–266, 333, 364; learning styles
    262–263, 265, 333, 334, 416; MED NORD
    inventory 266–267; Model of Domain Learning
    31–37, 40–43, 49–51, 90–91, 277–278, 279, 335,
    421; multiple text use 135; outcomes 85–86,
    260, 271, 326–327, 345, 357; Overlapping Waves
    Model 50; person-centered approaches 365,
    366, 367; project-based 76–77; science 178, 179,
    180–181, 187, 188, 189–190; social emotional
    71–72, 78; strategy definition 275–276;
    studies 32; subgroup profiles 364; surveys and
    retrospective self-reports 259–274, 333–334;
    verbal protocol analysis 375–376; video games
    302; visible 38, 64, 78; *see also* self-regulated
    learning
learning analytics (LA) 302–311, 338
Learning and Study Strategies Inventory (LASSI)
    263, 334
learning communities 69, 71, 72, 74

442 • Index

learning environments 84–85, 269, 410; person-centered approaches 365, 367; science 177–178; socially shared strategic processing 67, 69; student-centered 337; technology-mediated 305–308
learning management systems (LMSs) 306–307, 309
learning through reading (LTR) 73
Lee, D. 63, 70, 77
Lee, H. Y. 128, 130–131, 287
Lee, P. J. 202
Lee, S. 284
Lefevre, P. 163
Lei, C. L. 302
Leinhardt, G. 197
Lentz, L. R. 285
Leopold, C. 396
Leutner, D. 396
levels of processing 1, 29–46, 276, 337, 414; conceptualization of 30–38, 39; contextual factors 42; future directions for research 42–43; implications for practice 43–44; individual factors 41–42; operationalization of 38–39; systematic effects 39–41; see also deep-level strategies; surface-level strategies
Levin, J. R. 277
Levy, L. 163, 173
Li, D. 380
lifelong learning 47–48, 49, 58, 94
lifespan perspective 47–62
Ligorio, M. B. 306
Lindblom-Ylänne, S. 267
linear regression 396–397
Lipson, M. 111
List, Alexandra: levels of processing 31, 34; Model of Domain Learning 278; multiple text use 3, 119–140, 250, 287, 418
Liu, Y. 308
LMSs see learning management systems
Lobczowski, N. G. 38
Lockhart, R. S. 321, 336
Loken, E. 365
Lombardi, Doug 3, 177–194, 250, 412–413
longitudinal studies 24, 55, 94, 362, 365, 366, 368–369
Lonka, K. 266, 269, 339
Lortie, D. 189
Loughlin, S. M. 38, 39
Loyens, Sofie 5, 332–341
LPA see Latent Profile Analysis
LPTA see Latent Profile Transfer Analysis
LTA see Latent Transition Analysis
LTR see learning through reading
Luciw-Dubas, U. A. 130, 401
Lutz Klauda, Susan 4, 216–233, 416

Macagno, F. 207
MacArthur, C. A. 207
machine-generated data 298
machine-learning models 15, 44
Magliano, Joseph P. 5, 275–295, 334–336
Maier, J. 127, 133
Mailer, Norman 141
Mäkinen, J. 339
Malhotra, B. A. 181
Malone, A. S. 161, 162
MANOVA see multivariate analysis of variance
Manz, E. 184
Margolin, G. 400
Markman, Ellen 218, 222, 406
Martens, R. 355
Martin, E. 365
Martinez-Pons, M. 279
Marton, F. 37, 42, 261–262
Marzano, P. 110
Mason, L. 86, 149
Massively Online Open Courses (MOOCs) 307, 309
mathematics 3, 12, 159–176; executive functions 221; eye movement cued self-reports 283; growth curve modeling 355–356; levels of processing 42; monitoring learning 236; studies 33
Matthews, J. M. 166–167
Mayer, R. E. 48
McClure, R. 69
McCrudden, M. T. 349
McCune, V. 267
McCutcheon, A. L. 361
McGee, A. 224
McMaster, K. L. 282
McNamara, D. S. 86, 308
McNeil, N. M. 166–167, 173
McNeill, K. L. 183
MDL see Model of Domain Learning
meaning: meaning making 120, 380; reading comprehension 104–105, 107, 111, 115; socially shared strategic processing 68, 71–72, 73, 76, 78
measurement 4–5, 31–36, 254, 332–341, 411–412, 415; concurrent and task-specific self-reports 38, 276, 280–291, 334–335; domain-generality 14; levels of processing 38, 39, 43; Model of Domain Learning 278; person-centered approaches 368; physiological 5, 24, 38, 43, 56, 317–331, 336–337, 415–416; qualitative methods 277; self-regulated learning 279; strategy development 56; surveys and retrospective self-reports 38, 259–274, 333–334, 336; verbal protocol analysis 380; see also data collection; qualitative approaches; quantitative approaches
MED NORD inventory 266–267, 269, 334

MEL *see* Model-Evidence-Link diagram
memory: brain imaging 322; collaborative learning 239, 240; deep-level strategies 321; long-term 87, 88, 144–145, 240; mathematics 162; mnemonics 88, 90, 92–93; multiple text use 131–132; reading comprehension 112; short-term 377; task-specific self-report inventories 287; transactive 239, 242, 243; writing 144–145; *see also* working memory
Mendonça, P. C. C. 185
mental images 147
mental models 384; shared 239, 242, 243; verbal protocol analysis 280–281
mental representations 222, 319, 320, 375, 377, 388
Mercer, N. 268
Merchie, Emmelien 2, 47–62
Merkt, M. 204
Mesmer-Magnus, J. R. 239
metacognition 2, 4, 48–49, 84, 147, 196, 276, 374; choice of strategy 251; conceptual boundaries 414; conceptual fogginess 408, 412; conditional knowledge 114; definition of metacognitive strategies 259–260; EDM/LA impact on 311; executive functions 219, 221; gender differences 349; Good Strategy User Model 49, 277; growth curve modeling 399; history 199, 208; ILS 265; learning strategy inventories 263–264; levels of processing 29, 413; measurement issues 39; metacognitive-reflective processing 120, 121, 122, 123, 126–127, 132; Model of Domain Learning 40–41; MSLQ 264; multiple text use 120, 121, 133; reading comprehension strategies 100–101, 217; regression 397; science 177, 184, 185, 189; self-regulation 89, 90, 235; socially shared metacognitive regulation 241–242, 243; socially shared regulation of learning 241; socially shared strategic processing 73; studies 32, 34–36, 37, 38; surveys and retrospective self-reports 333; verbal protocol analysis 280, 281, 286, 374, 377, 378
Michaels, S. 70
Miller-Cotto, D. 165
Miller, M. 69, 75, 77
Millis, K. K. 282, 283
Minnaert, A. 399
misleading information 418
mixed effects models 324–325
mixed methods 357
Mixture Modeling 368
mnemonics 17, 88, 90, 91, 92–93
mobile devices 297–298, 299, 300
model essays 209
Model-Evidence-Link (MEL) diagram 186–189
model evolution 179
Model of Domain Learning (MDL) 31–37, 40–43, 49–51, 90–91, 277–278, 279, 335, 421

Model of Strategic Learning (MSL) 49–50
modeling 72–73, 104, 151, 152; history 209; science 184–186, 187, 189–190
Moeller, K. 173
monitoring: diary methods 289; EDM/LA 338; levels of processing 413; path model analysis 353–354; self-regulated learning 234, 235–239, 240, 243; socially shared regulation of learning 241, 243; task complexity 244; verbal protocol analysis 374, 380–381; *see also* comprehension monitoring
Monte-Sano, C. 208–209
MOOCs *see* Massively Online Open Courses
Morin, A. J. S. 363, 368
Moshman, D. 121
Moss, J. 324
Motivated Strategies for Learning Questionnaire (MSLQ) 264, 354
motivation 335, 421; Approaches to Study Inventory 261–262; autonomy support 226, 227, 228, 229; beliefs 36; choice of strategy 251; collaborative learning 239; conceptual change 179; executive functions 219, 220; Good Strategy User Model 277; ILS 265; individual differences 11; learner characteristics 319; learning strategy inventories 263; levels of processing 41, 42; MED NORD inventory 266–267; path model analysis 353, 356; person-centered approaches 363, 367; reading comprehension 115; science 178; self-regulated learning 278, 279; socially shared strategic processing 66; strategy development 148
motivational-affective strategies 48–49, 89, 90
Moulding, B. D. 185
MSL *see* Model of Strategic Learning
MSLQ *see* Motivated Strategies for Learning Questionnaire
MTSI *see* Multiple Text Strategy Inventory
Mukala, P. 307
multi-method designs 325–326, 335, 337
multidimensional models 421
multimedia learning 86, 411; click traces 363; eye movement cued self-reports 283; history 209; individual differences 131–132; multiple text use 129–130, 133, 134, 135, 418; reading comprehension 103
multiple linear regression (MLR) models 350–351
Multiple Text Strategy Inventory (MTSI) 127, 128
multiple texts 3, 119–140, 411, 418–419; history 202–203, 206; reading comprehension 103; task-specific self-report inventories 287
multivariate analysis of variance (MANOVA) 349, 368, 398
Muñoz, Pamela 141–158
Murphy, P. K. 365, 366, 410

music 17
Myers, M. 219

NAEP *see* National Assessment of Educational
   Progress
Najmaei, A. 35, 37
Nakajima, T. 308
Namkung, J. 162
Narens, L. 235
National Academies of Sciences 180
National Assessment of Educational Progress
   (NAEP) 104, 105–107, 162
National Council of Teachers of Mathematics 170
National Reading Panel 100
National Research Council (NRC) 181, 182, 184,
   187, 190
navigational supports 409–410
Nelson, T. O. 235
Netflix 300–301
neuroscience 222, 320–321; *see also* fMRI
Newton, Kristie 3, 159–176, 250, 251, 413, 414
Next Generation Science Standards (NGSS) 182
Nguyen, Q. 307
Nistal, A. A. 171–172
Nokes, Jeffery D. 4, 195–215, 250
NRC *see* National Research Council
number lines 161–162, 167, 169, 170

Oakhill, J. 224
Obersteiner, A. 173
Ochoa, X. 310
Oga-Baldwin, W. L. Q. 367
Okolo, C. M. 207
Olkinuora, E. 339
online learning 211–212, 296–297, 304, 306–307,
   309; *see also* internet
open-ended collaborative activities 76–77
origination 198, 200
Osborne, J. 189
outcome expectations 251, 252
outlining 17, 90
Overlapping Waves Model (OWM) 49, 50, 160
overt strategies 49

Paas, Fred 4, 234–247, 250
Pan, Y. 355
Panadero, E. 242
Panaoura, A. 170
Parakh, A. 302
paraphrasing 91, 122, 281, 283
Paré-Blagoev, E. J. 164
parents 227–228, 229
Paris, S. G. 35, 41, 111, 219
Pariser, E. 311

Park, S. 112
Parkinson, Meghan M. 1–8
Parpala, A. 267
Pask, G. 262
path analysis 351–354, 356, 363, 394, 397, 404
Paulson, N. 185
PBL *see* project-based learning
pedagogical practices 67, 78
peer-assessment 90
peer learning 264
performance 408–409; cyclical model of self-
   regulated learning 278; Good Strategy User
   Model 49; levels of processing 39–41; socially
   shared regulation of learning 242; task-specific
   self-report inventories 287
Perry, N. E. 69, 72–73, 285
person-centered approaches 5, 346–347, 356,
   361–372, 401–402, 403, 415
personality 261, 319, 333
personalization 309, 409, 414
Personalized Education Through Analytics on
   Learning Systems (PETALS) 304–305
perspective taking 207, 208, 211, 212
PETALS *see* Personalized Education Through
   Analytics on Learning Systems
Philipp, R. A. 168
physical models 167
physics 178
physiological measurements 5, 24, 38, 43, 56,
   317–331, 336–337, 415–416; *see also* eye tracking;
   fMRI
Phythian-Sence, C. 217
Piaget, Jean 88, 91, 92, 93, 178, 179, 217–218
Pike, K. 148
Pintrich, P. R. 30, 36, 37, 41, 264
planning: history 208; socially shared regulation of
   learning 241; writing 142, 146, 147, 149, 150,
   151, 152
Plumley, Robert D. 5, 345–360
Porat, D. 206–207
positive self-talk 90; *see also* self-talk
Posner, G. J. 179
POW strategy 150, 151–153
practicing problems 236
prediction 105, 107, 108–109, 123
Pressley, Michael 102, 109, 335; Good Strategy User
   Model 49, 218, 277, 279; reading strategies 374–
   375; verbal protocol analysis 281, 375, 376–377
previewing 103
Pribram, K. H. 219
prior knowledge 101, 216, 374, 409; diagrammatic
   learning 132; domain-general strategies 21;
   effectiveness of strategy use 135; learner
   characteristics 319; levels of processing 37, 41;

mathematics 171, 173; multiple text use 123, 126, 127, 131, 134; path model analysis 354; reading comprehension 109, 110–111, 114, 115, 130, 224; science 177; writing strategies 150–152

privacy 309, 310–311

problem-solving strategies 90, 236–237; concurrent and task-specific self-reports 290; intelligent tutoring systems 306; mathematics 159, 171, 172, 173; video games 308

procedural knowledge 57, 87, 88, 92, 147; domain-generality 13–14, 15–17, 19, 23; history 210; mathematics 171, 173; reading comprehension 110, 111, 114; science 113–114; strategy definition 275

process-oriented approach 19–20

professional development 58, 271, 420; Inventory of Teacher Learning 268; science 189, 190; writing strategies 155

proficiency 51, 52, 53, 57, 277–278; see also expertise

project-based learning (PBL) 76–77

Project READI 210–211

Prosser, M. 365, 366

psychophysiological measures 5, 56, 317–331, 415–416

qualitative approaches 5, 277, 357; conceptual frameworks and methods 384; data collection 362–363; process data 403; theoretical integration 369; transparency in data collection and analysis 389; verbal protocol analysis 373–392, 416–417

quantitative approaches: person-centered 5, 346–347, 356, 361–372, 401–402, 403, 415; variable-centered 5, 345–360, 362–363, 365–366, 369, 394–400, 403–404, 415

question answering/generation 100–101

questioning 13–14, 72–73, 101, 102, 211, 287–288

Quintana, C. 181

Ramey, J. 284

Ramsden, P. 261, 266, 365

randomized controlled trials 253

Rapp, D. N. 282

Rawson, K. A. 237

RCD see reading comprehension deficits

read-and-repeat strategy 49

reading 3, 99–118, 250; attentional resources 327; biometric data 24; domain-general strategies 23; epistemic processes 383, 385; executive functions 217–229; eye tracking 283, 318–320, 363; fMRI 323–324; history 197–198, 199, 200, 202, 204, 206–207, 208, 211–212; importance of analyzing strategic processing 373–375; intertextual knowledge elaboration 348; learning through reading 73; levels of processing 32, 42;

task-specific self-report inventories 286–287; verbal protocol analysis 280–283, 373–389; see also comprehension

reading comprehension deficits (RCD) 4, 216–217, 221–222, 224–225, 229

Reading Rockets 100–101

reasoning: claims-evidence-reasoning 183–184; collaborative learning 239; relational 22, 416; scientific 181, 185; verbal protocol analysis 374–375, 376, 379, 384–387, 388

rebuttal 208

reconciliation 124–125

Reed, C. 207

regression 350–354, 394, 396–397, 403–404

rehearsal 142, 264, 334

Reigeluth, C. M. 63

Reinecker, H. 289

Reisman, A. 206, 207

relational reasoning 22, 416

Remnet, M. A. 304

Renkl, A. 134

representational flexibility 170, 171–172

rereading 90, 101, 103, 320, 375; eye tracking 319; history 202; verbal protocol analysis 281; working memory capacity 238

researcher positionality 389

retrospective self-reports 4–5, 38, 259–274, 333–334, 336

revision 142, 143, 146, 147, 149

rewards 90, 142

Reynolds, R. E. 22

Richardson, J. T. E. 337

Richter, T. 127, 133

Riel, Jeremy 5, 296–316, 337–339, 419

Rienties, B. 307

Rinne, L. F. 402

Risemberg, R. 143

risk-taking 90

Rittle-Johnson, B. 171

Robertson, J. 355

Roebers, C. M. 219

Roelle, J. 350–351

Rogiers, Amélie 2, 47–62, 83–84, 86, 91, 93, 94, 421

Rouet, J. F. 125–126, 131, 197, 203

Ruckpaul, A. 284

Ruffing, S. 349

Ruohoniemi, M. 267

Russo, J. E. 284

Sadeghinejad, Z. 35, 37

SAL framework 37, 40, 42–43

Säljö, R. 37, 42, 261–262

Salmerón, Ladislao 5, 275–295, 334–336

sample size 364, 393, 396, 398, 399, 404

Sampson, V. 189
Samuelsson, J. 204
Samuelstuen, M. S. 286
Santangelo, T. 147
SAQ *see* Strategy and Attribution Questionnaire
scaffolding 76, 355, 410; history 208; science 181, 183, 184, 186–189, 190; self-regulated learning 72–73; video games 302, 308
Scardamalia, M. 146, 276
Schallert, Diane 22, 83, 89, 406
Schappelle, B. P. 168
Schatschneider, C. 217
Schauble, L. 185
Scheiter, K. 132, 134, 135
schemas 145, 197, 250, 252
Schmeck, R. R. 260, 262–263
Schmelzer, D. 289
Schmidt, E. M. 350–351
Schmitz, B. 289
Schneider, J. 203
Schneider, Wolfgang 218
Schnellert, Leyton 2, 63–81, 84, 92, 94
Schoenfeld, A. H. 70, 73
Schraw, G. 121
Schumacher, R. F. 162
Schwartz, D. L. 167
Schwarz, B. B. 206–207
Schwarz, C. V. 185
Schwonke, R. 133
science 3, 177–194; disciplinary knowledge 113–114; executive functions 221; monitoring learning 236; multimedia learning 130; reading comprehension strategies 108; scientific method 180; self-regulation 38; studies 34
searches 129, 133, 283
second language proficiency 282
second-order concepts 205–206
Segers, M. 355
Seixas, P. 202, 211
SEL *see* social emotional learning
selection 334
self-assessment 90, 134, 151
self-determination theory 226
self-efficacy: levels of processing 36, 41; Model of Domain Learning 335; motivation 89; MSLQ 264; reading comprehension 115; science 178; self-regulated learning 279; task-specific self-report inventories 287
self-evaluation 147
self-explanation 90, 253, 378, 403; as deep strategy 91, 92; mathematics 162, 165, 167; monitoring learning 236; strategy selection 93
self-instruction 142
self-questioning 12, 92, 375, 379

self-reflection 278
self-regulated learning (SRL) 2, 4, 37–38, 40, 42–43, 64–66, 84, 234–247; cyclical model of 278–279, 287, 335; data aggregation 348; influence on tactics and strategies 254–255; measurement issues 39; MSLQ 264, 354; path model analysis 353–354; research 252; socially shared strategic processing 67, 68, 71, 72–73, 74; strategic learners 248–249; structural equation modeling 355
self-regulated strategy development (SRSD) 149–154, 155, 156, 410
self-regulation 2, 64–66; autonomy support 227–228; collaborative learning 67; conceptual fogginess 408, 412; definition of strategic processing 87; EDM/LA impact on 311; effectiveness of strategy use 135; executive functions 221, 222, 228–229; ILS 266; individual differences 11; learning gain 267; levels of processing 29, 413; metacognitive-reflective processing 121; Model of Domain Learning 40–41; Model of Strategic Learning 49–50; person-centered approaches 365, 366–367; research 1; science 180; self-regulated cycles 93–94; studies 32, 34, 36, 37, 38; task-specific self-report inventories 287–288; types of strategies 89, 90; verbal protocol analysis 385; writing strategies 148, 149–154, 156; *see also* co-regulation
self-reinforcement 142, 151
self-reports 317, 318, 339, 356–357; combined with eye tracking 319, 322, 326; concurrent and task-specific 38, 276, 280–291, 334–335, 417; dominance of 333; Model of Domain Learning 278; retrospective 4–5, 38, 259–274, 333–334, 336, 416; self-regulated learning 279; structural equation modeling 354–355; student learning 307
self-talk 90, 151, 228, 229, 378
SEM *see* structural equation modeling
semantic organizers 100–101
sense-making 163, 164, 168, 198
Sesma, H. W. 222
Seufert, T. 134
Shanahan, C. 197
shared mental models 239, 242, 243
Shellings, G. 286
Shen, C. 349
Shin, M. 161
Shum, Alex 5, 361–372, 401
Shumka, E. 69
Siegler, R. S. 160
Simon, H. A. 196, 286, 376, 377
Simon, S. 189
Simons, K. D. 69, 76–77
Skemp, R. R. 163
skepticism 112, 197, 199, 200, 211, 212, 250

skills: automaticity 277; collaborative 63; cooperative learning 75; defining 99–100; domain-generality 14, 23; efficacy expectations 251; history 195; Model of Strategic Learning 49; science 180; strategies distinction 2–3, 13, 31, 32, 83, 99, 275, 334, 408
Skrzypiec, G. 350
Sleegers, P. 268
SLR *see* Structured Learning Report
Smith, J. P. 169
Smith, M. 211
Snow, E. L. 308
Snyder-Hogan, L. E. 130, 401
social emotional learning (SEL) 71–72, 74, 78
social interaction 239
social media 3, 300, 417–418
social network models 15
social skills 77
social strategies 89, 90, 93
socially shared metacognitive regulation (SSMR) 241–242, 243
socially shared regulation of learning (SSRL) 67–68, 241–243, 244
socially shared strategic processing 63–81, 84, 92
Soloway, E. 306
Sommer, J. 130
source evaluation 129, 133–134, 380–381
Sourcer's Apprentice 206
sourcing: Comprehensive Strategy Framework 122; history 120, 196–197, 199–200, 202–204, 206–207, 209, 210, 211–212; multiple text use 125–126, 130, 133–134
SRL *see* self-regulated learning
SRSD *see* self-regulated strategy development
SSMR *see* socially shared metacognitive regulation
SSRL *see* socially shared regulation of learning
Staarman, J. K. 70, 75–76
Stadtler, M. 125, 127, 128
Stafylidou, S. 160
Stahl, S. A. 202
Star, J. R. 159, 170, 171, 251
statistical power 393, 397, 400, 403–404
Stephens, L. A. 131
Stern, E. 168
stopping 101
story maps 100
strategic action 65, 67, 69, 71, 73, 74
strategic processing: Adaptive Model of Strategic Processing 177; Big Data 308, 337–338; conceptualizations of 333; concurrent and task-specific self-reports 280–291, 334–335, 336; defining 83–84, 85–87, 92–94; EDM/LA 305–306, 307, 308, 309; executive function 222; eye tracking 283, 317–320, 321–327;

fMRI 317–318, 320–324; history 204; ILS 266; individual differences 216–233; learning outcomes 345, 357; levels of 1, 29–46, 276, 337, 414; lifespan perspective 47–62; measurement 276, 332–341; multidimensional nature of 327; multiple text use 120–121, 130, 133–134; person-centered approaches 5, 361–372, 401–402, 415; psychophysiological measures 317–331, 336–337; reading 373–375; research 1–2, 406–424; science 177; socially shared 63–81, 84, 92; surveys and retrospective self-reports 38, 259–274, 333–334, 336; theoretical models 276–279; variable-centered approaches 5, 345–360, 362–363, 365–366, 369, 394–400, 403–404, 415; verbal protocol analysis 373–392; writing 145; *see also* cognitive processes; metacognition
strategic repertoires 49, 50, 52–53, 58
strategies: Big Data 299; choice of 251–252; conceptualizations of 2–4, 48, 250, 259, 407–408; defining 83–84, 87, 88–89, 99–100, 159, 249, 275–276, 334, 338, 412–413; domains of learning 11–28; educational psychology 11–12; executive functions 221; growth curve modeling 399; history 195–215; lack of research on 248; mathematics 159–176; multiple texts 119–140; operationalizations 4–6; PETALS 304; reading comprehension 99–118; research 1–2, 406–424; science 177–194; skills distinction 2–3, 13, 31, 32, 83, 99, 275, 334, 408; training programs 87; transfer of 12, 21, 23, 53, 57, 64, 188; types of 89–92, 259–260; verbal protocol analysis 380; writing 141–158; *see also* cognitive strategies; deep-level strategies; domain-general strategies; domain-specific strategies; surface-level strategies
Strategy and Attribution Questionnaire (SAQ) 266
stratification 198, 200
Strauss, A. L. 383
Strømsø, H. I. 124, 125, 127, 128, 131, 287, 349
structural equation modeling (SEM) 354–355, 356, 363, 398, 403–404; Latent Transition Analysis 402; path analysis 397; person-centered approaches combined with 368; pros and cons 394; sample size 393
Structured Learning Report (SLR) 268
structures, underlying 165, 169, 170
Student's t-test 348–349; *see also* t-test
Study Process Questionnaire (SPQ) 260–261, 270
Subramaniam, M. 302
substantiation 200, 206–207, 208
Sumfleth, E. 396
summarization 334, 375; Comprehensive Strategy Framework 122; history 202; intertextual knowledge elaboration 348; monitoring learning

236; reading comprehension 100–101, 103, 105, 107, 108–109; writing 143

Sun, C. T. 308, 338

supposition 198, 199, 200

surface-level strategies 29, 31–37, 43, 91, 334, 336; brain imaging 320–321, 322; Children's Perceived Use of Self-Regulated Learning Inventory 355; conceptual boundaries 413, 414; definition of strategies 276; developmental perspective 49, 53, 56; epistemic processes 383; formative assessment 357; growth curve modeling 399; key sentences 327; learner characteristics 319; Model of Domain Learning 41, 277–278; path model analysis 354; person-centered approaches 367; task-specific self-report inventories 286, 287; verbal protocols 417

surveys 4–5, 38, 259–274, 333–334, 336, 416

Sword, S. 165

t-test 348–349, 394, 395, 403–404

Taboada Barber, Ana 4, 216–233, 250, 253, 416

tactics 178, 250–251, 253, 254–255, 412–413

Tanes, Z. 304

TAPs see think-aloud protocols

task-specific self-report inventories 285–288, 290, 291, 333–335

task-specific strategies 88, 277, 317

tasks 16–17, 18; complexity of 237, 240, 243, 244, 255; eye tracking 319–320; goals 92; interpretation of 65; MSLQ 264; multiple text use 132–133; task-specific strategies 21, 24

Taub, M. 37

TC see transactive communication

teacher education 155, 189, 190; see also professional development

team cognition 239, 240, 242, 243, 244

technology 84, 296–297, 337–338, 417–418, 419; computer-supported collaborative learning 75–76; data collection 43–44; digital devices 415; strategy development 56; technology-mediated learning environments 305–308; see also Big Data; internet

text anxiety 264

text connections 101

theoretical convergence 366–367

think-aloud protocols (TAPs) 38, 39, 270, 317, 411; behavioral data 356; count data 351, 356; data aggregation 348; data collection 362–363; domain-general strategies 19; history 196, 208; Latent Class Analysis 401; multi-faceted measurement 24; multiple text use 123, 124, 126–127, 129; qualitative analysis of data 403; reading comprehension instruction 102–103; retrospective 319, 326; validity 285,

324; verbal protocol analysis 280–283, 286, 376–377, 416–417

Thorndike, E. L. 420

time management 142, 349

time/study environment 264

timers 90

Timperley, H. 73

Torre, D. M. 13, 70

Toulmin, S. E. 183, 385

Trabasso, T. 281, 282

trace data 254, 255, 307, 308, 351, 353, 356

Trach, J. 69

training programs 87, 155, 408–409, 414; see also instruction

transactive communication (TC) 75

transactive memory 239, 242, 243

transition analysis 395, 400; see also latent transition analysis

Treagust, D. F. 179

TREE strategy 150, 151–153, 156

triangulation 271, 333, 335–336, 339–340, 388–389

Trigwell, K. 365

Tsai, C. C. 306

Tsai, M.-J. 306

Tsang, J. M. 167

Tusubira, F. F. 70

validity 393, 420; construct 364; diary methods 288, 289–290; eye movement cued self-reports 284–285, 290; person-centered approaches 367; physiological measurements 323–324, 415–416; self-reports 270, 271, 286–287, 290, 333, 335; verbal protocols 282–283, 380, 417

van Boxtel, C. 205

Van Der Aalst, W. M. P. 307

Van der Werf, G. 399

Van Dooren, W. 171–172

van Drie, J. P. 205

Van Gog, T. 238

Van Keer, Hilde 2, 47–62

Van Meter, Peggy 3, 82–96, 130

Van Rijswijk, F. A. 266

VanSledright, B. A. 113, 210, 211

variable-centered approaches 5, 345–360, 362–363, 365–366, 369, 394–400, 403–404, 415

Varma, S. 324

Vasilyeva, M. 349, 357

Veenman, M. V. J. 286

verbal protocol analysis 280–283, 286, 373–392, 416–417

Vermeulen, M. 355

Vermunt, Jan D. 4–5, 36–42, 259–274, 333–334, 336, 337, 366, 416

Verschaffel, L. 171–172

Vidal-Abarca, E. 131, 133
video 130–131, 209, 270, 283–285, 307
video games 301–302, 308, 338
Vignoles, A. 267
visible learning 38, 64, 78
visual representations 163, 167, 169
visualization 20, 101, 287
visuospatial reasoning 132
Vlassis, J. 167
Vosniadou, S. 160
Voss, J. F. 133
Vrikki, M. 268

Wach, F. 349
Wagner, R. K. 217
Wagner, W. 204
Wallace, R. M. 306
Walton, D. 207
Wampold, B. E. 400
Wang, A. 162
Wang, D. Y. 308
Wang, Y. 128, 287
Warwick, P. 268
web analytics 299–300
Webb, N. M. 74–75
Weinstein, Claire Ellen 48, 49, 263, 406
Wendell, J. 204
Werner, B. 129, 134
Werner, M. 204
Whitacre, I. 168
Wiebe, E. N. 132
Wiese, B. S. 289
Wijnia, Lisette 4, 234–247, 250
Wiley, J. 128, 129, 133
will 49–50
Willingham, D. 108
Windschitl, M. 185

Wineburg, S. S. 119–120, 125, 130, 196–197, 199, 202, 211–212
Winne, Philip H. 4, 248–256, 285
Winograd, P. 104
Wissinger, D. 207, 209
Wittrock, Merle 407–408
Wixson, K. 111
Wolfe, M. B. 123, 126–127, 135
Wolters, C. 36
Woodward, Lindsay 5, 373–392, 416–417
word problems 163–164, 169
worked examples 164, 165, 167, 168–169, 171–172, 236
working memory 4, 21, 131–132, 216, 220, 253; cognitive load theory 237–238; collaborative learning 240, 244; eye tracking 283, 318–319; mathematics 162; reading comprehension 112, 222, 223, 224–225; socially shared regulation of learning 243; verbal protocol analysis 280, 281, 282, 286; writing 144
Writer(s)-within-Community (WWC) model 143–145, 148
writing 3, 141–158, 250, 413; domain-general strategies 23; executive functions 221; history 199, 201, 203, 204, 206, 208–209
Wu, H. H. 161

Ye, A. 402
Young, K. M. 197
Young, R. 148
Yuill, N. 224

Zakai, S. 203
Ziegler, E. 168
Zimmerman, B. J. 65–66, 143, 278–279, 287–288, 335, 348
Zwaan, R. A. 282